"Armour and Levitt walk the reader th [...] in baseball history, using a rare co [...] lively storytelling. If *Moneyball* is the tale of how a modern front office works, *In Pursuit of Pennants* is the prequel that ably sets the stage."
Jonah Keri, author of the best-selling *The Extra 2%* and *Up, Up, and Away*

"Armour and Levitt have given the reader an inside look at the different cultures and challenges facing professional sports executives. While executives' management styles might differ, the objective never changes: 'Be a consistent winner.'"
Pat Gillick

"Exceptionally well researched, reasoned, and argued, and also exceptionally well written."
Rob Neyer, *Just a Bit Outside*, Fox Sports

"A great source of well-researched front office stories. . . . Armour and Levitt give an insider's look at the teams' efforts to innovate in this highly competitive industry."
Sig Mejdal, director of decision sciences for the Houston Astros

"This is an interesting, well-written, and well-researched behind-the-scenes look at how certain winning clubs have been constructed by notable baseball executives and the philosophies employed."
Tal Smith, baseball executive

"A rare combination of a must-have reference book and engaging storytelling by distinguished baseball historians Armour and Levitt."
Vince Gennaro, president of the Society for American Baseball Research and author of *Diamond Dollars: The Economics of Winning in Baseball*

"By far the best treatment of the building of baseball teams. It belongs in easy reach on every baseball researcher's desk or bookshelf, and it's going to be there for a very long time."
Jan Finkel, *Inside Game*

"Read this book for its treasure trove of baseball history and because it is a damn good read."
G. Louis Heath, *Arete*

IN PURSUIT OF PENNANTS

IN PURSUIT

OF PENNANTS

Baseball Operations from
Deadball to *Moneyball*

MARK L. ARMOUR &
DANIEL R. LEVITT
With a new epilogue by the authors

University of Nebraska Press
Lincoln and London

© 2015 by Mark L. Armour and Daniel R. Levitt
Epilogue and appendix B © 2018 by Mark L.
Armour and Daniel R. Levitt

All rights reserved
Manufactured in the United States of America

Library of Congress Control Number: 2017961641

Set in Chaparral Pro by Lindsey Auten.

To the late Leonard Koppett, whose distinctive, wide-ranging examination of baseball inspired our own interest in the sport, particularly the matters that we address in these pages.

CONTENTS

List of Illustrations   ix

List of Tables   x

List of Charts   x

Acknowledgments   xi

Introduction   xiii

PART 1. PROFESSIONAL MANAGEMENT

1. Owner-Operator   3
2. Field Manager   29
3. General Manager   53
4. Executive   62
5. Farm System   70
6. Organization   80

PART 2. GENERAL MANAGER ASCENDANT

7. Dodger Way   97
8. Dynasty   120
9. Integration   135
10. Commitment   140
11. Excellence Rewarded   162
12. Amateur Draft   188
13. The Machine   198

PART 3. NEW ORDER

14. Long Road Back   233
15. Expansion   249
16. Free Agency   274
17. The Zoo   281
18. Many Rivers   300

PART 4. BUSINESSMEN

    19. Winning Now   321
    20. Analytics   352
    21. Post-*Moneyball*   362
    22. Modern Game   385

       Epilogue   401
       Appendix A: Front Office
       Awards and Recognition   415
       Appendix B: The Top Thirty
       General Managers   423
       Notes   429
       Index   459

ILLUSTRATIONS

Following page 190

1. Barney Dreyfuss and Garry Herrmann
2. John McGraw
3. John McGraw and Christy Mathewson
4. Bill Veeck Sr. with Rogers Hornsby and William Wrigley
5. Jacob Ruppert and Miller Huggins
6. Ed Barrow and Joe McCarthy
7. Walter O'Malley, Bob Hunter, and Buzzie Bavasi
8. Al Campanis and Jim Wynn
9. Walter O'Malley, Buzzie Bavasi, and Fresco Thompson
10. Branch Rickey and Larry MacPhail
11. Larry MacPhail, Del Webb, and Dan Topping
12. August Busch Jr. with Warren Giles
13. Dan Devine
14. Jim Campbell
15. Harry Dalton
16. Dick O'Connell, Haywood Sullivan, and Dick Williams
17. Bob Howsam
18. Larry, Lee, and Bill MacPhail
19. Mike Burke
20. Cedric Tallis with Dick Sisler
21. Ewing Kauffman
22. Frank White and other Kansas City prospects
23. Ewing Kauffman and Syd Thrift
24. Charlie Metro, Lou Gorman, and Cedric Tallis
25. Cedric Tallis's acquisitions
26. Gabe Paul
27. Peter Bavasi
28. Pat Gillick
29. Billy Beane
30. Bill Neukom, Larry Baer, and Brian Sabean
31. Ben Cherington and John Farrell

TABLES

1. Pittsburgh club, 1900   16
2. McGraw's young players   35
3. Team builders, 1938   60
4. Payments by Majors to
   Minors, 1909–14   73
5. 1923 Yankees   90
6. 1927 Yankees   91
7. 1939 Yankees   92
8. Red Sox All-Star draftees   193
9. Orioles All-Star draftees   195
10. Key Cedric Tallis trades   272
11. Key 2001 contributors   347
12. Number of free agents   366

CHARTS

1. The farm system from 1920 to 1960   78
2. Percentage change in
   African Americans and Latinos   136
3. African American and Latino
   player value   137
4. MLB WAR from drafted players   190
5. Average MLB salaries   278
6. WAR from players who have been
   through free agency   279

ACKNOWLEDGMENTS

We began talking about this book soon after we published our last book, *Paths to Glory*, in 2003. Several projects intervened in the past twelve years, but we continually explored and shaped the themes in these pages via conversations, emails, and research. By the middle of 2012 we had both finally cleared the decks so that we could focus on this effort.

To provide us with an inside view, a number of current and former front-office executives generously spent time discussing baseball management and how it has evolved: John Schuerholz, Roland Hemond, Peter Bavasi, Pat Gillick, Bill Neukom, Tal Smith, and Sig Mejdal. Bill Fischer and Dr. Steve Korcheck offered firsthand insights into the Kansas City Baseball Academy. We also need to thank Marc Appleman, Adele MacDonald, Ethan Morss, and Rob Garratt for helping coordinate our interviews.

Several people read early drafts of one or more chapters: Vince Gennaro, Marc Gullickson, Bill Lamb, John Mathew IV, Tom Simon, Lyle Spatz, Steve Steinberg, Stew Thornley, Steve Treder, Mike Webber, Arnold Witt, and Mark Witt. Their comments helped immeasurably, and we hope they will agree that the version in these pages is an improvement.

We also acknowledge the efforts of Gabriel Schechter, who retrieved files from the Baseball Hall of Fame Library several times over the years for each of us. When we spent two days in Cooperstown in 2013, we were treated royally at the hall by Tim Wiles, Tom Shieber, Freddy Berowski, Maura Coonan, and Paul Vinelli.

Some of our research on the pace and shape of baseball's integration, and the demographics of the game over the past seventy years (discussed in chapter 9), has been published on the Society for American Baseball Research (SABR) website (most recently in 2013). Subsequently, we received quite a bit of useful feedback and suggestions from several people, including Michael Teevan and Pat Courtney (both from Major League Baseball's Commissioner's Office), Tyler Kepner (*New York Times*), Paul Hagan (mlb.com), Adam Reiss (CNN), and Bob Nightengale (*USA Today*). Our presentation here is better for it.

Pat Kelly at the Baseball Hall of Fame, Sarah Coffin with the Boston Red Sox, Dennis Goldstein, David Eskenazi, and Howard Starkman eased the process of finding relevant photographs. Curt Nelson provided both images and insights for the Kansas City Baseball Academy. Cliff Blau provided an expert, professional fact-checking review.

We are both active members of SABR and have been continually educated by hundreds of conversations or email correspondences with fellow members. Those who have helped answer a question or two over the years specific to this book include Ron Antonucci, Dave Baldwin, Sam Bernstein, Jeff Bower, Sean Forman, Steve Gietschier, Tim Herlich, Bill Hickman, Kevin Johnson, Jonah Keri, Bruce Markuson, Gary Mitchem, Peter Morris, Rod Nelson, Rob Neyer, Bobby Plapinger, Jacob Pomrenke, Tom Ruane, John Stahl, Brad Sullivan, Mark Wernick, and Joe Williams.

Rob Taylor, Courtney Ochsner, Tish Fobben, Joeth Zucco, Annette Wenda, and the rest of the team at the University of Nebraska Press have been helpful and encouraging throughout the process.

Finally, we would like to thank our families—Jane, Maya and Drew; Suzy, Charlie and Joey—for their support through the many years of this project.

INTRODUCTION

When the St. Louis Cardinals and Boston Red Sox met in the 2013 World Series, the twenty-five players on their respective rosters rightfully took center stage. The composition of these rosters, though, was the result of the efforts of dozens of people in baseball operations positions who had scouted, drafted, developed, signed, or acquired the players. All of their decision making is analyzed and graded like never before by fans and writers, many of whom feel comfortable second-guessing not just Major League trades but also the drafting of high school prospects. In the end—at least for 2013—the Cardinals and Red Sox front offices found the right players more effectively than their counterparts on the other twenty-eight Major League teams.

Building a championship baseball team, 140 years after the start of the first professional league, remains a challenging task. Regardless of the strengths of any Major League organization, its management is generally competing against other smart, well-motivated people with significant resources of their own. In a direct competition, where every action draws a reaction, there can be no easy recipe for success. Moreover, in an industry where people shift between organizations on a regular basis, it is not possible to maintain trade secrets for more than a short period of time.

Organizations are also dealing with imperfect information when constructing their teams. Which eighteen-year-old draftee will add five miles per hour to his fastball, and which will hit for more power? Which player is ready to be promoted to the Majors, which declining player is over the hill and which will rebound, and which free-agent pitcher is least likely to break down due to arm troubles? The list of things one cannot know, at least precisely, is endless. Nevertheless, teams must make decisions.

Robert R. Bowie, a Harvard professor and a former director of Harvard's Center for International Affairs, discussed the problem of having insufficient information in a slightly different context: "The policy-maker, unlike the academic analyst, can rarely wait until all the facts are in. He is acutely aware of the contingency of both the setting and the results of his action. He thinks in terms of odds and probabilities, rarely in terms of carefully reasoned analytical judgments or certainties. He is very often under strong pressure to *do* something, to take *some* action, even if all the facts are not yet available to him or where a careful assessment of current data would provide useful results."[1]

Most baseball franchises recognize these limitations and spend time and money to improve their analysis and decision making, some more successfully than others. However, there is still much that can be learned from studying the history of baseball team building. Looking carefully, one can often identify differences between teams that consistently succeed and teams that struggle. Between evolving organizational frameworks and expanded or better sources of information, some teams have performed demonstrably better than others.

In this book we evaluate a number of successful teams throughout baseball history, along with the significant changes to the landscape that have affected how all teams have operated. We believe that the differentiating advantages that have led to their success, divided broadly between the organizational and the informational, can be grouped into four classes, which are not mutually exclusive.

The first advantage, which could result from luck or design, comes from having a creative, innovative, or simply brilliant person as the team's key decision maker. New York Giants manager John McGraw was not a great leader or organizer by almost any usual criteria, and it is hard to imagine anyone successfully emulating his style, but he was among baseball's most successful active baseball executives for thirty years. This may not be a particularly satisfying explanation, and this advantage is certainly less feasible with today's much more complicated baseball organizations. But once in a great while, a person like McGraw simply has the intuitive feel, internal drive, or overwhelming personality needed to build a collection of players into a champion without a clear organizational or informational advantage.

A second advantage comes about when a team creates a better-designed or better-managed organization. Around 1920 New York Yankees owner Jacob Ruppert was one of the first owners to introduce professional management by hiring what we now call a general manager (GM) and presided over one of baseball's best-administered organizations for the next twenty years. Similarly, George Weiss with the Yankees of the 1950s, Bob Howsam with the Cincinnati Reds of 1970s, and Bill Neukom with the San Francisco Giants of the late 2000s presided over streamlined front offices with a commitment to excellence from top to bottom. Central to building a top-notch baseball organization are finding, motivating, and listening to savvy scouts, player-personnel people, and, more recently, analytics and video staffs. Almost all great teams have done this better than their competition.

A third advantage comes when a team quickly grasps that there is a shift in the landscape, when new talent or new information is freshly available. In *Only the Paranoid Survive*, Andrew S. Grove, a onetime Intel chief executive officer (CEO), dubs these transitions "strategic inflection points," a point in time "when the balance of forces shifts, from the old structure, from the old ways of doing business and the old ways of competing, to the new."[2] Changes within the technology industry, where Grove worked, are usually more dramatic and momentous than those in baseball, but the concept he describes is certainly useful for thinking about changes in baseball.

A final class of advantage can come when a club creates a new approach to managing its baseball operation or takes advantage of circumstances unique to the team (including superior financial resources)—in effect generating one's own strategic inflection point. To highlight these last two opportunities—taking advantage of a shift in the landscape or effectively finding one's own new advantage—we devote six chapters to inflection points that are among the most significant in baseball history.

1. the creation of the general manager role in the 1920s
2. the establishment of the first farm systems in the 1920s and '30s
3. the integration that followed Jackie Robinson's 1947 debut
4. the advent of the first-year-player draft in 1965
5. the start of player free agency in 1976
6. the rise of baseball analytics in the 2000s

We also discuss several other inflection points that had important consequences, such as the baseball stadium boom in the 1990s, the acceleration of player signings in the Dominican Republic in the 1980s and Asia in the 2000s, and the recent marriage of video technology and high-speed computing.

Many of the most successful teams in baseball history have been ones that either best reacted to the changes to the game or created their own new approach. The best teams in the 1930s (the Yankees and Cardinals) were those that built productive farm systems. Many of the best teams in the 1950s (the Dodgers, Giants, and Braves) were ones that best took advantage of the newly admissible African American or Afro-Latino players. Pat Gillick built the Blue Jays after systematically scouting the Dominican Republic more aggressively than most of his competitors and then put his team over the top by smartly exploiting free agency.

Gabe Paul, blessed with his own experience and great scouts, combined these advantages with the Yankees' monetary edge to create a great team in New York. Simply having a better idea, such as the incorporation of analytics by the *Moneyball* A's of the early 2000s or the early adoption of video technology by the recent Giants, can also provide an advantage, although generally a transitory one, since good ideas will sooner or later diffuse throughout baseball. The more a successful new approach goes against the conventional wisdom and the harder it is to implement, the longer the advantage can last.

As teams have tried to implement the changes discussed above by building stronger, more efficient organizations or by taking advantage of changes in the environment in which they did business, the structure of their organizations evolved as well. Moreover, as baseball has grown as a business, with large increases in both total revenues and the number and variety of sources of those revenues, an increasingly sophisticated organization has been required to manage them. A second and related theme of our book is how the demands of building and managing a better organization inexorably led to increased complexity and size in baseball front offices.

Barney Dreyfuss, owner of the Pittsburgh Pirates from 1900 to 1932, personally kept a journal, or "dope book," filled with information on young players around the country, and he would often travel to see them play and sign or purchase those he liked. Jacob Ruppert built the Yankee dynasty in the 1920s after creating an organization of talented executives. From the 1930s to the 1970s, men such as Branch Rickey, George Weiss, and Bob Howsam presided over similar organizations, with much success.

Eventually, with the increasing complexity of the business side of the franchise, a team president or CEO typically emerged as ownership's top front-office employee, and the general manager's role was relegated to the baseball side. In many front offices the relationship between these two executives became the most important in the organization. The baseball side itself (which is now dubbed "baseball operations") has become much more sophisticated and complicated with the introduction of advanced data analytics, video technology, and player physiological applications.

The teams we have chosen to examine in this book were not necessarily the best or only example of a particular class of success, but were selected because we felt they best illustrated the way a particular organization at a particular time succeeded in overcoming the prevalent challenges. These teams are among the most successful in history, and in most cases the people who ran them did something new and interesting that was adopted by their competition. Not surprisingly, some of the approaches with which these teams met their particular challenges cannot automatically be extrapolated to a different time and place. Nevertheless, we believe that the stories of these winning teams can offer useful ideas or frameworks for future success.

IN PURSUIT OF PENNANTS

PART 1 • *Professional Management*

1 Owner-Operator

A survey of veteran baseball historians to determine the game's greatest talent evaluator would likely result in numerous mentions of Branch Rickey. Bob Quinn, who knew Rickey for fifty years and was an excellent judge of talent himself, thought Rickey might have suggested another candidate. "I'd say that Rickey's greatest ability was his tremendous judgment of players," Quinn recalled to historian Lee Allen. "In this, he patterned himself after Barney Dreyfuss, the owner of the Pirates. He often told me that Dreyfuss was the best judge of players he had ever seen."[1]

When Quinn spoke these words Dreyfuss had been dead for almost forty years and was nearly forgotten except by a few baseball historians. He had never been a scout, farm director, player-development coordinator, or general manager—none of those jobs, as we know them today, yet existed when he started in management. Unlike Rickey, Dreyfuss had never seriously played the game. He did not see his first baseball game until he was an adult. He obviously did not own a computer or a cell phone. In his early years he had to travel by train to see potential players. He did not have an organization of people to whom he could delegate work—if something needed to be done, Dreyfuss did it himself. He relied on friends and contacts throughout the country, a few newspaper subscriptions, an ever-present notebook in which he recorded everything he learned, a brilliant business sense, a large capacity for work, a superior intellect, and as keen an eye for spotting baseball players as the game has ever seen. Armed with all of this, he built the Pirates into one of history's greatest teams and was one of the most powerful men in the sport for more than thirty years.

Before baseball teams employed people we now call "general managers," major personnel decisions were made either by a team executive—typically the team president with an ownership stake—or by the field

3

manager. Baseball front offices were little more than one executive with a minimal staff to help oversee the financial accounting and the necessary back-office functions such as arranging travel and managing ticket sales. Farm systems did not yet exist. Teams typically landed young talent by purchasing or drafting players from independent Minor League teams. Dreyfuss proved to be a master in this environment.

Barney Dreyfuss's journey toward baseball began in 1882 when the seventeen-year-old emigrated from Freiburg, Germany, to Paducah, Kentucky, to live and work with relatives who operated the Bernheim Distillery, a maker of fine whiskey. Later described by sportswriter Fred Lieb as "a little energetic man of 125 pounds," Dreyfuss spoke with a heavy German accent throughout his life.[2] In Paducah he began as a barrel washer before becoming a bookkeeper, a skill he had learned in school in Germany. Within a few months he became credit manager, maintaining a grueling schedule, working long days and learning English at night.

Dreyfuss soon took a liking to the odd American sport of baseball, playing the game for recreation and ultimately organizing his own teams, using workers at the distillery and, later, local semipro players. When Bernheim moved its company headquarters to Louisville in 1888, Dreyfuss relocated and soon convinced his relatives to join him in investing in the local Louisville Colonels of the (Major League) American Association. By 1890 the twenty-five-year-old Dreyfuss served on the team's board of directors as treasurer.

The Colonels had been a mediocre team in the association for several years, but in the chaotic 1890 season (when the rebel Players League took most of the best players from both the American Association and the National League [NL]), the Colonels won their only pennant. When the Players League folded after that single season, the Colonels returned to their losing ways. Dreyfuss continued to increase his holdings in the team and soon was named secretary-treasurer. The management of the Louisville club was fluid in the 1890s, and at a time when buying into baseball franchises was still open to men of more modest means, Dreyfuss became the largest stockholder and gained further control. Because he still held a full-time job with Bernheim, often traveling overseas for the company, his hands-on role with the Colonels was limited by his own schedule.

Dreyfuss had been an avid fan of the game for many years and later told a writer that he had a complete run of the *Sporting Life*, a Philadelphia-based weekly devoted mainly to baseball, going back to the mid-1880s.[3] Once he got involved with the Colonels, he was not just reading the articles for pleasure, but using them to learn about the players. He devoured this publication, as well as the *Sporting News*, a rival newspaper published in St. Louis. In the days before teams had full-time scouts, Dreyfuss wrote everything in a dope book, which he carried with him everywhere.

Dreyfuss would develop a genius for finding ballplayers, but he also built a proto-organization. As opposed to a staff of scouts such a club might have today, Dreyfuss made and kept contacts throughout the country—former Louisville players who were now coaching in the Minor Leagues or newspapermen he had met during his travels. He communicated with these people regularly, via letter or telegraph, and supplemented the knowledge in his dope book. If one of the baseball papers was touting a Minor League player, or if Dreyfuss got a tip from someone in his network of baseball people, he often decided to look the player over. Dreyfuss usually worked at the distillery during the week, leaving the weekend for his baseball travels. If the occasion warranted, he might schedule a midweek business trip in conjunction with his scouting mission. And he had a prodigious memory. "At any time," recalled his longtime manager Fred Clarke, "he could quote current hitting averages without looking them up."[4]

Beginning in 1892, when four teams from the American Association were absorbed by the National League, and continuing for eight seasons, the "major leagues" consisted of a single twelve-team league, often called the "Big League." The 1890s were a historically crucial period in the development of the game. Most important, in 1893 the NL established the pitching rubber, raised it up on a mound, and placed it sixty feet and six inches from home plate; following many years of experimentation, this pitching distance took hold and has remained

ever since. In addition, many innovative teams and players began playing "scientific baseball," leading to more stolen bases, bunts, hit-and-
runs, and other innovations that came to define the game for the next
thirty years.

Off the field, however, the game was in disarray. The league owners—
who came to be called "magnates"—now had a monopoly and no longer needed to concern themselves with the interests of the players
or the league as a whole. Under the ineffectual leadership of league
president Nick Young, the owners broke into factions, wrangling for
the benefit of their narrow interests. New York owner Andrew Freedman, the wealthiest and most despised owner in baseball, worked
his own agenda for his personal benefit; large-market owners Arthur
Soden (Boston), John I. Rogers (Philadelphia), and James Hart (Chicago) schemed to take advantage of the lesser capitalized franchises;
the smaller-market teams, led by John Brush (Cincinnati), survived
by banding together to force an even split of gate receipts. This deli-
cate balance of power would not hold up for long.[5]

One thing all the owners could agree on: the players made too much
money. The owners instituted salary caps, tightened their hold on their
players' contracts, and codified strict behavioral rules. Salaries plum-
meted. The league also became grossly imbalanced. Boston and Baltimore won the first seven pennants of the Big League, and the other
ten teams generally spent the last three months of each season well
out of contention. Upon joining the NL in 1892, Louisville became one
of the also-rans and remained so for most of the decade. While Dreyfuss was gradually accumulating stock, his team was not winning many
games. But the talent on the team was slowly improving.

Early in the 1894 season, the *Sporting Life* mentioned a young left
fielder playing for the Savannah Modocs of the Southern Association:
"Fred Clarke is playing a phenomenal game, both in the field and at
the bat."[6] This one sentence was buried in a story about the Savannah club, but it is likely that Dreyfuss read this and made a note in his
dope book, probably adding to what he already knew about Clarke. As
a teenager Clarke, from Winterset, Iowa, had played on an amateur
team managed by Ed Barrow, near the start of Barrow's long and distinguished career. Clarke had then begun his professional career in

1893 with St. Joseph (Missouri) of the Western Association and was hitting .346 in twenty games when the league folded. He next hooked up with the Montgomery (Alabama) club of the Southern Association, hitting .306 over thirty-five games to close out the season, and then moved on to Savannah the next spring. Not long after, Dreyfuss arranged a business trip to Memphis when Savannah was playing there.[7]

Dreyfuss later recalled the journey. "A young, thin, rawboned little fellow was playing left field for Savannah; going after everything in sight and hitting the Memphis pitcher out of the lot." When the Savannah catcher became ill, Clarke donned the equipment and took over, showing himself to be both the toughest and the most talented player on the club.[8] According to a later account by Lieb, Savannah manager John McCloskey informed Dreyfuss that his team was broke and ready to disband and that McCloskey did not even have enough money for train fare to get his team back to Savannah. Dreyfuss offered McCloskey two hundred dollars—enough to get his team home—in exchange for Clarke's contract.[9] What we know for sure is that Dreyfuss purchased Clarke, and the twenty-one-year-old entered the Colonels' lineup immediately. In his first game Clarke had four singles and a triple. After the season a grateful Dreyfuss hired McCloskey as Louisville's manager.

Clarke soon became the best all-around player on the Colonels: an excellent hitter, a fine left fielder, and a ferocious base runner, one of the fiercest competitors of his era. Fred Lieb later recounted in Clarke's obituary: "With the possible exception of [Ty] Cobb and John McGraw, baseball never knew a sturdier competitor than Clarke."[10] Indeed, Clarke was often engaged in physical encounters on the field. The 1894 Colonels were a bad team (finishing fifty-four games behind the Orioles) and, except for Clarke, a team filled with disappointing veterans with no future.

Clarke later admitted that he developed some bad habits hanging around with some of his teammates early in his career. "Barney Dreyfuss recognized it too," he recalled, "and he called me into his office. He didn't lecture me, he merely said: 'Fred, you know if a man goes into any kind of business and neglects it, it will surely go the dogs.'" Dreyfuss walked out of the office, leaving Clarke to ponder what he had said. The next day Clarke returned and vowed to right the ship. "I do not think any employer ever gave a young player better counsel," he remembered.[11]

Clarke hit .325 and .347 with extra-base power and great base running in his first two full seasons, but the Colonels finished last twice more. They briefly added a second promising youngster in 1895 when the Boston Beaneaters loaned them outfielder Jimmy Collins after he had begun his first season hitting .211 in eleven games. McCloskey turned him into a third baseman, and he became a great one—soon one of the best in the game. Unfortunately for Louisville, after the season Boston asked for Collins back and withstood Dreyfuss's repeated attempts to gain his rights. Boston was willing to let Collins go only in exchange for Clarke, an offer Dreyfuss rebuffed. At the league meeting that December, Louisville was besieged with other offers for Clarke, including a seven-thousand-dollar bid from the New York Giants.[12]

After yet another last-place finish in 1896, Louisville started the next season 17-24 when Dreyfuss decided to jettison his latest manager, Jim Rogers. The problem with Rogers was not his managing—it was that he was hitting .144 in 153 at bats. During an era when most teams used playing managers to save money, Dreyfuss did not want to pay a manager to sit on the bench, so Rogers was released. Surprising most everyone, he hired the twenty-four-year-old Clarke to take Rogers's place. Clarke responded to his new authority by hitting .390 with fifty-nine steals as Louisville posted a 52-78 record. At the time he took the reins, Clarke was the only good offensive player on the team other than thirty-five-year-old first baseman Perry Werden. The situation soon improved considerably.

The closest thing Dreyfuss had to a coworker with the Colonels was Harry Pulliam, a reporter and city editor for the *Louisville Courier* who had also served as secretary of the American Association in its waning days.[13] In the early 1890s Pulliam became the business manager for the Colonels, working, like Dreyfuss, on a part-time basis, but by 1895 he had left his newspaper and become a full-time employee of the team. Two decades later a writer would say, "Harry Pulliam might be called the first of all Scouts."[14] It would be more accurate to say that everyone actively associated with a ball club—a group that generally numbered no more than a handful in addition to the owner and manager—performed scouting duties when time allowed, and Pulliam and Dreyfuss spent most of their free time during the season looking for players. As it happened, Pulliam garnered everlasting fame for his role in landing one of the best prospects any scout ever landed, though it took a fair bit of serendipity.

Honus Wagner grew up just outside of Pittsburgh and played for several Minor League teams before signing with Ed Barrow's Atlantic League club in Paterson, New Jersey. Wagner was a large, awkward-looking man who did not seem to have a position but hit .313 for Barrow in 1896. He returned the next season and hit even better. One of his opponents took special notice: Claude McFarlan, a pitcher-outfielder who lived in Louisville but played for Norfolk. After watching Wagner go eight for twenty-one with two home runs and two triples in the season's first few weeks, McFarlan wrote to Pulliam, who ignored the letter.[15]

McFarlan persisted, tracking down Pulliam in early June when Norfolk was playing in Newark and the Colonels were in New York. Ten years later Pulliam told the story at a banquet. "Fifteen years ago, down in my old home, I did a favor to a good fellow who was in hard luck," Pulliam related. "He never forgot my kindness, which was very small. . . . For three nights the man I referred to visited the old baseball headquarters in New York, the Stuyvesant House, in order to see me. Two nights he missed me, but on the third he remained at the hotel until I returned, a very tired young man. He said, 'You did me a good turn one time, and I am going to do you a good turn, for I have the greatest ball player in America for you in Paterson, and his name is Hans Wagner. The beauty of this man is that not only can he play ball, but he has the best disposition of any fellow you ever knew.'"[16]

Suitably impressed, the next day Pulliam went to see Wagner for himself, and both Clarke (soon to be named manager) and Dreyfuss joined Pulliam over the next few days. Pulliam began negotiations with Barrow that dragged on for several weeks, with other teams joining the bidding. Wagner helped Barrow's cause considerably on July 11, when he hit three home runs, a triple, and a double in a win over

Norfolk.[17] Pulliam pressed his case. "I told [Barrow] of the struggle we were having in Louisville to get on our feet and begged him to let me have the man," said Pulliam. "My efforts were successful, and he sold me the release of Wagner for $2,000 [sic]. I drew a draft on the Louisville club immediately for that sum, which I had my doubts was in the treasury, and wired Barney Dreyfuss, the moneyed man of our concern."[18] In fact, before selling Wagner to Pulliam, Barrow contacted the Pittsburgh Pirates, to whom he had earlier promised the first shot at his star. After hearing this Pulliam pleaded for more time and wired Dreyfuss for permission to up his bid. Dreyfuss agreed, and when the Pirates failed to counter, Dreyfuss and Pulliam landed their star for twenty-one hundred dollars.[19] Wagner, hitting .375 for Paterson, stepped right into the Colonels' lineup on July 19.

Wagner still had no position, but his .335 average over the rest of the season ensured that Clarke would keep him in the lineup. Wagner played mostly center field in 1897, first and third base in 1898, right field and third base in 1899, and right field in 1900. In fact, Clarke was often criticized for not finding a permanent place for Wagner, especially when Honus went into a (rare) batting slump. But wherever he played, Wagner was a star and with Clarke gave the Colonels two of the National League's best players as the team slowly gained respectability.

After the 1897 season Pulliam, increasingly directing the club, traded pitcher Bill Hill to Cincinnati for outfielder Dummy Hoy, pitcher Red Ehret, and shortstop Claude Ritchey. Although Hoy was a fine player, he was thirty-five years old, and Ehret was at the end of the line. Ritchey proved to be the key player in the trade. As a twenty-three-year-old rookie with the Reds in 1897, Ritchey had hit a respectable .282 but fielded poorly. He struggled with Louisville in 1898 as well, but in midseason Clarke moved him to second base, which he handled much better, becoming one of the NL's top second basemen for the next decade. Louisville inched forward again, to a 70-81 record and a ninth-place finish.

The Louisville management structure remained in flux throughout this period. The president of the team in the mid-1890s was Thomas Hunt Stucky, a local doctor who was apparently uninvolved in player acquisitions. Pulliam remained the secretary and worked full-time with the club. In early 1898 Dreyfuss, who now held a controlling share of the team's stock, resigned as club treasurer, citing poor health.[20] Pulliam took on the new duties, while Dreyfuss still spent many weekends scouting for baseball talent.

In late August he purchased twenty-year-old third baseman Tommie Leach from Auburn in the New York State League. Leach was a small man (five foot six, 150 pounds) who had surprising extra-base power for the time. Auburn had sent Leach to the New York Giants for a two-week trial, but Giants owner Andrew Freedman returned him immediately, saying, "Take your boy back before he gets hurt. We don't take midgets on the Giants."[21] Dreyfuss paid $650, and although it took a few years for Leach to become a regular player, he would fully justify the price and effort.

After the 1898 season Dreyfuss landed another future star, drafting pitcher Charles Phillippe from the Minneapolis club in the Western League. Although the twenty-six-year-old Phillippe was no kid, with only two years of Minor League experience behind him, he had proven to be a workhorse, finishing 22-18 in 363 innings in 1898, and Dreyfuss had been logging it all in his book. Still, he remained a businessman at heart, and when Phillippe did not accept the proffered contract, Dreyfuss was ready to walk away. After the barn on Phillippe's South Dakota farm burned down, the pitcher was ready to reconsider. "Sign with me and you will not regret it," said Dreyfuss. Phillippe signed.[22]

Just one year after he felt that he no longer had the energy to maintain an official position with the club, Dreyfuss reversed course. After the 1898 season ended, he resigned his position with the distillery and become a baseball man full-time. As he now held a majority of the stock in the team, he became team president, with Pulliam remaining as secretary. Reportedly, the other stockholders had been trying to persuade Dreyfuss to take over the team for some time. He had had a major influence in team affairs, especially the acquisition of players, for many years. But now, for the first time, he had complete authority to run the club as he saw fit.[23]

Meanwhile, the twelve-team National League had become even more dysfunctional and mismanaged. Frank Robison and his brother Stanley owned the generally competitive but poorly supported Cleveland Spiders, and then bought the moribund St. Louis Browns after the 1898 season. Frank Robison then transferred all of the best players from the Spiders (including Cy Young, Jesse Burkett, and player-manager Patsy Tebeau) to the Browns, creating an excellent team in St. Louis, its best since joining the NL, while destroying his Cleveland club, which finished the 1899 season with 20 wins and 134 losses.

In a similar vein, Brooklyn's Gus Abell and Charlie Ebbets combined forces with Baltimore's Harry von der Horst and Ned Hanlon, each taking an ownership stake in the other's club while moving most of the better Orioles players to Brooklyn. Von der Horst had reportedly resisted similar overtures from New York and Philadelphia before finally succumbing to the promise of great profits from the new combine. The Orioles had been a great club for many years, but in 1899 manager Ned Hanlon and stars Willie Keeler, Joe Kelley, Hugh Jennings, Bill Dahlen, Dan McGann, Doc McJames, Jim Hughes, and Al Maul joined the Dodgers, in exchange for much less accomplished players. The Brooklyn club, rechristened the Superbas, became the best club in the league while maintaining a virtual farm club in Baltimore, romping to its first pennant since the muddled 1890 season.[24]

At the same time, rumors were rampant that the NL was poised to eliminate four teams and return to its preferred eight-club circuit. The depleted Cleveland and Baltimore clubs were obvious elimination candidates, but Washington and Louisville were also considered to be in danger. Dreyfuss could read the tea leaves, and there were continual rumors that he was soliciting offers for the Colonels. In December 1898 Dreyfuss was reportedly negotiating with New York's Freedman. The Giants owner offered twenty-five thousand dollars for Clarke, but Dreyfuss had no interest in selling off his stars and being left with a shell of a ball club. Instead, he bought more stock in the Colonels and prepared to field a team for 1899.

The next sign of trouble for Dreyfuss came just prior to the 1899 season when a leaked version of an NL schedule showed that Louisville had lost most of its coveted Sunday dates, a clear sign that the Colonels were being pressured to leave the league. Louisville was one of the few NL cities that allowed their clubs to play home games on the

Christian Sabbath, and the Colonels counted on a lot of home Sundays to partially make up for their small market. Dreyfuss headed off this obvious challenge and got most of his Sundays restored, but for the remainder of his years in baseball he made sure to be involved in the annual schedule-making process.

Though Dreyfuss believed his team to be on the rise, the Colonels started poorly in 1899, and stories of disgruntled players caused Dreyfuss to travel with the club in June. When it became clear that catcher Malachi Kittredge was one of the complainers and was angling for Clarke's job, Dreyfuss released him and signed Chief Zimmer to catch. Coincidence or not, after sitting at just 16-38 on June 20, Louisville went 59-39 the rest of the way to nearly finish .500 (75-77), its best record since joining the league. Besides Wagner (.341) and Clarke (.340), the team was bolstered by fine years from second baseman Ritchey (.300) and supersub Leach (.288), whose fine play at third base forced Wagner back to the outfield. On the mound, newcomer Phillippe began his Major League career with twenty-one victories. With Louisville well out of the race, the Superbas tried to acquire Clarke and Wagner late in the season, forcing Dreyfuss to state publicly that no players would be sold under any circumstances.[25]

One of the more colorful characters for Louisville in the late 1890s was pitcher George Waddell, later universally known as "Rube" because of his childlike immaturity and personality. Waddell had pitched for various semipro teams in Pennsylvania before signing with Louisville and appearing twice in September 1897. Though his tenure was brief, Waddell had so annoyed Clarke that the manager sold him to Detroit in the Western League after the season, while retaining the right to recall him. After just nine games in Detroit, Waddell jumped the club and spent the rest of the summer pitching semipro ball. He returned to the Western League in 1899 with Columbus and Grand Rapids, where he fashioned a 26-8 record before Clarke finally decided to give him another shot. Waddell was excellent in this second stint, finishing 7-2 for the Colonels down the stretch, but he continued to drive the straitlaced Clarke batty by showing up late or not at all, drinking heavily, and not taking much of anything seriously. The Waddell-Clarke mismatch ultimately became more problematic, as time would tell.

Louisville's 1899 season was dramatically marred on August 12 when a large fire destroyed the grandstand of Eclipse Park. Dreyfuss worked quickly to erect temporary stands, but they were uncomfortable and provided no shade against Kentucky's brutal summer sun. After a twelve-game home stand ended on September 2, an unsentimental Dreyfuss announced that the remaining Louisville home games would be played on the road. Louisville ended the season on a thirty-eight-game road trip, during which they compiled a 24-13-1 record. Dreyfuss later claimed that the team would have been profitable for the first time in years, but the fire cost him his surplus. Little did anyone know that Louisville had seen its last Major League game.

Among its myriad difficulties, the NL of the 1890s was plagued by rowdyism: players fighting with umpires or other players, using profane language, and skirting the rules of the game. Fans were often no better, and brawls in the stands or attacks on umpires were common and often unpunished. Dreyfuss deplored such behavior and acted to stop it in Louisville. In early 1899 he announced that rowdy fans—including those shouting obscenities at opposing players—would be removed from Eclipse Park and not allowed to return.[26] By the end of that season, the *Sporting Life* was singing his praises: "Anyone who has taken to follow President Dreyfuss closely has noted the fact that he has kept his Louisville club free from the 'tough' element in making up his team and the Colonels come nearer filling the bill of gentlemen ball players than any team playing the game professionally. Everyone on the team is well educated and knows how to use his native language."[27]

Nevertheless, Dreyfuss knew his gentlemen team was in danger. After the 1899 season he renewed efforts to either sell his assets or find a way to stay in the league. Besides Wagner and Clarke, who were two of the more coveted players in the NL, he now had Ritchey, Zimmer, Phillippe, and Leach, all of whom were valuable players. At a minimum Dreyfuss negotiated with Robison of the Browns and James Hart of the Chicago Colts. In early November he struck a deal with William Kerr of the Pittsburgh Pirates, an agreement that briefly fell through before being resuscitated a month later. In the final arrangement Dreyfuss paid seventy thousand dollars for half of the Pirates and was installed as team president. As part of the transaction Dreyfuss engineered a "trade" to send Wagner, Clarke, Phillippe, Leach, Ritchey, Waddell, Zimmer, and six other players to the Pirates, in exchange for Jack Chesbro, George Fox, John O'Brien, Arthur Madison, William Gould, and twenty-five thousand dollars.[28] Harry Pulliam remained behind to run the depleted Colonels.

This last move was only temporary, as in March the NL finalized its plan to drop four teams, dissolving the Baltimore, Washington, Cleveland, and Louisville franchises. Pulliam came to Pittsburgh as the club secretary, and a few other Colonels followed, including Chesbro. Dreyfuss sold Patsy Donovan, who had been Pittsburgh's player-manager, to St. Louis, and installed Clarke.

Like the Colonels, the Pirates had not contended in the NL for several years, but the 1899 club had finished 76-73, two and a half games ahead of Louisville. They had a few promising young players, and the combined club appeared young and strong. The two best position players from the 1899 Pirates—center fielder Clarence Beaumont (.352) and third baseman Jimmy Williams (.354)—were both just twenty-two years old. Beaumont in particular was Dreyfuss's kind of player: he did not drink or smoke and spent much of his free time coaching baseball to local kids. It was Dreyfuss who gave Beaumont his enduring nickname of "Ginger," either because of his red hair or perhaps his hustle on the diamond. He was known as Ginger Beaumont for the rest of his life.[29]

The Pirates also had two good starting pitchers: twenty-seven-year-old Sam Leever (with a 21-23 record) and twenty-four-year-old Jesse Tannehill (24-14). "I am more than pleased with the deal," said Clarke, not surprisingly, in December. "I am satisfied that the Pittsburgh Club next season will become one of the strongest ever known in the National League."[30] Indeed, the new club seemed to have just about everything covered, as table 1 shows. Only first base seemed like a weak spot, but with Wagner on board Clarke had the flexibility to solve any such problem.

Table 1. Pittsburgh club, 1900

POSITION	PLAYER	AGE	1899 CLUB	1899 STATS
C	Chief Zimmer	39	Louisville	.298
2B	Claude Ritchey	26	Louisville	.300, 21 stolen bases
SS	Bones Ely	37	Pittsburgh	.278
3B	Jimmy Williams	23	Pittsburgh	.354, 27 triples, 28 doubles
3B	Tommy Leach	22	Louisville	.288
LF	Fred Clarke	27	Louisville	.340, 49 stolen bases
CF	Ginger Beaumont	23	Pittsburgh	.352, 31 stolen bases
RF	Tom McCreery	24	Pittsburgh	.324
UT	Honus Wagner	26	Louisville	.341, 45 doubles
P	Jesse Tannehill	25	Pittsburgh	24-14, 2.82 ERA, 322 innings
P	Deacon Phillippe	28	Louisville	21-17, 3.17 ERA, 321 innings
P	Sam Leever	28	Pittsburgh	21-23, 3.18 ERA, 379 innings
P	Jack Chesbro	26	Pittsburgh	6-9
P	Rube Waddell	23	Louisville	7-2, 3.08

Source: http://BaseballReference.com.

C. B. Power of the *Pittsburgh Leader* did have one concern. "Fred Clarke is one of the grandest ball players the game has ever known," wrote Power, "but I have serious doubts as to his abilities as a manager. Unfortunately Fred has never had the opportunity to play under a competent National League manager, and when he was placed in charge of the Louisville club he had no very clear idea of what constitutes the duties of a manager."[31] He cited Clarke's problems with some of his charges in 1899 and credited the acquisition of Zimmer with righting the ship. On the other hand, having players solve their own problems was not atypical for the time. As Clarke's managing style matured, he advocated personal responsibility, on and off the field, and relied on his players to learn to carry themselves properly.

With the combined Pirate team in 1900, it was thought that Clarke might play Wagner at first base, but he decided instead to position him in right field. Clarke ended up with Duff Cooley and Tom O'Brien, neither of whom hit well, at first, while both Tom McCreery and Leach, two fine players, were on the bench. The team ended up with a mediocre offense, as many of their star performers, including Clarke, Beaumont, and Williams, had off years. Wagner had the first of his many tremendous seasons—leading the league with a .381 batting average, forty-five doubles, and twenty-two triples—but no other player hit .300 or had more than twenty-two doubles. The team averaged 5.24 runs per game in a league that averaged 5.21.

The pitching staff, however, was the best and deepest in the league, though Clarke's problems with Waddell briefly made it less so. "We all loved Rube," Clarke later recalled. "But I knew I couldn't stay manager long if I let him take French leave whenever he wanted. During one of his absences I went to Barney Dreyfuss and said: 'Life is too short to monkey around with this guy. Suspend him and mail him his check.'" The Pirates instead loaned him to Connie Mack, managing the Milwaukee club in the (then minor) American League (AL), where Rube went 10-3. In September Clarke brought Waddell back, and he finished his split season with an 8-13 record for the Pirates but with a 2.37 earned run average (ERA) that led the National League. When Rube was around Clarke used five starters (Phillippe, Leever, Tannehill, Chesbro, and Waddell) in rotation, and all of them had excellent seasons. The team had started slowly (just 23-26 on July 17) but played well the rest of the year and ended up 79-60, in second place and just four and a half games behind the Superbas.

Bearing in mind the previous years' struggles and the slow start, the 1900 season was considered a success. With much of the attention and credit landing on Dreyfuss, and with the makings of a great Pirates team in place, William Kerr, who still owned half of the club, wanted to get back in the limelight. Right after the season he offered Tannehill to Cincinnati, but made an even bolder move in December when he attempted to fire Harry Pulliam, who he believed was too loyal to Dreyfuss. This led to a contentious board meeting in December, at which Kerr and his ally Phil Auten demanded that Dreyfuss either buy them out or sell. Dreyfuss gained an advantage when Kerr and Auten made a procedural error at the meeting, and he was able to pay thirty-five thousand dollars and gain complete control of the club.

In the meantime, Dreyfuss needed a first baseman. After scouring his baseball periodicals and his dope book, he purchased the contract of Kitty Bransfield from Worcester in the Class A Eastern League, one level below the Majors. Bransfield had been a catcher who played five games for the 1898 Boston Beaneaters before being sold to Worcester. After hitting .315 in 1899, he was converted to first base and in 1900 had hit .369 to lead the EL.

During the 1900–1901 off-season, when the American League announced that it would compete as a major league beginning in 1901, Dreyfuss and his fellow National League magnates faced their first significant player-procurement challenge in many years. After a decade-long NL monopoly, big-league players once again had competition for their services, driving up salaries and changing the way teams needed to compete for players. The AL put teams in Washington, Cleveland, and Baltimore—three of the recently vacated NL cities—and signed several topflight NL stars like Cy Young, Jimmy Collins, and Nap Lajoie, with the promise of many more to come. The new reality first affected the Pirates in March when Jimmy Williams jumped the club to sign with the new Baltimore AL club. Williams had a change of heart after a few weeks and told Dreyfuss he would return to the Pirates if

Dreyfuss would protect him from any legal action from Baltimore. Dreyfuss refused. Honus Wagner was reportedly offered a staggering twenty thousand dollars by the Chicago AL club (an amount possibly exaggerated), and Jack Chesbro was wooed by the Boston Americans. Both stayed put. Other than Williams, Dreyfuss managed to keep his team in the fold for 1901.

Clarke was not particularly bothered by the loss of Williams; he had Tommy Leach, at least Williams's equal, ready to step in. With Bransfield at first, the club had a steady infield for the first two months of the season. But Clarke was growing frustrated with shortstop Bones Ely's on-field struggles (hitting .208) and an attitude that grated on the manager. After Ely asked out of the lineup with a minor injury, Clarke told him, "Fred, if you don't play for me today, you will never play for me again."[32] When Ely reiterated that he could not play, Clarke benched him and soon had Dreyfuss release him. Clarke played shortstop himself for a day, then asked Wagner, who instead insisted that Leach get first crack at it. Eventually, Clarke put Leach back at third and moved Wagner to shortstop for the rest of the season. Wagner had previously played six positions on the diamond, but not until the middle of his fifth season did he play the position he would come to define.

After Waddell lost his first two starts in 1901, Clarke finally decided that the circus was not worth it, and Dreyfuss sold the pitcher to the Chicago Cubs in early May. In June Dreyfuss signed outfielder Lefty Davis, formerly of the Superbas; Davis was hitting just .209 in his rookie season and rarely playing, but with the Pirates he stepped into Wagner's old right-field post and hit .313 the rest of the year.

The 1901 Pirates played .500 ball for a few weeks, but took over first place in early June and cruised the rest of the season, finishing 90-49. Unlike the 1900 club, this team had outstanding offense to match its pitching. Wagner hit a predictable .353 with power, but Clarke, Beaumont, Davis, and Leach also hit over .300, while Ritchey and Bransfield were just under. The team finished second in the league in runs scored, while its defense allowed the fewest.

Typical of the Pirate staffs, none of the pitchers had gaudy win totals for the era because Clarke usually used four or five starters in rotation. Phillippe (21-12, 2.22), Chesbro (21-10, 2.38), Tannehill (18-10, 2.18), and Leever (14-5, 2.86) were nearly interchangeable, while Ed Doheny, picked up in July to take Waddell's spot, finished 6-2, 2.00. In the decade of 1901–10 there were sixty-nine pitcher seasons of 300 or more innings pitched in the National League, but a Pirates pitcher accomplished this feat only twice. The Pirates did, however, have four of the best ten ERAs in 1901.

No one was happier over the success of the Pirates than Barney Dreyfuss, in his first season of full control. The newspapers often remarked that he stood out among his fellow owners as much more than a businessman. "He never misses a game played at Exposition Park," raved *Baseball Magazine* a few years later, "and he never fails to keep a detailed score of the contest." He often discussed plays with the official scorer after the game, and he told Clarke if there was a managerial decision during the game with which he differed. In fact, he and his manager often had heated disagreements. Years later Clarke recalled: "Once I talked nasty to him and went back to try to apologize the next day. He stopped me. 'Fred,' he said, 'I wouldn't give a damn for any guy who always tries to agree with me.'"[33]

"So much has been said of Barney Dreyfuss as a wise owner," recalled Wagner, "a smart trader and a man who understands every angle of the baseball business that few know of him as a fan. If you ever sat next to him in a grandstand in the old days, though, you know him by sight and you'd never think the rooter next to you was the owner of the Pittsburgh club. Mr. Dreyfuss would travel with the team, mix up with the players and engage in many of their games, their amusements. He would mix up in practical jokes and give and take. But above all things, he was crazy to see his ball club win."[34] His ball club was winning now.

The American League was a magnificent success in 1901, matching the NL in attendance and getting through the season without overt financial difficulties. After the season the Milwaukee AL club was replaced by St. Louis, giving the upstarts a fourth city directly competing with the established NL. There were persistent rumors that the AL would move the Detroit club to Pittsburgh, but Dreyfuss worked to ward this off by renting plots of land where a stadium might be built. He also again managed to keep his players in the fold for the 1902 season amid further raiding of the NL by the new league.

Among the AL's advantages in the war were united owners, the strong leadership of league president Ban Johnson, and the significant financial backing of Cleveland magnate Charles Somers. The NL, meanwhile, remained in chaos. The feud between the league's two strongest owners, Brush of Cincinnati and Freedman of New York, often had league-wide ramifications. Brush was deeply involved in every aspect of the league and had been responsible for the NL's somewhat united efforts to keep salaries down. He resented Freedman's place as owner of the New York Giants, since Brush had wanted the New York franchise himself.

Freedman, closely connected with the corrupt Tammany Hall organization that ran the local Democratic Party and New York politics, had made a fortune selling real estate in New York based on those connections. He did not much care about baseball or the Giants—he enjoyed the power and prestige that he held by virtue of owning the team in the nation's largest city—and he resented that he had to share his gate receipts with teams from lesser cities. He was extremely unpopular with his fellow owners, his players, his team's fans, and the press. At one point when a league decision went against him, he reacted by deliberately letting his team deteriorate, figuring, with some justification, that the league needed a strong team in New York. "Base ball affairs in New York have been going just as I wished and expected them to go," he said in 1898. "I have given the club little attention and I would not give five cents for the best base ball player in the world to strengthen it."[35]

Brush and Freedman had reconciled a year or so before Johnson officially launched his Major League venture, with even more chaotic results. Brush proposed that the NL operate as a single trust company, dividing profits and losses (and players) according to market size. Freedman approved of the plan, which would allot him 30 percent of the league profits. Brush and Freedman recruited Soden of Boston and Robison of St. Louis, but the group could not find the fifth owner they needed to implement the scheme.

In particular, the plan seemed to target the upstart Dreyfuss, who had both the best players and the most profitable team. The league's owners were split into two factions, and the dispute played out at the 1901 league meetings over the naming of a new league president. The protrust forces wanted to reelect the hapless Young, while the others supported the stronger Albert Spalding. With no one willing to break the impasse, a compromise put the league in the hands of a three-man commission led by Brush. The trust concept, at least, was dead.

As good as the 1901 Pirates were—a club hardly challenged over the last four months of the season—the dominance of the 1902 team was extraordinary. The Pirates began the season 30-5, and hardly slowed down until season's end. They finished 103-36, twenty-seven and a half games ahead of the second-place Superbas—the largest margin ever in the years of the eight-team leagues. The club scored 5.5 runs per game, a run more than anyone else and 1.5 more than the league average. They allowed only 3.1 runs per game, by far the best mark in the league. Beaumont paced the NL with a .357 average, Leach led in triples and home runs, and Wagner in nearly everything else (runs, runs batted in [RBI], doubles, stolen bases, and slugging percentage, among others). The pitching was outstanding and deep. Chesbro finished 28-6, while the team's fifth starter, Ed Doheny, was 16-4 with a 2.53 ERA.

One reason for the Pirates' dominance was that they had been relatively unaffected by the American League's continued raiding, a condition that changed dramatically during the 1902 season. In midsummer Dreyfuss learned that Ban Johnson and Charles Somers had come to Pittsburgh and, with the aid of backup catcher Jack O'Connor, met with several Pirates. Dreyfuss suspended O'Connor immediately, but eventually determined that some of his players, including Chesbro, Tannehill, Davis, and Leach, had received salary advances from the rival league. The players initially believed that they would be playing for a new American League team in Pittsburgh but soon discovered that the new AL team was to be located in New York.

When the regular season ended, Dreyfuss released Chesbro, Tannehill, and Davis prior to a lucrative postseason series the team had planned against an American League all-star squad. Chesbro tried to make amends and return to the fold, but Dreyfuss would have none of it. "Chesbro is gone, and I am glad of it," Dreyfuss said of his twenty-eight-game winner. "I wish the American League luck with him, but no more of him in Pittsburgh."[36]

Tommy Leach, on the other hand, returned the money and told Dreyfuss he wanted to stay. Dreyfuss took him back and considered the matter closed. Ban Johnson disagreed, which touched off the largest skirmish to date between the two leagues. "Johnson is too much of an artistic prevaricator for me," said Dreyfuss. "I do not care about wrangling with him when he will not stick to the truth—does not, in fact, show any indication of ever hovering near same."[37]

At this time the relationship between the leagues was at its nadir due to even more dramatic events in New York. Brush and Freedman, thwarted in their plans to form a league trust, instead devised a plan to undermine the American League by destroying the AL's Baltimore Orioles franchise. First Brush convinced manager John McGraw, who was feuding with Johnson over the new league's efforts to eliminate umpire abuse and rowdyism, to jump to the NL to manage the Freedman's Giants, which McGraw did in the middle of the 1902 season. Meanwhile, Freedman maneuvered via friendly operatives to gain control of the Baltimore club. He soon released all the best Orioles, who then signed with either the Giants or Brush's Reds. Ban Johnson retaliated by having the league take control of the Baltimore franchise and soon announced that a franchise would be given to New York in 1903 to directly compete with the Giants.

The next step in the drama might have been the most important, as it laid the groundwork for the eventual peace settlement. In September Freedman threw in the towel and sold the Giants to Brush, who sold the Reds to a group of wealthy businessmen. Minority stockholder Garry Herrmann was named Cincinnati's team president and shortly emerged as one of baseball's key executives. Brush and McGraw soon built the New York Giants into a great team, and both would be unfriendly rivals to Dreyfuss. But the removal of Freedman from the ownership ranks, and the addition of Herrmann, had an immediate calming effect on the rest of the league.

Barney Dreyfuss, sensing an opportunity, stepped out of the shadows. At the league meetings in 1902, he proposed Harry Pulliam as the next NL president. Dreyfuss had undoubtedly done the necessary lobbying before the meeting, and his friend and longtime employee was quickly confirmed. The NL soon agreed to peace talks with the AL; along with Herrmann, Dreyfuss played a central role in the negotiations for the National League. In just a few weeks the warring factions recognized the AL as a major league, divvied up all of the disputed players, and cemented an agreement to respect each other's contracts. Of most importance to Dreyfuss: Tommy Leach would remain a Pirate, and the AL agreed to scrap any plans to put a team in Pittsburgh. Brush, for one, felt Dreyfuss had come out just a little too well and actually opposed the settlement until pressured by his fellow owners. "It's all right for me to have to buck an American League club on Manhattan Island," Brush complained, "so long as he is saved any opposition in Pittsburgh."[38] Nonetheless, peace was at hand.

Newly triumphant on and off the field, heading into the 1903 season Dreyfuss still had to replace an outfielder and two pitchers. Late in the 1902 season Dreyfuss acquired twenty-year-old Jimmy Sebring from Worcester, and the outfielder played 19 games in September, hitting .325 in 80 at bats. For 1903 Sebring replaced Davis in right. Replacing Tannehill and Chesbro was another matter. After using five great pitchers to start 134 of 141 games in 1902, Clarke needed twelve different starters in 1903. Brickyard Kennedy, acquired to be the fourth starter, managed only fifteen starts. Third starter Ed Doheny was in the midst of another excellent season in 1903 when a series of bizarre behavioral incidents sent him to a rest home for a few weeks in July and then ended his season in September. Unfortunately, he deteriorated further. In October he attacked both a doctor and a nurse and spent the rest of his life in mental asylums.

Due mainly to their pitching concerns, the Pirates regressed by 12.5 games from 1902, but they still finished 91-49 and won the pennant by 6.5 games. Their league-leading offense carried them, especially Wagner (.355, 30 doubles, 19 triples), Clarke (.351, 32 doubles, 15 triples), Beaumont (.341, 209 hits, 137 runs), and Leach (.298, 17 triples). The two remaining star pitchers—Leever and Phillippe—each won 25 games, with Leever posting a league-leading 2.06 ERA. In June, when

Doheny was still healthy, the Pirates threw a record six consecutive shutouts, with Leever and Phillippe contributing two each.

Late in the 1903 season, Dreyfuss met with Henry J. Killilea, owner of the AL champion Boston Americans, and agreed to a postseason series between the two teams. Although the leagues had made peace in January, it was the playing of this first (AL versus NL) World Series that cemented the partnership. Unfortunately for Dreyfuss, the Pirates were not at full strength when the best-of-nine World Series commenced. Already down to just two pitchers in September, late that month Sam Leever hurt his arm skeet shooting and could manage just ten painful innings in the Series. Deacon Phillippe, the team's sole remaining healthy and effective pitcher, remarkably started (and completed) five of the eight games, winning three times. It was not enough, as he went down to defeat in both Game Seven and Game Eight, and the Pirates fell five games to three.

Far from despondent, Dreyfuss donated his entire share of the Series gate receipts to his team, meaning that the Pirates players ended up making more money from the World Series than the victorious Americans. Moreover, the postseason Series was not steeped with the same significance as it would be with later generations of baseball fans. The Pirates were three-time NL pennant winners and widely hailed as one of the greatest teams ever assembled.

Just five years after Dreyfuss was nearly forced out of baseball, he stood at the very top of his sport. He had astutely foreseen extermination of his Louisville franchise and outfoxed his fellow magnates to end up with a better team in a larger city. By successfully anticipating and countering the impact of the American League's challenge, proving more adept than any of his fellow NL magnates, Dreyfuss warded off the most serious attempted inroads from the new league, leaving his Pirates the dominant NL franchise. Although his fellow owners may have resented his success for a time, thanks as much to Dreyfuss as anyone, the NL was immeasurably stronger and healthier in 1903 than at any time in its past.

Over the next three decades Dreyfuss ran the Pirates smartly and effectively, competitive nearly every season. Although well respected for his intelligence and diligence, he was not always an easy boss. "At times he could be severe, dominating, critical and stubborn," wrote Fred Lieb. "Many ball players felt he was a hard man to get along with. Yet he befriended many of the men who worked for him."[39] Many of his former players became his managers and coaches.

To remain competitive Dreyfuss continued to track baseball talent throughout the country and to know in detail the workings of his own team and most others. He coordinated this knowledge with his manager—Clarke through 1915 and others thereafter—in acquiring players to fill needs on the team. He picked up catcher George Gibson from Montreal in 1905, pitcher Vic Willis from the Boston Beaneaters in 1905, and pitcher Babe Adams from Denver in 1907. When Adams told Dreyfuss about Owen "Chief" Wilson, a Des Moines outfielder who had given Adams fits, Dreyfuss promptly bought him. Those players helped the Pirates capture the 1909 pennant and their first World Series.

Dreyfuss remained, first and foremost, a businessman. As Gibson later related, during negotiations after the 1909 World Series, Dreyfuss told him to fill in whatever salary figure he felt was fair. Gibson told Dreyfuss he wanted $12,000, one of baseball's highest salaries, and the right to be released as a free agent when Dreyfuss no longer wanted him, not placed on waivers to be claimed by any team for the $1,800 waiver price. "Gibby, I'll write it in the contract," Dreyfuss agreed. "No," Gibson demurred. "You've always been a man of your word with me." And Dreyfuss promised to release him when the time came.

Seven years later Dreyfuss placed Gibson on waivers, and the New York Giants claimed him. Gibson complained to Dreyfuss and Giants manager John McGraw, and the latter agreed to pay Gibson an additional $1,800 to get him to report. In 1919 when Dreyfuss asked Gibson to manage the Pirates, the player reminded his former owner of his broken promise. Dreyfuss grumbled and offered Gibson the $1,800 he received from the Giants as a peace offering. Gibson accepted both the manager's job and the money, which he had "already gotten . . . from John McGraw. But Barney Dreyfuss didn't know that."[40]

Dreyfuss made another lasting contribution to Pittsburgh and to baseball in 1909 with the opening of Forbes Field, the Pirates' spectacular new ballpark. Rather than erecting another rickety wooden structure, Dreyfuss built a three-tiered ballpark out of steel and concrete, much like Philadelphia's Shibe Park, which opened the same year. Spending roughly $1 million, Dreyfuss built the stadium on seven acres he had purchased in the Oakland neighborhood, a ten-minute trolley ride from downtown. Ignoring skeptics who thought Forbes Field too remote, too big (it originally seated twenty-three thousand fans), and too expensive, Dreyfuss forged ahead and in June 1909 opened a park that many considered the finest in the land.

With the increased revenues from Forbes Field and his generally well-run team, Dreyfuss continued to spend money on increasingly expensive talent that he or one of his contacts thought could help his club. In July 1911 Dreyfuss shocked the baseball establishment by purchasing hurler Marty O'Toole from St. Paul, a club in the American Association, for $22,500. This almost doubled baseball's previous high-dollar purchases: Rube Marquard by the Giants in 1908 for $11,000 and Lefty Russell by the Athletics in 1910 for $12,000.[41]

Unfortunately, O'Toole never panned out; Dreyfuss later believed he had been sold damaged goods, that O'Toole had been overworked. To Dreyfuss's credit, he understood that scouting and bringing in new players was an inexact science, and he continued his search for players. He bought Max Carey from South Bend in 1910, Wilbur Cooper from Columbus in 1912, Carson Bigbee from Tacoma in 1916, Pie Traynor from Portsmouth in 1920, Kiki Cuyler from Bay City (Mississippi) in 1921, and Glenn Wright from Kansas City in 1923.

In 1912 Dreyfuss purchased the contract of George Sisler from Columbus. Typically, he first scouted Sisler himself after receiving a recommendation from one of his friendly contacts. Unfortunately for the Pirates, Dreyfuss lost a bitter fight for Sisler's rights when the National Commission, baseball's governing body, awarded him to the St. Louis Browns, ruling that Sisler's father had not signed off on the youth's Pittsburgh contract.[42]

By the 1920s most of the Pirates' talent hunting was done by hired scouts, but Dreyfuss still kept his dope book, still knew who all the best Minor League players were and what the major newspapers had to say about them. In 1923 Dreyfuss hired Joe Devine to scout California, and within a few years Devine had landed Joe Cronin, Paul Waner, Lloyd

Waner, and Arky Vaughan. All four of those players ended up in the Hall of Fame, as did Wagner, Clarke, Carey, Cuyler, and Traynor. The Pirates won two more pennants in the 1920s, including the 1925 World Series.

In 1919 Dreyfuss's only son, Sam, graduated from Princeton and began working for the Pirates. Sam started on the business side, becoming treasurer in 1923, and by 1929 he was vice president (VP) and had become, like his father, one of the most respected and well-informed executives in the game.[43] In 1930 the elder Dreyfuss stepped aside to let his son run the team. Sam's sudden death from pneumonia in early 1931, at age thirty-four, was a crushing blow to Barney both personally and professionally. A year into semiretirement, Barney again took over the Pirates before his own death less than a year later in February 1932.

"I cannot tell you how deeply I feel the loss of Barney Dreyfuss," said NL president John A. Heydler. "He discovered more great players than any man in the game, and his advice and counsel always were sought by his associates." Jacob Ruppert, the owner of the New York Yankees, spoke for many of his colleagues when he said, "He was first and always a sportsman of the highest class."[44] Lieb summed up Dreyfuss's legacy: "He was one of the game's greatest and most far-seeing club owners."[45]

Dreyfuss operated the Pittsburgh Pirates for thirty-two seasons, winning six pennants and finishing in the first division twenty-six times. The Pirates ownership passed to his widow, Florence, and the club was run by son-in-law William Benswanger for the next fourteen years. In the eight decades since Dreyfuss's death, the Pirates have provided occasional joy to their fan base, but have won only three pennants.

Dreyfuss succeeded in this era because his unique attention to detail combined with his competitive fire, a knack for negotiating the charged politics of his league, and his ability to engender loyalty from his players created an organization one step ahead of most of the competition. At a time when the man in charge needed to be a jack-of-all-trades, Dreyfuss effectively understood both the detail and the general to assemble one of the great franchises of the early twentieth century.

But a century ago a man in charge like Dreyfuss did not need to be a representative of ownership. A strong, secure manager could also build and run a consistently successful organization, as we will see with John McGraw.

2 Field Manager

I don't know what he had, but he had a lot of it.—BOBBY MARKS, assistant
football coach, on his legendary boss, Paul "Bear" Bryant

In May 1905 manager John McGraw and his New York Giants hosted
the Pittsburgh Pirates for a four-game series. On May 19 McGraw got
into an argument with an umpire, as he was wont to do, and accused
the arbiter of being in the pocket of Barney Dreyfuss, the Pittsburgh
owner. As McGraw saw it, Harry Pulliam, the league president who
hired the umpires, was Dreyfuss's friend and former employee. Dreyfuss was seated nearby and overheard the remarks. The next day Mc-
Graw got into another heated exchange and was kicked out of the
game. On his way to the clubhouse, he ran into Dreyfuss, who was
talking with some friends.

"Hey Barney!" McGraw shouted sarcastically and repeatedly, and
when Dreyfuss could no longer ignore him he yelled, "Barney Dreyfuss bet $2,200 against $1,800 that the Pittsburgh club would beat
us." He followed up loudly and abusively that the Pittsburgh owner
owed money to a bookie and was welshing on bets. According to one
account, McGraw may have "caused aspersions upon the Jewish race,"
all while using language that was "constantly full of profanity, vulgar
words and epithets." Dreyfuss was embarrassed by the public exchange
and filed a formal complaint with the league. Pulliam, who had been
crusading to clean up the game during his three years as president,
suspended McGraw for fifteen days, while the league mildly rebuked
Dreyfuss for engaging with a rival manager.

McGraw and John Brush, the Giants owner, took the league to court,
where a judge ruled in favor of the Giants, overturning the suspension.
John McGraw had long lived his life according to his own set of laws,
and he certainly did not believe that anyone, including the president

of the National League, had any power over him. And in this instance among many others, he proved to be correct.[1]

While Dreyfuss had for many years embodied the powerful and brilliant baseball owner, one of the first who had never played the game but learned it so thoroughly that he could build and lead a great team and organization, John McGraw was one of the last and most successful embodiments of a different sort, a veteran field manager who also performed the duties that would later be associated with a general manager. After his own great playing career, McGraw became not just a legendary manager but also a man who completely controlled the running of his team on and off the field. McGraw never owned more than a minority interest in the Giants, but his bosses let him run baseball operations without interference. McGraw often did his own scouting, made trades, signed contracts, and generally told his players how to play and how to act. His owners could be content to sit back and watch the pennants and profits pile up.

Pittsburgh's Fred Clarke, talking years later about his own managerial style, which called for players learning the game well enough that they could make their own decisions on the field, said, "McGraw changed that in his early days with the Giants, when he began to run the whole game, and call every pitch, and every move of the batsman. That was a style peculiar to McGraw, one of the great managers. It is not a style fit for the whole of baseball, and I believe that dictation from the bench is the cause of so many players failing as managers in recent years. They have been brought up to lean on somebody else."[2] While Clarke was willing to take a backseat to all of the talented players on his team, John McGraw never took a backseat to anyone. McGraw *was* the New York Giants, who were one of the best teams in baseball for all of McGraw's reign. Outside of New York they were baseball's most hated team and McGraw the most hated manager.

Sportswriter Frank Graham described the feisty McGraw as "five feet, seven inches tall, dark-haired, dark-eyed, and slightly built. Restless, aggressive, and quick tempered, he would fight anybody—and frequently did."[3] McGraw played the bulk of his big-league career in the 1890s for the National League's Baltimore Orioles. Just eighteen when he joined Baltimore (then part of the American Association) in

1891, he was one of the building blocks of a team that captured three straight NL pennants beginning in 1894. The Orioles were led by brilliant manager Ned Hanlon, who acquired several little-used players from around the league—including Hughie Jennings, Willie Keeler, and Joe Kelley—and turned them into topflight stars. Despite his young age, McGraw quickly became one of the leaders on a club known both for its innovative brilliance and for its rowdy lawlessness.

The Orioles of the era closely mirrored McGraw's on-field personality. The team was known for its "inside baseball" and heady play. As we explored in *Paths to Glory*,[4] the 1890s Orioles team has been credited with inventing or popularizing the hit-and-run, the pickoff, cutoff plays, and the suicide squeeze, among other strategic ploys. Although they may not have actually been first, the team certainly used these plays, often to great advantage. On the other hand, the Orioles would resort to almost any tactic to win, including hiding balls in the outfield, vicious verbal and physical intimidation of umpires and opposing players, cutting across the diamond from first to third when the umpire was not looking, and tripping or grabbing opposing base runners to slow them down. This brand of baseball—clever play combined with purposeful violence—would define McGraw's teams throughout his managerial career.

In 1899 the owners of the Brooklyn and Baltimore teams formed a syndicate, and Hanlon and most of his best players moved to Brooklyn. The twenty-six-year-old McGraw stayed behind and was named manager of the gutted Orioles, earning acclaim for bringing his team in fourth despite the talent attenuation. After the season Baltimore was contracted as part of the NL reduction to eight teams, and McGraw ended up with St. Louis, as a player only, for the 1900 season.

In 1901 McGraw hooked up with Ban Johnson, who was in the process of turning his American League into a second major league. Johnson offered McGraw the stewardship and part ownership in the AL's new Baltimore franchise. McGraw brought his team in fifth, but often clashed with league president Johnson over umpire abuse and general rowdyism. One of Johnson's goals was to keep the NL hooliganism out of his league, making his selection of McGraw an odd one, and one ultimately doomed to fail.

In 1902, still just twenty-nine, McGraw found himself in the middle of one of the key battles of the war between the two leagues. As recounted in the previous chapter, McGraw's decision to bolt to the New York Giants led to the destruction of the Baltimore club, the creation of what would become the New York Yankees, and ownership changes for two NL teams. The Giants had been a bad team for several years, due mainly to the petty and destructive leadership of owner Andrew Freedman. But Freedman's final act as owner—the hiring of John McGraw—put the team on its path to greatness.

The Giants were coming off a seventh-place finish in 1901 and wound up last in 1902 despite the midseason acquisition of several released Orioles, including two future Hall of Famers, Joe McGinnity and Roger Bresnahan, plus Jack Cronin and Dan McGann. McGraw's restructuring of his roster, however, took effect quickly, and the team jumped all the way to second in 1903 and a pennant in 1904. The only member of the starting lineup left from the pre-McGraw days was catcher Jack Warner, but the strength of the early McGraw teams was the pitching of Christy Mathewson, whom he inherited, and McGinnity. McGraw also continually looked for tactical advantages within the game. He greatly expanded the practice of relief pitching: from 1903 to 1909 the Giants had 102 saves (as retroactively calculated), nearly twice as many as the second-ranked NL team (54).[5] In the latter year McGraw also began using Doc Crandall as baseball's first recognized relief ace.

Unlike Dreyfuss, Giants owner John Brush gave his manager complete authority over the design of his roster, a role that would fall to the general manager in the decades ahead. After McGraw captured the NL pennant in 1904, he and Brush refused to play the AL champion Boston Americans—McGraw hated Johnson from his time in the AL, and Brush was still angry that Johnson had put a franchise in New York. When the Giants repeated in 1905, they acceded and played the Philadelphia Athletics, beating them in five games. Over the next several years the NL was dominated by three clubs—Pittsburgh, Chicago, and New York—who combined to win all thirteen pennants between 1901 and 1913 and often finished in the top three slots in the league. McGraw's teams lost a few tight races while rebuilding, before breaking through for three consecutive pennants from 1911 through 1913. Other than the great Mathewson, McGraw rarely had superstars on his team; instead, he had an ever-changing group of players from whom he managed to wring two or three good years. The best position players on his 1911–13 teams were second baseman Larry Doyle and catcher Chief Meyers. When this Giants club began to slip, McGraw again restructured his team and won the flag with a different core in 1917. He rarely became attached to his players, even those he took pride in developing. When a player lost effectiveness, or McGraw felt they were about to, he replaced them. He dealt Doyle in 1916 after a strong 1915 season.

Brush and McGraw also succeeded in turning the Giants into baseball's most valuable and successful franchise. From 1903 to 1917, McGraw's Giants won six pennants, finished second five times, and regularly led the league in attendance. According to an article in *McClure's*, "The Giants now constitute the most valuable baseball property in the country, being held at more than a million dollars not including the grounds, which are leased. Brush has made immense profits from the team, ranging from $100,000 to $300,000 or more annually."[6]

In order to understand how McGraw built his teams, it is instructive to consider how he managed them. McGraw believed in aggressive, heady play. Leonard Koppett described seven ideas that McGraw learned from the great Ned Hanlon, manager of the Orioles. These ideas became McGraw's "bible":

1. Tactics can be employed to gain a small edge: the bunt, hit and run, steals, etc.
2. Conditioning and personal discipline are important [although McGraw employed notable exceptions].
3. The manager's authority is absolute.
4. Aggressiveness is a primary asset.
5. Speed helps you win.
6. Deciding where and when a man should play is as important as his generalized abilities.
7. It's us against them.[7]

McGraw worked hard to instill two distinct and, to a large extent, contradictory characteristics in his charges. On the one hand, he demanded absolute obedience and loyalty. McGraw felt any challenge to his authority would lead to the team losing its focus and drive, and he could be extremely unpleasant, abusive, and vindictive in trying to instill this single-mindedness. On the flip side, he also demanded a quickness of mind on the ball field. McGraw carried this need for intelligent ballplayers to its logical conclusion and spent the effort instilling, in the words of Koppett, "high morale and a sense of self-respect."[8] A player was required to learn the McGraw way to play, to play well, and to remain obedient; if he did all this, McGraw would show him loyalty and pay him well.

Many of McGraw's longtime charges tolerated his abuse, and possibly even felt a certain affinity toward him, because they recognized his approach could lead to pennants, higher salaries, and their own improved performance. This faith was most evident in players McGraw signed at a young age as amateurs or from the Minors, players he could more easily mold. Because he did not become attached to players, he also did not play favorites. It may have rankled the veterans who had put up with him for so long, but McGraw was completely evenhanded when selecting his team. The players McGraw clashed with—like Edd Roush or Billy Southworth—generally had prior big-league experience or a strong independent or unconventional streak. Although McGraw recognized the value in some of these players, he often became frustrated and traded them away.

McGraw was extremely confident in his ability to recognize talent. Because of this conceit, and his desire to be able to mold his charges, McGraw often introduced players to the Major Leagues at an extremely young age and, if they performed well, made them regulars. After all, he had debuted in the Major Leagues at only eighteen and was a star soon thereafter. McGraw was willing to live with youthful mistakes as long as he recognized a full effort. The famous 1908 "Merkle Boner" was a base-running error made by a nineteen-year-old kid whom McGraw thereafter publicly and consistently defended. Table 2 lists several young players that debuted for McGraw. The final six are now members of baseball's Hall of Fame.

Table 2. McGraw's young players

NAME	AGE	DEBUT YEAR	REGULAR YEAR
Fred Merkle	18	1907	1910
Larry Doyle	20	1907	1908
George Kelly	19	1915	1920
Ross Youngs	20	1917	1918
Frankie Frisch	21	1919	1920
Travis Jackson	18	1922	1923
Fred Lindstrom	18	1924	1925
Mel Ott	17	1926	1928

Source: http://BaseballReference.com.

To illustrate McGraw's team-building approach, in this chapter we explore the years after his club captured the 1917 pennant, when the Giants won ninety-eight games and topped the league in both runs and ERA. Despite the club's gaudy statistics, McGraw realized that it was not built to last.

As McGraw set out to rebuild his pennant winner, he was operating in an environment well suited to his skills. During the late teens and early 1920s, the rules governing the Major League–Minor League draft favored the high Minors, giving them unprecedented control over their players and consequently driving up the price of top Minor Leaguers. Once a few top amateurs recognized that signing with a high Minor League team might be more restrictive of their career, McGraw utilized his network of scouts to sign several who might earlier have gone to a Minor League team, such as those identified in table 2. He also used his team's financial advantage to purchase Minor Leaguers at their inflated prices.

The ownership of the Giants changed twice in the 1910s. John Brush, who had owned the club since 1903, died in late 1912. Control of the Giants then passed to Brush's son-in-law Harry Hempstead, who had little experience as a baseball executive. He maintained a cordial relationship with McGraw, who had hoped to secure an executive role in the reorganization after Brush's death. Hempstead enjoyed the prestige that came from running baseball's premier franchise, although he never really warmed to the task.[9] In early 1919 he sold a controlling interest to Charles Stoneham, a Manhattan stock trader.

Stoneham made his fortune operating what was known as a "bucket shop," something of a cut-rate stockbrokerage that played fast and loose with both the rules and their investors' money. Stoneham loved horse racing, had part ownership in a racetrack, and enjoyed gambling of all stripes. He cavorted with a number of New York's more unsavory characters, including underworld financier Arnold Rothstein, who arranged the fix of the 1919 World Series. Stoneham generally let McGraw have his way on player transactions, kept him highly paid (he was in the midst of a five-year contract worth forty thousand dollars per year that would be bumped significantly upon expiration), and loaned him the money to buy into a minority ownership position.[10]

At the start of 1918 McGraw traded Buck Herzog to reacquire aging favorite Larry Doyle and also landed pitcher Jesse Barnes in the swap. Barnes became a mainstay of the Giant pitching staff for several years, winning a total of seventy-three games from 1919 through 1922.

The Barnes deal was one of several between the Giants and Boston Braves over the next few years. Although not as infamous as the Yankees' pillaging of the Red Sox in this same period, the Giants acquired several stars from the Braves using a similar combination of cash and marginal ballplayers. This process accelerated when New Yorker George Washington Grant led a syndicate that purchased the Braves in 1919. Grant was a pal of both McGraw and Stoneham and, to the consternation of Boston's NL baseball fans, frequently did the bidding of his New York friends. Although Grant denied it, Stoneham likely loaned Grant around one hundred thousand of the four-hundred-thousand-dollar purchase price.[11]

In a year heavily affected by the world war, the 1918 Giants fell to second place, ten and a half games behind the Chicago Cubs. In one bright spot, McGraw installed twenty-one-year-old outfielder Ross Youngs as the team's regular right fielder. The Giants had acquired Youngs back in 1916 for a "fancy price," on the recommendation of

Dick Kinsella, one of baseball's first full-time scouts.[12] Kinsella had joined McGraw in 1907 and for the next couple of decades, with a few interruptions, remained McGraw's key lieutenant in digging out prospects.[13] The Giants optioned Youngs to Double-A Rochester and made him an outfielder. His .356 mark convinced McGraw the youngster was ready, and Youngs went on to become a Giants mainstay and one of the league's top players.

Along with his willingness to play youngsters, McGraw had a habit of acquiring players with character issues. Years earlier he had coaxed a couple of good seasons out of two players with alcohol problems, Larry McLean and Bugs Raymond, though neither proved to be a long-term solution. In July 1918 McGraw purchased pitcher Fred Toney, a man with a rather unusual set of problems, from Cincinnati. After a dominant 1917 season (24-16, 2.20 ERA, with a ten-inning no-hitter), Toney was arrested for claiming his wife and children as dependents to escape the military draft, though he had not lived with them for three years. Although his trial resulted in a hung jury, his troubles were not over. He was subsequently arrested for violating the Mann Act by traveling with a young woman who was not his wife. Passed in 1910, the Mann Act was designed to prevent "white slavery" (the forced prostitution of women). Under the austere moral climate of the time, even noncommercial sex became subject to the act.

At the time of his sale to the Giants, Toney had a 6-10 record and was awaiting trial. The opportunistic McGraw saw a chance to buy low and received a strong second half from Toney. After the season Toney was found guilty and spent time in prison before rejoining the club on May 1, 1919. Toney subsequently turned in three excellent seasons for McGraw's club.

McGraw picked up an even more troublesome player in 1919. Hal Chase, one of the era's greatest defensive first basemen and one of baseball's most nefarious crooks, had been suspended by Cincinnati during the 1918 season because Reds manager Christy Mathewson believed he was throwing games. At a hearing in January 1919 NL president John Heydler cleared Chase of any wrongdoing. Though there were several witnesses who testified to Chase's malfeasance, the absence of Mathewson (he was in France with the American Expeditionary Force [AEF]), the ambiguity of the evidence, the effective advocacy of Chase's three attorneys, and the lack of recent precedent in dealing with crooked players all combined to influence Heydler's decision.

McGraw always liked Chase as a ballplayer and believed, as he always had, that he could get him to play. But by the end of the 1919 season, McGraw benched Chase due to his own suspicions and more damaging information uncovered by Heydler's continuing investigation. Though not formally banned, Chase never again played in Major League Baseball.[14]

In July 1919 McGraw gambled again, sending outfielder Dave Robertson to the Cubs for Shufflin' Phil Douglas, one of the biggest (six foot three, 190 pounds) and most intriguing players in the game. Douglas came from Cedartown, Georgia, and grew up in Tennessee. Playing semipro ball by the age of fourteen, he soon developed into a topnotch pitcher. His best pitch was the (then legal) spitball, but he also threw a fastball, curve, and changeup. Giants catcher Frank Snyder later called him "the best right-handed pitcher I ever caught."[15]

Douglas was also a chronic alcoholic, a condition so severe that he often went AWOL from his team. He was never really able to accept the regimen of Major League life and its daily grind. "In his younger days in the south, in country-town baseball, Douglas pitched about once a week; between games he loafed, for the most part, and drunk corn whiskey," John Lardner recounted.[16] By the time McGraw acquired Douglas, he was twenty-nine years old and had already pitched for four different Major League teams. Typically, McGraw believed he could harness Douglas's obvious talents. For a while, he did. In both 1920 and 1921 Douglas hurled more than two hundred innings and won fourteen and fifteen games, respectively.

A week after picking up Douglas, McGraw acquired Art Nehf, an untroubled pitcher, from the Braves for four players and about fifty thousand dollars. Late-season trades often aroused consternation during a pennant race—the Giants were just a game and a half behind first-place Cincinnati at the time of the deal—but the trading deadline of August 1 would remain for several more years. Only 8-9 with Boston, Nehf pitched well down the stretch for the Giants (9-2), although the Reds ended up pulling away in the race. Over the next five years Nehf won eighty-seven games as the anchor of the Giants staff and one of the National League's top left-handers. With Nehf, Barnes, Toney, and Douglas, in less than two years McGraw had assembled one of the league's better starting rotations without surrendering much value.

With the exception of Youngs, the regular 1919 position players were all twenty-nine or older. In July McGraw acquired catcher Frank Snyder from the St. Louis Cardinals for Ferdie Schupp, a once-great pitcher who had set the single-season record for lowest ERA in 1916, then finished 21-7 in 1917, but could not regain his effectiveness after the war. Snyder was twenty-five at the time of the deal and became the Giants' best catcher since Chief Meyers was in his prime several years earlier.

More important, in the spring of 1919 McGraw held a tryout for a young infielder from Fordham University named Frankie Frisch, dubbed the Fordham Flash for his speed and overall athletic ability. Frisch, a three-sport star, had come recommended by Fordham coach Art Devlin, who had played for McGraw with the Giants. McGraw hoped to sign the youngster after his graduation, but first had to contend with Frisch's father, a wealthy linen merchant who expected his son to follow him into the family business. The youngster chose baseball, signing for a relatively meager two-hundred-dollar bonus and four-hundred-dollar per month salary. Frisch did secure an atypical clause in his contract requiring the Giants to give him his unconditional release if he did not succeed in his first two years.[17] The twenty-year-old Frisch played sparingly for a couple of months before earning regular playing time split between second and third bases over the last six weeks of the season. McGraw's 1919 Giants had three promising young players in the lineup (Youngs, Snyder, and Frisch) and four talented pitchers (Toney, Barnes, Douglas, and Nehf).

In 1920 McGraw gave the first base job to George Kelly, who had had several trials with the Giants and Pirates since 1915. Still just twenty-four, the San Franciscan earned a starting role and kept it for seven years. Kelly was a great defensive first baseman, a decent hitter, and smart enough to figure out how to get along with McGraw: "McGraw was all business, not much of a sense of humor; he relied on discipline and smart baseball," Kelly recalled. "You were expected to be watching, thinking, learning all the time."[18] But he also insisted on doing it his way. "You would never go up to him and say, 'Well I thought . . . ,' because he'd brush you off with, 'You just go out and play. I'll do the thinking.' And he believed that, too!"[19]

The Giants played terribly at the start of the 1920 season and were just 18-25 on June 7. On that day McGraw dealt aging shortstop Art Fletcher to the Philadelphia Phillies for Dave Bancroft, the league's best shortstop. Although the deal was announced as a straight-up trade, penurious Phillies owner William Baker actually received about a hundred thousand dollars from the Giants.[20] Still just twenty-nine, Bancroft had starred as a rookie for the Phillies pennant winner back in 1915. After a couple more first-division finishes, Baker began selling off his stars, and by the early 1920s the Phillies were beginning a twenty-year run as one of the most hapless clubs in Major League history. In New York Bancroft anchored the shortstop position for the next four seasons.

Although the Giants played much better over the second half (50-27), they had to settle for their third consecutive second-place finish, this time trailing their bitter rivals, the Brooklyn Dodgers. The Giants were led by three twenty-game winners (Barnes, Toney, and Nehf) and by the breakthrough of Ross Youngs, who hit .351. But McGraw's high tolerance for off-field problems, both for himself and for his team, reached new lows in 1920. The team had to deal with Douglas's repeated absences and unreliability and more than its share of rumors about various team members fixing games. But there was more.

The Giants had purchased outfielder Benny Kauff back in 1916 after the collapse of the Federal League. Kauff had been the FL's biggest star, leading the circuit in batting average and stolen bases in both years of the league's Major League seasons. Somewhat surprisingly, McGraw liked the fast-living, flashy-dressing Kauff, and he had tried unsuccessfully to get him to jump to the Giants in April 1915 before the league's demise. The off-season peace settlement allowed the Federals to dispose of their player contracts, and Newark owner Harry Sinclair sold Kauff to the Giants for thirty-five thousand dollars.

The trouble began in December 1919 when Kauff, an early automobile enthusiast with a small vehicle sales business, was arrested and indicted for auto theft. He played the entire 1920 season with the trial pending. Meanwhile, late in the season Kauff was called to testify in front of the Chicago grand jury investigating baseball game fixing. Kauff told the jury that he had been offered money in late 1919 by teammate Heinie Zimmerman to help lose games. Fred Toney also testified that he had also been approached by Zimmerman. The next day McGraw testified that while he had tossed Zimmerman and Chase off his club, Kauff was innocent of any wrongdoing. In March 1921 Zimmerman struck back by claiming in an affidavit that he was actually carrying an offer from a gambler to Kauff, who may have been more interested than he had acknowledged. McGraw continued to defend Kauff.[21]

Commissioner Kenesaw Landis did not share McGraw's confidence and declared Kauff ineligible in April 1921, just before the start of his car theft trial. During the trial two of Kauff's employees claimed that they and Kauff stole a car, sold it for eighteen hundred dollars, and split the proceeds. Kauff maintained he had bought the car and resold it but that when he was notified it was stolen returned the money. He added that he was the victim of employees who were running an auto theft ring without his knowledge. Kauff's defense produced several character witnesses, including McGraw. The jury found Kauff not guilty after a short deliberation. Not surprisingly, the acquittal had no effect on Landis's decision. Kauff challenged his suspension in court and received a temporary injunction that would reinstate him. On appeal, however, Landis's suspension was upheld, and Kauff never played organized baseball again.

In 1920 McGraw had another off-field distraction—this one of his own making. The bizarre series of events surrounding a midseason fracas at New York's Lambs Club testifies to the complexity of McGraw's character, how the self-discipline he preached to his players was missing from his own life, and how he rarely suffered any serious consequences for his self-destructive behavior.

After losing to the Chicago Cubs on Saturday, August 7, the Giants remained in fourth place in the NL with a record of 53-46, three games behind the Brooklyn Dodgers. After the ball game McGraw went out on the town with some friends. Although Prohibition had recently become the law of the land, McGraw and his society pals—he was popular with the Wall Street and Broadway crowds—had no intention of giving up alcohol or the associated nightlife.[22] Late in the evening the group reasoned that it was still too early to call it a night and stopped by the Lambs, a prestigious theatrical club on West Forty-Fourth Street in which McGraw was a member. Although the quarrelsome McGraw had been suspended from the Lambs three months earlier for fighting, in his intoxicated state he thought nothing of walking in.

Several fellow members welcomed McGraw and his small party. After drinking all night, around six in the morning a brawl broke out with McGraw at the center. James Slavin, a well-known comedian, helped break up the fight and pile the beaten McGraw into a cab. When they arrived at McGraw's apartment, Slavin tried to help McGraw to the door of his building. The next anybody knew, Slavin was lying unconscious with two missing teeth, a cut lip, a damaged tongue, bruises on his face, and a fracture at the base of his skull, obviously thrashed by McGraw but without witnesses. Conscious but still delirious a couple of days later, Slavin could not remember what had happened, and the police concluded that Slavin must have simply fallen down and hurt himself. He remained hospitalized for two months.

Meanwhile, McGraw holed up in his apartment with two black eyes, lacerations of the scalp, bruises on his face, and a possible concussion. He sneaked down to the Polo Grounds to put coach Johnny Evers in charge of the Giants and let the team know he would be unavailable for some time. He did not appear on the bench that day but hid out in the clubhouse. Back at his apartment, he refused to admit anyone connected with law enforcement. When a representative of the Prohibition enforcement office came by, McGraw refused to see him. The assistant district attorney (DA) received little better treatment, complaining that the door had been slammed in his face.

In the heat of a pennant race with the Giants very much alive, McGraw was unavailable to his club and ignoring law enforcement in a high-profile case. McGraw finally gave a statement to the DA on August 14, six days after the incident, acknowledging that he was drunk at the Lambs and would not have fought otherwise. That same night McGraw sneaked out of town to join the Giants in Chicago. The Giants managed a 7-4 record while their manager was hiding and remained two and a half games behind Brooklyn.

The investigation into McGraw's altercation with Slavin, along with the liquor charge against the Lambs Club, died out because no witness would testify under oath about a situation during which they had been drinking. Nevertheless, on October 29 McGraw was indicted for illegal possession of a bottle of whiskey. His attorney managed to delay the trial until May 1921, when a jury acquitted McGraw in less than five minutes.

Incredibly, McGraw had spent the final two months of the 1920 season and the start of the off-season in the midst of legal wrangling due largely to his own poor judgment. Of all the remarkable aspects of John McGraw, perhaps nothing is more remarkable than that he lived this wild lifestyle—staying up all night drinking and fighting, dealing with all of the legal fallout from his own actions—and still found time to build a great team, a team on the verge of dominating the National League.

After three consecutive second-place finishes, most observers felt the Giants had a good chance to win in 1921. The pitching staff was both solid and deep. To the top four McGraw added Rosy Ryan, signed in 1919 and optioned for two sensational seasons to the International League (IL). Ryan had often been accused of illegally doctoring the baseball but never got caught. To throw his trick pitch legally, Ryan appeared to dig his thumbnail into the seam of the ball to get it to move unpredictably.

McGraw was happy with three-fourths of his infield: Kelly at first base, Bancroft at shortstop, and Frisch, who had played out of position at third base in 1920 while aging favorite Larry Doyle held down second. Doyle was released after the season, and McGraw purchased third baseman Goldie Rapp from St. Paul of the American Association for fifteen thousand dollars. The catching position was manned by a platoon of Snyder and Earl Smith. Ross Youngs starred in right field, and steadfast George Burns, the lone holdover from the 1917 pennant winner, played left. Without Kauff, McGraw tried Eddie Brown and Curt Walker in center field to start the year.

Though the Giants played well early, it had become clear that Rapp was not the answer at third base. In Cincinnati Heinie Groh, whom

McGraw coveted, was holding out for a better contract. McGraw offered the Reds one hundred thousand dollars and three players for their
disgruntled star. Groh was willing to sign for a salary of ten thousand
dollars with the Giants, rather than the twelve thousand dollars he
was demanding from Garry Herrmann, and the Reds were more than
happy to make the deal.[23]

Commissioner Landis scuttled this rosy scenario by ruling that Groh
must finish the season for Cincinnati. Although players had occasionally forced trades this way, Groh's case caused protests from other
clubs, and Landis ruled that it would be detrimental to the sport if "by
the hold-out process a situation may be created disqualifying a player
from giving his best service to a public that for years has generously
supported that player."[24]

Denied his first choice, on July 1 McGraw sent Rapp and two other
players to Philadelphia for second baseman Johnny Rawlings and outfielder Casey Stengel. For the rest of the 1921 season, McGraw shifted
Frisch back to third and installed Rawlings at second.

In late July, with the Giants running second behind the Pirates,
McGraw acquired Philadelphia's star left fielder Irish Meusel, surrendering thirty thousand dollars and two players. Phillies owner William Baker had been gutting his ball club; at the time of the trade they
stood 25-62, and Meusel was one of the few stars left from what had
been a fine team before the war. To make room for Meusel, McGraw
shifted Burns to center field.

While not prohibited, late-season deals involving contenders were
understandably frowned upon. To shield himself from the ire of his
fellow magnates, Baker charged Meusel with "indifferent" playing
and claimed he had suspended Meusel several days before the trade.
Suitably riled, Landis investigated and determined that Meusel had
not been suspended or accused of malingering by his manager; Baker
had fabricated the story. Nevertheless, Landis allowed the deal to
stand, leading to a fracturing of his relationship with Barney Dreyfuss, owner of the league-leading Pirates. After a controversial late-
season trade a year later involving third baseman Joe Dugan and the
New York Yankees, the magnates moved the in-season trade deadline
back to June 15.[25]

The day after the Meusel trade was announced, the city of Pittsburgh got some measure of revenge. On July 26 a deputy sheriff arrested the manager in his Pittsburgh hotel room. A man named George Duffy accused McGraw of attacking him and knocking him unconscious back in June, when he had gone to a drunken McGraw's assistance. Although the complaint was a civil matter, the court required that McGraw post a three-thousand-dollar bond to ensure he would return in the fall for the trial. Duffy was suing for twenty thousand dollars, claiming he had been confined to his home under the care of a physician for a week and had still not fully recovered. No settlement amount was ever announced, but McGraw biographer Charles Alexander estimated it at five thousand dollars.[26]

At the time of the Meusel trade the Giants stood four games back of the Pirates. By August 23 the Giants had dropped to seven and a half games back, with the Pirates coming to New York for a five-game series. The two teams did not particularly like each other, and the Pirates were acting as if they had already clinched the pennant.[27] The Giants swept the five-game series and took over first place a few weeks later. In a particularly maddening sidelight for Pirate fans, Meusel keyed the sweep by going 8 for 16 with 4 extra-base hits. The Giants ended up winning the NL by four games, their first pennant since 1917 and McGraw's seventh in nineteen years in New York. Besides the typically great starting pitching, Frankie Frisch had his first big year (.341, 17 triples, 49 steals), Youngs hit .327, and Kelly drove in 122 and socked a league-leading 23 home runs.

The 1921 World Series pitted the Giants against the New York Yankees, who won their first-ever pennant behind the slugging of Babe Ruth and a great pitching staff. Because the Yankees also called the Polo Grounds their home park (they rented it from the Giants), the games would all be played there. Phil Douglas started the first game for the Giants and Nehf the second, but the Giants were shut out in both. The club quickly rebounded, winning five of the final six games to take the Series—McGraw's first since 1905—five games to three.

In December 1921 McGraw turned his attention back to Heinie Groh, whom he soon landed in exchange for Burns, journeyman catcher Mike

Gonzalez, and about a hundred thousand dollars. For many years baseball's top third baseman, Groh gave McGraw three years of solid service. Although Groh was a fine player, paying one hundred thousand dollars for a thirty-two-year-old third baseman was a luxury that no other NL club could afford.

That same off-season McGraw purchased Jimmy O'Connell from the San Francisco Seals for seventy-five thousand dollars—the highest price yet paid for a Minor League player. McGraw viewed O'Connell as a long-term center-field solution but agreed to leave him in San Francisco for the 1922 season. After briefly trying rookie Ralph Shinners in center, McGraw ultimately platooned Casey Stengel and Bill Cunningham. Despite tremendous hype, O'Connell never panned out as hoped and was later implicated in a game-fixing scandal.

The Giants led the 1922 pennant race for most of the summer, despite dealing with more off-field drama. McGraw had kept a rein on Phil Douglas for a few years by hiring detectives to follow him around, though the pitcher gave them the slip on occasion. In 1922 McGraw asked scout Jesse Burkett to keep an eye on his pitcher. Burkett began rooming with Douglas, a situation that surely pleased neither. Burkett's nickname during his playing days had been "the Crab," a moniker that was well earned. Douglas was in the middle of his best season in 1922 (11-4 with a league-leading 2.63 ERA) when things finally unraveled permanently.

After pitching a game against the Pirates on July 30, Douglas disappeared on another drinking binge. The police tracked him down two days later and on McGraw's orders transported Douglas to a sanitarium. Douglas claimed that the police had threatened force and that he was given "knockout stuff" in the sanitarium and held against his wishes. He was finally released August 5. In his addled state Douglas sent a letter to his friend Les Mann, an outfielder for the St. Louis Cardinals. He told Mann that he did not want McGraw to win the pennant and offered instead to leave the team if Mann gave him some money. As baseball was still going through a gambling panic in the wake of the Black Sox revelations, Mann reported the situation to his team, who turned the letter over to baseball commissioner Landis. Not surprisingly, Douglas was banned forever from organized baseball. When McGraw claimed that "without exception he was the dirtiest player I have ever seen," he was obviously letting his anger get the better of him—he had been around many more flagrant game-fixers.[28] But McGraw had reason to be angry. He did not need another scandal, especially one that cost him one of his better pitchers upon whom he had spent years of effort.

While this was going on, and with the Cardinals right on the Giants' heels, McGraw packaged a fading Toney, two other players, and one hundred thousand dollars to the always-accommodating Braves for twenty-six-year-old hurler Hugh McQuillan. Although he had yet to record a winning record in a full season with the weak Braves, McQuillan had pitched more than two hundred innings in both 1920 and 1921 and would be a solid contributor over the next several years. On August 1 McGraw took a flier on Jack Scott, a former Braves hurler who (as a member of the Reds) had retired back in April with a sore arm. Scott finished the year 8-2 and threw a four-hit shutout in the World Series. He went on to several more excellent seasons as a valuable swingman for McGraw.[29]

As accomplished as McGraw was in developing young players, none of the phenoms in table 2 were pitchers. Although he had purchased future Hall of Fame hurler Rube Marquard in 1908 for a then-record eleven thousand dollars, his great 1920s teams featured veteran pitchers that he picked up from other teams. "Much as I admire McGraw's great abilities," said Art Nehf, "I am convinced that his system does not tend to develop star pitchers."[30] He added:

[The] system is hard for a pitcher not merely because he is called upon to obey orders exactly all the time and is expected to pitch an uncommon number of curves, which are hard on the arm, but there is also the mental side which is harder still. McGraw does not confine his efforts to bossing the details of the ball game. He rides his players individually and collectively, particularly when things are not going well. This results in a mental strain that really gets upon a players nerves. . . . There is little room for the individual on his pitching staff. The player is merged in the welfare of the club.[31]

New York went on to capture the 1922 flag by seven games over the Reds. The Giants again had a well-balanced offense, with six regulars (Snyder, Kelly, Frisch, Bancroft, Youngs, and Meusel) and the center-field platoon all hitting .320 or better. In the World Series the Giants again met the Yankees, this time in a best-of-seven affair. The Giants won the title four games to zero, though there was one tie. The big story was the poor hitting of Babe Ruth (.118). As with 1921, a narrative formed that Ruth's power game was no match for the smarter inside baseball of John McGraw. McGraw had his third Series title, but Ruth would be heard from shortly.

Though McGraw seemed to have enough on his hands leading his team to its second consecutive championship and living the life of a New York celebrity, he always found time to scout for players who would some-day replace the ones winning for him today. During the 1922 season he signed three who would make a name for themselves: Bill Terry, a semi-pro first baseman from Memphis; Travis Jackson, an eighteen-year-old shortstop playing for Little Rock in the Southern League; and third base-man Fred Lindstrom, a sixteen-year-old amateur from Chicago. Terry was twenty-three, had a good job at Standard Oil, a wife, a young son, and a mature appreciation of his situation. McGraw wanted to farm Terry out to Toledo, but Terry agreed only after being assured his sal-ary would be the same as originally negotiated.[32] Jackson played three games in 1922 but became a key reserve the next season. Lindstrom joined the Giants in 1924 and starred soon after. In both of the latter two cases, McGraw was not afraid to give teenagers key roles on his teams.

McGraw's Giants also won pennants in 1923 and 1924, making them the only NL team ever to win four consecutive league titles. The 1923 team was largely unchanged, save for the addition of Jack Bentley, a pitcher–first baseman that McGraw purchased from the Interna-tional League Baltimore Orioles for sixty-five thousand dollars. When Barnes failed early in the season, Bentley took his place in the rota-tion. The best players on the 1923 club were again Frisch (.348) and Youngs (.336). For the third straight year the Giants faced off in the World Series with the Yankees, who had left the Polo Grounds for their own new stadium in the Bronx. This time the Yankees finally bested the Giants, winning their first championship, four games to two, with Ruth hitting three home runs in the Series.

On a scouting trip near the end of the 1923 season, McGraw discovered Hack Wilson playing for Portsmouth of the Virginia League. Wilson took over as the Giants' center fielder in 1924 and had a fine rookie season (.295 with 41 extra-base hits in just 107 games). The other change to the 1924 lineup was the ascension of shortstop Jackson. Late in the year McGraw found playing time for both Lindstrom and Terry, with Lindstrom often replacing Groh and Terry forcing Kelly to the outfield to get another left-handed bat in the lineup. McGraw's integration of all of this young talent while successfully defending his league title was typical for the great skipper.

The 1924 Giants were led again by Frisch and Youngs and a great year from George Kelly (.324 and a league-leading 136 runs batted in). One of the team's best pitchers turned out to be twenty-seven-year-old Virgil Barnes, brother of Jesse, who had toiled mostly in relief over the past couple of years. The team played well all year despite missing its manager for much of May and June after McGraw fell off a high curb in Chicago, badly injuring his knee.[33] He returned on July 8 with the Giants five games up. With McGraw back in the dugout, the Giants held off Brooklyn to win the pennant by a game and a half, before losing a thrilling seven-game World Series to the upstart Washington Senators. In the final game the Giants were victimized by two bad-hop singles past Lindstrom—one in a game-tying rally in the eighth and the other ending the game in the twelfth. The great McGraw, still just fifty-one years old, would never again win a pennant.

Much of John McGraw's success could be attributed to his genius and force of personality. He had a knack for recognizing good ballplayers, signing future stars at young ages, and rarely making bad trades or being without a competent player at a position. McGraw could usually compel his charges to bend to his will, somehow without causing them to freeze from the pressure. McGraw's drive, along with his high-level connections, also helped him avoid the consequences of his often odious behavior. While this helps explain his success, genius remains elusive.

McGraw did have one significant organizational advantage over the majority of his competitors: the Giants were the league's most profitable franchise, and throughout the early 1920s, before he ran into legal difficulties, Charles Stoneham let McGraw reinvest most of the profits in the Giants. McGraw also created another organizational advantage: he had one of baseball's first full-time scouts, Dick Kinsella, uncovering talent throughout the country.

McGraw managed the Giants for seven more seasons before retiring in mid-1932 due to poor health. The 1924 core included a group of young players—among the major contributors only Groh was older than thirty-one, and the Giants had his replacement (Lindstrom) ready to go. McGraw also continued to discover young players. In 1925 he brought up pitcher Freddie Fitzsimmons from Indianapolis. Later in the decade he secured Hall of Famers Carl Hubbell—recommended by Kinsella—and Mel Ott, probably the two best players McGraw ever found. McGraw signed Ott as a sixteen-year-old and made him a regular at nineteen in 1928. McGraw purchased Hubbell and his famous screwball out of the Texas League for forty thousand dollars in midseason 1928 and immediately inserted him into the Giants rotation. With all this young talent, why did his team stop winning pennants?

In the late teens and early twenties McGraw had done a great job building a pitching staff that won four pennants, but these pitchers (Toney, Douglas, Nehf, McQuillan, and others) were all three- or four-year solutions. This was well and good, but it meant that McGraw had to find pitchers like this almost every year, and he spent the rest of the decade a pitcher or two short. Finding someone like Carl Hubbell, someone who could contribute at a high level for a decade or more, would have helped considerably a few years earlier.

The offense also fell off after 1924. After leading the league in runs (twice by large margins) during three of the four pennant-winning years, the Giants topped the league only once between 1925 and 1930. The biggest blow was the tragic kidney disorder suffered by Ross Youngs, which ended his career in 1926 and his life a year later. Youngs was the best hitter on the pennant-winning teams and obviously not easily replaceable. The Giants also lost Hack Wilson due to a procedural blunder. When Wilson went through an off year in 1925, McGraw intended to option him to Toledo, thus preserving the Giants' rights to the player. Due to a clerical error, however, the Giants failed to maintain control. After the season the Cubs drafted Wilson, and he went on to several years of stardom in Chicago. George Kelly later made the Hall of Fame based on his fine contributions to the four pennants. His selection is often criticized because these four years represent most of his quality seasons, and his days of contributing were over by 1926, when he was just thirty.

The Giants' falloff might also be attributed to some off-field distractions that robbed much of McGraw's focus. First, he had been living with sinusitis and its associated complications for many years, and McGraw was now feeling increasingly uncomfortable. Moreover, by the mid-1920s McGraw's life was brimming with other interests. Right after the 1924 World Series, McGraw and Chicago White Sox owner Charles Comiskey took a number of players on a hastily organized baseball tour of Europe, much like the one the pair had organized in 1913. This much less successful trip lasted nearly seven weeks and cost McGraw around twenty thousand dollars. McGraw also lost close to a hundred thousand dollars on a Florida real estate venture called "Pennant Park." McGraw spent many hours on the new venture to the exclusion of baseball matters. *New York Times* reporter John Kieran later remarked, "Some of his old spirit died away in the collapse of the Florida land boom."[34]

While McGraw found several excellent young players in the late 1920s and picked up future Hall of Famers Rogers Hornsby and Burleigh Grimes in 1927, he could not quite get his squad over the hump. When Hornsby and Grimes were rashly dealt away at the end of the season, mostly at the insistence of Stoneham, it testified to McGraw's waning emotional energy.[35]

That he was also becoming increasingly cantankerous, perhaps due to his health problems, and uncommunicative with an increasingly mature brand of ballplayer did not help, either. Moreover, by the mid- to late 1920s the baseball enterprise had grown too big and too complex for just one man, no matter how driven and brilliant, to run a team on and off the field.

But at his peak, and with the money to back him up, no one was ever better than McGraw in finding good young players, integrating them onto his roster, and surrounding them with accomplished veterans. He might not have had the topflight stars that Barney Dreyfuss had, but he had an astonishing ability to get the best out of his charges. His ten NL pennants, and eleven second-place finishes, attest to his skills as a builder and leader of teams.

3 General Manager

As we have seen, the Pittsburgh Pirates and New York Giants were two of the best-run franchises in the game in the early years of the twentieth century, though they were run very differently. Pittsburgh's Barney Dreyfuss was a hands-on owner who established a respectful working relationship with his field manager to build and run the club. The Giants' owners, on the other hand, gave John McGraw complete authority to create and manage his team. Both examples—the hands-on baseball-savvy owner and the strong, energetic manager—were destined to be overtaken eventually by a new model, one that has dominated baseball front offices for the past nine decades.

Prior to World War I baseball franchises were generally owned not by the wealthy upper class, but by men who had modest wealth outside of baseball. Only two teams, the Cincinnati Reds, principally owned by the wealthy Fleischmann family of the Fleischmann Yeast conglomerate, and the Detroit Tigers, partially owned by Michigan lumber and mining heir Bill Yawkey, had owners near the top strata of American wealth. Neither spent their private riches on their team, and both delegated the management of the franchise to a minority owner—Garry Herrmann in Cincinnati and Frank Navin in Detroit. Most teams had a couple of principal backers, with the most interested large investor operating the club as the president.

Baseball management reflected the way American businesses had been run in the mid-nineteenth century. "The largest firms," wrote business historian Alfred Chandler, "were directed by a general superintendent and a president or treasurer. The general superintendent personally supervised the labor force."[1] Sixty years later baseball teams were still being run this way: with a president who represented the ownership syndicate, a business manager (for back-office functions such as travel arrangements, ticket sales, and uniforms), and a general superintendent in charge of the labor force (the manager). The relative influence and power of the president and manager in assembling the team depended on the relationship between the two and the president's desire and belief in his own baseball acumen. Owners such as Charles Comiskey in Chicago and Dreyfuss in Pittsburgh either made most of the key player-personnel decisions or played a large role in them. The Giants, on the other hand, allowed McGraw pretty much a free hand, with his oversight restricted mainly to budgetary limits.

In 1914 and 1915 the Major Leagues faced a new competitor, the Federal League, which bid for the best players and competed in the same cities with many established teams. Facing fresh competition, organized baseball needed to bolster some of its more poorly capitalized franchises. In one of his big successes, AL president Ban Johnson recruited millionaire brewer Jacob Ruppert to purchase the New York Yankees along with partner Tillinghast L'Hommedieu Huston. Bringing deep-pocketed owners to Gotham also helped provide a safeguard against Federal League threats to relocate a team there.

The Federals recruited some wealthy owners of their own: bread manufacturer Robert Ward in Brooklyn, ice-plant builder Phil Ball in St. Louis, and oilman Harry Sinclair in Indianapolis. When the Federal League folded after the 1915 season, Ball was allowed to purchase the American League's St. Louis Browns. Similarly, Chicago Federals owner and restaurateur Charles Weeghman, backed by a moneyed syndicate that included chewing-gum magnate William Wrigley, purchased the Chicago Cubs. When Weeghman ran into financial difficulties several years later, Wrigley gained control of the franchise. These new owners, Ball and Wrigley, boasted two things many of the previous owners lacked: a lot of money and an understanding of how to run a business.

Meanwhile, American business management had evolved considerably in the past half century. "At the close of World War I," wrote Chandler, "most larger industrial companies whose executives paid any attention to organizational matters were administered through much the same type of organization—the centralized, functionally departmentalized structure."[2]

Professional management soon came to baseball as well, and its importance can hardly be overstated. "It is management, and management alone," wrote the late management guru Peter Drucker, "that makes effective all this knowledge and these knowledgeable people."[3]

Because the new breed of baseball owners had little background in their new field, they recognized that they needed professional help in running their new baseball companies. Moreover, because of their wide experience in large industrial enterprises, they also realized that the effort of both finding players and managing the team had become too overwhelming for one man. Accordingly, over the next several years, baseball executives took the logical step of hiring veteran baseball men to run their front offices, to oversee the business of the ball club, and to take responsibility for finding players and building a team. Confined principally by the owner's budget, these men were in charge of purchasing or drafting players in the Minor Leagues, trading or acquiring players from other teams, and assembling a competitive roster for the field manager.

For many years there was no generally accepted title for the men (thus far, they have all been men) who performed this role. Eventually, he came to be called the "general manager" or "GM," though even today teams are not consistent about this. In the early days the breakdown of duties between the owner-president, the GM, and the field manager was imprecise. As this new model evolved, both the team president and the manager were often involved to a much larger degree than they would be when the front offices became larger and more complex.

Frank Navin could lay claim to having been baseball's first general manager, though he never had that title. In 1904, while working as business manager of the Tigers, Navin identified and recruited William Clyman Yawkey, a lumber and mining baron and one of the wealthiest men in Michigan, as a potential purchaser for the franchise. Before negotiations were finalized, however, Yawkey suddenly died. Undaunted, Navin pursued the idea with Yawkey's son, the twenty-five-year-old William H. (Bill) Yawkey, who had reportedly inherited ten million dollars. (Bill Yawkey was the uncle of Tom Yawkey, who in 1933 bought the Boston Red Sox with *his* inheritance.) Bill Yawkey paid fifty thousand dollars for the franchise, allocating five thousand dollars' worth of stock to Navin and twenty-five hundred to field manager Ed Barrow.

Though nominally still the business manager, Navin soon became involved with the player-procurement functions typically associated today with a GM. In 1908 Navin assumed the presidency of the team as Yawkey retreated to the background, and shortly thereafter he acquired a larger share of ownership and assumed its oversight. As head of the franchise, Navin became active in league matters, taking on more of a presidential role. But while Yawkey was still involved with the franchise, Navin acted very much like a general manager.

The newer owners who entered the game in the 1910s and 1920s acted to solidify this new function. When Phil Ball bought the Browns in 1916, he inherited field manager Branch Rickey. Ball brought the popular Fielder Jones from his St. Louis Federals squad to manage the Browns, but he kept Rickey, who had signed a long-term contract under the previous regime, to focus mainly on the players the Browns controlled in the Minor Leagues.[4] After the 1916 season, when the crosstown Cardinals' new ownership syndicate was looking for someone to run their organization, they offered Rickey the opportunity to buy a small ownership interest and become team president. Rickey chafed under Ball's direction, so he eagerly accepted and moved to the Cardinals.

To replace Rickey Ball hired Minor League business manager Bob Quinn and granted him the powers of a modern-day general manager—a role Quinn had successfully filled for a number of years with his team in Columbus. While there Quinn had even briefly affiliated with two clubs in the lower Minor Leagues, creating a rudimentary farm system.[5] The Browns, perennially one of the American League's worst teams, experienced some of their best seasons under Quinn's oversight. Like Rickey, Quinn eventually grew tired of Ball's meddling and jumped at the chance to lead an investor group in buying the struggling Boston Red Sox in 1923.[6]

Meanwhile, new Chicago Cubs owner William Wrigley brought in sportswriter Bill Veeck Sr. as vice president and treasurer and soon promoted him to president with control of team operations, a role similar to Quinn's. At the time of his hiring, Veeck was one of the highest-paid sportswriters in Chicago and considered his prospects carefully before leaving his profession. Veeck alleviated his financial concerns by negotiating a small percentage of the Cubs' profits.[7] Under Veeck's administration (and Wrigley's open checkbook), the Cubs returned to being perennial contenders. The team won four pennants and did not finish in the second division from 1926 until 1939, long after Wrigley's death.

As we discuss in the next chapter, New York Yankees owners Ruppert and Huston first tried to oversee the baseball side of their new club with the help of field manager Bill Donovan and business manager Harry Sparrow. The team improved immeasurably with the hiring of manager Miller Huggins for 1918 and the purchase of Babe Ruth after the 1919 season. When Sparrow passed away in May 1920, the two owners were forced to take on a larger hands-on role than they wanted. Accordingly, after the season they reached out to Ed Barrow, manager of the Boston Red Sox, to oversee their Yankees' front office.

Barrow had won the World Series in the war-shortened 1918 season and had spent twenty-five years in baseball in virtually every capacity except player: Minor League owner, Minor League president, Minor League manager, and Major League manager. Under Barrow's leadership (and that of capable field managers Miller Huggins and Joe McCarthy), the Yankees developed into one of the greatest dynasties in American sports: they won their first pennant the next year, and during Barrow's reign the Yankees won fourteen pennants and ten World Series. With the Yankees Barrow formally instituted the separation between the front office and the manager's domain of the clubhouse, a concept that has survived to the present. "As a front office man, he never interfered in the playing end of the game," wrote one sportswriter. "His field manager was the boss on the field, the bench and in the clubhouse."[8]

Of all the early general managers, Branch Rickey had the greatest impact. After two years overseeing the Cardinals off the field, in 1919 Rickey put on a uniform and managed the club for six years, while still serving as the (de facto) GM. Rickey shouldered a dual role that only a few others took on after World War I, with only Connie Mack, John McGraw, and Bill Terry having notable success. In 1920 wealthy auto dealer Sam Breadon purchased control of the Cardinals from the nearly bankrupt ownership group and assumed leadership of the franchise, while leaving Rickey in his two jobs. It was not until 1925 that Breadon separated the roles and returned Rickey full-time to the front office. "In time Branch, you will see that I am doing you a great favor," Breadon told a distraught Rickey. "You can now devote yourself fully to player development and scouting."[9] Among his many future contributions, Rickey introduced baseball's first sophisticated farm system and broke baseball's color barrier.

When Cleveland Indians president Alva Bradley hired Billy Evans to run his front office in 1927, the longtime umpire became the first person actually given the title of "general manager." Evans signed one of the era's most lucrative contracts, covering three years at thirty thousand dollars per year.[10] The *Reach Guide* remarked on the significance of this emerging position: "This is a new office in a ball club and Evans will act as buffer between players and the owners, exercising some of the powers of a club president."[11] The GM role was coming into its own.

By 1930 the GM job was largely recognized as a vital role. "[These new owners] with their huge investments, they can't afford to take a chance of directing the club with their own slim knowledge of the baseball business," wrote John Kieran. "They need men who know baseball from a business standpoint and business from a baseball standpoint. . . . Thus—and at last the heroes of the story appear—Colonel Ruppert has Ed Barrow . . . Mr. Wrigley has William L. Veeck . . . and Mr. Bradley has Billy Evans."[12]

Like most institutions, however, baseball progresses deliberately, and there were a few teams that resisted the new model. Connie Mack, a hybrid in that he was both the principal owner and the manager of the Philadelphia Athletics, had intermittent periods of considerable success through 1931 before a lack of financial resources led to two decades of struggle. Clark Griffith, like Dreyfuss, a hands-on owner with Washington, won his final pennant in 1933 and had trouble competing for the next twenty years. McGraw fielded competitive teams throughout the 1920s, and his successor, Bill Terry, also served as the primary team builder and won three pennants in the 1930s. By the end of the decade, however, Terry recognized the merits of the new organizational structure and asked to be relieved of his field-manager duties to focus solely on overseeing the club off the field. Young owner Horace Stoneham, who remembered the glory days of his father and John McGraw, insisted that Terry handle both positions.[13]

Nevertheless, baseball front offices inexorably progressed toward professionalism. The general manager, by whatever title, continued to catch on throughout the 1930s, particularly in the American League. "On many major league clubs today it is the general manager who directs the team's affairs," wrote John Drebinger, who lamented the new model. "Moving quietly behind the scenes, usually in the seclusion of a 'front office' and behind a big desk, he hires not only players but the manager as well. He makes all deals and trades, handles the player manipulations between parent club and its farm connections and, in short, has reduced the once-powerful manager to a position that is little more than a field captain, giving signals from the bench, yanking pitchers and sending up pinch hitters with the fervent hope that they deliver and thereby help save his job."[14]

Table 3 lists the 1938 executives primarily entrusted with building a team's roster.

The three teams with a full-time GM in the National League (the Cardinals, Reds, and Dodgers) were the best teams in the league in the late 1930s and early 1940s. The AL was dominated by Barrow's Yankees, with Eddie Collins's Red Sox usually finishing second. The teams that operated without a GM were generally not as successful by the late 1930s. After Veeck's sudden death in 1933, Phil Wrigley (who had recently taken over the team after the death of his father) kept the team competitive for a few years without a GM, though he struggled with defining front-office roles and experimented with other management structures. "What he was striving for, from the moment he took over the Cubs," wrote sportswriter Warren Brown, "was a compact organization which would run the baseball property, make its own decisions, and not bother him with every minute detail. Unhappily it was many years before he was to have his hopes realized."[15]

Because most teams still did not have extensive Minor League systems requiring a farm director, or formal scouting systems—as late as 1938 eight of the sixteen teams still officially employed two or fewer scouts—general managers still operated with only skeleton staffs.[16]

Table 3. Team builders, 1938

TEAM	LEAGUE	TEAM BUILDER	ROLE
Boston	AL	Eddie Collins	GM
Chicago	AL	Jimmie Dykes	Manager
Cleveland	AL	Cy Slapnicka	GM
Detroit	AL	Mickey Cochrane	Manager
New York	AL	Ed Barrow	GM
Philadelphia	AL	Connie Mack	President-manager
St. Louis	AL	Bill Dewitt	GM
Washington	AL	Clark Griffith	President
Boston	NL	Bob Quinn	President
Brooklyn	NL	Larry MacPhail	GM
Chicago	NL	Phil Wrigley	President
Cincinnati	NL	Warren Giles	GM
New York	NL	Bill Terry	Manager
Philadelphia	NL	Gerry Nugent	President
Pittsburgh	NL	Bill Benswanger	President
St. Louis	NL	Branch Rickey	GM

But the structure had been established. As baseball revenue exploded after World War II, the attendant leap in operating specialization and new departmental responsibilities fell under the aegis of the general manager. How he handled all his charges would often determine the fate of the franchise.

As the sport evolved, most successful baseball owners understood the importance of professional management, both on the field and in the front office. Perhaps no other action could be as influential in the success or failure of a franchise as hiring the right person as GM.

The owner needed to provide a budget and remain engaged but otherwise let the general manager do his job. The relationship between the owner and his GM arguably became the most important one in a baseball organization, with the potential to create a first-rate organization and consistent on-field success.

4 Executive

The greatest single quality of a championship baseball club is a collective, dominating urge to win.—BRANCH RICKEY, baseball executive

When the American League put a baseball team in New York in 1903, it did so with the hope that it could challenge the National League's Giants and become one of the AL's flagship franchises. Instead, the new club (called the Highlanders until 1913, and then the Yankees) floundered both on the field (no pennants and just three second-place finishes in their first dozen years in New York) and off. The tipping point for the club, the event that caused their fortunes to change, came when Jacob Ruppert and Tillinghast L'Hommedieu Huston bought the club in 1915. Within a few years the American League had its strong New York team—stronger than anyone could have imagined, in fact.

Jacob Ruppert Jr. was born into a German brewing family in New York City in 1867. His father ran the Ruppert Brewery, while his mother came from another brewing family. Not surprisingly, Ruppert's parents directed him into the family beer business, where he started at the bottom as a nineteen-year-old barrel washer. Ruppert proved himself a personable yet determined young man and was rapidly promoted through the company ranks. A perfectionist who often lapsed into a German accent when agitated, he soon proved a skilled executive.

Of medium height and a stocky 170 pounds, Ruppert cultivated an imperial appearance. Often lamenting that men did not dress as well as women, he dressed impeccably, wearing his hair slicked back and sporting a well-trimmed mustache.[1] He led an active social life but did not drink much beyond beer and remained free of public scandal. He had unusual interests and hobbies. He collected jade and Chinese porcelain, decorative books, and oil paintings. At his country estate in Garrison, New York, he had a large collection of exotic animals, including small monkeys and unusual birds. Like many of the upper class at the turn of the last century, he also enjoyed horses. Before he left the hobby, Ruppert had purchased and raced some top racehorses and ran the Ruppert Stables. He later became a leading breeder of St. Bernards and was most proud of his champion, Oh Boy.

Ruppert never married and throughout his life remained one of New York's most eligible bachelors. Over the years Ruppert developed deep friendships with several of his subordinates, particularly Al Brennan, his secretary, and George Perry, a business confidant and Yankees public relations man. Ruppert was also very close to New York mayor Jimmy Walker. Ruppert once lent Perry to Walker's mayoral campaign for four months while still paying Perry's salary.[2]

In 1886 Ruppert joined an upper-class regiment of New York's National Guard. A few years later he was appointed aide-de-camp to Governor David Hill and given the rank of Colonel, a largely ceremonial title. Ruppert took great pleasure in this title and for the rest of his life liked to be addressed by it. Later, with the support of Tammany Hall, Ruppert spent four terms in the U.S. Congress. Ruppert then retired from politics and concentrated most of his energies—aside from his various hobbies of the moment—on the brewery business.

In 1914 the forty-seven-year-old Ruppert became interested in purchasing a baseball team. At the same time Huston, an engineer who had made his fortune in Cuba after the Spanish-American War, had been independently rummaging around baseball's boardrooms for a team to buy. Ruppert and Huston decided to join forces. They consulted Huston's friend New York Giants manager John McGraw for advice on finding and buying a team. The two quickly learned that the American League was seeking a new owner for its New York club.

The Yankees were controlled by a couple of the city's more disreputable characters, though they had mostly reformed over the previous decade: Frank Farrell, a onetime operator of gambling venues, and William Devery, a multiply indicted former police chief. Huston secretly agreed to pay McGraw $5,000 for his help making the connection, and in January 1915 he and Ruppert closed on the purchase for $463,000, assuming roughly $20,000 in debts.[3] With the sale Ruppert became one of baseball's first owners from America's upper crust, a society within which he moved easily and comfortably.

Ruppert and Huston wasted no time in aggressively trying to acquire talented players, relying on Ruppert's wealth and their own limited knowledge of the game, albeit with significant input from manager Bill Donovan. Detroit president Frank Navin honored the league's pledge to make some capable players available to the new owners, selling them little-used first baseman Wally Pipp. Cash-strapped Philadelphia owner Connie Mack later sold pitcher Bob Shawkey to the Yankees for only $3,000. When organized baseball and the Federal League reached a settlement after the 1915 season, Ruppert spent $40,000 buying four players from the Federals (including outfielder Lee Magee and twenty-two-game winner Nick Cullop), though none panned out as hoped. More successfully, Ruppert went back to Mack and landed star third baseman Frank "Home Run" Baker for $37,500, at the time one of the highest prices ever paid for a player.[4]

After three years of finishing well behind the American League leaders, Ruppert and Huston grew dissatisfied with field manager Donovan. In late 1917, while Huston was away in France with the AEF (he would return a lieutenant colonel), Ruppert hired Miller Huggins, who had managed the Cardinals during the just completed season. Huston had championed his friend Wilbert Robinson, the Brooklyn Dodgers' manager. Ruppert's hiring of Huggins led to a serious and long-lasting disagreement between the two owners and fueled Huston's excessive and unreasonable dislike of Huggins.

With their new manager in place, the Yankees redoubled their efforts to purchase Major League stars. Though Connie Mack had run out of stars to sell, the Yankees soon found a new supplier. The Boston Red Sox had just won the 1918 World Series and, with good players returning from the war, believed they had a surplus of talent. Moreover, owner Harry Frazee was in a financial squeeze, needing money to cover the debt now coming due from his purchase of the team and Fenway Park and for his theatrical interests. Serendipitously for the Yankees, Frazee was a New Yorker and a social friend of Huston, and Ruppert had the funds necessary to buy the players. Over the next half-dozen years the Yankees sent Frazee about $450,000 (roughly the equivalent of what they paid for the entire franchise in 1915), plus Ruppert made Frazee a personal loan for $300,000 secured by a mortgage on Fenway Park. In return for this outlay, the Yankees received one of the greatest hauls of players in baseball history, most prominently Babe Ruth, Joe Dugan, Everett Scott, Carl Mays, Joe Bush, Waite Hoyt, Sam Jones, Wally Schang, and Herb Pennock. When the Yankees won their first World Series in 1923, former Red Sox made up four-fifths of their starting rotation and four of their starting eight position players.

Even before the advent of modern free agency, when a player was effectively tethered to his team, money mattered: a wealthy owner could invest personal funds into his ball club, and team revenues could be reinvested in the team. The most savvy baseball executives recognized this. "After several years of unsuccessful experimentation," wrote J. G. Taylor Spink, "[Chicago Cubs president William] Veeck became convinced that a championship team could not be welded together without spending money."[5] The wealthiest teams often ended up with the best players, by paying more to sign the top amateurs or paying more to Minor League teams for their best players.

Many economists apply to baseball an eponymous theorem developed by Ronald Coase, which states that subject to several limiting assumptions, "parties will bargain to an efficient outcome" and that "the same outcome will be achieved regardless of property rights."[6] Thus, free agency should not affect the distribution of playing talent, but only who receives the benefit: prior to the advent of free agency (which began in 1976), the value of the property rights (i.e., rights to the players' services) went to the owners; post–free agency it mostly stays with the players, but the players still generally end up with the teams most willing to pay for them. In other words, because Babe Ruth in 1920 was more valuable to the surging Yankees than to the declining Red Sox, he inevitably ended up moving from Boston to New York. Before the advent of free agency he would be sold or traded to the Yankees; post–free agency he would sign with them for the highest contract. But the result, according to the Coase theorem, would be the same.

Ruppert's huge investment in the team is all the more remarkable in light of the onset of Prohibition, which banned the manufacture or sale of alcoholic beverages in January 1920. To remain in business Ruppert shifted to producing near-beer (essentially nonalcoholic beer), a much less desirable and less profitable beverage—the brewery's annual output fell from 1.25 million barrels to 350,000.[7] In 1920 Ruppert sold a collection of rare books, reportedly to help cover roughly $1 million in losses on mortgages he held on bars no longer able to service their debts.[8] That Ruppert was willing to pay record prices for players and build Yankee Stadium, baseball's most expensive venue, amid such uncertainty and declining revenues in his main business testifies to his passion for his baseball team and his competitive drive.

Furthermore, Ruppert was not taking distributions from the Yankees; he was reinvesting all of the team's profits. From 1920 through 1924 four American League clubs distributed at least $200,000 to their owners, reducing the funds available for investing in Minor League talent. In contrast, the Yankees plowed more than $1.6 million in profits back into the franchise; no other American League team retained even $700,000. The NL rival Giants, the Yankees' landlord through 1922, were also clearing large profits, but by the middle of the decade owner Charles Stoneham needed money. Between 1924 and 1930 the club distributed as dividends more than $1.5 million in profits, money that was not reinvested in the ball club.

Jacob Ruppert was not the first man to enter baseball willing to spend his money. What made Ruppert's efforts so historically effective was the combination of his wealth and the professional administration he brought to the club. Ruppert hired Huggins in 1918 and let him run the team on the field. Perhaps more significantly, after the 1920 season he and Huston hired Red Sox manager Ed Barrow to be their general manager, one of the first men to hold the role in baseball. Ruppert, owner of a large brewery operation, recognized the importance of sound oversight and administration. Once in place it was Barrow who made most of the fruitful acquisitions from his old club. Just as Ruppert would let Barrow do his job, Barrow provided Huggins similar support.

Ed Barrow lived up to his half of the bargain: he and his scouts found the necessary players, and he let Huggins run the team. Whenever Huggins had to deal with an insubordinate Babe Ruth, which was often, Barrow backed his manager. The combination of their financial advantage and superior organization put the Yankees on the path to become one of America's greatest sports dynasties. The Yankees won three straight pennants beginning in 1921, including the 1923 World Series.

Between the costs of all the players and the stunning new Yankee Stadium, which opened in 1923, the Yankee owners made a huge capital infusion into their franchise. As their investment grew, Huston had become increasingly concerned that virtually his entire net worth was tied up in the Yankee franchise. Coupled with his continued disapproval of Huggins, he eventually decided he wanted out. In 1923 Ruppert bought Huston's share of the team for $1.25 million, leaving Ruppert, with the able Barrow and Huggins, free to develop the franchise as he saw fit.

The Yankees' rise to the top was attained largely by their purchases from Frazee and the Red Sox. As the Boston well inevitably ran dry, and as no other American League team had any interest in selling off its stars, Barrow recognized that the club needed to find another source of talent to keep winning. With organized baseball's top stable of scouts, Barrow turned his focus to the high Minor Leagues, who were selling, though not cheaply. Fortunately for Barrow, Ruppert kept his checkbook open, allowing his GM to buy some of the Minor Leagues' most expensive players.

One of Barrow's greatest contributions to the Yankees was his hiring of topflight scouts. While still with the Red Sox Barrow employed a former catcher named Paul Krichell to do some talent hunting for him, and when Barrow joined the Yankees in 1920 he brought Krichell along. Krichell mainly scouted colleges and semipro clubs, making his biggest mark on baseball history in 1923 when he signed Columbia first baseman Lou Gehrig to a Yankee contract. Krichell would still be employed as a Yankee scout when he died in 1957, having discovered and signed many players, including several future Hall of Fame players.

Barrow relied on Krichell not just for top scouting missions, often directed on short notice, but as his most trusted assistant and adviser. When Lou Gehrig was struggling with Hartford in 1923 and considering quitting, Barrow dispatched Krichell to boost his confidence. When Babe Ruth developed his famous "stomachache" in the spring of 1925,

Barrow dispatched Krichell to Florida to bring Ruth back on the train. During the off-season Krichell often traveled to the Yankees players' residences to check up on their conditioning and health. In 1928, when the Yankees purchased their first farm club, in Chambersburg, Pennsylvania, it was Krichell who finalized the deal. When Ruppert and Barrow pursued Joe McCarthy as manager after the 1930 season, Krichell went to Philadelphia to accompany him back to New York for a job interview. Though he remained a topflight scout, Krichell operated as a member of the front office, as Barrow's top assistant.

After the team fell back in 1924 and 1925, and the Yankees needed some younger, hungrier players, Barrow's Minor League initiative began to pay off. Between 1924 and 1925 the Yankees purchased several top Minor Leaguers, including catcher Pat Collins, second baseman Tony Lazzeri, shortstop Mark Koenig, and outfielder Earle Combs. All four of these players started for the 1926 club that began a second run of three straight pennants, and two of them (Lazzeri and Combs) were future Hall of Famers.

It is worth noting that the Yankees also had many misses. The club recognized that scouting is an inexact science: a team needed to sign as many talented young players as possible because some inevitably did not live up to expectations. But Ruppert did not scrimp when it came to his ball club; he trusted Barrow and his scouts. The eventually wasted cost of Ben Paschal (twenty thousand dollars from Atlanta in 1924) was part of the price the Yankees were willing to pay so that they could land a Tony Lazzeri or an Earle Combs.

After the 1925 season Barrow added two more scouts to his staff: Eddie Herr, who would scout the Midwest, and Bill Essick, manager of the Vernon club in the Pacific Coast League (PCL) for the previous eight years, would now scout the West Coast. Essick did not get off to a great start—his first big recommendations led to the purchases of shortstop Lyn Lary and second baseman Jimmy Reese from Oakland for $125,000. Lary and Reese never panned out, eventually leading owner Jacob Ruppert to become disillusioned with this method of talent acquisition. Fortunately for Essick, in 1929 he purchased pitcher Lefty Gomez from San Francisco and the next year landed shortstop Frank Crosetti from the same club. Two years earlier, at the urging of scout Johnny Nee, Barrow had paid $12,000 for Minor League catcher Bill Dickey.

Meanwhile, Krichell was still scouting the college ranks and local New York teams. In 1929 he signed Fordham pitcher Johnny Murphy, who spent a few years in the Minors before having several excellent seasons beginning in 1934. Krichell had less luck with Hank Greenberg, who grew up in the Bronx and was playing semipro ball in the area when Krichell first scouted him. When he brought Greenberg to Yankee Stadium for a visit, he tried to downplay Greenberg's concerns about trying to beat out the great Lou Gehrig for playing time. Krichell told the youngster that Gehrig was nearly washed up, a prophesy with which Greenberg correctly disagreed.

While the great Yankee teams of the early 1920s had been built largely through a series of purchases from Harry Frazee's Red Sox, the late 1920s teams had been rebuilt by scouting and purchasing top Minor League players. The Minor League players were not purchased for the future—for the most part they were expected to step onto the team and play. When Krichell recommended Lazzeri, he was suggesting not that Lazzeri would someday be able to help the Yankees, but that he could help them immediately.

But even Jacob Ruppert began to realize that he needed a less expensive way to find players. One thousand miles away, in St. Louis, Branch Rickey was facing the same problem and trying a new model.

5 Farm System

The Minor Leagues of the 1920s were still mostly unaffiliated with the Majors. There were usually procedures in place that prevented the Minors from holding on to star players for long, but the Major League teams still had to scout them and outbid other suitors. Moreover, player acquisition and development were much more haphazard and less efficiently regulated. Along with deep pockets, Major League teams needed connections, hustle, and skilled scouts.

Prior to the advent of modern farm systems, teams acquired talent in four ways: trades or purchases from other Major League teams, trades or purchases from the independent Minor Leagues, drafting from the Minor Leagues, or signing amateur free agents. In terms of quality players acquired, the Minor League draft was the least utilized of the four methods, but the ever-changing draft rules exerted pressure on the system that affected the importance and cost of the other three.

Minor League teams before the 1930s were usually run by local operators, who needed first to make a profit and, if possible, to win games. Many of the top Minor League teams played in large cities with enthusiastic followers who cared as much about winning as their Major League counterparts. The rules and arrangements governing how players moved between the Major and Minor Leagues evolved continually.

The Minor Leagues were overseen by the National Association, an umbrella organization that grouped the Minors into five "classes," Double-A to D, and provided territorial protection for the individual teams. The National Association and the two Major Leagues were governed by the National Agreement, and the leagues covered under this agreement became known as organized baseball.

The National Agreement established a draft both within the Minor Leagues and between the Minor and Major Leagues. The draft allowed teams to select players from teams in lower classification leagues. The exact rules would be in flux for many years, but teams could typically draft from lower-classification clubs and lose one or two players to the leagues above. The Major Leagues sat at the top of the pyramid and could draft players from the highest Minor Leagues. Teams paid a draft price, which rose steadily throughout the era but was still less than a straight purchase would be, to the team from which they selected the player. Nearly all players who reached the Majors, however, did *not* do so via the draft. Instead, Minor League teams recognized which players would likely be drafted and sold them before season's end, receiving more than the draft price. So although the top players were not getting drafted, the presence of the draft kept their careers advancing.

The lower Minor Leagues supported the draft because it provided much-needed revenue. Players in the lower Minors were less skilled and less widely scouted, resulting in less opportunity for the clubs to sell their players. The Major Leagues also favored the draft, which gave them access to all the best Minor League talent at reasonable prices. The draft was also good for the players, who had a systematic procedure for advancing their careers and earning more money.

However, the three highest-classification (Double-A) Minor Leagues—the International League, American Association, and Pacific Coast League—fervently fought against the draft. Most significantly, the owners knew that the draft price was generally much lower than what they could charge in a true open market. In addition, these teams and their fans often did not consider themselves to be "Minor League" at all and wanted to hang on to their players just as the Major League teams did.

After the wartime 1918 season, beset with broad losses throughout the Minors, the National Association declared itself opposed to the draft and other sections of the National Agreement. The Majors and the Minors agreed to let the agreement lapse, while separately and informally arranging to respect each other's territories and the reserve clause, giving teams complete control of their players. But the Minors were satisfied in their key demand that there be no draft by Major League clubs.

Over the next few years, as prosperity returned to the game, the leagues met after each season to try to hammer out a new National

Agreement. But more significant problems facing baseball—the Black Sox scandal, unresolved litigation from the Federal League settlement, and a bitter fight among the AL owners and league president Johnson— deferred the necessary focus and energy from the negotiations. The appointment of Kenesaw Landis as commissioner in November 1920 brought some stability back into the game, helping lead to a new National Agreement in early 1921. The new agreement reestablished the draft, but one of its provisions allowed five Minor Leagues, including the three Double-A circuits, to opt out.

After the 1923 season the draft was again revised, and only the International League continued to hold out. The modified draft included only players who had once been the property of the Major Leagues and had been demoted to the Minors. Players acquired either as amateurs or through lower leagues were exempt. The new draft allowed the higher Minor Leagues to find their own players and keep them, and also allowed them access to the lower Minors. After the 1924 season the International League finally relented, and all the Minor Leagues were once again subject to the draft. Owing to this short-term relaxation of the draft rules, however, teams such as the IL's Baltimore Orioles established some of the greatest Minor League teams in history.

Prior to the suspension of the draft in 1918, Minor League teams earned a significant portion of their income through the draft or by selling their top players. Major League teams at the time spent about $16,000 per team per year to acquire Minor League talent, with the high figure for one player being the $22,500 that Barney Dreyfuss paid for Marty O'Toole in 1913. Table 4 summarizes the total amounts paid to the Minors by the Majors from 1909 through 1914.

By the early 1920s, with the temporary absence of the baseball draft for Double-A leagues coupled with postwar prosperity, prices exploded past those of the previous decade. From 1922 to 1924 an annual average of just over $50,000 per team was paid by Major League teams to the Minors. The Baltimore Orioles, to cite one example, sold four players to the Philadelphia Athletics—Lefty Grove, George Earnshaw, Max Bishop, and Joe Boley—for a total of $245,000. In this period annual Major League team expenses, exclusive of player-acquisition costs, to-

Table 4. Payments by Majors to Minors, 1909–14

METHOD	1909	1910	1911	1912	1913	1914
Draft	$100,550	$84,500	$83,850	$103,000	$117,550	$56,500
Purchases	$145,000	$152,000	$158,000	$196,350	$188,250	$167,870
Total	$245,550	$236,500	$241,850	$299,350	$305,800	$224,370

Source: *Sporting News*, November 26, 1914, 3.

taled around $600,000, so the explosion in prices to buy Minor League players suddenly represented a significant share of a team's budget.

For the most part, Minor League teams were "developing" players. Major League clubs usually bought players who were ready to contribute in the big leagues, as they did not have a mechanism for controlling many still developing players. By the early 1920s Major League teams were limited by the same twenty-five-man (active) roster and forty-man (under control) roster still in use today. Subject to several technicalities, most of the fifteen nonactive players were sent to Minor League teams but remained under Major League–team control. The most common mechanism for this placement was the "optional assignment": the sale of a player to a Minor League team with the option to buy him back at a later date for a higher price. Merely "farming" a player—sending him to a Minor League team with the right to recall him at any time—was prohibited in the 1920s.

Part of the story of the Major League–Minor League relationship between 1900 and 1930 centered around Major League teams trying to evade these limitations and control extra players through covert agreements with friendly Minor League owners. In the 1910s several teams tried to either establish working relationships with Minor League teams or even directly own them. Some Minor League teams, such as Bob Quinn's Columbus team in the American Association, even created working relationships with nearby clubs in lower leagues.[1] Although the practice was limited in scope compared to what would come later, in 1913 the National Commission (the governing body of organized baseball) ruled that these affiliations violated the no-farming rule, and the teams would have to cease their Minor League relationships. The Federal League war during 1914 and 1915 effectively eliminated all restrictions on roster sizes and ownership, as the Majors and Minors banded together to freeze out the outlaw Federals. Once the Federal League folded in December 1915, the roster limits returned, though the ownership restrictions remained in limbo.

Branch Rickey, the general manager of the impoverished St. Louis Cardinals, first envisioned an organized "farm system" as a solution to the high cost of buying Minor League players. In Rickey's scheme a team could instead sign amateur players (for much less money than Minor League stars) and then assume the cost of developing the players on Minor League teams under its control. While living in Ohio years earlier, Rickey saw the success of Quinn's Columbus team and the value of its affiliations with lower-classification teams.[2] "We owed $175,000," Rickey later testified before a congressional hearing. "And we finished in last place in 1918. And I said to myself 'what can I do about it?' I have no money. We have a reserve list of 23 players [of the forty men allotted under the roster rules, the Cardinals controlled only twenty-three],' only three of whom were with the club two years later, for they did not rate. Clubs usually finish last on merit, because they do not have enough good players."[3]

"I had coaching friends," Rickey continued. "Coaches of college teams, and they would tell me about players, and they were not ready for the major leagues, but they were prospectively able to become members of a major league club."[4] For a relatively cheap price, Rickey purchased an interest in a team in Fort Smith, Arkansas, followed shortly thereafter by interests in clubs in Houston (Texas League) and Syracuse (International League). "The whole basic secret of it . . . is that the farm system is the only vehicle that a poor club has available to it to use to mount into respectability competitively."[5] While rudimentary compared to what would come later, Rickey's relationships with Minor League teams in the 1920s proved to be groundbreaking.

An interesting historical question is why Judge Landis, who had officially become baseball's commissioner in January 1921 and would prove to be a staunch critic of farm systems, did not work harder in his early years to ban ownership interests in Minor League teams. Landis always felt that such an arrangement would act to restrict the upward mobility of players and, if Major League teams recalled players during the season, destroy the legitimacy of Minor League pennant races. Landis's fears would be justified on both counts.

"Judge Landis consulted the two oldest men in baseball," recalled his secretary Leslie O'Connor. "The most experienced and very sensible, intelligent men, Barney Dreyfuss of the Pittsburgh Club and Frank Navin of the Detroit Club. And both of those gentlemen assured him that he need have no worries about it because it was financially destructive to a club to undertake to operate Minor League clubs, and that the thing would fall of its own weight. . . . He [Landis] was dissuaded from taking any action originally by the advice given him by Dreyfuss and Navin, which turned out to be inaccurate."[6] Moreover, Landis may simply not have wanted to confront his owners too directly on a matter he knew was important to them. Although he was firmly entrenched in his role, he remained ultimately beholden to the owners for his position.

Most of the other Major League teams were as skeptical of Rickey's idea as Dreyfuss and Navin. "It's the stupidest idea in baseball," said John McGraw. "What Rickey is trying to do can't be done."[7] As of the end of the 1927 season, the sixteen Major League clubs controlled very few farm teams, and these men had ample reason for skepticism.[8] Most significantly, investment in Minor League teams did not change the prevailing fact that a Major League team was still limited to controlling only forty players. One of the ways Rickey tried to circumvent this rule was to structure an option to purchase one or two players from a Minor League club without identifying them. Given that a Minor League team would be unlikely to have more than one or two Major League–ready players anyway, this would effectively allow Rickey to control well beyond forty players. The legality of this interpretation was debatable.[9]

While Rickey's early attempts at a Minor League organization helped restock his team on the field—the Cardinals won four pennants and two World Series between 1926 and 1931—owner Sam Breadon was unhappy with his financial return. In 1932, despite his four pennants,

Breadon looked into moving the Cardinals to Montreal, traveling there twice to investigate possible ballpark sites. Though Breadon backed off the move once the costs of relocation became apparent, he remained disappointed with his profits in St. Louis. He also considered a transfer to Detroit, an embryonic idea that was quickly vetoed by Tiger owner Frank Navin.[10] The Cardinals' Minor League system was exacting a cost on Breadon's finances, and the rest of baseball remained cautious. Furthermore, as historian Henry Fetter has pointed out, "Rickey's astute trades were far more responsible for replenishing the Cardinal talent pool after 1926 than the farm teams, but in 1931 this changed."[11] The Cardinals' farm system then began producing quality Major Leaguers, helping them to another Series victory in 1934. Other teams soon began to catch up.

Even the New York Yankees, who had the best scouts and the most money and were consequently the dominant team in the Majors, with successive four-game sweeps in the 1927 and 1928 World Series, were becoming frustrated with the high cost of purchasing Minor League players. Jacob Ruppert, who had recently paid $125,000 to the Oakland Oaks for Lyn Lary and Jimmy Reese, the highest single transaction price to date for Minor Leaguers, only to discover that neither looked likely to be a star, vented his frustration at winter meetings in December 1929:

> I do not know whether a major league club owner makes money or loses money on the clubs he owns, and I do not care. That is not my business. I know I am going to be forced into owning minor league clubs and so is every other major league owner in this room, for the simple reason, as was stated before by Mr. Breadon and Mr. Navin, where are we eventually going to get our ballplayers from? I do not know which club—I don't care which ballclub it is—can afford to pay the prices for the minor league ballplayers that we are paying for them now. The minor leagues have got us just where they want us. I for one am opposed to owning minor league ball clubs. As I said repeatedly, and I will say again, I for one am going to own a minor-league ballclub, although it is against my own idea, but at the same time I must do something to develop my own players.[12]

Ruppert continued to push his concerns over the next two years, and by the time of the 1931 meetings, the environment had changed. The Great Depression had devastated the Minor Leagues, which sent a representative to the big-league meetings, begging for financial support. After a long, confusing discussion of existing roster rules involving several club officers, notably Ruppert and Rickey, the owners agreed that Major League teams could invest in and provide financial assistance to Minor League clubs. In return a Major League team could secure the rights to the players on the Minor League team, and those players would not count against their forty-man roster. This measure was originally considered temporary and applicable only to Class B leagues and below, but, much to Landis's chagrin, the new understanding was soon applied to all Minor Leagues and made permanent.

It is to Ruppert's credit that he recognized the transformative impact of this rule change, as most owners saw it as evolutionary and not truly revolutionary. Ruppert immediately embarked on building baseball's best and most organized system. In the fall of 1931 he had purchased Newark's International League franchise, and in February 1932 he announced that the Yankees intended to own or control four Minor League teams in different classifications.

Chart 1 illustrates the evolution of the farm system as Minor League teams became affiliated with Major League franchises. The top line indicates the number of Minor League teams in organized baseball each year between 1920 and 1960.[13] It has three dips: during the early years of the Great Depression, a trend that reversed after the Major Leagues changed the roster rules; during World War II, when nearly all young American men were in the service; and in the late 1950s, a drop usually blamed on television. This last reduction was permanent, though the expansion of the Major Leagues created a need for more Minor League teams today (more than two hundred) than there were in the late 1950s.

The bottom line indicates the number of Minor League teams that had some form of affiliation with a Major League team. In the early years these might have been informal arrangements, whereby a big-league club could option a few players to the Minors for the year. Once Major League teams could control a virtually unlimited number of

Chart 1. The farm system from 1920 to 1960

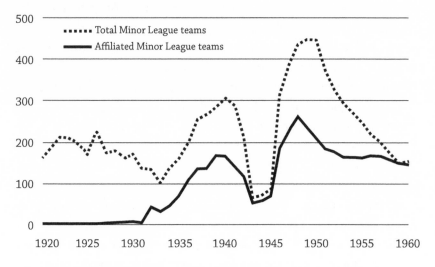

Source: U.S. House of Representatives, *Hearings Before the Subcommittee on the Study of Monopoly Power of the Committee on the Judiciary: Organized Baseball*, 82nd Cong., 1st sess. (1952); Lloyd Johnson and Miles Wolff, eds., *The Encyclopedia of Minor League Baseball*, 3rd ed. (Durham NC: Baseball America, 2007).

players, however, the Major League team often controlled most or all of the players on a Minor League team, perhaps even owning the team outright. By 1960 nearly every Minor League club was affiliated with a Major League organization.

Major League organizations set up their farm systems at vastly different speeds. In the first ten years of the relaxed rules (1932–41), the Yankees averaged 9.5 affiliations per year, which was the highest total in the American League. Rickey's Cardinals, however, had more than twice that total, averaging more than 20 farm teams a year. The smallest farms were those of the Phillies and Athletics, who averaged fewer than 3. After the war the totals were higher, and nearly all organizations had at least 10-team farms for several years.

The introduction and evolution of the farm system were the most significant changes to the nature of team building and talent acquisition during the first half of the twentieth century. The ability to sign virtually unlimited numbers of teenage players and systematically train and develop them over a period of years changed the way teams acquired and advanced talent. No longer did a team need to risk spending huge amounts of money on Minor League players, nor were they more than temporarily inconvenienced when a player was injured—another could always be promoted from the Minors. Moreover, the ability to standardize training methods and in-game tactics allowed teams to instill a sense of organizational pride throughout the system.

6 Organization

The emergence of management has converted knowledge from social ornament and luxury into the true capital of any economy.—PETER DRUCKER, management consultant

As New York Yankees owner Jacob Ruppert prepared to attend the winter meetings after the 1935 season, he was not a satisfied man. His team had just finished in second place for the third straight season, and as he had told Joe McCarthy upon hiring him five years earlier, "I'll stand for finishing second this year, McCarthy. But remember, I do not like to finish second."[1] Over the previous seven seasons the Yankees had won only one pennant, with a dominant 107-win team that captured the 1932 World Series in four games.

The 1929–35 teams had been regularly competitive—in their six non-pennant-winning seasons the Yankees had finished second five times and third once—but Ruppert wanted more. Although he had not actively participated in the annual "trading mart," leaving the baseball matters to general manager Ed Barrow, at the 1935 winter meetings in Chicago Ruppert tried to take matters into his own hands. A year earlier Boston's new owner, Tom Yawkey, had purchased shortstop Joe Cronin from the Washington Senators for an astounding $250,000—an amount greater than the entire player payroll of fourteen of the sixteen teams. A year later Ruppert mimicked Yawkey's strategy with Washington owner Clark Griffith, making an offer for second baseman Buddy Myer, the 1935 AL batting champion. But Griffith considered the Cronin sale a onetime thing and had no interest in selling more players. Still, Ruppert demanded that Griffith name a price. Flippantly, Griffith told Ruppert that he wanted $500,000. "And do you know that Ruppert almost made a deal with me," Griffith recounted. "He actually was going to give the Washington club $400,000 and second baseman Tony Lazzeri for Myer, until Ed Barrow, his business manager, stopped him. If Barrow hadn't been around that night, I'd have made a $400,000 sale."[2]

Though Ruppert did not bag the star, his worries would soon be over. The Yankees were about to embark on one of the greatest stretches of winning baseball in the history of the sport. The credit for this success has been given to many people over the years, but no one deserves it more than Ruppert. The Yankees won because they had an extraordinary organization of talented people—from the general manager, to the farm director, to the field manager, to the players. The person who created this incredible organization, deliberately and brilliantly, was Jake Ruppert.

Beginning in 1932 Major League teams were free to establish tight affiliations with Minor League teams, controlling most or all of the players on the team's roster. As mentioned in the previous chapter, Jacob Ruppert recognized better than almost anyone the sweeping impact that a farm system could make and was determined to build the biggest and best. There was no blueprint on how to design, organize, and manage a farm system. Ruppert could have simply piled the job onto the existing front-office structure of Barrow and his scouts and let Barrow figure out how to staff and run it. But Ruppert knew that he needed a new kind of executive to run this new, complex organization.

Barrow recommended former Yankee scout Bob Connery, by then the owner of the St. Paul Saints of the American Association. Connery was only forty-eight, but Ruppert decided that he wanted a younger man. He probably viewed the hire for this position as an understudy for the sixty-three-year-old Barrow. Moreover, Ruppert had paid Connery's St. Paul club around three hundred thousand dollars for players, and other than shortstop Mark Koenig, none had developed into more than a passable Major Leaguer. Additionally, Ruppert suspected he had been treated unfairly in the high-priced acquisition of a player whose rights he believed he already controlled.[3] In any event, after a thorough investigation Ruppert chose longtime Minor League operative George Weiss, then the general manager of the Baltimore club in the International League. A native of New Haven, Connecticut, Weiss was only thirty-seven, but had already spent nearly two decades in baseball. Like Barrow, Weiss was a workaholic who had begun his career in baseball promotion while still in his teens. Also like Barrow, Weiss proved to be a brilliant hire.[4]

While Ruppert was restructuring his organization, he also had to deal with transitions in the dugout. Miller Huggins, his handpicked manager who had justified Ruppert's confidence with six pennants and three world championships in twelve seasons, fell ill late in the 1929 season and passed away on September 25 at the age of fifty. Babe Ruth, who had never liked or respected Huggins, made it known that he wanted to replace him. Ruppert and Barrow never seriously considered Ruth, still the greatest player in the game, and offered the job to three other people before settling on Bob Shawkey, their former star pitcher. Shawkey's club finished third in 1930, with eighty-six wins, eighteen games behind the Athletics.

After a single season Barrow dismissed Shawkey in favor of Joe McCarthy, recently deposed manager of the Cubs. McCarthy was a serious man, suspicious with the press, but he got along well with his bosses and his players. Ruth never stopped thinking that the job should be his, and the big star generally behaved however he wanted, but he and McCarthy managed to coexist for four productive seasons. In McCarthy's second year, 1932, the Yankees returned to the World Series and easily defeated the Cubs in four straight games.

Though Ed Barrow and George Weiss both reported to Ruppert, in reality they, and Joe McCarthy, all worked together. Ruppert maintained an office in his brewery but talked to Barrow nearly every day. Barrow often called in the late morning to give Ruppert an update of the day's business. On days without a game, Barrow met with the press on many afternoons to fill them in on those items with which he felt they could be trusted. On game days Barrow would head over to the stadium about one o'clock and eat lunch with McCarthy at the commissary, providing an opportunity for the two to catch up on issues and concerns. Barrow would then retire to his box to watch the game, usually in the company of a couple of friends. When Ruppert went to a game he was notoriously nervous when watching from his field box, fidgeting and anxious unless the Yankees held a big lead. Weiss focused principally on operating the Newark club and overseeing and expanding the farm system. In November, when Ruppert and Barrow headed off to French Lick and its famous sulfur springs for some rest and relaxation, Weiss frequently managed the office in their absence. Often he would follow to Indiana a week or two later, as would McCarthy. The foursome would spend much of their vacation discussing how to improve the ball club.[5]

The Yankee scouts reported to Barrow, who now redirected his staff to intensify their focus on amateurs rather than experienced Minor Leaguers. After the unproductive $50,000 purchase of Danny MacFayden from the Red Sox in June 1932, the Yankees significantly curtailed their purchases of ready-made ballplayers, whether from the high Minors or other American League ball clubs. Instead, they concentrated on finding players for their own Minor League teams. The timing of this philosophical change was interesting, because in the early 1930s, with the Depression severely affecting baseball, a new source of Major League players suddenly became available. Connie Mack, fresh off three straight pennants from 1929 to 1931, was dumping his stars, as he had in the 1910s.

In his first transaction after the 1932 season, Mack sent Al Simmons, Jimmy Dykes, and Mule Haas to the Chicago White Sox for around $150,000. This represented a huge expenditure for the Chicago owners, the heirs to team founder Charles Comiskey, who were not independently wealthy. Mack seemingly spurned the Yankees when marketing his players, though Ruppert and Barrow were likely not as interested as they would have been in previous years. Other than the Yankees, however, no AL team had much money in those difficult times. Mack's luck improved considerably when thirty-year-old multimillionaire Tom Yawkey bought the Red Sox and announced his intentions to spend money. The impatient Yawkey soon gave Mack $125,000 for future Hall of Fame pitcher Lefty Grove and a couple of other capable ballplayers.

Meanwhile, the Yankees were tiring of Ruth. His habit of showing up whenever he pleased was tolerated when he was hitting .340 with forty-five home runs every year, but in 1933 the thirty-eight-year-old Ruth, increasingly overweight, slipped to .301 with thirty-four home runs. Much of his happy-go-lucky youthful energy had given way to surliness, particularly with respect to McCarthy. After the season Ruppert offered him the managerial position at Newark, as a possible stepping-stone to a Major League job, but Ruth's ego would not let him accept anything less than a big-league spot. Ruppert had another chance to appease Ruth when Detroit's Frank Navin, looking to fire up his fan base, asked if he could have Ruth as his player-manager. Ruppert and Barrow agreed to let Ruth go, particularly since they might receive a useful player in return. Believing the opportunity would remain open, Ruth ignored Navin's request to meet him in Detroit and went off on his scheduled Hawaiian trip. Navin, with no desire to wait and now having observed Ruth's lack of self-discipline firsthand, chose to move in a different direction. He cobbled together $100,000 to purchase Mickey Cochrane from Mack's Athletics to be his player-manager. With Cochrane on board, the Tigers captured the American League flag in both the 1934 and the 1935 seasons.

The Ruth problem continued to fester—he further tumbled to .288 and twenty-two home runs in 1934—and when he returned from a baseball tour of Japan after the season, Ruth publicly declared he would come back only as a manager. Although Ruppert liked Ruth, he and Barrow had no intention of acquiescing. To alleviate the problem once and for all, the two orchestrated the transfer of Ruth to the Boston Braves, where he would have the titles of vice president and assistant manager, while also playing. Braves owner Judge Emil Fuchs hoped that by returning Ruth to the city where he had debuted as a Major Leaguer, he could rekindle some fan interest in his Depression-ravaged team.

The Ruth saga tells us a lot about how Ruppert wanted his organization to run. All of his important hires—starting with Huggins and continuing with Barrow, McCarthy, and Weiss—were highly skilled men who offered very little drama or personality. Highly competitive and laser-focused on doing their jobs, they gave nothing to the hungry New York press corps other than winning teams. Many of the best Yankee players, especially Lou Gehrig, were much the same way. Babe Ruth, of course, was the great exception to this rule, and part of his larger-than-life story is that Ruth was surrounded by highly accomplished people perfectly willing to let him have all the attention. No matter how well Huggins or McCarthy managed, or how well Barrow provided talent, the Yankees were always going to be Ruth's team. Had Ruth played for a different sort of manager, someone like John McGraw, things might not have gone so smoothly.

Ruth's massive ego and irresponsible personal habits were a small price to pay for having the greatest player in the world on one's team. But the idea of this man being the Yankee manager seems completely incongruous from what we know about Ruppert and, particularly, Barrow. The two executives might have wanted the likable Ruth to get a chance to manage in the Major Leagues—but certainly not for the Yankees.

The first Yankee season without Ruth, 1935, went much the same as their previous two with him: second place, this time just three games behind the Tigers. These Yankees had a lot of young talent. Of the starting eight position players on the 1935 squad, only 1920s holdovers Gehrig and Lazzeri were over thirty. Shortstop Frank Crosetti and catcher Bill Dickey had been purchased from the Minors in the late 1920s. Among the top starting pitchers, Red Ruffing and Johnny Allen were the old men at thirty. Ruffing had come from the Red Sox in 1930, while fellow ace Lefty Gomez had been purchased from San Francisco. Solid midrotation starters Monte Pearson and Bump Hadley were acquired via trade after the 1935 season.

What turned this good team into a great team was George Weiss's new farm system, which began to bear fruit. Third baseman Red Rolfe, signed by Krichell off of the Dartmouth campus, had been one of the first amateurs signed for the system, and outfielder George Selkirk, although purchased from the Minors, had spent several years on Weiss's farm. Starter Johnny Broaca had been signed by Krichell from Yale University and also spent time in the system. All three were key performers on the 1936 squad.

Another pitcher, Johnny Murphy, used his fine curve ball to earn a total of twenty-four wins over the 1934 and 1935 seasons. McCarthy believed a starter could not be successful with only one Major League–caliber pitch and felt Murphy would never develop another one. Rather than casting his pitcher aside, he turned Murphy into an ace reliever, a role no high-quality pitcher had held since Firpo Marberry several years earlier.

But the greatest addition to the 1936 Yankees was acquired the old-fashioned way. In November 1934 Yankee scouts Bill Essick and Joe Devine convinced Barrow and Ruppert that a knee injury suffered by San Francisco outfielder Joe DiMaggio was not chronic. DiMaggio had been one of the brightest prospects in the country before he got hurt that season, causing most teams to back away from pursuing the youngster. Before the injury Seals owner Charley Graham had hoped for a huge payday, but with his team badly hurt by the Depression, he chose not to wait for a better deal.

"Development of our farm system does not mean we are not open for purchases," Ruppert said a few years later. "It was in the open market that we found Joe DiMaggio with the San Francisco Seals. A bad knee had scared everybody else off DiMaggio. But we risked $25,000 in cash and five players, and landed a star whom I would not sell for $250,000."[6] As part of the deal, the Yankees allowed DiMaggio to spend another season with the Seals. He hit .398 over 172 games in 1935, showing now jealous suitors what they had missed out on.

In 1936, with the twenty-one-year-old DiMaggio in their outfield, the Yankees exploded from the gate. After sweeping a July 4 doubleheader in Washington, the Yankees' record stood at 51-22. Boasting six future Hall of Famers all having good seasons—Gehrig, Lazzeri, DiMaggio, Dickey, Ruffing, and Gomez—the team finished 102-51, 19.5 games in front of the second-place Tigers. The powerhouse club excelled both at the bat and in the field, scoring 1,065 runs, the second-highest total in league history, while leading the league in ERA. In the World Series the Yankees beat their bitter crosstown rivals, the New York Giants, four games to two.

Ruppert, Barrow, and Weiss did not rest on their laurels. During the following off-season the team brought the Kansas City franchise (American Association) into the Yankee fold. The Yankees now possessed a ten-team system: four by outright ownership and six by working agreement. Only Branch Rickey's St. Louis Cardinals could boast a larger chain, and no other Major League organization was at the level of these two.

By early in the 1937 season it was clear that Ruppert, Barrow, and McCarthy had created something special. That season played out much like the previous one, quashing any hope by their AL rivals that the 1936 runaway had been a fluke. DiMaggio led the league in home runs and hit .346. Gomez won 21 games and led the league in ERA. McCarthy continued his brilliant use of ace reliever Murphy, who started only 4 games but finished 13-4 in 110 innings pitched. Their most important addition was rookie Tommy Henrich, who joined the team early in the season from Newark. The Yankees had signed Henrich just prior to the season after Judge Landis voided his Indians contract, ruling that Cleveland had conspired to keep him hidden in their farm system. Henrich hit .320 in 67 games and promised more. The Yankees again won 102 games, while leading the league in runs scored and fewest runs allowed. And again the Yankees dispatched their New York rivals in the World Series.

What made the Yankees' dominance even more disheartening for their fellow American League franchises was the amount of talent they had in the Minor Leagues, nearly ready to join the powerhouse in New York. The Yankees' top farm team in Newark compiled a winning percentage above .700 and won the International League title by a record 25.5 games. It boasted a number of future Major League regulars, including Joe Gordon, Babe Dahlgren, Charlie Keller, George McQuinn, Atley Donald, and Marius Russo.

These players testify to the successful change of focus by the Yankees' scouts from the high Minors to the amateur ranks. Bill Essick signed Gordon from the University of Oregon and assigned him to Oakland for the 1936 season, before bringing him to Newark. Krichell signed Russo, a collegiate star at Long Island University who had also pitched semiprofessionally. Donald pitched for Louisiana Tech and was so determined to join the Yankees that he rode the bus to St. Petersburg for a chance to try out during spring training and was signed by scout Johnny Nee. Another top-notch scout, Gene McCann, landed University of Maryland star Keller. "I have just signed the greatest prospect I have ever seen," McCann wired Barrow afterward.[7] McCann also signed McQuinn.

Prior to the 1938 season DiMaggio engaged in a bitter contract dispute that kept him away from the team for several weeks. When he finally signed in late spring, the Yankees arranged a publicity event. Ruppert uncharacteristically hurried through the affair, saying that he had some important business. In fact, Ruppert had a doctor's appointment to treat phlebitis, an inflammation of the veins in his left leg. Although the condition was not thought to be serious, Ruppert was confined to his home for several days.

With DiMaggio in the fold, the 1938 Yankees won their third straight pennant and World Series, sweeping the Cubs, and again led the league in both runs and ERA. The Yankees were again unafraid to integrate high-quality young players into their lineup, bringing up Gordon to replace Lazzeri at second base and handing the full-time right-field job to Henrich. Gordon and Henrich went on to become vital components of the Yankee lineup for several years.

Ruppert and the Yankees did experience an embarrassing episode that exposed how far the Yankees, baseball, and America had to go on racial matters. In late July, while on a road trip to Chicago, reserve outfielder Jake Powell was asked on a radio show how he kept in shape over the winter. He replied, "Oh, that's easy. I'm a policeman and I beat n———s over the head with my blackjack while on my beat."[8] In 1938 organized baseball was still several years away from employing black players. Because African Americans were denied access to most of the fruits of American society, baseball owners, players, fans, and the mainstream media did not concern themselves much with the all-white nature of their sport.

Nevertheless, blacks attended Major League games and listened on the radio, and many of them immediately deluged the Yankees and the Commissioner's Office, demanding punishment for Powell and a statement repudiating his offensive remarks. The vehemence of the reaction surprised and confused the baseball establishment. The mainstream press had minimized and underestimated the impact of Powell's comment on the black community.

As a sop baseball commissioner Landis suspended Powell for ten days in the hope of defusing the situation. Both McCarthy and Landis blamed the press. McCarthy ruled that he would no longer allow radio interviews with his players unless from a prepared script. This suspension and halfhearted response from baseball and the Yankees did little to placate black Americans.

Ruppert no more understood the anger than the rest of white America. For the time, the Yankees had a generally good relationship with the black community. To preserve some of this goodwill, Ruppert and Barrow ordered Powell to make amends by visiting black newspapers, businesses, and bars. Powell dutifully toured these establishments and apologized for his remarks. Some accepted his apology as sincere, but the controversy lingered, with a significant share of New York's black community calling for Powell's exile via trade or sale. In the end it turned out Powell had never actually been a policeman in Dayton. In 1948 while in police custody for passing bad checks, Powell committed suicide by shooting himself.

Although the Yankees and the rest of baseball did not know it, the days of half measures to appease the black community would soon come to an end. As the Powell controversy was playing out, Jackie Robinson was a nineteen-year-old star athlete in Pasadena, California.

In 1939 the Yankees captured their fourth straight pennant—tying a record held by the St. Louis Browns of the old American Association and, more important, by John McGraw's New York Giants. But Ruppert would not live to see it. Throughout 1938 Ruppert had struggled with his phlebitis and its complications. On January 13, 1939, after dropping in and out of a coma for several days, the seventy-one-year-old Ruppert died at his home. Nearing the end, he emerged from a coma to see Barrow standing by his bed. "Do you think we will win the pennant again?" he asked. "We'll win again, Colonel," Barrow reassured him.[9]

The 1939 Yankees were their best team yet. For the fourth consecutive season the Yankees led the league in most runs scored and fewest allowed. The club finished with a winning percentage above .700 and a record of 106-45. At first base Babe Dahlgren adequately replaced Gehrig, tragically deteriorating due to (as yet undiagnosed) amyotrophic lateral sclerosis, or ALS. The rest of the infield—Gordon, Crosetti, and Rolfe—carried over from 1938, and Dickey still anchored the team behind the plate. The team boasted four excellent outfielders: DiMaggio,

Table 5. 1923 Yankees

C	Wally Schang	Acquired from Boston (AL)
1B	Wally Pipp	Acquired from Detroit (AL)
2B	Aaron Ward	Minor League purchase
SS	Everett Scott	Acquired from Boston (AL)
3B	Joe Dugan	Acquired from Boston (AL)
LF	Bob Meusel	Minor League purchase
CF	Whitey Witt	Acquired from Philadelphia (AL)
RF	Babe Ruth	Acquired from Boston (AL)
P	Sam Jones	Acquired from Boston (AL)
P	Joe Bush	Acquired from Boston (AL)
P	Herb Pennock	Acquired from Boston (AL)
P	Bob Shawkey	Acquired from Philadelphia (AL)
P	Waite Hoyt	Acquired from Boston (AL)

Source: Daniel R. Levitt, *Ed Barrow: The Bulldog Who Built the Yankees' First Dynasty* (Lincoln: University of Nebraska Press, 2008).

Selkirk, Keller, and Henrich. Ruffing and Gomez anchored an extremely deep pitching staff. In the World Series the Yankees easily topped the Cincinnati Reds in four games, capturing their fourth straight title.

A comparison of the 1939 team with previous champions from 1923 and 1927 highlights the Yankees' adjustment to the circumstances of the time. Of the 1923 team's top thirteen players—eight position players and five pitchers—all but two came from other American League teams. The Yankees purchased eight of them, including four of their top pitchers, from Harry Frazee.

By 1927 the Yankees had retooled with players purchased at high prices from the high Minor Leagues. Combs, Lazzeri, and Koenig cost the Yankees around $150,000 in the mid-1920s. The team still relied on

Table 6. 1927 Yankees

C	Pat Collins	Minor League purchase
1B	Lou Gehrig	Signed as amateur
2B	Tony Lazzeri	Minor League purchase
SS	Mark Koenig	Minor League purchase
3B	Joe Dugan	Acquired from Boston (AL)
LF	Bob Meusel	Minor League purchase
CF	Earle Combs	Minor League purchase
RF	Babe Ruth	Acquired from Boston (AL)
P	Urban Shocker	Acquired from St. Louis (AL)
P	Waite Hoyt	Acquired from Boston (AL)
P	Herb Pennock	Acquired from Boston (AL)
P	Dutch Ruether	Acquired from Washington (AL)
P	Wilcy Moore	Minor League purchase

Source: Levitt, *Ed Barrow*.

Major League veterans for its starting rotation, but five of their eight position players debuted as rookies with the Yankees.

The 1939 roster underlines the success of the Yankees scouting staff and farm system in the changing era.

Only three of the top fifteen players on the 1939 squad were purchased from other Major League organizations. Four were purchased from the high Minors, and unlike those acquired in the mid-1920s, many spent time seasoning in the Yankee farm system subsequent to their acquisition. Six were signed as amateurs and developed in the Minor Leagues. And many were recent young promotions to the big leagues. The Yankees introduced new All-Star-caliber players every year, bringing in Joe DiMaggio (1936), Tommy Henrich (1937), Spud Chandler (1937), Joe Gordon (1938), and Charlie Keller (1939) in only four seasons.[10]

Table 7. 1939 Yankees

C	Bill Dickey	Minor League purchase
1B	Babe Dahlgren	Acquired from Boston (AL)
2B	Joe Gordon	Signed as amateur
SS	Frank Crosetti	Minor League purchase
3B	Red Rolfe	Signed as amateur
LF	Charlie Keller	Signed as amateur
CF	Joe DiMaggio	Minor League purchase
RF	Tommy Henrich	Signed as Minor League free agent
OF	George Selkirk	Minor League purchase
P	Red Ruffing	Acquired from Boston (AL)
P	Lefty Gomez	Minor League purchase
P	Bump Hadley	Acquired from Washington (AL)
P	Atley Donald	Signed as amateur
P	Marius Russo	Signed as amateur
P	Johnny Murphy	Signed as amateur

Source: Levitt, *Ed Barrow*.

Major League contenders often resort to finding aging Major League veterans to fill in holes in the club. The Yankees had enough confidence in their scouts and their Minor League system to instead promote their own players. The quality of the Yankee scouting and development system and Ruppert's willingness to spend made this strategy highly successful.

Jacob Ruppert was a model baseball owner, whose achievements the Baseball Hall of Fame finally recognized with induction in 2013. As a businessman Ruppert understood the importance of professional management, and after a few years of trying to run the team with Til Huston, he brought in Ed Barrow and gave him the budget and authority to make baseball decisions. Ruppert took no financial distributions from the team and paid the highest salaries in baseball. He aggressively pursued the players his executives and scouts recommended, paying top dollar for both Major and Minor League stars. Ruppert also recognized and shaped baseball's trends. When the price of Minor League stars escalated beyond reason, Ruppert lobbied to amend the roster rules and grasped the long-range implications of the changes. He understood that the changing environment called for an organized farm system, and he hired a new type of executive, George Weiss, who ultimately built baseball's best.

Ruppert had an almost unerring eye for hiring key personnel. "Pick the right people to pick the right people," Hall of Fame general manager Pat Gillick once said.[11] Ruppert did so magnificently. During his ownership tenure, he hired four managers. Two, Huggins and McCarthy, encompassing twenty of the twenty-four years he owned the club, became legendary managers and are in the Baseball Hall of Fame. Ruppert had similar success with his front office. His two key hires, Barrow and Weiss, are also in the Hall of Fame, two of the greatest executives in baseball history. Moreover, Ruppert had the conviction to hire Huggins and Weiss over the objections of a trusted partner and adviser, respectively. Barrow followed Ruppert's lead by hiring the best staff, including some of the most acclaimed scouts in baseball history.

Once he had a crack team in place, Ruppert supervised it flawlessly. He pushed, he asked questions, and he demanded results, but he rarely interfered with his hires' spheres of authority and backed them up when needed. His men cared little for getting their names in the paper, obsessed only with winning. Ruppert committed most of his own energy and most of his money to the effort. Ruppert had several exotic hobbies, but baseball was more than an avocation. He crafted and oversaw his team with passion and commitment and created the greatest baseball organization of his generation.

PART 2 • *General Manager Ascendant*

7 Dodger Way

Between 1938 and 1967 three men held the job of Brooklyn (later Los Angeles) Dodgers general manager. The first two—Larry MacPhail and Branch Rickey—are among the most celebrated team architects in baseball history. Together they won a total of three pennants, though no World Series titles, with the Dodgers. The third, the less famous Buzzie Bavasi, won eight pennants and four World Series in eighteen years of running the club. Of course, MacPhail and Rickey won championships with other teams and are justly credited with profoundly changing the way baseball organizations functioned, how and when and for whom the game was played, and who was allowed to play it. MacPhail and Rickey were more than general managers in Brooklyn— they were team presidents who ran the entire operation. Bavasi, on the other hand, worked for a powerful and accomplished owner—Walter O'Malley—who was always the public face of the team.

O'Malley hired Bavasi to run the Major League team and generally left Bavasi alone and watched the pennants pile up. To be sure, Bavasi had some advantages. "[Bavasi] learned [baseball] under Larry MacPhail and Branch Rickey," Jim Murray once wrote. "That was like learning war under Genghis Kahn and Machiavelli. And Bavasi never knew what it was to work under a dilettante owner, some millionaire who wanted a ball club instead of a yacht."[1]

If Bavasi is overlooked today, it may be partially because he did himself no favors. In a series of articles he wrote for *Sports Illustrated* in 1967, he repeatedly downplayed his own role in his club's success. "Running a ball club is 10% skill, 40% having the right men working for you and 50% dumb luck," he wrote.[2] One cannot imagine Rickey or MacPhail voicing such an opinion. Likewise, Bavasi's 1987 memoir is a collection of funny stories in which the author is often the butt of the joke, along with stories of all his lucky trades.[3] Still, few general managers win eight pennants.

MacPhail turned the Dodgers around in his frenetic, aggressive, haphazard way; Rickey brought structure and a farm system; and Bavasi made the entire system even better. Along the way the Dodgers created an unparalleled organization: brilliant, innovative scouts and scouting techniques, plus a strong farm system staff instilled with standardized training methods. In addition, the Dodgers, better than most, took advantage of the two main transformations after World War II in the sourcing of talent—the availability of African American players (a change the Dodgers initiated) and the free-spending pursuit of top amateurs.

When Leland Stanford "Larry" MacPhail took over the Dodgers in early 1938, he already had a fair bit of fame. Born in Michigan in 1890, he earned a law degree from Georgetown, ran a department store in Nashville, served as an artillery captain in France during the Great War, and practiced law in Columbus, Ohio. In 1931 he helped broker the sale of the (American Association) Columbus Redbirds to Branch Rickey, and the club became part of the growing Cardinals farm system. MacPhail became the president, and the team enjoyed much success on and off the field.

After the 1933 season MacPhail was asked to run the struggling Cincinnati Reds franchise. He quickly turned the business around, making it profitable in a few years. He spent money fixing up the ballpark and staged many promotions and events. He hired a college football announcer named Red Barber to broadcast Cincinnati games, greatly expanding both the number of games and the reach of the radio network at a time when most of baseball was leery of the new medium. He installed lights at Crosley Field and staged the first-ever Major League night game in 1935. The Reds improved on the field, advancing from eighth (last) in 1934 to fifth (74-80) in 1936.

Into the bargain with his obvious business genius, MacPhail could be abusive and abrasive when he drank, which he did often. After the 1936 season Cincinnati owner Powel Crosley decided that MacPhail's positives were no longer worth the embarrassment and fired him. Crosley hired the talented but comparatively dull Warren Giles, who made a few astute trades and won pennants in 1939 and 1940.

While the Reds were on the rise, the Brooklyn Dodgers had become a laughingstock, losing ball games and bleeding money. The 1925 deaths of both Charles Ebbets and Ed McKeever, who between them owned 75 percent of the team, had left club ownership in the hands of squabbling heirs and, once the Depression hit, impatient bankers. By late 1937 the Dodgers were $700,000 in debt and losing more than $100,000 a year.[4] In desperation, the club asked Branch Rickey, who was running the Cardinals, if he would come to Brooklyn and take over the Dodgers. Rickey turned them down but suggested MacPhail, who took the job.

MacPhail's transformation of the Dodgers was rapid. He began by cleaning, repairing, and repainting Ebbets Field, again installing lights so that the Dodgers could play some night games. He brought Barber from Cincinnati and abrogated a three-way agreement among the Dodgers, Giants, and Yankees by broadcasting Brooklyn's games. Home attendance increased from 482,000 in 1937 to a league-leading 976,000 in 1940 and then to a franchise record 1,215,000 in 1941. By 1940 the Dodgers were turning a profit and by 1941 were out of debt.

At least as importantly (and, of course, a key driver for the turnaround at the turnstiles), MacPhail greatly improved the product on the field. He bought slugger Dolph Camilli from the Phillies for $45,000 in early 1938 and Whitlow Wyatt from the Indians a few months later. In 1939 MacPhail promoted shortstop Leo Durocher to player-manager.

MacPhail landed Pete Reiser in 1938 after baseball commissioner Landis freed a number of Minor Leaguers, including Reiser, from Rickey's Cardinal farm system for the circumvention of various rules. MacPhail and Rickey had apparently negotiated a secret agreement whereby the Cardinals could reacquire him at a later date, but Reiser remained a Dodger.[5] That same year MacPhail drafted Hugh Casey from Memphis, and in 1939 he purchased Pee Wee Reese from Louisville. These new acquisitions soon paid dividends. Dixie Walker was claimed off waivers from Detroit in July 1939 and became one of the most popular Dodger players ever. With Durocher at the helm, the 1939 team won 84 games and finished third. The next year they won 88 and finished second.

As the team became profitable MacPhail poured even more money into the club. In June 1940 he sent four players and $125,000 to the

Cardinals for pitcher Curt Davis and slugging outfielder Joe Medwick, who both provided excellent production for a few years. After the season he sent three players and another $100,000 to the Phillies for pitcher Kirby Higbe, who won 22 games in 1941. The 1941 club, made up mainly of men MacPhail had brought into the organization over the previous three years, broke through and won 100 games and Brooklyn's first NL pennant since 1920. After the season MacPhail acquired Arky Vaughan from the Pirates for four players. The 1942 Dodgers won a franchise record 104 games but were overtaken by a Cardinal club that won 38 of its final 44 contests.

Despite his success, after five years MacPhail had again worn out his welcome due to his personality and his profligate spending. In September 1942 MacPhail, probably sensing that his time was up, entered military service. During MacPhail's five years at the helm, the Dodgers had evolved from a pathetic franchise to one of the best teams in baseball. The Dodgers again offered the presidency to Rickey. This time they got their man.

Branch Rickey was sixty when he joined the Dodgers in late 1942. By the age of thirty, he had retired from his brief Major League playing career and had received a law degree from the University of Michigan. The practice of law did not appeal to Rickey, and by 1913 he was back in baseball, where he remained for the next five decades. Rickey managed parts of ten seasons with the Browns and Cardinals without much success but made his mark as general manager (under various titles) with the Cardinals from 1917 to 1942. In the mid-1920s Cardinals owner Sam Breadon gave Rickey the go-ahead to create affiliations with several Minor League teams, the start of what became a full-scale farm system, the first of its kind.

Soon after Rickey created his system, he realized that he needed a cohesive philosophy of scouting, instruction, and coaching. As discussed earlier, prior to the 1930s most Major League players were acquired via purchase or the draft from the high Minors, and most of these players were assumed to be big league ready. Now, since the players being scouted were so raw—essentially just coming out of high school and occasionally college—scouts were no longer simply finding the best players but the players who were projected to be the best. Rickey's scouts looked for raw athletic skills, especially speed, one skill that could help on both offense and defense. Certain scouting principles became law. Defense could be taught, but an overstriding hitter could not be corrected.

For similar reasons the new model required much more coordinated instruction. The Cardinals were not signing ready-made players; they were signing boys who needed to be taught how to play. Every part of the game—bunting, sliding, run-down plays, and so on—Rickey wanted to be taught consistently throughout the organization. And Rickey wanted the scouting and player-development parts of the system to work hand in hand. As Kevin Kerrane wrote in his classic book on scouting, "Rickey applied scouting insights to teaching, and vice versa."[6]

For his part, Rickey became a legendary talent evaluator, able to make decisions quickly on players. Besides speed, he also valued youth. No sentimentalist, he tried to trade players before they started to decline rather than after. With his huge farm system, he believed he could fill the holes created when he traded his veterans away.

From 1926 to 1942 the Cardinals won six pennants and four World Series, then captured three more pennants and two Series titles in the four years after Rickey left. Rickey had not been getting along with owner Sam Breadon, who had become disenchanted with how much Rickey was earning under his incentive-laden contract. When the Dodgers offered a job with more authority in October 1942, Rickey jumped to a team that had just won 104 games. But the team he joined was not the type of team that Rickey particularly liked.

Larry MacPhail ran his clubs like a man in a hurry, like he needed to win today because he might not be around tomorrow. The 1942 Dodgers included several key players in their thirties—Camilli, Medwick, Walker, Vaughan, Billy Herman, Curt Davis, Wyatt, and Johnny Allen—all acquired by MacPhail, and all now at an age beyond which Rickey would have looked to offload them. As good as the 1942 Dodgers were, only a few first-rate players—Reese, Reiser, Higbe, and catcher

Mickey Owen—were in their twenties. But although MacPhail's team was not built to last, he had overseen such a dramatic improvement in the Dodgers' financial position that Rickey had the resources to build the organization that he wanted. He wasted no time getting to work.

With the war going on, the Dodgers, like every other team, could not really count on anyone. During the next three years, with most players in the service and teams scrambling to find able-bodied players to take the field, the Dodgers managed two third-place finishes. More important, Rickey's scouts were stocking the farm system with prospects who would be ready when the war inevitably ended. In 1943 alone the Dodgers signed Rex Barney, Duke Snider, Gil Hodges, and Ralph Branca. Over the next couple of years Brooklyn added Carl Erskine and Clem Labine, two other mainstays of Dodger teams to come.

The most important event of Rickey's career, of course, was the signing of Jackie Robinson in October 1945, the first step on the road to ending the Major Leagues' decades-long prohibition on dark-skinned players. Rickey has been justifiably praised for this courageous and ethical act and his related decisions to sign other black players in the coming years. What interests us here is what this meant for the Dodgers, which was plenty. When Robinson was signed it effectively opened up a huge new source of talent for the Major Leagues, the biggest new pool in history. As baseball soon discovered, there were dozens of good players, some of them among the greatest players ever, ready to sign cheaply with the first team that asked them.

By the end of the 1940s eleven black players had made their debuts in the Major Leagues, eight of whom ended up playing at least five full Major League seasons. Among them were three Dodgers—Jackie Robinson, Roy Campanella, and Don Newcombe—whose extraordinary play helped define an era and one of history's most beloved teams.

The integration of the Dodgers went pretty smoothly, likely helped a great deal by how good these three players were. Rickey traded away several southern players during and after the 1947 season, but most of these deals were classic Rickey moves that helped the ball club. In December he dealt Dixie Walker, one of the team's best and most popular players, to the Pirates, a deal many have interpreted as an indication that Rickey wanted Walker off the team. In fact, it was a great baseball trade: Rickey acquired infielder Billy Cox and pitcher Preacher Roe, who played huge roles on the coming teams. Eddie Stanky was dealt the following March, allowing Robinson to move to second base and Gil Hodges to play first, another very solid baseball move.

After losing a pennant playoff in 1946, the Dodgers won NL pennants in 1947 and 1949 and then lost in 1950 on the season's final weekend. Unlike the prewar teams, by 1950 the Dodgers had several good players in their twenties and more on the way.

In 1944 Rickey, John Smith, and Walter O'Malley joined forces to purchase 25 percent of the Dodgers and bought another 50 percent in 1945. Rickey, the baseball man, remained the face of the team and always held control over baseball decisions subject to an occasional vote on large expenditures. In late 1950 Rickey began to sense that his position had weakened with his partners and decided to cash in his stake and take a job running the Pittsburgh Pirates. O'Malley bought Rickey's share and gained control of the club.

O'Malley had been largely in the background in the past few years, with Rickey representing the Dodgers at league meetings and acting as the face of club management. Many Dodger fans likely did not know who O'Malley was before he became the principal owner. They soon found out.

Walter O'Malley controlled the Dodgers for the next twenty-nine years, until his death in 1979. Unlike Rickey, he was not a baseball man; he was a lawyer and a businessman, and his primary interest in owning the Dodgers was to run the club as a business. He and Rickey had clashed over Rickey's purchase of ballplayers, on a new spring-training facility, and his investment in the Brooklyn Dodgers of the All-American Football Conference. Unlike Rickey, O'Malley did not rely solely on the team to bring fans and revenue—he cultivated the local press and promoted his team.

O'Malley knew as well as anyone that he was not qualified to run the ball club. Accordingly, he turned to Buzzie Bavasi, who had been the general manager of the Dodgers' top farm club in Montreal. "[Ford] Frick said Buzzie has exceptional 'mental agility,'" O'Malley later said. "The wheels are always turning in Buzzie's head. He'll work for you 24 hours a day. This is because the man doesn't sleep."[7]

For the next seventeen years O'Malley gave Bavasi the freedom and money to run the club virtually without interference. He would not regret it.

Emil Joseph Bavasi was born in Manhattan in 1914, the son of a French immigrant who became a very successful newspaper distributor. By the late 1920s the Bavasis were living in the wealthy suburb of Scarsdale, in a house with many rooms and servants. Emil picked up the nickname "Buzzie" as a child, and no one ever called him anything else again. As a youth he played and loved baseball and often attended Giants games at the Polo Grounds. One of his high school classmates was Fred Frick, the son of Ford Frick, the National League president. The elder Frick was an alumnus of DePauw University in Indiana, and both Buzzie and Fred likewise spent four years there and became roommates. Soon after Bavasi graduated with a degree in business, the elder Frick introduced him to Dodger boss Larry MacPhail, who gave Bavasi a job as a "glorified office boy."[8] This was 1939.

The next year Bavasi was sent to Americus, Georgia, to operate a Dodger farm club. "It was a grand experience," Bavasi recalled. "I learned a lot about human relations and about baseball at the same time. Larry used to fire me every day and then forget about it."[9] Bavasi had to do everything for the Class D club, even playing second base for four games. Bavasi also spent two years in Valdosta, Georgia, and then a year at Durham, North Carolina. In 1943 he was drafted into the army and spent eighteen months as a staff sergeant in a machine-gun unit in Italy, earning a Bronze Star.

After his discharge Bavasi was named business manager of the Dodgers' club in Nashua, New Hampshire, where his field manager was Walter Alston. The Brooklyn organization was now in the hands of Branch Rickey, who called Bavasi in early 1946 to ask how he felt about having a couple of black players on his club. "Can they play ball?" asked Buzzie. "Oh, my, yes," said Rickey. "Then send them up. We've got plenty of white folks up here, but not nearly enough ballplayers."[10] The new players were Roy Campanella and Don Newcombe, both of whom played outstanding ball in Nashua. It was not always easy. One day, after listening to an opposing manager heap abuse on his two black players, the six-foot, 190-pound Bavasi challenged the manager to a fight after the game. Nothing came of it, other than additional respect from his team.

In 1948 the thirty-three-year-old Bavasi took over the Montreal club in the International League. This was the top of the Dodgers' great farm system, and several future stars passed through during Bavasi's tenure: Newcombe, Duke Snider, Sam Jethroe, Carl Erskine, and many others. The Royals won two pennants and finished third in Bavasi's three years with the club.

After the 1950 season Rickey went to Pittsburgh, and O'Malley promoted both Bavasi and Fresco Thompson to vice president. In effect, Bavasi ran the big-league team and the two Triple-A clubs (Montreal and St. Paul), while Thompson ran the rest of the farm system. Both men reported to O'Malley. Bavasi was just thirty-five and running one of the best teams in baseball.

Unlike Bavasi, Thompson had been a big-league player, including four seasons (1927–30) as the starting second baseman for the Philadelphia Phillies. After his long Minor League playing career ended, he managed for several years before joining the Dodger organization in 1941. In 1946 Rickey named Thompson assistant farm director, and by 1950 Thompson ran the system. With Rickey's departure, O'Malley hedged his bets somewhat by giving Bavasi and Thompson the same title and prestige. Their spheres were distinct, but they worked closely together for eighteen years.

Unlike MacPhail, Rickey left behind a great team filled with young talent. Many of the best players from the 1950 club—Robinson, Campanella, Snider, Reese, Newcombe, Furillo, Erskine, and Hodges—later came to be known as "the Boys of Summer," famous not only for their deeds on the diamond but for staying together as the core of a great team for so long. All of these players were still contributing when the Dodgers played in the 1956 World Series. Rickey's club had won pennants in 1947 and 1949, and the same group added flags in 1952, 1953, 1955, and 1956.

"[Bavasi] sets a league low for trades," Jim Murray once wrote, "because he thinks the Dodger organization has more and better talent than they can get." Or, as Bavasi put it, "Why play poker when you're the only one in the game with any money?"[11] During his initial years with the club Bavasi's principal job was to find complementary players to fill in a hole or two every year.

Bavasi did this job ably. The 1951 Dodgers that led from the start were bolstered by Bavasi's June acquisition of outfielder Andy Pafko from the Cubs. Pafko gave the Dodgers a virtual All-Star team for a lineup, but they were still caught by the Giants, who beat the Dodgers in a best-of-three playoff to decide the NL pennant.

The 1952 and 1953 clubs featured powerhouse offenses, but a pitching staff that had to withstand the loss of Newcombe, who spent two years in the army. Both clubs won pennants and lost the World Series to the Yankees. The two key additions in these years were pitcher Joe Black and infielder Jim Gilliam. In 1950, while he was still running the Montreal club, Bavasi had purchased the contracts of Black and Gilliam from the Baltimore Elite Giants of the Negro American League. "I made the deal for $11,000, and if you can beat that, call me collect," said Bavasi years later.[12] Black had a fabulous year out of the bullpen for the Dodgers in 1952 (15-4, 2.15), though arm trouble limited his effectiveness thereafter. Gilliam took over at second base in 1953, moving Robinson to left field, and was a key member of the club for another decade.

Bavasi's best move in his long tenure with the Dodgers might have been with a managerial hire. Chuck Dressen had lost his job after the 1953 season when he demanded a long-term contract from O'Malley. Bavasi then gave the position to the relatively unknown forty-two-year-old Walter Alston, who had a single Major League at bat in 1936 (a strikeout) and had spent thirteen years managing in the Minors. Bavasi had worked with him in both Nashua and Montreal, and many of the current Dodgers had played for him. Alston managed the Dodgers for the next twenty-three seasons, and his eventual election to the Hall of Fame is testament to how well he did his job.

When the Dodgers captured their first World Series title in 1955, the most important young contributors were outfielder Sandy Amoros and pitcher Johnny Podres. The Cuban Amoros was signed by scout Al Campanis in 1952 after a tip from coach Billy Herman, who had seen Amoros play in the Cuban Winter League. Podres was signed in 1951.

Amoros's spectacular catch and Podres's pitching keyed the Dodgers' Game Seven victory over the Yankees, making the pair lifetime heroes in Brooklyn.

In May 1956 Bavasi surprised everyone by purchasing the contract of pitcher Sal Maglie from Cleveland. The surly and competitive Maglie had turned in a number of excellent seasons with the New York Giants and had been the hated rival of many Dodger players and fans. Over the remainder of the 1956 season Maglie won them over with his spectacular pitching (13-5, 2.87), helping lead the Dodgers back to the World Series. This time the team lost to the Yankees in seven games.

Looking back, it was inevitable that this great team would decline. "We had the misfortune," said Fresco Thompson in 1961, "if you want to call it that, of a whole team jelling at the same time. For ten years a sportswriter could sit down at Christmas and pick our Opening Day lineup."[13] The "misfortune" came when the Dodgers had to replace these men, not one or two a year but seemingly all at once. Robinson was gone after 1956. A year later Campanella was involved in a terrible car accident that left him paralyzed for the rest of his life. Reese, Furillo, Newcombe, Erskine—suddenly the great team had left the scene.

Even more amazingly, the Dodgers left Brooklyn altogether. O'Malley had spent a few years trying to find a place to build a new stadium in Brooklyn and finally gave up and moved the operation to Los Angeles, California. The Boys of Summer, Branch Rickey's team, were gone. If the Los Angeles Dodgers were going to win, it would be with Buzzie Bavasi's players, three thousand miles from Ebbets Field.

During Branch Rickey's tenure with the Dodgers, a concept that later became known as "the Dodger Way" first took hold. Rickey's philosophies on scouting and instruction, along with those of many of his scouts, came with him from the Cardinals to the Dodgers. He instilled a systematic approach to scouting and training throughout the organization. His acolytes in Brooklyn, including Bavasi, Thompson, Alston, and Campanis, expanded and enhanced the Dodger Way for another four decades.

In 1948 Rickey leased part of an old naval base in Vero Beach, Florida, and converted it into Dodgertown, the principal spring-training facility for the organization for the next sixty years. O'Malley initially chafed at Rickey's outlay, but he grew to thoroughly believe in its effectiveness. The camp was large enough to house all seven hundred players in the organization, plus all other personnel, in dormitory-like facilities. Diamonds, pitching mounds, batting cages, and other baseball structures were added. Prospects reported to the camp in mid-February, giving them a solid month of training prior to the start of exhibition games. Besides the hands-on instruction, the prospects were taught the game in traditional classrooms, led by instructors who were experts in the chosen field. Of importance in the segregated South of the time, the facility allowed both white and black players to live, eat, and work together.[14]

It was Al Campanis, more than any one person, who came to be associated with the Dodger Way. Campanis spent several years in the Dodger organization as a player (getting into seven big-league games in 1943) and manager, before becoming a scout in 1951. In that role Campanis created a numerical vocabulary, ranking players' skills with a number between 60 and 80. A score of 70 represented the Major League average. Sandy Koufax, whom Campanis scouted in 1954, was given a 77 for his fastball and a 72 for his curve.

Meanwhile, Campanis also became the field director at Dodgertown, where he often led the recruits in calisthenics, designed and taught lectures, and conducted batting and fielding clinics. In an organization filled with teachers, Campanis was both the lead instructor and the principal.

In 1950 Campanis, a fluent Spanish speaker, conducted his first clinic in Puerto Rico and soon was doing so throughout Latin America. "They're baseball crazy down there," Campanis said. "I would say that the biggest drawback right now is the lack of elementary instruction in schools and on the sandlots."[15] As Campanis knew, the clinics had the added benefit of making the Dodgers popular in the region. After a late-1952 visit, with the Dodgers having already signed Cubans Chico Fernandez and Sandy Amoros, Campanis could report, "Everywhere I went the fans were anxious to know how the Dodgers were making out."[16]

In 1954 he turned his lectures into a book, *The Dodgers' Way to Play Baseball*.[17] The book was divided into sixteen chapters, focusing on defense at each position on the field, all aspects of pitching, batting, bunting, sliding, and managing, among other topics. The book went through numerous printings, was translated into four languages, and was taught by the Dodgers as well as amateur teams throughout the country. The "Dodger Way" came to take on even greater meaning, as the organization began to stand for excellence from top to bottom.

In the generation before the first amateur player draft in 1965, organized baseball made several attempts to reduce the size of bonus payments to amateur players. In the late 1940s a rule provided that any player who received a bonus of more than $6,000 from a Major League team could not be optioned to a lower level without clearing waivers. Although there were a few successful bonus players in this period, such as the Phillies' standout pitching tandem of Robin Roberts and Curt Simmons, both Major and Minor League officials began agitating to eliminate the rule soon after it was enacted.[18]

With the shackles of the rule cast aside, Major League clubs engaged in a feeding frenzy, signing a succession of unknown players to five- and six-figure bonuses. One source estimated that the Major Leagues spent upwards of $4.5 million on signing bonuses in 1952.[19] The Dodgers stayed away—they had a large farm system and were confident that their scouts and development people would find plenty of good prospects. For everyone else, this free market inevitably led to a clamoring for a return to some sort of bonus rule, which suddenly did not seem so bad.

In December 1952 a new rule was enacted, tougher than the previous one. Any player who received a bonus of more than $4,000 had to remain on the active Major League roster for two full seasons.[20] Since each team would not want to use more than one or two roster spots on bonus players, the rule had the intended effect of reducing the number of bonus players.

The Dodgers, a contending team unwilling to sacrifice roster spots for untried amateurs, did not play a large role in the bonus wars during this period. In fact, over the five years covered by the rule, they gave out only two bonuses that exceeded the limit. But these two were something special.

In late 1952, while the new rule was being worked out, Dodger scout Al Campanis conducted a clinic in Puerto Rico that drew many youngsters from the Puerto Rican Winter League. One of them, eighteen-year-old Roberto Clemente, impressed Campanis tremendously. "He ran the 60-yard dash in 6.4, and then threw strikes from centerfield to home plate. I said to myself: 'If this kid can just hold a bat in his hands, we've got to sign him.' He hit one line drive after another."[21] He was still in high school, and the Dodgers did not actually sign Clemente until February 1954, when Campanis gave the nineteen-year-old a $10,000 bonus. Under the new rule, Brooklyn had to either put him on the Dodgers' roster or risk losing him in the Rule 5 Draft after the season. The Dodgers, two-time defending league champs, decided to send him to Montreal and take their chances.

This proved to be a mistake. The 1954 Dodgers had two outfielders who played nearly every day (Snider and Furillo) and two who split time in left field (Amoros and Robinson, who also played the infield). Had Clemente been retained on the roster, it would have been at the expense of someone like Walt Moryn or George Shuba, who between them started twenty-eight games in the outfield.

The Dodgers, therefore, were in the unusual position of having a great prospect whom they did not want to look too great to anyone else. "We ordered Montreal to keep him under wraps any way they could," recalled Bavasi.[22] Playing behind the likes of Jack Cassini and Ken Wood, Clemente managed just 155 plate appearances and hit just .257 with two home runs. Unfortunately, his talent was too obvious to keep hidden. Clyde Sukeforth, the longtime Dodger scout who had followed Rickey to Pittsburgh, loved Clemente and let Bavasi know that he was not fooled. The Pirates, who finished in last place in 1954, had the first pick in the December draft. The Pirates took Clemente and had the benefit of his stellar eighteen-year career.

Once Clemente became a star, this story became something Bavasi was asked about often, and his explanation continued to evolve. In later years he claimed that he had gotten Rickey to agree not to claim Clemente, only to have the deal fall apart when O'Malley and Rickey had a fight about an unrelated matter. But the details hardly mattered, and Bavasi was smart enough to realize that. "Am I admitting that we blew it?" asked Bavasi. "I certainly am."[23]

Meanwhile, the Dodgers signed their second bonus player in December. Sandy Koufax grew up in Brooklyn and had attracted some attention as a basketball player, earning a scholarship to the University of Cincinnati. In baseball he was a first baseman who did not hit much, and it was not until the summer after high school that a few coaches thought he should try to pitch. He played on the freshman team at Cincinnati and on the Brooklyn sandlots the following summer. During a tryout with Campanis at Ebbets Field that summer, Koufax apparently stunned everyone. Though no one affiliated with the Dodgers had ever seen Koufax pitch in a game, he was eventually offered a fourteen-thousand-dollar bonus. Having learned their tough lesson with Clemente, Koufax stepped right onto the Major League team beginning in 1955. To that point, he had pitched fewer than twenty games in his life.

The Dodgers continued to sign players, of course, taking care to keep their bonuses under the threshold. In 1954 scout Lefty Phillips nabbed Don Drysdale, a highly sought-after six-foot-five pitcher from Van Nuys, California. His bonus was four thousand dollars, the maximum they could give him without making him a bonus player, but the Dodgers also gave his father a job as a bird-dog scout in the Los Angeles area.

In 1956 the Dodgers signed seventeen-year-old Tommy Davis, another Brooklynite. Davis starred in basketball (with future National Basketball Association Hall of Famer Lenny Wilkins), track, and baseball at Boys' High. He was on the verge of signing with the Yankees, when a phone call from his hero, Jackie Robinson, changed his mind. Davis received four thousand dollars when he signed with Campanis, and the outfielder spent four years working his way through the farm system.

The Major Leagues finally voted to repeal the bonus rule at their meetings in Colorado Springs in December 1957. In the five years of the regulation there were sixty bonus players, twenty-one of whom had not fulfilled their two-year commitment at the time the rule ended. Among the sixty were four eventual Hall of Famers—Detroit's Al Kaline, Washington's Harmon Killebrew, Clemente, and Koufax.[24]

With the bonus rule abolished, the Dodgers' top executives gathered at the big-league meetings in December 1957. Bavasi, backed by his top aides, urged O'Malley to open his wallet and allow Dodger scouts to outbid the competition. The reasoning was twofold: the current club was aging and in need of wholesale replacements, and the Dodgers were headed to Los Angeles and expected to reap bigger profits playing to a new and excited audience. The Dodgers had never been big spenders on amateurs, but now was surely the time to change that. "All right, let's do it," said O'Malley.

"The toughest job a general manager has is to find good players," Bavasi once said. "That means he has to find good scouts to find those players."[25] Al Campanis was named scouting director, a formalization of a role he had taken on a few years earlier. His scouts were given the freedom to find good players and sign them. Over the next three years (1958 through 1960), the Dodgers spent more than two million dollars on amateur players in a bold attempt to create the next great Dodger team.[26]

While scouts had always been asked to learn a lot about a player's life off the field, the Dodgers under Campanis might have taken it to a new level. "Our scouts talk to the family, to friends, to the local barber, to the man at the soda shop," said Campanis. "We know whether the kid's marks are good in school."[27] The Dodgers believed that mental agility would help the player get through inevitable slumps and difficult times.

Campanis put the scouts through role-playing sessions to teach them how to sell the Dodgers in a prospect's living room. Senior scouts would pretend to be parents or kids, asking for more money or inquiring about their path to the big leagues. Everything was rehearsed— "the knock on the door, the greeting, the ice-breaking chit chat"—to ensure that the Dodgers were presented in the best possible light. The scout was instructed, for example, not to use the father's first name unless the father asked him to.[28]

Moreover, the Dodgers were not afraid to innovate, introducing some protoanalytics in studying other clubs. "Our scouting methods are new and different," Campanis said in describing their scouting of the Yankees for the 1955 World Series. "We do not rely on notions, on impressions. We look for cause and effect." On large sheets of paper the Dodger scouts tracked opposing pitchers and hitters. "The space represents the strike zone. I put down in each of those locations the nature of the pitch, and what the batter did against it. At the end of the game I have before me a definite pattern on each batter, and complete information on every pitcher." This was simply a carryover from what they had been doing during the season. "We keep scouting the seven other clubs in the National League," he said. "You'd be surprised how we run into valuable tipoffs."[29]

Kenny Myers, who scouted Southern California for the Dodgers, was known for seeing things in players that others overlooked. When Myers first saw Willie Davis play for Roosevelt High in Los Angeles, Davis was a right-handed hitting first baseman and outfielder and a sidearm-throwing left-handed pitcher. "When I first saw Willie Davis," said Fresco Thompson, "I wouldn't give you a quarter for him."[30] He was also an extraordinary athlete, a basketball and track star who ran the 100-yard dash in 9.5 seconds and broad jumped more than twenty-five feet. Intrigued, Myers worked with Davis on his fielding, hitting, and throwing to determine whether his raw athleticism could be honed for baseball. In June 1958 Myers signed Davis for a small bonus.

Once Davis was in the fold, Myers taught Davis to throw (by having him throw while lying on a floor) and to hit left-handed to better utilize his speed. Davis hit .352 and .346 in his two Minor League seasons and was in the Majors by the end of the 1960 season. "He taught me everything I know about baseball," Davis acknowledged. "I practiced batting left until my hands were blistered raw. I was a terrible thrower until he taught me. That man can teach anyone to hit and be a ball player."[31]

In addition to the many future Major League players he signed, Myers became an unofficial instructor for many in the organization. John Roseboro, who spent five years in the Dodger system before taking over as catcher in 1958, said, "Myers was sensational; he had revolutionary ideas about batting and how to teach it."[32] But he did not just coach hitting. Pitcher Roger Craig, another longtime member of the system, said of Myers, "He helped me more than anyone with whom I came into contact in baseball."[33] Norm Sherry, who played and coached in the Dodger organization for twenty years, considered Myers "the most knowledgeable baseball man in all phases of the game."[34] The Dodgers' commitment to having the best organization in baseball showed up in many ways.

While the biggest benefactors of the Dodger Way were the Dodgers, it is telling how many future managers came through their system in the 1950s. Sparky Anderson, Dick Williams, and Tommy Lasorda all became Hall of Fame managers after undistinguished playing careers; all spent years in the Dodger system. Other future managers in the system included Preston Gomez, Lefty Phillips, Don Zimmer, Gene Mauch, Clyde King, Danny Ozark, Roger Craig, Larry Shepard, Bobby Bragan, Cookie Lavagetto, and Gil Hodges. This list is not exhaustive and does not count the coaches, scouts, and instructors who spread through the game and inevitably taught the Dodger Way.[35]

A more traditional recruitment than Willie Davis's was that of Frank Howard, a huge (six-foot-seven) college basketball star at Ohio State whom Dodger scout Cliff Alexander began following in 1956 when Howard was a sophomore. The next year Alexander filed a telling report: "Good arm. Fielding below average. Hitting below average (good potential). Running speed slightly below average. *Major league power*. Definite follow." Although Howard had many suitors, he got to know Alexander so well that he never really considered any other team. Howard stayed in college until the end of basketball season his senior year, then signed in the spring of 1958 with Alexander for $108,000.[36]

In the meantime the Dodgers were watching another collegian, University of Southern California (USC) center fielder Ron Fairly, who had grown up in Long Beach and led the Trojans to victory in the 1958 College World Series. Fairly was highly sought after by many teams, but chose to sign with Lefty Phillips, the Dodgers' area scout. Of great importance was the Dodgers' recent move to Los Angeles. "I definitely took less to stay close to home," Fairly recalled.[37] In addition to their usual scouting prowess, the Dodgers were also taking advantage of their huge popularity in Southern California with several of their more promising local signings.

Along with Fairly, Howard, and Willie Davis, the Dodgers signed a fourth future All-Star in 1958 (pitcher Pete Richert), then Al Ferrara,

Ken McMullen, Jack Billingham, and Jim Lefebvre (along with many players who did not become regulars, of course) over the next few years. The Dodgers were betting that Fresco Thompson's farm system could mold all this young talent into the next great Dodger team in the 1960s.

Meanwhile, Buzzie Bavasi's Major League club, freshly moved to Los Angeles, fell all the way to seventh place in 1958, their first year out of the top three since 1944. Many of their remaining stars did not acclimate well to the LA Coliseum, with its makeshift dimensions that included a 42-foot screen fence in left field, just 251 feet away on the foul line, and an enormous right field that reached 440 feet in the power alley. Right-handed hitting Gil Hodges fell to .259 with just 22 home runs, while left-handed hitting Duke Snider dropped from five consecutive 40-homer seasons to just 15 in his new home.

The 1959 Dodgers surprised nearly everyone by capturing the NL pennant despite winning just eighty-eight games. They finished 86-68 in their scheduled games and then won two more in a pennant play-off with the Braves. It was the worst pennant-winning record in NL history prior to the advent of divisions. Unlike the recent Brooklyn clubs, these Dodgers won without stars. Snider and Hodges enjoyed comeback seasons of a sort, though certainly not to their previous levels. Jim Gilliam and Charlie Neal had good years in the infield. Don Drysdale, just twenty-two years old, broke out with 17 wins and a 3.46 ERA, and Sandy Koufax, twenty-three, won eight games and showed glimpses of what he might become.

The biggest star might have been twenty-nine-year-old outfielder Wally Moon, whom Bavasi had acquired from the Cardinals for Gino Cimoli the previous December. Though Moon was left-handed, he learned to adjust his stroke to hit long fly balls over the short left-field screen and had three excellent seasons in the Coliseum. In 1959 he hit 19 home runs and 11 triples and did most of his damage at home.

The 1959 Dodgers were not built to last, and Bavasi and Alston did not allow their surprising success to slow the rebuilding plan. Frank Howard, after hitting .341 in parts of three Minor League seasons, was the Dodgers' primary right fielder by 1960, when he won the NL Rookie of the Year Award. Tommy Davis hit .337 in his four Minor

League seasons and was also in the Dodger outfield in 1960. In Willie Davis's two Minor League seasons, he hit .349 while averaging 42 doubles, 21 triples, and 14 home runs. In late 1960 he joined the Dodgers, completing the young outfield. Ron Fairly also had a fine Minor League résumé, hitting 27 home runs for Spokane in 1960, but ultimately had to be moved to first base because of the outfield log jam (and Howard's inability to play first competently).

In 1962 the Dodgers moved into Dodger Stadium, in Chavez Ravine, near downtown Los Angeles. In sharp contrast to Ebbets Field and the LA Coliseum, Dodger Stadium was an extreme pitcher's park, one that helped define the team that the Dodgers came to be, while also distorting the value of some of their best players. The Dodgers broke through to finish the regular schedule 101-61, before losing to the Giants in a three-game playoff.

Their four best hitters were Tommy Davis (.346 with 27 homers and 153 RBI), Willie Davis (21 home runs and 32 steals), Howard (31 homers and 119 RBI), and Fairly (14 home runs). The biggest story on the club was shortstop Maury Wills, whose 208 hits came with a then-record 104 stolen bases (and only 13 caught stealing). Signed in 1951, Wills spent nine years in the Minor Leagues before joining the Dodgers during the 1959 season. He had limited offensive skills, but once he got on first base he could take over a game.

The Dodger team was a testament to the work of Bavasi. He had overseen Rickey's club through its glory years and decline, won two World Series, been named baseball's top executive (in 1959), and was now sitting atop a promising team built completely on his watch. But it was not without stress. "[Bavasi]'s the one who turns green at any home game the Dodgers are losing," reported Jim Murray. "He can also be recognized by his bow tie and his hairline which has not been receded, it's been routed. Buzzie Bavasi always looks as if you're interrupting him on the way to catch a train. Ballplayers wear out two sets of gloves per season, but Buzzie Bavasi wears out new sets of stomach linings."[38]

"The general manager of the Dodgers," said another writer, "is a 5-foot 11½-inch, 194 pound, balding, moon-faced saucer eyed man who, on a typical day, is on the move no longer than an average river. He looks like a guy who started out with a good case of nerves and liked it so much that he sent away for an extra case. For a quarter century, he has been acting as though his wife is going to have her first baby in five minutes."[39]

Besides Bavasi, credit for the new Dodgers must also be given to Thompson's system, Campanis's scouts, and O'Malley's money. They had accomplished the mission they had embarked on several years earlier. "We paid out $2.5 million, roughly $800,000 per year, for the past three years," Campanis said in 1961. "In the past four or five years the kids who got the most money were the ones who went to the big leagues. There were, of course, exceptions, but a fairly consistent pattern is evident now. The pattern indicates that if a club keeps signing high bonus boys, as a steadfast policy, it will have a much higher proportion of kids who made the grade than a club concentrating on the hopeful bargains in the low bonus prospects."[40]

The signature element of the 1960s Dodgers was their power pitching, especially the duo of Sandy Koufax and Don Drysdale. Koufax was plagued by inconsistency and wildness in the early years of his career, but his talent was obvious. He struck out a record-breaking eighteen men in a 1959 game against the Giants, led the league in strikeouts per nine innings in 1960, and won eighteen games with a league-leading 269 strikeouts in 1961. But it was the move to Dodger Stadium that made him a legend. In mid-July 1962 he was 14-4 and leading the league in both ERA and strikeouts, before an arm injury shut him down for two months and limited him to just one inning in the three-game playoff with the Giants. He came back with a vengeance in 1963.

Don Drysdale had a much quicker ascent, winning seventeen games as a twenty-year-old in the final season in Brooklyn. Drysdale threw hard fastballs without Koufax's control problems, and leading the league in hit batters five times abetted his reputation as an intimidator. After several fine seasons, he broke through in 1962 to finish 25-9 with a third strikeout title.

In 1963 the Dodgers won ninety-nine games and captured the NL pennant. Koufax was the big star, finishing 25-5 while leading the league in wins, strikeouts, and ERA. He capped his season with two dominant victories in the Dodgers' four-game World Series sweep of the Yankees, including a record 15 strikeouts in Game One. Many of the Dodger hitters had good years, a situation masked by Dodger Stadium and the new larger strike zone in 1963, which created a second Deadball era over the next six years.

The Dodgers also won pennants in 1965 and 1966, winning the 1965 World Series. Arm injuries prematurely ended the careers of Koufax and Drysdale, conspiring to drop the Dodgers back for a few years, but the overall excellence of the organization continued with five pennants and two more World Series victories in the 1970s and 1980s.

Through it all, Bavasi remained a very popular and respected man around baseball. "You can write anything good about Buzzie and say I said it," Chub Feeney, an executive with the rival Giants, told a writer. "Buzzie is a guy with great integrity. He has a good sense of humor and he's a very warm person. He's fun to be with. And it's pretty obvious from what the Dodgers have done what kind of general manager he is."[41]

Fresco Thompson, who knew Bavasi as well as anyone, offered just one semiserious complaint. "He makes me do the firing," Thompson reported. "If we're going to fire a scout, he'll say, 'I think you better get rid of that guy, Fresco.' But if the scout is going to get some more money, he'll say, 'Fresco, I think I'll give that guy a raise.'"[42]

The Dodger Way endured, in part, because of the stability of the organization. Despite numerous opportunities to leave, Bavasi remained GM until 1968, when he was lured away to run the expansion San Diego Padres, for whom he would be president and part owner. To replace Bavasi, O'Malley turned to Thompson, who had run the farm system for eighteen years and been in the organization for three decades. Tragically, Thompson died of cancer just six months later.

To replace Thompson, the Dodgers promoted Campanis, who remained the Dodger GM for eighteen years, building his own great championship clubs largely with players scouted, signed, and developed by the Dodgers. O'Malley turned the presidency over to his son, Peter, in 1970, and Peter became the principal owner when his father died in 1979. Walter Alston managed the club for twenty-three seasons, and, upon Alston's resignation, Tommy Lasorda took over for another twenty years.

This stability indicates both the loyalty these brilliant men felt for O'Malley and the organization and the faith both O'Malleys had in the Dodger Way. In the rare cases where a top hire was necessary, the club always promoted from within the deep ranks of talented executives and coaches. The Dodgers had become the gold standard for baseball organizations and would remain so for many years. They had a brilliant owner, excellent executives and managers throughout the system, great scouts, and a productive player-development system.

O'Malley ran a family-oriented franchise and would host a big retreat for his employees and their families—part work, part vacation—at the end of every season.[43] Besides O'Malley's own son, the Dodgers also employed the sons of Bavasi (Peter, a Minor League general manager) and Campanis (Jim, signed as a catcher, played parts of three years with the Dodgers). The Dodgers had their own luxurious airplane, housed the players in first-class hotels, and generally developed a reputation for treating their players and other employees with class.

Other organizations would later develop sophisticated, effective front offices and scouting bureaus, often underneath an all-powerful general manager. The teams that most smartly managed the transition to this new structural paradigm would be the most successful on the field for the next several decades.

8 Dynasty

The key to any successful business operation is outstanding personnel . . . productive, well-trained, dedicated employees.—BOB HOWSAM, baseball executive

The death of Jacob Ruppert in January 1939 kicked off a period of uncertainty and turmoil in the Yankee front office that would last for nearly nine years. Ruppert had no children; he left his entire estate, including his brewery and the Yankees, in a trust for the benefit of two nieces and the daughter of a deceased friend. Ed Barrow, George Weiss, and manager Joe McCarthy continued to ably run the organization and Major League club, and the team made four more World Series appearances (winning three) in the next six years.

Meanwhile, Ruppert's trustees faced a large estate-tax burden and not enough cash to settle it. For these reasons the sale of the team was inevitable, though the start of the Second World War and the subsequent shutdown in non-war-related financial activity delayed things considerably.[1]

One interested buyer was Larry MacPhail, the former general manager of the Cincinnati Reds and Brooklyn Dodgers, now working in the War Department. In early 1943 MacPhail put together a syndicate to bid on the Yankees. The most prominent moneyed member of his group was John Hertz, a taxicab and rental-car mogul in Chicago. In February 1944 baseball commissioner Landis scuttled any hope of a deal because Hertz owned several thoroughbred racehorses, and Landis wanted to avoid the appearance of any relationship between baseball and gambling interests. When MacPhail backed away, Ed Barrow looked for another buyer.

Now seventy-five years old but still running the club and wishing to continue, Barrow had two big reasons to disapprove of a sale to a MacPhail group. First, Barrow owned 10 percent of the Yankees, and

MacPhail's offer ($2.8 million for the 96.88 percent of the stock owned by the Ruppert estate and Barrow) provided little return on Barrow's small investment made more than two decades earlier. The team had enjoyed tremendous financial success in the intervening years, with Ruppert pouring its profits back into the ball club. The franchise now included several Minor League teams and Yankee Stadium as well. Second, MacPhail was a loud, domineering man who would surely want to operate the club himself. Barrow countered unsuccessfully by courting both Tom Yawkey, who owned the Red Sox, and James Farley, the former postmaster general.

As the pressure grew on the trust to pay the estate tax, MacPhail reorganized his bid, lining up two investors from his original syndicate to put up most of the money: Dan Topping, a sportsman playboy who owned a professional football team in Brooklyn, and Del Webb, a construction and real estate tycoon from Arizona. Once Barrow realized the sale was inevitable, he arranged separate meetings with Topping and Webb to stress the importance of maintaining stability in the very successful organization. Both men assured him they intended to keep the team running as it always had.

The sale of the Yankees to MacPhail, Webb, and Topping was announced in January 1945. Shortly thereafter, the trio acquired the nominal remaining interests held by others, giving the three men complete ownership. MacPhail borrowed most of his share of the purchase price from his two partners and, as the baseball man in the group, was named club president. Topping, Webb, and Weiss were elected vice presidents. Barrow was made chairman of the board, an empty title with no duties. MacPhail was in charge.

During the long reign of Ruppert and Barrow, the Yankees were a businesslike, drama-free operation. Ruppert let Barrow run the team, and the two men kept any disagreements they may have had out of the newspapers. Despite the assurances to Barrow by Topping and Webb, Larry MacPhail made news wherever he went and would not change just because he was taking over the hallowed and conservative Yankees. He had little patience or tolerance for administrative structure. He was an outgoing, frenetic man—the antithesis of Ruppert and Barrow and a shock to Weiss. MacPhail got to work.

With a war going on and many baseball players in the service, MacPhail's considerable energies were directed toward the day-to-day activities of the team, which did not sit well with Joe McCarthy, who had won seven World Series as the Yankees' manager. McCarthy had always been a drinker, but during the relatively calm days working with Barrow he had managed to keep his consumption in check. In 1945, however, McCarthy's drinking problems worsened. He left the club on July 20 to return to his Buffalo home. (The press was told he was battling health issues.) He tried to resign, but MacPhail encouraged him to stick it out, and McCarthy returned on August 9.

During his manager's absence, MacPhail sold Hank Borowy, the club's most effective pitcher, to the Chicago Cubs for ninety-seven thousand dollars. This was somewhat shocking, as the Yankees did not seem to be in need of money. MacPhail feebly noted that Borowy was a poor second-half pitcher, but the hurler finished 11-2 for Chicago and helped lead them to the National League pennant.[2] MacPhail, it was assumed, just wanted to shake up his team and to show there was a new boss in town. The Yankees were four games behind the Tigers at the time of the sale and finished six and a half back.

In 1946, with the war over, MacPhail was ready to make more of an impact. He installed lights at Yankee Stadium, as he had done in Cincinnati and Brooklyn. He added a new Stadium Club (which offered more luxurious seating and brought in five hundred thousand dollars before the season even started), reinstalled 15,000 seats, and added more promotional events. The Yankees played before an all-time record 2,265,512 customers in 1946. All of baseball experienced an attendance boom that year, but the Yankees were easily the biggest draw.

On the field the 1946 Yankees won eighty-seven games, well short of the powerful Boston Red Sox. Manager McCarthy again had to leave the team for "health" reasons, and this time he did not return. Longtime catcher Bill Dickey took over the club in May, but quit in September when he realized that MacPhail would not renew him for 1947, admitting that getting along with MacPhail was a challenge.[3] Johnny Neun finished out the year, but left after the season to manage the Cincinnati Reds. MacPhail then selected Bucky Harris, a twenty-year managerial veteran.

MacPhail made two important moves during the following off-season. First, he traded second baseman Joe Gordon to the Indians for pitcher Allie Reynolds. The thirty-one-year-old Gordon had hit just .210 in 1946, and MacPhail probably thought he would not recover his pre-war form. In fact, Gordon did bounce back to give the Indians a few excellent seasons and helped lead them to their 1948 pennant. Nonetheless, Reynolds's eight stellar years anchoring the team's pitching staff made this an excellent deal. In January 1947 MacPhail signed veteran first baseman George McQuinn to take over for the disappointing Nick Etten. McQuinn was nearly thirty-seven and was coming off a poor year with the Philadelphia Athletics, but he still had one excellent season left.

Somewhat surprisingly, the 1947 Yankees won ninety-seven games and a fairly easy pennant. After their dramatic World Series victory over the Dodgers, ending with a Game Seven win in Yankee Stadium on October 6, the Yankee owners had every reason to feel satisfied with their accomplishment and their future. Yet MacPhail's bizarre reaction to the club's victory would ultimately take over the story.

Just minutes after the final game, MacPhail stormed into the team's clubhouse and announced his resignation, a decision first thought to be fueled by emotion (he was reportedly crying) and alcohol. A few hours later MacPhail arrived at the Biltmore Hotel in Manhattan, where the three owners were hosting a lavish "Victory Dinner." The press was waiting for him, but he angrily shouted, "Stay away or get punched." Sportswriter Sid Keener of the *St. Louis Star-Times* managed to capture a few MacPhail quotes. "I'm simply tired of it all," said MacPhail. "Too much worry. The critical New York press gets me down. Besides, there are a lot of guys in baseball I don't like—and don't care to associate with." He specifically mentioned baseball commissioner Happy Chandler and Brooklyn general manager Branch Rickey. "Well, I gave New York another championship, didn't I? And what are they saying about it around here? That I'm nothing but a big popoff. Maybe I am, but I deliver the goods, don't I?"[4]

It later came out that MacPhail had been flustered by a brief exchange with Rickey just before MacPhail entered the Yankees' locker room. MacPhail offered his hand, which Rickey took while saying,

"I'm shaking hands with you because a thousand people are looking on, but I don't like you." Rickey later acknowledged this conversation.[5]

When he finally worked his way inside to the dinner, MacPhail only made things worse. He stumbled drunk around the dining room, alternating between bouts of sentimental crying and irrational raging. He slugged John McDonald, former traveling secretary with the Dodgers, who had made a complimentary remark about Rickey.

MacPhail lurched over to George Weiss's table, where the Yankee farm director was dining with his wife, Hazel, as well as Barrow and several others. MacPhail started cursing Weiss and berating his work, eventually working himself into a frenzy and demanding that Weiss had "48 hours to make up your mind what you are going to do." Weiss remained as calm as possible and suggested, "Larry, I don't want to make a decision here tonight. We have all been drinking. I would like to wait until tomorrow and discuss this with you." MacPhail, in no condition to be mollified, responded by firing Weiss on the spot. As MacPhail walked away Hazel Weiss chased after him to appeal for her husband's job, without effect. A shaken Weiss went outside to cool down. Hazel returned to the table in tears.[6]

When Dan Topping tried to intervene, MacPhail shouted at his partner, "You're just a guy who was born with a silver spoon in your mouth and never made a dollar in your life." As MacPhail walked away Topping grabbed him, saying, "Come here you. . . . I have taken all of this I am going to take." Topping forced MacPhail into an adjoining kitchen and closed the door.[7]

Now Mrs. MacPhail was in tears. "What's Danny doing to him?" she cried. "He's a mighty sick, nervous man." Topping emerged alone, having forced the somewhat calmer MacPhail out a side door. MacPhail returned sometime later, freshened up, with neatly combed hair. He berated at least one Yankee player after his return, but the drama was largely over.[8]

Topping and Webb assessed the situation and concluded that they could not leave their investment in the hands of the obviously unstable MacPhail. The following day the Yankees announced Webb and Topping had bought out MacPhail's shares for two million dollars. Topping was elected president, and Weiss was named general manager. "MacPhail's connection with the Yankees is ended," said Topping. MacPhail had turned his small initial investment into two million dollars in less than three years, but he would never work in baseball again.

Dan Daniel, writing in the *Sporting News*, summarized the dramatic events this way: "After three years of turbulence and equivocation under the sometimes inspired, and often much less than that, administration of Col. Leland Stanford MacPhail, the Yankees have returned to quiet and the peaceful pursuit of baseball happiness."[9] MacPhail's frenetic style might briefly succeed, especially when backed by the wealth of Webb and Topping. However, in the growing complexity of baseball businesses in postwar America, neither the small streamlined front office of the Barrow years nor MacPhail's crazed genius could expect to run a successful club for long. But the new partnership of Webb, Topping, and Weiss would create a professionally managed franchise that remained in place for thirteen years, capturing ten pennants and seven World Series titles.

When Topping and Webb named Weiss general manager, the Yankees were undisputedly baseball's preeminent organization. In the aftermath of the war, however, the pecking order among AL teams was as fluid as it had been for many years. Nearly all of baseball's top stars had been away from organized baseball for two years or more, and top prospects had lost valuable developmental time supporting the war effort. The talent was not as concentrated as it had been before the war. From 1944 to 1948 five different American League teams won the pennant. When George Weiss took control of the Yankee ship, there was more parity in the AL than there had been in decades.

The two co-owners were an odd couple—Topping, educated in an East Coast boarding school and expensive colleges, had little in common with Webb, a Californian who grew up in the construction business and played semipro ball—but established a surprisingly smooth working relationship. Topping's role generally was to oversee the club's business, while Webb assumed an active role in league affairs. The two owners recognized they had a talented general manager and generally left Weiss alone to mastermind one of baseball's greatest organizations.

Weiss began his career in baseball in New Haven, Connecticut. After high school graduation, Weiss reorganized his school baseball team, brought in a couple of new players, and promoted his squad as a semi-pro club. He leased a field just outside the city limits and began playing games on Sunday, a practice prohibited in New Haven proper. By promising a guaranteed purse, Weiss brought in stars such as Ty Cobb and Walter Johnson, with whom he became friends, to play Sunday exhibitions with his team. Weiss parlayed this success into taking over New Haven's team in the Eastern League. He quickly turned around that club's on-field fortunes, and New Haven won the Eastern League pennant in 1920.

Weiss's baseball career almost ended before he became famous. In December 1923 Weiss and New Haven manager Wild Bill Donovan set out for the winter meetings in Chicago aboard the 20th Century Limited. Tragically, the train crashed, killing Donovan and eight other passengers. Badly injured with lacerations to his back, Weiss spent the next month hospitalized in Erie, Pennsylvania, followed by a long convalescence at home.

Weiss understood that the financial survival of Minor League operators required selling their players to higher leagues. Redirecting his promotional skills to negotiating player sales, he sold twenty-six players for around $300,000 while keeping his team highly competitive on the field during his tenure with New Haven. From 1920 through 1928 New Haven won three Eastern League pennants and had only two losing seasons. After the 1928 season Weiss sold the New Haven team and took over the International League's Baltimore Orioles, a storied franchise that had fallen on hard times. Over the next three seasons Weiss rebuilt the struggling club and earned another $242,000 on player sales.[10] In 1932, at age thirty-seven, he joined the Yankees as director of their fledgling farm system.

Jacob Ruppert's 1939 death placed constraints on club spending. Weiss was directed to try to sell some of the unneeded talent in the system, a practice Branch Rickey had mastered in St. Louis. Weiss managed to peddle a number of players for prices in the $20,000 to $40,000 range. He also often garnered a Minor Leaguer in the deals, and the quality of the Yankee scouts meant that these afterthoughts occasionally developed into valuable ballplayers.[11] In one oft-chronicled series of transactions, Weiss sold Willard Hershberger to the Reds after the 1937 season for $20,000 and shortstop Eddie Miller. He later sent Miller to the Boston Braves for $10,000 and several players, including Vince DiMaggio and Gil English. Weiss sold DiMaggio to the Reds for $20,000 and two players, Nino Bongiovanni and Frenchy Bordagaray, the latter later sold to the Dodgers. Weiss also received $7,500 in exchange for English when he sent him to St. Paul in the American Association.[12] Weiss had learned well in New Haven.

Weiss succeeded in running one of the great dynasties of American sports because he understood the importance of a strong organization. He was unafraid of having strong, intelligent men working for him. As his top assistants Weiss at various times had Bill Dewitt, a once and future baseball GM and owner, and Lee MacPhail, a future GM and American League president whose father, Larry, had gone on the tirade against Weiss in 1947. Weiss held regular meetings at which he "invited open discussion from all department heads, and weighed each suggestion carefully before reaching a decision."[13] He was a perfectionist and detail oriented but would allow trusted associates to make decisions. "The entire organization bears down all the time. Every day, 12 months a year," Weiss remarked. "There's a restaurant in New York which advertises that it threw away the key when it opened for business. That's the picture I carry of the Yankees."[14] In today's world of twenty-four-hour sports channels and football coaches sleeping in their offices, this may seem unremarkable. But in the 1950s, with family ownership and sportsmen owners, Weiss's professional approach was groundbreaking.

Red Patterson worked for Weiss for many years as a public relations director. "Weiss was a great detail man," Patterson recalled. "He always had an old envelope in his pocket. On the back he had written himself notes and details he wanted taken care of. If he gave you something to do he would keep reminding you of it until it was done and he could cross out the note."[15]

By the time Weiss took over the Yankees at age fifty-three, he looked and acted the part of an executive. He dressed in conservative suits, wore little jewelry, and had put on weight. Generally soft-spoken, but firm and confident, the round-faced Weiss had the "odd habit of thrusting his hands into his jacket pockets, with the thumbs on the outside when engaging in standup conversation."[16] He was often cold and unemotional to those outside of his closest circle. This was both a conscious effort to keep his distance from players and subordinates and a case of extreme shyness.

"George Weiss always seemed like a guy who never had fun," one writer recalled years later, "but that wasn't so. They say he swung pretty good in his younger days, and there were signs in his latter days with the Yankees that this was so. He liked to bet a horse, but he could bet and then watch the race as excitedly as if he were watching the grass grow. He liked a drink, but he was a washout at any kind of party because small talk was impossible for him and any kind of talk was improbable. There were times, though, when a couple of beakers of grog would loosen him up in a boys-will-be-boys situation."[17] But to the public he looked the part of a conservative businessman.

One of the keys to the Yankee success was their remarkable farm system. A May 1958 *Baseball Digest* study of ballplayers showed that of the 318 regulars and top reserves in the Major Leagues (approximately 20 per team), 43 had originally been signed by the Yankees, nearly one-seventh of the total. The Dodgers, the National League's top franchise at the time, ranked second with 36.

The Yankees were landing quality as well as quantity. Yogi Berra joined the club when Weiss was still farm director. Mickey Mantle and Whitey Ford graduated to the Yankees early in Weiss's tenure as general manager. These three were among the best half-dozen players in the AL in the 1950s, which begins to explain the Yankees' ongoing dominance. Weiss and his scouts also filled the roster with other stars and capable regulars.

By the postwar period few players in the dwindling independent Minor Leagues were sufficiently skilled to play in the Majors—most Minor League teams were affiliated with Major League organizations, who were stocking their farm systems by signing amateur talent. The price for the top talent skyrocketed after the war, although the Yankees' role in this market was minimal (notably their 1950 signing of Andy Carey for sixty-five thousand dollars). Weiss believed his scouts could outhustle their competitors and dig up players others might miss. The scouts proved him right: Mantle, Berra, and Ford, plus future stars Bill Skowron, Gil McDougald, Hank Bauer, Bobby Richardson, and Tony Kubek, all cost less than seven thousand dollars per signing.[18]

The Yankee farm system also innovated. When Lee MacPhail and scout Joe Devine suggested a fall gathering of top prospects for additional coaching and evaluation, with input from the Major League coaches, Weiss approved the idea. The Yankees expanded the venture over the next couple of years, and other teams eventually followed suit. Today, this experimental initiative has matured into the Fall Instructional League.[19]

The postwar Yankee farm system proved more successful at developing position players than pitchers. Other than Ford and Vic Raschi, most of the best Yankees pitchers during Weiss's tenure came via trades. The farm system's surplus and Weiss's trading acumen allowed the Yankees to pick up Eddie Lopat, Allie Reynolds, Don Larsen, and Bob Turley, among others. Weiss trusted his scouts to find good pitchers who were struggling with poor records on second-division teams. He then acquired these hurlers by surrendering prospects and occasionally cash. The Yankees were wealthier than most teams and willing to use this advantage.

Weiss's first acquisition turned out to be his worst. After the 1948 season Weiss sent three players and one hundred thousand dollars to the St. Louis Browns for pitcher Fred Sanford, a deal that Weiss remembered with dismay for the rest of his career. Weiss later claimed that he had succumbed to pressure from the press and co-owner Dan Topping. Though Sanford won just twelve games over the next two-plus seasons, the deal did not sour Weiss on using cash in future transactions.

Weiss became a master of the midseason trade, often adding a valuable veteran to bolster the always-contending Yankees for the stretch drive. "Our trading philosophy," said Weiss, "has been one of trying to get a man to fill a needed gap, often short-term, without helping the opposition too much and without trading away a star."[20] Late in the 1949 season Weiss purchased aging veteran Johnny Mize, who still had a couple of good years left, for forty thousand dollars. At the 1950 trading deadline he picked up pitchers Tom Ferrick and Joe Ostrowski for several players and forty thousand dollars. "They weren't stars," Weiss explained, "but they helped us considerably." The next year Weiss made another poor trade—sending pitcher Tommy Byrne and twenty-five thousand dollars to the St. Louis Browns for Stubby Overmire—which he again blamed on Topping's influence. Byrne was a pretty good pitcher, but Topping said he could not watch him because of his wildness. While pleasing Topping, Weiss angered manager Casey Stengel, who still thought he could harness Byrne's potential. A couple of years later Weiss reacquired Byrne, who turned in several good seasons for Stengel. Other midseason acquisitions included Johnny Sain, Johnny Hopp, Ewell Blackwell, Harry Simpson, and Ryne Duren.[21]

The Kansas City Athletics famously proved to be a willing trade partner. Topping's close friend Arnold Johnson had purchased the Athletics after the 1954 season and moved them from Philadelphia to Kansas City. Johnson used very little of his own money to buy the club, and throughout his tenure the organization was consistently woeful. While forty-three Major League regulars or semiregulars in 1958 had been originally signed by the Yankees, only eight had been inked by the Athletics. Weiss made numerous deals with Kansas City general manager Parke Carroll, who, predictably, had also once worked for the Yankees. In aggregate, however, the trades were not nearly as one-sided as often remembered. Kansas City needed to find players somewhere, and the Yankees reputedly had good ones. Weiss summarized Johnson's typical response to the criticism, which was to argue that he was "out to improve the A's whether it helps the Yanks or not."[22]

To some degree the legacy of all postwar general managers and owners is heavily determined by their response to integration. Weiss and the Yankees have been rightly criticized for their hesitancy in this area. No black player made the Yankees' regular-season roster until Elston Howard in 1955, eight years after Jackie Robinson broke the color barrier in Brooklyn. Weiss was certainly not alone in either baseball or American society in his dawdling on integration. Ten of the sixteen teams were still all-white as late as September 1953. Moreover, most teams did not integrate solely due to a sense of responsibility or morality. Teams signed black players because they wanted to win, and once Robinson had broken down the door and played so well, integration was the best (and cheapest) way to find top talent. As we shall see in the next chapter, this huge supply of available baseball stars was unique in baseball history, and the way teams responded to this opportunity changed the balance of power in baseball for the next twenty years. The Yankees, uniquely, continued to win without aggressively signing black talent.

By the late 1940s the Yankees were actively scouting the Negro Leagues. In addition to Howard the Yankees made a couple of notable acquisitions, including Vic Power and Luis Marquez. Weiss was later criticized for trading Power before he appeared in the Majors with the Yankees, and many believed Weiss was actively delaying the team's integration. On the other hand, Weiss was livid when baseball commissioner Happy Chandler awarded Marquez to Cleveland because of a dispute over which Negro League club held his rights. "This decision soured George Weiss on Chandler," Lee MacPhail later wrote. "Del Webb was already against him and the Yankees then took the lead in putting together enough votes to eventually unseat Chandler as commissioner."[23]

Weiss had a reputation as a hard negotiator with his players, which made him little different from most front-office executives of the time. Before free agency, players had little leverage other than refusing to sign a contract and hoping the team would relent, at least a little. Relative to the rest of baseball the Yankees paid respectable salaries. In 1954, one of the few Weiss years the Yankees failed to win the pennant, the team paid a league high $674,622 in player salaries. Pennant-winning Cleveland was second at $592,660; the rest of the league ranged from $357,329 to $450,796. The Yankees had a payroll 50 percent greater than all but one team, a level befitting their unparalleled success.[24]

One of the more controversial moves Weiss made in his Yankee years came with his lone managerial hire. When the 1948 club, the first with Weiss in charge, slipped to third (albeit with ninety-four wins), Weiss fired Bucky Harris, who Weiss felt was "an old-style, 'book' manager who couldn't fit in with the many experiments the Yankees wanted to make with new young players."[25] Harris had been hired by Larry MacPhail, and Weiss wanted his own man in the dugout.

Weiss surprised baseball pundits by hiring Casey Stengel, who in nine years managing in the National League had never finished higher than fifth. Weiss and Stengel had been friends for many years, dating back to Stengel's brief managing stint in the Eastern League. Stengel had just won the PCL pennant in Oakland, which had helped restore his reputation somewhat, but his hiring was still a shock to the New York sportswriters, many of whom portrayed the colorful Stengel as a clown.

With Stengel in charge on the field, the team won a record five consecutive World Series from 1949 through 1953. After the 1953 Series crusading U.S. congressman Emanuel Celler of Brooklyn, whose beloved Dodger squad the Yankees had just defeated, penned a verse complaining about the Yankees' dominance, partially in jest.

> It's time that Congress investigate.
> The time is short, the hour is late,
> Five times running; it's more than fate,
> The Yankees have a monopoly!
> The Dodgers are artful, courageous the Braves,
> The Giants have stature, the Phillies earn raves,
> Must they now all take to caves?
> The Yankees have a monopoly!
> They can't flout our laws; the trust must be bust.
> We'll subpoena the witness and answer he must.
> The cry has been heard; the verdict is just
> The Yankees have a monopoly![26]

The next season the Yankees won 103 games, the high-water mark during Weiss's tenure, but fell to second behind a Cleveland Indians team that won a then league record 111. The Yankees' success in the nation's largest metropolis generally led to the league's largest profit. For the years for which we have data, 1952–54, the Yankees outearned their competition in two of the three years. In 1952 the Yankees booked $224,000 in net income, Cleveland was second at $204,000, and four teams lost money. The next year the Yankees made $622,000, the White

Sox were second at $205,000, and three teams lost money. In 1954 Baltimore (their first year in the new city), Cleveland, and Chicago all made more than the Yankees' $174,000.

After four more pennants from 1955 to 1958, the Yankees fell to third in 1959. The team, the press, and the fans spent much of the off-season trying to understand how the Yankees could have fallen from their rightful place atop the league. "Injuries ruined the team," Weiss explained, but he also thought that his players "maybe weren't hungry enough . . . maybe they had too many outside interests on their minds. All the key men are independently wealthy from the high salaries and the World Series shares they've been getting for a long time. They've invested their money in business propositions."[27] The team rebounded in 1960 to capture the pennant before losing a heartbreaking seven-game World Series to the Pirates.

In the aftermath of the 1960 Series, Topping forced both Stengel and Weiss out of their positions. At Topping's request both the seventy-year-old manager and the sixty-six-year-old general manager announced their retirements at press conferences. Though he mainly kept his remarks evasive, Stengel conveyed that he was not quitting voluntarily. Weiss was a little less transparent, but the New York Times reported that he "did not sound altogether happy, despite his protestations to the contrary."[28] Exactly why the Yankee owners fired Weiss and Stengel remains murky. The team's claim that they were instating a sixty-five-year-old retirement age probably contained a grain of truth. More likely, the Yankee owners questioned whether the club was still moving in the right direction. In addition, Topping wanted to get more directly involved in the operation of the franchise and wanted a position for his son Dan Jr., desires that would have been much trickier with the imperial Weiss still in charge.

From 1949 through 1960 the New York Yankees won ten pennants and seven World Series. In recognition of his retooling of the Yankees into the 1960 pennant winner, the Sporting News named Weiss Executive of the Year, the fourth time he had been so honored. No one has been awarded this prestigious accolade more often. The team Weiss had built went on to win the next four pennants as well, giving the Yankees an incredible fourteen in sixteen years.

Weiss spent his formative baseball years as a successful Minor League operator at a time when it took smarts, hustle, and a good eye for ballplayers. He successfully transferred his skills to the Yankees, first to the farm system, then to the entire operation. Once in charge Weiss proved a skilled administrator: he was not afraid to hire strong men as subordinates, maintained the crack scouting staff organized under Barrow, and, most important, trusted and listened to his staff. The professional organization over which Weiss presided influenced many of baseball's more recent championship clubs.

9 Integration

In April 1947 Jackie Robinson played his first game for the Brooklyn Dodgers, bringing an end to a sixty-year ban on black players in the Major Leagues. The story of Robinson and the brave men who followed his lead and helped change the game has been told often and well over the succeeding years in articles, books, and movies. Robinson's bravery and outstanding play combined to right baseball's great wrong and led the way for many other players who followed.

Although baseball's belated foray into social justice is worth all the attention it has received, the issue that concerns us here is that the integration of the game had an extraordinary impact on how a team could be built. Jackie Robinson improved baseball ethically and morally, but he also made it better because he was a great player, and his playing time came at the expense of someone who was a lesser player. Robinson opened the doors for a vast new source of baseball talent, and that talent could not help but dramatically improve the game.

Robinson paved the way for all dark-skinned players, whether they were African American or Latino. Although light-skinned Latinos occasionally played in the Majors before 1947 (making up less than 1 percent of all players), the integration of the game led to the gradual acceptance of all Latinos, not just those who were adequately light-skinned. Chart 2 illustrates the speed with which the game integrated.[1]

In 1950 only five teams had integrated. As more and more teams, however, became willing to incorporate dark-skinned players and began scouting the new talent pool, the ratio of nonwhite players increased until it reached 20 percent in the early 1960s and 30 percent by the mid-1970s. Although the twenty-first century has seen a decline in African American players, the large number of Afro-Latinos has kept the overall percentage well over 30 percent since 1990.

Moreover, the mere number of players understates their value. From 1947 to 2013 African American players have won 47 MVP awards and

Chart 2. Percentage change in African Americans and Latinos

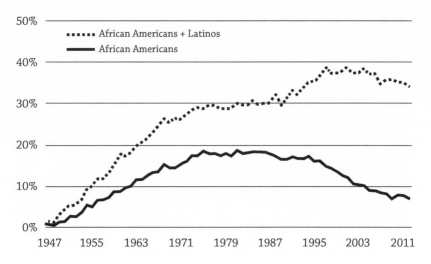

Source: Database owned and maintained by the authors.

Latinos another 21, totaling more than one-half of the 134 awards given in the period, much more than their proportional representation suggests they should have won. Chart 3 illuminates, alternatively, the percentage of total wins above replacement contributed by this group of players. Despite their still modest numbers, nonwhite players were contributing one-third of the WAR in baseball by the early 1960s and have been well above that ever since.

Although all sorts of inferences can be drawn from the data, what we will focus on here is the impact of this newly accessible talent pool on a Major League organization trying to build its team. When baseball integrated in 1947, most teams were likely oblivious to how much talent had just become available. There were not just a handful of players who could play in the Majors, but dozens of them, many of them among the greatest players ever to play the game: Willie Mays, Henry Aaron, Ernie Banks, Roberto Clemente, and Frank Robinson were discovered and signed within a five-year period.

In order to take advantage of this extraordinary point in time, a baseball team needed both moral courage (although this arguably became less important by the mid-1950s when blacks were excelling

Chart 3. African American and Latino player value

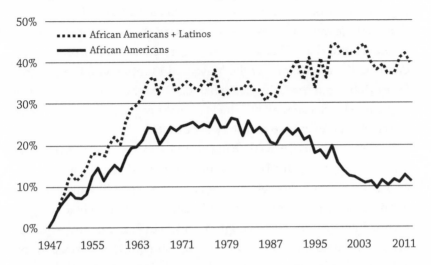

Source: Database owned and maintained by the authors.

in the game) and the willingness to expend the additional time and money to find and scout these players. If a team employed a dozen scouts spread over a still largely segregated country, chances are they would not have seen many dark-skinned players unless they were instructed to do so, to go see different games in different towns and cities. In a similar vein, as the previous figures illustrate, the Major Leagues did not really efficiently mine the talent in Latin America until the 1990s.

Jules Tygiel, the preeminent scholar of baseball's integration period, pointed out that it was not enough that a team express a willingness to integrate, or even to have a legitimate willingness to do so. A team had to redirect its scouts or hire new ones, including Latino scouts for Mexico and the Caribbean.[2] The Boston Red Sox often claimed to be looking for black players in the 1950s, and they made a few high-profile attempts to acquire established blacks, but they were the last team to actually field a black Major League player, in 1959. They had the money—their owner, Tom Yawkey, might have been the richest man in the game—but when faced with one of history's great talent windfalls, they sat on their hands.

The pace of integration moved slowly in the early years; through 1953 only nine of the sixteen teams had fielded a black player. But although there were only twenty-four blacks in the game, these included several future Hall of Famers: the Dodgers' Jackie Robinson and Roy Campanella, the Giants' Willie Mays and Monte Irvin, the Indians' Larry Doby, and the Cubs' Ernie Banks. Over the next few years the pace quickened, especially in the National League, where there were thirty-six blacks in 1956 and sixty-six in 1960.

Importantly, these players changed the balance of power in baseball, especially in the NL. The Dodgers and Giants, both heavily integrated, won all six NL pennants between 1951 and 1956. The Milwaukee Braves, fortified by Henry Aaron in 1954 and reinforced by other black players such as Billy Bruton, Wes Covington, and Juan Pizarro, won pennants in 1957 and 1958. Competing with these teams without black players, at least in the National League, proved to be nearly impossible.

The American League trends were much different. The Yankees had so much talent already, and were competing with so many dysfunctional AL franchises, that they were able to ride three great white stars—Mickey Mantle, Whitey Ford, and Yogi Berra—to eight pennants in the decade without aggressively pursuing the new market. Elston Howard was their first black player, in 1955, and he played a big role in several pennants. The Yankees' toughest regular-season competition came from the Cleveland Indians and the Chicago White Sox, the two most integrated teams in the AL.

As examined in the next chapter, the St. Louis Cardinals experienced the other side of this revolution. Initially, their response to integration was embarrassing. Stories that players on the team tried to strike rather than play against Robinson have persisted to this day, though all the principals have denied them. More important, the organization did not employ any blacks for more than seven years after Robinson's 1945 signing and did not field a black on the big-league club until 1954.

Fred Saigh, the team's owner until 1953, told interviewer Bill Marshall years later, "I think we were thought of as a team from the South." He claimed the club sold more tickets "largely because of the mail we'd get—'Well, we're glad you're not scumming.'" Saigh also claimed a difference between the writers that covered the Cardinals and the eastern writers, who were "Jewish boys" and "minority minded."[3] The National Association for the Advancement of Colored People threatened to boycott Cardinal games in 1952 if they did not sign a black player. Saigh responded that the team was trying to integrate and that the team was actively scouting the Negro Leagues for players.[4] Nonetheless, the club had signed no blacks before Saigh sold the team.

Prior to Jackie Robinson's debut, the Cardinals had been the dominant team in the National League, winning nine pennants and six World Series in twenty-one years. The all-white Cardinals gave the Dodgers a tough fight in 1949, losing by a single game, but the problem began to catch up with them—they did not receive a notable contribution from a black player until 1959. Not coincidentally, they spent a decade out of contention, watching their well-integrated competition represent the NL in the World Series every year.

By the 1960s the advantages gained by the early integrators had dissipated, and the ever-increasing numbers of black stars were being distributed more equally throughout the Major Leagues. But the lesson of this period—that teams can gain an advantage from a newly discovered (or newly permitted) talent source—would play out again (to a lesser degree) in Latin America in the 1980s and in Asia around 2000. In 2013, after an increasing number of their players had defected and found riches in U.S. baseball, Cuba announced that it would now allow its baseball players to sign contracts with U.S. teams.[5] How this will affect the vast talent on that Caribbean island is not known at the time of this writing, nor is how the various Major League teams will deal with this new reality.

10 Commitment

You get a feeling of how the club interrelates with each other. You make a move, you better try to bring in somebody who's going to relate to the guys you have.—PAT GILLICK, baseball executive

When Gussie Busch, the newly minted owner of the St. Louis Cardinals, visited spring training in 1953 to see his club in action, he asked of his coaching staff, "Where are our black players?" After an uncomfortable pause, he was told that there were none. Busch responded, "How can it be the great game if blacks can't play?"[1] Knowingly or not, Busch had hit on the question of the age. An extraordinarily accomplished businessman, his company had sold plenty of beer to African Americans over the years, and he understood both the moral and the economic ramifications of the situation.

August "Gussie" Busch Jr. was the grandson of the cofounder of Anheuser-Busch and assumed control of the company in 1946 when he was forty-seven. One of St. Louis's best-known citizens, Busch lived on a 281-acre palatial estate just outside the city, where he hosted wild parties for hundreds of friends. Harry Caray, the longtime Cardinal announcer, called Busch "a beer-and-broads man," which Caray meant as high praise. In February 1953 Anheuser-Busch purchased the Cardinals, and the fifty-four-year-old Busch named himself president of the team. His title evolved over the years, but he ran the Cardinals until his death in 1989.

The Cardinals had become available because previous owner Fred Saigh had run afoul of income tax law—his no-contest plea to evading $50,000 in taxes led to a fifteen-month prison term. Saigh had several offers from parties who wanted to move the team out of St. Louis, but he held out for a local buyer. A couple of bankers pressured Busch to have Anheuser-Busch buy the club, convincing him that it would help both the city and his beer business.[2] The company paid $3.75 million for the Cardinals and nine Minor League teams. As Busch's fortune was estimated at $60 million, the price was well within his means.[3] The team soon bought Sportsman's Park from the American League's St. Louis Browns and renamed it Busch Stadium. A year later the Browns moved to Baltimore, and the Cardinals had the city to themselves.

Busch knew little about the baseball business at the time. "I've been a fan all my life," said Busch, "but I've been too busy to get out to the park in recent years unfortunately. However, the brewery has a box reserved for its use each season."[4] Many observers doubted Busch's motivations. "Probably there has never been another owner in the Major Leagues with less personal interest in the game than Gussie Busch," wrote Red Smith, "or one who used his baseball connection more blatantly to shill for his product."[5] All ad space at the park was used to sell beer, the Budweiser jingle was played between innings, and, on occasion, the company Clydesdales drove a beer wagon around the ballpark. The company was fourth in national beer sales in 1947, but first within a few years after Busch bought the Cardinals.[6]

Though he knew little about the game, Busch took a hands-on approach in his early days as owner. Soon after Anheuser-Busch bought the team Busch reportedly asked at a meeting of brewery executives whether anyone present knew anything about baseball. Dick Meyer, a vice president at the brewery, offered that he had played first base as a student. Hearing this, Busch named Meyer the club's general manager. This was in 1954; the prior year Busch had run the club himself, deferring to manager Eddie Stanky on personnel matters. With his experience running a brewing empire, Busch slowly realized that he needed to build a more professional front office, although he never really established the harmonized structure of the Dodgers or Yankees.

One directive Busch was firm on was the need to field some black players. A few weeks after taking over the team Busch signed Quincy Trouppe, a longtime Negro League star, as a full-time scout. In May the Cardinals signed their first black player—outfielder Leonard Tucker from Fresno State College—and assigned him to their Fresno farm club. Busch sent Tucker a telegram, saying, in part, "I hope your professional record is a credit to all of us."[7] The team signed at least two more blacks to Minor League contracts that summer. In October Busch pledged that the team would sign more. "It is ridiculous to close the door to any minority, especially when our competitors owe so much of their success to members of this minority group."[8]

Busch's comments reveal his various motivations. He likely genuinely believed that blacks deserved the opportunity to play on his team, but he was not afraid to voice another obvious fact: the Cardinals were getting soundly beaten every year by the well-integrated Giants and Dodgers. Busch wanted to win and knew that he needed to field the best players—regardless of race—to do so.

In January 1954 the Cardinals acquired Tom Alston from the then–Minor League San Diego Padres. Alston was a navy veteran and a former collegian (North Carolina A&T) and was already twenty-eight years old when the Cardinals bought him. He had hit .297 with twenty-three home runs for the Padres, and his purchase price of one hundred thousand dollars (plus two players) was believed to be the most money yet spent to acquire a black player. Alston started on opening day and played fairly regularly, but ultimately proved to be overmatched by big-league pitching. He hit .246 in sixty-four games, before being demoted to Rochester in July. He had shorter trials the next three years before drawing his release.

The Cardinals also used two black pitchers in 1954. Bill Greason, recalled at the end of May, lasted just three outings, but Brooks Lawrence, who came up in late June, had a fine year, finishing 15-6 for a Cardinal club that finished in sixth place at 72-82. Lawrence struggled in 1955, leading to his trade to Cincinnati, but bounced back to have a few more fine seasons. The Cardinals continued to sign and play young black players, though they did not find any stars immediately.

In other ways Gussie Busch's early years were marked by impatience. A brilliant success as a brewer, Busch fully expected the same results in baseball. He started out by asking the most basic of questions to his manager, Eddie Stanky: what do you need to make this team a contender? Stanky suggested a first baseman and a third baseman. What player in baseball would you most want? Stanky liked Dodger star Gil Hodges, whereupon Busch offered Brooklyn owner Walter O'Malley five hundred thousand dollars for Hodges. O'Malley reminded Busch that the Dodgers also needed Hodges. Busch received similar responses elsewhere.[9]

After a 1955 season in which the Cardinals posted their worst record (68-84) since 1924, Busch finally realized that relying on his manager for personnel decisions and offering huge amounts of money for good but not great players were no way to run a franchise. Accordingly, he promoted Meyer to executive vice president and hired Frank Lane to be the club's general manager. "Trader" Lane had a long career in the game as a GM and became particularly famous for his obsessive trading. He made his mark with the Chicago White Sox, who gave him the GM job in late 1948. In just a few years Lane made dozens of deals of little consequence but a few that turned out brilliantly. Three largely unknown acquisitions—pitcher Billy Pierce, second baseman Nellie Fox, and outfielder Minnie Minoso—became immediate stars and remained so for a decade while the White Sox enjoyed an extended run of contention. By 1955 Lane's relationship with the White Sox had soured, and Busch was able to hire him away.

After his early success Lane seemed to have become so enamored with his own genius that he made trades for the sake of creating news. ("Frank Lane was a great trader," Buzzie Bavasi once remarked. "But, when I say that, I don't mean the trades he made were great.")[10] While Lane's White Sox deals had seemed part of a larger design, there seemed to be no purpose to his actions in St. Louis. The 1955 Cardinals still had two veteran holdovers from their 1940s clubs—Stan Musial, thirty-four, and Red Schoendienst, thirty-two—but also a core of young position players with promise. Rookie Ken Boyer had hit eighteen home runs and played a fine third base, and the outfield of Rip Repulski (twenty-three home runs), Bill Virdon (seventeen homers, an excellent center fielder, and 1955 Rookie of the Year), and Wally Moon (nineteen home runs and 1954 Rookie of the Year) was one of the league's youngest and most promising.

A month into the 1956 season Lane dealt Virdon for two mediocrities—outfielder Bobby Del Greco and pitcher Dick Littlefield. In June Lane traded the popular Schoendienst in a nine-player deal; the principal returns were veterans Al Dark and Whitey Lockman. After the season Repulski was sent to the Phillies for thirty-two-year-old outfielder Del

Ennis, who had several fine years in his past but just one in his future. Busch, still looking for a quick fix, encouraged Lane to offer five hundred thousand dollars for Ernie Banks and one million dollars for Willie Mays. Both their teams turned him down.[11]

Under Lane the team improved to seventy-six wins in 1956 and eighty-seven in 1957, but the principal cause of the gain was the performance of the players already in place when Lane arrived. Before the 1957 season Lane attempted to trade Musial to the Pirates; Busch got wind of the deal and overruled it. After the 1957 season Lane decided he could not handle the interference and quit. At the urging of Dick Meyer, Busch hired Bing Devine to replace Lane, and the real building of the team began.[12]

Vaughan Pallmore "Bing" Devine, a soft-spoken, modest man, could not have been more of a departure from the loud and brash Frank Lane. Born and raised in St. Louis, Devine played basketball and baseball at his hometown Washington University. Upon his graduation he went to work for the Cardinals as a general office boy and batting-practice pitcher. These were the Cardinals of Sam Breadon and Branch Rickey, though Devine's menial work did not get him much face time with his famous bosses. In 1941 the twenty-five-year-old Devine became the GM for one of the Cardinals' many Minor League teams, an Appalachian League club in Johnson City, Tennessee. Faced with a roster shortage due to the military draft, Devine played twenty-seven games at second base. After hitting just .118, he hung up his uniform permanently. In 1942 he ran the Fresno club in the California League. When the league folded Devine finished the season in Decatur, Illinois.

After four years in the navy, Devine returned to the Cardinals, spending two seasons in Columbus, Georgia, and seven in Rochester, New York (the Cardinals' top club). In Rochester Devine worked not only with many future Major League players, but also with managers Johnny Keane and Harry Walker, both future big-league managers with whom Devine would remain close. After a successful run, including two league championships, Devine became Lane's assistant, a job that did not give Devine much to do. Lane did not involve advisers in his deal making. "If Frank Lane didn't make a deal in a month," recalled Devine, "he'd be nasty, just like a smoker who needed a cigarette." Lane, Devine felt, resented Musial and Schoendienst getting all of the attention around the club, and this led to Lane's need to try to deal them.[13]

Just before Lane quit in 1957 he had worked out a trade with the Pirates, leaving only the final approval for Devine: the Cardinals would send Ken Boyer to Pittsburgh for outfielder Frank Thomas and third baseman Gene Freese. Boyer had a fine sophomore season in 1956 (.306 with twenty-six home runs), but both Lane and manager Fred Hutchinson questioned his determination and effort. Lane, in fact, suggested that Boyer should have hit .360. After an early slump at third base and at the plate in 1957, Hutchinson moved Boyer to center field (a weak spot ever since Lane had traded Virdon), and Boyer regressed. While Devine was contemplating the Boyer deal, Hutchinson said of Boyer, "He has the potential all right, but I don't know whether he's determined enough to reach that potential." Rival NL infielder Johnny Temple disagreed, saying, "I think Lane had him all shook up. He didn't know what he was doing."[14] Just days into his new job, Bing Devine called off the deal.

The Boyer nondeal would prove to be one of Devine's best decisions. Hutchinson originally planned to keep Boyer in center field, but decided late in spring training that he needed Boyer back at third base. After a fine 1958 season—twenty-three home runs, ninety RBI, a .307 average, and his first Gold Glove award—the St. Louis writers honored Boyer at their winter banquet. "My thanks to Bing Devine," said Boyer, "for not trading me when, I know, there was considerable pressure to do so."[15] Boyer became one of the best players in the game for the next several years, winning five Gold Gloves and appearing in ten All-Star Games.

In his memoirs Devine credits Lane for instilling in him the willingness to take a chance, to be aggressive in making trades. Devine would never be a deal maker like Lane, but he thought Lane's example allowed him not to be afraid to make a trade that might be unpopular.[16]

Unlike Lane, Devine sought and received a lot of input on his potential trades and credited other people for his successful ones. Eddie Stanky worked for several years scouting other Major League clubs and became an important Devine adviser, as did Harry Walker. Devine "was very methodical," remembered Lee Thomas, who later worked for Devine. "He gave everybody a chance to voice his opinion. You were not afraid to speak up. He wanted to hear what you had to say. . . . But we knew he was the boss." Devine could also be tough when he needed to be. "Bing intimidated a lot of people," Thomas added. "In a good way, not a mean way. They respected him. I know I did. He was very free to give credit to everybody when things went well. And when things didn't he took the blame."[17]

Devine also had to consult with Meyer, who would run major decisions past Busch. Unlike Lane, Devine developed a good relationship with Meyer, and the two became close friends. Devine felt that Busch had every right to be notified on possible deals, and the owner rarely interfered. In fact, if Busch expressed any misgivings, Meyer would likely as not lobby on Devine's behalf to get the deal approved.[18]

Devine made his first trade in December 1957, dealing three pitchers—only one of whom, reliever Willard Schmidt, had Major League experience—to the Cincinnati Reds for outfielder Joe Taylor and infielder-outfielder Curt Flood. Both acquisitions had shown promise—Taylor as a slugger, Flood as a hitter and defensive player.

In Flood's 1970 memoirs he blames racism for this trade, suggesting that the Reds did not want to have three black outfielders. Frank Robinson was already one of the league's best players, though Vada Pinson, whom Flood names as the other outfielder, would not play regularly until 1959. In a 1962 magazine story written after Flood had become a star, but long before his memoirs, Flood was asked about this very issue. "As far as the Negro situation in Cincinnati," Flood said, "I don't know. It came up quite a bit early in my career, but I never felt that was why I was traded." Birdie Tebbetts, the Reds' manager, took full responsibility: "We needed pitching with that club. We had the power. The thing with Flood was he had a hitch in his swing. We knew he'd be a good one, but the reports were that he wouldn't arrive for several years and we needed pitching help right away." Flood agreed: "Birdie was right about the hitch. I had to work hard to correct it."[19]

Flood was just nineteen at the time of the deal and (other than a handful of games with the Reds) had not yet played higher than Single-A. He was a slight man, just five foot eight and 150 pounds at this stage, and had played third base for Savannah in 1957. "I'll play where they put me," allowed Flood. "All I want to do is play, and play every day if possible." Manager Hutchinson decided he was an outfielder. "Flood can run and has good range in the outfield. He has batted in every league he's been in, but he is only a baby and we don't know what he will do against strong pitching."[20] Flood was sent to Omaha to start the season, but returned at the end of April after hitting .340 in 15 games. He played almost every day in center field the rest of the season, hitting .261 with 10 home runs.

The 1958 Cardinals fell to 72-82 and fifth place. The principal problem was the offense—only Musial, Boyer, and first baseman–outfielder Joe Cunningham (.312 with 82 walks in just 337 at bats) could be considered even average hitters at their positions. The starting pitching, led by Sam Jones, Larry Jackson, and Vinegar Bend Mizell, was unspectacular but far from the problem.

As the season wound down Busch decided that he no longer wanted Hutchinson to manage his team. He instead wanted Solly Hemus, then an infielder for the Phillies. Hemus had played parts of seven seasons with St. Louis before being dealt by Lane in May 1956. After the trade Hemus wrote Busch a letter, thanking him for treating him so well during his years with the team and asking that he be considered down the road for a manager's job in the organization. Three years later Busch had Devine reacquire Hemus and make him the team's manager.[21]

Devine made several other moves in the off-season. In October he dealt two starting players—shortstop Eddie Kasko and right fielder Del Ennis—to the Reds for shortstop Alex Grammas and first baseman George Crowe. Grammas took over at short, while the African American Crowe would provide veteran bench strength and leadership, especially for the team's growing pool of young black players. Five days later Devine pulled off a five-player deal with the Giants, which netted the Cardinals pitching prospect Ernie Broglio, who would be one of the more important members of the pitching staff for the next several years. In December Wally Moon was sent to the Dodgers for outfielder Gino Cimoli, who would have a decent 1959 season. Finally, just prior to the start of the season, Sam Jones was traded to the Giants for first baseman–outfielder Bill White.

White had been caught in a logjam with the Giants. As a rookie in 1956 the twenty-two-year-old White hit 22 home runs and seemed to be one of the more promising hitters in the league. White was drafted into the army and missed all of 1957 and most of 1958. When he returned the Giants were using rookie Orlando Cepeda, a twenty-year-old who hit .312 with 25 home runs and won the Rookie of the Year Award at White's first base position. White was relegated to pinch-hitting the last two months of the season. The next spring manager Bill Rigney said he wanted to keep White as bench strength, but White repeatedly demanded a trade, finally getting his wish.[22]

Unfortunately for White, he faced a similar situation in St. Louis, where the incumbent first baseman was Stan Musial, the team's biggest star and still the best in the league at the position. The Cardinals were already playing Joe Cunningham, an excellent offensive player, out of position in right field in deference to Musial. The team had also just acquired Crowe, who had hit 31 home runs just two seasons earlier. It took a few weeks for things to settle, but eventually Hemus kept Musial at first base, played Cunningham in right, and put White in left. Musial's season-long slump got him benched a few times, allowing White to start 40 times at first base. White hit .302 and Cunningham .345 with a league-best .453 on-base percentage. Along with another fine year from Ken Boyer (.309 with 28 home runs), the club now had three good hitters in their mid- to late twenties. Curt Flood, still just twenty-one, was mainly used as a defensive replacement and fourth outfielder, hitting just .255 in 208 at bats.

Also arriving in 1959 was Bob Gibson, a fire-balling right-hander from Omaha, Nebraska. The Cardinals signed Gibson after his graduation from Creighton University in 1957, and he spent a year and a half in the Minor Leagues. He toiled most of the 1959 season with the Omaha Cardinals (9-9, 3.07), but made nine starts for St. Louis (3-5, 3.07). Gibson threw hard, but was beset with control problems that delayed his advancement.

The 1959 Cardinals fell to 71-83, a game worse than the previous year, but followed up with an 86-76 season in 1960. The principal improvement came from the fine pitching of Ernie Broglio (21-9, 2.74), Larry Jackson (18-13, 3.48), and nineteen-year-old rookie Ray Sadecki (9-9, 3.78). In May Devine picked up pitcher Curt Simmons, who had been released by the Phillies after a decade of solid pitching. He had been suffering an arm injury, and the Phillies thought he was finished. With the Cardinals he went 7-4, with a 2.66 ERA.

Despite the improvement on the field, these were not happy years for many of the Cardinal players, mainly because of dissatisfaction with Hemus. Many thought that manager Hemus, a scrappy, overachieving player, tried to overcompensate for his own shortcomings by screaming at and ridiculing his players, often for small miscues on the field. Although this style might have been tolerated a generation or two earlier, many of the younger players resented him. In particular, Bob Gibson and Curt Flood despised him and believed him to be a racist. Gibson later wrote that "either he disliked us deeply or he genuinely believed that the way to motivate us was with insults." Flood was less equivocal, saying, "Hemus acted as if I smelled bad."[23]

The most egregious incident came during a game in Pittsburgh in 1959. Hemus played himself against Bennie Daniels, a black pitcher. When a pitch hit Hemus on the leg, he yelled at Daniels, calling him a "black bastard." In a later at bat Hemus took a swing and flung his bat at the pitcher, leading to both benches emptying. After the game Hemus held a team meeting to explain himself and admit what he had called Daniels. He did not apologize. Bill White, who was less sure than his teammates of Hemus's racism, later said that Hemus never regained the team's trust. Thirty years later Hemus told David Halberstam that his comments had been misinterpreted, that he had been raised in a game when players called each other "Jew bastard" and similar things, but the world had changed and he had not. He took the blame for what had happened with the Cardinals.[24]

Both Gibson and Flood later wrote that Hemus did not give them a chance and played inferior players in their place.[25] In 1960 Flood, still just twenty-two, played 132 games in center field, including 116 starts. Although his defense drew high praise, he hit a woeful .237 with little power and just 35 walks. Whatever Hemus might have been like to deal with, Flood got quite a bit of playing time and did not hit. Gibson pitched in 27 games, including 12 starts, and finished 3-6 with a 5.61 ERA. Gibson would become a great pitcher, and Hemus might not have properly recognized this, but Gibson also did not deliver when given the ball.

Hemus lasted until the middle of the 1961 season, when Devine finally approached Gussie Busch and said a change was necessary. Busch agreed and allowed Devine to offer the job to Johnny Keane, who had managed in the organization for many years and knew many of the current players. In particular, the black players felt like a weight had been lifted off their shoulders.

Although Keane's tactical changes have been overstated over the years, there is no doubt that the team as a whole responded by playing better baseball. The team was 33-41 and in sixth place when they changed skippers, but Keane brought them up to 80-74. Many of the Cardinal players have pointed to the change of managers as a pivotal event in the club's evolution. Johnny Keane was very well liked and respected by his players.

Bing Devine deserves credit for recognizing that with the integration of his ball club, he needed a skipper who could manage black players with dignity and respect. Taking advantage of the availability of African American players was, of course, the first indispensable step. But the teams that created a positive environment for these new players could gain an additional advantage. Devine went beyond the admittedly low bar of the era to pair an integrated team with a skipper all the players respected. He had wanted to hire Keane instead of Hemus in 1958, and the team might have been better off had Busch allowed him to.

In 1962 the NL expanded to ten teams, resulting in a longer schedule and two new terrible teams. After a 14-4 start the Cardinals' slow march forward stalled, and the club finished 84-78. That said, there were many hopeful signs as their good young players made progress. Bob Gibson (15-13, 2.85 ERA, 208 strikeouts), Ernie Broglio (12-9, 3.00), and Ray Washburn (12-9, 4.10) were all under twenty-seven years old. Veterans Larry Jackson (16-11, 3.75) and Curt Simmons (10-10, 3.51) joined them, forming a solid starting pitching core. The offense was led by Bill White (20 home runs, 102 RBI, .324 batting average), Ken Boyer (24, 98, .291) and forty-one-year-old Stan Musial (19, 82, .330) in his last hurrah. Flood batted .296, and second baseman Julian Javier (a 1960 acquisition from the Pirates) hit .263 and played a fine second base. The team's offense was dragged down by its substandard production at shortstop and right field.

One observer decidedly unimpressed with the team's progress was Gussie Busch. "As far as I'm concerned," said Busch in August, "I'm almost at the point where I'd trade just about everybody. They're going to be a hungry club—or there won't be anyone around next spring. I'm so disgusted I can hardly think straight." Busch absolved manager Keane of blame, but allowed that Bing Devine and the rest of the organization were on thin ice.[26] In the end Busch's chosen course was to hire Branch Rickey, the legendary eighty-year-old executive who had built great teams in St. Louis and Brooklyn, but had not worked for a team since leaving the Pirates in 1955. Rickey reported to Busch and was supposed to advise Busch, Meyer, Devine, and Keane. Bing Devine, who had not resented the presence of Dick Meyer as Busch's adviser, very much resented the presence of Rickey. One evening shortly after Rickey joined the club, he asked Devine, "Are we going to have trouble if I'm here to run the club?" Devine boldly replied, "Mr. Rickey, we're not *going* to have trouble. We *have* trouble right now." Devine knew that his career was on the line, but he had no interest in playing second fiddle after so many years in charge. According to Devine, they did not speak much after that. When a writer asked about the reported feud, Dick Meyer said, "Bing Devine is still the general manager."[27]

Rickey overplayed his hand almost immediately. He told Devine that it was time for Musial, fresh off his .330 season, to retire. Word leaked to Musial himself, who said he was not retiring and would play elsewhere if the Cardinals did not want him. Devine and Keane wanted him to stay. Gussie Busch stepped in and said that Musial could play as long as he wanted and would have a job with the organization when he was through playing. Busch reiterated that Bing Devine was in charge of the team.[28]

Devine made two deals in the fall in an attempt to plug the team's two positional holes. In one he dealt pitchers Larry Jackson and Lindy

McDaniel and reserve catcher Jimmie Schaffer to the Cubs for All-Star outfielder George Altman, pitcher Don Cardwell, and catcher Moe Thacker. This turned out to be one of Devine's worst trades. The thirty-year-old Altman had hit over .300 with power the previous two years, but would have just one mediocre season with the Cardinals before moving on. Meanwhile, Jackson, who was thirty-two years old, would average 265 innings over the next six years, including two especially fine years in 1963 and 1964, and McDaniel had thirteen years left as a capable reliever.

Devine's next deal was more successful, though it got him in more trouble with Rickey. Devine worked out a deal with Pittsburgh to trade twenty-three-year-old Julio Gotay, who hit .255 in his first full year as the Cardinal shortstop, along with the just-acquired Cardwell, for thirty-three-year-old shortstop Dick Groat. Devine knew that Rickey would disapprove—he loathed dealing young players for older ones. To press his case Devine invited Rickey to a meeting that also included several of Devine's advisers, including Harry Walker and Eddie Stanky. Rickey looked around the room and said, "You've kind of loaded this meeting for me, haven't you?" Rickey finally agreed to take the deal to Busch, along with his own negative opinion. Busch, likely swayed by Dick Meyer, gave his approval, and the deal was made.[29] Groat, who had several fine years with the Pirates, including winning the Most Valuable Player award for the 1960 season, would hit .319 and finish a strong second for the MVP award in 1963.

When the team gathered in St. Petersburg for spring training in 1963, Johnny Keane discovered that Rickey believed his consultant job also covered matters on the playing field. One day Rickey came onto the field and asked Keane why he had sent rookie shortstop Jim Harris to the Minor League camp. Keane told Rickey to get off the field, that he was the manager of the team and needed no help. Rickey left. In a magazine article that spring, Rickey picked the Cardinals to finish fifth. He was especially critical of the team's young pitching staff. Keane shot back, "Our pitchers are not as young as the 1942 Cards [who won the World Series]. I'd like to know who assembled them." It was Rickey, as Keane knew.[30]

Despite the distractions the 1963 Cardinals finally took a leap forward, finishing in second place at 93-69. The Cards drew to within one game of the Dodgers with twelve to play but then lost three straight to Los Angeles on the way to losing six in a row and finished six games out. The credit for the success of the team fell largely on Devine, whose trades were seen as the key to the team. This was especially on display in the All-Star Game, which featured all four Cardinal infielders (White, Javier, Groat, and Boyer) starting the game for the National League—three of them acquired by Bing Devine and the other saved by him several years earlier. After the season he was named baseball's Executive of the Year by the *Sporting News*.[31]

The club was led by the great all-around play of White, Boyer, Groat, and Flood. There were five players in the Major Leagues who had 200 hits in 1963, and three of them were Cardinals—Flood, White, and Groat. White, Flood, and Boyer won Gold Gloves for their fielding. White and Boyer combined for 51 home runs and 220 RBI. The team also had an excellent quartet of starters—Bob Gibson (18-9), Ernie Broglio (18-10), Curt Simmons (15-9), and Ray Sadecki (10-10), supplemented by the excellent relief work of Ron Taylor and Bobby Shantz. Stan Musial fell to .255 and retired, the one down note to a year otherwise filled with progress.

A key arrival in 1963 was catcher Tim McCarver. A three-sport high school star, McCarver turned down football scholarships from Notre Dame and Tennessee (he had been an all-state end) to sign in 1959 for a reported bonus of seventy-five thousand dollars. He was only seventeen when he debuted in the Majors that September and spent most of four seasons in the Minor Leagues. In March 1963 Keane finally told the twenty-one-year-old that he had nothing left to prove, that he would be the third-string catcher, behind Carl Sawatski and Gene Oliver, with Oliver the incumbent starter.

McCarver impressed in his occasional appearances, and by late May he was platooning with Oliver. In June the Cardinals needed another pitcher, and Devine traded Oliver to Milwaukee for Lew Burdette. Just like that, McCarver was the everyday catcher. "It was a big break for me when they traded Oliver," said McCarver. "I had no reservations about getting in there. That's what I trained for." He played nearly every game the rest of the season and hit .289 with excellent defense.

From the day he arrived, the rookie was aggressive and cocky. For the Cardinal pitching staff, this was crucial. "When McCarver was put into the lineup," said Broglio, "it was a big thing, a big question. I want my catcher to call my game for me. He has to take charge." McCarver took charge. Johnny Keane recalled going out to the mound late in a game to talk with Lew Burdette, who had not looked comfortable. Before Keane could decide to take him out, McCarver stepped in and convinced both the manager and the pitcher that they were going to get out of this jam. "I can't say enough about that kid," said Dick Groat after the season. "I've never seen a guy take over the way he did. He's the best-looking catcher I've seen in baseball." Groat marveled at how quickly the rookie catcher instilled faith in his pitchers. "Give the credit to McCarver, he's been great," said Bill White.[32] Said McCarver:

> I knew when I took over that it was a great opportunity, and I realized, too, that everyone was saying I was so young that it would be a problem. No one in the world realized just how young I was any better than I did. I knew when I got in there that I couldn't let the pitchers run all over me. You have to earn their respect, treat each and every one of them like he was your own flesh and blood. You have to be stern with them yet go along with them. You should only go out to the mound to talk to them when it is needed. You can't keep running out there and make a useless thing out of it. With some pitchers you know right away that a walk will shake them up and your job is not to let them get bothered, so you go out.[33]

His relationship with the fiery Gibson was especially important. Gibson later admitted that he was initially cautious about McCarver, the white bonus player from the heavily segregated city of Memphis. A great prospect in his own right, Gibson's four-thousand-dollar bonus paled next to the seventy-five thousand that McCarver had received. For his part, McCarver has acknowledged being uncomfortable around outspoken black men like Gibson and Flood, people who confronted the prejudices of his upbringing. (Both men have told the story of Gibson approaching McCarver on the team bus while the catcher was drinking a soda. "Can I have a sip?" asked Gibson, knowing a white southerner would be reluctant to share a bottle with a black man. "I'll save you some," responded McCarver.) To the credit of both men, they grew into the best of friends. Both fiercely competitive team leaders despite their relative youth, their friendship would help bind the entire team together.[34]

Looking ahead to 1964, the Cardinals appeared set in the infield, at catcher, in center field, and on the mound. The problem spot was in the corner outfield spots—Musial had retired, and Altman had been traded to the Mets for Roger Craig, who would add depth to the team's bullpen. Devine's other key off-season acquisitions were Carl Warwick, an outfielder obtained from Houston, and Bob Uecker, a backup catcher received from the Braves for two young players—Gary Kolb and Jimmie Coker. On his first day in the Cardinal clubhouse in the spring, Uecker met the great Branch Rickey. "Mr. Rickey, I'm Bob Uecker, and I've just joined your club." Rickey responded gruffly, "Yes, I know, and I didn't want you. I wouldn't trade a hundred Bob Ueckers for one Gary Kolb."[35] Little wonder that Uecker would develop a much-beloved Rodney Dangerfield attitude regarding his baseball skill set.

Keane spent the first two months of the season trying to find adequate production from left and right fields. Charlie James, who had hit .268 with 10 home runs in half-time play in 1963, started the season in a slump and never shook it, hitting .223 on the season. Rookie Johnny Lewis started the year as the regular right fielder, but was back in the Minor Leagues by mid-June. Warwick served as an adequate fourth outfielder and pinch hitter. Doug Clemens had experienced annual trials since 1960 and hit .205 in 33 games.

The Cardinals began the season playing well and were just a game behind the first-place Giants on May 22. Then St. Louis slumped badly, dropping 17 of 23 games by June 15 and falling 7 games behind the front-running Phillies. More important, the Cardinals were in eighth place in a very competitive pennant race. June 15 was the trading deadline, and Bing Devine had spent the previous few weeks desperately looking for outfielders. Two days earlier Devine had traded a Minor Leaguer to Cincinnati for Bob Skinner, a thirty-two-year-old former All-Star who was hitting .220 and had lost most of his playing time with the Reds. As a sign of how desperate Keane was, he immediately installed Skinner in right field, a position he had last played, briefly, eight years earlier. Skinner held the job only a couple of weeks.

The man Devine and Keane most wanted was Chicago Cubs outfielder Lou Brock, whom they had tried to acquire the previous winter. Brock was an odd player—small and extremely fast with occasional power. He was not a good defensive player and was particularly miscast in Wrigley Field's sunny and challenging right field. The Cubs were a team bloated with power, and they wanted Brock to get on base, bunt whenever possible, and limit his base running. In two and a half seasons with Chicago he had hit .257 with 20 home runs.

Devine and Keane had come to believe that the one asset the club most needed was speed—the game was getting faster, and many of the most successful National League teams of the era employed fast base running in their arsenal. Brock, Keane felt, might be the fastest man in the league, despite his pedestrian stolen-base totals. The continuing struggles of the team's outfielders made the team's interest even stronger. The Cardinals were in Los Angeles on June 14 when Devine again contacted Cubs general manager John Holland. With Brock hitting his usual .251, and the Cubs short of pitching, this time the teams were able to make a six-player deal: Broglio, Clemens, and Shantz for Brock and pitchers Jack Spring and Paul Toth. The key players were Broglio, who won 18 games the previous year and was pitching well in 1964, and Brock.

"None of us liked the deal," admitted Bill White years later. "We lie and say we did, but we didn't like that deal. In my opinion, Lou had a lot of talent, but he didn't know anything about baseball. . . . But somehow, when he came to us, he turned everything around."[36] Keane told Brock that he would play left field every day, that he would not be asked to bunt, and that he should steal bases anytime he thought he could make it. In Gibson's words, "Presto, we were transformed." Batting second behind Flood, Brock hit .348 with 42 extra-base hits in 103 games to finish out the season.

The Cardinals still had seven teams to catch, but they slowly inched toward the fringes of the pennant race. They were in seventh place at the end of June and sixth at the end of July though just 7 games behind the first-place Phillies. Devine and Keane finally settled on a right fielder by recalling Mike Shannon from Jacksonville and handing him the job for the duration. Shannon was a local kid who was signed by the Cardinals in 1958 and had brief trials in 1962 and 1963.

Meanwhile, Gussie Busch was becoming more and more restless. The Cardinals seemed to have regressed from their strong 1963 season and looked no closer to winning than they were when Busch took over a decade earlier. By midsummer Busch was talking about replacing both Devine and Keane. According to Harry Caray, the club's radio voice and Busch's frequent drinking companion, Busch asked him if he wanted to be the team's general manager. When Caray turned him down, Busch apparently asked both Bill Veeck and Branch Rickey if they wanted the job. On August 18 Busch finally fired Devine and hired Bob Howsam, a longtime Minor League operator in Denver, at Rickey's suggestion.[37]

An incident involving Keane and Groat in July might have helped trigger the dismissal. Keane had given Groat the freedom to call a hit-and-run play when he was batting, but after it failed a few times early in the season, Keane revoked the privilege. According to Gibson, Groat stopped talking to Keane for a while, and their feud divided the team. Devine asked Keane to hold a team meeting where Keane confronted Groat directly, and Groat apologized to the team and everyone moved on. Weeks later Busch heard about the meeting and concluded that Devine was keeping problems from him.[38]

Devine, for one, believed that he was dismissed mainly because of Busch's frustration over the performance of the team.[39] Devine had been running the ball club for nearly seven years, and only once, the previous season, had it won more than eighty-six games. With 1963's fine second-place finish appearing more like a fluke than a real step forward, Busch made the move. In retrospect, it might be considered surprising that Devine held onto his job as long as he did given all the different opinions that Busch listened to and the lack of concrete successes on the playing field.

On the other hand, Devine was the reigning Executive of the Year and just two months earlier had made what would become the signature trade of his career. Devine was very popular with the players and also enjoyed a close relationship with Keane and Meyer. He soon took a job with the Mets, and by the end of September Eddie Stanky, director of player personnel, and several of the Cardinal scouts had followed Devine to New York.

At the time the press blamed Rickey for the shakeup. Bob Broeg, the dean of St. Louis sportswriters, referred to Rickey as "Branch Richelieu" (a reference to the seventeenth-century French cardinal who acted with the king's authority). Rickey denied any involvement in the firing and claimed that he tried to talk Busch into at least waiting until after the season. But if Rickey did not force the change, he was guilty at the very least of "poisoning the well." In the twenty-two months since he had been hired, he had continually disagreed with Devine's player moves and was advising Busch accordingly.

As for Howsam, with just six weeks left in the season there was very little work for a general manager to do. The Cardinals, it was assumed, were playing for 1965.

Less than two weeks after Devine's dismissal the Los Angeles Dodgers were playing a series in St. Louis. On his pregame show Caray interviewed Dodger coach Leo Durocher, who had managed the Dodgers and Giants to three pennants and the 1954 championship, and asked him whether he wanted to manage again. Durocher replied frankly that he was not getting many offers. Busch heard the show and asked Caray to bring Durocher out to Busch's estate the next morning. Busch offered Durocher the manager's job for the following season. Despite the cloak-and-dagger treatment, the story was widely reported, and Keane himself was well aware of it.[40] As Keane and Devine were good friends, most assumed Keane's days were numbered.

In the midst of all this scheming, something extraordinary began happening on the field. When Durocher and the Dodgers left St. Louis at the end of August, the Cardinals were still seven and a half games behind the Phillies. Their record was a fine 43-28 (.606) since the Brock trade, but they appeared to have dug themselves too deep a hole. Twenty days later the Cardinals were 83-66, still six and a half back with thirteen to go, tied with the Reds and a half game ahead of the Giants. Then the Phillies had their historic collapse, losing ten consecutive games and throwing the race into total chaos heading into the final few days. The Cardinals took over first place with three games to go and then survived losing two of three to the lowly Mets to pull out a miraculous pennant on the last day of the season.

The Cardinals' final record, 93-69, was unchanged from 1963. The Cardinals were loaded with fine players, many acquired by Devine in trades. Ken Boyer (24 home runs, 119 RBI) had a typical year and won the league MVP award. Bill White drove in 102. Brock hit .348, Flood .311, Groat .292. McCarver hit .288 and was a rock at catcher. Sadecki finished 20-11, Gibson 19-12, and Simmons 18-9. Devine's trades had brought Flood, White, Javier, Groat, and, finally, Brock to the offense, plus Simmons and an effective and flexible bullpen. When the season finished, Devine's role in creating the club began to take over the narrative.

In the World Series the Cardinals faced off against the Yankees, who had also held off three teams to capture the pennant by a single game. In a tight but not especially memorable World Series, the Cardinals defeated New York in seven games. In the finale a clearly struggling Bob Gibson withstood two solo ninth-inning home runs to hold off the Yankees, 7–5. After the game, when asked whether he had considered removing Gibson, Keane replied, "I made a commitment to his heart."[41] For Gibson, who had endured what he believed to be degrading treatment at the hands of Solly Hemus, it was "the nicest thing that can be said about an athlete."[42] Keane's statement, coupled with other heroic World Series efforts in the years ahead, is a central part of Bob Gibson's legend.

Bob Howsam was unequivocal in placing credit for the 1964 Cardinals. "Of course, it was Bing Devine's team," he wrote. "He built it. I was just the caretaker for the last third of the 1964 season."[43]

Busch, Devine, and Keane had created something truly remarkable in a city that until recently had been Major League Baseball's southernmost location. At the height of the nation's civil rights struggles, the Cardinals had not only been integrated, but fashioned an enlightened, harmonious team. "Our triumph was not a product of hitting and fielding and pitching skills alone," Gibson recalled, "but, in an almost tangible sense, of the mental, social, and spiritual qualities that made the Cardinals unique—of intelligence, courage, brotherhood, and faith."[44] Though the lion's share of the credit must go to the players themselves, Busch had demanded the integration, and Devine and Keane had created the atmosphere.

For Gussie Busch, the Series victory was the culmination of a dream and one of the happiest days of his life. Things would soon unravel. After the remarkable comeback and Series win, he realized that the club had better re-sign Johnny Keane. He called a press conference on October 16, the day after the Series ended, to announce Keane's return. Fifteen minutes before the conference was to begin, Keane walked into Busch's office and handed him a resignation letter. The letter was dated September 28, six days before the end of the season when the Cardinals were one game behind the Reds. Keane later said he and his wife began discussing it about ten days before that. A much different press conference went forward as scheduled. "This has really shocked me," allowed a visibly flustered Busch.[45] Keane said he never wavered after writing the letter, that his decision was based on a lot of things, including the firing of Devine. He told the press that he had no plans, other than to go fishing.

Three days later Keane dropped the other shoe, signing a contract to manage the Yankees, who had just dismissed Yogi Berra. Keane had apparently talked with the Yankees about the job before the Series, when both teams were thick in pennant races. This sequence of news events, spread over just a few days, shocked the baseball world and pushed the Cardinals' great victory off the nation's sports pages. Busch had his World Series, but now people were laughing at him. And there was more to come. Branch Rickey "resigned," although it was later revealed that Busch had ordered Howsam to fire him. The *Sporting News* named Devine the Major League Executive of the Year, as they had in 1963. United Press International (UPI) named Johnny Keane the NL Manager of the Year.

After leaving the Cardinals Bing Devine spent three years with the Mets, two as George Weiss's assistant before succeeding Weiss as team president in 1967. Devine played a key role in helping assemble the team that would win the World Series in 1969. In early 1966 William Eckert, baseball's commissioner, ruled that the Atlanta Braves had improperly signed USC pitcher Tom Seaver to a contract after his college season had begun. Eckert announced that any team who wished to assume the terms of the contract, which included a bonus of fifty thousand dollars, could enter into a drawing. Devine successfully lobbied Weiss to enter, and the Mets were selected from the three interested teams. Devine made several key trades and kept the organization focused on the development of its young players. He also lured Gil Hodges from the Senators to manage the Mets. Although the team was not yet winning, the pieces were coming into place.

In St. Louis Bob Howsam ran the Cardinals for the next two seasons. After a disappointing 1965 Howsam made the unpopular decisions to trade mainstays Groat, White, and Boyer, players in their thirties whom Howsam deemed—correctly—to be nearing the end of the road. His acquisitions of Orlando Cepeda and Roger Maris restocked a team that would win two consecutive pennants and the 1967 World Series. Before that happened, however, Howsam resigned his post to take a similar position, with far more autonomy, with the Cincinnati Reds. Howsam was replaced by Musial, who won the championship in his one and only year in charge.

After Musial resigned Meyer suggested to Busch that he rehire Devine, and the owner, who had long regretted his decision to fire Devine, quickly agreed. Convincing Devine was not difficult—he had been born and raised in St. Louis, and his family had remained there while Devine commuted to New York for three years.

Many of the ballplayers Devine had assembled were still Cardinals when he returned. He, and then Howsam, had built a celebrated team, not just of ballplayers but of men, and Devine was reluctant to make significant adjustments, even as some of his star players were fading. While he remained at the helm for another ten years, the club gradually faded from contention. The unique changing circumstances that Devine had mastered more than a decade earlier—recognizing the influx of black talent and building an organization in which they were respected—offered a onetime opportunity. In the decade after his last championship, Devine could neither take advantage of the contemporary changes taking place in talent procurement, such as the amateur draft, nor create another enduring advantage for the ball club.

11 Excellence Rewarded

When the New York Yankees were winning pennant after pennant (fourteen of sixteen from 1949 to 1964), they had the good fortune of playing in a league filled with dysfunctional franchises—teams that were undercapitalized or beset with front-office incompetence or turmoil. As well managed as the Yankees were, they needed considerable help from their fellow franchises to stay on top every year. When the Yankee dynasty came to a sudden end in 1965, several league franchises had revived and put themselves in a position to take advantage of a suddenly wide-open league.

In this chapter we take a closer look at three of these teams and how they had righted their ships by the mid-1960s. The Boston Red Sox, the Yankees' chief rival after the war, were beset with organizational incompetence and slowly fell to the bottom of the league. The Detroit Tigers hit bottom in the 1950s in the midst of extensive ownership and management turmoil. The St. Louis Browns, the epitome of a downtrodden club, moved to Baltimore in 1954, becoming the Orioles, and then spent several years building an organization while dealing with squabbling between two brilliant executives.

During their respective years in the wilderness, the clubs each employed a talented but relatively anonymous functionary who was slowly given more and more responsibility. Eventually, having tried everything else, the club owners rewarded their loyal charge with control of baseball operations. In a way their paths followed the model of George Weiss—a longtime team employee who had been comfortable working in the background until given control of the team. For all three men, their days of anonymity would be over.

Prior to their long-overdue 2004 World Series victory, the Boston Red Sox had played eighty-five seasons without winning a world championship, and many lifelong fans had never witnessed their team capture the ultimate prize. The club did, however, experience a legion of near misses, creating stories that have filled several books: four World Series losses in the seventh game, two lost playoff games for the pennant or division, and several other seasons in which they fell short on the final weekend. Recollections of these seasons are almost universally negative, focusing not on all of the victories that brought the Red Sox to the final day, but on why the team again fell short. What did they do wrong? Who screwed up?

In this long story arc there is one oasis, one season that has been immune from criticism. The 1967 Red Sox, who lost the seventh game of the World Series to the St. Louis Cardinals, carry no such "what-might-have-been" burden—they remain, even after the recent championships, the most beloved team in club history. The 1967 team has been honored many times on the field before games, and people of a certain age can recite details from dozens of games throughout the season. Before the pennant had been won, people were already calling it "the Impossible Dream," after a song from the hit Broadway musical *Man of La Mancha*, and the name has been associated with the team ever since. This label carries an implication that the season was miraculous, that credit was due to a higher power. Ken Coleman and Dan Valenti, in their 1987 book, *The Impossible Dream Remembered*, wrote: "The real miracle of 1967 is that it happened, not as the conscious effort applied to a preconceived plan, but in spite of just about everything."[1]

On the contrary, much conscious effort was applied. In fact, Dick O'Connell, the team's principal architect, was honored with the *Sporting News* Executive of the Year award that season. The team's performance was no fluke. In a powerful indication that the club was well constructed, the previously downtrodden Red Sox ran off sixteen consecutive winning seasons, still one of the longest such stretches in baseball history. The season is considered miraculous because no one, outside of perhaps the Red Sox themselves, saw it coming. *Sports Illustrated* came the closest to expressing optimism that spring: "If [manager Dick Williams] can find some pitching, the 1967 Sox may revive baseball in Boston."[2] But there were other signs, if one had known where to look, that the team was on the rise.

The roots of the Red Sox' problems extended back more than a decade. The team had a nice five-year run in the late 1940s (featuring a pennant and three near misses), fueled by players signed and nurtured by the organization. But the club subsequently frittered away the 1950s, the last decade of Ted Williams's great career, because they could not develop or acquire enough good players. Under Joe Cronin, the club's genial general manager from 1948 through 1958, the talent in the organization deteriorated considerably, despite millionaire owner Tom Yawkey's willingness to spend money. During this decade the Red Sox more or less treaded water, usually finishing third or fourth in a league filled with struggling franchises, but never sniffing a pennant race.

As discussed in previous chapters, two historic team-building opportunities presented themselves in the late 1940s, and the Red Sox' response to each led to their decline. The first was the signing of highly touted high school and college players to ever-larger signing bonuses. The second, more historic, was the integration of the Major Leagues, which opened (as a practical matter) the largest and most talented pool of freely available talent in the game's history. The Red Sox chose to be big players in the first market (bearing little fruit) and small players in the second—twin decisions that, whether due to a moral failing or mismanagement, eventually dragged the club to the bottom of the league.

The Red Sox finally cratered in 1960, Williams's final season, finishing seventh of eight teams at 65-89, their worst record in twenty-seven years. The next six seasons were similarly dreary, with placements between sixth and ninth in the new ten-team American League. The club was also unpopular, playing before crowds of eight or ten thousand people (although many other teams were not drawing much better; only four AL clubs reached one million in attendance in 1965). The Red Sox were playing in what was seen to be an old, decaying ballpark, and their owner, Tom Yawkey, was trying desperately to hitch a ride on the new stadium bandwagon sweeping the game.

Not only did the team play poorly, but it was also filled with "colorful" mediocrities. When Dick Williams finished his playing career with the Red Sox in 1963 and 1964, he complained about the lazy, careless attitudes of the veterans, which he believed were rubbing off on the young players. They were a lousy team loaded with funny stories—

Dick Stuart butchering ground balls or pestering manager Johnny Pesky; pitcher Gene Conley getting drunk, walking off a team bus in New York, and trying to book a flight to Jerusalem; among others. The team's general manager, Mike Higgins, was an old drinking buddy of Yawkey, having been a player (twice) and manager (twice) for the team before taking formal control of the organization in 1962.

A turning point took place on September 16, 1965, on a day that Dave Morehead no-hit the Indians at Fenway Park. Morehead did not live up to the promise he showed that day, and he was upstaged after the biggest game of his life when it was announced that Higgins had been cashiered and that Dick O'Connell, a little-known business executive in the front office, would assume control of the team.

As in most organizations, Boston's general manager had tended to be a well-known baseball man. The club's four previous occupants of the role—Eddie Collins, Cronin, Bucky Harris, and Higgins—had been well-known players and managers before getting the top post. By turning to O'Connell, Yawkey seemed to recognize that the job now required skills beyond being able to play the game well. Or else he had run out of ideas.

Richard Henry O'Connell grew up in Winthrop, Massachusetts, just north of Boston, and played football and baseball at Boston College in the 1930s. After earning two degrees at BC, he spent a few years as a high school athletic director before joining the navy at the onset of World War II. An intelligence officer for three years, he earned the Bronze Star for his efforts in helping plan invasions in the Pacific. He met a few employees of the Red Sox during his years in Hawaii and was urged to come see them after the war for a possible job. After his discharge O'Connell followed up, and the Red Sox made him business manager of their new farm club in Lynn, not far from where he had grown up. He held this job for three years, until the New England League collapsed. But O'Connell had impressed the Red Sox' front office, and the club kept him on in a variety of positions over the next decade.[3]

In 1960 O'Connell became an executive vice president, running the day-to-day operations of the team and ballpark, though he had little say in player-personnel matters. The team had no official general manager, leaving manager Higgins in charge of trades and the team's roster. After the 1962 season Johnny Pesky replaced Higgins in the dugout, while the latter was promoted to "executive vice-president in charge of baseball." Higgins was considered little more than a drinking crony of Yawkey, and his promotion further solidified Boston's reputation as a risible organization. The team had done nothing but lose ball games for the past three years, and here was Yawkey giving Higgins even more power.

After the 1964 season Higgins replaced Pesky with Billy Herman (not surprisingly, a close friend of Higgins), and the team sank even further. In 1965 the team had its first one-hundred-loss season since 1932 and recorded its lowest peacetime attendance (652,000) since 1933. This dismal performance finally convinced Yawkey that he needed to fire Higgins. Somewhat surprisingly, Yawkey turned the entire club over to O'Connell, largely unknown to the fans of the region despite his long association with the club. Outside of the limelight the fifty-one-year-old O'Connell had spent the previous several years working with farm director Neil Mahoney in strengthening the long-neglected Minor League system.

The Red Sox' improved farm system was little remarked upon at the time, as the Major League Red Sox were going through one dreadful season after another, and the fans and press had endured too many failed phenoms in the 1950s to get too excited about the latest rookies. Nonetheless, the club had begun to produce talent. Signed in late 1958, Carl Yastrzemski tore up two Minor Leagues and took over left field in 1961. He was seen as a disappointment by many who had wanted him to be the next Ted Williams, but he won the 1963 batting title, led the league in on-base and slugging percentage in 1965, and had won two Gold Gloves. Fellow outfielder Tony Conigliaro, an immensely popular swinger from nearby Revere, burst on the scene with twenty-four homers in 111 games as a nineteen-year-old in 1964 and followed up with a home run title in 1965. Shortstop Rico Petrocelli was a 1965 rookie who showed promise on both offense and defense. For O'Connell, these three players represented the core around which he needed to build a team. The other five position players were mediocre or on the downside of their careers.

The pitching staff was in rougher shape. The team's best pitchers for the past few years had been Earl Wilson and Bill Monbouquette, two workhorses good for 200 or more innings but without the impressive won-loss records they might have had elsewhere. Wilson had finished 13-14 in 1965 with a 3.98 ERA in 230 innings, valuable production in Fenway Park, while Monbouquette was 10-18, 3.70. The rest of the starters, Jim Lonborg, Dave Morehead, and Dennis Bennett, were young and not yet particularly good.

Although he never articulated it as such, O'Connell's strategy might as well have been: discard all players older than twenty-six. The Red Sox had repeatedly failed by bringing in veterans, even productive veterans, who groused about playing time while the team finished near the bottom of the league every year. O'Connell cleaned house of all but the promising young players, opening roster spots for the Minor League prospects in whose ability he believed.

O'Connell began revamping his team immediately; in October 1965 the Red Sox traded Monbouquette to the Tigers for two utility players, George Smith and George Thomas. Frank Malzone, who had had a fine eleven-year career with the club, was released in November (he caught on with the Angels, but hit just .206 as a backup and retired). O'Connell traded Lee Thomas and pitcher Arnold Early for two pitchers, one of whom, Dan Osinski, would be one of their better relievers the next two seasons. Just before the start of the 1966 season, O'Connell dealt Felix Mantilla, who had hit forty-eight home runs over the previous two years, to the Astros for veteran utility infielder Eddie Kasko.[4] The crop of players O'Connell got in return was not particularly impressive—he was mainly collecting role players or young pitchers. The primary purpose of many of the deals was to open positions for their Minor Leaguers. Manager Herman had no choice but to play the youngsters, because now that was all he had.

For 1966 the Red Sox' most interesting ready prospects played the infield corners. Tony Horton, just twenty-one, was a big (six-foot-three, 210-pound) power-hitting first baseman from Santa Monica, California, who had been called up in 1965 and hit .294 with seven homers in sixty games. With Lee Thomas gone, manager Herman announced that Horton would take over at first base. Joe Foy, a twenty-three-year-old third baseman from the Bronx, had hit .302 with fourteen home runs in Toronto, winning the International League batting title and MVP award, and was named the Minor League Player of the Year by the *Sporting News*. With Malzone out of the picture, Foy seemed to have third base locked down. Complicating matters, however, was twenty-two-year-old George Scott, another third baseman, one level down from Foy at Pittsfield in the Eastern League, who had won his league's Triple Crown.

All three players had fine springs, and Herman kept all of them on the Major League roster. After Horton started poorly (three for twenty-two in just six games), he was demoted to Toronto, Scott moved to first base, and Foy claimed third. Scott began the season on a tear, and actually started the All-Star Game, before cooling off to hit .245 with twenty-seven home runs. Foy was even better. He hit .262 in a league that hit .240, and his ninety-one walks were second in the AL, giving him the league's eighth-best on-base percentage at .364. Foy improved substantially during the year; he hit only .213 with four home runs over the first half, .303 with eleven home runs thereafter. It was a great rookie year, and Foy looked to be a rising star.

Catcher Mike Ryan was a third newcomer to the starting lineup. Unlike Scott and Foy, Ryan did not come with impressive press clippings. He had hit just .236 for Toronto in 1965 and .159 in 107 at bats in Boston, although he had a fine defensive reputation. Manager Herman compared his defense favorably to that of Yankee catcher Elston Howard.[5] Ryan's promotion was consistent with O'Connell's strategy: nothing could be gained by continuing to start undistinguished veteran Bob Tillman.

With the three youngsters added to Yastrzemski, Petrocelli, and Conigliaro, only second base and center field remained unclaimed by young players. Veteran George Smith received most of the playing time at second base but hit just .213. Five players started between eighteen and fifty-one games in center field, none of whom appeared to be more than a stopgap solution. In mid-June O'Connell dealt Earl Wilson to the Tigers for veteran center fielder Don Demeter, who hit .292 while getting the bulk of the playing time in the second half.

The Wilson-Demeter deal later became one of the more controversial of O'Connell's tenure. Wilson, the club's second black player back in 1959, had been one of the better players on several bad Red Sox teams. Because of other Red Sox problems dealing with black players over the years, the trade has often been lumped in as an indication of the club's racism. O'Connell does not deserve this smear, and the Wilson-Demeter trade, on its face, seems pretty even. Wilson was a thirty-one-year-old pitcher who had proven capable of throwing two hundred league-average innings—a valuable commodity. Demeter was also thirty-one but represented a team need: a center fielder capable of hitting. In any event, Wilson had a great second half for Detroit (13-6, 2.59) and then won twenty-two games in 1967. Demeter played well for the Red Sox in 1966, but Wilson would have been more help for the next couple of seasons.

Two other June 1966 trades by O'Connell paid dividends the following season. On June 2 he traded Dick Radatz, their former star workhorse reliever, to the Indians for pitchers Lee Stange and Don McMahon, both of whom became important contributors. O'Connell then dealt three unneeded players for John Wyatt, the team's best relief pitcher over the next two years, and Jose Tartabull, a valuable reserve outfielder and pinch runner.

While the team now had promising youngsters at most positions, the outlook for the pitching staff appeared less rosy. The two 1965 starters O'Connell kept were Morehead, who never put it together, and Jim Lonborg, a promising but erratic hard-throwing right-hander. By midseason Herman was using Jose Santiago (twenty-five), Stange (twenty-nine), Dennis Bennett (twenty-six), Darrell Brandon (twenty-five), and Lonborg (twenty-four), without ever establishing a set rotation. While not a great group, the youngsters looked much improved over their recent predecessors.

The 1966 Red Sox improved by ten wins, but still finished ninth at 72-90, a half game better than the last-place Yankees. In late September O'Connell fired Herman as manager and replaced him after the season with Dick Williams, who had piloted their Triple-A Toronto farm club the past two seasons. O'Connell had inherited Herman but wanted his own man, someone as committed to the young players and to the system as he was.

Williams was an inspired choice who became a crucial cog in the Red Sox' rebuilding plan—like O'Connell, he wanted to rid the organization of veteran troublemakers and believed in the farm system. Williams had grown up in the instruction-rich Brooklyn Dodgers organization and put together a thirteen-year big-league career mainly as a fourth outfielder. He spent the 1963 and 1964 seasons with the Red Sox and was appalled at what he saw. "Players showed up when they felt like it," recalled Williams, "and took extra hitting when it didn't interfere with a card game."[6] Williams did not hide his frustrations, which found sympathetic ears in O'Connell and Mahoney. After the 1964 season Williams was released as a player but offered the job as manager of their Triple-A farm team in Toronto.

Williams wanted his ballplayers to be young, hungry, and as angry after a loss as he was. His 1965 squad, led by Foy and shortstop Mike Andrews, won the International League championship. Horton and Reggie Smith joined the club in 1966, and they and Andrews led Toronto to its second consecutive league title. Williams also managed a number of promising young pitchers, notably twenty-four-year-old right-hander Gary Waslewski (18-11, 2.52) and twenty-year-old lefty Billy Rohr (14-10, 3.55).

The handling of Smith and Andrews in 1966 further illustrates O'Connell's deliberate thinking. Smith had been taken from the Twins in the first-year player draft after the 1963 season and sped through three levels of the Red Sox system before reaching Toronto, just twenty-one years old, in 1966. As he climbed through the Minors, Smith played three infield positions and all over the outfield without ever settling at one spot. Williams and O'Connell, looking ahead to the needs of the Major League team, made him Toronto's full-time center fielder in 1966. Smith responded by winning the league's batting title and hitting eighteen home runs. Andrews, just twenty-two, was a fine shortstop but blocked in Boston by Rico Petrocelli. The organization shifted Andrews to second base, and he responded with an excellent season, hitting .267 with eighty-nine walks, fourteen home runs, and a league-leading ninety-seven runs scored. Both Smith and Andrews also played excellent defense at their new positions. The Major League team's biggest positional needs were second base and center field, and, thanks to the two position switches, the organization now had quality solutions ready to go.

Now that Williams was the big-league manager, he made it known in the spring of 1967 that he had no loyalty to any of the incumbent players—all had to earn their jobs. Tony Horton, demoted in 1966 only because of the logjam of corner-infield prospects, had hit twenty-six home runs and batted .297 for Williams in Toronto. Williams had not managed Scott in the Minors and declared the first base job wide open, despite Scott's All-Star season. Williams even used Scott in the outfield in the spring. As it turned out Scott outhit Horton and kept his job. In other camp news Andrews hurt his back and missed the final week of the exhibition season. In response Williams shifted Reggie Smith to second base for the first week of the regular season. When Andrews returned he reclaimed second, and Smith moved to center. As with Foy and Scott in 1966, Smith and Andrews did not have mediocre veteran players to displace—they filled gaping holes on the team.

To summarize, entering the 1967 season the Red Sox had good or promising young players at seven of the eight positions. Outfielders Yastrzemski (twenty-seven) and Conigliaro (twenty-two) were established stars. Infielders Scott (twenty-three) and Foy (twenty-four) were two of the better young players in the league. Petrocelli (twenty-four) was making progress, and Smith (twenty-two) and Andrews (twenty-three) were prized rookies. Only at catcher, where Ryan (twenty-five) and Russ Gibson (twenty-eight) shared the load, was the solution less encouraging. Remarkably, all nine of the aforementioned players came out of Neil Mahoney's farm system, all but Yastrzemski in just the last three years. The pitching staff began the season with the same young arms as had ended the previous year—Jim Lonborg (twenty-five), Dave Morehead (twenty-four), Darrell Brandon (twenty-six)—plus Billy Rohr (twenty-one), another rookie from Toronto. It was a tremendously young team.

Though most observers conceded the 1967 pennant to the powerful Baltimore Orioles, the defending champs, they suffered a slew of injuries and finished tied for sixth. With a surprising vacancy at the top, four teams spent much of the summer locked in a legendary pennant race, won by the Red Sox on the final day of the season.

Only one of the team's young hurlers took a step forward, but that pitcher, Lonborg, won twenty-two games and led the league with 246 strikeouts. Brandon, who had pitched well in 1966, regressed, and Rohr lasted only a few starts (the first of which was a memorable near-no-hitter in Yankee Stadium). Williams had no regular starting rotation, using a revolving cast to surround Lonborg. In early June O'Connell dealt his two best bench bats, Horton and Demeter, to the Indians for Gary Bell, who became the team's second-best pitcher. This trade further testified to the depth of the team's system—Horton was a good player who had no job in Boston but became one of the Indians' best hitters over the next few seasons. Without Horton, a fine prospect who had not been able to beat out other fine prospects, the Red Sox would not have landed Gary Bell and likely would not have won the pennant.

O'Connell also picked up some very important position players during the season. On June 2 he dealt McMahon to the White Sox for veteran infielder Jerry Adair, who played semiregularly the rest of the season at second, short, and third, hitting .291 while providing experienced leadership without the baggage of some of the previous Boston veterans. In early August the club acquired veteran catcher Elston Howard from the Yankees; Howard could no longer hit, batting only .196, but was considered an excellent defensive catcher and handler of pitchers. Substituting for the overmatched Ryan, Howard started throughout the pennant race and World Series.

In late August O'Connell found himself in need of another outfielder when Conigliaro was hit in the left eye by a pitch, costing him the remainder of the season and all of 1968. Coincidently, Kansas City outfielder Ken Harrelson had just been released by owner Charlie Finley in a fit of pique and was now a free agent. O'Connell outbid and outhustled several other suitors to sign Harrelson. Taking over right field, Harrelson played a key role for the Red Sox over the final month of the season and the World Series.

O'Connell deserves credit for a very bold and productive roster turnover in the eighteen months leading up the 1967 season. If one had just looked at the standings, 1966 felt much like the other recent Red

Sox seasons. Their ninth-place finish matched their 1965 result, which had followed finishes of eighth, seventh, and eighth. On closer inspection, though, the 1966 club was far ahead of where it had been a year earlier, even more than their ten-game improvement suggested. The average age of their hitters, only 24.9, was the youngest in the league. And these players were not just young; they were also excellent ballplayers. In Scott and Foy the 1966 club had two of the finest rookies in the American League, and the rest of their core was equally talented.

Another factor largely overlooked from the Red Sox' escape from the cellar in September 1966 was their remarkable turnaround during the second half of the season. The team stood at 29-51 on July 4 but finished 43-39, only one half game worse than the champion Orioles over the same period. While it should not be ignored that this club was hopelessly out of the pennant race in the second half, an eighty-two-game sample size can be evidence of genuine improvement. The 1967 team's promising start was really just a carryover from the previous year.

The pitching staff fueled much of their mid-1966 improvement, as the team's ERA improved from 4.41 in the first half (easily the worst in the league) to 3.40 in the second half (basically the league average), while playing in the worst pitcher's park in the AL. Lonborg (6-3, 2.91), Lee Stange (6-5, 2.53), and Darrell Brandon (7-6, 3.31) were collectively much better in the second half of 1966.

As further evidence of the team's quality, the improvement occurred despite the fact that the Red Sox suffered several setbacks in 1967. Joe Foy, one of the best young players in baseball in 1966, regressed, and Williams benched him much of the second half in deference to Dalton Jones and Jerry Adair. Foy had on-base skills that were unappreciated in his time, and his career petered out while he was still a productive hitter. Conigliaro, a twenty-two-year-old star, was in the midst of perhaps his finest season when it was brutally terminated. Brandon had finished 1966 with a flourish and broke camp as the team's number-two starter but finished 5-11, 4.17. Rohr, the rookie who began the season as the number-three starter, was back in the Minor Leagues by June.

Of course, Petrocelli, Scott, Lonborg, and especially Yastrzemski did break out with big years. Yaz's Triple Crown season (.326, 44 home runs,

121 RBI, and many dramatic late-season heroics) might have been the best by any player in the 1960s and was likely responsible for a good chunk of the twenty-game improvement. But the team had so many young players who had either shown ability in the Major Leagues or in the high Minors that it did not need every player to break out.

Finally, the best evidence that the season was not a miracle may simply be what happened next. Conigliaro missed the entire 1968 season due to his eye injury. Lonborg broke his leg in December, stalling his career for several years. Scott suffered through a ghastly season (.171 with 3 home runs). Despite getting virtually no contribution from three of its best players, in 1968 the team finished 86-76, a drop of just six games, an accomplishment every bit as impressive as their "Impossible Dream."

Reporter Clark Booth said years later:

> The guy who finally made sense of it all was Dick O'Connell. He was a drinker too. But he had a business mind. He took the race issue head on, signed Reggie Smith, Joe Foy, George Scott, Elston Howard. It was as easy as that. No more race issue. He had a saying . . . some young reporter like Peter Gammons [who became the dean of baseball reporters over the next several decades] would be asking him a lot of questions and leave and O'Connell would turn to you and say, "He thinks this fucking shit is real." He said that all the time: "He thinks this fucking shit is real." But he's the one who turned it around.[7]

What Mahoney and O'Connell had done was establish a new baseline for the organization. By bringing professionalism to the front office, valuing talent over experience, and putting his faith in a young manager and even younger players, O'Connell turned the franchise around. After 1967 the fans of New England would no longer deplore their incompetent ball club but instead lament that they were not winning the World Series. This was progress.

As moribund as the Red Sox franchise had been in the 1950s, the Detroit Tigers had been even worse. After contending in 1950, the Tigers finished no closer than fifteen games back for the next decade and finished as low as 50-104 in 1954. The organization produced a number of excellent players, including Hall of Famers Al Kaline and Jim Bunning and stars Harvey Kuenn and Frank Lary, but was never able to fill out a roster that could compete with the Yankees.

Like the Red Sox and most of their American League counterparts, the Tigers initially shunned the largest source of newly available talent in baseball history—the black players made eligible with the ending of the unwritten color barrier in 1947. The Tigers were the fifteenth team (of sixteen) to integrate, when Ozzie Virgil played forty-nine games at third base in 1958. By the late 1950s no team other than the Yankees flourished on the field without actively pursuing black players. The Tigers eventually seemed to recognize this, and by 1961 the team had three black starting position players (Chico Fernandez, Jake Wood, and Bill Bruton) and turned in their best season in many years.

In contrast with well-managed and successful organizations like the Yankees and Dodgers, ownership and executive-level turnover also combined to impede the development of any sort of long-term strategy. In January 1952 longtime owner Walter Briggs died, leaving the Tigers to a trusteeship, with his son Spike as team president. In 1956 the trustees put the team up for sale and orchestrated a spirited bidding contest, won by a complicated group led by radio-station operator Fred Knorr. He was helped in his offer by Spike Briggs, an investor in one of Knorr's companies, who was ineligible to bid for the team himself. The new eleven-person syndicate named Knorr president and Briggs general manager.

Over the next few years the personnel of the team was overseen by a succession of general managers, including Briggs, John McHale (1957), Rick Ferrell (1959), Bill DeWitt (1960), and Ferrell again (1961). Complicating the front office, a number of the syndicate's members held executive positions in the Detroit organization. In 1960 John Fetzer, part of the original syndicate and a Kalamazoo, Michigan, radio and television operator, acquired a controlling interest in the franchise and by the end of 1961 had the entire team. Fetzer owned the Tigers for the next twenty years, and his most important decision was naming Jim Campbell to run the organization.

"I set up a chain of command and found the most talented person I could to run each section or department," Fetzer explained. "I allowed each department head a great deal of autonomy and allowed each the leeway to think through a problem. I didn't allow any department head to come to me and say here's a problem. He came to me with a recommendation. I might not agree with that recommendation, but then we worked out some sort of solution. . . . I put a baseball man [Campbell] in charge and he ran the ship. I guess you could call that designed anonymity."[8]

After three years in the navy, Campbell had starred for the Ohio State baseball team in the late 1940s. A friend landed him an interview with the Tigers, and in December 1949 he was named business manager of their club in Thomasville, Georgia. As with George Weiss and Buzzie Bavasi before him, and Dick O'Connell at roughly the same time, the Minor Leagues proved a fertile training ground.

After the first home game of his first season, his ballpark burned to the ground. "I thought that was it for me," he later related.[9] Instead, Campbell got the park rebuilt, borrowed uniforms, and carried on. He held similar posts for Toledo and Buffalo the next two seasons, and in 1952 he became business manager of the Tiger system at age twenty-eight. Over the next several years, while the team was floundering amid front-office turnover, Campbell rose through the organization. He was named the club's farm director in 1956, and by 1961 he was vice president in charge of Minor League operations and scouting.

When Fetzer took control in 1961 he began a search for the long-term general manager he felt the club needed. Baseball GMs in those days often had tremendous power, presiding over the entire organization—the stadium ushers, ticket sellers, the public relations staff. Fetzer later said that he thought Campbell was "ten years away" from taking on such a job, but the more he searched, the more he was intrigued by the brilliant thirty-eight-year-old executive. Campbell, Fetzer felt, "demonstrated an ability to take charge. He knew our whole system. He knew the game. And more than anything else, Jim Campbell was probably the most honest man I had ever encountered."[10] Fetzer also discovered that Campbell's scouting and development organization had been doing its job well during the years of management turmoil.

From 1957 to 1962 the Tigers' scouts had a phenomenal period of signing amateur free agents who would become the core of their squad.

Even earlier, scouting director Ed Katalinas teamed with John McHale in 1953 to sign right-field mainstay Al Kaline. Some of the more productive scouts included Bernie DeViveiros, Lou D'Annunzio, Edwin (Cy) Williams, and Katalinas. Of the top sixteen players on the eventual 1968 world championship team (the nine position players with at least 100 games, six pitchers with at least 70 innings pitched, and pinch-hitter extraordinaire Gates Brown), eleven were signed during this six-year time frame: infielders Dick McAuliffe, Ray Oyler, and Don Wert; outfielders Jim Northrup, Gates Brown, Willie Horton, and Mickey Stanley; catcher Bill Freehan; and pitchers Mickey Lolich, Pat Dobson, and John Hiller.

Bill DeWitt helped immeasurably in April 1960 with a couple of great trades, acquiring twenty-five-year-old first baseman Norm Cash from the White Sox and twenty-six-year-old outfielder Rocky Colavito from the Indians. In 1961 the pair combined for 86 home runs and 272 RBI, and the team unexpectedly won 101 games but fell short of the Yankees. Neither had a year quite that good again, and in 1962 the team fell back to a respectable 85 victories, a level more representative of the talent on the team.

Over the next several seasons Campbell and his field managers successfully integrated their young players onto the roster of an already good team. The Tigers were consistently close enough in the pennant race that they must have been often tempted to trade prospects for veteran stopgap solutions, but Campbell kept his players. Dick McAuliffe became a regular by the end of 1961; Don Wert in 1963; Bill Freehan, Mickey Lolich, and Gates Brown in 1964; Willie Horton, Denny McLain (claimed from the White Sox two years earlier), and Joe Sparma in 1965; and Jim Northrup in 1966. The Tigers also introduced two light-hitting, good-fielding farm products into part-time roles: shortstop Ray Oyler and center fielder Mickey Stanley.

In June 1966, as the Tigers battled at the edge of the pennant race, Campbell helped unclog a crowded outfield and addressed a need by swapping Don Demeter to Boston for hurler Earl Wilson. The Tigers went on a six-game winning streak to climb within a game and a half of league-leading Baltimore, but they could inch no closer; Baltimore pulled away from the field. The 1966 season was also marred by tragedy—

manager Charlie Dressen experienced a heart attack on May 16, and his replacement, Bob Swift, was soon hospitalized with a suspected case of food poisoning and later diagnosed with cancer. By October both men were dead.

To skipper the team for 1967 Campbell hired Yankees scout Mayo Smith, who, on the surface, did not seem a particularly inspired choice. Smith had last managed in the Major Leagues in 1959 and had not distinguished himself in either Philadelphia or Cincinnati. The Tigers also hired brilliant pitching coach Johnny Sain, who had just been fired by the Twins.

The Tigers remained in the pennant race until the final day of the 1967 season, ultimately finishing a game behind the surprising Red Sox. The Tigers were a very good team, good enough to compete for a championship during a period in which the league had no dominant club. Freehan was the AL's best backstop. Cash was a very good first baseman. In his most important decision Smith shifted power-hitting McAuliffe to second base to make room for slick-fielding Oyler at short. Wert, like Oyler a fine fielder but weak hitter, continued to hold down third. In the outfield Smith rotated Kaline, Horton, Northrup, and Stanley, depth that allowed Smith to deal with injuries to Kaline and Horton that season. Smith and Sain retained the established pitching rotation of McLain, Wilson, Lolich, and Sparma. Dressen had earlier complained about the bullpen, but by 1967 Campbell had delivered his new manager a pretty good one: three of their relievers—Mike Marshall, Pat Dobson, and John Hiller—would go on to long, productive careers.

Campbell essentially stood pat over the 1967–68 off-season, believing that with a healthy Kaline and Horton the team could win. The biggest hole on his club was at shortstop: Oyler, Dick Tracewski, and Tom Matchick were woefully inadequate hitters even in a low-offense era, and the Tigers likely could have addressed this problem with its surplus in the outfield and on the mound. In 1968 the Tigers had five quality Major League outfielders (counting Brown, who hit .370 mainly pinch-hitting), while the team's shortstops combined to hit just .163, a situation for which Campbell must take some blame. Smith dealt with this problem by moving Mickey Stanley, an outstanding defensive center fielder, to shortstop with a week to go in the 1968 season, a bold and unpopular move. "Ernie Harwell, the Tigers broadcaster openly complained that it was 'a bad move,'" wrote baseball author Tim Wendel. "And [he] went so far to ask twenty-five so-called experts what they thought about Stanley at short. They all agreed it was a misuse of personnel."[11] Stanley finished out the season at short (hitting .313 in nine games), then started all seven games in the victorious World Series. That this move worked out is to Smith's credit, but one wonders whether he should have been placed in this situation in the first place.

In the Tigers' 1968 championship season the core of players signed and developed over the previous decade delivered a world championship. The team featured the best offense in the league and a solid pitching staff led by McLain's remarkable 31-6 season and seventeen wins from Lolich. After years of contention, Campbell's homegrown ball club had finally come together. Many observers felt that this would be the start of a great run, with an organization that had proven itself capable of churning out talent. The core of the 1968 team was already middle-aged, but surely the talent would keep coming.

When twenty-five-year-old Harry Dalton, just home from the Korean War in late 1953, called the Baltimore Orioles looking for a job, the club had just relocated from St. Louis. Dalton's timing proved fortuitous, and he was hired as an assistant to farm director Jim McLaughlin. The job paid so poorly that Dalton had to drive a taxi at night to pay off his debts.

The club had lost one hundred games in 1953, their last in St. Louis, and would lose a hundred more their first year in Baltimore. The new Orioles had little talent in the Majors and none in the Minors. After the 1954 season the club hired Paul Richards, the White Sox' manager, to run the organization as both field manager and general manager. Richards summoned McLaughlin, who had worked with the Browns for seventeen years, and the latter assumed he would be fired. "When I got there, he must have expected me to defend the farm system, but I told him the truth: it was horseshit. We didn't have anything, because we hadn't been able to spend enough money."[12] Surprising his new underling, Richards chose to retain McLaughlin. Their relationship defined the organization for the next several years.

"As much as anyone," Dalton later said, "[McLaughlin] helped get the Orioles off the ground. His legacy was organizing the scouting and farm department, and helping establish strong pride in the organization. The Orioles became well respected, not only because of their success on the field, but a lot of baseball people thought the organization was run very well."[13]

McLaughlin developed a pie chart that he labeled "The Whole Player." The top half of the circle had sections devoted to traditional player skills such as speed, hitting, and arm strength, while the bottom half dealt with intangibles such as intelligence, personal habits, and attitude. McLaughlin instructed his scouts to stress the bottom of the chart when finding players. He hired Federal Bureau of Investigation (FBI) agents to teach scouts how to conduct background checks and sent Minor League managers to communications seminars. "He was years ahead of his time," said famed scout Jim Russo. "A brilliant baseball guy."[14]

Over the next several years McLaughlin and Richards each worked to transform the organization but unfortunately at cross-purposes. They did not get along at all—McLaughlin had assembled a great team of scouts and thought Richards should stay out of the farm department, while Richards wanted to control everything. Even worse, Richards hired his own scouts and sent them out to see players without involving McLaughlin's organization.

When Richards took over in 1955, the prevailing "bonus rule" required any player receiving more than four thousand dollars to spend two seasons in the Major Leagues before he could begin his seasoning in the Minors. Richards (generally without the input of McLaughlin's scouts) was very active in this market, signing six bonus players in 1955 alone. One of them, pitcher Bruce Swango, was released just a few months after receiving thirty-six thousand dollars in May 1955. "To me, it was a mystery why he was ever signed," recalled coach Al Vincent. "He just did not have any grasp of what was going on."[15] Swango had not yet appeared in a game when he was let go, and though he spent a few years in the Minors with other clubs, he never played in the Majors. Of Richards's eight bonus signings during the 1955–57 period (before the rule was rescinded), only Wayne Causey, who emerged as a good player years later in Kansas City, and Jerry Walker, who had one excellent season, had any success.

In addition to all the bonus players, Richards signed several other amateurs to Major League contracts. While keeping their bonuses at four thousand dollars or below allowed these prospects to be farmed out, their contracts required that they be placed on the club's forty-man roster, where they took up valuable space. All were promoted to the Majors their first season. One of them, future Hall of Famer Brooks Robinson, played briefly with the Orioles at age eighteen but was not a useful contributor until four years later. "Paul wasn't really an organizational guy," Dalton remembered. "He was in the sense that he'd work with young players, especially pitchers. But as far as signing them and waiting five years for them to be ready to help in the big leagues, that was too far off as far he was concerned. But he had the owners bamboozled."[16]

The Orioles had established a Minor League camp at an old veterans rest home in Thomasville, Georgia. Richards brought all his Minor League managers and coaches to camp early each spring to teach them how the players should be instructed. When the players arrived, Richards would lecture hundreds of them for hours at a time, walking around the diamond to explain everything from how to walk up to the plate to how to lead off the bases and how to run from first to third. Defense and pitching, Richards's passions, took even longer.

In 1955 Richards wrote the book *Modern Baseball Strategy*, a thorough treatise on the game for the general public, a condensed version of which became the basis for the club's instruction at Thomasville. The manual continued to evolve throughout Richards's tenure with the club, and many of the Minor League managers became versed in his instructional philosophies.

By the end of the 1957 season the Orioles owners, a group led by Joe Iglehart, had tired of Richards's lavish spending on amateur ballplayers. Accordingly, they hired Lee MacPhail, the Yankees' farm director, to be the Orioles' general manager, leaving Richards as field manager only. The result was an end to the huge bonuses and a general calming of the organization. MacPhail was the son of former Reds, Dodgers, and Yankees boss Larry MacPhail, but as different from his father as one could be. "Bringing in MacPhail was the best decision the owners ever had," recalled Bob Brown, a longtime Oriole front-office man. "Lee built morale."[17]

Meanwhile, the talent in the organization grew. Infielders Brooks Robinson, Ron Hansen, and Jerry Adair, along with pitchers Milt Pappas, Jerry Walker, Jack Fisher, Chuck Estrada, and Steve Barber, all came through the farm system by 1960. The Orioles reached .500 in 1957 for the first time and in 1960 shocked everyone by finishing 89-65 and staying in contention well into September. The club was led by its young pitching, dubbed "the Kiddie Corps," a group of twenty-one- and twenty-two-year-old pitchers who started 117 of the club's games.

After the 1960 season MacPhail finally gave up thinking that his two talented subordinates could get along and fired McLaughlin. "It got to the point," MacPhail recalled, "where you were either a 'McLaughlin player' or a 'Richards player' in the organization, and there were decisions made on that basis. Paul and Jim just never could get along. I finally told Jim we were going to have to do something. I hated to do it."[18] Harry Dalton, the thirty-two-year-old assistant, took over the farm system.

The dismissal may have been unnecessary because less than a year later, in August 1961, Richards resigned to join the expansion Houston Colt .45s as general manager. His success in baseball was destined to be in the dugout, though his personality and ego would never be satisfied with the limited power of field manager. Luman Harris finished the season as the Orioles' manager, and the club won 95 games and finished third.

With MacPhail and Dalton firmly in charge, the rivalries and factions in the organization ceased. McLaughlin had assembled a great team of scouts who now became known as "the Dalton Gang." The Orioles might have been the first team to employ national cross-checkers, men who would go everywhere to check on players who had been recommended by the area scouts. Jim Russo, known as "Super Scout," and Arthur Ehlers, who had been the club's GM before Richards, filled this role under Dalton. "Dalton had brain power," recalled longtime scout Walter Youse. "He was a smart boy. He was the one who really believed in the Minor Leagues and built up the farm system. He was a great believer in scouts."[19]

Already a good Major League team, the Oriole scouts now brought even more talent into the organization. In a five-year period beginning in 1959, the Orioles signed Boog Powell, Dave McNally, Jim Palmer, Mark Belanger, Dave Johnson, Dean Chance, Tom Phoebus, Andy Etchebarren, Darold Knowles, Larry Haney, Eddie Watt, Wally Bunker, and Dave Leonhard, along with several other future Major Leaguers (and, of course, many who never made it). They lost Chance in the 1960 expansion draft, but Paul Blair was drafted from the Mets organization in 1962. For Palmer, a highly recruited pitcher from Scottsdale, Arizona, the choice came down to an offer from Russo and Houston's Richards. "It wasn't that Richards was a bad guy. He just had a certain arrogance. And my parents said, 'You know, the Orioles seem like a better organization.'"[20]

Dalton kept a close watch on the team's success in procuring amateur prospects. "In the past three years, the Orioles have signed 25 players for bonuses of $15,000 or more," Dalton wrote in an internal budgeting memo in early 1961. "Of these, only five were signed during 1960. This figure has reduced from eight in 1959, and 12 in 1958. We must remain competitive in this money group." Dalton added: "If we expect to improve our player strength, we must sign slightly more prospects each year than our competition. We can only do this if we approach each major case in an aggressive manner and stay in active competition to the point where our judgment on ability dictates we should stop."[21]

Unlike the crop from the 1950s, these players did not have to join the Orioles right away and instead began their careers in the Minors under the tutelage of the Orioles' coaches and instructors. Their managers included many who worked in the organization during the Richards era—Earl Weaver, George Staller, Billy Hunter, Cal Ripken Sr.— and who remained many years after he left.

As Oriole manager MacPhail hired Billy Hitchcock, who had had a nine-year career as an American League infielder before a six-year stint as the Tigers' third base coach. After dropping back to seventy-seven wins in 1962 and then eighty-six in 1963 (eighteen and a half games from first), MacPhail fired Hitchcock and hired Hank Bauer, ex-Yankee star and A's manager.

As Earl Weaver later related, the strict adherence to an organizational philosophy softened during the post-Richards years. Neither Hitchcock nor Bauer came from the Oriole system, and both took more of a hands-off approach to instruction. "Hank was from the Yankee school," Weaver remembered. "'Just get talent, put the ball and some bats on the field, and let's go get 'em.' There wasn't a hell of a lot of program."[22]

To supplement all of the youngsters coming out of the system, MacPhail proved adept at finding useful players from other organizations who contributed some excellent seasons. He acquired Jim Gentile from the Dodgers in 1959, and the first baseman provided some good power for a few years (especially in 1961, when he hit forty-six home runs). He picked up center fielder Jackie Brandt from the Giants in 1959, relief pitcher Stu Miller from the Giants in 1962, and pitcher Robin Roberts (who had been released by the Yankees) also in 1962. In early 1963 he acquired veteran shortstop Luis Aparicio from the White Sox for four good players: infielders Ron Hansen and Pete Ward, outfielder Dave Nicholson, and veteran relief ace Hoyt Wilhelm. The cost proved to be steep, but Aparicio provided outstanding defense and base running for several years in Baltimore.

The 1964 Orioles, Bauer's first club, led the AL for most of the summer before settling for ninety-seven wins, two games behind the Yankees. Powell broke out as a slugger, while Barber, Pappas, and Wally Bunker emerged as the best of the crop of homegrown pitchers; Aparicio anchored the defense; and Robinson won the league MVP award. The same crew helped the club win ninety-four games the next year.

After the 1965 season baseball hired a new commissioner, retired air force general William Eckert, a man who knew little about how the baseball business worked. To help ease his transition the owners enticed MacPhail to accept a new job as Eckert's assistant. A change in Oriole ownership created just enough uncertainty to push MacPhail to make the move. Jerry Hoffberger, the president of the National Brewing Company, had been a silent partner in the club since 1953, but gradually accumulated enough stock (through his company) to gain control.

Like fellow brewer turned owner Gussie Busch, Hoffberger wanted a trusted intermediary between himself and his ball club. He hired Frank Cashen, the brewery's advertising chief, to oversee the team for him, and both men urged MacPhail to remain as general manager. "I appreciated their words," MacPhail recalled, "but somehow I felt it was time to move on."[23] As his successor MacPhail recommended Dalton, the farm director, and Hoffberger and Cashen agreed.

As his final act as the Orioles' GM, MacPhail attended the 1965 winter meetings and held talks with Cincinnati on a trade that would bring star outfielder Frank Robinson to Baltimore in exchange for pitchers Milt Pappas and Jack Baldschun and outfielder Dick Simpson. "I told [Reds GM Bill] Dewitt that I was leaving and would have to clear it with Harry Dalton, the general manager-to-be."[24] Dalton, in his first act as GM, approved the deal.

It was the arrival of Frank Robinson, more than any other player, who turned the Orioles from a consistent contender into a great team. Robinson was a superb all-around player who became the leader both on and off the field. Brooks Robinson, the Orioles' top star at the time, enthusiastically welcomed his new teammate, and the rest of the team came on board. "You talk about teams that hoped they could win," remembered Palmer. "That was the Orioles before Frank. After he got here, we expected to win."

The 1966 Orioles made quick work of the AL pennant race, leading by seven on July 4 and cruising from there, finishing with ninety-seven wins, nine games ahead of the Twins. Frank Robinson, the first black superstar in the American League, won the league's Triple Crown. The team continued to incorporate farm-system players into the mix, giving full-time jobs to two rookies: catcher Etchebarren and second baseman Davey Johnson. The Orioles also continued to churn out good young pitchers, even as others, particularly Chuck Estrada, Steve Barber, and Wally Bunker, were hampered by early career injuries and never fulfilled their initial promise. Their two biggest winners in 1966 were twenty-three-year-old McNally, who had debuted in 1962 and finally earned a regular-rotation job in 1965, and twenty-year-old Palmer, a top prospect who needed just a single season in the Minors before his 1965 debut. The Orioles swept the Dodgers in the World Series and finished the Series with three straight complete-game shutouts from Palmer, Bunker, and McNally.

In 1967 the Oriole ship hit rocky waters. Powell had a down season, Frank Robinson was injured much of the year, and the team's two best pitchers, McNally and Palmer, got hurt, the latter's great career derailed for two full seasons. When the club failed to rebound adequately in 1968, reaching the All-Star break at 43-37, Dalton fired Bauer and gave the job to Earl Weaver, who had spent many years in the organization as a Minor League manager.

The thirty-seven-year-old Weaver's Major League experience consisted of just a few months as first base coach, but he had the self-confidence to make changes right away. He took two little-used players—utility man Don Buford and catcher Elrod Hendricks—and expanded their roles. In his first game as manager Weaver installed Buford in center field and batted him leadoff. Buford walked and scored in the first and homered in the fifth, and the Orioles beat Washington 2–0. Buford led off every game the rest of the season, and he responded by hitting .298 with eleven home runs and forty-five walks over the final eighty-two games of the season. In 1968 these were star numbers. "Don Buford is the spark plug," said Frank Robinson after the season, "the guy who always gets on base, who doesn't scream or yell, but when you see him out there on a sack, you just have got to bring him home."[25]

The ascension of Weaver also brought the return of the standardization of instruction within the organization. "When I finally got there [in 1968] I still had the Richards influence. So it was, 'Let's get back to that.' As well as using some of the other stuff I'd learned along the way in the Cardinals organization [where Weaver had played in 1950s]. The Dodgers had their way, the Cardinals had their way, and now OK, the Orioles were going to have our way."[26]

"It was my idea to put it on paper so everybody would be responsible for knowing," recalled Dalton. "And then it became a manual instead of a leaflet. A lot of people wrote. I asked them to commit it to paper and give it to me."[27] The author of the first formal manual, *The Oriole Way to Play Baseball*, was Don Pries, who had become the director of player development. "In spring training," said Pries, "each person at various positions was required to take the manual and in an evening classroom atmosphere write down everything the manual said. My feeling was, if they write it, they remember it."[28] Like the Dodgers in the National League, the Orioles became known for instruction and organizational excellence.

Led by Dalton and Weaver, the Oriole Way carried over into every aspect of the organization. The team had a detailed scouting manual containing rules, forms, tips, and an organizational overview. Additionally, Baltimore distributed another comprehensive manual to guide Minor League managers and instructors. At a time when some teams still ran an informal spring training, the Orioles established detailed schedules for the drills at each defensive position, including specific goals for certain players. They also prepared analyses of other teams' prospects and players and solicited the opinions of multiple organizational scouts.[29]

For the 1969 season the Orioles, Red Sox, and Tigers—the previous three American League pennant winners—joined the new AL East. Each had recently rebuilt their organizations behind strong general managers and strong scouting staffs, and each had high hopes that they could ascend to the top of their new division. The amateur talent for the next decade, however, would no longer be procured by scouts hustling to sign the best players they could within their budget. Beginning in 1965 all American amateur players were subject to a draft.

12 Amateur Draft

Everybody thinks they can be a GM or president of baseball operations. It comes with the territory.—THEO EPSTEIN, baseball executive

After several ill-fated attempts to curtail huge bonuses given to amateur players, at the 1964 winter meetings baseball owners agreed to create an amateur draft, officially the Rule 4 Draft but usually called the "first-year player draft." In the succeeding five decades, the amateur draft has been the primary mechanism for Major League teams to acquire high school and college players from the United States, U.S. territories (such as Puerto Rico as of 1989), and Canada (as of 1991). Originally, there were three drafts: the largest one in June and others in August (for players who played American Legion ball) and January (for players who finished high school or college in the fall). As of 1987 there has been a single June draft.

The purpose of the draft was obvious: owners were tired of giving out large bonuses to amateur players and had been unable to stop even in the face of rules that essentially penalized themselves for doing so. In June 1964 the Los Angeles Angels gave more than $200,000 to twenty-one-year-old University of Wisconsin outfielder Rick Reichardt, and soon after Kansas City owner Charlie Finley disclosed that he had disbursed $634,000 to eighty players that year.[1] When the two leagues responded by finally approving the draft, they were taking a step already embraced by both the National Football League (in 1936) and the Basketball Association of America, a forerunner to the National Basketball Association (in 1947).

The draft dramatically changed the way teams brought players into their organizations. Gone were the days when a wealthy team could outbid the competition for top talent. The Angels were able to sign Reichardt not because they had outscouted the other nineteen teams—

everyone was well aware of Reichardt's talent—but because the Angels ponied up the most money. Had the draft been in place in 1964, Reichardt might very well have been the first selection by either the Mets or the Senators (the two last-place teams in 1963).

Moreover, because a team was limited by its draft position, its scouts could no longer sign as many top prospects as the ownership would afford or they could hustle. Finley or Buzzie Bavasi could no longer replenish their systems by pursuing a large class of amateurs all at once. And traditional winners like the Yankees could no longer lure a prospect with the Yankee mystique and the promise of World Series riches down the line.

Nevertheless, once one got past the first handful of players—the blue-chip prospects that everyone generally agreed on—the draft still afforded an advantage to teams that could identify future regulars and stars and develop them. As an illustration: In the first thirty drafts (through 1994) Major League teams drafted eighty-six players, just fewer than three per draft, who would go on to earn fifty or more WAR in their careers.[2] Although twenty-three of these were selected within the first ten picks in their draft year, another twenty-eight were drafted after the fourth round. There is an unmistakable advantage to getting one of the top picks, but there is still plenty of room for good scouting to make a difference. In the very first draft, in June 1965, there were no fifty-WAR players taken in the first round, but Johnny Bench went in the second (the 36th overall pick) and Nolan Ryan in the twelfth (the 295th pick).

As a way to study the history of the draft, we created a database of every Major League player who has played since 1965, noted how they first entered organized baseball, and recorded their yearly "wins above replacement" totals. When using WAR at the team level, the reader should keep in mind that a team whose players accumulate 0 WAR in a season would be expected to have a record of around 47-115. In order to compete for a division title or a playoff berth, a team would need its players to accumulate somewhere around 40–45 WAR.

We first calculated how much on-field Major League talent, year to year, originally came into organized baseball via the draft. Chart 4

Chart 4. MLB WAR from drafted players

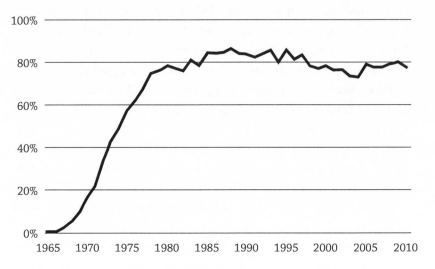

Source: Database owned and maintained by the authors.

illustrates for the forty-six seasons from 1965 to 2010 the percentage of WAR accounted for by players who were drafted and ultimately
signed.

It took a few years for the talent from the early drafts to make an
impact, but by 1971 fully 20 percent of Major League talent had come
from the draft and more than half by 1975. It generally takes a few
years for drafted players to reach the Major Leagues and perhaps six
to eight years for the best players to reach their peak value. In the past
twenty years the draft has become slightly less important (though still
dominant) because of the influx of non-American players who have
been either signed as amateurs or acquired from non-U.S. leagues.

Although teams can find talent in other countries or acquire developed talent from other teams through trading or midcareer free-agent
signings, history has shown that they can put themselves at a big advantage by drafting astutely and developing these draftees.

In the history of the draft a typical team in a typical year drafts players who, collectively, are destined to produce 25 to 30 future WAR. In
1965 the Reds drafted 122 future WAR (mostly Bench), and then followed that up in succeeding years with 18, 6, 13, 63, and 32. No team

1. (*top*) Barney Dreyfuss (*right*) built some of history's great teams in Pittsburgh and teamed with Garry Herrmann (*left*) to forge a lasting peace with the upstart American League in 1903. Library of Congress, Prints and Photographs Division, LC-DIG-ggbain-04424.

2. (*bottom*) John McGraw relied on his own genius and force of personality to build numerous pennant winners with the New York Giants. Library of Congress, Prints and Photographs Division, LC-DIG-ggbain-11245.

3. (*opposite*) Christy Mathewson (*right*) was McGraw's opposite in temperament and lifestyle, but he provided many spectacular seasons for his skipper. National Baseball Hall of Fame Library, Cooperstown NY.

4. (*above*) The Chicago Cubs' Bill Veeck Sr. (*left*) was one of the first to serve as a baseball general manager. Here he is with his manager (Rogers Hornsby, *center*) and his owner (William Wrigley) in the early 1930s. The Dennis Goldstein Collection.

5. (*above*) Jacob Ruppert (*left*) hired many brilliant men while building his dynasty, starting with manager Miller Huggins in 1917. National Baseball Hall of Fame Library, Cooperstown NY.

6. (*opposite top*) Jacob Ruppert hired Ed Barrow (*left*) in 1920 to run the team. In 1931 Joe McCarthy (*right*) came aboard as manager, and the championships kept coming. National Baseball Hall of Fame Library, Cooperstown NY.

7. (*opposite bottom*) Walter O'Malley left the management of the Dodgers to Buzzie Bavasi, who rewarded his boss with four World Series titles. At this off-season banquet they flank longtime LA sportswriter Bob Hunter. Courtesy of the Los Angeles Dodgers.

8. (*above*) Al Campanis (*right*) served the Dodgers as scout, instructor, scouting director, and, beginning in 1968, general manager. Here he poses with Jim Wynn, one of his many great acquisitions. Campanis is holding a "toy cannon," which was Wynn's nickname. Courtesy of the Los Angeles Dodgers.

9. (*opposite top*) Walter O'Malley inspects some plans with (*clockwise from front left*) Brooklyn Borough president John Cashmore, farm director Fresco Thompson, general manager Buzzie Bavasi, and Mary Smith, widow of minority owner John Smith. The Dennis Goldstein Collection.

10. (*opposite bottom*) In 1942 Branch Rickey (*right*) succeeded Larry MacPhail, his onetime protégé, as Dodger president. The two men grew to loathe each other. National Baseball Hall of Fame Library, Cooperstown NY.

11. (*opposite top*) The triumvirate of Larry MacPhail, Del Webb, and Dan Topping (*left to right*) purchased the Yankees in 1945. After his famous meltdown at the World Series victory party, MacPhail's partners bought him out. The Dennis Goldstein Collection.

12. (*opposite bottom*) Beer magnate August Busch Jr. (*left*) integrated the Cardinals after purchasing the team in the early 1950s. He is seen here with NL president Warren Giles (*right*), at one time a pennant-winning general manager with the Reds. National Baseball Hall of Fame Library, Cooperstown NY.

13. (*above*) Bing Devine (*left*) spent years running the Rochester Red Wings before getting his shot as general manager of the Cardinals. National Baseball Hall of Fame Library, Cooperstown NY.

14. (*above*) Longtime Tigers general manager Jim Campbell built the 1968 World Series champion but failed to integrate younger players into his aging team, allowing the team to fall from contention by the mid-1970s. National Baseball Hall of Fame Library, Cooperstown NY.

15. (*opposite top*) Harry Dalton took the reins of the Baltimore Orioles in 1965 and oversaw one of history's greatest teams over the next six years. National Baseball Hall of Fame Library, Cooperstown NY.

16. (*opposite bottom*) Dick O'Connell (*right*) took over a struggling Red Sox franchise in 1965 and built a surprise pennant winner in just two off-seasons. One of his best moves was the hiring of manager Dick Williams (*center*) in 1966. Assistant GM Haywood Sullivan (*left*) shares the optimism. Courtesy of the Boston Red Sox.

17. After many years honing his skills in the Minor Leagues and a stint with the American Football League, Bob Howsam became one of baseball's most successful general managers. Most notably, he assembled Cincinnati's Big Red Machine, which boasted perhaps baseball's best-ever eight-man lineup. National Baseball Hall of Fame Library, Cooperstown NY.

18. Father and son Hall of Famers Larry (*left*) and Lee (*center*) MacPhail could not have been more different. The competent, thoughtful Lee contrasted strikingly with his boisterous, impetuous father. Another son, Bill (*right*), was a longtime president of CBS Sports. National Baseball Hall of Fame Library, Cooperstown NY.

19. Two years after CBS bought the Yankees, it tapped worldly, dashing business executive Mike Burke to run the team. He lost his position soon after George Steinbrenner purchased the team in January 1973. National Baseball Hall of Fame Library, Cooperstown NY.

20. The architect of the expansion Kansas City Royals, general manager Cedric Tallis (*right*) learned his craft by serving many years in the Minors. He is seen here in 1960 with Seattle Rainiers manager Dick Sisler. From the David Eskenazi Collection.

21. (*above*) The owner of the expansion Kansas City Royals, the highly competitive Ewing Kauffman was also one of baseball's most thoughtful and original thinkers. National Baseball Hall of Fame Library, Cooperstown NY.

22. (*opposite top*) Kansas City's future star second baseman Frank White (*center*) was the top prospect to come out of the Baseball Academy, the brainchild of owner Ewing Kauffman. Courtesy of the Kansas City Royals.

23. (*opposite bottom*) Ewing Kauffman (*left*) named iconoclastic scout Syd Thrift (*right*) to run the Kansas City Baseball Academy. Thrift later spent time as the general manager of the Pirates and Orioles. Courtesy of the Kansas City Royals.

24. Kansas City general manager Cedric Tallis (*right*) built a great front office, which included longtime baseball man Charlie Metro (*left*) and several future general managers, including Lou Gorman (*center*), Herk Robinson, and John Schuerholz. Courtesy of the Kansas City Royals.

25. The Royals owed much of their quick ascent to general manager Cedric Tallis's great trades. Seen here with many of his acquisitions, Tallis landed five of the starting-nine position players on the 1976 division winner through swaps. Courtesy of the Kansas City Royals.

26. After spending a lifetime in baseball generally overseeing undercapitalized ball clubs, Gabe Paul finally got his chance to spend some money with the Yankees. Starting from the solid base built by Mike Burke and Lee MacPhail, Paul assembled the Yankee juggernaut of the late 1970s. National Baseball Hall of Fame Library, Cooperstown NY.

27. (*top*) As the president of the expansion Toronto Blue Jays, Peter Bavasi hired Pat Gillick to run the baseball side of the operation. Bavasi also became one of the first baseball executives to consciously incorporate professional management concepts and practices. Courtesy Toronto Blue Jays.

28. (*bottom*) Hall of Fame general manager Pat Gillick succeeded brilliantly in all four of his stints as general manager. He built world champions with two different franchises and made it to the League Championship Series with the other two. Courtesy Toronto Blue Jays.

29. Oakland A's general manager Billy Beane became famous with the 2003 publication
of Michael Lewis's *Moneyball*. When Brad Pitt played Beane in the movie adaption,
baseball general managers entered the mainstream of American culture. National
Baseball Hall of Fame Library, Cooperstown NY.

30. Managing general partner Bill Neukom (*left*), president Larry Baer (*center*), and general manager Brian Sabean (*right*) rebuilt the Giants into the team that won the 2010, 2012, and 2014 World Series. © 2010 S.F. Giants.

31. Boston Red Sox general manager Ben Cherington (*left*) and manager John Farrell (*right*) have embraced modern analytical approaches to build one of baseball's most successful recent franchises. Courtesy of the Boston Red Sox.

has figured out how to find a superstar every year; most team histories are a mix of good drafts and bad drafts. Teams that can put a few good drafts together in a short window usually have contending teams several years later when these players develop.

In June 1965 the Kansas City Athletics, with the first pick in the first draft, selected Arizona State outfielder Rick Monday. By picking Sal Bando and Gene Tenace the same year, the Athletics put together a draft class (141 WAR) that still ranks as the eighth best in history. They built on this the next two years with two drafts that are in the top 10 percent of all drafts, nabbing Reggie Jackson in 1966 and then Darrell Evans and Vida Blue in 1967. Though they lost Evans in the Rule 5 Draft a year later (because he was not placed on their forty-man roster), the A's (relocated to Oakland) built upon these three excellent draft classes, made a few astute trades, and won three World Series in the early 1970s.

The greatest single draft class was that of the 1968 Los Angeles Dodgers, who selected and signed 234 future WAR. This group included Ron Cey, Dave Lopes, Steve Garvey, Doyle Alexander, Joe Ferguson, Geoff Zahn, and Bill Buckner. The Dodgers' top pick that year—Bobby Valentine—had a promising career snuffed out by an injury, but the depth of this draft remains unprecedented even decades later. The Dodgers had drafted Bill Russell, Charlie Hough, and Steve Yeager over the previous two years, and most of this group stayed together to help win four pennants and a World Series over an eight-year period. The nature of scouting had changed, but the Dodgers, led by their brilliant scouting director Al Campanis, could still find tremendous value where other teams had not.

In the previous chapter we discussed three American League teams—the Boston Red Sox, Detroit Tigers, and Baltimore Orioles—that won pennants in the late 1960s and began competing with each other in the new AL East in 1969. The talent-acquisition revolution caused by the draft played a large role in determining how these teams, and all other teams, performed on the field in the 1970s.

The Boston Red Sox won the pennant in 1967 with an extremely young team. Their best players were Carl Yastrzemski (twenty-seven), Jim

Lonborg (twenty-five), Rico Petrocelli (twenty-four), Joe Foy (twenty-four), George Scott (twenty-three), Mike Andrews (twenty-three), Tony Conigliaro (twenty-two), and Reggie Smith (twenty-two). Their oldest important contributors were midseason pickups Gary Bell and Jerry Adair (each thirty).

That said, this core of players met with quite a bit of misfortune. Conigliaro's beaning cost him more than a season, and he had just two full years left in his once-promising career. Lonborg never attained the heights of 1967 after his skiing accident. Foy, so promising in 1966, never repeated that season and was out of baseball by 1971. Scott had a gruesome 1968 and several inconsistent years thereafter. Only Yastrzemski, Petrocelli, and Smith stayed on track, helping the club into the 1970s.

Although GM Dick O'Connell could not have known this at the time, his team was going to need reinforcements much sooner than the ages of their stars would otherwise have indicated. The Minor League system that had produced the great bounty in the middle 1960s was going to have to keep supplying it, only this time via the amateur draft. Remarkably, the system delivered. Table 8 lists players selected and signed by the Red Sox in the first nine drafts who became All-Stars. The table lists their future WAR and their number of All-Star selections.

The Red Sox lost Otis to the Mets in a Minor League draft after just two years, but the best of the rest joined the Major League club two or three years after they were drafted. Not surprisingly, this was enough to keep the club contending for another decade, winning a pennant in 1975 and nearly winning a few others.

Looking at table 8, one might reasonably ask why the team did not perform even better than they did in the 1970s. One problem is that the talent the Red Sox produced in the 1960s and 1970s was not evenly distributed; the team was generally loaded with outfielders and first basemen but did not have enough good pitchers or infielders. O'Connell was tasked with the job of making trades to balance the team, and he did not trade particularly well. Beginning in 1969 he dealt Ken Harrelson, Conigliaro, Scott, Smith, Ben Oglivie, and Cecil Cooper, all outfielders and first basemen, and did not recoup nearly

Table 8. Red Sox All-Star draftees

YEAR	PLAYER	WAR	ASG
1965	Amos Otis	43	5
1966	Ken Brett	17	1
1967	Carlton Fisk	69	11
1968	Cecil Cooper	36	6
1968	Ben Oglivie	26	3
1968	Bill Lee	22	1
1968	Lynn McGlothlen	15	1
1969	Dwight Evans	69	3
1970	Rick Burleson	23	4
1971	Jim Rice	47	8
1972	Don Aase	15	1
1972	Ernie Whitt	18	1
1973	Fred Lynn	50	9

Source: http://BaseballReference.com.

the equivalent value. The latter four all had multiple All-Star seasons ahead of them, while the best of the acquired players (pitchers Sonny Siebert, Marty Pattin, and Rick Wise) had a handful of good seasons in the rotation.

O'Connell's worst sequence of deals involved the first base position. After the 1971 season O'Connell packaged the frustrating Scott and Lonborg (who, it turned out, was finally about to turn things around) in a deal with the Brewers mainly to get more pitching (Pattin) and speed (Tommy Harper). Of the ten players in the deal, Scott had the best future, putting together five good years with the Brewers, winning a home run title and five Gold Gloves. The Red Sox hoped to give the vacated first base job to Cooper, a top prospect, but when manager Eddie Kasko determined he was not ready in the spring of 1972,

O'Connell dealt pitcher Sparky Lyle to the Yankees for veteran first baseman Danny Cater. Lyle became a star in New York, Cater was awful, and the Red Sox moved Yastrzemski to first while they waited for Cooper to develop.

Meanwhile, the club kept developing outfielders, keeping Yastrzemski in the infield and seriously delaying the career of Cooper, who played part-time for a few years and showed promise. After the 1976 season O'Connell, unaware of what he had, traded Cooper and Bernie Carbo, another good-hitting outfielder, to the Brewers to get Scott back. Scott was now thirty-three and had just one decent season left, while Cooper went on to star in Milwaukee for a decade. All told, these few decisions cost Boston the prime years of Scott, Cooper, and Lyle, with little to show for any of it.

O'Connell got away with these poor trades because the club drafted and developed so well. In 1977 the homegrown club had an outfield of Yastrzemski, Lynn, and Evans (who missed time with a knee injury), with Rice serving as the designated hitter (DH) and Scott having his last good year. The team did not miss Smith, Cooper, and Oglivie directly, at least not yet, and remained competitive for several more seasons.

The Baltimore Orioles, made up mainly of predraft players signed and developed in their organization, burst through to dominate the AL East from 1969 to 1971, winning three AL pennants and the 1970 World Series. The Orioles had also made some great trades, acquiring Frank Robinson in 1965, Don Buford in 1967, and Mike Cuellar in 1968. Harry Dalton also dealt for Pat Dobson in 1971, and the right-hander teamed with Cuellar, Dave McNally, and Jim Palmer to give the club four twenty-game winners. It was a tremendous team, well balanced and filled with stars.

The Orioles did not select as well as the Red Sox did in the early drafts, but they found a few gems, as table 9 shows.

During this period the Orioles added on average just over thirty future WAR through the draft, scarcely more than the overall average. When factoring in that the Orioles' success on the field meant they rarely had a high draft pick, their drafting results appear more impressive.

Table 9. Orioles All-Star draftees

YEAR	PLAYER	WAR	ASG
1967	Bobby Grich	71	6
1967	Don Baylor	28	1
1968	Al Bumbry	24	1
1970	Doug DeCinces	42	1
1973	Eddie Murray	68	8
1973	Mike Flanagan	26	1

Source: http://BaseballReference.com.

After the Orioles lost the 1971 World Series, Dalton left Baltimore to take a job with the lowly California Angels. Dalton had played a large role in building this great team, but now itched for the challenge of starting from scratch and assumed the reins of a team that had struggled on and off the field for several years. Frank Cashen, the Orioles' president and Dalton's boss, took over the general manager duties himself.

On October 19, just two days after losing the final game of the 1971 World Series to the Pirates, Dalton prepared a memorandum for Cashen outlining his "thoughts on possible trades." Many of these involved strengthening the bullpen and upgrading the bench, but the most important item stressed making room on the club for Minor League stars such as Baylor and Grich. In particular, Dalton suggested trading the face of the team, star outfielder Frank Robinson. "I might even consider a good prospect and some cash or a young Major League player who has potential but has not matured yet," wrote Dalton. "It will be tough to get much else for him, but I now feel it is absolutely essential to trade him if we can, and I would like to trade him to a club which pleases him. This would probably be the Dodgers, a New York club, and maybe any of the other clubs in California."[3]

Whether this influenced Cashen is not known, but on December 2 he traded Robinson to the Dodgers for four prospects, one of whom, Doyle Alexander, won 194 games over nineteen big-league seasons.

The trade shocked the Oriole players and fans, many of whom blamed this deal for the club's dreadful offensive performance in 1972, when they dropped from a league-leading 4.7 runs per game to an eighth-best 3.4 and consequently to third place.

This proved to be an aberration, as the team regrouped to win division titles the next two seasons and won 90 or more games in nine of the next eleven years. Cashen made several outstanding trades in the 1973 and 1974 off-seasons, acquiring pitchers Ross Grimsley and Mike Torrez, first baseman Lee May, and outfielder Ken Singleton without losing a single player the Orioles needed. These deals, along with the draft picks noted in table 9, were enough to keep the Orioles near the top in the mid-1970s. Within a few years the team had different ownership and management, and the organization gradually began to lose some of its shine. After eighteen winning years, the club finally finished under .500 in 1986.

The 1968 Tigers, consisting almost entirely of players signed by their scouts and developed in their system, won 103 games and the World Series. The heart of this team was mainly in its prime: only three regulars (Al Kaline, Norm Cash, and Earl Wilson) were over thirty, and many of their best players were in their midtwenties. But other than a fluky title in a weak division in 1972, these Tigers never contended again and were in last place by 1974. What happened? The answer is simple: the Tigers drafted miserably in the first several drafts and were unable to replace their 1968 core as it aged.

In 1965 the Tigers selected and signed three players who would eventually play in the Major Leagues: Gene Lamont (with the thirteenth overall pick), Gary Taylor, and Bill Butler. This turned out to be one of their better early drafts. In fact, the Tigers did not land an impact Major Leaguer until 1974 when they selected catcher Lance Parrish. By that time, when nearly half of the WAR in the Major Leagues was generated by players who had come through the first nine drafts (1965–73), the best Tiger draftees had been Elliott Maddox, Vern Ruhle, and Leon Roberts. It is no wonder that the Tigers fell to last place. When their roster began sprouting the inevitable holes, the Tigers lacked qualified replacements down on the farm.

In fact, the Tigers of this era had the most stable roster in baseball history. Nine Tigers—Gates Brown, Norm Cash, Bill Freehan, Willie Horton, Al Kaline, Mickey Lolich, Dick McAuliffe, Jim Northrup, and Mickey Stanley—were together for the entire decade of 1964 to 1973, easily a record. John Hiller just missed this list, joining the club in 1965 and staying on for fifteen years. Loyalty of this sort has its merits, but by the early 1970s several of these players were barely contributing and the team was alarmingly old. Brown, certainly capable of holding down a regular job somewhere in these years, spent thirteen seasons with the Tigers competing for playing time with the same four outfielders. The Tigers inexplicably chose to hang on to Brown rather than using him as trade bait to acquire an infielder and giving him a chance for a more rewarding career.

Tigers GM Jim Campbell chose to allow his team to age while he waited for the fruits of his farm system, help that had arrived so impressively throughout the 1960s. When reinforcements failed to arrive, his aging regulars had no competition for jobs, and Campbell had little to offer other teams in trade. Ultimately, the Tigers would have to wait until the late 1970s, when Lance Parrish, Alan Trammell, Lou Whitaker, and Kirk Gibson, all astute Tiger draft picks, helped usher in another great period of Tiger baseball.

How teams adapt to changing circumstances can affect their fortunes for years to come. The Red Sox, Orioles, and Tigers, dormant franchises in the 1950s, all successfully revamped their front offices and became regular contenders by the late 1960s. The three clearly diverged, however, when the first-year player draft became the principal means of acquiring amateur talent. Some of the most important skills of the predraft era—money, hustle, and the ability to sell the benefits of one's Major League franchise—no longer mattered to the same degree. The remaining skill—talent evaluation—was all that mattered now, and teams needed to adapt to the new reality.

13 The Machine

After their triumphant 1970 pennant-winning campaign, the wheels came off the Big Red Machine the next year, as the Cincinnati Reds fell to seventy-nine wins and a fourth-place tie in the NL West. One could have concluded that their 1971 regression was something of a fluke—injuries would heal, young stars would recover from their off-years—and that the club, if left intact, would ride its core of talent back to contention in 1972. Bob Howsam, the team's general manager and architect, felt differently. He knew that the flaws in his team—among other things, it was too slow, too defensively challenged, and too right-handed—were real and that the team needed to be revamped in order to get back on top.

Howsam was a problem solver and a successful businessman, and he proceeded as any good leader would. He gathered his top advisers to solicit their honest views about the club and to brainstorm possible solutions. A brilliant organizational manager, Howsam had a team of people that he trusted and whose advice he valued. Each of these men had real and specific responsibilities and spoke with Howsam regularly. Howsam listened to everyone's opinion, allowed for disagreement, and then made the final decisions himself.

Howsam's annual organizational meetings, held over several days in September, followed a pattern. He first went over his club position by position, asking his staff for honest evaluations. How did everyone feel about the team's starting shortstop? What if he got hurt—what would the Reds do then? How was the team's organizational depth at third base? Every position and the pitching staff received the full treatment, with Howsam listening and taking notes. Next, with the help of his inner circle, Howsam put together a position-by-position ranking of all the regular players in the Major Leagues to gauge where the Reds players ranked. "This is a lot of work," recalled manager Sparky Anderson. "Ain't no flying in and flying out. But when you're done—

and this was Bob's theory and he was right—if your club had the lowest numbers, then you had the best team."[1]

Howsam not only expected his staff to thoroughly know the players in the Reds organization, but also required that they know all the other teams and their farm systems as well or better than the teams themselves did. He would ask his people: What do the Phillies need? What do the Astros need? What players do they undervalue? Which up-and-coming players are blocked from advancement? When he talked to a fellow general manager, he would start by explaining to his counterpart what their team needed and where they had a surplus and how the Reds could help solve their problems. Howsam wanted to be the most informed person in every interaction with other teams, and he relied on his staff to make this so. With full control over the organization, he had the authority to create this culture of baseball intelligence and organizational excellence.

Howsam grew up in Colorado helping his father run a profitable honey business and graduated from business school with the intention of working in the family trade. After World War II he moved to Washington to act as administrative assistant for his father-in-law, U.S. senator Ed Johnson. When Johnson was appointed the unpaid president of a reincarnated Western League in 1947, he asked Howsam to move to Denver to run the league as executive secretary. As the league's sole employee, Howsam wrote the league's constitution, helped to arrange stadium repair and construction, prepared the league schedule, and hired the umpires. He traveled all over the region, from Denver to Lincoln to Pueblo, helping new owners run their new teams.

Though Howsam undertook the job assuming it was a six-month assignment, by the end of the season he knew he wanted to remain in the game. With support from his brother and father, after the season he purchased the Denver Bears, one of the league's struggling clubs. He bought an old dump site and built Bears Stadium, later Mile High Stadium, the principal facility for baseball and football in Denver for more than fifty years. The Bears led the league in attendance in 1948 and would for the rest of their tenure in the league. In 1949 the Bears drew more than 450,000 fans, more than the St. Louis Browns of the

American League and one of the highest totals in Single-A history. In 1951 Howsam was named the *Sporting News'* Single-A Executive of the Year. The next year the Bears won their first league championship and copped a second pennant in 1954, before losing in the playoff finals.

In the early 1950s the Bears were an affiliate of the Pittsburgh Pirates, allowing Howsam to work with legendary general manager Branch Rickey. Howsam learned many lifelong baseball lessons from Rickey by following him around during spring training as he conducted clinics and spoke to the Pirates' Minor League players. Rickey preached the tenets that would guide Howsam in the decades ahead: look for size in pitchers, speed in position players, power in hitters, and youth in everyone. "Rickey was the great teacher," Howsam recalled.[2]

After the 1954 season Howsam bought the Kansas City Blues of the American Association and moved them to Denver, where they became the New York Yankees' Triple-A affiliate and displaced his Single-A club. Now part of the Yankees chain, Howsam worked with their renowned general manager, George Weiss. Like Rickey, Weiss became a major influence on Howsam's career. Unlike Rickey, Weiss had not played or managed in the Major Leagues, but he had been organizing baseball teams since he was a teenager and knew how to run one. He surrounded himself with baseball people he could trust, and he listened to their advice. Rickey once said that Weiss "couldn't tell a bull from a cow," but he employed people who could, and he relied on them.[3] "Mr. Weiss was not a one-man show like Mr. Rickey," said Howsam. "He was the ideal corporate man, hiring good people such as [farm director] Lee MacPhail, delegating authority, and keeping all the buttons on his desk at his fingertips."[4] Howsam was a quick learner, as MacPhail related in his own memoirs: "In many ways, [Bob] was a little like George Weiss. He watched costs very carefully and was very concerned about the reputation and image of the team."[5]

Howsam's great success continued, as the new Bears, managed by Ralph Houk, led the American Association in attendance during their first three seasons. Howsam won the *Sporting News'* Triple-A Executive of the Year award in 1956 and then watched his Bears win the league title and the Little World Series the next year. By 1957 he was doubling as president of the American Association, while still running the Denver club. Many Minor League teams struggled mightily in the 1950s, but Howsam's thrived.

In the late 1950s Howsam aligned with Rickey and others in the ultimately failed effort to create the Continental League, a third Major League that hoped to operate cooperatively with the existing American and National Leagues. He also founded the Denver Broncos of the American Football League, but after their inaugural 1960 season, heavy financial losses convinced Howsam to sell not only the Broncos but also the Bears and the stadium. "It was not fair to my family," recalled Howsam, "to keep a debt that was considerably more than I could handle. We had spent so much enlarging the stands and it just didn't pay off as quickly as I thought. That first season of football, we lost two home dates to snow-outs. It was sad to leave sports."[6]

Howsam spent the next three years selling mutual funds before he received a call from Gussie Busch, at the behest of Branch Rickey, asking him to run the St. Louis Cardinals. Howsam was forty-six and had thought his baseball career was behind him, but his decision, especially considering the presence of Rickey, was not difficult. As recounted in chapter 10, the Cardinals put on a dramatic drive for the pennant and ultimately won the team's first World Series since 1946.

The change in general managers was met with derision in St. Louis. Bing Devine, a St. Louis native, was popular with the local fans, his players, and the media, most of whom blamed Rickey for his dismissal. Howsam was blameless, but he was in a very uncomfortable situation when the team he inherited won the championship.

A less confident man might have considered himself fortunate to be the caretaker of this championship team and quietly tinker to keep the club contending while slowly earning the respect of the team's rabid fan base. Howsam, on the other hand, intended to run the team the way he had run teams for twenty years, even if it was far different from the way Bing Devine had. Howsam found the front office to be in disarray, an amateur operation when compared with what he had run in Denver. There was no mechanism for selling season tickets or for promotion (beyond the close tie-in with Busch's brewery), and some of the ticket takers were stealing tickets from the club. In effect Devine had concentrated solely on the Major League team, while Howsam, who came from a background of running entire organizations, believed that the team and business operated hand in hand. The people working in the office were mainly Devine loyalists who resented Howsam's presence and his obvious plans to institute change.

Later, Howsam regretted that he had not asked for the resignations of the entire front office after the season, hiring back as he saw fit. Instead, he went about this process slowly, "gradually changing [the] staff by hiring new people and cutting dead wood adrift. For the dead wood it is slow and painful whereas the quick cut would be merciful." Soon after Howsam arrived farm director Eddie Stanky came into his office and proceeded to tell Howsam just how he expected things would be run. Howsam calmly told Stanky to clear out his desk and that he was through with the Cardinals. Howsam also fired two women who he believed were responsible for leaking a memo that proved embarrassing to Rickey.[7]

On the flip side, when Howsam found people he valued and trusted, he gave them authority and respect. To replace Stanky Howsam promoted Sheldon "Chief" Bender, previously Stanky's assistant. Bender had been in the organization since the late 1930s, as a player, manager, executive, and scout, before taking his position as assistant farm director. A bright and respected baseball man, he carried a toughness earned in Pacific combat during the Second World War. Bender was tasked with teaching Howsam the Cardinals system, the strengths and weaknesses of every player and manager from the bottom up. Bender and Howsam became close friends and worked productively together for the next twenty years.

To run the business side of the club, overseeing marketing, promotions, and sales, Howsam hired Dick Wagner, whom he knew from his years in the Western League. Howsam believed Wagner to be bright, hardworking, and tough. Wagner started in baseball at age nineteen in 1946, when he was named business manager of a Detroit Tigers affiliate in Thomasville, Georgia, and held various Minor League posts over the next twelve years in the Tigers and Pirates organizations. Wagner had been out of baseball for a few years, working first with the Ice Capades and most recently running a radio station in Kansas. He joined the Cardinals in the spring of 1965 and, like Bender, remained with Howsam for most of the next two decades. While running promotions and sales, Wagner played a key role in moving the Cardinals into their new facility, the second Busch Stadium, in 1966. "Such a move," said Howsam later, "like any operation—major or minor—is a series of logical moves, putting one foot in front of another. That takes organization. I am an organizer. So is Dick Wagner. We are both do-ers."[8]

Whereas Devine had been personal friends with many of the players and spent time on the field before games, Howsam mostly stayed away, other than occasionally sending word that someone was not wearing his uniform properly. Like Rickey, Howsam was considered a calculating negotiator at contract time, which was often the only time his players saw him. Considering his roster, Howsam saw a club filled with aging stars who were fortunate to grab a single pennant and unlikely to grab any more. They had won just ninety-three games, benefiting from the Phillies' collapse, and their core included Ken Boyer (thirty-three), Dick Groat (thirty-three), Bill White (thirty), Curt Simmons (thirty-five), and Barney Shultz (thirty-seven).

Howsam hired Red Schoendienst to manage for 1965, figuring that the local hero would help soothe the fans still reeling from the Keane debacle. Howsam kept the team intact for a year but was probably not too surprised when they fell to eighty wins and seventh place in 1965. After the season he traded Boyer to the Mets and Groat and White to the Phillies, receiving considerably less famous players in return. This was a shocking turn of events in St. Louis, whose fans knew that Bing Devine would not have dealt these popular players, his friends, for little return. Howsam confidently deflected the criticism. The team would be improved, he felt, with more team speed, better defense, more pitching depth, youth, and a more balanced offense. "And there will be strong competition for several positions," he said. "Competition adds a lot—in aggressive play and hustle." He also pointed out that the Cardinals' planned move in 1966 to the new Busch Stadium, a much bigger facility, emphasized the need for younger and faster players.[9]

"My player moves were mostly youth oriented," he later wrote. "Mr. Rickey used to say that it's better to trade a player one year too early than one year too late. I think that makes sense, although I realize the wrench of the fans hearts when a longtime favorite is traded or released but often it's necessary for the continued success of the team."[10] At the time of the deals, Groat and Boyer were thirty-four, and White was thirty-one. White charged that the Cardinals had spread rumors that he was actually thirty-seven and remained bitter at Howsam decades later. Howsam did not mention the allegation in his memoirs, and it is unclear what he would have gained by devaluing his own player.

The 1966 Cardinals improved slightly, to eighty-three wins, aided considerably by the early May trade of pitcher Ray Sadecki for slugging first baseman Orlando Cepeda. With his cleanup hitter on board, after the season Howsam acquired Roger Maris from the Yankees to bat third, precipitating the move of Mike Shannon from right field to third base, thereby completing the core of the club that would win two pennants in 1967 and 1968. Howsam, however, would not be around to celebrate the fruits of his rebuilding effort.

Although Howsam had a good relationship with Gussie Busch, things were not as smooth with Dick Meyer, Busch's adviser who acted as the required go-between to get Busch's approval for personnel moves. Devine had accepted this arrangement and befriended Meyer, but Howsam was used to being in charge and acting quickly if he needed to make a deal. The trade for Cepeda almost fell through because Meyer was concerned with the state of Cepeda's knee even after Howsam had the Cardinals' doctor examine the player and voice his approval. Howsam, supremely confident in his own decisions, chafed at the unwanted bureaucracy.

Meanwhile, the Cincinnati Reds, who had lost the pennant to the Cardinals on the final day of the 1964 season, had been sold in 1966 by Bill DeWitt to an eleven-man group headed by Francis Dale, the publisher of the *Cincinnati Enquirer*. DeWitt had previously been the general manager of the St. Louis Browns, Detroit Tigers, and Reds, before buying a majority stake in the team in 1962. He had wanted to build a ballpark in the suburbs and received several offers to move the team to another city. Dale's group bought the Reds primarily to save the team for Cincinnati. The men did not know baseball and needed someone who did.

The new Reds owners contacted Howsam and offered him complete control over the ball club, a substantial raise, and a three-year contract.

Howsam was happy with the Cardinals and felt they were moving in the right direction, but he could not turn down either the money or the total freedom. In announcing the hiring Dale said the Reds valued Howsam's experience as general manager, his focus on being "promotion minded and dedicated to making baseball exciting, interesting and a family occasion," and his desire to build an extensive farm system.[11] The Reds also needed someone who knew how to move into a new ballpark, which the Reds were planning to do by 1969. Howsam took over the club on January 22, 1967.

With the Cincinnati Reds, Howsam had license to set up the organization as he saw fit, and it did not take him long to restructure the front office. He doubled the size of the staff, adding an advertising director, a sales department, and more promotions people. He also brought aboard some of his most trusted people from St. Louis. Wagner, who had left the Cardinals because he could not work with Meyer, was operating the Los Angeles Forum. Howsam lured him back as his assistant, with the same role but answering only to the general manager. Together they opened ticket offices throughout the region, created souvenir stores, set up a Reds-controlled radio network, and created a speakers bureau. Wagner also was not afraid to ruffle feathers if necessary. "He's tough, abrasive and often completely without tact and compassion," writer Earl Lawson once wrote. "If he were entrusted with the duties of the Secretary of State, the United States undoubtedly would be constantly at war. . . . Howsam swears by him."[12]

Although Howsam had developed a reputation in the press as a cold employer, it is telling that many Cardinal employees followed him to Cincinnati, including Bender, who had worked in the Cardinal organization for more than twenty years. Bender became the Reds' farm director, a lateral move, though within a couple of years he was the player-personnel director. The Cincinnati owners allowed Bender and Howsam to hire many more scouts and expand the farm system. Howsam also replaced much of the office staff, putting more focus on advance ticket sales and keeping the ballpark and its environs spotless, as he had done in St. Louis. Howsam and Bender hired managers who were instructors. "You'd be surprised how many ex-big leaguers given a Minor League managerial job take everything for granted and teach nothing," Howsam said. "We're building a new breed and it must start at the Minor League level."[13] Among Howsam's Minor League managers in his early years in Cincinnati were future big-league skippers Don Zimmer, Sparky Anderson, and Vern Rapp. Howsam visited his affiliates every year, usually without warning, watching the team play before showing up in the clubhouse and taking everyone to dinner.

After sitting through his first amateur draft with the Reds in June 1967, Howsam was dissatisfied with the performance of scouting director Jim McLaughlin, who tried to overrule scouts who had spent months scouring the country and recommended pitcher Wayne Simpson. "And here was McLaughlin asking about a player he had seen only a couple of times in a tournament," Howsam remembered.[14] McLaughlin, a key man in the Orioles' organization in the 1950s, had clashed there with Paul Richards. McLaughlin returned to Baltimore, where he remained for many years.

Soon after the draft Howsam replaced McLaughlin with Rex Bowen, who had held the same role with the Pirates. Like Howsam and Bender, Bowen was a Rickey man, having played in the Cardinals' organization and then scouted for Rickey with the Cardinals, Dodgers, and Pirates. Among his more famous signings were Maury Wills, Bill Mazeroski, and Dick Groat. He also ran tryout camps and Minor League instructional clinics for Rickey, before becoming scouting director in 1957. Howsam had worked with Bowen in the Minor Leagues and had tremendous respect for his talent evaluation and judgment.

Bowen brought along his younger brother Joe, who had scouted for the Pirates for the previous fifteen years, signing Gene Alley among others. Rex Bowen had a strong personality and was comfortable arguing forcefully for his point of view—a trait Howsam appreciated. Joe had a gentler personality and enjoyed organizational management. Howsam and the Bowens soon realized that Joe should stay in the office and run the scouting department, freeing Rex to work for Howsam as a special-assignment scout. If Howsam needed someone to check on a player, in the Majors or the Minors, he sent Rex. In fact, by the early 1970s Bowen's field had grown considerably, as he was asked to immerse himself in the understanding of such topics as hypnosis and motivational psychology. Although most of this came to nothing, Bowen's study of the effect of light reflection on the human eye led Howsam to change the Reds' hats so that the underside of the bill was medium gray instead of dark green.[15]

Another crucial member of Howsam's inner circle beginning in 1968 was Ray Shore, who had a brief Major League career with the Browns in the 1940s and had spent five years with the Reds as a Major League coach. Howsam made Shore one of baseball's first advance scouts, sending him on the road to watch the team the Reds were going to play next and preparing reports that would help the Reds get ready for each series. Information from Shore was relayed to the pitchers, the hitters, and even the third base coach who needed to know how opposing outfielders were throwing. Howsam also sent Shore to scout players the Reds were considering acquiring. Like Wagner, like Bender, and like the Bowens, Shore remained with Howsam for many years and played a vital role in the organization.

Howsam depended on all of these men and counted on them to tell him the truth. "'Yes' men do you no good," he said. "The rule I had was say what you want, I may not agree with you, but say it. But when you go out that door, don't you ever talk about how that isn't the way you would have done it. We're a team and once we decide what we want to do, nobody's going to second-guess it, or you won't be around long."[16] He had begun his Major League career by walking into a soap opera in St. Louis, but there would be no such drama, ever, in Cincinnati.

When Howsam joined the Reds in January 1967, it was too late to do much to the team other than get everyone signed up and ready for another season. The 1967 club improved from seventy-six to eighty-seven wins with essentially the team that Howsam inherited. Manager Dave Bristol, just thirty-four years old, impressed Howsam enough to get a two-year extension during the season.

Howsam and Bristol had some talent on hand. Pete Rose, a switch-hitting twenty-six-year-old leadoff hitter and one of the game's best young players, was moved to the outfield in 1967 and hit .301. Vada Pinson, still just twenty-eight, had manned center field capably for nine years, sporting a .299 lifetime average with extra-base power. Third baseman Tony Perez had broken through at age twenty-five, stroking

26 home runs with 102 RBI and a game-winning home run in that year's All-Star Game. Tommy Helms, a defensive-minded second baseman, had won the Rookie of the Year Award in 1966. Young first baseman Lee May received his first extended playing time in 1967, hitting 12 home runs in 438 at bats. The pitching staff included a solid core of starters: Jim Maloney, the staff ace for the past several seasons; Gary Nolan, 14-game winner at age nineteen; Milt Pappas, a dependable 15-game winner; and Mel Queen, a converted outfielder who won 14 games in his first year of full-time pitching. Among all of these players, Pappas was the oldest, at just twenty-eight.

The Reds also had some talent in the farm system, including a nineteen-year-old catcher in Buffalo named Johnny Bench. Early in the 1967 season Howsam dispatched scout Charlie Metro to go take a look at Bench. Metro had managed for Howsam in Denver, managed in the Minors for him in St. Louis, and then jumped to the Reds when Howsam moved to Cincinnati. Metro journeyed to Buffalo and reported back that Bench was the best prospect in baseball and one of the best catchers anyone had ever seen. In late August Howsam brought him to the Reds, and he played regularly over the last few weeks of the season. Bench hit only .163 but showed everyone he was ready to play.

With the 1967 season completed Howsam had his first real chance to begin creating the team that he thought could win. Armed with his own belief in the type of team he wanted, plus faith in his talent evaluators, Howsam went to work. Over the next several off-seasons Howsam and the Reds put together an enviable series of deals and built one of history's greatest teams. An examination of these deals and how they came together helps illustrate Howsam's philosophies of team building.

October 10, 1967—Traded corner infielder Deron Johnson (twenty-nine) to the Atlanta Braves in exchange for outfielder Jim Beauchamp (twenty-eight), Mack Jones (twenty-nine), and pitcher Jay Ritchie (thirty-one).

With this deal Howsam relieved a logjam in the Cincinnati infield. Johnson had had a great 1965 season (32 home runs and a league-leading 130 RBI) playing third base, but had regressed considerably the next two years, hitting just .224 with 13 home runs in 1967. Bristol had tried him in left field so that he could play Perez at third and when that failed tried him at first base, which only served to block May. In this exchange Howsam acquired Mack Jones, as good a hitter as Johnson but athletic enough to play all three outfield positions. Beauchamp was a utility player, and Ritchie bullpen depth, but this was also typical of Howsam trades, as he obtained an additional player or two in what seemed like a fair swap without them.

November 21, 1967—Traded outfielder Tommy Harper (twenty-seven) to the Cleveland Indians in exchange for pitcher George Culver (twenty-four), Fred Whitfield (twenty-nine), and outfielder Bob Raudman (twenty-five).

Harper had been a starting outfielder for the Reds since 1963 but, like Johnson, had regressed from a fine 1965 season (18 home runs, 35-for-41 stealing bases, a league-leading 126 runs). The recently acquired Jones appeared to be an upgrade to Harper in right field, and Howsam again managed to get a collection of useful players: Culver had won 7 games as a rookie relief pitcher and could also start, Whitfield would be a powerful left-handed pinch hitter and backup for Lee May at first base, and Raudman provided organizational depth.

January 11, 1968—Traded outfielder Dick Simpson (twenty-four) to the St. Louis Cardinals in exchange for outfielder Alex Johnson (twenty-five).

On talent alone this swap of outfielders was a steal for the Reds. But in the previous four years Johnson had been, to be kind, an enigmatic player who had worn out his welcome in both Philadelphia and St. Louis. He appeared to have All-Star talent but had displayed a notable lack of effort and poor attitude, infuriating managers Gene Mauch and Red Schoendienst. At first blush he seemed like precisely the kind of player Howsam would avoid, but Howsam knew what he was getting—he had traded for him with the Cardinals and had seen his problems up close. Charlie Metro had managed Johnson at Tulsa in 1966, when he hit .355, and gave a solid recommendation. For the cost of Simpson, a reserve outfielder, Howsam decided Johnson's talent was worth another try.

February 8, 1968—Traded catcher Johnny Edwards (twenty-nine) to the St. Louis Cardinals in exchange for Pat Corrales (twenty-six) and infielder Jimy Williams (twenty-four).

Edwards had been the principal catcher for six years, though he had slumped badly the last two seasons (.191 and .206). But this trade was all about clearing the way for Bench, their twenty-year-old prospect. This deal also allowed Howsam to shed Edwards's veteran salary; Howsam never wanted to pay starting-player wages to a bench player if he could help it. Corrales was a solid backup who was paid like one and another player Howsam had acquired during his days as the Cardinals GM. Williams had 14 Major League plate appearances in his past and none in his future.

June 11, 1968—Traded pitcher Milt Pappas (twenty-nine), outfielder Ted Davidson (twenty-eight), and infielder Bob Johnson (thirty-two) to the Atlanta Braves in exchange for shortstop Woody Woodward (twenty-five) and pitchers Clay Carroll (twenty-seven) and Tony Cloninger (twenty-seven).

After the assassination of Robert F. Kennedy, President Johnson declared Saturday, June 8 (the day of the funeral), to be a national day of mourning. When the Reds decided to go through with their scheduled doubleheader against the Cardinals, several of the Reds players, apparently led by Pappas and outfielder Vada Pinson, tried to organize a boycott of the games. Manager Bristol and an irate Howsam talked them out of it, and three days later Pappas, a 16-game winner in 1967 and a successful pitcher for many years before and after, was traded. Pappas had a reputation with Howsam as clubhouse lawyer before this event, mainly due to his role as player representative. "The players elected me their representative," reasoned Pappas, "so I tried to do my best." Howsam denied Pappas's role had anything to do with it, of course.[17]

Given the size of the deal it is unlikely that the attempted boycott was the sole impetus—the trade was likely formulated over several weeks—but Howsam did not hesitate to rid the Reds of rebellious players, as he would show again and again. Davidson and Johnson were little-used utility men. In return, the three acquisitions would be useful parts of the team. Woodward was a great fielder who had lost his starting second base job early that season. Carroll and Cloninger were right-handers coming off poor years but still young enough to turn it around. Ray Shore had strongly advocated for Carroll. "We're pleased with the trade and feel both Cloninger and Carroll will be a tremendous asset to our pitching staff," said Howsam.[18] Dave Bristol later said that Reds scouts thought that Carroll alone was worth the three players the Reds surrendered.[19]

After all the wheeling and dealing, the Reds put up another fourth-place season in 1968, winning 83 games. The biggest disappointments were the arm injuries suffered by pitchers Gary Nolan (sore shoulder) and Mel Queen (forearm, then shoulder). Though the Howsam reign in Cincinnati would be marked with great success, the team struggled to keep its young pitchers healthy. Some of this was simply bad luck, injuries unrelated to the pitching arm, but some of their pitchers broke down after workloads that would be considered excessive decades later. Queen was a former outfielder who pitched 7 innings, the first of his professional career, in 1966. His conversion to pitching began in earnest in Venezuela over the winter, after which he threw 195 2/3 innings (with a solid 2.76 ERA) in 1967. He later related that his arm was sore the entire season, and he showed up the next year unable to pitch. He threw just 30 innings the next two years for the Reds. Nolan, who threw 226 innings as a nineteen-year-old in 1967, would battle a sore arm for the next decade, with several excellent seasons along the way.

On the plus side, Bench took over at catcher and excelled immediately, hitting 15 home runs and earning the first of ten consecutive Gold Glove awards. Pete Rose hit .335 and won his first batting title. Perez and May hit well at the infield corners, and Alex Johnson surprised everyone by winning the left-field job and batting .312. The Reds had far and away the best offense in the league but also the worst ERA. It was the pitching injuries, many observers believed, that kept the Reds from contending.

October 11, 1968—Traded center fielder Vada Pinson (thirty) to the St. Louis Cardinals in exchange for center fielder Bobby Tolan (twenty-two) and pitcher Wayne Granger (twenty-four).

In many ways this was the classic Howsam trade. Pinson was a longtime star and a local favorite, having reached 200 hits four times and holding a .297 lifetime average in an era of low offense. But he appeared to have lost a step on offense (just .271 in 1968) and defense, and Howsam, like Rickey, generally wanted players to grow old on someone else's team. Howsam understood that thirty-year-old players were prone to decline and generally much more expensive than their future production was going to warrant. He did not keep veterans around very long unless they were playing at a star level.

In exchange, he received a promising center fielder who was eight years younger than Pinson and a relief pitcher with a great sinkerball. "With his tremendous speed, Tolan can become a very exciting player," said Howsam.[20] This would prove to be one of Howsam's best trades, and one of his favorites.

November 21, 1968—Traded shortstop Leo Cardenas (twenty-nine) to the Minnesota Twins in exchange for pitcher Jim Merritt (twenty-four).

Cardenas was a veteran who had won a Gold Glove and made four All-Star teams, including the one just four months earlier, but Howsam did not think he was the solution. "I had always heard that Cardenas was an outstanding shortstop. But he had to play in so close, his arm was weak, that he couldn't go in the hole and throw anybody out."[21] The Reds had acquired Woodward five months earlier and felt he could do the job as well as Cardenas. The hidden actor in this story is Darrel Chaney, a slick-fielding twenty-year-old shortstop who had hit 23 home runs in 1968 in the Southern League and looked ready to take over. Again, Howsam was willing to deal the higher-priced veteran to make way for the prospect, trading the veteran before his decline rather than after.

In exchange, Howsam received Merritt, an above-average workhorse who had averaged more than 230 innings the past two seasons. As usual, Howsam got the younger player. The only two members of

the 1968 lineup older than twenty-seven—Pinson and Cardenas—
were now gone.

The Reds were first called the Big Red Machine in 1969, in deference
to their league-leading offense. Bench hit .293 with 26 home runs in
his sophomore season, while Perez (37 homers) and May (38) filled
out a great middle of the order. Rose hit .348 to win another batting
title, Alex Johnson hit .315, and newcomer Tolan hit .305 with 21 home
runs—a season right out of Vada Pinson's prime. The Reds were in
contention in the new NL West all season and in first place as late as
September 8, eventually finishing third with 89 wins.

Ultimately, the club again came up short in pitching: Jim Merritt
won 17 games but with a mediocre 4.37 ERA, while Cloninger was 11-17,
5.03. Maloney was their best hurler (12-5, 2.77) but battled a sore arm
much of the season. "I think we should have won it," recalled Howsam.
"After I reviewed all the clubs in contention, I concluded that we had
the ballclub to win it all."[22]

Howsam, though, did not believe he had the manager to win it all.
Dave Bristol had led the club to three above-.500 finishes and an 89-
win season in 1969. But Howsam thought the club had peaked with
Bristol, and he wanted his own guy. He had long favored Charlie Metro,
who managed for him at Denver and had scouted for Howsam in 1967
before jumping to Kansas City to help put together the expansion
Royals. As it happened, Metro was named the Royals' new manager
literally the day before Howsam convened his inner circle to consider
candidates. The group eventually settled on Sparky Anderson, a longtime Dodger farmhand who played one year for the Phillies in 1959.

Howsam and his advisers knew Anderson well. He had managed for
three years in Howsam's Cardinals organization and in 1968 for the
Reds' club in Asheville, North Carolina, winning two pennants under
Howsam's watch. Howsam visited his Minor League affiliates every
year and spoke with his Minor League managers regularly. Anderson
had left the Reds in 1969 to serve as a coach for the expansion San Diego Padres and had just been hired for 1970 to coach for the California
Angels. Instead, he would manage the Reds.

Howsam received quite a bit of criticism for hiring the unknown Anderson, but he wanted a communicator and an instructor and thought Anderson fitted the bill. "I had seen Sparky many times over the years," remembered Howsam. "He liked young ballplayers; he was willing to work with them. We had some very good young players, but they needed to know how to do certain things. We thought they needed to work on fundamentals. Sparky was extremely capable of that. Sparky was a good family man. He was willing to work and wouldn't be thinking about other things."[23] Like Branch Rickey and George Weiss before him, Howsam did not seem concerned with how other people might judge him. "You just have to make a decision; there are too many people, general managers in particular, that are more interested in their jobs than doing a good job. But if you do a good job, you don't have to worry, that's the thing."[24]

Like Howsam, Anderson was a leader not afraid to delegate authority to the men on his staff. Anderson hired Larry Shepard as pitching coach and allowed him to get his pitchers conditioned and ready to pitch. George Scherger, Anderson's very first professional manager at Santa Barbara in 1953, acted as a key adviser and ran most of the drills in spring training. Ted Kluszewski worked with the hitters, and Alex Grammas worked on defense. All of these men coached for Anderson for years and helped keep the Reds well conditioned and well prepared.

November 25, 1969—Traded outfielder Alex Johnson (twenty-six) and infielder Chico Ruiz (twenty-nine) to the California Angels in exchange for pitchers Jim McGlothlin (twenty-six), Vern Geishert (twenty-three), and Pedro Borbon (twenty-two).

In his two seasons with the Reds, Johnson had hit well (.312 and .315 with midrange power) and had gotten along with manager Bristol and his teammates. This deal was not about getting rid of Johnson; it was about trading surplus offense for some much-needed pitching. The team had two fine outfield prospects in Hal McRae and Bernie Carbo, and Johnson was clearly less valued than fellow outfielders Rose and Tolan.

Jim McGlothlin was the prize: a 200-inning pitcher who had made the 1967 All-Star team and was still young. "We decided there were only 20 pitchers in the American League that interested us," remembered Howsam. "McGlothlin made the list based on his ability, temperament, poise, attitude and behavior on and off the field." Borbon and Geishert were untested and represented Howsam's usual practice of getting an extra player or two in hopes of striking gold. Ray Shore, who had managed Borbon in winter ball, lobbied for the youngster. "I always liked him. He could throw every day and he was tough in relief. I always brought Borbon's name up when we were talking trades. The Angels just didn't hold him up that high."

Although the club had first earned the nickname "the Big Red Machine" locally in 1969, it was their 1970 club that first made it famous, as they soared to 102 wins and an easy division title. Bench, their twenty-two-year-old all-world catcher, took another step forward (45 home runs, 148 RBI, MVP award) to become the best player in the game. Third baseman Tony Perez (40 homers, 129 RBI) was not far behind, while May (34 home runs), Rose (.316), and Tolan (.316 with 57 steals) also had big years. The Reds introduced three rookies on offense: shortstop Dave Concepcion (.260 in half-time play), a Venezuelan signed as an amateur free agent in 1967, and the left-field platoon of Carbo (21 homers and a .454 on-base percentage) and McRae (.248 with 8 homers).

Another rookie garnered even more headlines in 1970: starting pitcher Wayne Simpson, who was 13-1 with a 2.27 ERA in the season's first half. In late July he tore his rotator cuff and was ineffective in limited action the rest of the year, never again attaining stardom. Nolan had a fine year (18-7), as did Howsam acquisitions Merritt, McGlothlin, Cloninger, Granger, and Carroll as well as yet another rookie, nineteen-year-old Don Gullett. The Reds beat the Pirates in the National League Championship Series (NLCS), before falling to the Orioles in the World Series.

One of the high points of the 1970 season for Howsam was the July opening of Riverfront Stadium, which hosted the All-Star Game just two weeks later. The park was already being planned when he arrived in Cincinnati, but it was Howsam who insisted upon a spotless facility, clean restrooms, friendly ushers, and efficiency everywhere. "Our fans range from infants in the arms of their parents to old-timers who might hobble into the park with the aid of canes," he said. "This pleases me."[25] He also had artificial turf installed, part of an ongoing trend with new facilities. Howsam, like Rickey, believed in team speed—a skill that helped on both offense and defense—and his new ballpark would place an added premium on speed afoot, creating a better brand of baseball in the bargain.

Howsam earned widespread praise for the Reds' pennant and for the character of the team he had created. "Bob Howsam traded away 80 percent of the people he found when he got here," marveled Anderson, "and 60 percent of those were clubhouse lawyers." An unnamed player said, "You know why we won the National League pennant? Because there were no cliques on this ball club."[26] The Reds were great, and they were also remarkably young. Rose, at twenty-eight, was the oldest regular player or pitcher on the team. The future was very bright indeed.

On January 6, 1971, Tolan ruptured his Achilles' tendon playing basketball, an injury originally expected to sideline him until June but eventually costing him the entire 1971 season. Both Howsam and Anderson were angry about the injury: Tolan played on a team with several other Reds players, including Rose, Bench, and May, and they had been asked not to play. In 1971 teams typically had no contractual way to forbid such off-season activities. For Howsam, this was an event for which his dogged preparedness had no answer. Tolan had been a vital piece of his grand design.

May 29, 1971—Traded shortstop Frank Duffy (twenty-four) and Vern Geishert (twenty-five) to the San Francisco Giants in exchange for outfielder George Foster (twenty-two).

Without Tolan, Anderson had to scramble to find a center fielder. He first tried Hal McRae, who had formed a great left-field platoon with Bernie Carbo in 1970. He then turned to Ty Cline, Buddy Bradford (acquired in early May), Rose, and even Concepcion (who started five games in center). The team was struggling generally, but center field was one of the larger aggravations.

Duffy forced the team's hand by refusing to report to Triple-A when the Reds optioned him in mid-May. Howsam began looking for a trading partner and sent his scouts out on the road looking at prospects. The Giants offered Minor League outfielder Bernie Williams, leading both Howsam and Shore to visit Phoenix to scout him. When the Reds agreed to accept a trade for Duffy, the Giants backed off, instead offering Foster, who was showing promise (.267 with signs of power) with the Major League club. Shore was stunned, as he much preferred Foster. "He was raw, but he showed some power," he recalled.[27] Howsam took the opportunity to add Geishert to the deal, and it was done. A few days after arriving Foster started in center field.

In a season beset with injuries and off-years, the Reds fell back to fourth place. Besides the Tolan injury, both Simpson and Merritt battled arm woes, and each was finished as an effective Major League pitcher. The offense fell off dramatically, from 775 runs scored to 586. Bench hit just 27 home runs with 61 RBI, while Perez, Carbo, and McRae all saw their production decline. On the plus side, twenty-year-old Gullett stepped forward (16-6, 2.65) to become the best pitcher on the staff. But when Howsam and his inner circle met in September 1971, they knew they had work to do.

The men on whose advice Howsam relied huddled over several days of meetings that September: Chief Bender, Ray Shore, Rex Bowen, Joe Bowen, and Sparky Anderson. "I worked somewhat like Branch Rickey," Howsam recalled. "I wanted my scouts to be able to tell me everything I needed and put it all together, and as a group we would talk about it. And we got everyone in priority."[28]

The group determined that the club's biggest needs were more speed, more left-handed hitting, and better defense. Pete Rose led the 1971 club with only 13 stolen bases, and this overall lack of speed was more glaring in their new stadium. The Reds had lived with Perez out of position at third base in Crosley Field, but the speedy new artificial surface at Riverfront magnified his poor range. Without Tolan, Howsam spent the season watching balls continually find the gaps and roll unimpeded to the distant fences. "I started bearing down in my scouting on outfielder's defense," remembered Shore. "At Crosley, you could get by with slower guys, but boy, the minute you moved to turf, if you don't have speed, you can get killed."[29] Moreover, the Reds' own hitters were often too slow to take the extra base when their hits skipped through the opposing defense.

To correct the imbalance on the team, the Reds were willing to sacrifice some right-handed power. The man Anderson wanted, he told Howsam, was Houston second baseman Joe Morgan. Morgan, twenty-eight years old, was a left-handed hitter and a great base stealer (40 or more steals for the past three seasons) who hit more than most middle infielders—just a .251 average in 1971, but with 51 extra-base hits and 88 walks. He would either replace or supplement Bobby Tolan's speed game, depending on whether Tolan could make it back.

It was no secret that Morgan did not get along with Astros manager Harry Walker. Morgan has maintained that Walker was a racist who did not appreciate any of the black players on the Astros. Jimmie Wynn, in his recent memoirs, backs this up. Some other black players of the period, such as Bill White, liked Walker. What is not in dispute is that Walker and Morgan disagreed on how Morgan should play baseball. They disagreed on how to hit, when to run the bases, and what strategies to use to try to win the game. Morgan often grumbled about it, and Walker would respond by asking Morgan to bunt more.

Howsam asked Ray Shore to look into the matter further and report back. This sort of scouting was routine for the Reds. "You want to make sure you have the right person," Howsam recalled. "If you don't go to great lengths to find out what is right and how to do it, then you are not doing your job. One reason we were successful [is that] we knew about the players we were going to trade for; we knew them on and off the field; we knew them and their backgrounds."[30]

Ray Shore spent the last few weeks of the 1971 season with the Astros, scouting Morgan. Shore knew everyone and knew how to get the information he needed. One of his sources was Harry Kalas, a radio broadcaster for the Astros at the time. Kalas liked Morgan, thought him bright and competitive, and believed that Walker mismanaged him. Shore concluded that Morgan would be a great addition to the club and further believed that he might be available. Howsam knew that Houston wanted a power hitter and, with the group's blessing, said he would contact Astros general manager Spec Richardson and offer Lee May straight up for Morgan. One of the further benefits of the contemplated deal was that it would allow the Reds to move Perez back to first base and Helms to third, shoring up their defense considerably.

Francis Dale, the Reds' president, was impressed by the thoroughness of Howsam and his staff. "He could go to [Astros' general manager Spec] Richardson, and Richardson so respected Bob's judgment that Howsam could sit down with him and say, 'I've studied and analyzed your team and here are my reports on what your team needs. What your team needs is this, and so on.' And he so convinced the Houston team about what they needed that he was then able to say, 'I just happen to have what you need.' It was thorough professionalism."[31]

The Houston Astros played in the Astrodome, one of the most extreme pitchers parks in modern history, particularly after they moved the fences out in 1966. The Astros hit just 18 home runs at home in 1971. Another reason for the club's lack of power was that Walker did not value the young power hitters he had, such as John Mayberry and Bob Watson, and tried to get them to hit the ball to the opposite field. Meanwhile, Houston's most common first baseman in 1971, Dennis Menke, hit .246 with 1 home run.

Richardson did not accept Howsam's offer, instead shopping Morgan around to other clubs. The Reds and Astros kept in touch over the next several weeks, until Richardson said he wanted to expand the deal to include Helms (who would replace Morgan for the Astros) and Menke (whom the Reds could play at third base). Howsam, who always worked alone once his course had been set, anticipated this sensible balancing and used it as an opportunity to ask for more. His scouts had thoroughly scoured the Houston roster and found two players that were largely unnecessary to the Astros. Jack Billingham was a workhorse (228 innings in 1971) league-average starting pitcher somewhat lost among a group of younger and more talented pitchers. Cesar Geronimo was a brilliant defensive center fielder with a great throwing arm who was playing behind the best young center fielder in the game, Cesar Cedeno. Howsam boldly asked for both players.

Further negotiation added two more players, and the trade was announced on November 29, two months after Howsam had first placed the call.

November 29, 1971—Traded first baseman Lee May (twenty-eight), second baseman Tommy Helms (thirty), and utility man Jimmy Stewart (thirty-two) to the Houston Astros in exchange for second baseman Joe Morgan (twenty-eight), infielder Denis Menke (thirty-one), pitcher Jack Billingham (twenty-eight), outfielder Cesar Geronimo (twenty-three), and outfielder Ed Armbrister (twenty-three).

The reaction to the trade was mostly pro-Houston. May and Helms were very popular players in Cincinnati, while many observers thought of Morgan as a worse fielding version of Helms. This judgment would prove wildly incorrect. Over the next five seasons Morgan would be the best player in baseball, averaging .303 with a .431 on-base percentage, 22 home runs, 113 runs, 62 steals, and winning four Gold Gloves. He had two spectacular MVP seasons in 1975 and 1976, capping off one of the best five-year peaks in baseball history, comparable to those of Willie Mays and Mickey Mantle.

Howsam later estimated that the Reds spent three thousand man-hours working on the Astros deal, the equivalent of a single person working forty hours a week for a year and a half.[32] The effort more than paid off for Howsam and his team.

December 3, 1971—Traded pitcher Wayne Granger (twenty-seven) to the Minnesota Twins for pitcher Tom Hall (twenty-four).

With the emergence of Clay Carroll as the team's right-handed relief ace in 1971, the Reds swapped the still-effective Granger for another reliever who was younger, threw harder than anyone on the Reds staff, and was left-handed. The Reds had been looking for a left-handed pitcher for several years.

The 1972 Reds won 95 games and returned to the World Series. Tolan's effective return, Bench's comeback MVP season, and Morgan's ascent to stardom gave the team even more firepower, and it was an upset when they lost the World Series to the Oakland Athletics. This matchup came to be known as the "Hairs against the Squares," a battle between the rough and scruffy A's and the clean-cut and gentlemanly Reds. Howsam was unapologetic about his team and its image. "Some people have accused me of being old fashioned," he wrote in his memoirs. "They felt that none of this made a difference as long as the players can play the game. I felt that it made a lot of difference to a lot of fans, particularly in a solid community as Cincinnati, and it made a lot of difference to me personally. We took a lot of adverse criticism for it because these were the 70's . . . but we filled a lot of stadium seats, and I'm convinced that our concept of entertainment as well as the excellence of our team is what brought the people in."[33] As Howsam was aware, his Reds outdrew the A's by two to one, even while Oakland was winning three consecutive championships.

We discussed the Oakland A's at some length in our previous book, *Paths to Glory*,[34] but a short digression may be of some value here. Owner Charles Finley built a team that won three consecutive World Series without a coherent organization. A man without any baseball experience, he essentially operated as his own general manager, while giving front-office roles to his wife and his brother. Given the lack of talent and experience in management, his success is remarkable. That he had success while antagonizing nearly everyone he came in contact with, from the other owners to the players to the press, makes his accomplishment truly astonishing.

Finley may have been tactless, rude, and vulgar, but he also outworked nearly everyone and had more ideas and imagination than any other owner. He spent countless hours on the phone, usually with someone who would rather have been doing anything other than talking to Finley. He was a professional salesman, and he worked his fellow owners by browbeating them until they might give in. Finley built the A's precisely the way a great team ought to be built: he signed or drafted dozens of quality players, sifted through them for a few years until a bunch of them developed, made a couple of key trades to redistribute the talent, and provided depth with veteran role players.

Finley did well both before and after the advent of the amateur draft. In late 1964 Finley claimed that he had spent $634,000 during the past year for eighty players, one of the largest totals in baseball. When the amateur draft began in 1965, Finley immediately landed another bumper crop of players—partly because the A's poor records led to high picks—but also because they selected the right players. In these three signing years, from 1964 to 1966, Finley invested perhaps

$2 million in two hundred players. This group included three future members of the Baseball Hall of Fame (Catfish Hunter, Rollie Fingers, and Reggie Jackson) and several other future All-Stars (Rick Monday, Joe Rudi, Gene Tenace, Blue Moon Odom, and Sal Bando).

The A's cut back dramatically on their scouting and signing activities at this point and, in fact, received only limited contributions from players signed after 1966 (with Vida Blue a notable exception). Finley made a couple of key trades over the next few years to reconfigure his talent and assemble the bulk of the squad that would go on to such success. Finley's genius may not be duplicable, but his recognition and reaction to the changing source of amateur talent need to be acknowledged. As the owners discussed ways to limit the free-for-all for amateur prospects, Finley outworked and outspent his rivals to grab as many as he could. His further success in baseball's first two drafts testifies to his ability to take advantage of this dramatic change in the method of amateur talent sourcing.

November 30, 1972—Traded Wayne Simpson and Hal McRae to Kansas City Royals in exchange for Roger Nelson (twenty-eight) and Richie Scheinblum (thirty).

The same methodical procedure that culminated in the Morgan trade in 1971 led to this less successful deal twelve months later. Howsam and his staff wanted to trade some of their outfield excess for a starting pitcher, and Ray Shore recommended Nelson as one of the best pitchers in the American League. When the Reds staff assembled to rank all the pitchers in baseball, Nelson came in eleventh (Philadelphia's Steve Carlton was first). After years of promise the Royals' first pick in the 1968 expansion draft came through in 1972 with an 11-6 record 6 shutouts and a 2.06 ERA that was fifth in the league. Scheinblum was a journeyman outfielder coming off a surprising .300 season that had earned him a trip to the All-Star Game.

To get these two players the Reds dealt Simpson, who had been hurt for two and a half years, and McRae, whose defensive struggles had made him a poor fit for the Reds. This deal stands out for Howsam because it was a rare case where he acquired players who were at the peak of their perceived value, and, in fact, he was very close to walking away from this trade in its final configuration. Royals GM Cedric Tallis was selling high, and the Reds were betting that their new players' recent advances were real. McRae had many years of stardom in Kansas City, albeit serving as a designated hitter, a spot not available in the Reds' National League.

June 12, 1973—Traded outfielder Gene Locklear (twenty-three), pitcher Mike Johnson (twenty-two), and cash to the San Diego Padres in exchange for pitcher Fred Norman (thirty).

By mid-June the Reds, the defending league champions, were struggling. Roger Nelson began the season in the rotation and had pitched well (2.06 ERA at the end of May) but had developed a sore arm that would plague him for the remainder of his career. With the continued absence of Gary Nolan (who would start just two games) and the ineffectiveness of McGlothlin (who would be traded in August), the Reds were desperate for a starting pitcher. Norman had been a dependable starter for a few years but was struggling (1-7, 4.26) with a terrible Padres team. Howsam's scouts liked his stuff, and Anderson had been impressed by Norman's lone victory: a complete-game 6-hit 3–1 victory over the Reds at Riverfront Stadium.

Howsam had little difficulty convincing the Padres that they had no need for Norman, especially when he was willing to send some money along to the financially strapped San Diego owners. Anderson stuck Norman into the rotation immediately, and he responded with complete-game shutouts in his first two starts. Locklear was a valued prospect who had no place to play, while Johnson was in the Minor Leagues.

From July 1973 onward the club was dominant again, finishing 60-26 over the final 86 games and winning 99 games overall, the best record in baseball. Rose won his third batting title and the MVP award, while Bench, Morgan, and Perez had fine years to lead a solid offense. Bobby Tolan (.206) had a lost season, culminating in emotional and disciplinary issues. When added to Denis Menke at third (.191) and Geronimo in center (.210), Anderson had three holes in the lineup, causing Howsam to reach into the Minor Leagues to bring up Dan

Driessen (.301 in 366 at bats) to play third and Ken Griffey (.384 in 86 at bats) to play right field. Gary Nolan could pitch only 2 games, but Billingham (19 wins), Gullett, Norman, and Ross Grimsley made up a fine rotation.

Surprisingly, the Reds lost a 5-game League Championship Series (LCS) to a New York Mets team that had won just 82 games during the season. The Reds were beaten mainly by the great pitching of Tom Seaver, Jon Matlack, and Jerry Koosman. For Howsam, the loss was doubly bitter because he had to endure "the worst experience, the darkest day I ever had in baseball." Late in the fifth and final game, which the Mets won easily, 9–2, the Mets opened the gates and let thousands of people come into the stadium to prepare for the celebration. Instead, many of the "young hoodlums" seized upon Howsam and his party, including dignitaries from Ohio, screaming profanities, grabbing the ladies' hair, and spitting on them. "I am convinced to this day," Howsam recalled years later, "remembering the crazed faces of those monsters, that most of them if not all were under the influence of drugs."[35] Howsam's group had to climb onto the field to escape the mob and leave via the Reds' dugout. The event only solidified Howsam's pride in his own stadium and fans.

After the season the *Sporting News* named Howsam its Major League Executive of the Year for the first time, though he had won the award twice in the Minor Leagues. He did not have a Morgan deal on his 1973 résumé, but his acquisitions of Norman and bench players Andy Kosco and Phil Gagliano were cited as moves that kept the Reds on top. Upon hearing the news Howsam typically pointed out that running the Reds was anything but a one-man operation.[36]

November 9, 1973—Traded outfielder Bobby Tolan (twenty-seven) and pitcher Dave Tomlin (twenty-four) to the San Diego Padres in exchange for Clay Kirby (twenty-five).

After a fine comeback season in 1972, Tolan had seemed a big part of the Cincinnati Reds. In the spring he expressed how happy he was to be on the team. "I don't know what it's like on the outside of this organization, but there is absolutely no trouble here. With a Rose, a Johnny Bench, Joe Morgan, there can't be. These are highly paid players and they could stick to themselves. But they don't. They take in the kids. We're all together. There's no black or white on this team."[37] But as his long summer slump in 1973 dragged on, he became more and more distant. Growing tired of the verbal sparring his teammates engaged in, Tolan began sitting by himself in the dugout, grew a beard and kept his Afro long (both in defiance of team rules), missed scheduled appointments, and engaged in a physical confrontation with Chief Bender. He was fined and suspended in September. "I liked Bobby Tolan," Howsam lamented later, "admired him as a man and as a ball player, and wanted him to be a continuing part of our big future. But it wasn't meant to be."[38]

Kirby had been the Padres' best pitcher for several years, though he had not pitched well in 1973 (8-18, 4.79). The Reds hoped he could blossom with a better team behind him, as had Norman when liberated from the same Padres five months before.

December 4, 1973—Traded pitcher Ross Grimsley (twenty-three) and catcher Wally Williams to the Baltimore Orioles in exchange for outfielder Merv Rettenmund, infielder Junior Kennedy, and catcher Bill Wood (twenty-two).

Howsam and Anderson had very conservative views about the look and decorum of their players. They were insistent that the Reds wear their uniform a certain way—not too baggy, socks visible up nearly to the knee, low stirrups, black shoes—and that their uniforms were clean and pressed each day. In an era of increasing facial hair in the culture generally and baseball specifically, the Reds stood out for their short hair and lack of facial hair. Off the field the club wanted players to act professionally, both to protect the team's image and to ensure that the players were fully prepared to come to work each day at full strength.

One player who resisted these protocols was Grimsley, a highly talented young left-handed pitcher who had been a steady member of the starting rotation for three seasons. Anderson did not appreciate Grimsley's flaunting of team rules, with his long hair and supposedly wild lifestyle. In the team's end-of-the-year meetings, Anderson requested that Grimsley be traded. "Bob probably listened to me more when it was a player on our staff," Anderson said.

"I liked Ross," recalled Shore, "but I didn't try to protect him. One thing I told Sparky was I will argue abilities with you, but I'm not going to argue personalities. You live with them. If you say this guy disrupts my clubhouse, he's uncoachable or whatever, I can't argue the point."[39] The Reds' traditional approach worked because the leaders on the team, like Rose, Morgan, and Bench, agreed and went along. If the approach cost them a Ross Grimsley, Howsam and Anderson believed it gained them more than that. What would have happened had one of the team's stars balked is an interesting question.

In the era before free agency, general managers were more often judged by their ability to make trades, which was the best way to improve the big-league roster. As our detailed analysis of his trades highlight, Howsam proved a master of using this approach for both tactical and strategic advantage. In his dozen years at the helm in Cincinnati, Howsam surrendered 258 future WAR and received 332, a net gain of 74 WAR. Given that an average draft class supplies roughly 30 WAR, his trades netted the equivalent of two and a half draft classes. More important, however, Howsam successfully used his trades to build the team he wanted: he added speed, youth, and character players; he addressed position shortcomings and pitching weaknesses; and he did this all without surrendering any of his core players.

The 1974 Reds had another outstanding season, winning 98 games—the second most in the game. Unfortunately, it was 4 games fewer than the Los Angeles Dodgers, who beat them out in the NL West. Kirby stepped up to replace Grimsley, Driessen took over at third (though his defensive struggles would keep him from staying there), and Foster and Griffey shared right field. It was a fine team that had the misfortune of being in the same division with a Dodger team that put together a great season.

For the first time since he had become a general manager, Howsam did not make significant changes to his team after the 1974 season. The Reds had a handful of stars, several very good players, and a farm system that kept cranking out regulars. Howsam was apparently at a loss for how to improve his creation. In Morgan, Bench, and Rose, he had three of the very best players in baseball. Perez and Concepcion were All-Star performers. Geronimo, Foster, Griffey, and Driessen provided defense, speed, and versatility. The starting rotation (Billingham, Gullett, Norman, and Kirby) was solid, and the bullpen (mainly Carroll and Borbon) was excellent.

The club did have one obvious missing piece: third base. Anderson finally abandoned the notion that Driessen could play there and concluded that the recently acquired John Vukovich could not hit. In early May 1975 Anderson made the bold decision to shift Rose to third base, a position he had briefly played nine years earlier. Anderson consulted with Rose, but not with Howsam, who was reportedly alarmed when he read about it in the paper. The new alignment allowed Anderson to play Foster in left field and Griffey in right field, solidifying what has come to be regarded as the greatest eight-man lineup in Major League history. Coupled with a fine pitching staff, especially Gullett and a dominant bullpen (supplemented by rookie Rawley Eastwick and youngster Will McEnaney), the Reds ran away with the division, winning 108 games and beating the Dodgers by 20 games. An easy NLCS victory over the Pirates followed, before a grueling, and ultimately victorious, seven-game World Series against the Boston Red Sox.

The enduring nickname "the Big Red Machine," forged during the years 1969 and 1970 when they led the league in home runs and featured three right-handed sluggers, stuck with the club even after the term no longer fitted the same way. The 1970 team hit a league-leading 191 home runs and stole 115 bases. The 1975 team hit a respectable 124 homers, but led the league with 168 steals against only 36 caught stealing. (The next year they stole 210 with only 57 caught stealing.) Because they had both the best base runners and the best defensive catcher, they dominated this aspect of the game. As an illustration, in the 1975 postseason Cincinnati base runners were successful in 20 of 22 attempts to steal, while Reds opponents were 0 for 2. Sometimes the stolen base was not even necessary: in the final NLCS game the Reds scored the winning run in the tenth inning when Griffey singled, advanced to second when he got the Pirate pitcher to balk, moved to third on a ground ball, and scored on a fly ball.

In 42 postseason games between 1970 and 1976 with Bench catching, the Reds outstole their opponents by an incredible 53-2. Bob Howsam loved the running game, and no one ever did it better than his Cincinnati Reds. As Howsam learned from Rickey, this speed helped even more on defense, where the Reds won four Gold Gloves in 1975, all at the crucial up-the-middle positions: catcher Bench, second baseman Morgan, shortstop Concepcion, and center fielder Geronimo.

The Reds, virtually unchanged outside of their reserves, won again in 1976, and these two teams are ranked among the greatest baseball teams ever. The 1976 team swept the Yankees in the World Series, the crowning achievement of Howsam's career. He later said that he felt some sadness knowing that no team would ever be put together the way his team had. Howsam was referring to the onset of player free agency, which led to available star players in the upcoming off-season for the first time. Howsam was one of baseball's most vocal hawks on labor matters, speaking out for holding the line during the 1972 strike and the 1976 lockout.

Howsam and the Reds did not adjust well to the changing landscape. They lost star pitcher Don Gullett to free agency after the 1976 season and several others in the coming years, foremost among them Rose and Morgan. After a slow start in 1977 Howsam acquired pitcher Tom Seaver from the Mets. Despite Seaver's great second half, the Reds could not catch the Dodgers. After the season Howsam resigned, taking a position as vice chairman of the board, while appointing Dick Wagner as his successor. Wagner's regime was contentious, and he became the scapegoat with the fans and the press for losing the well-known players and the deteriorating performance of the team. The club contended for a few years before falling to last place in 1982.

Midway through the 1983 season Howsam returned as general manager, a position he held for two years. Howsam's biggest move was to reacquire Rose in August 1984 and make him the player-manager of the team. Rose helped turn the team around, as they finished in second place for four straight seasons beginning in 1985. Howsam retired, as planned, effective July 1, 1985. His insistence on keeping to his retirement date was solidified by the sale of the team in late 1984 to Marge Schott, with whom Howsam did not get along. While

Howsam had stayed busy with the team during his five years as vice chairman, this parting was a real retirement. Howsam's long career in the game had ended.

Howsam had more power than most general managers, as both Francis Dale and later Louis Nippert (who bought a controlling interest in 1973) let him represent the club at ownership meetings. Dale held the title of president even though he did not meddle much, but during the Nippert years Howsam received that title as well. By the time he joined the Reds, most contemporary GMs, and certainly all GMs in the years since his retirement, worked for an active team owner or president who was the face of the team. Howsam represented one of the last of a breed.

PART 3 • *New Order*

14 Long Road Back

Sometimes it's painful, and balancing what's best for the future and now isn't easy. People are patient to an extent, but it's not going to last very long. You have to stay strong in your convictions and believe in what you're doing.
—DAVE DOMBROWSKI, baseball executive

When New York Yankees owner George Steinbrenner died in 2010, having presided over the franchise for thirty-seven years and seven championships, his obituary in the *New York Times* credited him for taking over a "declining Yankees team" and building it into a powerhouse.[1] In the *Washington Post*, it was said that he "transformed a team failing at the box office and on the field," while the *Wall Street Journal* suggested that he turned "a moribund franchise" into the most powerful team in sports.[2] Although there is no denying the accomplishments of the Yankees on Steinbrenner's watch, the degree of disarray he inherited has been exaggerated. The man who inherited a Yankee team in disarray was Mike Burke, who had been team president for six years when Steinbrenner took charge and who had begun the process of turning the ship around.

Unlike the other teams we explore in this book, the Yankees during the reign of Burke and general manager Lee MacPhail never reached the postseason. Nevertheless, their story is interesting because it illustrates the difficulty even competent baseball men, even in baseball's largest and most prestigious market, had in rebuilding a franchise under the unique circumstances of the era.

Before 1965 the Yankees could use their money and prestige to land the best Minor Leaguers and later the top amateur talent, helping them stay on top for decades. After 1976, with the advent of baseball free agency, a team with deep pockets had the advantage of being able to afford the best veteran Major Leaguers on the market. In the intervening years rich teams like the Yankees had neither advantage.

In order to get the best amateur players, a team had to outscout and outdevelop the competition. The top black players were by this time all in organized baseball. There were no poor teams forced to sell their stars. To acquire the best Major League talent took astute scouting and trading. Building a team, even a team like the Yankees, would take brains and a fair bit of patience.

As we have seen, by 1960 the New York Yankees had been owned for thirteen years by the partnership of Del Webb and Dan Topping, with Topping serving as president, George Weiss as general manager, and Casey Stengel (since 1949) as manager. Under the direction of Weiss, a superb cadre of scouts, and a great development system, the team kept churning out star after star, hardly missing a beat as Joe DiMaggio, Tommy Henrich, Allie Reynolds, and Phil Rizzuto made way for Mickey Mantle, Yogi Berra, Whitey Ford, Gil McDougald, Elston Howard, and plenty more. Weiss also made a number of shrewd acquisitions, adding the likes of Eddie Lopat, Johnny Mize, Clete Boyer, and Roger Maris, all of whom helped win multiple titles. The team won ten pennants and seven World Series in twelve years under the Weiss and Stengel regime.

After losing the 1960 World Series Topping forced out Weiss and Stengel, replacing them with Roy Hamey and Ralph Houk. After three more pennants and two world championships, in 1964 Houk moved upstairs to replace Hamey and hired Berra as manager. The club captured another pennant, its fourteenth in sixteen years. Like all Yankee teams of the previous four decades, this club was an effective blend of experience and youth. Mantle and Ford, two of the league's best players, were thirty-two and thirty-three, respectively, but still playing well. Maris, Tony Kubek, and Bobby Richardson were in their late twenties. In just the past few years the Yankees farm system had produced shortstop-outfielder Tom Tresh (now twenty-five), already a two-time all-star; pitcher Jim Bouton (twenty-five), the winner of thirty-nine games in the previous two years; pitcher Mel Stottlemyre (twenty-two), who was called up in mid-1964 and finished 9-3 in twelve starts; pitcher Al Downing (twenty-three), winner of thirteen games each of the past two seasons; and first baseman Joe Pepitone (twenty-three), who had just hit thirty-one home runs. The only key old player was Howard (thirty-five), though he was coming off his best two seasons. The Yankees had stayed on top for decades by continually producing young talent, and the latest crop looked typically promising.

In November 1964 Webb and Topping sold 80 percent of the Yankees to the Columbia Broadcasting System for fourteen million dollars. Although the sale caused worry in some quarters, and near panic in the media and around baseball, CBS claimed no intention of influencing the running of the team, and there is no record that they did so. The purchase was part of a concerted diversification effort for the company—in this period they also purchased magazine publishers, toy companies, and the electric guitar company Fender. The Yankees were a famous and successful enterprise, and their continued success would only further enhance CBS's brand. To run the Yankees, Topping and Houk remained as president and GM, respectively, though Houk fired Berra after the 1964 World Series in favor of Johnny Keane.

And, just like that, the 1965 Yankees collapsed to sixth place, their worst showing since 1925.

The team declined principally for the same reasons most teams decline: injuries (to Mantle, Maris, Kubek, and Bouton, among others) and aging (especially Elston Howard, who suddenly played like the thirty-six-year-old catcher that he was). They were also somewhat unlucky (they outscored their opponents but still finished 77-85). In reality, the collapse was "shocking" only because they were the Yankees, who had finished over .500 for thirty-nine consecutive seasons. Several other pennant winners from the period dropped to the second division the following year, including the 1960 Pirates and the 1966 Dodgers and Orioles. But such a result was not supposed to happen to the Yankees, who had survived the losses of Babe Ruth and Lou Gehrig and Joe DiMaggio without missing a beat. Many observers, including perhaps the people running the Yankees, believed that they would "replace" Mickey Mantle and Whitey Ford the same way. The early 1960s Yankees were a fairly top-heavy team, with much of their talent tied up in a handful of stars. When Maris, Howard, Ford, and Mantle got hurt or old (or both) at the same time, no farm system could have realistically filled such huge holes.

One might reasonably wonder why some of the promising young Yankee players from the early 1960s did not have better careers than they did. Jerry Coleman, a former Yankee infielder and a team broadcaster by the 1960s, offered one explanation: "They slid into a degenerate-type thing. That's why they went downhill."[3] Jim Bouton's classic book *Ball Four*,[4] released in 1970, detailed stories of the Yankees' off-field drinking and women chasing and his admiration for how Mickey Mantle could drink all night and play the next day. Mantle later owned up to this behavior that likely shortened his own great career (and life).

"Don't do what I do," Mantle once told Pepitone. Unfortunately, as Jane Leavy detailed in her biography of Mantle, the young players revered Mantle and wanted to do nothing so much as hang out late at night with the Mick. "I didn't care if I slept at all in New York," outfielder Steve Whitaker, a once-promising prospect, later said. "It's open 24/7, and, trust me, I closed it." Unfortunately, the fun came at a price. "In fact," he says, "it was probably the end of my career." Bouton pointed out to Leavy that the team drank and caroused just as much when they were winning as when they were losing, but admitted, "We weren't as good at it in 1965. We didn't have the energy for it."[5]

In the years after Weiss left the organization the club made very few player transactions, apparently confident that they could keep winning with their own players. "We'll get the edge again, the way we always have," farm director Johnny Johnson said in 1965. "With superior scouting."[6] Houk made no material deals either prior to or during the 1965 season. That fall he acquired thirty-year-old shortstop Ruben Amaro from the Phillies to try to replace Kubek, whose injuries had forced his retirement. Otherwise, the Yankee strategy seemed to be to wait for their players to return to their previous levels. After the 1966 team started 4-16, Topping convinced Houk to return to the dugout as manager. Keane was fired, and Topping's son Dan Jr. was anointed as the interim GM. The Yankees played better briefly (winning thirteen of Houk's first seventeen) before sinking to finish 70-89, in tenth (last) place. It was not a terrible team—their run differential was 611–612—but the Yankees had not finished last since 1912. More important, the team did not have anyone who looked likely to get any better and many players who appeared finished. Their future looked bleaker than their present.

One of the reasons for the Yankees' decline was their lack of African American talent. They had developed just one quality black player, Elston Howard, in an era when these men were making huge inroads in the game. In the two decades after Jackie Robinson's 1947 debut, there were seventeen black Hall of Famers who debuted in the Major Leagues. For the most part, the teams who actively signed and developed these players became the strong teams, and the teams that did not struggled to compete. The Yankees were the exception, as they rode stars like Mantle, Berra, and Ford to pennant after pennant. Now, perhaps, the problem was catching up with them.

In September 1966 Topping Sr. sold his remaining 10 percent stake to CBS (Webb had sold out the year before) and resigned as president after nineteen years, most likely with the encouragement of his employer. Though Topping had enjoyed tremendous success with the Yankees, the task ahead was unlike any he had faced in his wildly successful tenure. "My family lives permanently in Florida, and I have many other outside activities," he said at the time. "I think it is in the best interests of the Yankees as well as for myself to leave at this time."[7] To replace Topping Sr., CBS appointed Mike Burke, who had been an executive at CBS for several years and on the Yankee board for the past two.

By the late 1960s many of the most successful franchises, such as Detroit, Cincinnati, and Boston, were overseen by a strong general manager. As the off-field business became more complex and baseball ownerships became more corporate, teams began installing a nonbaseball man, often with little or no equity in the franchise, as the senior executive. Not surprisingly, a large conglomerate like CBS, with vast business holdings in a variety of industries, turned to a versatile business executive like Burke to run the Yankees.

Burke, who wore tailored suits made in Rome, cut a dashing figure, especially compared with the staid and conservative Yankees. He had been a football star at Penn, a war hero, a drinking buddy of Ernest Hemingway, an agent with the Office of Strategic Services, and an executive with Ringling Brothers circus, before joining CBS. His job now was to restore a legendary baseball team to its proper place of glory. "I won't be satisfied," he said, "until the Yankees are once again the champions of the world."[8]

His first public act, on September 27, was to fire beloved broadcaster Red Barber. Burke said that the decision predated his tenure (Topping had described the broadcasting crew as "horrible" in a May memo),[9] but the public and press reacted harshly and considered this a poor beginning. Red Smith, satirically praising the Yankees for their foresight in firing "the best reporter that ever covered baseball on the air," wrote, "A guy that honest had to get canned. The chump was telling the truth about the Yankees."[10]

Burke did better in his second act, hiring Lee MacPhail as general manager on October 13, replacing Dan Topping Jr. MacPhail's father, Larry, had run the Yankees in the 1940s, but Lee had more than bloodlines on his résumé. He had started working for his father in Brooklyn and New York and later served George Weiss's Yankees as farm director from 1948 to 1958, highly productive years for the organization. He left the Yankees to become general manager of the Baltimore Orioles, helping build the team that won the 1966 World Series. MacPhail left the Orioles in late 1965 when he was asked to serve as the assistant to new baseball commissioner William Eckert. After just a single year in the job, MacPhail wanted to get back to running a team, and he answered Burke's plea. "This is not a tenth place club, but we've got a long row to hoe," admitted MacPhail.[11] Soon after MacPhail took the Yankee job, the *Sporting News* named him Executive of the Year for his work building the Orioles and hand-holding Eckert.

One person who did not approve of Lee MacPhail's new job was Larry MacPhail, retired to his Maryland farm but never one to shy away from a story. "I advised Lee several times not to take the job," said Larry. "CBS doesn't know anything about baseball. Certainly Burke doesn't. I've got great confidence in Lee's ability, but someone's got to call the shots. I doubt [the Yankees] can win a pennant in five years. The damned club was allowed to deteriorate." Twenty years earlier Larry MacPhail had had a free hand running the Yankees, but the new management team was a triumvirate: Burke, MacPhail, and Houk. "Larry is a free man living in a free world and a very lively spirit," Burke said.

"At the same time he has nothing whatsoever to do with the Yankees. We recognize we have problems, but there's an enormous opportunity here for the Yankees."[12]

In an interview with sportswriter Joe Falls soon after taking over, Lee MacPhail was asked why he thought the Yankees had fallen. "There have been problems in the organization, like George Weiss leaving and a general turnover at the top . . . and frankly, I think their scouting staff got a little old," he said. "The farm system stopped producing the kind of players they needed to stay on top and down they went."[13] During the years MacPhail ran the Yankees' farm system, it had produced not only several stars but enough surplus talent to allow the team to acquire the likes of Lopat and Maris. By 1965 there was no surplus—whatever talent the system produced needed to play.

In December MacPhail negotiated a deal to acquire Maury Wills, the Dodgers' star shortstop. National League president Warren Giles, however, was so upset at the outcome of the Frank Robinson trade, one year earlier, that he "used the weight of his office and also his personal powers of persuasion" to block trades of National League stars to the American League. "I heard the Yankees and the White Sox were especially eager to get Wills," Giles said. "This was during the winter meetings. So I went to Buzzie [Bavasi] and asked him not to rush into such a deal, because he had until December 15 [the trading deadline]. . . . As a matter of fact, Mike Burke and Lee MacPhail could have killed me when they lost out on Wills. Burke told me, 'Thanks for sabotaging our deal.'"[14] Bavasi instead swapped Wills to the Pirates.

One of the problems Burke faced right away was how unpopular the Yankees had become. In the George Weiss years the Yankees made no effort to promote the team or involve fans in the game. They did not need to sell anything other than a championship ball club, which they delivered regularly. In 1964 the two-year-old New York Mets began playing in brand-new Shea Stadium in Queens, and the cellar-dwelling club beat the league champion Yankees in attendance by five hundred thousand. The Mets went out of their way to cater to young people and families, while the Yankees were seen as a dull corporate team of an earlier generation. Now that a corporation actually owned the team, and now that the team was losing, the long-neglected press and fans saw no reason for loyalty. Burke set out to change this image, inviting the press to call him anytime, staging days at the park for various city groups, and inviting local citizens (not just dignitaries) to throw out the first pitch.

The Mets had long allowed fans to bring banners to the game to show their support for their lovable heroes, a practice the Yankees had once haughtily disallowed. In early 1967 a Yankee loyalist unfurled a banner at the stadium that said "MIKE BURKE IS THE GREATEST," as much to get on television as anything else.[15] "Whether the Yankees were really cold or not," thought Burke, "or cared about the fans or not, was not material. What was important was that fans felt the Yankees were cold."[16] Burke distributed pamphlets to all employees to spell out how they needed to behave with the fans.[17]

Burke was once asked whether previous Yankee administrations had taken the game and the team too seriously. "In my measure, yes," said Burke. "I cannot knock the successful approach of another man *in his time*, but in this time I believe we need to inculcate a sense of humor. How? By example, not by ukase. You have to communicate your own philosophy, and humor is part of my philosophy."[18] No, these were not the old Yankees.

The new Yankee management team agreed that recovery would not come without action. The old stars were not going to return to their past glory, and the young prospects were not going to "replace" them. Pepitone had stalled as a one-dimensional slugger, Tresh had not built on his early success, and Bouton's sore arm was not going to heal. MacPhail, with his experience in player development, got to work cleaning house. A week into the job he released Hector Lopez. By the end of the year he had traded Clete Boyer, Roger Maris, and Pedro Ramos, receiving untried youngsters in return. Like most untried youngsters, this group did not help much, let alone replace Mickey Mantle. There would be no quick fix.

Whitey Ford, still pitching well when his sore arm allowed him to take the mound, quit early in the 1967 season. MacPhail dealt Howard to the Red Sox in August, promising Elston a job with the Yankees as soon as he finished his career. Houk moved Mantle to first base in 1967, and the Mick provided two seasons of productive offense, though nothing like the all-around game he once boasted. He retired after the 1968 season. Pepitone, Downing, and Tresh were discarded in 1969.

Slowly, the Yankees began developing talented players. Mel Stottlemyre was the one youngster from the 1964 team who lasted into the 1970s, providing the team a decade of solid pitching. Outfielder Roy White debuted in 1965 and took a couple of years to hit, but by 1968 he was an underrated star. Left-handed pitcher Fritz Peterson came up in 1966 and won 109 games over the next eight seasons. Righty Stan Bahnsen won 17 games and the Rookie of the Year Award in 1968. Bobby Murcer was expected to win the shortstop job in 1967 but was instead drafted into the army. When he came out two years later, the Yankees shifted him to center field, the hallowed turf of DiMaggio and Mantle, and he became one of the league's best players. All of these players would have fitted in on the great 1950s teams just fine. The 1968 club finished 83-79 and in fifth place; two years later they finished second at 93-69.

Along the way they almost lost Mike Burke, who was a candidate to become baseball commissioner in late 1968. "Only Mike Burke," wrote Jimmy Cannon, "has the kind of personality which suggests an eccentric fairness and also a contempt for the protocol of selfishness maintained by the franchise owners."[19] Burke nearly got the job, which eventually went to Bowie Kuhn.

One of the positive side effects of the Yankees' dropoff was that it led to relatively high positions in the annual amateur draft. In 1965 the Yankees nabbed Bahnsen in round 4 but had less luck the following year. In his first year in charge MacPhail had the number-one overall pick in 1967. "It wasn't simple to determine your pick with different area scouts strongly plugging for the best player in their territory," MacPhail recalled. In the old days the Yankees would have been free to sign all of these players, rather than just one. "We narrowed our choice down to Greg Luzinski, Ted Simmons, and Ron Blomberg," he said. [Luzinski wasn't actually eligible for the draft until the following year.] "Unfortunately, we picked Blomberg. . . . He could run and had outstanding power; moreover he was a left-handed pull hitter with the ideal Yankee Stadium stroke. He seemed to have a good temperament, showed great hustle, and really should have been a star. But it turned out he was not willing to fully dedicate himself to his work." Blomberg had a few functional seasons with the Yankees before succumbing to injuries.[20]

The Yankees struck gold in 1968, taking catcher Thurman Munson with the fourth pick in the draft. MacPhail and scout Gene Woodling traveled to Ohio to convince Munson to give up a college scholarship and start his baseball career.[21] The Yankees also drafted outfielder Charlie Spikes in 1969, pitcher George "Doc" Medich in 1970, pitcher Ron Guidry in 1971, and pitcher Scott McGregor in 1972. By the early 1970s the Yankees' farm system had gone from a weakness to a strength.

In 1970 the Yankees offense featured three stars from the system: White (twenty-two home runs, .293), Murcer (twenty-three homers), and Rookie of the Year Munson (.302), destined to be their cocky leader. The club also featured three very good starters—Stottlemyre, Peterson, and Bahnsen (all homegrown)—and a great bullpen of Lindy McDaniel, Jack Aker, and Ron Klimkowski (all acquired in MacPhail trades). Before the 1971 season MacPhail acquired veteran Felipe Alou from Oakland, a sign that he felt the team was ready to compete. But the 1970 season turned out to be a mirage: the offense was not deep and would need more reinforcement.

After falling to 82-80 in 1971, MacPhail made his worst trade with the Yankees, dealing Bahnsen to the White Sox for infielder Rich McKinney. The Yankees intended to move McKinney from second to third base, which had been a trouble spot, and MacPhail felt that he could afford to surrender a starting pitcher from their deep stable. Bahnsen remained a valuable league-average workhorse and won twenty-one games his first year in Chicago. McKinney did not take well to his new position, hitting just .215 in thirty-seven games before being demoted to the Minors and then traded after the season.

The improvement in the Yankees during this period occurred in the shadow of a much larger story on the other side of the East River. When the Miracle Mets broke through in 1969, winning the World Series, they drew more than twice the attendance of the Yankees. "While the new, lightweight Yankees were being built," *Sports Illustrated* wrote in 1970, "New York fans slipped away in hordes to watch the Mets, and the loss has begun to show significantly at places other than just the gate, where it has been plenty noticeable." The Mets were winning the battle for television and radio contracts as well.[22]

But although MacPhail's conservative approach to rebuilding the team required time and patience, he thought it was close to paying off. "I don't believe it is possible to build a winning team by trades," he said in 1972. "It is a must to develop your own players for the key spots, then possibly fill in here and there by trading. I feel our program of development is coming along and will eventually pay off."[23] Nonetheless, MacPhail made his best two trades in 1972, one just before the season and one just after. In March the club swapped singles-hitting first baseman Danny Cater and Minor League infielder Mario Guerrero to the Red Sox for left-handed relief pitcher Sparky Lyle. The Yankees' depth at the position (they had both Blomberg and Alou available to play first) gave them no need for Cater, and Lyle became a sensation, finishing 9-5 with 35 saves and a 1.92 ERA. By August he was on the cover of *Sports Illustrated* ("Damn Yankees Again," said the headline),[24] and the Yankees were in the pennant race. "You know," MacPhail said late in the season, responding to his disgruntled fan base, "the Yankees are in a strange spot. They are not competing against the Tigers, Orioles and the rest of the league. They are competing against ghosts and that's a battle you can't win."[25]

In November MacPhail again took advantage of the team's rebuilt organizational depth in two deals. First he traded McKinney and pitcher Rob Gardner to the Athletics for thirty-three-year-old outfielder Matty Alou, Felipe's brother. A few days later MacPhail dealt four of the farm system's recently developed players—Charlie Spikes, John Ellis, Rusty Torres, and Jerry Kenney—to the Indians for third baseman Graig Nettles and reserve catcher Gerry Moses.

Nettles was a perfect fit for the club: a defensive star who hit with power from the left side, a skill particularly valued in Yankee Stadium with its short right-field porch. Spikes was the big prize for Cleveland, a twenty-one-year-old slugger (26 homers, .309 at Double-A West Haven) and the jewel of the Yankees' revamped system. "We've been talking to Cleveland since last season," admitted MacPhail, "but the answer was always the same—they wanted Spikes. We finally decided there was no way to get Nettles without giving him up, even though he was the best prospect we've had in years. Now we have as good a club as anybody in baseball." Ralph Houk was excited. "I'm not worrying about youth," he said. "It's time to go out and win it. Our lineup should be the best since our winning teams of 10 years ago."[26] Burke rewarded both Houk and MacPhail with new three-year contracts.

Meanwhile, Burke made his most lasting contribution to the future of New York and the Yankees when he came to a deal with Mayor John Lindsay for the city to thoroughly remodel Yankee Stadium. The fifty-year-old ballpark had been deteriorating without significant upkeep for many years until Burke had the interior and exterior painted in 1967. Five years later he talked Lindsay into backing a twenty-four-million-dollar renovation, the same cost the city had borne to build Shea Stadium for the Mets in 1964. Burke had been aggressively pursued by the officials building new facilities right across the Hudson River in New Jersey and smartly used this leverage with the city. The football Giants, the Yankees cotenants in Yankee Stadium, ultimately decided to abandon New York and move to New Jersey, but Burke had no desire to do so. "Yankee Stadium is the most famous arena since the Roman Coliseum," he said.[27]

The renovation ended up costing the city more than a hundred million dollars (largely due to major road redesign), but Burke can be said to have saved the Yankees for New York. He worked out a deal to play both the 1974 and the 1975 seasons in Shea Stadium, allowing the contractors nearly two and a half years for construction. Ultimately, the renovation removed the 105 columns that reinforced the three-tiered grandstand (which had obstructed many views) and replaced the roof and all the seats. The stadium reopened on time in 1976, but by then another man was in charge to reap the benefits. The additional revenues from the revamped ballpark would be critical in helping underwrite the team's aggressive approach to the coming free agency.

As the calendar flipped to 1973, many observers believed that the Yankees were the best team in the AL East and in position to regain some of their former glory. The club had added Nettles and Matty Alou to an attack that featured Murcer, White, Munson, and Felipe Alou. Stottlemyre, Peterson, and Steve Kline formed an excellent front three start-ers, and Lyle and McDaniel headed one of the game's best bullpens. Burke and MacPhail were finally poised to take the last step on their journey, in their sixth year in charge. Oddsmakers in Las Vegas made the Yankees the 9–5 favorite to win the AL East.[28]

Notwithstanding all of the progress on and off the field, the Yankees' parent company, the Columbia Broadcasting System, decided to sell the team. Having purchased the most famous franchise in sports just eight years earlier, CBS was reportedly losing money on the Yankees, though that was not the primary motivation for selling. CBS had bought the team for its famous brand, in order to bring additional prestige to their hugely successful media company. Instead, the team fell from glory, and many fans tended to blame the largely unseen corporate managers for the change in fortune. "CBS came to the conclusion," said a spokesman, "that perhaps it was not as viable for the network to own the Yankees as for some people. Fans get worked up over great men, not great corporations. We came to the realization, I think, that sports franchises really flourish better with *people* owning them."[29]

In mid-1972 CBS chairman William S. Paley asked Burke to put together a group to buy the club, and Burke looked for a purchaser that would allow him to continue running the team. Cleveland Indians general manager Gabe Paul introduced Burke to George M. Steinbrenner, the forty-two-year-old CEO of the American Shipbuilding Company who had recently come very close to purchasing his hometown Indians. A decade earlier Steinbrenner had taken over the small Great Lakes shipping company from his father, bought out most of his competitors, and built an empire.

Although hardly a household name, Steinbrenner had been involved with sports teams for many years. Once a track star at Williams College, he was later a football graduate assistant to Coach Woody Hayes at Ohio State and had held football coaching positions at Northwestern and Purdue. In the early 1960s he bought the Cleveland Pipers, a team in the short-lived American Basketball League, and made an immediate splash by signing the most coveted college player in the country, Ohio State's Jerry Lucas. The league soon folded, but a few years later Steinbrenner bought a stake in the Chicago Bulls and began acquiring racehorses.

Burke and Steinbrenner came to a deal quickly, and the formal announcement was made on January 4, 1973. Steinbrenner and several other general partners put up a total of ten million dollars in cash, four million less than CBS had paid eight years earlier. With the stadium about to be substantially renovated, a team coming into contention, decades of tradition to fall back on, and sitting in the biggest marketplace in the country, it was an extraordinary deal. Burke reportedly could have received more money from other bidders, but with Steinbrenner's group he would be a general partner. More important, Burke was led to believe he would continue to run the club as chief executive. MacPhail and Houk also remained in their posts.

Just six days after the deal was announced, Steinbrenner held a press conference to introduce the other limited partners, including Gabe Paul, who had been running the Cleveland Indians. The news stunned Burke, who realized that Paul, with more than three decades' experience running baseball teams, would be no mere adviser. Steinbrenner had withheld the news of Paul's inclusion from Burke, without whom he would not have secured the team. Burke resigned a few months later, after it had become clear that his control would be much more limited than he had anticipated. He would not be the last person to underestimate George Steinbrenner.

Within a few months of leaving the Yankees, Burke was named chairman of Madison Square Garden and soon the president of the New York Knicks (basketball) and New York Rangers (hockey) teams that played there. He later retired to Ireland, and when he died in 1987 he was championed by his many friends in the press as the savior of the Yankees. "I remember the early '70s and the [football] Giants' desertion of New York," wrote one. "Mike Burke would have none of it, none of the attempts to lure the Yankees across the river."[30]

The 1973 Yankees led the AL East for several weeks, as late as July 31. With a pennant in sight, MacPhail acquired pitchers Pat Dobson and

Sam McDowell, giving Houk four recent twenty-game winners. But it was the hitting of Murcer, Munson, Nettles, and the rest that made the manager smile. "Just about the entire difference between our team now and in the last couple of seasons," he said, "is the hitting. It's fun to sit back and see our hitters do their job." Murcer, who been through much of the rebuilding, was thrilled. "I have a feeling about this team," he said, "a feeling that all the bad things are in the past, that we can win just like the Yankees are supposed to."[31]

They could not, collapsing in August and finishing seventeen games behind the streaking Orioles. At the end of the season, a frustrated Houk resigned and soon took the managerial post with the Tigers. MacPhail served the year out but resigned in October, becoming AL president. Both men were highly respected around baseball and in New York and had many years ahead of them in baseball, but neither would be able to work with the constant interference of the new majority owner.

"The general impression of people today," wrote MacPhail years later, "is that CBS did not provide good ownership—that it would not spend money to improve the team. Actually CBS did everything in its power—under the baseball rules in force at the time—to improve the club. Scouting and player development budgets were increased and it gladly would have purchased players had there been good players available for purchase. And actually, the team did improve. Nor was CBS any problem with respect to broadcast matters."[32]

Shortly after the conclusion of Yankees' final game on September 30, construction crews began removing the famous girders and frieze of Yankee Stadium. When the Yankees next played a game on the site, thirty months later, both the stadium and the team had been considerably revamped.

As Burke and MacPhail learned, from the introduction of the draft until modern free agency may have been the most difficult period in baseball history to build a championship team. The paths available for talent acquisition were as limited as they were at any time in memory, putting pressure on the team's skill in scouting, drafting, and player development and the GM's expertise trading. The Burke-MacPhail-Houk triumvirate ran the Yankees for nearly seven years and failed in their goal to bring the Yankees back to their glory years. The organization they left behind, however, was immeasurably improved from its state in 1966.

In the next few years the Yankees would reap the benefit of two huge off-the-field events: the opening of the remodeled Yankee Stadium and the beginning of player free agency.

15 Expansion

After decades of stability the 1950s and 1960s saw a flurry of long-standing teams moving to new cities and baseball expanding three times, adding two AL teams in 1961, two NL teams in 1962, and two in each league in 1969. Each of these eight new clubs was initially stocked with largely unwanted or unvalued players from other teams and then patiently built piece by piece by the team's management.

The 1969 expansion was precipitated when Charlie Finley moved the Kansas City Athletics to Oakland in October 1967. Facing legal pressure, the American League responded by awarding franchises to Kansas City and, eventually, Seattle. Unlike later expansions in the 1990s, baseball chose the cities first and then searched for ownership groups.

A leading candidate to own the new Kansas City franchise was Ewing Kauffman, a wealthy Kansas City entrepreneur who had made his fortune as the founder and chairman of Marion Laboratories, a pharmaceutical company. As he contemplated his bid, Kauffman traveled to Anaheim to meet with California Angels owner Gene Autry and team president Bob Reynolds, who had been through the process with their 1961 expansion team. While on the trip Kauffman was greatly impressed by Angels executive Cedric Tallis. As Kauffman finalized his bid for his team, he invited Tallis to join his group as its general manager. Kauffman not only thought Tallis a smart baseball man, but also considered him as someone who could be a champion and overseer for the new stadium complex under consideration in Kansas City.

As we have seen, many of the most successful teams of the 1960s operated with a dominant general manager atop the organization, and Kauffman recognized the merit of this model. Additionally, Tallis felt comfortable dealing with the press and enjoyed the limelight, key attributes for someone who would be an important face of the team. Years later when Tallis was working in the Yankees' front office, owner

George Steinbrenner was looking for him. When told that Tallis was giving an interview, Steinbrenner joked, "Hell, we'll never get him out of there. You know how Cedric loves those TV cameras."[1]

With the January 11, 1968, announcement awarding the team to Kauffman, the fifty-three-year-old Tallis had a four-year contract and a new Major League team to build. "Outside of finances, he will run the club,"[2] Kauffman told reporters. Marvin Milkes, Tallis's colleague with the Angels, was soon named the new general manager for the Seattle club.

A highly competitive, enthusiastic, and generous self-made millionaire, Kauffman had formulated his first drug—"There was nothing original in it"—from "pouring over medical journals," and concocting a pill for chronic fatigue.[3] At least as importantly, he developed new ways to motivate his sales force, including profit sharing and sophisticated recognition programs. With a restless and creative mind, Kauffman read up to twenty books a week as an eleven-year-old while laid up with rheumatic fever and learned to quickly perform complicated mathematical calculations in his head.

"Kauffman did not dabble in day-to-day team management," wrote his biographer. "He had decided early in his involvement with baseball that he would either have to trust the executives he hired or fire them. That had been his policy at Marion Laboratories where he understood the pharmaceutical business."[4] But Kauffman was an attentive and demanding boss who built his company as much on his sales and management skills as on the products themselves. "His cardinal rule of business is: 'Produce or get out,'" wrote Allan Demaree in *Fortune*. "Sometimes if a salesman fails to increase the volume of business in his territory, says Kauffman, 'we call him in and say, "Before we leave this room one of three things is going to happen. Either you're going to get fired, or you're going to quit, or you're going to change."' The first time a salesman hears this pitch it constitutes a warning; the second time he's canned."[5]

At the ballpark he could be similarly engaged, sitting behind the dugout at home games and dissecting his manager's decisions. "I'd have taken out the kid [Hedlund] and brought in Moe [Drabowsky] a little sooner than Joe [Gordon] did," Kauffman remarked after one game in 1969. After learning that Drabowsky was not "completely warmed up," Kauffman backpedaled, "That's why he's the manager and I'm the owner."[6] But he remained attentive and unafraid to demand explanations from his senior management.

In early 1948, after seven years in the army, thirty-three-year-old captain Cedric Tallis decided it was time to look for a life beyond military service. A native of Penacook, New Hampshire, Tallis had spent two years coaching basketball at Fort Benning, Georgia, where his squad had won the Southeastern Amateur Athletic Union championship. Switching to baseball, Tallis got a job as general manager at Thomasville in the Class D Georgia-Alabama League, the lowest rung in organized baseball and a perfect place to learn the baseball business from the ground up. At this time a Minor League GM was responsible for just about everything: finding players, managing the business affairs, and once for Tallis helping to contain a pack of unruly fans trying to attack the umpire while waiting for the police.[7]

Tallis spent several years running Minor League teams, interrupted by a two-year army recall during the Korean War. In 1953 he was overseeing a Single-A Detroit farm club in Montgomery, Alabama, two notches below the Major Leagues. His first year there was a disaster on and off the field. The club finished last, and Tallis was forced to sell off several players, including former Major Leaguers Kirby Higbe and Grady Wilson. The team improved and in 1955 made it to the Southern League finals. While in Montgomery Tallis formed a long-term bond with his manager Charlie Metro.[8]

After the 1955 season owner Brick Laws moved the financially stressed Oakland Oaks, his Pacific Coast League club, to Vancouver. Laws selected Tallis to run his team, and Tallis signed a working agreement with the Baltimore Orioles. After one year in Vancouver, and a last-place finish, Laws decided to sell, and Tallis spearheaded a group of local businessmen to finance the $150,000 purchase price and an additional $125,000 in operating funds. He brought in Metro to manage, and the team jumped to second place and led the league in attendance.[9]

Despite its Baltimore affiliation, in those days a Minor League club like Vancouver still needed to find many of its own players. Tallis organized a six-day tryout camp for seventeen- to nineteen-year-olds. The Mounties accepted forty-two candidates for the clinic, where youngsters received instruction from several former Major Leaguers, including outfielder Earl Averill and pitcher Earl Johnson.[10]

When the Orioles terminated their agreement with Vancouver after the 1959 season, Tallis moved to the Seattle Rainiers, another PCL team, who affiliated with the Cincinnati Reds. Tallis brought in a new manager, and the team improved from seventh to fourth. When the Boston Red Sox purchased the Rainiers after the 1960 season, Tallis again moved on. Now forty-six and with more than a decade as a Minor League general manager, he was ready for a Major League challenge.[11] He had hopes of landing the GM job in Cincinnati, where Gabe Paul had just resigned. "I would be honored to have the opportunity to appear before Powel Crosley, Jr. and the Cincinnati club's board of directors," Tallis told the press.[12] There were several candidates ahead of Tallis, however. The Reds chose Bill DeWitt and went on to win the 1961 pennant.

Determined to get into the Major Leagues, Tallis accepted a job as an assistant to general manager Fred Haney with the expansion Los Angeles Angels. Marvin Milkes, a onetime *Sporting News* Minor League Executive of the Year, was named as the administrative assistant to both Haney and Tallis. Over the next few years Tallis's role evolved into that of business manager, while Milkes shifted over to the assistant GM job.[13]

Tallis was an avid golfer and often used the game to deal with stress or uncomfortable situations. To avoid an unpleasant conversation with an office visitor, he was known to pull out a putter and talk about his grip or practice his putting. Alternatively, a difficult day could lead him to grab a club, head down to the field, and drive golf balls into the bleachers.[14]

"Tallis was a gentle bear of a man," one of his subordinates later said.

He was kind, personable, compassionate and fun-loving. He could be stubborn when he made up his mind and it would take a great deal of tactful persuasion to change. However, he was always willing to listen to your point of view, argument or opinions. He loved life and truly loved having a good time. He had a marvelous sense of humor, which made it fun to work for him. He was not afraid to delegate responsibility or authority, nor was he afraid to stand his ground on any issue he felt strongly about—no matter what the pressures brought to bear upon him. I admired his guts and also his compassion in dealing with subordinates.[15]

Tallis worked for the Angels for six years, successfully overseeing the club's 1966 move to Anaheim and its new stadium. In early 1968 he answered the call from Ewing Kauffman.

Longtime baseball GM Gabe Paul believed that Tallis "was probably the best in baseball when it came to details and trivia."[16] In Kansas City Tallis did not just sit on his hands waiting for the October 1968 expansion draft, which would get him his first players. He brought in two trusted lieutenants: Charlie Metro, recently the chief scout for Cincinnati general manager Bob Howsam, as director of scouting, and Lou Gorman, from the well-respected Orioles organization, as director of Minor League operations. Taking a page from the Orioles and the Dodgers before them, Tallis, Metro, and Gorman put together the *Kansas City Royals Instructional Manual* to highlight how each defensive play should be executed. Gorman, with his Oriole background, advocated consistent instruction throughout the Royals' organization.[17]

Metro was the quintessential baseball scout, a great judge of talent and an active, enthusiastic instructor. He also had strong opinions and many time-honored biases on what makes a ballplayer. During one workout Metro pointed at a player and told Gorman, "Release that player."

"Charles, he hasn't even thrown a baseball yet," Gorman responded.

"He has a bad face," said Metro.

"Charlie, let's take a look at his physical skills first, you can't judge a player solely on his looks," Gorman concluded.[18]

But Metro also boasted a creative mind. He claimed to have invented the batting tee using rubber tubing when he played for the Heisley Coal Company team in the 1940s.[19] He gave players true-false tests to make sure they knew the rules. While a manager he installed a pitching machine and batting cage at his home park so that his pinch hitters could warm up before batting and carried both right- and left-handed batting-practice pitchers.[20]

Tallis let Gorman bring along an assistant from Baltimore named John Schuerholz, just two years removed from teaching junior high school. Schuerholz would go on to become one of baseball's greatest general managers, first in Kansas City and later in Atlanta. One of Schuerholz's early duties in KC was to determine how other organizations assessed the amateur draft. "Get as much information as you can," Metro advised the young assistant, "but don't give them anything."[21]

Two other future general managers also joined the Royals. Syd Thrift, an original thinker who later ran the Pittsburgh Pirates and Baltimore Orioles, started as a scout. Herk Robinson, also from the Baltimore organization, became Metro's assistant. Years later Robinson led the Royals front office for a decade.

Like George Weiss earlier in New York, Tallis hired strong, intelligent baseball men with different outlooks, men who did not necessarily like or even respect each other. Tallis felt secure enough in his position to search out the best staff and deal with their quirks and disagreements. Traditionalist Metro, free-thinking Thrift, and nice-guy Gorman could not have been more different, and Metro did not really respect either associate, but in sum they brought a broad and deep perspective to the task of building the team. As Schuerholz remembered, the disparate group worked very well together.[22] Tallis utilized and amalgamated their skills and judgments masterfully.

To manage the Royals Tallis hired Joe Gordon, who had previously led three Major League teams, though none since 1961. "My main aim," Tallis had said, "is to pick a man who can motivate young players." Tallis gave Gordon free rein to pick the coaching staff, subject only to his final approval.[23]

Shortly after being awarded their franchise, the Royals petitioned the other owners to be allowed to participate in the June 1968 amateur baseball draft, a request that was not part of the original expansion arrangement. When the owners relented (although the four new teams were not allowed to select until the middle of the fourth round), the Royals drafted two future quality Major Leaguers, Paul Splittorff and

Dane Iorg; none of the other expansion teams landed any with a significant big-league career. Tallis established two Minor League working relationships to place his draftees and Minor League free agents.[24]

On October 15, 1968, the Royals and Seattle Pilots had their chance to draft players from the other American League ball clubs. (The NL held a separate draft for their new teams.) The ten AL teams could each protect fifteen players, after which Kansas City and Seattle would draft ten players—five each—one from each AL team. The clubs could then protect three more players, and the Royals and Pilots could pick another ten players. In all there were six rounds, with the American League teams allowed to protect another three after each round, so that each expansion team in the end had drafted thirty players.

Tallis and Milkes both had ringside seats for the Angels' expansion draft in 1960, making the fact that they learned diametrically opposed lessons all the more fascinating. Milkes concentrated on veterans with name recognition, while Tallis focused almost exclusively on young players. As researcher Steve Treder has pointed out, the first ten picks for the Pilots averaged 27.6 years old, 1,920 Major League at bats, and 247 Major League innings. The Royals, on the other hand, averaged 24.2 years old, 332 Major League at bats, and 164 Major League innings.[25] Tallis's first two selections were pitcher Roger Nelson (24) from the Orioles and third baseman Joe Foy (25) from the Red Sox.

Around the twentieth pick the Royals changed their strategy to also look for older players with trade value, realizing that many of the better younger players had been protected by that point in the draft. (Their most famous draftee, veteran relief pitcher Hoyt Wilhelm, was traded to the Angels for two young players a few days later.) For the day Kansas City selected a number of players who still had meaningful Major League seasons in front of them; measured by WAR, they ended up with nearly 50 percent more future talent than the Pilots. Kauffman was a driving owner, and Tallis and staff had made a great start.

Despite the relatively successful draft, Metro later lamented that it could have been better. "When Lou Gorman came over to the Royals, I asked him about this young guy Palmer [future Hall of Famer Jim, just 23 but having missed nearly two full years due to injury]. Some of my friends had told me he had a great arm," Metro wrote. "Lou said, 'Oh, he's got sore arm . . . he can't pitch.'" Metro also blamed Gorman for missing on Bobby Grich, a future great second baseman. "Aw, he can't play shortstop. He's too fat, too big," Gorman told him. "I can't say too much for old Louie," Metro concluded. "He talked a lot but didn't do much. He didn't know a ballplayer from a hole in the ground."[26] By the time Metro wrote this he had seemingly become bitter toward many in baseball, and the accuracy of his recollections should be taken with some skepticism. Moreover, Gorman was a key contributor to this very successful front office, remembered by Schuerholz as a man of "remarkable ability,"[27] and would go on to a couple of stints as a general manager in his own right. But at the very least, Metro's comments give some sense of the tension, some of it productive, within the Royals' organization.

Metro also blamed Thrift for missing on future star infielder Toby Harrah. "[He] did a terrible job of covering the Washington Senators organization," Metro huffed, and "we blew a chance to get Harrah." The traditionalist Metro clearly did not like Thrift. "We signed [Thrift] to a contract and three days later he was dissatisfied, and we had to give him another contract," Metro complained. "He cried—not my type of guy."[28]

Though Ewing Kauffman allowed his baseball men to build his team, he was unafraid of thinking outside the box with his own ideas. He kept on his desk a copy of Earnshaw Cook's *Percentage Baseball*, the first serious statistical look at the game written by an outsider. Though many of Cook's specific conclusions have since been shown to be in error, the book convinced Kauffman that analytical thinking could offer a competitive advantage. Kauffman also introduced one of baseball's first computer systems, which by the end of the 1971 season contained statistics such as "the nature of every pitch thrown by a Royal . . . what happened to every ball hit . . . [and] even the humidity." One writer who witnessed Tallis and his staff reviewing some of this information exclaimed, "I felt I had walked in on a conclave of madmen. Here were six or seven grown men around a table piled high with computer cards, mulling over every pitch thrown and every ball hit in what is supposed to be a game." This information was fed to the manager so that it could be applied. Thirty years before Michael Lewis wrote *Mon-*

eyball, Kauffman believed that statistical analysis could provide a competitive advantage when added to traditional evaluation methods.[29]

Kauffman also had ideas on how the team should find talent. He had publicly stated that he wanted a pennant within five years, a wildly aggressive prediction given the development of the four expansion franchises in the early 1960s. To accomplish this goal Kauffman realized that the usual methods of finding players would not be sufficient: the amateur draft offered all teams equal access to top prospects, Latin and Caribbean countries were being scouted, and Japan was not yet considered a source for Major League players.[30]

Kauffman was said to spend two hours a night smoking his pipe and thinking, and after consultations with his baseball executives, one night this led to an inspiration. He would create a Baseball Academy, operating separately from the traditional farm system, where great athletes with little baseball background could learn the game, thus tapping into a potentially new pool of baseball talent. Kauffman planned to apply a scientific approach: figure out which raw skills best translated into baseball success and then how to best develop and hone those skills to create ballplayers. Most baseball men thought the Baseball Academy a waste of time, money, and coaching resources. "Of all the people in baseball," Kauffman said, "only Bob Howsam of the Cincinnati Reds thought the Academy was a good idea. He offered to share expenses and share results. Of course, I wanted all the results to myself and I turned him down, which was probably a mistake."[31]

Kauffman purchased a 121-acre site in Sarasota, Florida. The complex cost roughly $1.5 million and required a further $500,000 to $600,000 or so in annual operating expenses. Kauffman named Thrift, then a senior Royals scout, to run the academy.[32] Thrift and his staff held the first tryout camp in early June 1970; over the summer the Royals held 126 tryout camps throughout the country, evaluating more than 7,000 potential ballplayers between sixteen and twenty-one years old, most with little previous baseball experience.[33]

To identify prospects Kauffman enlisted Dr. Raymond Reilly, a young research psychologist, to measure the physical skills of 150 players. Reilly established four in particular that correlated to baseball success: foot speed, which was thought to be the best indicator of muscle twitch and required superior body control; eyesight; fast reflex actions; and body balance. From the research Thrift also came to believe in the importance of a player's throwing arm.[34]

From the tryout pool Thrift and his staff selected 42 recruits. These young men spent ten months at the academy engaged in intense training, playing roughly 150 games, and taking general studies in the morning at a nearby junior college. Kauffman and Thrift insisted on an open-minded, scientific approach to training as well as scouting. Players spent extra time in batting practice against both live pitching and machines, pitching machines were used for fielding practice, new techniques were used to teach speed on the base paths and how to lead off a base, stopwatches were used at a time before they became ubiquitous throughout sports, players exercised in water—to increase resistance—when coming back from injury, videotape replays were introduced, body-building sessions were used selectively long before they became popular, and players were coached on improving their mental approach to the game.[35]

In mid-June 1971 the academy faced its first public test, when they placed a team in the seven-team, rookie-level Gulf Coast League, pitting the recruits against drafted ballplayers in other organizations. The players more than validated their nine months of training: the team won the pennant with a record of 40-13 and led the league in both scoring and ERA. Next to the two American League pennants the Royals later won, this 1971 pennant was Kauffman's greatest thrill in baseball. The team stole 103 bases, while no other team had more than 55. Even more astonishingly, their 16 caught stealing was tied for the second fewest in the league. This emphasis on speed and its application would carry over to the Major League club and was a key component of the team's success in the latter half of the 1970s.[36]

Yet the academy had detractors within the organization, as Tallis, Gorman, and Metro begrudged the huge allocation of resources to something outside of their development system, and Metro in particular believed many of the nontraditional teaching methods silly. What Thrift described as teaching a forty-five-degree bunting angle, Metro ridiculed as, "One guy had the batters holding the bat straight up and down for bunting. I thought, 'the first time a guy foul tips a bunt attempt inside and it hits him between the eyes, that'll be the end of that.'" Gorman, however, was more sympathetic to the training: "The Academy staff developed some excellent methods of instruction and solid theories in teaching certain skills at all levels of the game. The players in the Academy program were all fundamentally sound and well drilled."[37]

In tandem Tallis and his staff had also built a first-rate scouting and development system and wanted to integrate the academy into their organization, including rotating players from the farm system through the academy and revising some of the instruction. Tallis recognized the value of keeping an open mind to new training techniques, including "purchasing a new stop action camera to help our hitters and pitchers. This camera can stop any action without blurring or fuzzy lines. It's expensive, but we feel it will be of considerable help to both our pitchers and hitters."[38] Accordingly, the Royals began sending some of their Minor Leaguers to the academy.

Unfortunately, a true integration was not really possible given the different philosophies and the animosity between many of the academy staff, particularly Thrift, who wanted to run the academy as an independent enterprise, and the more traditional front office. The academy's second class, which participated in the 1972 Gulf Coast League season, consisted of twenty-six young men between seventeen and nineteen years old, reduced due to the difficulty of finding qualified prospects and so that the academy could also accommodate the traditional Minor Leaguers. Thrift became so frustrated with the meddling from the front office that he resigned. Kauffman appointed Gorman the new director, reporting directly to him on academy matters.[39]

By 1973, although the academy had produced several prospects, it had become clear that Kauffman's brainchild needed to be revamped. For that season's class Gorman's staff uncovered only fourteen athletes meeting their admission criteria. The Royals' original thesis—that great young athletes with little baseball background could be molded into Major League Baseball players—had not proven out. Despite all its creative ideas and intense testing, the academy could not create ballplayers from raw, unskilled athletes. The top prospect in the academy, infielder Frank White, had baseball experience. He also fitted into the academy model because of his tremendous speed. White had been extensively scouted and passed over because most scouts believed he would never learn to hit adequately.[40] As White later said, "I was lucky because I came into the Academy knowing the basic fundamentals of the game."[41]

The other significant problem with the academy was the huge cost. By 1973 the school cost about $700,000 per year to operate, a massive outlay for the time. In 1974, the closest year for which we have data, the cost of running a Major League farm system was about $900,000. Assuming that the Royals pulled in close to the league average in revenue ($6.25 million), the academy absorbed about 11 percent of their total proceeds. In Kansas City's smaller market, this percentage was probably even greater.[42]

The academy had its successes, just not enough: White developed into a longtime star for the Royals; U. L. Washington—the only raw athlete turned into a quality regular—anchored shortstop for several years; Ron Washington played ten seasons, mostly as a reserve, and later led the Texas Rangers to two American League pennants as manager; and several other academy signees appeared in the Major Leagues, though none as contributing regulars. But the cost of the academy became prohibitive and the demands for integration with the regular farm system dilutive of some of the more experimental ideas.[43]

The Baseball Academy challenged many standard assumptions of scouting and instruction. First, the academy was predicated on the idea that there was untapped Major League–caliber baseball talent inside of young athletes who had little exposure to the game. Second, the academy theorized that these athletes could be identified not only by watching them play baseball, but by observing and testing their skills. Much like today's NFL Scouting Combine, specific physical and mental traits could be measured and used to project future success in baseball. Finally, a more scientific approach could be brought to instruction and training, to improve how prospects were developed into Major League players.

The academy did not succeed in turning athletes into baseball players, suggesting that traditional scouting was already finding most—though not all—of the potential Major Leaguers. However, Kauffman's philosophy of always looking for new sources of talent is one of the foundations of successful organizations. Of the academy's innovations in scouting and player development, some were transferred to the Royals' farm system, and many others were carried by the academy's coaches and trainers as they migrated to other teams. Like most successful organizations, Kauffman's Royals showed a sincere willingness to experiment with new ideas and methods. As a result they found a few valuable players and learned useful player development and scouting lessons.

Just prior to the 1969 season Tallis made the first in a series of deals that would ultimately build a contending club. The Royals had drafted outfielder Steve Whitaker from the Yankees, only to discover that he was beset with off-field problems. "He had a good year [in 1967], but the Yankees exposed him to the draft," Metro wrote. "We took him and we found out why."[44] Tallis sent him to the Pilots for Lou Piniella, who would go on to win the AL Rookie of the Year Award that season.

Joe Gordon proved to be a fine manager for a young expansion team, as he liked working with young players. He spent considerable time salvaging the confidence in the batter's box of third baseman Paul Schaal, a player he had recommended the Royals draft from the Angels, despite a near-career-ending beaning in 1968. Gordon's work paid off with Schaal and others, and the young 1969 team played surprisingly well.

"I will be an angry man if we don't finish third," Milkes, Tallis's counterpart in Seattle, boasted in August. "If Kansas City finishes ahead of us, it would be the worst disgrace I could think of." In fact, the Royals finished fourth, five games ahead of the last place and "disgraced" Pilots, and Tallis knew that his team also had a brighter future. "We're trying to do as well as we can this year," Tallis said, "but we're also looking ahead to 1970, and I'm not going to worry about who is ahead of us or behind us."[45] The 1969 Royals were led by their young league-average pitching, especially the rotation of Wally Bunker, Roger Nelson, Dick Drago, and Bill Butler, none older than twenty-five.

Though Gordon was credited with much of the team's progress, after the season he decided that the stress of the job was too much for him and chose to resign. Tallis named Metro manager for 1970 and reassigned Gordon, at the latter's request, to the Kansas City Minor League system.[46]

In December 1969 Tallis made one of his most famous deals, securing twenty-two-year-old outfielder Amos Otis from the Mets for third baseman Joe Foy. Foy had played well in his one season with the Royals, but Otis would become Kansas City's first star, holding down center field for the next fourteen seasons. "The Mets wanted a third baseman and they were trying to get Ken McMullen from Washington," Tallis later related. "Washington wanted two starting pitchers and the Mets didn't want to give that much. When they saw they couldn't make the McMullen deal, they turned to Foy."[47]

"[Foy] wasn't taking good care of himself," Metro later wrote. "He was smoking marijuana, and he was just losing control." Metro remembered watching Otis in spring training—when the Mets were trying to make him into a third baseman—and thinking that the Royals should keep him in mind as a future acquisition target.

If the trade was not yet good enough, Tallis also got the Mets to include starting pitcher Bob Johnson. "We insisted on getting Johnson in the deal and they didn't want to give him up. We met with some of the Mets officials one night trying to get the thing wrapped up. Johnny Murphy was the general manager then. I told him we had to have Johnson if we were going to make the deal. He said they couldn't give up Johnson. About 45 seconds went by without a word being said, I was really sweating. Finally he said okay, they'd put Johnson in." Tallis also thought he might be able to get the Mets to include Jon Matlack, soon to develop into one of the league's top hurlers, but backed off at the last moment for fear they were "pushing [their] luck."[48] Johnson had one good year with the Royals and proved a valuable asset the next winter.

In June 1970 Tallis sent a Minor Leaguer to the Cardinals for thirty-one-year-old second baseman Cookie Rojas. Tallis did not generally look for older players, but second base had been a gaping hole on the club, and Rojas seemed a reasonable stopgap. In fact, Rojas rejuvenated his career, playing in four All-Star Games for the Royals.

Unfortunately, new manager Metro proved to be a disaster. He ran spring training like boot camp, and the players, only half-jokingly, referred to it as "Stalag 17." With the Royals at 19-33 in early June, Tallis fired Metro, promoting another longtime friend, pitching coach Bob Lemon. Metro was bitter over his firing and in later years blamed his poor performance ("to the extent I did a lousy job") on a bleeding ulcer that he kept to himself.[49] Metro returned to coaching and scouting, but he never got another shot as manager.

After the 1970 season Tallis and his staff recognized that the team needed to improve at shortstop and decided that one of their targets should be Freddy Patek, an undersized, underappreciated player backing up Gene Alley in Pittsburgh. Tallis, Gorman, and Metro met with a Pittsburgh contingent of GM Joe Brown, farm director Pete Peterson, manager Danny Murtaugh, and two scouts. As the multiplayer trade was being negotiated, Metro suggested that Kansas City should also get pitcher Bruce Dal Canton. As Gorman recalled, Brown looked to his manager, who shrugged and replied, "Bob Johnson is the pitcher we want." For Johnson, displaced shortstop Jackie Hernandez, and a Minor Leaguer, Tallis landed Patek, Dal Canton, and a decent catcher in Jackie May.[50] Patek held down shortstop for nine years in Kansas City, teaming with Rojas as one of the league's top double-play combinations.

The 1971 Royals astonished everyone by finishing second with a record of 85-76, although sixteen games behind the powerful Oakland A's. For his efforts, Tallis was named Executive of the Year by the *Sporting News*. Kauffman believed the team was on the verge of the playoffs, but the club had overachieved in 1971, and the talent was not really ready to capture a division title, even in the weaker West Division. Kauffman, however, now felt that the Royals should be in contention annually. This sentiment placed Tallis in the difficult position of knowing he needed more talent to win, but also trying to fill specific holes to give him the best chance to win each particular season. A brilliant trader, Tallis walked this thin line remarkably well.

One of the stars of the Royals' 1970 club, first baseman Bob Oliver, fell from twenty-seven home runs and ninety-nine RBI to just eight and fifty-two in 1971. Accordingly, Tallis looked for a power-hitting first baseman that winter. He initially targeted Boston's George Scott, but the Red Sox asked for Dick Drago, a hurler Tallis was unwilling to surrender. His scouts liked Houston's young first baseman John Mayberry, who had struggled in a few trials, so Tallis explored that option at the winter meetings. Dealing from strength, Kansas City sent two young pitchers to Houston for Mayberry, who broke through in 1972 with twenty-five home runs and one hundred RBI and had several more fine seasons for the Royals.

The 1972 season was marred by a players strike that began during spring training and lingered into the season, canceling a week's worth of games. As the players' union had never taken such an action before, the events stunned many longtime baseball people, including Lemon. "We asked the players to get on a bus, and they refused," Tallis said, recounting the start of the strike. "Then Lemon and I went into our office and Bob began to cry. He could not believe what was happening to his game."[51]

The Royals backslid in 1972 to 76-78, though the fall to fourth place likely overstated their regression. They were a young team that experienced a few off years and were still well ahead of the other three 1969 expansion teams. Nonetheless, the impatient Kauffman, disappointed that the club's 1971 improvement had not been sustained, decided to fire Lemon. In August Lemon had benched Otis and Patek for not hustling, an incident that Kauffman later said was mishandled.[52]

Tallis disagreed, feeling that Lemon had done a fine job managing the club for three years. In the October 3 press conference, Kauffman made the announcement, while Tallis, when asked, indicated his disapproval. As justification, Kauffman mentioned the August benching and also suggested that he wanted to hire someone younger. This last comment exposed Kauffman to age-discrimination laws, causing him to have to pay Lemon an extra year's salary. Kauffman's impatience and unrealistic expectations were laid bare. "Starting in 1974," Kauffman bragged, "we expect to win it [the American League Championship] five out of ten years."[53]

Kauffman further exasperated Tallis by hiring Jack McKeon, the manager at Triple-A Omaha, with whom Tallis had quarreled in the past. In particular, McKeon was a vocal advocate of the Baseball Academy and hence a favorite of Kauffman's. McKeon recalled:

When Mr. Kauffman asked me if we had any prospects in the Academy, I mentioned Frank White, Ron Washington, and a few others because Sid and I had talked about those guys. Sid knew talent and was my right-hand man. Kauffman told Tallis about this, and Tallis called me into his office. In front of Lou Gorman, Tallis said, "Jack, don't you ever lie to Mr. Kauffman again. You told him there were prospects in the Academy."

Now I was really steamed and I told Tallis and Gorman there were prospects there. Gorman said his scouts didn't think so. I told them maybe they could find someone who would tell them what they wanted to hear, but this was the way I saw it.[54]

The presence of the academy had created bickering fiefdoms from the beginning, but Kauffman's hiring of McKeon, knowing the feelings of Tallis—in theory the person in charge of running the baseball team—drove a further wedge in the organization. McKeon would go on to a successful career in baseball as both a manager and a general manager, but in 1972 he owed his allegiance to Ewing Kauffman alone. The impatient Kauffman had journeyed a long way from the putatively hands-off owner of 1969.

At the winter meetings in November, Tallis targeted Reds outfielder–third baseman Hal McRae, a player the Royals scouts felt could hit but lacked a viable defensive position. Reds GM Bob Howsam was reluctant to give up on McRae, despite his defensive liabilities. After some negotiation Tallis offered Roger Nelson, their first pick in the 1968 expansion draft who finished 1972 at 11-6 with a 2.08 ERA. The Royals' brain trust was not really sold on Nelson's ability to stay healthy. "He had a concave chest," Metro recalled. "Those guys always come up with sore arms and shoulders." To sweeten the pot Tallis also proposed outfielder Richie Scheinblum, coming off an All-Star season in which he had hit .300, though he was already twenty-nine and 1972 was his first season as a big-league regular. Tallis asked for Wayne Simpson, a young pitcher with a history of arm problems, to help balance the expanded trade.[55]

Tallis thought he had a deal, but in the end Howsam demurred. As Howsam and his staff were leaving, Tallis sarcastically remarked,

"Thanks for the visit." At that point one of Howsam's entourage asked his general manager, "Could we caucus a minute and ask the Kansas City people to wait?" Howsam agreed and returned a little later. "I've been persuaded to change my position." In Kansas City McRae struggled for a year as a platoon right fielder, before turning into one of the league's best designated hitters for twelve years. There is no record of what happened to the staff member who coaxed Howsam into one of the few bad trades of his career.[56]

The Royals opened the 1973 season strong, sitting at 30-23 on June 3, but after four straight losses McKeon vented his frustration to the press. He felt the team was close but that Tallis had failed to land several key pieces that had been available earlier in the season. Veterans Deron Johnson and Jim Ray Hart had been traded from NL teams to the AL in this first year of the designated hitter, and McKeon felt the Royals could have used either. McKeon also wondered why the club had not bid on veteran hurler Sam McDowell, who had been sold to the Yankees. McKeon's actions were unusual. Here was a first-year manager publicly berating one of the game's most respected GMs, less than two years removed from an Executive of the Year award. "I've been mad for two or three days. Every time you look up, some team or other has picked up another guy and we're standing still. The scouts keep saying these guys are through," McKeon complained regarding the two veteran designated hitters. "What have [Hart and Johnson] played, a month each in this league? They both have had six or seven home runs."

Tallis was in an awkward situation. His rebellious manager had been imposed by the owner, limiting his disciplinary options and the chance of creating a harmonious relationship. Instead, Tallis gave a surprisingly blunt and honest public explanation:

> It would have been possible for us to get Hart last year, but there was no designated hitter rule then. He had a bad record with his knee and all. Even now he can't move well. We sent a scout out to see him and did not get a favorable report. He was not offered to us this year. We double checked Johnson and decided he was too much of a gamble. We were not aware that McDowell was available.

I'm not sure whether McDowell was offered to anyone other than the Yankees. Sam and Gabe Paul have a very good relationship. We tried to get [Pat] Dobson, but we couldn't get waivers on one of our players. In the case of Mike Kekich, we felt he had been to the well once too often and had been found wanting. If Jack wants to gamble, we have two players, Lou Piniella and [Hal] McRae, who are not hitting well now, but who have hit in the past and are good gambles.

In this, Tallis was correct. Both Piniella and McRae, who was hardly playing, proved to have much more to offer than Hart or Johnson.

"After losing a game a manager may say things that he will regret later. I hope this is what happened in Jack's case," Tallis added, trying to defuse the matter. He then gave his views of the state of the team:

We spent five years developing a farm system and bringing our club along and we're going to proceed in what we think is a proper manner. Any number of things could happen to turn our situation around. I've always said that we have to have a healthy infield if we're going to win and right now our infield isn't healthy. The type of trade you make ahead of the trading deadline is one in which you get a player with a big salary who isn't producing or one that a club wants to let go for some other reason. You don't make big trades ahead of the trading deadline. You make them in the winter.[57]

The team's solid finish validated Tallis's approach. The Royals finished the season 88-74, six games behind the eventual world champion A's. The club had great years from Mayberry (26 homers, 100 RBI, .294 batting average) and Otis (26, 93, .300) and excellent starting pitching from Paul Splittorff and Steve Busby. The club opened Royals Stadium, whose spacious outfield and artificial playing surface placed a premium on speed, something that players like Otis, Patek, and Rojas—all Tallis additions—had brought to the club.

The club also began to feature some of the talent they had selected in the annual June draft. Both Splittorff (1968) and Busby (1971) were draftees, as was George Brett (1971), a twenty-year-old third baseman from El Segundo, California, who debuted in August. Brett joined the lineup in 1974 and soon became the face of the franchise. To mine Southern California Metro had hired scout Rosie Gilhousen, who boasted a network of bird-dog scouts.[58]

After the 1973 season Tallis was typically active in the trade market, though he did not find any stars. In one of his few unfavorable deals, Tallis sent Piniella and Ken Wright to the Yankees for Lindy McDaniel, a thirty-seven-year-old relief ace who had pitched 160 innings in 1973, his most since 1957. Piniella appeared washed up after a poor season at twenty-nine, and the team had a surplus of good outfielders. Piniella, however, went on to several productive years with the Yankees, while McDaniel provided little to the Royals.

Despite the Royals' strong second-place finish in 1973, Kauffman became frustrated with his mounting financial losses. Between the financial drain of the academy and the Royals' top-notch Minor League system, the team reportedly lost hundreds of thousands of dollars annually. Notwithstanding a strong season on the field, the opening of their new stadium, and a near doubling of attendance, Kauffman lost roughly nine hundred thousand dollars in 1973. The strain of these losses triggered a rift between Tallis and the Royals' vice president on the business side, Charles Truitt, leading to further divisions in an already inharmonious front office.[59]

Late in the 1973 season Truitt retired, and Kauffman hired Joe Burke to replace him. This was an ominous hire for Tallis—Burke had spent years in the front office of the Washington Senators and, after the club's move to Texas, two years as the club's GM. "With Mr. Burke directing the business operations and Mr. Tallis directing the baseball operations, plus having Lou Gorman to direct our Minor League and scouting operations," Kauffman told the press, "I believe we have the best men possible for each area of responsibility."[60]

By the middle of the 1974 season, as the Royals hovered near .500, "Kauffman's irritation with the costs of owning a baseball team was beginning to show."[61] He had sunk somewhere around twenty million dollars into the club and had yet to turn a profit in any season. Although Kauffman was a very rich man, he was beginning to feel a financial pinch, particularly because Marion Laboratories' stock was sinking amid the deepening recession. Moreover, he was becoming disenchanted with the dysfunction—much of it of his own making—in the front office.

In mid-June Tallis felt compelled to offer a defense of the team he had assembled, placing the blame for the team's struggles on the players' lack of effort and, by implication, McKeon's handling of them: "I'm not entirely satisfied that every effort is being extended by all of our players. Some of them seem to be letting down a little here and there. Players like [Cookie] Rojas and some others have given everything they have, that's not true of everybody."[62]

Kauffman apparently disagreed and soon promoted Joe Burke to general manager, giving him full control over both the baseball and the business sides, demoting Tallis to an unidentified position and firing him shortly thereafter. In another cost-saving move, after the season Kauffman directed Burke to join the newly formed Major League Scouting Bureau, enabling the Royals to lay off twenty full-time and fifty part-time scouts.[63]

Kauffman never publicly identified why he fired Tallis, but it seems clear that his frustration had been building for some time. He knew that he was going to have to abandon his beloved academy for financial reasons and surely resented Tallis for never fully embracing it. When he fired Lemon and imposed McKeon as manager—an early sign of his growing irritation—Tallis, rightly or wrongly, would not publicly buy in to the decision. The continuing friction between Tallis and McKeon led to a situation where Kauffman had to choose one or the other. With Joe Burke already on board, Kauffman had an executive ready to step into the position. In a further attempt to foster harmony and stability, Burke gave McKeon a two-year contract extension.

McKeon, however, never received Burke's harmony memo. With only days left in the 1974 season, McKeon dismissed hitting coach Charlie Lau, beloved by many of his players, including Patek, McRae, and star rookie George Brett, who reportedly cried in the dugout when he heard the news. Even star pitcher Steve Busby ripped his manager: "We'll never win a pennant if this is the type of thinking the organization is going to continue to show." McKeon was unhappy with the players' loyalty to Lau, whose somewhat unconventional approach to hitting differed from his own. Nevertheless, making the move before the end of season was an arrogant power play that was bound to fail.[64]

And in fact it did. A team that Kauffman and Burke expected to contend in 1975 was 50-46 in late July, eleven games back. Moreover, McKeon appeared to have lost the respect of his players, exemplified most notably in May when Busby had threatened to leave the team. In late July Burke fired McKeon and hired Whitey Herzog. Herzog had managed for Burke in Texas and at the time was the third base coach for the California Angels. Herzog got the players on his side right away by reinstating Lau, who had remained in the Royals' Minor League system after his release. The team went 41-25 for Herzog down the stretch.

After four seasons of pursuing the A's, in 1976 Kauffman's team finally broke through with a 90-72 record and won the division title. In a tightly contested American League Championship Series (ALCS), the Royals fell in the fifth and deciding game when the Yankees' Chris Chambliss led off the bottom of the ninth inning with a game-ending home run off Mark Littell.

For the team's success the *Sporting News* named Burke Executive of the Year, edging Paul Owens of the Phillies and Gabe Paul of the Yankees. In truth, Burke's key decision was the hiring of Herzog. He made one excellent trade—dealing backup catcher Fran Healy to the Yankees for pitcher Larry Gura—but otherwise did not alter the team that Tallis had left him. In fact, this core would win three more division titles over the next four years, finally reaching the World Series in 1980. By this time the Royals had rightly earned a reputation as one of baseball's best organizations, one that could compete with the larger market franchises in this new era of free agency.

By the time Kauffman forced him out, Cedric Tallis had assembled the nucleus of players that would carry through to the Royals' 1980 pennant. In particular Tallis made his mark with an extraordinary series of trades over a four-year period, usually at baseball's winter meetings. "Your look must be not lascivious, but eager," Tallis described his trading face.[65]

Tallis believed that deal making was an organizational process. "I've always had a horror of people who are 'I' people," he once said.

Our trades have been a cooperative effort, I'm no genius. That's a lot of junk about anyone being a magician in making trades. We have competent knowledgeable scouts I have confidence in. We have an owner who will permit us to have an extensive scouting system. My job is to study the scouting reports and attach the proper weight to each man's judgment. I have to take into consideration how many games they have seen a player in. Some scouts are conservative in judging players, others are more enthusiastic. If possible, I like to see a player myself, but mainly my job is that of a coordinator. After all the information is weighed a final decision has to be made. I'm the one responsible for that decision. I'm not patting myself on the back, but if you spend 13 years in the minors, you learn about talent.[66]

"I think there are three main reasons why we have been successful trading," he continued. "First, we've been fortunate enough to have players available at positions other people were trying to fill. . . . Second, I think we've benefited from the cross-checking we've had our scouts do. When we start thinking about making a deal, we like to have more than one report to go on. Third, if we didn't have an owner like Ewing Kauffman who says, 'Go ahead, let's go,' we might have been more cautious and more inclined to stand pat."[67]

Five of the starting-nine position players on the 1976 pennant winner came via Tallis's deal making: catcher Buck Martinez (acquired shortly after the expansion draft from the Astros), first baseman Mayberry, shortstop Patek, center fielder Otis, and designated hitter McRae.

To evaluate Tallis's trading a little more tangibly, we examined each of his deals and calculated how much WAR each of the involved players accumulated over the remainder of their careers. The trades made by the Royals during Tallis's tenure as general manager brought in 184 future WAR while surrendering only 97. Table 10 summarizes the major trades and the future WAR of each player included in those trades. Tallis is right to credit others in the organization for the evaluation involved in making each of these deals, but the final decision rested with the general manager, and Tallis was the one who bears the ultimate responsibility for the deals' success or failure.

Table 10. Key Cedric Tallis trades

DATE	TO KC (KEY PLAYERS)	REM WAR (ALL PLAYERS IN TRADE)	FROM KC (KEY PLAYERS)	REM WAR (ALL PLAYERS IN TRADE)
December 12, 1968	Ed Kirkpatrick	9.3	Hoyt Wilhelm	3.7
April 1, 1969	Lou Piniella	12.5	Steve Whitaker	1.7
December 3, 1969	Amos Otis	50.0	Joe Foy	2.9
June 13, 1970	Cookie Rojas	7.2	Fred Rico	0.0
December 2, 1970	Freddy Patek	27.3	Bob Johnson	1.0
December 2, 1970	Tom Hilgendorf	3.5	Ellie Rodriguez	13.0
December 2, 1971	John Mayberry	24.4	Two young pitchers	-1.6
October 25, 1972	Gene Garber	17.7	Jim Rooker	17.2
November 30, 1972	Hal McRae	26.7	Nelson/ Scheinblum	1.8
April 2, 1973	Fran Healy	5.7	Greg Minton	17.9
October 24, 1973	NA	0.0	Tom Burgmeier	16.6
December 7, 1973	Lindy McDaniel	0.8	Lou Piniella	9.3
Total		185.1		83.5

Source: http://BaseballReference.com.

The rest of the nucleus of the 1976 team also arrived under Tallis's reign. Second baseman Frank White was a product of the Baseball Academy, while right fielder Cowens and third baseman Brett were drafted. Three of the starting pitchers (Splittorff, Leonard, and Doug Bird) came from the draft, as did ace reliever Mark Littell, while starter Al Fitzmorris was still around from the 1968 expansion draft.

In order to make good trades one first needs to build a solid base of talent. At the very beginning of his tenure, Tallis targeted young and tradable players in the expansion draft; he did not worry about getting veteran "name" players who might provide an ephemeral boost at the gate. He built one of baseball's largest and best group of scouts. He hired smart baseball men for his front office and farm system and did not shy away if they were strong willed (four of his top staff eventually became Major League general managers).

In Ewing Kauffman Tallis had a tireless and innovative owner with an open checkbook. Of the eight expansion teams that began play in the 1960s, the Royals attained and sustained success the quickest, and Kauffman's willingness to hire good baseball people and put money into his team is a big reason. Although he eventually closed down the Baseball Academy, Kauffman's brainchild provided several lasting evaluation and training techniques and a couple of quality ballplayers. His early embrace of the computer and numerical analysis also offered a competitive advantage.

A smart, engaged owner can be a tremendous advantage by letting the staff know they are both supported and accountable. But to be successful the general manager must feel secure in his position. Kauffman's impatience, exemplified by his unrealistic prediction that the Royals would win a pennant within five years, kept him from appreciating how much progress was being made and prevented Cedric Tallis from being around when the team finally broke through.

16 Free Agency

If you don't have solid, committed and supportive ownership, even the best and brightest front office will be doomed.—PETER BAVASI, baseball executive

On December 23, 1975, arbitrator Peter Seitz forever altered the balance of power between baseball players and their clubs and how a general manager could build his team. In a high-profile arbitration hearing involving Los Angeles Dodgers pitcher Andy Messersmith and Montreal Expos pitcher Dave McNally, Seitz ruled that the infamous "reserve clause" in the standard player contract did not in fact bind a player to his club endlessly and that the two players were now free agents.

Messersmith and McNally had played the 1975 season without contracts, their teams having renewed their 1974 contracts under what was commonly referred to as the reserve clause, a provision that allowed a club to re-up the player for one year. The two claimed that their clubs now had no right to them for the following year because both their contract and the option year had expired. Seitz sided with the players, ruling that the wording of the clause, which had been in every player's contract for decades, applied only to the year following the end of their signed contract. Team building had changed forever.

The players had been striving for modifications to the reserve clause for many years without success. Most famously, in early 1970 longtime St. Louis star Curt Flood, in reaction to a late 1969 trade to Philadelphia, filed suit against baseball in an attempt to invalidate the clause and give him the right to sign with any team he wished. Flood lost his case in the U.S. Supreme Court, but his struggle, and the obvious panic it induced in the owners, helped to strengthen the players' resolve and persuade many in the media of the merits of his case.

Besides a desire to choose their employer, the players had also become increasingly aware of how much money they might make in an open market. In August 1967 Kansas City Athletics owner Charlie Finley released outfielder Ken Harrelson in a fit of pique. Finley had fired manager Alvin Dark, and Harrelson responded by calling Finley "a menace to baseball." When Harrelson refused to apologize, Finley set him free. Harrelson was initially shocked, fearing that he would be blacklisted from the game, but his shock abated once he started getting phone calls from general managers offering him contracts at significantly more money than he had been making. A good player but by no means a star, when Harrelson signed with the Red Sox for a reported $75,000 (Harrelson later claimed $150,000, which likely included a sizable bonus), he became one of the highest-compensated players in the game. The ramifications of Harrelson's free agency so disturbed Major League owners that they strengthened the rules so that a released player had to pass through waivers before becoming a free agent.[1]

Seven years later Finley gave the players another glimpse at a possible future. On the eve of the 1974 World Series, which the A's won for the third straight year, a story broke that star pitcher Jim "Catfish" Hunter would file a "breach of contract" grievance against the A's because Finley had failed to pay a $50,000 annuity as stipulated by Hunter's contract (which totaled $100,000 for the season). Soon after the A's beat the Dodgers in the final game, Hunter followed through. Two weeks after a lengthy November 26 hearing, arbitrator Seitz found for Hunter, voiding his contract and freeing him to sign with any club. The baseball world went crazy. Never before had a player of Hunter's caliber at the height of his career been available to the highest bidder.

A three-week battle ensued involving nearly every team in baseball. The Yankees landed him with a five-year deal totaling $3.35 million, about three times the going rate for the game's top stars. Players union chief Marvin Miller had been telling the players for years what the free market might mean, and now they knew. "This had shown everybody," said Lee MacPhail, now the AL president, "exactly what free agency could amount to."[2]

San Diego Padres president Buzzie Bavasi, who reportedly bid higher than the Yankees for Hunter, likely spoke for many owners in expressing his fear of what had transpired. "What we saw happen here," he said, "fully demonstrates the importance of the reserve rule. The richest clubs would offer the top players the biggest salaries and the biggest bonuses."

Marvin Miller disagreed. "Buzzie Bavasi is a smart man," he said, "educated and all of that, but he obviously didn't learn anything about economics. What he is saying is economic idiocy. The Hunter case establishes zero about what would happen in a free market. Here we had a supply of one and a demand of 24. Obviously, when the supply is one and the demand is great, prices will go up dramatically."[3]

A year later Seitz's ruling in the Messersmith case meant that any player could play the upcoming 1976 season, or any future season, without signing a contract, making potentially hundreds of players free agents at the end of every season. The stunned owners and giddy players' union spent the next several months negotiating a new collective bargaining agreement that restricted free agency to players with six or more years of Major League service. In order to give every current player at least one chance at the free market, the service-time provision did not apply for 1976. (Also, if a player had already signed his 1976 contract, he could become a free agent at the end of that contract, without regard to service time.) There would be widespread free agency for the first time after the 1976 season.

Many baseball men, understandably, were shocked and angry, notably Cincinnati general manager Bob Howsam. "Arbiters weren't intended to rule upon baseball's reserve clause," he said, though Seitz had repeatedly but unsuccessfully asked the owners to negotiate the issue with the players' union. Howsam had the best team in baseball at the time, and he feared that teams would no longer have any incentive to build the way he had built his Reds. "Why spend money developing players if you may lose them when they're ready to produce?"[4]

Miller had no sympathy for the owners' suddenly vulnerable position. "For 10 years, the owners' view has been 'go to hell' when any talk of modifying the reserve clause arose. And for 10 years, I have been telling the owners, 'That's silly. Don't wait until you've been hit on the head.' Now they've been hit on the head." To the claims that baseball teams would go broke, Miller offered that the reserve system had led to incompetent team management. "I think if owners knew that players weren't bound to them for life, they would run more efficient operations. For example, who's to say they can't run player development programs just as efficiently at a lower cost?"[5]

Free agency dramatically changed the way baseball ran its business. For starters, it shifted the balance of power in collective bargaining. Since the Messersmith ruling most labor negotiations have hinged on the owners attempting to reduce the freedoms that Seitz had given the players—by limiting free agency to six-year veterans, by requiring some sort of compensation going to the team that lost the player (the details of which have changed many times), or by taxing team payrolls.

Not surprisingly, free agency has led to dramatically higher salaries for players—not just for the free agents, but for players who could use each new signing in their own negotiations. Chart 5 recaps the average player salary back to 1961.[6] As indicated by the chart, player salaries began their dramatic rise in the late 1970s and have hardly stopped. In the 1985–87 period the owners secretly agreed not to bid on free agents, a violation for which they later had to pay the players $280 million in damages. In the mid-1990s baseball went through difficult financial times, both before and after a long player strike that lasted from August 1994 into April 1995.

At the time of the Messersmith decision, many observers predicted that salaries would skyrocket and that baseball would suffer terrible harm. "Without a reserve system," baseball commissioner Bowie Kuhn testified in the hearing, "our vast array of minor leagues would hardly survive. It is not hard to imagine that we could even lose a major league."[7] But many also believed that the owners were little concerned with principle. "It is the *price* of human flesh that has scandalized the baseball establishment," Red Smith wrote, "not the *barter* of human flesh."[8] And, in fact, the owners were right that the players would get a larger piece of the pie: the players' percentage of revenue jumped from near-historic lows in the mid-1970s of roughly 20 percent (it had been around 30 percent in 1939) to 63 percent by 2003. As of 2012 it had come back down to around 42 percent.[9]

In the end, of course, the game did not crumble. Baseball revenues (bolstered by enormous television, stadium enhancement, merchandising, and advanced media income) have skyrocketed beyond what

Chart 5. Average MLB salaries

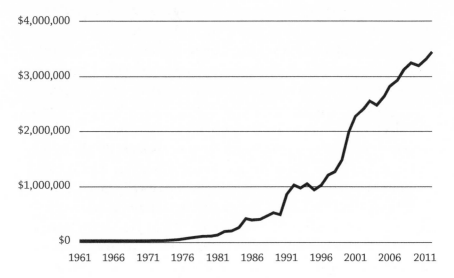

Source: Mike Haupert, Haupert Baseball Salary Database, private collection.

could have been imagined in 1975. Roughly $161 million in 1975, baseball revenues grew to $1.2 billion by 1992 and $7.5 billion in 2012,[10] more than forty-six times higher than thirty-seven years earlier before free agency. Moreover, the associated massive escalation in franchise values has more than offset the jump in salaries.

Not surprisingly, player contract status quickly became an important factor in managing a baseball roster. Chart 6 shows the percentage of WAR in the Major Leagues that was earned by players who had previously been through free agency. This includes players who signed as free agents and then later were traded to other teams. The graph is designed to distinguish players who presumably are being paid "free market" rates for their services.

Because players with fewer than six years of service, and especially those with fewer than three (who have not yet earned the right to have their salary determined through arbitration), are usually much less expensive, even the richest teams can generally not afford to have a roster filled with veterans. The Yankees of the 2001–12 period maintained the largest payroll every year, not only because they

Chart 6. WAR from players who have been through free agency

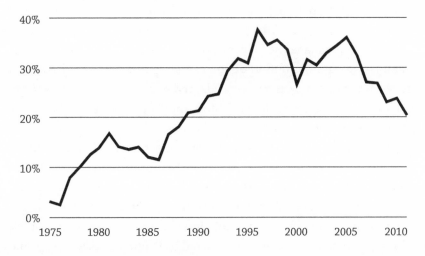

Source: Database owned and maintained by the authors.

had good players but because more than half of the team's WAR was earned by players who had been free agents. For most teams this is not a sustainable practice. In order to compete with a free-spending club like the Yankees, a team needs substantial production from pre–free agency players.

The recent downturn in the percentage of WAR attributed to former free agents can be attributed to at least two factors. First, teams are often using younger, cheaper Minor League veterans instead of aging Major Leaguers as role players. Additionally, teams often try to sign their young star players to long-term contracts before they are eligible for free agency. For example, the Minnesota Twins signed reigning MVP Joe Mauer to an eight-year, $184 million contract after the 2009 season to prevent his impending free agency a year later. According to a study by the *Pittsburgh Tribune-Review*, 108 players on Major League rosters in 2013 had had at least one free-agent season bought out through a multiyear contract.[11]

Much like the creation of the amateur draft in 1965, the advent of free agency required front offices to adapt to a new reality. If a team wanted to keep one of its players in the fold, it had to make sure that he was well treated and well compensated in accordance with the newly emerging market. In order to attract another team's player, the team needed to persuade the player of the benefits of a new environment and be prepared to outbid other teams. As with all such changes in the game's history, some teams adapted more quickly and effectively than others. How well they adjusted would be a key determinant of a team's success over the next forty years.

Because the change was thrust upon them, rather than well planned, many 1976 teams suddenly had players that they could not, or at least would not, pay to retain. The first few months of the 1976 season were played while a new collective bargaining agreement was being negotiated, and many players did not sign contracts in hopes of cashing in after the season. Some clubs reacted by trading stars with expiring contracts—Reggie Jackson, Don Baylor, Bert Blyleven, Ken Holtzman (twice)—in order to salvage something before the player became free at the end of the year. Charlie Finley took this one step further, selling Vida Blue to the Yankees and Rollie Fingers and Joe Rudi to the Red Sox for a total of $3.5 million, deals that were controversially voided by baseball commissioner Kuhn.

The great Cincinnati Reds, whose consecutive World Series titles straddled the Messersmith decision, slowly deteriorated in part because they refused to participate in the annual free-agent derby. The club lost star pitcher Don Gullett after the 1976 World Series and Pete Rose and Joe Morgan within a few years. Bob Howsam, a man who had proved to be a genius at building a club in the reserve-clause era, recognized that those days were over. As the Reds celebrated their 1976 Series sweep of the Yankees, just days before the start of the first free-agent signing period, Howsam was asked in the wild clubhouse celebration to say a few words. "This may be the last time you see a club win that has been built this way," he said. As one writer later observed, "It was a sober moment, like announcing at a birthday party that someone's mother had died. The announcer hardly knew what to say."

But if Bob Howsam feared the future, George Steinbrenner did not. His Yankee team had just won the AL pennant, had just opened their remodeled stadium, and was eager to compete in this new free market.

17 The Zoo

Gabe Paul's career in baseball began in 1928. He was covering high school sports for a Rochester, New York, newspaper when Warren Giles offered him an office job with the Rochester Red Wings, a farm club of the St. Louis Cardinals. Paul eventually became road secretary, and when Giles moved to Cincinnati to run the Reds in 1936, he brought Paul along as public relations director. When Giles became NL president in 1951, Paul replaced him as general manager.

Paul ran the Reds for nine seasons, and only in 1956, when they finished two games behind the Dodgers, did they contend for a pennant. Paul left after the 1960 season because he feared owner Powel Crosley might move the team. His successor, Bill DeWitt, made a couple of key trades, but when the Reds won the 1961 pennant, they did so predominantly with the team Paul had assembled. Paul moved first to the expansion Houston Astros and then to Cleveland, where he ran the Indians for twelve years. Like the Reds, the Indians were an also-ran while Paul was there, beset with financial woes that almost caused the team to leave the city. Paul and George Steinbrenner knew each other well in these years, and when Paul had the chance to come to New York with the promise of a free-spending owner, he did not hesitate.

After the departures of Mike Burke and Lee MacPhail, Gabe Paul ran the Yankees as team president for the next four eventful seasons. Steinbrenner admired Paul and respected his long history in the game, and early on he allowed Paul significant latitude in hiring and making deals. As we shall see events would conspire to keep Steinbrenner in the background for much of Paul's reign, but behind the scenes Paul had to deal with a strong-willed and often abusive boss. Though Steinbrenner was a full twenty years younger than Paul, he did not hesitate to reprimand or belittle him in front of friends or strangers. As the club became more successful, and especially as Paul received much of the credit for that success, Steinbrenner did whatever he could to elbow himself into the story. Paul never seemed to let any of it bother him. "Gabe would get red in the face," wrote Ed Linn, "but he'd take it and talk George out of doing something foolish. He took it because after [thirty] years in the game he was being given the chance to operate in the Big Town, with an unlimited amount of money. And that was irresistible."[1]

"He is a marvelously energetic man," wrote Steve Jacobson. "His hair is silver, his nose prominent and red, and his complexion a normal shade of pink. He has a bag packed with a shirt, a razor, and a toothbrush at all times, ready to go off and make a deal." About Paul's search for unappreciated players, Jacobson wrote, "Paul has a saying: 'One man's shit is another man's ice cream.' He is saying, let me make up my own mind."[2]

Paul knew just about everyone in baseball, and over the next few years he brought to New York some of baseball's best front-office executives, both proven veterans and young up-and-comers. To Paul's credit he was not afraid to hire senior executives with an established track record. In November 1973 Paul hired Tal Smith as executive vice president and Clyde Kluttz as scouting director. Smith had been the director of stadium operations for the Astros and had worked with Paul in Cincinnati. He ostensibly replaced MacPhail, though Paul handled the GM duties himself under the new structure. Kluttz managed the scouts, who led the charge to bring new talent into the system, often amateurs and more often players from other organizations.

Paul's first order of business was to find a manager to replace Ralph Houk, who, unhappy with Steinbrenner's second-guessing and criticism of veteran players, announced his resignation in the pressroom after the final game of the 1973 season.[3] Paul's effort to find a replacement turned into the biggest soap opera of the off-season. Some in the press favored Elston Howard, the team's first base coach, who would have been the game's first black manager. Paul preferred Dick Williams, who had just resigned his post with the A's moments after his team had won their second straight World Series. Williams had spent three years dealing with the meddling of owner Charlie Finley and had decided that was enough. Williams said that he still wanted to manage and in fact might be interested in the vacated Yankees job. Everyone assumed that the Yankees would hire him within a week.

A few days later Finley announced that Williams still had a contract with the A's, that the Yankees could not sign his manager without paying adequate compensation, and that he would lodge a protest with the league if any team tampered with Williams. A shaken Williams claimed he had been told by Finley that he would not stand in his way if he sought another job. Finley's comments also stunned Gabe Paul, who now decided he should have compensation from the Tigers for their signing of Houk. Both cases were soon thrown in the lap of outgoing AL president Joe Cronin.

Finley assured the press that he was not standing in Williams's way—he was merely asking to be compensated, something that had happened several times in recent history. When the Mets hired Gil Hodges in 1968, for example, they gave the Senators, his previous employer, one hundred thousand dollars plus a player. The Yankees saw the strength of Finley's position and attempted to negotiate a deal, but they could not reach terms.

Undeterred, and tired of waiting for a decision from Cronin, the Yankees went ahead and signed Williams on December 13. "We feel we waited long enough," said Paul. "We conferred with our attorneys and they told us we had a right to sign Williams."[4] Finley filed an injunction in federal court, which was upheld. On December 20 Cronin ruled against the Yankees in both cases. Houk belonged to the Tigers and Williams to the A's. Paul tried again to work out a deal with Finley but failed. On January 3 Paul hired ex-Pirates manager Bill Virdon to lead the club.

In the meantime Paul started work on the playing roster. His first big deal came in early December when he traded Lindy McDaniel to Kansas City for outfielder Lou Piniella and pitcher Ken Wright. McDaniel, one of MacPhail's best acquisitions, had given the Yankees six quality seasons in the bullpen, but he was now thirty-eight years old. Piniella was thirty but would play the next decade in Yankee pinstripes. In March Paul purchased outfielder Elliot Maddox from the Rangers and watched Maddox hit .303 and play an outstanding center field.

Paul made his most dramatic move on April 26, two weeks into the 1974 season, when he shipped four pitchers—Fritz Peterson, Steve Kline, Fred Beene, and Tom Buskey—to the Indians for first baseman Chris Chambliss and pitchers Dick Tidrow and Cecil Upshaw. Paul craved the offense the left-handed hitting Chambliss could bring ("You don't get an opportunity to get a star ballplayer every day," he reasoned), but the price of four pitchers from the Major League roster was steep. "I can't believe this trade," said Murcer. "It just means they don't think we have a winning club." Stottlemyre added, "You just don't trade four pitchers, you just don't." Angrier still was Thurman Munson: "I'll go to Cleveland. They can trade me there now. How can they trade Beene? They've got to be kidding."[5]

The Yankees spent much of the summer near the bottom of the division and did not pass .500 for good until August 21. Paul made several moves to try to plug the leaks on his team, picking up pitchers Mike Wallace, Rudy May, and Larry Gura (who combined to finish 19-4 with the Yankees) as well as Sandy Alomar, who took over as the starting second baseman. The Yankees were seven games behind the Red Sox on August 23 but caught fire and finished 26-12 from that point forward. This was good enough to pass the Red Sox, but both were overtaken by the Orioles, who went 28-8 over the same stretch. Still, the Yankees finished 89-73, just two games back. The team was led by the strong pitching of Dobson and Medich (who each won nineteen games) and Lyle and the hitting of Maddox, Piniella, Munson, and Nettles. After the season Paul was named Executive of the Year by the *Sporting News*.

Steinbrenner, meanwhile, spent the 1974 season dealing with serious legal difficulties. In April he was indicted on fourteen felony charges, most stemming from his illegal contributions to the reelection campaign of President Richard Nixon. Although Steinbrenner tried to whitewash his offenses in later years, the facts of the case were pretty clear then and now. In order to circumvent campaign donation limits, Steinbrenner devised a fraudulent laundering scheme at American Shipbuilding: the company gave large "bonuses" to several employees, who were then required to donate that money (less taxes) back to Steinbrenner to funnel to Nixon's people. Furthermore, Steinbrenner coerced these same employees to file false expense reports and backdated memorandums to cover up the illegal activities. Two of his workers made full confessions to the grand jury, and in April 1974 Leon Jaworski, the Watergate special prosecutor, served Steinbrenner a fifteen-count indictment. He faced six years in federal prison.[6]

In late August Steinbrenner's lawyer, Edward Bennett Williams, worked out a generous deal for his client. In exchange for pleading guilty to both authorizing twenty-five thousand dollars in illegal contributions and conniving to cover up his crimes, Steinbrenner paid fifteen thousand dollars in fines but avoided jail. In November baseball commissioner Bowie Kuhn suspended Steinbrenner from day-to-day operations of the Yankees for two years. The suspension had little teeth—Steinbrenner could not represent the club at league meetings or conduct business deals with other teams, but he remained very much in charge. "Unless Bowie Kuhn has the telephones bugged," wrote Red Smith, "there will be nothing to prevent him from consulting with Gabe Paul every hour on the hour."[7] Kuhn himself recognized this: "Of course I knew, and I couldn't object to his involvement in big money decisions. So long as he didn't flaunt it."[8]

Paul was the central public Yankee figure in the next two off-seasons, ones just as eventful as the last. Things heated up right after the World Series when Paul swapped Murcer to the San Francisco Giants for outfielder Bobby Bonds. Although both players had had subpar seasons in 1974, Murcer was the Yankees' biggest star and most popular player, and Bonds had been called the best player in baseball as recently as 1973.[9] Bonds promised more speed and better defense and, perhaps most important, was a right-handed hitter on a club that had become far too left-handed. "He'll bat third and play right field," said Virdon. "He's got great speed and great power. There isn't anybody who wouldn't argue that he's one of the super players in the game."[10] Murcer's left-handed power had been curbed by Shea Stadium, the Yankees' temporary home, and he had sulked when Virdon, a great defensive outfielder from an earlier generation, moved him to right field in deference to Maddox.

The deal proved to be merely a warm-up to the big drama ahead. As recounted in the previous chapter, the Yankees were the winners of the Catfish Hunter derby, signing the star pitcher on December 31. If anyone had been wondering if the Yankees would be handicapped by the suspension of their principal owner, the signing of Hunter provided the answer. Paul flew down to Tampa, Florida, to meet with the banished Steinbrenner, who provided the go-ahead to do whatever it took. The Yankees' wild card, it turned out, was scouting director Kluttz, who lived near Hunter and had signed him to his first contract with the A's ten years earlier. Kluttz visited Hunter first and then returned with Paul a couple of days later to sign him.

The acquisitions of Bonds and Hunter, added to what had already been a contending team, made the Yankees one of the World Series favorites for 1975. "We know the Yankees stand for class," said Paul. "We think we have it now. We think we have a winning team. And the one tradition we are most anxious to reestablish is winning. You know, it's easy to have class when you are winning and you have the wherewithal."[11]

The 1975 Yankees started slowly but caught fire in May and led the AL East for several days in late June. Ultimately, a succession of injuries derailed this promising team. On June 7, not quite a third of the way through the season, Bonds was leading the league with fourteen home runs and forty-one RBI. That day in Anaheim he tore cartilage in his right knee while making a running catch and hobbled through the rest of the season. (He still led the club with thirty-two home runs and thirty stolen bases and in slugging percentage.) A more serious injury struck just six days later, when Elliott Maddox, hitting .307 with walks and providing great center-field defense, collapsed on the wet field at Shea Stadium making a catch against the White Sox, tearing ligaments in his right knee. He missed the rest of the season and most of 1976 and was never again the same player. If that were not enough, Lou Piniella suffered an ear infection and hit .196, and Ron Blomberg tore the rotator cuff in his shoulder and dropped to .255—both had hit over .300 the previous season. Hunter won twenty-three games (completing thirty of thirty-nine starts) in his first year in New York, but ultimately the team dropped out of the race and finished twelve games behind the surprising Red Sox.

During his "suspension," Steinbrenner sat in his owner's box at Shea Stadium and could be seen yelling into the dugout if he disagreed with something Virdon was doing. When the Yankees started losing in mid-summer, the yelling became a frequent occurrence. As if willed by the fates, in late July the Texas Rangers fired manager Billy Martin, who had starred for the Yankees in the 1950s. A few days later the Red Sox came into Shea Stadium and won three out of four to put the Yankees ten games back, whereupon Steinbrenner ordered Paul to make a change. Paul's first choice was Bobby Cox, managing for the Yankees Triple-A affiliate in Syracuse. Paul sent his top scout, Birdie Tebbetts, to Syracuse to scout Cox. Tebbetts reported back that Cox was not ready. Steinbrenner suggested Martin, whom Paul quickly hired. Martin had experienced short-term success in Minnesota, Detroit, and Texas, but he also brought quite a bit of baggage with him, something that Paul and Steinbrenner would learn soon enough.

By 1975 the Yankee front office had added a couple of significant new faces. In August 1974 Tal Smith hired Pat Gillick, with whom he had worked in Houston, as coordinator of player development and scouting. "He works harder than anybody I've ever seen in baseball," said Smith at the time. "No lead is too small or too insignificant when it comes to checking out a free agent."[12] Still just thirty-seven, Gillick was considered one of the bright young minds in the game and a big coup for the Yankees.

When Smith left New York in 1975 to become Houston's general manager, Paul hired a man he knew from his days in the Cincinnati organization, Cedric Tallis, who, since his dismissal from the Royals, had been a consultant for a group trying to bring an expansion team to New Orleans. With Yankee Stadium due to reopen in April 1976, Tallis, who had overseen the building of both Anaheim Stadium and Royals Stadium, watched over the complicated details of the grand remodel. In effect Paul continued as the team's general manager, in charge of the Major League team, while Tallis became vice president of baseball operations, assisting Paul on all baseball matters.

Tallis tried to lure John Schuerholz, an assistant in Kansas City's front office since their 1969 creation, to be New York's farm director. Royals general manager Joe Burke granted Tallis permission to talk to Schuerholz, and the young executive accepted Tallis's offer, which was a promotion. When Schuerholz informed the Royals, Burke counteroffered with an expanded role (also farm director) and presumably more money. Schuerholz decided to stay in Kansas City. "Cedric was irate," Schuerholz recalled, telling him, "'I can't believe you would go against your word.'" Although Schuerholz felt he had made the right decision, he never managed to rebuild his relationship with Tallis.[13]

With Tal Smith gone Gillick became a crucial adviser to Paul, and the two were destined to play a starring role in yet another eventful off-season. Just after the 1975 World Series Paul met with Gillick (with the suspended Steinbrenner listening over a speakerphone) to go over the scouting director's views on the entire organization and what the Yankees might be able to do to improve it. Gillick had spent the season watching the Yankees' Major and Minor League teams and scouting other organizations as well.

The Yankees' biggest flaw, Gillick felt, was the performance of their up-the-middle position players other than Munson. Their most commonly used double-play combination had hit .152 (shortstop Jim Mason) and .229 (second baseman Sandy Alomar), while center fielder Maddox's recovery from his knee injury was far from certain. He also thought the team needed more starting pitching. The way to solve some of these problems, Gillick felt, was to trade Bonds. This suggestion surprised Steinbrenner, who considered Bonds, justifiably, their best player and biggest asset. According to Paul, however, Bonds was a heavy drinker, and his training habits were worrisome for the future.[14]

Gillick also lobbied for Willie Randolph, a twenty-one-year-old second baseman who had debuted for the Pirates in July and hit just .164 in thirty games. Randolph was blocked in Pittsburgh by Rennie Stennett, a twenty-four-year-old with similar skills. Gillick spent ten days that fall watching Randolph play in the Venezuelan Winter League, which only increased his interest in the youngster. As the *Sporting News* described it, "His heart palpitating, Gillick raved over Randolph's attitude, his makeup, his leadership, his desire, his range, and his bat."[15] Paul solicited other reports from his scouts and heard nothing but high praise. In December he offered pitcher Doc Medich to Pirates GM Joe Brown, in exchange for Randolph and left-handed starter Ken Brett. A couple of days later Brown said he would do the deal only if the Yankees also took Dock Ellis, a talented pitcher prone to erratic behavior. A startled Paul made the trade.

On the same day, December 11, the Yankees implemented the other half of Gillick's advice, trading Bonds to the California Angels for speedy center fielder Mickey Rivers, who had stolen seventy bases in 1975, and right-hander Ed Figueroa, who had won sixteen games for a poor Angels club. "It's run production that counts," said Paul. "I think we'll score more runs without the home runs than we did last season."[16] In a cab to the airport while leaving the winter meetings, Gillick said to Paul, "Well, boss, we pretty much filled just about all of our needs in two deals."[17] As the Yankees saw it, Figueroa replaced Medich, so the team essentially traded Bonds for Rivers, Randolph, Ellis, and Brett, which would prove to be an astounding exchange. The trade of Bonds, though, was a shocker at the time. The club had spent much of the previous off-season touting his greatness, and Bonds had lived up to the hype. Now he had been traded.

As we have seen, the future of the New York Yankees, and every other team in baseball, transformed dramatically in December 1975 when arbitrator Peter Seitz ruled against baseball in the Messersmith-McNally case. McNally had retired during the 1975 season, so he was personally unaffected by the case. Messersmith, like Hunter a year earlier, was a one-person free-agent class and, with a 39-20 record and a 2.43 ERA over the past two years, one of baseball's best pitchers. Because the owners fought the arbitrator's decision for several weeks, Messersmith was not technically free to sign until March 16.

It surprised no one a couple of weeks later when the Yankees announced signing Messersmith to a four-year one-million-dollar contract. What was surprising was that the pitcher angrily denied that he had signed and furthermore claimed he would now definitely not sign with the Yankees. "They agreed to certain things and then they came back and they were different," he said. "It's incredible. I can't believe what's going on. These are the people who run our country. It seems to me like it's a cute game."[18] Steinbrenner sent a threatening telegram to Messersmith, demanding that he live up to the agreement or suffer legal consequences, but after a hearing between all parties with commissioner Kuhn, the owner backed down. Using language base-ball fans would come to know, he said, "I have stated publicly many times how I feel about the great tradition of the New York Yankees and how I expect my players to feel about the privilege of being a Yankee and wearing the pinstripes. There can be no place in the Yankee or-ganization for any player who cannot find it in himself to feel this."[19] On April 10 Messersmith signed with the Atlanta Braves. But Stein-brenner had made it clear that the Yankees would be a big player in the upcoming free-agent bonanza.

The Yankee owner was able to take such a public stance because commissioner Kuhn had ended Steinbrenner's suspension on March 1, nine months before his two-year ban was due to end, reportedly be-cause the Yankees agreed to change their vote to renew Kuhn's con-tract. The end of the suspension changed little, of course, but Stein-brenner now took his place as the public face of the team, much more than he had before his suspension. His time away had taught Stein-brenner how popular the team could be and how famous he could be sitting atop it, especially with free agency coming to the game. Stein-brenner's first public foray in his return to the club, the Messersmith nonsigning, had gone poorly, but this setback would not slow him down in any noticeable way.

The key factor in what became the Yankees' renaissance might have been the opening of the remodeled Yankee Stadium on April 15. The Yankees had been outdrawn by the Mets the last ten years they played in old Yankee Stadium, in some years by more than two to one, and both years the teams shared Shea Stadium. In their remodeled home this reversed immediately. The 1976 Yankees drew more than two mil-lion fans for the first time since 1950 and led the league in attendance for their first six years back home. The Yankees under Steinbrenner and Paul had made several important moves to improve their ball club, but they benefited tremendously from two events neither man had anything to do with: the advent of free agency and the remodeling of Yankee Stadium. Former team president Mike Burke had spearheaded the deal with the city for the stadium, which once again became one of baseball's most famous venues. The revenues from the stadium gave Steinbrenner and Paul additional funds for the upcoming free market.

After a year of battling injuries, the 1976 squad finished 10-3 in April, had a ten-game lead by July, and won the AL East rather easily. The Yankees coasted to a 97-62 record and a ten-and-a-half-game margin over the Orioles. Led by Thurman Munson (.302 with 105 RBI and the league MVP award), the well-balanced offense also featured excellent years from Nettles (a league-leading 32 homers), Chambliss (.293 with 17 homers), Roy White (a league-leading 104 runs scored), and newcomers Rivers and Randolph (who combined for 80 steals in 99 attempts). The pitching featured 19 wins from Figueroa and 17 each by Hunter and Ellis.

The season included a bit of drama on June 15, the annual trading deadline. Paul first pulled off a huge deal with the Orioles, trading starting pitcher Rudy May along with four youngsters—pitchers Tippy Martinez, Scott McGregor, Dave Pagan, and catcher Rick Dempsey—for pitchers Grant Jackson, Doyle Alexander, Ken Holtzman, and Jimmy Freeman as well as catcher Elrod Hendricks. The Orioles were mainly interested in getting some value for pending free agents Alexander and Holtzman, who they believed they could not re-sign, while the Yankees were prepared to sign anyone and paid with young players they did not need at the moment. Over time this would become an excellent trade for the Orioles: May remained a good starter, while Martinez, Dempsey, and McGregor would have long careers and play key roles on pennant-winning Oriole teams.

Paul was not through. Just hours before the deadline, he announced the purchase of Oakland A's ace Vida Blue for $1.5 million, an extraordinary sum that, coupled with the Red Sox' purchase of Oakland's Joe Rudi and Rollie Fingers for $1 million each, sent shock waves throughout baseball. These sales were a natural outgrowth of the new era of free agency. Oakland owner Charlie Finley knew he could not sign the players and would otherwise lose them after the season. Getting cash now was an intelligent reaction to the new reality. "I'm going to use the money to buy players and I'm going to do it immediately," said Finley. When faced with charges that his team, already with a sizable lead in the division, was trying to buy the pennant, Paul offered, "It all depends on what side of the fence you're sitting."[20]

This all soon proved to be moot, as commissioner Kuhn voided the Finley sales as not being "in the best interests of baseball" and ordered the players returned to the A's. Finley sued and spent several months fighting the case in vain. As valuable as Blue was, the voiding of the sale was not decisive. The Yankees still had a starting rotation of Hunter, Ellis, Figueroa, Holtzman, and Alexander, which proved more than sufficient to win the division. Paul had already traded Brett (for designated hitter Carlos May) because Martin could find no work for him.

In 1976 the Yankees returned to the postseason for the first time in twelve years and won a thrilling five-game ALCS, culminating in Chris Chambliss's game-winning home run in the bottom of the ninth inning of Game Five. The ensuing celebration, with fans storming the field while Chambliss tried in vain to complete the circuit around the bases, was one of the wilder endings in Yankee history. This proved to be the end of the celebrating that season, as the Yankees were swept by the juggernaut Cincinnati Reds in the World Series in four relatively easy games. Unlike many of the seasons ahead, Steinbrenner did not rage at the loss. The season was a success by any reasonable standard, with a shiny new ballpark and a pennant-winning team, and he knew that the changing landscape was playing right into his hands.

Soon after the 1976 World Series, Steinbrenner assembled his brain trust to discuss the upcoming free-agent marketplace, the first of its kind in baseball history. The ground rules of the free-agent system have changed many times over the years, but in this first go-round each team was allowed to sign no more than two free agents or the number of players the club itself lost, whichever was higher. Baseball first conducted a dispersal draft, with each club selecting the right to negotiate with certain players. Teams could pick as many players as they wanted, but each player could be selected by only twelve clubs plus the one he was just on, effectively cutting his potential buyers by half.

When his front office gathered, Steinbrenner's opening words were: "We are not going to win a championship with Fred Stanley at shortstop."[21] Indeed, the Yankees fielded nearly a complete team of All-Stars in 1976, with Stanley clearly the weak link in the regular lineup. There was only one starting shortstop available on the market, thirty-four-year-old Bert Campaneris of the Oakland A's. Gabe Paul had another name in mind: Baltimore's Bobby Grich, an outstanding defensive second baseman who had played shortstop in the Minor Leagues. Grich was also a fine right-handed hitter. "We need right-handed hitting with authority," said Martin. "We have enough left-handed power." It was quickly agreed that Grich would be their top priority.

Their second choice was also an easy one, Cincinnati's twenty-five-year-old left-hander Don Gullett, who had beaten the Yankees in the first game of the just-completed World Series. Proving that they could operate in the new system, the club contacted Jerry Kapstein, the agent for both Gullett and Grich, and secured the right to make the last offer to each, essentially guaranteeing that they could top the highest bid. Their offer to Gullett, six years and two million dollars, was enough to land their prey, thereby angering several other teams who had not even had the opportunity to speak with the star pitcher.

Unlike the prolonged chess matches of twenty-first-century off-seasons, in 1976 the players acted as if they feared waking up from their dream. Don Baylor was signed by the Angels on November 16 and the following day brought contracts for Joe Rudi (also the Angels), Dave Cash (Montreal), Gary Mathews (Atlanta), and Bert Campaneris (Texas). The Yankees signed Gullett on the eighteenth and then asked Kapstein what it was that Bobby Grich wanted.

What Bobby Grich wanted, it turned out, was to play for the Angels, in his beloved Southern California. When he heard that Baylor, his best friend in baseball, had signed with California, he called Kapstein and asked him to contact Harry Dalton, the Angels' general manager, whom Grich knew well from their years together in Baltimore. California had selected Grich with their last pick in the draft and was the twelfth and final team to choose the second baseman. Dalton's priorities had been Baylor and Rudi, and he had quickly landed both.

The rule allowing each team to sign only two free agents contained an exception: a club could sign enough players to replace their own lost free agents. The Angels played the 1976 season with two unsigned players: seldom-used utility men Paul Dade and Billy Smith. On September 9 the Angels purchased infielder Tim Nordbrook from the Orioles, an unusual transaction for a team that was in fifth place, seventeen games behind the Royals. Nordbrook, as it happened, was a potential free agent. After the season the Angels made no effort to sign Nordbrook, bringing their "lost" free agents to three, albeit three who combined for only twenty-five at bats and four hits in the 1976 season.

Bobby Grich knew that the Angels could sign a third player. When Kapstein relayed Grich's interest to Dalton, Harry told him that the Angels had already spent more money than they had wanted and were out of the market. Grich persisted, telling Dalton that if the Angels made a decent offer he would take it without any bidding war. Dalton obtained permission from owner Gene Autry and invited Grich to Anaheim to negotiate a contract.

But first Grich had his promised meeting with George Steinbrenner. The Yankees put on quite a show, telling Grich that he would guarantee them the championship, that he would be an outstanding shortstop, the missing piece to a coming dynasty. Grich said he would think it over, that he was leaning toward the Angels but he was impressed with the Yankees' pitch. Of course, Steinbrenner was not used to people "thinking it over," so he told Grich that if he signed with the Angels he would lodge a protest with the commissioner about their suspicious purchase of Nordbrook. This proved to be a mistake. Grich left the meeting, called his friend Dalton to ask whether the Yankees had a case, and quickly worked out an agreement with the Angels.[22]

The Yankees did not want to be publicly spurned by anyone, so they leaked a story that they had soured on Grich's demands (though he had made none) and were wary of his ability to play shortstop. The guy they wanted all along, the new story went, was Reggie Jackson. This was convenient, since by this time there were only two free agents left on the Yankees' draft list: Reggie Jackson and Billy Smith. Apparently, Paul still did not want Jackson, due to both his skill set and his personality. Paul worried that Jackson would have a destructive effect on the team, and Martin agreed.[23] Steinbrenner overruled them and was heavily involved in the negotiations that landed the star outfielder for five years and a record three million dollars.

Gabe Paul finally got his shortstop in March, trading right fielder Oscar Gamble, now displaced by Jackson, a couple of prospects (one of whom, LaMarr Hoyt, would later win an AL Cy Young Award), and two hundred thousand dollars to the White Sox for Bucky Dent. Dent was no Bobby Grich, but Steinbrenner had become obsessed with upgrading the position, and he badgered Paul to make the trade. Paul was forced to make another deal in April after Dock Ellis publicly called out Steinbrenner for coming into the clubhouse where he did not belong. Paul traded him to Oakland for pitcher Mike Torrez.

Paul fought more successfully with his boss that off-season in the matter of young pitcher Ron Guidry. Paul's most trusted scout, Birdie Tebbetts, raved about Guidry, suggesting he could be the best pitcher in baseball in a few years. Based largely on Tebbetts's reports, Paul had protected the pitcher in the previous fall's expansion draft and resisted several opportunities to include him in trades. When Guidry pitched poorly in the spring, Steinbrenner raged. "The problem with you," he told Paul, "is that you believe everything Tebbetts tells you. There aren't any geniuses in this business." Paul's insistence on keeping Guidry almost cost them Dent, and then almost cost them Torrez. In both cases Paul had to come up with other packages to get the deals done.

Gabe Paul had built his team. The 1977 Yankees had an infield of Chambliss, Randolph, Dent, and Nettles and an outfield of White, Rivers, and Jackson, with Munson catching and Piniella serving as the designated hitter. Of these nine players Paul had inherited three, acquired five in trades, and signed Jackson. Of the most used pitchers he had inherited Lyle; saved Guidry; acquired Figueroa, Torrez, and Tidrow; and signed Hunter and Gullett. It was a remarkable series of moves spread over four off-seasons.

The 1976 team had successfully blended the egos and personalities of many talented players, even with a brilliant but mercurial alcoholic manager and an overbearing owner. But the acquisition of Jackson served to light the powder keg, leading to all manner of jealousies and hatreds and confrontations, both verbal and physical. Paul had spent the past thirty years dreaming of having a team with this much talent, but there were surely days during that 1977 season when he wondered whether it was all worth it.

Some of the problems were only indirectly related to Jackson. To start with there was the money. Several prominent Yankees were either holding out or publicly lobbying for larger contracts in the spring of 1977. "As soon as a good player becomes available," said Lyle, "there goes two or three million dollars to him. But the guys who won for him see very little of it." In fact, Thurman Munson had tried to protect himself a year earlier by signing a two-year contract with the oral understanding that he would be the highest-paid Yankee for the duration of the deal. Munson signed another contract in January, though he publicly accused Steinbrenner of lying to him about the terms of Jackson's deal. Nettles walked out of camp that spring, and Ellis ridiculed the boss both publicly and to his face. Jackson, meanwhile, talked about his contract daily and was known to sit on the team plane literally counting out the hundred-dollar bills in his wallet.

Jackson had been a tremendous player for eight seasons with Oakland and Baltimore: a power hitter who could run the bases and had good range and a fine arm in right field. He was also a man who loved talking to the press, especially about himself, a habit his teammates mocked in Oakland. He often talked of his supposedly superior intellect, or his money, or his collection of cars. His teammates and manager in New York, who had won the previous pennant without him, had no interest in putting up with a boastful new star. They wanted someone who hit home runs and shut his mouth. In the spring writer Robert Ward spent a few days with Jackson to do a *Sport* magazine story, which the baseball world read in late May. And thus the "Bronx Zoo" was born.

In Ward's article Reggie ruminated on how hard his life had become now that he was not just a "black athlete" but also a "tremendous intellect." In words that would make his life quite a bit harder, Jackson told Ward, "You know, this team . . . it all flows from me. I've got to keep it all going. I'm the straw that stirs the drink. It all comes back to me. Maybe I should say me and Munson . . . but really he doesn't enter into it. He's being so damned insecure about the whole thing." As he said these words Jackson had yet to play a game for the Yankees, while Munson was the league MVP on the reigning champions. The writer suggested Jackson talk to Munson, advice that was deflected. Munson was insecure and would deny the conflict, Jackson thought. But Jackson was too smart for him. "Let me put it this way: no team I am on will ever be humiliated the way the Yankees were by the Reds in the World Series. That's why Munson can't intimidate me. Nobody can." But Jackson was also obsessed with what his teammates had told Ward about him and laughed when told that Martin had said that Munson was the team's leader. "Don't you see," Jackson said, "that there is just no way I can play second fiddle to *anybody*. Hah! That's just not in the cards. . . . There ain't no way."[24]

His new teammates, not surprisingly, were horrified. "I just go out every day and play," said Munson. "I helped the Yankees win the pennant. I was MVP. What's so bad about that?"[25] The rest of the players and Martin agreed, and the clubhouse never recovered. One day Jackson refused to shake any of his teammates' hands after a home run, and a few days later Munson would not shake Jackson's hand. Playing the victim to the end, Jackson could never own up to how he had mistreated his teammates. When Jackson slumped over the first half of the season, Martin frequently batted him fifth or sixth in the order or benched him against left-handed pitchers, all of which Reggie believed was done to humiliate him. Martin also used Jackson as the designated hitter seventeen times, noticing that the slugger's defense seemed to have deteriorated.

With the aggrieved Munson staying quiet, Martin and Jackson became the chief protagonists, and the situation had another dramatic moment on June 18 in Boston, in front of a national television audience. It started when Jackson seemed to react slowly to a shallow pop fly by Jim Rice that fell safely and then weakly lobbed a throw to the pitcher's mound while Rice hustled into second base. Martin reacted by sending Paul Blair out to replace Jackson in the middle of the inning, and an enraged Jackson began yelling at his manager when he returned to the dugout. The two men had to be restrained from brawling in full view of the millions watching on television.

Steinbrenner, who was not in Boston, got a message to Paul, who was seated in a box seat near the Yankee dugout. The owner wanted Martin fired immediately. Paul talked him out of it, reasoning, correctly, that everyone would have blamed Jackson. Reggie later made the same case to Steinbrenner, and he (ironically) and Paul likely saved Martin's job. The boss eventually confronted Martin to read him the riot act, telling him that he had wanted to fire him. "It's in Gabe's hands," he told Martin. Not long after, Steinbrenner would claim sole credit for keeping Martin on, because, in Ed Linn's words, "the bane of George's life in those first years was that he knew he needed Gabe Paul and wished he didn't. And so, from time to time, it made him feel better to make believe he didn't." Paul was so distraught by the circus that he left the team for several days, forcing Steinbrenner to fly back to Tampa (where both men lived) to ask him to return.[26]

There were several other interpersonal dramas throughout the season, too numerous to recount here, and Martin was nearly fired a few other times. In fact, Paul offered the managerial job to coach Dick Howser in late July but was turned down. The Yankees had a few slumps in the first half of the season, but eventually their combined talents righted the ship. It was a very tough division—both the Red Sox (who led most of the summer) and the Orioles won 97 games—but the Yankees went 42-17 the last two months of the season to win 100 games and capture their second consecutive pennant. Jackson shook off his malaise to hit 32 homers and bat .287, Nettles added 37 homers, while Munson (.308, 100 RBI), Chambliss (90 RBI), Rivers (.326), White, Randolph, and Piniella made up a great offense. Ron Guidry won 16 games with a 2.82 ERA, while Figueroa, Gullett, and Torrez all had good years. Sparky Lyle finished 13-5 with 26 saves and won the Cy Young Award.

The postseason included its fair share of drama as well. The Yankees matched up with the Royals again in the ALCS and again went to the deciding fifth game. With Jackson struggling at 1 for 14 for the series, Martin benched him against the left-handed Paul Splittorff in the finale. Jackson came off the bench with a pinch single that helped the Yankees to their come-from-behind 5–3 victory. The Yankees then beat the Dodgers in a six-game World Series, their first championship in twelve years. Jackson, back in the lineup, hit home runs in the fourth and fifth games, and then tied a record with three in the finale. His five home runs in the Series set a new record, and he was a fairly obvious choice as the Series MVP.

Amid all the celebration, hostility remained. "Every member of that team hated and despised me," Jackson later said. This was an exaggeration, but not a large one. "How could I ever like that motherfucking sonofabitch after what he said about me?" asked Munson.[27] Martin clearly hated him, and many of the other Yankees did not hide their feelings in later memoirs.

Soon after the Series was over, Gabe Paul decided to call it a day, moving back to Cleveland to run the Indians. He had built the Yankees and watched them win, but he could clearly see that his boss's need to be on center stage was only going to grow. Steinbrenner had said in 1973 that he intended to stick to building ships, but those days seemed long ago.

To replace Gabe Paul, Steinbrenner promoted Tallis, and the Yankees repeated in 1978 with even more bizarre interpersonal drama. But the owner soon tired of Tallis too, and there followed a parade of Yankee general managers, nine in all over the next fourteen years, each one needing to respond to the boss's temper and whims. Despite a huge monetary advantage, the talent in the Yankees' organization slowly slipped away, not to return until the 1990s. In fact, it took a second Steinbrenner suspension, this one lasting from 1990 to 1993, to allow another general manager (Gene Michael) to keep the job more than a couple of years, and when Steinbrenner returned the club was back in contention again. Steinbrenner's money and commitment to excellence, when coupled with strong baseball people running the team, proved to be a formidable combination.

Paul could not turn the Indians around. As much as Steinbrenner needed Paul's baseball intellect, Paul needed Steinbrenner's bankroll. But weep not for Gabe Paul. "There was a line by Dave LeFevre, who once tried to buy the team in the 1980s," said Pete Franklin, a radio personality in Cleveland. "He said, 'I want to stand next to Gabe Paul when they drop the atomic bomb.' Boy, was that the truth. Gabe was the ultimate baseball survivor. He was a very intelligent man, a great self-promoter, and a guy who knew how to get next to people with money."[28]

As for Steinbrenner he never stopped trying to minimize the importance of Paul to his own legacy. "I like Gabe," the boss said later. "He had a great career in baseball. Of course, the poor guy was so shaky the last couple of years here that he really couldn't do much of anything."[29]

18 Many Rivers

You can't acquire or develop good players unless everyone in the front office is thinking alike, or unless there's one strong personality in charge. . . . You don't find an organization like that very often, but when you do, it's usually flying pennant flags.—WHITEY HERZOG, baseball manager

In 1976 the American League awarded two new expansion franchises: one to Seattle (which had lost the Pilots to Milwaukee in 1970 after just one season) and a second to a Toronto ownership group led by Labatt, the beer conglomerate, and R. Howard Webster, described by *Time* as a Montreal-based, publicity-shy bachelor multimillionaire.[1] While Toronto's new team owed its existence to the hard work and lobbying of many, Don McDougall, president of Labatt Breweries, a large subsidiary of John Labatt, Ltd., spearheaded the company's pursuit. McDougall, as part of a five-person board, oversaw the building of a new baseball organization.

Testifying to Labatt's business focus, the first executive hired by the board was Paul Beeston, a personable thirty-year-old accountant given wide responsibility on the administrative side of the organization. Early in his tenure with the Blue Jays, Beeston received some unwanted attention when he brashly claimed, "Anyone who quotes profits of a baseball club is missing the point. I could turn a $4 million profit into a $2 million loss and I could get every national accounting firm to agree with me."[2] Beeston proved a savvy hire. He went on to an illustrious career with the Blue Jays, eventually becoming president and CEO, and served a stint as president and chief operating officer (COO) of Major League Baseball. "I can't imagine anybody who saw the way Paul would develop," said attorney Herb Solway. "They might have thought he would be a good CFO [chief financial officer], but who in their right mind would have thought he would be the chief executive officer?"[3]

Labatt intended to run its baseball team as it had run its beer business. "It's the same as any kind of management," explained executive Peter Widdrington. "You get the most capable people you can and let them go to work, which means let them make mistakes. That's why there are erasers on pencils. It's not exactly a hands-off approach. We question and pursue things that should have happened and didn't, and we decide policy in terms of how many farm clubs we are going to have and why. We look at the budgets, the salaries. We don't negotiate salaries, but we sure as hell know how much they can spend. We leave it to them to work within that thing."[4] The board wanted to win, but they also wanted a solid financial foundation.

To lead their new franchise, McDougall and the board needed a strong baseball man with marketing smarts. They quickly settled on a short list of Bill Giles, a senior executive in the Phillies' front office; Frank Cashen, the longtime general manager with Baltimore, regarded as one of baseball's model organizations; and Peter Bavasi, the thirty-three-year-old GM of the San Diego Padres.[5]

The ownership group initially offered the job to Cashen, who demanded too much money and was uncomfortable jumping from his job at National Brewery, owned by Canadian brewing rival Carling O'Keefe.[6] McDougall felt Giles's background had been more administrative, a role they deemed already filled with Beeston. McDougall and the board turned to Bavasi.

Peter Bavasi had grown up in baseball. His father, Buzzie, spent nearly thirty years in the Dodgers' front office, the last eighteen as the general manager. When Peter graduated from St. Mary's College (California) in 1964 with a degree in philosophy, Buzzie hired him to be the business manager of one of the Dodgers' Minor League affiliates. After a few years of apprenticeship, the younger Bavasi became a Minor League general manager.

In 1968 the expansion San Diego Padres hired Buzzie Bavasi away as minority owner and president, and he took his son along as farm director. Peter Bavasi was sharp, personable, confident, and already thinking about the big-picture issues of marketing and business strategy. When Padres general manager Edwin Leishman died in late 1972, Buzzie promoted his thirty-year-old son to the position. The Padres were struggling both on the field and at the gate; in their first four seasons the team finished last in the NL West and trailed the league in attendance every year. By 1973 the franchise appeared ready to bolt for Washington DC, and Bavasi told his dad, "If your will says I get the ball club, please change it."[7]

San Diego received a late reprieve when Ray Kroc stepped forward to buy the club, and with the younger Bavasi at the helm the team's fortunes began to improve. In 1975 the team finished fourth in the six-team National League West and sixth in league attendance. Bavasi believed that for a bad team to be successful at the gate, "you've got to sell the sizzle before you can sell the steak."[8] Kroc, who had built the McDonald's hamburger chain into a behemoth, left a mark on Bavasi: "Ray always said to look at a product through the eyes of the consumer. He was a big fan of selling the sizzle if you don't have the steak ready. It works the same with baseball as it does with food."[9] And the surprising jump in attendance testified to his maxim, at least for this time and place. With an opportunity to run a team of his own, on June 18, 1976, Bavasi accepted the job as executive vice president of the Toronto Blue Jays.

"Pete's the most charming guy I ever met," Paul Beeston said years later of his former boss. "I mean, he can sell. First of all, he's brilliant. He's a very, very smart guy. Tremendous energy. One of the very few guys you'll ever meet in your life who has a hundred ideas a day. Maybe only one of them is any good, but I can find guys who won't have 100 ideas in their lifetime and who won't have one good idea in a year. This guy had one good idea a day."[10]

Bavasi understood that his initial charge was to generate interest and convince the faithful that the owners had a plan for the franchise. "The intense marketing of the Blue Jays coast-to-coast in Canada (even into English-speaking Quebec) was critical to the club's initial and long-term success," Bavasi wrote. "And it was a key objective of Labatt Breweries, our most visible owner. They wanted to sell beer, and the Blue Jays were to be an important marketing vehicle."[11]

Bavasi also embraced a formal management style. "We produced annual operating plans, budgets, cash-flow forecasts, business plans, marketing plans, strategy plans, short-term, long-term, medium term plans. It disciplined us."[12] Once the board recognized that Bavasi knew what was expected, they gave him room to operate. "They were great," Bavasi recalled. "They turned the whole operation over to me to organize from scratch. We had monthly board meetings and a spring training meeting for the directors in Dunedin, and other than seeing them at games during the season, they never bothered us—except to ask periodically, is there anything we can do for you. Once the annual budgets and the operating plans were approved, it was total freedom to operate. The best owners you could ask for."[13] Kansas City's Ewing Kauffman, who had started the Royals from scratch eight years earlier, later credited Bavasi with setting a sound organizational footing: "From a business point of view, Toronto has one of the best managed clubs in baseball. It's one of the very few financially solid clubs."[14]

Starting a new baseball franchise is obviously a huge undertaking, and it needed to be done quickly. "I preferred to recruit for the core group of senior department heads those who were experienced in their field, with a reputation for exceedingly hard work and for getting a lot of things done all at once without guidance or supervision," Bavasi wrote. "'Here's the Management By Objectives operating plan we all agreed to, let's go.' They would be collegial and collaborative, and fearless and optimistic and not easily discouraged. They would usually be recruited on the basis of consistently high recommendations from other senior executives within baseball, whose recruiting counsel I would seek." With only a couple of exceptions, Bavasi "never recruited anyone [he] had previously worked with, to avoid any perceived workplace favoritism issues, and in order to develop fresh ideas and new ways of looking at old methods."[15]

For back-office functions the competent Beeston could help immeasurably, but Bavasi had to assemble a front office to run the baseball functions. Experienced as a baseball man, Bavasi was not ready to surrender control over player-personnel decisions but recognized he needed someone to supervise and build scouting and farm departments while he oversaw the entire franchise. Bavasi canvassed his colleagues for suggestions, at least two of whom, Houston general manager Tal Smith and San Diego scout Bob Fontaine, recommended another longtime scout, thirty-eight-year-old Pat Gillick, currently serving as the New York Yankees' coordinator of player development and scouting.

"Both of them said, 'Pat's your man. Look no further,'" Bavasi remembered.

> Pat was living in Atlanta at the time and was under contract to the Yankees until October 31, 1976. The expansion draft was scheduled for November 5, 1976. Yes, I tampered with Pat. The way the baseball grapevine works, that secret didn't hold for very long. The president of Labatt received a blistering phone call from George [Steinbrenner], insisting that I should be fired, because I was tampering with and hiring away "the brightest young baseball mind in the business and the future general manager of the Yankees." "Fired?!," replied the Labatt president, "for hiring the brightest young baseball mind in the business? We're not going to fire Bavasi, but we will consider giving him a raise and a bonus." Years later, George would make me tell that story. He got a kick out of it.

Gillick would grow to be one of baseball's greatest executives. "From the moment I hired Gillick, it was his baby," Bavasi recalled, although he "did bother Pat rather often about roster stuff, which I should not have done."[16]

Pat Gillick was mainly raised by his maternal grandparents in Southern California. His mother, a minor silent-movie actress, and his father, a pitcher for several seasons in the Pacific Coast League who later became the sheriff of Butte County, divorced when he was just a baby. Gillick and his mother moved into her parents' home in Van Nuys. When he was nine his mother remarried and left to live with her new husband. Pat stayed behind.

Gillick's grandfather sent him to Ridgewood Military Academy in Woodland Hills, hoping to provide some structure and keep him out of trouble. At Ridgewood Gillick excelled in both baseball and football. On the gridiron Gillick played center and snapped the ball to quarterback Bobby Beathard, later to gain fame as general manager of the NFL's Washington Redskins during their Super Bowl years in the 1980s.

Ridgewood closed its high school after his junior year, and Gillick finished up at Notre Dame High School in Sherman Oaks.

Smart and ambitious, Gillick graduated at sixteen and enrolled at LA Valley Junior College, from where the left-handed pitcher was successfully recruited by USC's legendary coach Rod Dedeaux. In Gillick's 1958 senior season the Trojans, featuring future big-league stars Don Buford and Ron Fairly, won the College World Series. Dedeaux later related that Gillick "remembered everything I told him."[17] Over the years his incredible memory and recall became a recurring theme in his colleagues' descriptions of him. Some bestowed on him the nickname "Wolley Segap," which is "Yellow Pages" spelled backward.[18]

Gillick graduated from USC with a business degree but decided to give baseball a shot, first pitching semiprofessionally in Canada, before signing with the Baltimore Orioles' organization in 1959. "I wouldn't say Pat was a can't-miss prospect," said Earl Weaver, who managed him in the Minors, "but he was definitely a prospect."[19] Gillick pitched five years in Jim McGlaughlin's instruction-oriented farm system. "Last year he was mediocre pitcher," read one scouting report from August 1960. "This year has a very good curve and change. Has lots of moxie."[20] But Gillick could not get past Triple-A, and after the 1963 season, having just turned twenty-six, he decided to go back to school, possibly to become a high school coach.

Eddie Robinson, the farm director of the Houston Colt .45s, intervened, however. Robinson had known Gillick from his time in the Orioles' organization and offered him a job as his assistant in Houston. Gillick happily accepted, soon gravitating to the scouting side of the Astros' organization.

As the southernmost team in the Majors, Houston had already developed a Latin American presence, and Gillick spent much of his time combing the area for ballplayers. In the fall of 1967 Gillick and fellow Astros scout Tony Pacheco were in the Dominican Republic when native Epy Guerrero, a part-time scout, took them to see sixteen-year-old Cesar Cedeno. "We noticed this kid and liked the way he moved, his actions and size," Gillick recalled. "We saw him throw and then we saw him go up and get a hit and go up and get another hit." The scouts arranged a workout a couple of days later, sixty miles away so as to remain hidden from competing scouts. They liked what they saw and met with Cedeno's father to negotiate a signing bonus.

Once Gillick learned that the Cardinals had offered one thousand dollars, he offered twelve hundred, upping it to fifteen hundred when the elder Cedeno turned him down. Cedeno's father rejected this offer as well. As the dickering continued one of Houston's local bird-dog scouts came to warn him that a Cardinal scout was on his way. Gillick quickly raised his offer to three thousand dollars, and Cedeno's father agreed. As Gillick was leaving he saw his rival. Holding up the contract he said, "You're a few minutes too late." Cedeno would go on to become one of the top center fielders of the 1970s.[21] Partly because of the Cedeno signing, Gillick hired Guerrero as a full-time scout, and the two worked together for the next twenty-eight years with three organizations.

In 1974 Tal Smith, with whom Gillick had worked in Houston, brought Gillick to the Yankees as coordinator of player development and scouting. For most of Gillick's tenure in New York, owner George Steinbrenner was under suspension. Commissioner Bowie Kuhn reinstated Steinbrenner before the 1976 season, and the working conditions in the Yankees' front office deteriorated rapidly. Smith had moved back to Houston as general manager in 1975. When Bavasi came calling a year later, Gillick was ready to leave.

Gillick was initially named vice president of player personnel for the Blue Jays, but after one year became VP of baseball operations and general manager. He was allowed to build a top-notch scouting staff. Two of his most important hires were Al LaMacchia, a longtime scout for the Phillies and Braves, and Bobby Mattick, who had already signed Frank Robinson, Vada Pinson, Curt Flood, and Gary Carter by the time he joined the Blue Jays. "Scouts are the backbone of the organization," Gillick was fond of saying.[22] He joined a minority of teams that shunned the new centralized Major League Scouting Bureau. Gillick was going to build his own organization.

Bavasi showed a surprisingly sentimental side in the selection of his inaugural manager. When Bavasi was the business manager for Albuquerque years earlier, Roy Hartsfield was the team's field manager. Hartsfield took the young Bavasi under his wing, patiently teaching him the many intricacies of the game both on and off the field. Bavasi had promised Hartsfield that if he ever had an opportunity in the big leagues, he would name Hartsfield as his manager. More than a decade later, Bavasi honored this pledge. Even though Bavasi informed Hartsfield of his intent soon after his hiring, he delayed making the announcement to the press in order to give the appearance of a comprehensive investigation.

Bavasi and Gillick next needed to get down to the hard work of building a franchise and preparing for the expansion draft on November 5. The rules were similar to those eight years earlier. Each of the twelve established AL teams could protect fifteen players, after which Toronto and Seattle would draft twelve players—six each—one from each AL team. The AL teams could then each protect three more players, and Toronto and Seattle could pick another twelve players. This continued for a total of five rounds, with the AL teams allowed to protect another three after each round, except after the fourth round, when they could protect only two. In the end each expansion team had drafted thirty players.

Toronto and Seattle labored under additional handicaps when compared with the 1968 expansion, as the players had gained more rights in the intervening years. Most significantly, the fall of 1976 brought the first class of free agents, players who had played out their option and were free to sign with a new team. The two expansion clubs were not allowed to sign any of these players. Second, veterans with "ten and five" rights—those who had played ten years in the Major Leagues and five years with the same team—could not be forced to join an expansion team. If Seattle or Toronto drafted one of these players, he could decide to stay put, with no compensation to the drafting team. The established clubs could therefore leave these players unprotected without much risk. Finally, players who made their Major League debut in 1976 were exempt and did not have to be protected.[23] Each of these handicaps reduced the pool of available players to the expansion clubs.

During the draft the Blue Jays emphasized younger pitchers (nine of their first fourteen selections) while also mixing in a few well-known veterans. The Blue Jays drafted two players, pitcher Jim Clancy and catcher Ernie Whitt, who would become All-Stars and play prominent roles on the franchise's first division winner many years later.

Surprisingly, the Blue Jays also drafted Rico Carty, an aging slugger with bad knees, from the Cleveland Indians. "What do we need Carty for?" Bavasi asked Gillick before they made the pick. "Rico was Mr. Wahoo," Gillick told him. After a blank stare from Bavasi, Gillick continued, "The Indians Man of the Year. Let's take him. In Cleveland the writers and fans will kill the team if they lose Carty. Then they'll have to trade and get Rico back." Sure enough, in trading Carty back to Cleveland he extracted young catcher Rick Cerone, who played another sixteen years in the big leagues, plus longtime platoon outfielder John Lowenstein.[24]

Because the Blue Jays' home ballpark, Exhibition Stadium, featured an artificial playing surface (the first in the AL's Eastern Division), Gillick targeted athletic players. The game played faster on turf than on grass, and Gillick believed speed would make the team more competitive in their home games without sacrificing too much in their road games.[25] With their first pick Gillick took Baltimore shortstop-outfielder Bob Bailor, who had recently hit .300 and shown speed on the bases in Triple-A for the Orioles.

Just as importantly, the Blue Jays needed to create and fill a farm system. "It all came down to the money," Bavasi believed. "In San Diego, until Ray Kroc came in, we had very few resources to throw at the scouting and farm system operations. In Toronto, we had plenty of money from the very beginning."[26]

Bavasi and Gillick used their resources to cast a wide net for players. "There are five or six rivers flowing into one river—fish in all of them," Gillick said, describing his philosophy in finding players.[27] One river involved trading with other Major League teams, and Gillick was always on the lookout for unappreciated young talent. Two of his early deals landed shortstop Alfredo Griffin (from Cleveland) and second baseman Damaso Garcia (from the Yankees, for Cerone). Griffin won the 1979 Rookie of the Year Award, and the two made up the Blue Jays' double-play combination for several years.

At least one big fish got away. Just prior to the team's inaugural 1977 season, Gillick believed he had worked out a deal to trade veteran pitcher Bill Singer, taken in the expansion draft, to the Yankees for young pitcher Ron Guidry. "I knew [New York manager] Billy Martin wanted some veteran players and I knew he didn't like Guidry—because I came from over there," Gillick recalled later.[28] Bavasi, however, vetoed the trade because he had made Singer one of the focal points of the team's marketing. "We were selling the collective American baseball experience, not wins and losses," Bavasi wrote. "So much so that I turned Gillick down on a trade he had arranged with the Yankees. To Pat's everlasting credit, he never ratted me out on that one."[29]

Gillick had better luck with the Yankees in bringing over Epy Guerrero, possibly the greatest of all Dominican scouts. In 1977, using borrowed money, Guerrero spent nine thousand dollars on eighteen acres and some cinderblock buildings outside of Santo Domingo. He built a ballpark and created a rudimentary baseball school for youngsters. Several years later the Blue Jays began to fund the operation, expand it, and run it year-round.[30] Guerrero helped the Blue Jays sign several top Dominican players, enrich the organizational environment for Latin players, and identify worthwhile trade and draft targets. Other organizations soon followed, but Toronto established a prominent presence in the country, one that provided them an advantage for a decade or more.

Scouting and continuity were two key areas in which Toronto differentiated itself from Seattle, its sister expansion club. "The biggest reason Toronto passed us was that they had money to spend," said one Mariner scout. "We started pinching pennies. While the Blue Jays were opening up in Latin America and signing players to good contracts, we had the smallest scouting staff in baseball and were losing people like Julio Cruz and Floyd Bannister because we weren't paying them enough."[31]

In the fall of 1977 Gillick began to exploit a little-used "river" when he selected first baseman Willie Upshaw, whom he and Guerrero knew from the Yankees' organization, in the Rule 5 Draft. Generally held in December, this draft allows teams to claim veteran Minor Leaguers not protected on their club's forty-man roster. The catch was that the selecting team had to put the player on its Major League roster for the entire upcoming season. Oftentimes the player is not advanced enough to play for his current team, but perhaps good enough to play for a team like the expansion Blue Jays. Over the years Gillick mastered the Rule 5 Draft to uncover a number of valuable contributors, including George Bell, Manny Lee, Jim Gott, and Kelly Gruber.

Gillick was also willing to take risks with multisport athletes, accommodating them in ways other teams might not have. In 1977 Gillick drafted Eugene, Oregon, prep star Danny Ainge in the fifteenth round. Ainge was heavily recruited by big-name colleges to play football or basketball, so Toronto paid him a bonus of three hundred thousand dollars and allowed him to play college basketball at Brigham Young. Two years later Toronto drafted prep quarterback and baseball catcher Jay Schroeder in the first round, paying a bonus of one hundred thousand dollars and permitting him to play college football at the University of California–Los Angeles.

In the end neither panned out. After four years in the Blue Jays' organization, including 211 games in the majors, Ainge finished college after a decorated All-American basketball career. After contentious negotiations, the Blue Jays let him out of his contract so that he could sign with the Boston Celtics. Schroeder never learned to hit the breaking ball and went on to play quarterback for the Washington Redskins. Schroeder believed that several position shifts in the Minors hurt his development. Gillick instead blamed the lack of focus on baseball: "If he had devoted all his time to baseball instead of switching between the two sports, maybe things would have been different."[32] The same likely could be said for Ainge.

"It's a game of mistakes," Mattick told Gillick. "Don't pull in your horns. Keep firing."[33] Bavasi concurred: "We did things in Toronto that many clubs then could not afford to do. Pat gambled with multi-sport players and began the Blue Jays foray into international scouting— because we had the money and a wide margin for error. Gillick was always respectful of the budget, he never overspent. He created a terrific player development and roster development program."[34]

Despite the team's poor showing in 1977, this first season was widely viewed as a triumph for baseball in Toronto. Their attendance of 1.7 million surpassed expectations and ranked fourth in the league. For

Bavasi's success the Toronto and Montreal baseball writers named him baseball's man of the year in Canada. Moreover, the team turned a profit of about $1.5 million, as Bavasi successfully sold the sizzle before the steak. He clearly understood the profit imperative: "When the great scorer comes to mark against your name, it is not whether you won or lost, but how many paid to see the game."[35] In recognition of the team's off-field success, the board promoted Bavasi to president, also promoting Beeston to VP of business operations and Gillick to VP of baseball operations.

As Gillick built the ball club, Bavasi preached patience. "You realize the importance of patience when you handle a team like ours," Bavasi said.

> If you draft young as we did, you have to bite the bullet. You don't want to make wholesale changes too quickly. If you do you wind up mixing and matching and eventually rebuilding. The same goes for financing. In San Diego we had to trade three good pitchers—Pat Dobson, Fred Norman and Dave Giusti—for financial reasons. If we had bitten the bullet and made other financial adjustments, we would have been sitting pretty. But we had no other choice. Fortunately, we have the financial resources in Toronto to forestall any such difficulties.[36]

While Toronto was fielding poor Major League teams, Gillick was expending his energies creating the team he hoped would someday contend. In Toronto's first crack at the amateur draft, in 1977, he selected Illinois prep outfielder Jesse Barfield. The next year he nabbed high school first baseman Lloyd Moseby, whom Toronto turned into an outfielder, and Dave Stieb, who had starred at Southern Illinois. Stieb hoped to play the outfield, but after Gillick met his asking price, he agreed to switch to the mound.[37] He was one of baseball's best pitchers in the 1980s.

Meanwhile, the Major League team continued to lose games, finishing a woeful 53-109 in 1979. Moreover, their manager appeared to lose control of his team. "Hartsfield was a bitter man," wrote sports reporter Alison Gordon, "loathed by many of his players, ignored by his coaches, and the focus of the frustration of supporters who were impatient to win. It was not an enviable position, but he handled it badly."[38] In August relief pitcher Tom Buskey went public, saying, "We need a new manager. Roy Hartsfield just doesn't know how to handle a pitching staff. Nobody knows what he's supposed to be doing. Maybe you can see it in other parts of the game as well." Third baseman Roy Howell and pitcher Tom Underwood piled on, voicing their own frustrations.[39] Hartsfield, hired by Bavasi and never really a Gillick favorite, was let go after the season.

Knowing his club was not a contender, Gillick wanted a manager willing to sacrifice the present for the future as the team advanced its prospects to the Major Leagues. Gillick named Bobby Mattick, a career baseball man with limited managerial experience, who at sixty-four became the oldest rookie manager in Major League history. Under Mattick's watch the team turned in its best season, albeit by winning just sixty-seven games. "He didn't know beans about managing in the big leagues," Gordon wrote. But "he lightened up all around and gave players back the fun they'd been missing. He brought Hartsfield's enemies out of the doghouse and gave them a chance to play."[40]

Mattick could not sustain the improvement in 1981. The team stood at a horrific 16-42 when a players strike interrupted the season, and even a 21-27 second half could not save Mattick's job. "When the team began to lose in 1981," Gordon wrote, "the honeymoon ended. What had once been quaint suddenly seemed incompetent."[41] Gillick returned Mattick to his scouting and player-development role, where he remained a valued member of the organization. "Bobby Mattick was the most complete scout and player development man I've ever seen," Gillick later said.[42]

Despite the 1981 regression Gillick knew he was making progress. Several prospects from the system or the Rule 5 Draft had reached the Major Leagues, including Garcia, Griffin, Moseby, Bell, Upshaw, Barfield, and Stieb. "While the roots of the roster-development plan would remain in the farm system," Gillick wrote in his year-end report, "the emphasis for 1982 will shift to a future-is-now concept."[43]

For his new manager Gillick wanted Bobby Cox, who had managed in the Yankees' system while Gillick was there and had just been released as manager by the Braves. "I'd call him a player's manager," Gillick said. "By that I mean his approach is to build confidence. He can be tough when that's called for but basically, he gives the players the notion he's on their side. And he knows what it takes to play defensively and scratch out runs."[44] Beeston concurred: "Cox's biggest strength was the players loved to play for him. The guys never knew whether he liked them or didn't like them. But they all thought he liked them. And you know he was just mean enough and tough enough that you weren't going to take a chance."[45]

Bavasi, however, fought Gillick on the choice: "He's a friend of yours. That's why you want him."

"The hell it is," Gillick shot back.[46]

Bavasi eventually acquiesced, but Gillick had grown tired of Bavasi's management style, which he considered micromanaging and driven by an overgrown ego. Moreover, getting a decision out of Bavasi was becoming increasingly difficult. "You can't get your ass in a wringer if you say no," Gillick complained. "So anything you went to Bavasi for you'd have to fight him to make him say yes. It really got to be very tiring."[47] With lower subordinates Bavasi could be even more disagreeable. "He would just lose control of himself," recalled lawyer Herb Solway. "There were two things he could do. He could either lose control of himself completely or he would go into an act where he would try and embarrass somebody in front of somebody else. It was just awful behavior."[48] Most agreed Bavasi had built a fine organization but was no longer effective. "He had a brilliant mind," wrote longtime announcer Tom Cheek, "but had a grating obstinacy that made it difficult for those working under him. He was impulsive, at times egotistical, and he sorely lacked patience."[49]

Beeston was even more frustrated than Gillick. When he resigned to take another job as business manager of a law firm, board chairman Peter Hardy decided it was time to investigate the team's management. After talking with a number of people, he fired Bavasi on November 22, took over himself, and put Gillick in charge of the front office and Beeston the back.

With Bobby Cox leading the team in the dugout, Gillick continued to promote his prospects and make trades to fill in the positions not sufficiently addressed by the farm system. He traded veteran first baseman John Mayberry to the Yankees to open a spot for Upshaw, while Cox gave starting jobs to Barfield (right field) and Moseby (center field). Gillick also acquired two valuable platoon players: third baseman Rance Mulliniks and catcher Buck Martinez (obtained during the 1981 season). With a moderately revamped lineup and the same top-three starting pitchers—Stieb, Clancy, and Luis Leal—the 1982 Blue Jays finished a franchise best 78-84.

With his remarkably young team ready to break through, after the season Gillick acquired two older players—Cliff Johnson and Jorge Orta—to platoon at designated hitter. He also traded for thirty-year-old speedster Dave Collins to play left field. Gillick called this latter trade one of his favorites, not because of Collins, but for the additional prospect he wheeled out of the Yankees. Gillick initially negotiated with Bill Bergesch, the latest general manager in the Yankees' ever-changing and chaotic front office. The Yankees desperately sought Toronto's relief ace Dale Murray, and after several rounds of negotiations, Gillick agreed to take outfielder Dave Collins and pitcher Mike Morgan in exchange. But like any savvy trader, he wanted an additional prospect, particularly one with power. Gillick and his scouts liked eighteen-year-old first baseman Fred McGriff, still in rookie ball, but did not mention him right away for fear the Yankees would ask for more. Instead, Gillick mentioned Dan Pasqua and Don Mattingly, two prospects he knew the Yankees did not want to surrender. Finally, Steinbrenner stepped in and called Gillick, telling him that he would have to take McGriff as the third player in the deal or there would not be one. Gillick coyly said that he needed to check with his scouts and would call back in fifteen minutes. When he did so he got the player he wanted.[50]

Gillick's team stepped forward in 1983, leading the division as late as July and finishing 89-73. Upshaw (27 home runs, .306 average), Barfield (27 home runs), Moseby (18 home runs, .315 average, 27 steals), and Johnson (22 home runs) all had solid offensive seasons. The platoons of Whitt and Martinez at catcher, Mulliniks and Garth Iorg at third, and Johnson and Orta were all productive as well. Of the regulars only Griffin, who had been unable to replicate the success of his rookie season, struggled at the plate.

The team again had excellent starting pitching, with Stieb (17-12, 3.04 ERA) the big star. In late June Gillick signed veteran pitcher Doyle Alexander, whom the Yankees had released. Alexander could be ornery, but Gillick believed the thirty-two-year-old right hander still had something left, and over the last half of the season Alexander finished 7-6 to round out an excellent rotation.

"If you can always stay in that 85 to 90 win area," Gillick later said, "if you can stay injury free and somebody has a hot year offensively or a pitcher has a great year, you might get 95, 96, or 99 wins."[51] The Blue Jays, winners of 89 games, had a young core and were within Gillick's window, and, accordingly, he tinkered less with the roster.

The 1984 Blue Jays returned nearly an identical team and posted an identical record, 89-73. Yet because of the Detroit Tigers' phenomenal start (35-5 at one point), no pennant race ever developed; the Jays finished in second place, but 15 games out of first. The team's lineup underwent two significant changes. Tony Fernandez, signed out of the Dominican Republic by Epy Guerrero in 1979, finally wrestled the shortstop job from Alfredo Griffin late in the 1984 season. And George Bell, the former Rule 5 signee, finally earned regular playing time, hitting .292 with 26 home runs. The Blue Jays' young outfield—Bell, Moseby, and Barfield—was often ranked as the best in baseball over the next several years.

The most troublesome element of the team's performance continued to be the bullpen. For 1984 Gillick had signed veteran Dennis Lamp and promoted twenty-three-year-old Jimmy Key, drafted in the third round in 1982. Neither proved particularly effective, nor did holdover Roy Lee Jackson. "I learned a couple of things," Hall of Fame manager Whitey Herzog once wrote. "First, if at all possible, get yourself a great relief pitcher."[52]

Gillick resolved to do just that and traded Griffin and Collins, recently displaced by Fernandez and Bell, to Seattle for Bill Caudill, whose 36 saves in 1984 were second in the league. Cox was not fully sold on Caudill. "He placed his two index fingers about six inches apart," Cheek later wrote of a conversation with Cox during the trade negotiations, "and said 'Tom, he's lost about *that* much off his fastball.'"[53] Gillick also acquired left-handed reliever Gary Lavelle from the Giants for two Minor Leaguers and pitcher Jim Gott.

Otherwise, Gillick returned the same team in 1985, losing only DH Cliff Johnson to free agency. Of the eight position players, only catcher (where Whitt and Martinez platooned) was manned by a player who had reached thirty years old. On the mound Stieb (twenty-five) was a star, Clancy (twenty-nine) was still going strong, and Key (twenty-four) joined the rotation for the first time.

On the strength of its pitching staff (a league-leading 3.31 ERA despite playing in a hitter's park), in 1985 the Blue Jays broke through with a 99-63 record to win the highly competitive AL East. Stieb led the league in ERA, Key finished fourth, and Alexander went 17-10. The lineup was balanced and deep, led by the slugging of Bell and Barfield and the all-around excellence of Moseby and Fernandez. Cox worked all season to replace Johnson's DH production, before Gillick acquired veteran Al Oliver in July and then reacquired Johnson in late August.

In the bullpen Caudill and Lavelle pitched poorly during April, earning the scorn of the now impatient Jays fans and losing Cox's confidence. Although both pitched better as the season evolved, neither ever really gained the team's complete trust.

Fortunately, Gillick had again secured a key player from an unconventional source, a new river. For a few years in the 1980s, teams that lost a free agent (as the Blue Jays had lost Johnson) could select from a pool of players made available by teams that signed free agents. As compensation for losing Johnson, the Jays selected Tom Henke, a young, hard-throwing relief pitcher who had yet to break through with the Rangers. Henke started the 1985 season in the Minors, but Toronto promoted him in late July, and he thereupon pitched spectacularly, allowing no runs in his first eleven appearances. Henke ended the season with thirteen saves, blowing just one, and an ERA of 2.03. In recognition of his influence on the pennant race, Henke finished twentieth in the league MVP voting.

Cox deserves additional credit for the division title because he essentially played the season with just twenty-three players. While the Blue Jays scouts were successful in finding value in the Rule 5 Draft, these players needed to be kept on the Major League roster the entire next season. Because most of these players were generally not Major League ready—otherwise they would have been protected from the draft—they often just sat on their new team's bench for a season. When Toronto was still uncompetitive, the burden of carrying these players seemed a reasonable trade-off. But with a contending team in 1985, it is surprising that Gillick saddled Cox with two Rule 5 players, Manny Lee and Lou Thornton. Both appeared only sporadically, effectively leaving Cox with a much shorter bench than he would have liked. But one of the many things Gillick appreciated about his manager was that be bought into the overall program, even when it made his job a little harder.[54]

In the 1985 League Championship Series against Kansas City, the first year the Series expanded from best of five to best of seven, Toronto won three of the first four games. Then the offense went cold, and they scored only five runs in the last three games. In the end Kansas City prevailed in seven games, winning the pennant and, ultimately, the World Series.

In building the 1985 Blue Jays, Gillick lived by his "many rivers into one" metaphor, using, among others, the expansion draft, the amateur draft, the Rule 5 Draft, and even (in the case of Henke) free-agent compensation to build his team. One river that he fished in more productively than most other teams was the one representing Latin America. In 1985 Toronto allocated 2,068 plate appearances to Latino players, second only to the Giants, who had just 1 more. No other team had more than 1,600. The Blue Jays also had quite a few African Americans on their squad, resulting in the team receiving fewer plate appearances from Caucasian players than any team in the Majors. This tendency was much less pronounced on the pitching side, though there were comparably few nonwhite pitchers in that era.

Gillick had built a team he wanted: one that could be consistently profitable while winning 85–90 games, with the expectation of occasionally breaking through to 95-plus wins and a division title. The Blue Jays were loaded with talent, and Gillick had continued to integrate new young stars as the older ones lost effectiveness.

The Blue Jays suffered a setback when Cox resigned shortly after the 1985 playoff loss to become the general manager of the Atlanta

Braves, whose owner, Ted Turner, had realized his mistake in letting Cox go four years earlier. Cox would help rebuild the Braves' organization and later return to the dugout, where he would manage the club to one of the great multiyear runs in baseball history. As for Pat Gillick, he would need to utilize one more river before finally delivering a World Series to Toronto.

PART 4 • *Businessmen*

19 Winning Now

Pat Gillick's first division championship, with the 1985 Toronto Blue Jays, testified to the strong team and superb organization he had built. He was chosen to run the Blue Jays because of his record in scouting and player development, and he used those skills, plus creativity and a knack for leadership and management, to create a great farm system and developmental program. By the mid-1980s Gillick was no longer in charge of a developing expansion team, but head of one of baseball's model franchises.

Over the rest of Gillick's outstanding career as a baseball executive, a career that would be recognized in 2011 by induction into the Hall of Fame, he would never again be in charge of a new or struggling team. Because of what he did next in Toronto and then later in Baltimore, Seattle, and Philadelphia, Gillick became known for a different skill: using a large budget to take a talented team over the top, either by making the playoffs or by winning a championship. Gillick still needed to call on many of the same resources he had used so well in his early years: managing people, judging talent, and expanding his "many rivers" philosophy in finding players. For now, though, his work in Toronto was not finished.

Having reached the postseason in 1985, the Blue Jays' future looked promising. All of the key regulars, save catcher Ernie Whitt and designated hitter Cliff Johnson, were under thirty years old. Dave Stieb (twenty-five) and Jimmy Key (twenty-four) anchored the pitching staff, and only thirty-five-year-old Doyle Alexander was near the end of his career. Gillick replaced his great manager, Bobby Cox, by promoting third base coach Jimy Williams, a natural choice. Otherwise Gillick returned almost the same team that fell one game short of the World Series.

Nonetheless, the 1986 team struggled early, mostly due to a regression among its pitchers, whose ERA jumped from a league-leading 3.31

to 4.08, fourth in the division. With his team nine and a half games back in July, Gillick swapped Alexander, whose ERA was a run higher than the previous season, to Atlanta for twenty-two-year-old Duane Ward, who within a few years would become a key Toronto relief pitcher. The team climbed to within three and a half in early September but faded to 86-76, nine and a half games behind the Red Sox.

Williams appeared overmatched his first year on the job. "He dealt with players in a far less sophisticated manner than Cox, both strategically and emotionally," wrote Tom Cheek later. "His persona was difficult to penetrate and he often found himself hypersensitive to media criticism, which can be a killer in big-time professional sports."[1]

During spring training in 1987, a scout was watching the Blue Jays work out. "They remind me of one of those circus cars where all the clowns keep getting out," he said. "Toronto opens the clubhouse door and one potential star after another pops out."[2] The latest round included twenty-three-year-old Fred McGriff, newly installed as the designated hitter, since first base was still manned by Willie Upshaw, coming off a subpar season. At second base Gillick had tired of Damaso Garcia's relatively empty batting average and traded him to Atlanta, though Williams struggled to find an adequate replacement. More positively, Kelly Gruber joined the club and shared third base with Rance Mulliniks.

Gillick preferred to promote from within, a fine strategy as long as the farm system produces talent on a regular basis, but more limiting when it experiences an inevitable fallow period. The Blue Jays could have used a free-agent signing or two, but the team's budget combined with the baseball owners' collective collusion not to pursue other teams' free agents (an agreement that later cost owners $280 million in legal damages) limited Gillick's freedom of action. He also had difficulty convincing players to play in Canada. "There's a psychological barrier," he said. "There is a reluctance to go to a foreign country." Moreover, "there is absolutely no way we can overcome the taxes, even if we pay a 10 or 15 percent premium."[3]

The 1987 Blue Jays experienced a rebound thanks to their pitchers' league-best ERA and an MVP season from left fielder George Bell (47 home runs, 134 RBI, .308 batting average). In the end the Blue Jays won ninety-six games but unfortunately lost shortstop Tony Fernandez to an elbow injury and then dropped the last seven games of the season, finishing two games behind the streaking Detroit Tigers.

The next spring McGriff took over at first for Upshaw, who was sold to Cleveland; Rule 5 Draftee Manny Lee was installed at second; Fernandez returned at short; and Gruber was poised for full-time duty at third. Although now thirty-six, Ernie Whitt returned as the regular catcher, and Jesse Barfield, still only twenty-eight, remained anchored in right. More dramatically, Williams had grown unhappy with Bell's defense in left and wanted to shift him to DH, move Lloyd Moseby from center to left, and install one of the organization's young prospects, Sil Campusano or Rob Ducey, in center.

Complicating matters, Bell was due to become a free agent at the end of 1988 and said he would leave if not signed to a long-term contract. This threat worried the Blue Jays less than it normally would—with baseball teams still colluding, Bell might not find any bidders. Gillick and vice president Paul Beeston tried instead to sign Bell to a one-year deal.

In January 1988 Gillick convened several key executives, including Beeston, Williams, and scout Al LaMacchia, to meet with Bell and his agents. When negotiating potentially large contracts, Beeston often took a leadership role, with Gillick and assistant GM Gordon Ash also involved. Occasionally, this led to confusion: Whitt once called Gillick to accept a Blue Jay deadline offer, only to have Gillick initially demur because he was unaware of a concession made by Beeston.[4]

In this meeting Gillick told Bell that the team wanted him to play some games at DH, to save wear and tear on his knees. Bell interpreted this request to mean about ten or fifteen games at DH and acquiesced. Williams interjected that he actually wanted Bell to primarily DH. Not surprisingly, the twenty-eight-year-old Bell balked. "Fuck you, Jimy," Bell responded, and the conference broke up, with Williams feeling he had made his case and Bell believing he had agreed to DH about fifteen games.[5] Several weeks later Bell agreed to a three-year, $5.8 million contract, a healthy deal but less than his current market value and not enough, as time would tell, to convince him that he should leave the outfield.

The Blue Jays' 1988 spring training was dominated by the Williams-Bell feud. Things came to a head on St. Patrick's Day when Bell, in the lineup as the DH, refused to play. Bell was later informed that if he did such a thing again, he would be subject to a thirty-day suspension and fine. Bell seemed surprised by the uproar his action caused and subsequently begrudgingly agreed to Williams's plan. When the season opened Bell served as DH in five of the team's first ten games, while Campusano, the youngster upon whom this drama hinged, hit just .115. Williams and the Blue Jays thereupon abandoned the move, returning Bell to left and Moseby to center, but the tension festered.

In retrospect, Gillick could have managed this situation better. Most players of Bell's stature, in the prime of their career, would have been sensitive to such a slight, and the Blue Jays should have quietly lobbied their star or offered additional financial inducements. The controversy also likely put additional pressure on the young Campusano, who never did learn to hit in the big leagues.

With all the turmoil the Blue Jays came in at 87-75 in 1988, finishing two games behind the Red Sox in a very winnable division race. Gillick, who earned the nickname "Stand Pat" for his perceived reluctance to make trades or sign free agents to shake up his club, definitely lived up to this moniker in 1988. In fact, he did not make a single trade all calendar year, while the Red Sox (acquiring pitcher Mike Boddicker) and Tigers (outfielder Fred Lynn) added players during the pennant race.

Gillick was inactive again before the 1989 season, but with the team at 9-16 on April 30 he finally made a deal, trading Barfield to the Yankees for left-handed pitcher Al Leiter. Barfield and Moseby had declined rather suddenly from their mid-1980s stardom, and the deal opened up a spot for twenty-one-year-old Dominican phenom Junior Felix.

When the team's slump reached 12-24, Gillick fired Williams, a move most of the fans and media had been calling for. Gillick first hoped to land Lou Piniella, let go as Yankees manager at the end of 1988, but Piniella surprised Gillick by telling him he had a personal-services contract with George Steinbrenner (which involved scouting, doing TV work, and making a few speeches) and would need permission to join the Blue Jays. Steinbrenner well remembered Gillick leaving him thirteen years earlier and now demanded young hurler Todd Stottlemyre as compensation. Gillick wanted Piniella, but not at the price of the well-regarded pitcher.[6]

While he was deliberating Gillick had given the reins to batting coach Cito Gaston, who was eventually hired to finish the season. The well-liked and mild-mannered Gaston created a more relaxed clubhouse atmosphere, and the team responded with a 77-49 record after the change, enough to win the division by two games over Baltimore. Gillick helped out by acquiring Mookie Wilson from the Mets in late July, solidifying the outfield and the clubhouse. "He leads the way George Brett and Reggie Jackson lead," said Gillick. "By example."[7] McGriff had a great season (36 home runs and 119 walks), Stieb turned in another excellent year to lead a solid group of starters, while Henke and Ward anchored the bullpen. The team again fell short in the playoffs, losing the LCS to the A's in five games. Most people credited Gaston for the club's turnaround. "Sometimes teams with the most talent don't win," said Gillick. "Sometimes players like ours take a while to learn how to win. Cito has tried to teach them that."[8]

More significantly for the future of the club, on June 5 the Blue Jays opened SkyDome (now Rogers Centre), the start of what was to become a baseball stadium boom in North America. With the stadium funded by three levels of government (federal, provincial, and city) and by large corporate donations and prepaid luxury-box leases, the grand opening (two days before the Jays played there) was broadcast on Canadian television and featured performances from Canada's elite entertainers. With its one-of-a-kind retractable roof (Montreal's Olympic Stadium had one, though it had worked only sporadically), SkyDome was hailed as an engineering marvel and a new standard-bearer. Using SkyDome for two-thirds of the year, Toronto set the all-time attendance record (which they broke the next year) with more than 3.375 million fans.

Helped immeasurably by their new stadium, over the next five years Toronto consistently ranked among baseball's top three teams in total revenue.[9] Although ownership had generally provided Gillick with a competitive budget, in the early SkyDome years the Blue Jays were one of the wealthiest teams in the game, and his budget increased accordingly. Over the next twenty years high-revenue stadiums opened nearly every year, lessening the advantages, but the teams that built their parks in the first wave—Toronto, the Chicago White Sox, Baltimore, and Cleveland—had a financial advantage that could allow historically lower-revenue teams to leap ahead of their competitors. If a general manager could build a strong nucleus prior to the opening, he could use some of the revenue windfall on high-level free agents to augment the club. It would take him one more year, but Pat Gillick would prove a master of this strategy.

In the 1989 amateur draft Gillick selected Washington State pitcher–first baseman John Olerud in the third round. The *Baseball America* college player of the year as a sophomore in 1988 (when he hit 23 home runs while going 15-0 as a pitcher), before his junior season Olerud underwent surgery for a brain aneurysm, putting his future in doubt. Blue Jay scouts had been following Olerud closely, and Gillick sent him a get-well card during his recovery. Olerud played that spring, but told scouts he would return to college for his senior season. Gillick chose him anyway and visited him nine times before Olerud finally signed a contract. Along with a bonus of three hundred thousand dollars, Gillick agreed to start him in the Major Leagues, and Olerud got into 6 games that September, going 3 for 8. In 1990 he made the team and played 115 games mainly at designated hitter, becoming one of the team's most productive hitters (17 home runs, 68 RBI). Gillick always considered Olerud his favorite draft pick, enough so that Beeston often joked, "He cries every time Olerud gets a single."[10]

The Blue Jays returned most of their lineup (led by McGriff, Fernandez, Bell, and Gruber) and pitching staff (Stieb, Key, Henke, Ward) for 1990. Other than Olerud newcomer David Wells (11-6, 3.14) joined the pitching rotation and contributed, while Ernie Whitt, after a decade of solid service at catcher, finally gave way to Pat Borders. Despite the new talent the Blue Jays fell to 86 wins and finished 2 games behind the Red Sox.

For eight seasons, from 1983 to 1990, the Blue Jays had been remarkably consistent. In six of the eight years they had won between 86 and 89 games, over 95 in the other two, and had captured two division titles. Gillick had integrated a number of young stars in this period, one or two at a time, while continuing to win: Bell, Fernandez, Henke, McGriff, Ward, Olerud, Wells, and Borders gave the Blue Jays a young core in 1990.

In the following off-season Gillick shifted to a new gear. With baseball's ill-considered collusion finally a thing of the past, and an increased budget due to the new stadium revenues, Gillick was freed to enter the marketplace. Now fifty-four, he had been running the Blue Jays' front office for fourteen years and had experienced some health issues. He told Beeston he intended to retire in three years.[11]

Early in the 1990 winter meetings Gillick traded Felix to the Angels for twenty-eight-year-old Devon White, one of baseball's best defensive center fielders (a deal that also included several less notable players). Three days later he made much larger headlines when he swapped McGriff and Fernandez, two of his best players, to San Diego for second baseman Roberto Alomar and left fielder Joe Carter. McGriff and Fernandez would be missed, but the thirty-one-year-old Carter was a valuable run producer, and Alomar, the best player in the deal, was a great offensive and defensive player and still only twenty-three. Olerud took over at first base and replaced McGriff's production, while Manny Lee shifted from second to shortstop to complete the infield. With their rebuilt offense the Blue Jays seemed poised to retake the division.

The club suffered a huge setback in late May when Dave Stieb, an underappreciated pitching star for a decade, was injured in a collision with a base runner and never recovered his previous form. Rookie Juan Guzman joined the team in June and finished 10-3 with a 2.69 ERA, and a few weeks later Gillick landed knuckleballer Tom Candiotti from Cleveland. The reworked rotation of Key, Stottlemyre, Wells, Guzman, and Candiotti led the league in ERA, and Ward and Henke saved 55 games in 157 innings pitched between them. This great pitching led Toronto to a 91-71 record and their third division crown. Disappointingly, they again lost in the ALCS, this time to the Twins.

In the 1991–92 offseason Gillick made his first significant foray into the free-agent market, by signing thirty-seven-year-old Twins pitcher Jack Morris, a five-time All-Star fresh off a 10-inning complete-game shutout to win Game Seven of the World Series, and aging Angels slugger Dave Winfield. When Gillick called Beeston, recently named CEO, to tell him he had reached an agreement with Winfield, Beeston complained, "I didn't know we were even interested in this guy. I know where he ain't playing. He ain't playing here."

Gillick considered Winfield a leader and called Winfield's agent, Jeff Klein. "I'm going to be in the air," Gillick told him. "But I think you should talk to Paul. He really wants to talk to you. You'd better call him right away."

"The phone rings in my office," Beeston related. "The guy says, 'Hello this is Jeff Klein, Dave Winfield's agent. Pat Gillick says you want to talk to me.'" After his initial consternation, Beeston consummated a one-year deal with Klein for $2.3 million.[12]

By the 1980s most front offices included a team president or CEO, who ran the ever more complicated business and directed the general manager or head of baseball operations. Although Gillick and Beeston had grown up together in the Toronto organization, Beeston was now technically his boss, having been named president in 1989. Don McDougall, who was on the Blue Jays' original board of directors, later downplayed this hierarchy: "Paul Beeston is the heart of the Blue Jays. And Pat Gillick is the head."[13] The two maintained a smooth working relationship based on years of mutual respect.

Peter Bavasi described this shift: "Up until the late '70s, the 'general manager' ran both the business and baseball sides of the operation. Buzzie [Bavasi], Joe Brown, Jim Campbell, Gabe Paul, fellows like that. Most of those men came out of the minor league system, where they learned every aspect of the business—on and off the field—by running the minor league teams."

"Beginning in the early 80s I noticed that clubs were beginning to split the organization into baseball ops and business ops," Bavasi added. "With an executive vice president/general manager for baseball and an executive vice president for business, each reporting to a nonowner president who reported directly to the owner or the ownership board. Clubs began to take on a more corporate structure, in part because the economics of the business had become both fragile and complex. Owners didn't have the time or inclination to stay as deeply involved in day-to-day operations as they had once been."[14]

With essentially the same lineup the 1992 Blue Jays led the AL in slug-ging and were second in runs scored. Carter (119 RBI) and Winfield (108 RBI) received a good deal of the headlines, but Alomar's over-all excellence (.310 with 43 extra base hits, 88 walks, 49 stolen bases, and a Gold Glove at second base) led the club. Morris won 21 games, albeit with a 4.04 ERA, while Juan Guzman finished 16-5, 2.64. To re-inforce their rotation for the stretch run, Gillick acquired free-agent-to-be David Cone for three then-unneeded players. "Pat would always make a trade to put us over the top, and he was making a statement." Beeston recalled. "You're telling the team, 'We (the front office) are trying, too.'"[15] Gillick agreed: "One of the guys [we gave up] probably is a marginal Hall of Famer, Jeff Kent. We thought about it and said, 'David Cone is a guy we think can get us over the hump,' and at the same time a deal like that kind of deflates your competition."[16]

The 1992 Blue Jays won 96 games and their fourth division title, before finally breaking through in the ALCS, topping the A's in six games, then beating the Atlanta Braves in six games to give Canada its first-ever World Series championship. Winfield's two-run double in the top of the eleventh in the final game proved to be the deciding blow. "This is really a tremendous evening for everybody in the orga-nization," said Beeston, accepting the trophy.[17]

Gillick's strategy of signing or dealing for short-term solutions worked because he had a young core to build around and the money to find new solutions when the old ones left or declined. After the 1992 season Gillick faced just this problem when seven key Blue Jays became free agents: Key, Cone, Henke, Winfield, Carter, Lee, and left fielder Candy Maldonado. Of the seven Gillick re-signed only Carter.

Though he had entered the free-agent market a year earlier, Gil-lick still would not compete for the best midcareer players because he would not offer contracts longer than three years. He had hoped to re-sign Key, but the pitcher instead inked a four-year deal with the Yankees. Cone took three years from the Royals but received a nine-million-dollar signing bonus that Gillick would not match.[18]

His three-year limit instead led Gillick to short-term players in their midthirties. Gillick signed veteran Dave Stewart to bolster the pitch-ing staff and veteran Paul Molitor to replace Winfield at DH. The team also had a couple of prospects ready for regular roles: starting pitcher Pat Hentgen and third baseman Ed Sprague. The Toronto core, however, had gotten older. Only Olerud and Alomar were established stars under thirty, and among the pitchers only Guzman and Ward had significant remaining service time under Toronto's control.

Toronto's reliance on veteran players can be seen in the team's balance sheet. After ranking thirteenth in payroll in 1990, the team had climbed to ninth in 1991, it was third in 1992, and finally, in 1993, the team had the highest payroll in the game.[19] To Gillick's credit the money was well spent; he and his scouts correctly identified veterans—particularly Winfield, Morris, Molitor, Stewart, and Carter—who still offered valuable production. Money mattered, but one still needed to identify the right pieces.

By the middle of July 1993 the AL East was a wide-open pennant race, with five teams—Baltimore, New York, Toronto, Boston, and Detroit—within two games of first. With several of his pitchers, especially Morris, struggling, Gillick worked the phones to look for mound help. Gillick and Ash especially coveted Seattle ace Randy Johnson. In return, Seattle demanded Steve Karsay, one of the top pitching prospects in baseball. Gillick and Ash offered Todd Stottlemyre, but the two sides could not reach an agreement.

In June Gillick had traded struggling left fielder Darrin Jackson to the New York Mets to reacquire shortstop Tony Fernandez, whom the Blue Jays had never adequately replaced. To fill the hole in left the team had plugged in youngster Rob Butler, who tore a ligament in his thumb soon thereafter. As he had no luck finding an ace pitcher, Gillick called Oakland GM Sandy Alderson to inquire about Rickey Henderson, their star left fielder having another great season and in the final year of his contract.

Like the Mariners, Alderson demanded Karsay or another top pitching prospect. Gillick suggested instead that Alderson list three pitchers in the Toronto organization, allow Toronto to remove one, and then select either of the other two. Reportedly, Alderson listed Karsay, Jose Silva, and Paul Spoljaric. Gillick called an all-hands-on-deck meeting of his front office: Ash, Beeston, Al LaMacchia, Bobby Mattick, one-time pitching coach Al Widmar, and a few scouts. The group agreed that the deal was worth the chance to get back to the World Series. The A's ended up with Karsay. (In the end, none of the three pitchers had much of a career.) Alderson had to work on Henderson to waive his no-trade clause (giving Seattle another chance to revive a Randy Johnson deal), but Toronto and Oakland completed their trade on July 31.[20]

Though Henderson hurt his hands and struggled over the regular season's final two months, the trade did what it was supposed to do: solidify the outfield and leadoff spot of an already formidable team.[21] Unlike the 1980s teams this Toronto club was led by its extraordinary offense, especially Olerud (24 home runs, .363) and Alomar (17 homers, .326, 55 steals). The Blue Jays finished 95-67 to win the division easily and then dispatched the White Sox and Phillies to capture their second world championship.

Gillick reconfirmed that 1994 would be his last season, and he and Ash were hopeful that the roster of 1993 could win again. The club lost Morris, Henderson, and Fernandez, at the end of their contracts, but otherwise returned intact. Once the season began, both the offense and pitching took steps backward, and the team was only 55-60 in August when the players went out on strike, ultimately ending the season. In the fall Gillick formally retired, staying on only as a consultant.

Gillick's legacy in Toronto, besides his two championships, is the remarkable amount of talent he and his scouts managed to unearth. From 1983, when the team first became competitive, until 1993, the Blue Jays won eighty-six or more games every year. In order to do this, Gillick needed to continually feed new talent into his team, and until the last few years it was nearly always from his farm system. Over the thirteen-year period from 1979 through 1991, an average Major League team debuted players who went on to total 471 WAR over their careers. The Blue Jays introduced players who totaled 731, 55 percent more than the average club. That difference is the biggest reason they could win so consistently.

Using the same methodology, in the 1977–91 period the Blue Jays outperformed the average team in the amateur draft (617 WAR to 460) and in undrafted amateur free agents, mostly Latino players (156 WAR to 92). In the Rule 5 Draft, which rearranged players from the above categories, the Blue Jays brought in another 77 WAR.

In the twenty years following Gillick's departure, the Blue Jays finished over .500 ten times and have yet to return to the playoffs. The rest of baseball caught up in Latin America, and the wave of new stadiums curtailed the Blue Jays' brief revenue advantage. But the job Pat Gillick and his staff did to create a brand-new team and make it consistently one of the best in baseball deserves to be remembered.

While consulting for the Blue Jays in 1995, Pat Gillick drew interest from several teams looking for a GM, notably Arizona, Tampa Bay (two expansion teams that would start play in 1998), Florida, and the Cubs. While he expected to run a ball club again, he felt he could wait for the right opportunity. After the 1995 season Baltimore Orioles owner Peter Angelos reached out to Gillick, who again said he was not interested. But at the general managers' meetings in Scottsdale that November, Gillick ran into Davey Johnson, an old Minor League teammate who had recently become the Orioles' manager. Gillick congratulated Johnson on his new position and asked what he was doing in town. Johnson told Gillick he was helping Angelos find a general manager and convinced him to accept the job.[22]

Angelos gave Gillick a three-year contract for $2.4 million, one of the highest packages ever for a general manager. Moreover, Angelos promised Gillick complete freedom to run the baseball side of the organization, as he had in Toronto. "He has all the leeway a general manager should have and probably more. I don't tell the GM who to get, or the manager who to play, he knows that."[23]

Angelos had led a syndicate of investors in 1993 to purchase the Orioles for $173 million, the highest price ever paid for a baseball team. Angelos had made his fortune principally as a plaintiff's attorney in asbestos litigation, and his consortium bought the team at a bankruptcy auction necessitated by the financial problems of previous owner Eli Jacobs. The Angelos syndicate included Bill DeWitt Jr., who would later buy the St. Louis Cardinals, but Angelos was in charge. He promised to spend money and build a winning team.

Angelos retained the incumbent GM, Roland Hemond, who had twice been named Executive of the Year by the *Sporting News*, including as recently as four years earlier with Baltimore. The well-liked Hemond had overseen several teams that finished well above preseason expectations and believed that a GM should "always be positive and feel he has a chance to turn things around."[24] Angelos asked team president Larry Lucchino to stay on and run the baseball side of the operation as vice chairman (Angelos brought in Joe Foss to run the business side), which would have undercut Hemond. Lucchino declined, believing that Angelos would not allow him the freedom to run the team.[25]

Lucchino's belief proved correct. Angelos lived up to his promise to spend money, but he repeatedly intervened in the management of the team. Early in 1994, Angelos's first year, Hemond became so frustrated by his new boss that he decided to resign. Angelos talked him out of it, but the match was not destined to last.[26]

The Orioles had been a good club, finishing third in both 1992 and 1993. With the 1992 opening of their wildly successful and influential new home, Oriole Park at Camden Yards, the Orioles consistently drew more than three million fans, second in attendance only to Toronto's more spacious SkyDome. Armed with this revenue, Angelos allowed Hemond to sign several high-profile free agents: first baseman Rafael Palmeiro, third baseman Chris Sabo, DH Harold Baines, starting pitcher Sid Fernandez, and relievers Mark Eichhorn and Lee Smith.

When the 1994 strike hit the team was in second (in the new five-team AL East) with a record of 63-49. Angelos spent the year badgering manager Johnny Oates, repeatedly threatening to fire him.[27] At the end of the season he followed through, and his search committee, which included (but was not led by) Hemond, surprised most everyone by hiring Cleveland pitching coach Phil Regan. To lead the farm system Angelos hired Syd Thrift, the iconoclast who had run the Kansas City Baseball Academy in the 1970s and served as Pirates GM in the late 1980s.

When the strike ended in early 1995 Baltimore jumped in and landed starter Kevin Brown, relievers Jesse Orosco and Doug Jones, and outfielder Kevin Bass. The season highlight was the September 6 celebration for Cal Ripken breaking Lou Gehrig's consecutive-game streak, but the rest of the season was a disappointment. The Orioles fell to 71-73 and a distant third place.

After the season Angelos forced both Hemond and Regan out. "I wish I could have had more direct contact with [Angelos]," Hemond recalled. "He was a very busy man. I had to go through other people sometimes to pass on my thoughts. That was my only difficulty."[28] Unusually, Angelos hired his manager first: Davey Johnson, who had enjoyed great success managing the Mets in the 1980s and had just been let go by the Reds. Angelos then turned his attention to finding a general manager. With Johnson's help he hired Gillick, promising control.

Not everyone was convinced. "It's silly to believe that Angelos will simply sit back and watch Gillick run the operations without a few suggestions here and there," wrote sportswriter Bob Nightengale.[29] Prescient words, it would turn out.

The challenge ahead of Gillick was similar to that of his final years in Toronto: get into the playoffs by building on the team's revenue advantage and solid talent base. As his assistant Gillick brought in Kevin Malone, most recently general manager for the Montreal Expos. At Angelos's request he kept Thrift to run the farm system. Like in his later stops, Gillick did not bring an entourage with him; he evaluated the front-office staff just as he did his players and came to recognize that many were sound baseball men. The departed Hemond praised his successor: "He has an analytical mind, and he doesn't panic."[30]

Gillick inherited a team with several excellent players, including Palmeiro, Ripken, catcher Chris Hoiles, outfielders Bobby Bonilla and Brady Anderson, and pitchers Mike Mussina and Scott Erickson. The team's two biggest deficiencies were at second and third bases and the balance of its pitching staff. The farm system, ranked twenty-fourth of twenty-eight teams by *Baseball America*, did not offer much help.

Gillick filled many of these holes rather quickly and effectively, while still holding to the three-year contract limit he had used in Toronto. He signed free agents Robbie Alomar, his old Toronto standout, to play second, and Milwaukee veteran B. J. Surhoff to play third. To shore up the bullpen, he signed Randy Myers (with help from Thrift) and Roger McDowell (who had played for Johnson in New York).[31] Finally, to make up for the loss of departing free-agent hurler Kevin Brown, Gillick traded young outfielder Curtis Goodwin to the Reds for David Wells, another former Blue Jay.

Although many of these moves worked out quite well, the Orioles were hovering just over .500 around midseason in 1996, and Gillick wanted to cash in a couple of his veterans for younger players. He first worked out a trade of the underperforming Wells to Seattle. Gillick also hoped to move Bonilla, who had played well, offering him to Cincinnati for pitcher John Smiley and to Chicago for outfielder Brian McRae. Both teams turned him down, so Gillick eventually settled on a deal with Cleveland for twenty-seven-year-old Jeromy Burnitz, who Gillick thought could become a big home run threat in Oriole Park.[32]

Angelos stepped in and vetoed both trades, telling Gillick it was not a baseball decision but one that concerned his relationship with the city and the fans. Faced with the undermining of his position, "Gillick's appetite for the job was never the same," Tom Verducci later wrote.[33]

Vice chairman and chief operating officer (effectively club president) Joe Foss felt Gillick handled the situation poorly: "The problem was our baseball front office went public that Peter had disagreed with their recommendation. I personally was dumbfounded to read about that meeting the next day in the paper. I'd been in the business world for twenty-five years, and it's a normal occurrence to sit down and then, once the boss makes a decision, you jump on it and make it work."[34]

Angelos's meddling clearly stung Gillick, but once committed he went back to the trading block, this time looking to stock up for the stretch run. Accordingly, he traded pitcher Kent Mercker to the Indians for aging but still effective DH Eddie Murray and acquired slugging third baseman Todd Zeile, allowing Surhoff to move to fill a hole in left field.

Gillick's biggest frustration was that he could not land a frontline starter to strengthen the Orioles' mediocre rotation. He liked Florida's John Burkett and was furious when GM Dave Dombrowski traded him to the Rangers after telling Malone he was unavailable. "The guy lied to Kevin," Gillick fumed. Dombrowski shrugged off the accusation: "A good amount of time had passed from the time we spoke. They weren't even one of the teams I was talking to at the [July 31 trading] deadline. Things change all the time."[35]

Even without an additional ace, the team rebounded over the last two months of the season to finish 88-74, four games behind the Yankees but good enough to earn the AL's wild card. The Orioles overcame a mediocre rotation by slugging a then-record 257 home runs, including a remarkable 50 by Anderson. The Orioles defeated defending AL champion Cleveland to reach their first League Championship Series in fourteen years, before falling to the Yankees.

Despite a fairly successful year, Angelos fought with manager Davey Johnson throughout the season and off-season. For starters, Johnson had shifted the aging icon Ripken to third base in July for a few days, an act not appreciated by either the player or the owner. Angelos was also unhappy with Johnson's handling of the pitching staff, his moving of Bonilla to DH at the start of the season, and his response to a September incident when Alomar spit in the face of umpire John Hirschbeck. (Angelos wanted Johnson to go public that he thought Hirschbeck had used "motherfucker" in the exchange before Alomar spit on him.) Moreover, both sides were leaking matters to the press to the detriment of the other: Johnson that Angelos wanted to reduce the payroll from fifty to forty million dollars and Angelos that Johnson routinely arrived at the ballpark too close to game time.[36] In a show of authority Angelos fired pitching coach Pat Dobson and brought in Ray Miller. Johnson stayed on for 1997, but he was clearly unhappy with his situation.

The Orioles were a good team, though every key regular other than Alomar and Hammonds was over thirty. Johnson and Gillick both wanted to pursue younger players, but Angelos insisted that they not sacrifice the talent on the present team. The Orioles lost both Bonilla and Wells to free agency after the season, and Gillick responded by signing another of his old Toronto favorites, Jimmy Key, to replace Wells and veteran Eric Davis to replace Bonilla. "Personally, I like both Bobby and David, but they didn't respect authority," says Gillick. "Bobby didn't get along with the manager, and it got to the point where he was always upset. It got to be a distraction."[37]

More significantly, Gillick signed shortstop Mike Bordick, paving the path for Johnson to move Ripken permanently to third base. Though Ripken had initially been reluctant, he indicated that he would make the shift if Baltimore had a quality defensive replacement whose work ethic he respected. Bordick's presence helped Johnson convince Ripken to make the move, alleviating a potentially uncomfortable situation.[38] "We've got guys who I like to call just baseball players," said a pleased Gillick. "They're not concerned with peripheral stuff. They're not worrying about what the press says or whether the manager is going to DH them instead of play them in the field. They just play."[39]

Gillick's moves generally played out well for 1997. Key had a strong season, while a more unheralded signing, pitcher Scott Kamieniecki, turned in the best season of his career. Mussina and Erickson also had strong seasons, Myers saved forty-five games with a 1.51 ERA, and the pitching staff allowed the fewest runs in the league. The offense fell off by sixty-one home runs, but remained above average. Davis missed most of the season while being treated for colon cancer, but his return for the playoffs was one of the feel-good stories of the year. The Orioles finished 98-64, the American League's best record. The team dispatched Seattle in the Division Series, before falling to Cleveland in six games in the LCS. The Indians, winners of just eighty-six games, were not nearly the team they had been a few years earlier, so Baltimore's loss was particularly disappointing. Every Cleveland victory was by just one run, two in extra innings and one in the bottom of the ninth. Many Oriole players felt they should have won the series.

Johnson and Angelos continued to spar throughout the season, and this time Gillick could not prevent a final breakup. Johnson fined Alomar for missing a team function and an exhibition game during the season and directed his player to send the payment to a charity for which Johnson's wife worked. Angelos was angry that he had not been consulted about the fine and was further upset when news about the charity leaked out. Johnson admitted he had mishandled the situation, but not that Angelos should have been involved. Gillick reportedly brokered a truce, but when Johnson, whose contract expired at the end of 1998 and who had just been named Manager of the Year, threatened to quit without an extension, an incensed Angelos accepted his resignation.[40] Angelos named Miller the new manager, and Gillick, in the unfamiliar role of bystander in baseball matters, likely had no interest in staying beyond the remaining year of his own deal.

With his aging team, Gillick once again went back to the free-agent well for 1998, but this time his signings were over-the-hill veterans who did not produce: thirty-eight-year-old Joe Carter, who had little left, and pitchers Doug Drabek and Norm Charlton, who put up ERAs of

7.29 and 6.94. The club finally found some production from their farm system, as twenty-one-year-old Sidney Ponson pitched adequately in twenty starts and had several useful seasons ahead.

As Gillick knew, a team can be bandaged with free agents and other veterans only so many times. At some point a team needs to find young stars, players who could be long-term solutions and, importantly, perform at a lower salary than older players. By 1998 thirty-year-old Roberto Alomar was the youngest player of the eleven Orioles who received two hundred at bats. In the end the 1998 Orioles did not respond well to Miller, and the team fell to 79-83. Even worse, this mediocre team of veterans had the highest payroll in baseball.

In late September Malone left to take the GM job with the Dodgers, tellingly before waiting to see if the Oriole job would be available. A week later Gillick made his resignation official. In his three years with the Orioles he had performed the job he had been hired to do. Angelos wanted to put off a rebuild so that his team could win, and Gillick put together a team that played in two consecutive ALCS's, their first postseason appearances since 1983.

As a longtime proponent of scouting and player development, Gillick hoped to improve the farm system and produce young talent for the Orioles. In this he was less successful: according to the annual rankings by *Baseball America*, the system improved modestly from twenty-fourth out of twenty-eight when he joined the Orioles to nineteenth out of thirty when he left. Of their top prospects Jayson Werth and Jerry Hairston developed into quality Major Leaguers. On Gillick's watch the Orioles drafted a couple of multisport athletes and some other high-ceiling prep players who never developed as hoped. Moreover, several top-ranked pitchers suffered serious injuries. The Orioles paid the price for not rebuilding in the 1990s, as they finished below .500 for fourteen consecutive seasons beginning in 1998.

Joe Foss defended Angelos, his friend and boss, over his meddling in baseball operations: "Frankly I don't think you have owners delegating or abdicating all responsibility anymore. I think that's a dated model."[41] Speaking years later San Francisco Giants CEO Larry Baer defined ownership's role in slightly different terms: "What I've tried to do is to make sure people who do good jobs stay focused and intensify the focus even more. My job is to empower the good people here and provide the leadership and focus and be available."[42]

Dave Johnson later summed up Gillick's tenure with the Orioles: "He put the farm system back together, he created harmony in the office, and he really was just a wonderful human being and executive. . . . The bottom line is you knew what Pat was trying to do; he knew what we needed to do to be a real championship club, not just a good club. And Mr. Angelos didn't really use that knowledge."[43] Gillick would not have to wait long for another chance to use that knowledge.

Pat Gillick spent the 1999 season outside of Major League Baseball, enjoying what he called a "sabbatical." He and his wife, Doris, had settled in Toronto, where she had opened an art gallery. When the Seattle Mariners approached him about taking their GM position, he initially declined because he did not want to live apart from his wife. Eventually, Doris worked out an arrangement whereby she could spend three weeks a month in Seattle, allowing Gillick to take the job. "I'm really happy to be here and that they had patience with me," he said. The Mariners gave him a three-year contract at $750,000 per year.[44]

Eight years earlier, in early 1992, the Mariners had been sold to a local syndicate backed by Japanese national Hiroshi Yamauchi, the president of Nintendo, who delegated baseball matters to Nintendo of America's senior vice president Howard Lincoln. The group also included Microsoft executive Chris Lawson and John Ellis, CEO of Puget Sound Power & Light, who was named the team's chairman and CEO. The new ownership returned Chuck Armstrong to his former role of team president, where he actively oversaw the operations of the ball club, occasionally encroaching on baseball decisions.

At the time of the sale to Nintendo, the Mariners were not without assets: in 1991 the team posted its first winning season, and the club featured twenty-one-year-old center-field star Ken Griffey Jr., third baseman Edgar Martinez, right fielder Jay Buhner, first baseman Tino Martinez, and pitcher Randy Johnson.

When the Mariners fell back in 1992 general manager Woody Woodward hired manager Lou Piniella, who had recently led the Reds to the 1990 World Series title. After two mediocre Mariner seasons, the Mariners finally broke through in 1995 with a division title and a dramatic playoff win over the Yankees. Seattle fell in the ALCS to Cleveland, but this iconic club is credited with saving baseball in Seattle because, after much political wrangling, the team secured a deal to build what would become Safeco Field.

The next few years were awkward for Woodward. Ownership wanted to keep momentum while negotiating the details of their stadium, but they also wanted to limit payroll. The 1995 Mariners had finished nineteenth in revenue with the tenth-highest payroll in baseball. Woodward had acquired veterans Andy Benes, Vince Coleman, and Norm Charlton to help push the team to the playoffs. But after the season, to save money, Woodward dealt Tino Martinez and pitchers Jeff Nelson and Jim Mecir to the Yankees for young hurler Sterling Hitchcock and third baseman Russ Davis.[45] This disastrous trade left Seattle without its star first baseman and most effective relief pitcher. To his credit Woodward signed Paul Sorrento and Mike Jackson to replace the departed players, two moves that worked out very well.

In 1996 twenty-one-year-old Alex Rodriguez became the team's shortstop, giving the Mariners the two best players in the league with Griffey (49 homers, .303) and Rodriguez (36 homers, .358), but poor pitching (an injury to Johnson limited him to eight starts) kept the team to an 85-76 record. In midsummer Woodward made his best trade, sending outfielder Darren Bragg to the Red Sox for Jamie Moyer, who became one of the best pitchers in club history. A month later Woodward less successfully swapped Minor Leaguer David Ortiz to the Twins for Dave Hollins, who hit well down the stretch, while the Mariners ultimately fell short of the postseason.

After losing reliever Jackson to free agency, Woodward spent much of 1997 trying to fix a terrible bullpen that posted a 5.47 ERA on the season. At the July 31 deadline Woodward traded promising outfielder Jose Cruz Jr. for journeyman relievers Paul Spoljaric and Mike Timlin. Even worse, he followed this up by swapping two future stars, hurler Derek Lowe and catcher Jason Varitek, to the Red Sox for reliever Heathcliff Slocumb, who bombed with the Mariners.

Despite these disastrous deals, an all-time record 261 home runs and excellent starting pitching helped the Mariners to a 90-72 record and another division title. The Mariners were led by Johnson (20-4, 2.28) and league MVP Griffey (56 home runs). In the Division Series the Mariners faced Gillick's Orioles and dropped three out of four games.

At the end of the 1997 season the Mariner brain trust found itself at a self-imposed crossroads. The new stadium and its associated revenue would not open until mid-1999, yet the window to win with the current team appeared to be shrinking. Johnson's contract expired after the 1998 season and both Rodriguez's and Griffey's after 2000. Even with the coming stadium revenues, there was no guarantee that the team would be able to keep any of them. The Mariners needed to decide whether to expand their payroll to acquire the necessary players to get over the top or consider trading their stars for younger players and build a new team with the coming revenues. They could no longer trade prospects for veterans because their prospects were gone; over a twenty-six-month period from 1995 to 1997, the team had dealt seven former first-round draft picks.[46] These trades had denuded the farm system, ranked fifth by *Baseball America* in 1994 but last by 1998.

In the end the team decided to build for the future while hoping they could re-sign Rodriguez and Griffey, who were still in their twenties. "We were tearing down to get ready for the new park," Piniella recalled later. "You couldn't do it at once. It had to be done over a two-year period. We took our lumps, but it was the right thing to do. . . . No question there was a conscious decision."[47] Whether this was the right decision remains highly debatable; there have been few teams in history with as much topflight talent as the Mariners had, with Griffey, Johnson, Rodriguez, and Edgar Martinez in their prime. But the Mariners had made their choice.

When the team started poorly in 1998—they were 34-49 at the end of June—the Mariner ownership instructed Woodward to deal Johnson rather than lose him to free agency at the end of the season. Woodward did surprisingly well, shipping the Big Unit to the Astros for what proved to be three valuable players: pitchers Freddie Garcia and John Halama and infielder Carlos Guillen. Although the fans and media would eventually come to appreciate this good deal, at the time everyone was disappointed. The team appeared to be dumping salary after getting the public to fund an expensive new stadium. Worse, the team finished 76-85.

The Mariners finally opened Safeco Field in July 1999 to great fanfare, but once again the team finished below .500. Without Johnson, the pitching staff in particular pulled down the team's season, finishing with the league's second-highest ERA. Although Moyer, Garcia, and Halama pitched well at the top of the rotation, the club gave a remarkable 342 1/3 innings to pitchers with an ERA of 7.38 or higher.

At the end of the 1999 season John Ellis retired as CEO and was replaced by Howard Lincoln. With their two stars just a year from free agency, Woodward and the owners presented Griffey and Rodriguez with huge contract extensions—Griffey's would have made him the highest-paid player in the game—but both players declined. Woodward knew that he had unpleasant work ahead.

Lincoln made it clear that he was not a supporter of Woodward, the long-serving GM.[48] After the season Woodward resigned. Lincoln and Armstrong wanted a veteran baseball man who could produce a winner in their new stadium, and not surprisingly they turned to Pat Gillick.

Early in his Seattle tenure Gillick discussed his approach to player evaluation, stressing character, makeup, and chemistry. "When I'm scouting, I take character over physical ability every time." He also knew that the prevailing free-agent market might require him to move beyond his self-imposed three-year limit for players whose character met his test: "I hate to say I put makeup ahead of ability, but the more I'm around the more I believe you have to do this. With the multi-year contracts we give out, makeup becomes more important. When you're in the midst of a five-year contract, one side is going to be upset." Gillick also maintained, "Chemistry is unbelievably critical. If you come into the workplace, and there is inconsistency, there are disruptive employees or you don't know what to expect, then you won't be a motivated employee." Gillick extended this concept to the players' wives as well, because "there can be a lot of one-upmanship with the ladies."[49]

With Safeco Field open, Seattle's management finally agreed to increase payroll as a means to improve the team. Gillick knew that signing free agents was a risky strategy, because most available players tend to be overpriced and declining. Many teams have assumed that adding payroll would lead to success on the field, only to be surprised when it does not. Gillick was one of the few general managers who had proved capable of finding the right players and not overpaying.

One of Gillick's first chores, though, was to address the situation with his franchise's all-time greatest player. In November 1999 Griffey told Gillick and Lincoln that he planned to leave as a free agent after the 2000 season and asked to be traded. Wanting to avoid potential disruption from a disgruntled superstar, the Mariners reluctantly agreed. As a so-called ten-and-five player (a ten-year veteran, including five with his current team), Griffey had the right to approve any trade. When Griffey gave Gillick a list of only four teams to which he was willing to be dealt, the outfielder greatly hampered Gillick's leverage.

As Gillick went through his limited options, he mainly demanded top prospects. When it became clear that the Reds, Griffey's hometown team and his father's longtime organization, were the most likely suitor, Gillick initially asked for a mother lode of young ballplayers, including second baseman Pokey Reese, first baseman Sean Casey, starter Denny Neagle, reliever Scott Williamson, and a top prospect. Fortunately, this overreach did not derail negotiations, and in the end he was forced to settle for center fielder Mike Cameron, pitcher Brett Tomko, and two Minor Leaguers. Of the four only Cameron, who turned in four excellent seasons in Seattle, proved a valuable addition.

Back in Toronto Gillick had benefited from his "many rivers" approach to team building, being willing to use nontraditional sources to find talent. In Seattle Gillick fished a new river, signing Japanese relief pitcher Kaz Sasaki in December. A few days later he secured one of baseball's best left-handed relievers, Arthur Rhodes, with a four-year deal, helping to turn the club's biggest weakness into a strength.[50]

In finding a starter Gillick was the beneficiary of some good fortune. The Rangers' Aaron Sele, a solid midrotation pitcher, had agreed to a four-year, $29 million deal with the Orioles. After Sele took his physical, Baltimore scaled back its offer. The annoyed Sele instead signed with Seattle, in his home state, even though the terms were only two years and $15 million.[51] With Sele added to Jamie Moyer and twenty-three-year-old Freddie Garcia (acquired in the Johnson deal), the Mariners anticipated a stronger rotation in 2000.

Turning to the offense, Gillick again looked to the free-agent market. As he had in Baltimore, Gillick targeted one of his former Blue Jays, and one of his favorites, star first baseman John Olerud. He also signed infielder-outfielder Mark McLemore, a veteran with much-needed on-base skills. McLemore proved to be an extremely valuable player, filling in at a number of positions and regularly getting on base over the next few years. Finally, the club signed utility outfielder Stan Javier to bolster the bench. Piniella liked switch hitters, and McLemore and Javier provided him with two. With all the new additions the team's payroll increased only moderately, from $54.1 million to $60.5 million, because their two largest salaries from 1999—Griffey and pitcher Jeff Fassero—both came off the roster.

All six off-season free-agent acquisitions—Sasaki (the Rookie of the Year), Rhodes, Sele (17 wins), Olerud (103 RBI), Javier, and McLemore—delivered what the Mariners hoped for, as did trade acquisition Cameron. The team rebounded to 91 wins and a return to the playoffs, where they beat the White Sox in the Division Series before losing the ALCS to the Yankees. The revamped squad improved in all facets of the game: run scoring increased from sixth to fourth in the league, despite playing a full season in pitcher-friendly Safeco Field; the team improved from twelfth to second in fewest runs allowed; and the defense had become one of the league's best.

Gillick's second off-season in Seattle might have been even more dramatic than his first. The overriding story, once again, was the disposition of a Mariner superstar, this time free-agent shortstop Alex Rodriguez. Unlike the situations with Randy Johnson and Ken Griffey, the Mariners believed that they could retain their shortstop and worked to that end for a few months.

Meanwhile, Gillick turned back to Japan, where the Orix team in the Japanese Pacific League made star outfielder Ichiro Suzuki available to the U.S. Major Leagues. Although Ichiro was one of Japan's best players, there was some doubt regarding how he would perform, because a Japanese nonpitcher had yet to excel in the United States. Jim Colborn, the Mariners' director of Pacific Rim scouting, had been a pitching coach in Japan in the early 1990s when he had befriended the young outfielder, and he vouched for Ichiro's skills.[52] With this endorsement Gillick and the Mariners sought and landed Ichiro, first sending $13.125 million to Orix for the right to negotiate with the player and then, on November 30, signing him to a three-year deal for $14.088 million.

In December Gillick reinforced his bullpen by signing skilled setup man Jeff Nelson, whom the Mariners had traded away several years earlier. He also inked veteran second baseman Bret Boone, also a former Mariner, filling one of the larger holes on the team. McLemore returned to a multiposition role, primarily sharing left field with the returning Al Martin.

Gillick and ownership remained active in their pursuit of Rodriguez. When the team offered a three-year contract for $54 million plus a two-year option, bringing the contract value to $92 million—believing Rodriguez and his agent, Scott Boras, were looking for a short-term contract—Boras told the Mariner delegation, "You're not even close."[53] Boras was correct. In late January word came that the Texas Rangers had landed Rodriguez with a ten-year, $252 million contract, well beyond the terms of any previous baseball contract. Gillick knew that he could not possibly replace Rodriguez at shortstop, but he and Piniella decided to try young infielder Carlos Guillen, who had failed to win the third base job in 2000. Despite the loss of the league's best player, the off-season moves increased the team's payroll to $74.7 million.

Heading into the 2001 season the Mariners were seen as a good, but not great, ball club. Both *Sports Illustrated* and the *Sporting News* projected a second-place finish in the AL West. While the pitching was solid, the offense was considered suspect. Boone and Ichiro could not be expected to offset the loss of Rodriguez and the anticipated fall-off in production from the injury-plagued Jay Buhner. The experts turned out to have underestimated things considerably, as the team started quickly and never slowed down, reaching a high-water mark of 47-12 after the games of June 8. At the All-Star break the team sat 63-24 and led the division by nineteen games.

Gillick tried to improve his great team at midseason. First, he argued that "if you want to go to the end (the World Series) you basically have to have a number one starter." And while Gillick liked Freddie Garcia (who would lead the league in ERA that year), he thought him not quite ready: "Freddie Garcia might be at some point a number one starter, and hopefully he will be. He has the potential to be. (But) Freddie's 24 years old."[54] He tried to improve his offense, inquiring about San Diego third baseman Phil Nevin, New York Yankee left fielder Chuck Knoblauch, Toronto left fielder Shannon Stewart, and Detroit outfielder Juan Encarnacion.[55] In the end Gillick left his team alone.

The 2001 Seattle Mariners set the AL record and tied the 1906 Chicago Cubs' Major League record, with 116 wins. In addition to their 116-46 record, the Mariners led the league in runs scored, fewest runs allowed, and attendance. The team had several excellent individual seasons, especially from Bret Boone (.337 with 37 home runs) and Rookie of the Year and MVP Ichiro Suzuki (.350). In the playoffs the Mariners first squeaked by the 91-win Cleveland Indians, 3 games to 2 in the Division Series, before falling once again to the Yankees in the ALCS, a disappointing end to a historic season.

The 2001 Mariners dramatically highlight how free agency could be used as a tool for assembling a team. Table 11 summarizes how their most significant eighteen players were acquired.

Only Edgar Martinez and Bret Boone (who was traded away and reacquired) were products of the Mariner farm system. Just seven of these players were on the roster during the 1999 season, two of whom arrived via a trade-deadline deal in mid-1998. Nine free agents were signed during the two subsequent off-seasons. Several other players were acquired as an indirect result of free agency, in the forced trades of Johnson and Griffey.

The transformation of a mediocre 79-win team to the 116-win juggernaut in just two years was quite an accomplishment by Gillick and the front office, especially considering that they lost two of the greatest players in the game in the process. Prior to free agency such a dramatic leap forward would have required an unusually strong crop of rookies, a lopsided trade or two, or player purchases from a struggling franchise. Free agency changed this paradigm. Moreover, the newly

Table 11. Key 2001 contributors

POSITION	NAME	HOW ACQUIRED
C	Dan Wilson	Trade with Cincinnati, November 2, 1993
1B	John Olerud	Free agent, December 15, 1999
2B	Bret Boone	Free agent, December 22, 2000
3B	David Bell	Trade with Cleveland, August 31, 1998
SS	Carlos Guillen	Randy Johnson trade, July 31, 1998
LF	Al Martin	Trade with San Diego, July 31, 2000
CF	Mike Cameron	Ken Griffey trade, February 10, 2000
RF	Ichiro Suzuki	Free agent, November 30, 2000
DH	Edgar Martinez	Nondrafted free agent, December 19, 1982
UT	Mark McLemore	Free agent, December 20, 1999
UT	Stan Javier	Free agent, December 20, 1999
SP	Freddy Garcia	Randy Johnson trade, July 31, 1998
SP	Aaron Sele	Free agent, January 10, 2000
SP	Jamie Moyer	Trade with Boston, July 31, 1996; re-signed November 20, 1996
SP	Paul Abbott	Free agent, January 10, 1997; re-signed January 4, 1999
RP	Jeff Nelson	Free agent, December 4, 2000
RP	Arthur Rhodes	Free agent, December 21, 1999
RP	Kazuhiro Sasaki	Free agent, December 18, 1999

Source: http://BaseballReference.com.

available players from Japan provided Gillick another river to fish in. Teams today can add a lot of talent on short notice.

One of the pitfalls of this approach is that free-market players are generally nearing or past thirty, since they must have accrued six years of service time. For that reason they often need to be replaced quickly, requiring either a productive farm system or continually guessing correctly in a risky marketplace.

Gillick lost his magic touch during the 2001–2 offseason. He acquired three players to shore up his three weakest offensive positions—left fielder Ruben Sierra, third baseman Jeff Cirillo, and catcher Ben Davis— but none of them made an impact. On the pitching staff the Mariners lost Sele to free agency, and Gillick could bring in only James Baldwin, a bottom-of-the-rotation starter. With this new batch of free agents Seattle's payroll continued to climb, jumping to $80.3 million in 2002, the fourth highest in the league.

Even with an aging squad and a less than stellar offseason, the Mariners were 60-36 on July 18 with a four-game lead in the division. Gillick hoped to make one of his patented midseason trades, but ownership told him the budget was firm. "We could probably use a starting pitcher," Gillick remarked. "But from a standpoint of budget, we are more than maxed out."[56] Lincoln concurred publicly: "If you don't operate as a business, all sorts of bad things happen. People want us to do something exceptional, but what we want to do is have discipline and stick with our plan. . . . We absolutely have to make money. No question, end of story."[57]

The budget limitations surely frustrated Gillick because the Mariners had become extremely profitable. Lincoln confirmed to the press that the team made $9.6 million in 2000 and likely exceeded that amount in 2001. Total revenue for the Mariners was the second highest in baseball behind only the Yankees and had more than doubled from $82.67 million the last year in the Kingdome to $183.64 million in 2001.[58] Moreover, Lincoln believed Gillick could deliver the same product for less money: "I think we can actually spend less money with our Major League payroll simply because Pat Gillick and his staff are much more efficient than some general managers on how they spend money."[59]

Plus the owners had a long memory. Armstrong, conscious of the importance of financial matters in his position as team president, even kept a card in his pocket reminding him of the $77 million the club reportedly lost between 1992 and the opening of Safeco Field.[60] Without any midseason additions, the team slumped over the last two months, winning ninety-three games, a dramatic falloff from 2001 but still the second most in Seattle history and a record often sufficient to reach the postseason. In a very strong AL West, however, ninety-three wins was only third best, behind Oakland and Anaheim.

In retrospect, the talent on the 2001 Mariners was not as outstanding as its record implied—the club benefited from several players having the best season of their careers. Researcher Phil Birnbaum developed an objective method for measuring this phenomenon. After examining several factors, including how well a team converts its runs into wins and how players performed compared to previous and subsequent seasons, Birnbaum concluded several years ago that the 2001 Seattle Mariners were the "luckiest" team since at least 1965. None of this should detract in any way from the achievements of the team—the term *luckiest* is ill-suited, as the Mariners won the games and deserve the record. But in evaluating the potential for the following season, recognizing unaccountably strong seasons from players is essential. The thirty-two-year-old Bret Boone was a lifetime .255 hitter with a .312 on-base percentage and .413 slugging percentage, who recorded averages of .331, .372, and .578 in 2001, with 141 RBI. Looking forward, one should have expected a sharp dropoff, which is what transpired.

Gillick still believed he could deliver a title to Seattle and re-upped with the team for one year after the 2002 season. He believed ownership would allow him to hold on to several key players nearing the end of their contracts plus pursue a pitcher and outfielder.[61] For the most part his expectations held up, and for 2003 Gillick returned essentially the same squad, adding left fielder Randy Winn as compensation from Tampa Bay for the signing of manager Lou Piniella, who left after having developed a rocky relationship with Lincoln. "In my ten years in Seattle, the Mariners never got a left fielder for me," cracked an obviously relieved Piniella.[62] As his replacement Gillick and the ownership team brought in Bob Melvin, giving the ex-catcher his first Major League managerial opportunity. Gillick could not find a front-line pitcher, however.

At the July 31 trading deadline the Mariners were leading the division by four games. Once again Gillick made no moves. Though he returned with the hope of winning a title, he was not going to mortgage the future if they could not get over the top. "Don't read too much into this for the offseason, but there are certain players I won't give up, because it didn't make sense," Gillick recalled. "Legitimately there are eight to ten solid prospects, say eight, and I'd be willing to give up four. But of that four, I might be willing to give up one. I'm not going to give up two."[63] The team again won ninety-three games and fell short of the playoffs.

Though Gillick wanted to rebuild the farm system during his years in Seattle, that goal was secondary to delivering a title. He was hampered by the loss of draft choices from all his free-agent signings, another pitfall of relying heavily on free agency. In fact, the Mariners had only one first-round draft choice during his four years at the helm and failed to sign him (John Mayberry Jr.). Gillick's scouts remained active internationally, and the team signed four impact players (career WAR over 10) for the Minor League system during Gillick's tenure: outfielder Shin-Soo Choo, second baseman Jose Lopez, pitcher Felix Hernandez, and shortstop Asdrubal Cabrera. The farm system that ranked twenty-fourth when he took over had improved to twelfth by the start of the 2004 season (as rated by *Baseball America*).

By the end of 2003 Gillick had spent four years with the Mariners and was ready to move on. Gillick never really offered an explanation beyond "feeling it was time to give someone else a chance."[64] Most likely, he knew that his two talented free-agent classes had run their course, as most of these players were past their prime. Moreover, he was reportedly frustrated that the ownership group vetoed a couple of trade-deadline deals during the season.[65] The farm system was stronger than when he arrived, and the team had several quality young pitchers, but it was time for a new challenge. Once again, Gillick signed on as a consultant.

Getting a veteran team with core talent over the top is a much different challenge than building an expansion franchise. By correctly evaluating and sifting through his inherited players and using all available avenues to surround his nucleus with stars and capable role players, Gillick crafted a team that won Canada's first two World Series, went to two consecutive American League Championship Series in Baltimore, and won a record 116 games in Seattle. Along with his genius, Gillick had two advantages, although not unique, that he relied on: an ownership willing and able to occasionally outspend the competition and enough status that ownership was usually leery about meddling too directly in his baseball sphere.

20 Analytics

The one thing good leaders have in common is a willingness to let new evidence change their views.—The *Economist*, citing a study by the executive search firm Korn/Ferry

In the spring of 2003 author Michael Lewis created a sensation in the baseball community with the release of *Moneyball*, a book that relates the story of how Oakland A's general manager Billy Beane kept his undercapitalized team competitive. A onetime financial trader turned writer who had unprecedented access to Beane's activities, Lewis identified two related causes for the A's success: Beane understood the concept of market inefficiencies and the analogous benefit of finding undervalued players, and Beane believed that these players could be better identified using statistical and analytical techniques than by traditional scouting methods.

The second issue caused a fair bit of controversy. Lewis is a terrific writer, and much of the charm of his book came from the dichotomy he drew between the old-school scouts and the newfangled statistical analysts. As Lewis put it, "Billy had his own idea about where to find future Major League Baseball players: inside [assistant general manager Paul DePodesta's] computer. He flirted with the idea of firing all the scouts and just drafting kids straight from Paul's laptop."[1] The two most prominent statistical insights of the A's, as highlighted by Lewis, were that most organizations undervalued hitters with a high on-base percentage who did not otherwise stand out and that teams undervalued college players when compared to high school players in the amateur draft.

Baseball statistical analysis had been evolving and developing for roughly fifty years and had begun to find an audience with the writings of Bill James starting in the late 1970s, but this audience mainly consisted of independent researchers and a particular type of fan.

Sabermetrics, a word coined by James, did not prescribe a set of formulas and answers, as its critics might have thought. It is a process, a philosophy that teams should make decisions based on evidence and data. This was not a new idea—scouts had been using radar guns and stopwatches for decades rather than merely trusting their eyes—but sabermetrics suggested that baseball's vast statistical record could tell a team which players were actually helping the team score or prevent runs, which strategies would increase the team's chances of winning, which Minor Leaguers were likely to be good Major Leaguers, and more. Much more, in fact.

By the 1990s sabermetrics had begun to creep into some of the more progressive baseball front offices. For example, Yankee general manager Gene Michael stressed several key statistical areas, including on-base percentage, when he rebuilt the Yankees early in the decade.[2] More analytically, Rockies general manager Dan O'Dowd and Major League administrator Thad Levine were making sophisticated mathematical evaluations of the effects of their high-altitude Coors Field in 1999.[3] But most teams, before the publication of *Moneyball*, kept their analytical efforts out of the public eye. Not surprisingly, Lewis's portrayal of a general manager who seemed to be rejecting one hundred years of supposedly hidebound traditionalist scouting in favor of novel statistical methods created a rift between the proponents of traditional scouting and statistical analysis.

The escalation of data-driven analytics in the evaluation of players and game strategies created a new opportunity for baseball teams to gain an advantage over their peers. The team most associated with analytics after the A's was the Boston Red Sox, whose principal owner John Henry made a fortune as a commodities trader by taking the emotional element out of trading decisions. He hired James as a consultant and a young Yale graduate, Theo Epstein, as general manager. The Red Sox success—they won the World Series in 2004 and 2007—along with improvement in other analytically associated teams like the Cleveland Indians, led to a more widespread acceptance that analytics could offer important insights into both the understanding of a player's value and how that player's value was likely to evolve.

Pat Gillick, who had earned his formidable stripes as a scout, was not an early adopter of statistical analysis. For people like Gillick, Lewis's unflattering portrayal of traditional scouts poisoned even his more compelling statistical arguments. Because Gillick's Mariners were also competing directly with the A's in the AL West, Gillick managed to get himself into something of a feud with Beane and Lewis.

"I thought the way the writer treated people in the book was in poor taste," Gillick said. "That's why I wouldn't buy it. I'm very, very disappointed that anybody would take shots at people as were taken. They took a shot at one of my guys right here, Roger [Jongewaard, the Mariners' longtime vice president of scouting and player development, who originally scouted and signed Beane]." Gillick did not let Beane off the hook, either. When asked if Beane's interpretation might have been misrepresented, Gillick replied, "He was not misquoted for 200-and-some pages." To Beane's credit he did not run from his comments: "I never said I was misquoted. I don't feel the need to pacify others. Again, my energies, as they always have been, are on trying to compete, with the lowest payroll in the division."[4]

"You have to give them credit, but the test is going to be how they maintain it," Gillick said. "It's difficult, with that payroll, to maintain. We'll have to wait and see. Initially, they've gotten it done, but once [shortstop Miguel] Tejada and [third baseman Eric] Chavez are eligible (for free agency), if they can't pay them, you'll probably see a decline in their won-loss record."[5]

Lewis thought that Beane's advantage would dissipate for a different reason: because other teams were going to start mimicking his strategies. "He [Beane] may feel pretty happy with himself now, because his team reflects inefficiencies exploited in the past, and looks pretty damned good. He might even get through this whole year without having to use the trade deadline, one of his favorite things. But two, three years down the road, he has problems." More specifically, Lewis concluded, "I don't think [Beane] gave away all his secrets. They still have secrets; but I don't think they have secrets from the Red Sox. They certainly don't have secrets from the Dodgers. But the Dodgers may have secrets from the A's, because I don't think Paul [DePodesta, whom the Dodgers hired away as general manager] coughed up everything he knew to Billy."[6]

Beane, too, understood this predicament: "Time will tell. Listen, at some point, yeah, there will be a dip in the performance level. You don't have to be Nostradamus to predict that. But you know what? That's the case with every sports franchise. It doesn't take a genius to figure that out."[7]

Gillick also added his thoughts on some of Beane's specific theories as translated by Lewis:

> I think from the Double-A level up, statistical information is more pertinent than from Single-A down. At least when you get to Double-A, Triple-A and the Major Leagues, you have something to compare the statistics against. I'm not sure what the level of competition is at Class A, rookie or amateur level. I don't want to limit myself in one area. If we think the best player is from college, we'll take him; if we think the best player is a high-school player, we'll select that player. If we think we want to get a player from China, Japan or the Dominican Republic, those are all areas you have to investigate. Why limit yourself to one area? Why say you have to draft college guys and you have to fit this criteria? I think you're limiting yourself and not looking at the big picture. Baseball is full of exceptions and opinions. . . . They have a theory what they do, but I think what they're doing is limiting themselves, maybe because of economics. They think high-school kids are too much of a longshot, too much uncertainty. But the old saying is, if you want to hit it big, you'd better take a risk.[8]

For Gillick, this was another side of his "many rivers" philosophy of finding talent: be prepared to use all the information you have available to you.

But what Beane, through Lewis, was saying was not that high school players should not be drafted, but that they were currently *overdrafted*, and college players taken at the same draft position were a better risk. If all teams made this determination at once and shifted their strategies, high school players could suddenly become *underdrafted*, and a market-driven team would then shift its focus to high schools.

As with much of Lewis's book, this point was not sufficiently understood in the debates that ensued.

In the decade after the publication of *Moneyball*, analytics has gradually become much more sophisticated and ubiquitous. "We go after players we feel have a positive residual, guys we like better than everyone else," explained A's director of baseball operations Farhan Zaidi in 2013. However, Zaidi further points out that it is important to recognize "what data is commoditized, and what data really gives you a competitive advantage. Knowing that—knowing when you're using data that other teams have access to, versus data that is legitimately proprietary—is an important point to be able to recognize."[9]

Statistical analysis can also be used to evaluate in-game situations. The mountains of data rapidly becoming available allow comprehensive analysis of on-field events such as batter-pitcher matchups, strategic decisions such as bunting, and defensive positioning. As the front offices in some of the more statistically savvy organizations better understand these relationships, there has been a natural tendency to impose some of this knowledge on the manager. Not surprisingly, this has occasionally upset the barrier that has been observed between the front office and the field staff for nearly a century. "You're the manager and you're going to get no interference or second-guessing from me," Yankees general manager Ed Barrow told manager Miller Huggins in the 1920s. "Your job is to win, and my job is to see that you have the players to win with."[10]

Analytics has changed this relationship; the front office now has information that might contradict what a manager ordinarily would want to do. As one writer recently observed, "Teams don't want a seasoned, master tactician anymore so much as they want a manager with a small ego and an open mind. At the root of this change is the proliferation of statistical analysis, which can make decisions for managers if they're willing to embrace it."[11] Lewis described Beane's preferred approach in *Moneyball*: "Beane ran the whole show. He wasn't just making the trades and supervising scouts and getting his name in the papers and whatever else a GM did. He was deciding whether to bunt or steal; who played and who sat; who hit in which spot in the lineup; how the bullpen was used; even the manager's subtle psychological tactics."[12]

This was clearly the extreme, but other teams that put more emphasis on the statistical side also made in-game suggestions. In Boston, "in those first years they would have guys who would send me lineups," manager Terry Francona later complained. For example, "they would tell me not to hit David Ortiz against Scott Kazmir because chances are David's going to have a rough night. Well, I'm not sitting David. He's got a chance to be MVP, and you want me to start Doug Mirabelli at DH because Doug has better numbers against this guy?" After winning the 2004 World Series Francona had earned enough standing to push back. Nevertheless, his statistically inclined owner continued to pepper him with advice gleaned from an analysis of the team's statistical research. Henry would often send late night emails, "usually asking why certain decisions were made that ran contrary to the imposing database maintained by the baseball operations staff."[13] (We discuss the Red Sox at greater length in a later chapter.)

Over the next several years many teams employed a staff of analysts, and each club had to reach its own internal accord over its primacy. Some depended on it more than others, but nearly all recognized that scouting and sabermetrics were not mutually exclusive and that some level of analytics was valuable. The most statistically inclined teams often looked to hire managers who embraced the new techniques, perhaps illustrated most notably by Joe Maddon in Tampa Bay.

By 2014 every big-league team had wealthy ownership, smart professionals in the front office, and well-organized player-development systems. The new stadium binge that saw nearly every team in baseball get a new or remodeled ballpark, and its associated increase in revenues, had run its course. Toronto, Baltimore, and Cleveland, which won in the 1990s with smart organizations and new stadium revenues, can no longer boast either advantage over their competitors.

In the aftermath of *Moneyball*, most teams have staff dedicated to analytics looking for strategic advantages over their competition. An indicative, but far from comprehensive, survey of various teams and technologies testifies to the sophistication, variety, and ubiquitousness of the advanced analytical techniques and concepts. The New York Mets are one of seventeen organizations (as of 2013) that employ TrackMan, a ball-tracking technology that uses Doppler radar to track the baseball. Such 3-D tracking systems that can capture the location of the ball and players at near-continuous intervals are now scheduled for installation in all the Major League parks by 2015. "A guy could be throwing 90 miles per hour with 7 feet of extension, and he gets the ball to home plate quicker than a guy throwing harder that doesn't release the ball as close to home plate, essentially redefining velocity," said Josh Orenstein, the company's director of baseball operations and analysis.[14] Another baseball executive noted that his club was using the technology in scouting, Minor League instruction, and the Major Leagues.[15] Sandy Alderson, the Mets' GM and the man who hired Beane in Oakland, agrees: "This is quite simply going to add immeasurably to the amount of information that's available. To the extent that things become more granular, then we make fewer inferences as to what actually is going on. The critical thing is to be able to use the data in such a way that ultimately it can be used either in terms of player evaluation or even player education or instruction."[16] Such data-intensive video requires high-speed computers and new analytical methods to study the "big-data" output from this and other initiatives. One team, currently unidentified, purchased a Cray supercomputer, reported to cost a minimum five hundred thousand dollars, for analyzing the forthcoming data explosion.[17]

The Tampa Bay Rays, owned and managed by former Wall Street executives and investors, assembled a front-office staff tasked, in part, with uncovering market inefficiencies and unearthing new insights for finding, improving, and utilizing baseball players. As detailed in a recent book by Jonah Keri, the Rays' staff includes James Click, who created a sophisticated database to track all available information on each player; physicist and mathematician Josh Kalk to tease insights out of the PITCHf/x data (a new technology discussed in greater detail in the next chapter); and sports psychologist Dr. John Eliot to better understand the mental side of player-performance fundamentals and the nebulous concept of clubhouse chemistry. Some of their findings, notably in the area of defensive positioning and the results of batter-pitcher matchups, have become integrated into the team's on-field strategies.[18]

In 2012 the Orioles hired longtime big-league pitching coach Rick Peterson as director of pitching development, focusing on biomechanical studies of pitchers' motions. He has long been a proponent of understanding pitching mechanics and recently teamed with famed sports orthopedic surgeon Dr. James Andrews to better understand them. "It's based on Dr. Andrews research at ASMI (American Sports Medicine Institute)," says Peterson, "to get an MRI [magnetic resonance imaging] of the pitching delivery to make sure that the measurements in that delivery are falling into normative range to optimize performance and reduce the risk of injury."[19]

The struggling Houston Astros hired Jeff Luhnow out of the Cardinals' organization after the 2011 season, and he brought along others from St. Louis. He had video coordinator Jim Summers analyzing the vast amount of available video information. The team uses data generated by Inside Edge and runs it through a program made by Sydex Sports. For example, the Astros compile every pitch for the past few years thrown by opposing pitchers and scrutinize the data with the team's hitters. "The right-handed batters will say 'OK,' let me see this period of time against right-handed batters," Summers explained. "Now we're going on proper preparation to see the ball. We know what's coming. We know that on a 2–1 count, 37 percent of the time a pitcher is going to throw a fastball in a certain area. We can prepare for that. The statistics and video have broken it down."[20]

In Chicago new Cubs president Theo Epstein teamed with Bloomberg Sports to create a first-class player-evaluation system. "The management and analysis of data," said Epstein, "whether it be scouting reports, statistics, medical information or video, is a critical component of our operation. We look forward to developing a customized program that utilizes the most advanced and efficient technology available in the marketplace today to facilitate quicker, easier and more accurate access to all the sources of information we use to make baseball decisions."[21]

The Tigers hired a performance-enhancement instructor, as of 2011 one of only a handful of teams to employ such a specialist. In this role

Brian Peterson, who holds a master's degree in counseling psychology, tries "to help all of the players, in the entire organization, be clear of mind while they're going about their business." Peterson might be approached by a hitter who says, "Geez, I'm 2-for-50; what am I going to do?" As Peterson sees it, "The majority of time there is some sort of personal issue that is creating some type of emotion, and their coping mechanisms maybe aren't quite as good as they could be. I simply try to help them by giving them some good coping mechanisms and some good direction so they can be clear of mind while they're going about their business."[22]

In 2013 the Pittsburgh Pirates made the playoffs after twenty consecutive years of below-.500 finishes, one of the longest runs of futility in American sports history. Some of their turnaround is due to simply finally succeeding with their long run of high draft choices. But the Pirates actively secured this young talent by spending more money on amateur signing bonuses than any other team in baseball between 2007 and 2011.[23] The team also started applying thoughtful analytics to uncover possible competitive advantages. After studying the key elements of successful defense, the team began using more targeted defensive shifts and getting their pitchers to throw more pitches that could induce ground balls, an approach that required a buy-in from manager Clint Hurdle.[24] (In fact, a baseball executive told us in 2014 that convincing pitchers of the benefits of the new defenses was often a challenge.) Under their new program the Pirates improved their defensive efficiency from last in the league in 2010 to fourth in 2013 and surrendered the second-fewest runs.

Nationals general manager Mike Rizzo, the son of a baseball scout, expanded his organization's analytical capabilities. The widely second-guessed decision to limit pitching phenom Stephen Strasburg's innings in 2012, his first year after coming off Tommy John surgery, was the result of extensive study of previous cases. Another medical study led the Nationals to bring in a doctor to evaluate and monitor blood nutrients in the players.[25]

Rizzo also worked to integrate the scouting and analytics departments. During the 2012–13 offseason the Nationals were "looking heavily at the left-handed relief market," director of baseball operations

Adam Cromie told the *Washington Post*. One of the team's scouts framed the question: "What is the profile of a left-handed starter who has success after moving into a relief role?" To help answer the question Cromie and Samuel Mondry-Cohen analyzed both statistical information and scout-derived evaluations. "That's something that was very much driven by a scout," Cromie said. "A scout came to us and said, 'Look, this is kind of to me what a starter who fits into a relief role looks like. What does it look like to you? And how can we put those two things together and come up with a list of players who fit into that profile?' It was a very interesting project, and I would say the results are very interesting, too."[26]

In the decade after *Moneyball* most teams struggled with how deeply and broadly to embrace analytics. The debate in the immediate aftermath of the book was between those who supported the traditional scouting model and those who thought, as Beane did in Lewis's book, that sabermetrics could dramatically reduce the need for scouts. The smartest and most successful teams, as it turned out, grew their analytics staff to provide information that could enhance and augment what their scouts were telling them and that, in the ideal environment, the scouts and analytics staffs could work together and learn from each other. Scouting was not going away. Nor was analytics.

21 Post-*Moneyball*

The Philadelphia Phillies finished 88-74 in 2005, missing the playoffs by just a single game. The team's ownership, led by president Dave Montgomery and principal owner Bill Giles, had grown tired of the club's repeated failures to reach the postseason. The team had moved into the new Citizens Bank Park a year earlier, and general manager Ed Wade had assembled a competitive team with baseball's fourth-highest payroll. But ownership believed that with the new stadium and budget, the Phillies needed to be reaching the playoffs. "I believe he's done a good job. We're a better club than when he took over," Montgomery said of Wade. "However, we set goals for ourselves. We haven't achieved our goals. I think it's appropriate at this time to find a new GM."[1]

Montgomery turned to Pat Gillick, a man who had three times succeeded in just this situation—a new stadium and high expectations—and signed him to a three-year contract. As in Baltimore and Seattle, Gillick did not bring a bunch of his own men into the front office; he believed that under his leadership he could build an organization and win with the people on hand. In particular, Gillick worked with two well-respected front-office men from Wade's regime: assistant general managers Ruben Amaro Jr. and Mike Arbuckle.

At a time when *Moneyball* was all the rage, when many teams were looking for their own Ivy League wunderkind to model their team after the Red Sox, the Phillies instead hired a sixty-eight-year-old traditionalist, a man who had spoken out in defense of the scouts he felt had been disparaged by Michael Lewis's book. Gillick's philosophy had not changed: he believed in hard work and intelligent management.

"I don't know that I have a style or a way," Gillick said at the time.

I guess what I think is most important is hiring the right people to make the right personnel decisions, trying to get the best people to make those decisions. And you have to be consistent. That's why the Braves are so good. I don't think old way vs. new way. It's about getting your goals in place and running with them. Don't all of a sudden go off on a tangent. If you have to tweak your game plan, tweak your game plan, but stay consistent. I don't think anything gets an organization off track more than changing course all the time. Get a plan and stick with it.[2]

Gillick knew practically everyone in baseball—owners, general managers, other executives, agents, and scouts—and he spent a good part of every day talking to them on the phone, learning whatever he could. Moreover, he was relentless in this pursuit as in all others. "If Pat wants something, he goes and gets it," his wife, Doris, said. "He doesn't let up."[3]

The Phillies had finished second in the league in runs scored in 2005 but ninth in ERA, and the club had several young stars who had recently graduated from the team's farm system, most notably slugging first baseman Ryan Howard, the 2005 Rookie of the Year; second baseman Chase Utley; shortstop Jimmy Rollins; left fielder Pat Burrell; and pitcher Brett Myers. "Usually when you come into a situation like this," Gillick said, "it's not a club that has won the number of games that the Phillies have over the last five years. You're usually coming to a club that's rebuilding, reconstructing or remodeling. I don't think that's the case here. We've got some holes to fill. We need to add some starting pitching. If we do that, we have a chance to get to the playoffs." Gillick always believed that if he could structure his team to consistently win eighty-five to ninety games, the players could occasionally put together a few big years and break through. "My challenge," he said, "is to try and coax five more wins out of this team and get us into the playoffs. Once you get into the playoffs, anything can happen."[4]

Gillick hoped to land an ace pitcher, but knew how difficult that task was. "We need a No. 1 or No. 2 power guy right at the top, somebody that can stop a losing streak," he said. "The type of person we're looking for, they're hard animals to find."[5] He later added, "You look at the free agent list and there's not a lot of No. 1 starters out there. Most of the No. 1 starters, I've said this before, are developed by the club they signed with."[6] Instead, Gillick hoped to fill in around them with undervalued free agents and a few trade targets. He was very much a "character guy" when pursuing players, particularly role players. "If a team meets its goals," he said, "personal goals fall into place."[7]

"You get a feeling for how the club interrelates with each other," Gillick said later. "[If] you make a move you better try to bring in somebody who's going to relate to the guys you have. In other words, you bring in a bad apple, players begin to question your motives. The mental approach is almost more important than the physical. It's a matching game you've got to go through."[8] Because of this sentiment, he often reacquired players he had on previous clubs. That offseason he traded for Arthur Rhodes and signed Ryan Franklin, players he had at earlier stops.

The 2006 season started disappointingly. Despite the call-up of future ace Cole Hamels in May, the team was below .500 in July, and Gillick looked to shake up the team. At the trading deadline Gillick swapped star right fielder Bobby Abreu along with pitcher Cory Lidle to the New York Yankees for four players, none of whom ever panned out. Dumping Abreu opened up some payroll flexibility and transformed the team's leadership. "From a talent standpoint, it was the wrong decision because Abreu is still playing well," Gillick said several years later. "But I thought he set the tone for the club and he's not really a high-energy player. I thought I had to change the energy level, and when we made that trade guys like Utley, Rollins and [right fielder Shane] Victorino, their personalities energized the club."[9]

Several weeks later he swapped a couple of nondescript Minor Leaguers for another old favorite, veteran hurler Jamie Moyer. Mainly because the team began playing up to its talent level, the Phillies rebounded over the second half to win eighty-five games, still well short of Gillick's ninety-three-win goal to make them a playoff contender.

During the off-season Gillick used some of the money freed up from the Abreu trade to sign several free agents, most of whom produced below expectation. In his most successful move Gillick "took a flyer"[10] and signed free-agent outfielder Jayson Werth, who had been injured for the previous year and a half. Nevertheless, the team rebounded from its disappointing 2006 season due mainly to its young position players. First baseman Howard (47 home runs), second baseman Utley

(22 homers, .332), shortstop Rollins (30 homers, 20 triples, 41 steals, the MVP award), and outfielders Burrell, Rowand, and Victorino, backed by Werth (.863 OPS [on-base plus slugging] in 304 plate appearances) and Greg Dobbs (a waiver pickup who filled in at third), contributed to the team's league-leading 892 runs. Twelve-game winner Brett Myers was shifted to closer, and Hamels and Moyer anchored an improved rotation. It was enough to win eighty-nine games and, thanks to a collapse by the New York Mets in late September, the NL East title.

After the Phillies were swept in the Division Series by the Colorado Rockies, Gillick went back to work. Over the 2007–8 winter, Gillick had his greatest success building his bullpen. He first traded a package of players, including speedy young outfielder Michael Bourn, to Houston for closer Brad Lidge, allowing the Phillies to return Myers to the starting rotation. Gillick also signed free agent Chad Durbin and re-signed left-hander J. C. Romero, a free agent he had picked up over the summer.

The 2008 Phillies won ninety-two games, just three more than they had in 2007. Gillick preached that once a team got to the postseason, anything could happen, and the Phillies proved that by winning three postseason rounds. In the finale they beat Tampa Bay to win the Phillies' second-ever World Series.

None of Gillick's free-agent signings in Philadelphia had the impact of his earlier ones with Toronto, Baltimore, or Seattle. One theory for this would be that there simply were not as many quality free agents available—the best players in the 2000s were re-signing with their existing teams before hitting the market. In general, this does not appear to be the case.

Table 12 shows the number of players with at least 3 WAR (a good regular player or starting pitcher) in the first season following their free agency (including players re-signing with their current team). Using this arbitrary but reasonable cutoff, the number of impact free agents has not materially changed since the end of the strike and its aftermath in the mid-1990s, though the pool did appear to be somewhat smaller during the few years, 2006 to 2008, that Gillick was trying to bolster the Phillies.

Table 12. Number of free agents

YEAR	>=3 WAR
1997	12
1998	10
1999	18
2000	5
2001	11
2002	10
2003	19
2004	20
2005	18
2006	9
2007	10
2008	6
2009	13
2010	16
2011	14
2012	11

If Gillick made fewer impact-player transactions with Philadelphia than he had with Baltimore or Seattle, it is because he finally inherited a core of young talent. He had no young stars in Baltimore until he signed Roberto Alomar. In Seattle he had Ken Griffey, whom he had to trade immediately, and Alex Rodriguez, who left after one season. In contrast, the Phillies team he took over was filled with young talent, including Howard, Rollins, Utley, Myers, and Hamels. With Philadelphia he did not have to find the key players; he was looking for the players to augment a talented core.

Though outfielder Jayson Werth (twenty-four home runs) and hurler Jamie Moyer (sixteen wins), both important additions in 2008, had come cheaply, Brad Lidge had cost Michael Bourn, a pretty good prospect. The price proved to be worth paying, as Lidge gave the club a 1.95 ERA and forty-one saves and then added seven more in the postseason.

Earlier Gillick moves, such as the signing of pitcher Adam Eaton and a trade for pitcher Freddy Garcia, did not pan out, nor did a number of his lower-profile moves. Nevertheless, Gillick's persistence in fine-tuning the team paid off. "It's a crapshoot, but the thing about it is I think you have to—you can't lose your guts, let me put it that way," Gillick said. "If you lose your nerve or your guts, if you have a failure and you think you're doing the right things preparing to make that sign, if you've crossed all the T's and dotted all the I's and checked everything out and it just didn't work out, you can't let that stop you. You've got to go ahead and not lose you're nerve and go ahead and do what you think is best for the club."[11]

Gillick had bolstered a young nucleus with an excellent bullpen, a couple of veteran hurlers, and Werth. Moreover, he managed to do this without surrendering any of his key players—the core he inherited in 2005 was all on hand to celebrate the World Series victory in 2008. He also accomplished the championship without increasing the budget. The 2005 payroll of $95.5 had increased only slightly to $97.9 million in 2008, falling from fourth to twelfth in the Major Leagues.

With his three-year contract up and his third world championship earned, Gillick decided it was time to retire. He was seventy-one years old and had succeeded with a fourth organization, fully validating his credentials as a master team builder. But the *Moneyball* effect had brought many more young, statistically inclined young men (women were still a distinct minority) into baseball front offices. While Gillick believed that bringing in new ideas was healthy, he felt baseball needed to be careful not to let the pendulum swing too far.[12]

When asked in 2011 which current general manager reminded him most of himself, Gillick cited Jon Daniels, a New York–born and –raised Ivy Leaguer who became the Rangers GM when only twenty-eight, a significantly different career path than Gillick's. "Let me put it this way," he said. "I always kind of considered myself a little bit adventurous, [willing] to try out new ideas and I think . . . he's got a lot of the [new] nuances that you have in baseball. At the same time, he . . . looks back and says a lot of the things that worked years ago, you know, they're still valid."[13] Daniels's Rangers won the AL pennant in both 2010 and 2011 and have been a perennial contender.

In fact, Gillick's extraordinary success as an executive can be credited in part to his adventurousness, to his willingness to discover new ways of finding players. His exploitation of the Rule 5 Draft remains unprecedented and likely led to teams being much more careful about whom they left unprotected. His inroads into the Dominican Republic in the 1980s changed the game, as one look at the All-Star rosters and league leaderboards can attest. His acquisition of Japanese stars in Seattle, especially Ichiro Suzuki, ended any misconceptions Americans might have had about the talent there. If Gillick did not embrace *Moneyball*, it is not because he was afraid of change or of statistics. As a man who grew up in baseball, he believed the process should respect all of the people and traditions that he held dear.

With the Phillies Pat Gillick showed that he did not need to aggressively embrace analytics, even in the twenty-first century, because of all of the other skills he brought to the table. The Phillies' scouts and development system had drafted and delivered a talented core to build around. Gillick's willingness to listen to his scouts, his knowledge of the game, and his widespread contacts around baseball allowed him to surround the nucleus with enough talent to be successful. As the game continued to grow in complexity, however, an organization without Gillick's lifetime of contacts, insights, and success would need to incorporate all the new technological and analytical tools available.

The 2002 San Francisco Giants, behind thirty-seven-year-old Barry Bonds's fifth MVP season, came within one game of winning the World Series before falling to the Anaheim Angels. The Giants were an exceedingly old team, with second baseman Jeff Kent (thirty-four), catcher Benito Santiago (thirty-seven), and right fielder Reggie Sanders (thirty-four) also playing key roles. At twenty-nine third baseman David Bell was the youngest regular.

For the next several years general manager Brian Sabean did what one might expect with an aging superstar and an old team: he used veteran free agents to fill holes and try to win before his stars could no longer contribute. Bonds's tremendous late-career peak (he added MVPs at ages thirty-eight and thirty-nine), in effect, delayed Sabean from rebuilding. Sabean's strategy worked for a couple of years. In 2003 the team won one hundred games (losing in the first round of the playoffs), and in 2004 they won ninety-one, missing the postseason by a single game.

Inevitably, a win-now strategy with a veteran team can work for only a limited time and eventually comes with a cost. Without the necessary influx of young players, the Giants lost at least eighty-five games from 2005 to 2007, the final three seasons of Bonds's career. Bonds remained a great hitter even at forty-two, but the Giants finally decided that they needed to build a new team without him, and with the baggage surrounding accusations of his use of performance-enhancing drugs, no other team was interested. His storied twenty-two-year career, fifteen with the Giants, came to an end.

In May 2008 Peter Magowan, the Giants' managing general partner (equivalent to the principal owner) announced he would be resigning at the end of the season. He had led a group to purchase the team in 1993 and had a celebratory first decade or so in charge. The Giants opened their new privately financed stadium in 2000, made four playoff appearances, and nearly won the city's first World Series in 2002.

By 2008, however, Magowan and the Giants had struggled through some difficult years. On top of the three disappointing seasons on the field, he and the Giants' front office did not come off well in the December 2007 *Mitchell Report*, devoted to the prevalence of steroids in baseball. Moreover, in late 2006 the team had signed free-agent pitcher Barry Zito to a record-breaking contract (seven years, $126 million), and Zito had pitched poorly in his first season. Finally, the death of Harlan Burns, who held the largest block of Giants' stock, boded ill for Magowan. Burns had generally allowed Magowan to operate as he saw fit, but his wife, Sue, who was a regular attendee at PacBell Park, had less patience after the recent lapses.[14]

To replace Magowan the board named William Neukom, another Giants investor, to the post of managing general partner and promoted Larry Baer from executive vice president and COO to president.

A native of the Bay Area, Neukom had made his fortune as the general counsel for Microsoft. When he was a junior partner at Shidler, McBroom, Gates, and Baldwin in Seattle in the late 1970s, one of the senior partners, William H. Gates Sr., asked Neukom to advise a fledgling computer firm his son was moving from Albuquerque to Seattle.[15] As Microsoft grew, and Neukom's time became more and more focused on their affairs, he became a full-time employee in 1985. Neukom built Microsoft's legal department and fashioned their defense in the government's multiyear antitrust litigation. "The people in [Microsoft] were so smart and so young," Neukom said, "it felt like part of what I did was provide some adult supervision, just providing a good sounding board, a little bit of discipline, a little bit of structure and ideas. Not just legal concepts but just some common sense on how to run with this idea."[16] By the time he left Microsoft in 2001, he reportedly owned $107 million in stock.

Neukom grew up a San Francisco baseball fan before Major League Baseball reached the West Coast. His next-door neighbor was Charlie Graham Jr., son of the owner of the Pacific Coast League's San Francisco Seals, and Neukom often attended Seals games with Graham's tomboy daughter. When he grew to six feet four, Neukom naturally gravitated to basketball but injured his knee during his senior year in high school. After graduating as class president from San Mateo High, Neukom majored in philosophy at Dartmouth because "they were such rigorous thinkers"[17] and then returned home to attend Stanford law school.[18] Famous for his bow ties, in his midsixties Neukom still looked like the tall, athletic man he must have been as a teenager. His hair had turned white, but he still had a large shock of it above his long, still youthful face.

With the Giants Neukom was more than just a smart man who loved baseball. "My job," Neukom said, "is to see to it that as an enterprise, primarily on the baseball side but also on the business side, we have the right structure and the right culture so we can provide the resources and the guidance so our baseball experts can put a contending team on the field. And that buck stops with me."[19] He had a plan, gleaned from his many years following baseball and working with other executives, for how a baseball team should be run. He had also learned from his father, who managed the San Francisco office for McKinsey and Co., one of the world's premier business consulting firms. Neukom was a firm believer in strategic planning, and one of the first things he did upon taking over the Giants was to commission a study to "update us on our strategy going forward."[20]

As both the baseball and the financial operations of baseball franchises became more complicated, and as front offices evolved to become more corporate in structure, often including both a CEO and a team president, standard corporate management tools, such as management consulting, seeped into baseball as well.

One of the first to use a management consultant was Peter Bavasi, when he took over as president of the Cleveland Indians in 1985. Bavasi had long admired management specialist Peter Drucker and subscribed to his "management by objectives" philosophy. Upon joining the Indians, Bavasi prepared a 450-page MBO directive, covering everyone in the organization. He then hired Drucker to review the document and work with Bavasi and the staff on how to better administer the ball club. "He consulted by probing," recalled Bavasi, "asking layers of questions, our answers to which began to reveal new ways of approaching old problems."

Not every problem had a management solution. Cleveland manager Pat Corrales once asked Drucker about pitcher Ernie Camacho, who had a history of following a good season with a poor one. "'Patrick,' answered Drucker in his formal manner, 'the way I see it, there's only thing you can do.' Finally, after a long pause while the manager eagerly awaited his wisdom, Drucker said, 'You should consider trading this man as soon as you can.'"[21] Drucker's approach appeared to help. In 1986 the Indians recorded their only winning season between 1982 and 1994. When the club was sold after the season, Bavasi (and Drucker) were not retained, and the team returned to its losing ways.

The Giants' front office that Neukom inherited two decades later had evolved dramatically. No longer did a front office consist of a half-dozen or so former players and men who had grown up in the scouting or Minor League instructional departments. As revenue sources and payrolls exploded, the baseball business grew much more complex, requiring larger staffs and more specialists on both the business and the baseball sides of an organization. The following list, based on the Giants' media guides, chronicles these changes. By 2002 the team's baseball operations unit had grown to eighteen, and heading into the 2014 season the Giants' website identified thirty-five executives in the group. Running a baseball team had come a long way from the cozy days of a general manager and a small handpicked staff.

SAN FRANCISCO BASEBALL OPERATIONS EXECUTIVE POSITIONS

1983 (6)

Vice President, Baseball Operations (GM)
Assistant Vice President, Baseball Operations/Administrator
    of Minor League Operations
Director of Player Personnel and Scouting
Field Director of Player Development
Assistant Director of Player Personnel and Scouting
Minor League Consultant

1989 (9)

President and General Manager
Vice President, Baseball Operations
Vice President/Assistant General Manger
Vice President, Scouting Operations
Director of Player Development
Director of Minor League & Scouting Operations
Special Assistants to the President & GM (2)
Special Assistant for Player Development
(Special Assistants were Willie Mays, Willie McCovey, and
    Orlando Cepeda)

2002 (18)

Senior Vice President and General Manager
Senior Assistant (Willie Mays)
Senior Advisor (Willie McCovey)
Vice President and Assistant General Manager
Vice President, Player Personnel

Senior Advisor, Baseball Operations/Director of Arizona
   Operations
Special Assistant to the General Manager
Director of Player Development
Special Assistant, Player Personnel (3)
Director of Minor League Administration
Coordinator of Scouting
Coordinator of International Operations
Coordinator of Video Systems
Assistant, Baseball Operations
Assistant, Video Systems (2)

2014 (35)
Listed in the administrative section under the President and CEO
   Special Assistant (Willie Mays)
   Senior Advisor (Willie McCovey)
   Special Assistant (J. T. Snow)
   Special Assistant (Will Clark)
Listed in the baseball operations section
   Senior Vice President and General Manager
   Vice President and Assistant General Manager, Player
      Personnel
   Vice President and Assistant General Manager
   Vice President and Assistant General Manager, Scouting and
      International Operations
   Special Assistant to the General Manager
   Vice President, Pro Scouting and Player Evaluation
   Senior Advisor, Baseball Operations
   Director, Player Development
   Assistant, Player Personnel
   Director, Minor League Operations/Quantitative Analysis
   Senior Advisor, Scouting (5)
   Director, Dominican Operations
   Assistant Director, Dominican Operations
   Coordinator, Pacific Rim Scouting
   Senior Consultant, Player Personnel

Special Assistant, Player Development (2)
Director, Team Travel
Director, Arizona Minor League Operations
Manager, Player Personnel Administration
Coordinator, Video Coaching Systems
Coordinator, Video Coaching Systems
Coordinator, Medical Administration
Coordinator, Scouting Administration
Coordinator, Minor League Operations
Baseball Operations Assistant
Arizona Minor League Operations Assistant

As he considered his new challenge, Neukom outlined what he called the "Giants Way." Neukom first asked, "What business are we in?" In addition to the baseball business—obviously the principal concern—Neukom also recognized that the Giants were in the entertainment business, the information business, the customer relations business, the community service business, and the real estate business. A top-notch organization needed to excel in all of these.[22]

As Neukom saw the baseball side, "if you have that kind of clear message and you teach to that message and are consistent with it, you are just bound to get better results at the end of the day at every level and particularly the Major League level. So I think it's more than a reemphasis on it. It's some clarification and some commitment to teaching the Giants Way in a very consistent manner."[23] The Giants Way could be thought of as divided into two pieces: the players, their development, and the game on field; and the front-office and business side of the operation.[24]

Neukom defined the players' portion as "Job One . . . identifying the talent, teaching the talent and playing the game the right way."[25] He broke this section down into four parts:

- *The Players:* Neukom outlined at an early press conference that the Giants were going to be "emphasizing and investing even more in homegrown talent. We have to find the best baseball athletes we can find, through better scouting and better analysis of the amateur draft. We have to emphasize that part of our roster. At the same time, we have to be wise about making strategic trades when it will materially help our team in the medium run, at least, if not the long run, and we have to be willing to enter into the free-trade, free-agent market every now and again, where there is an opportunity to materially improve our competitiveness as a ballclub."[26]

- *The Teachers:* Neukom demanded that the Giants have the "best coaches that allow that talent to go from great athletes into great baseball players."[27] He also stressed having the best trainers to make the Giants players the best conditioned and to maximize the players' potential for strength and speed.[28] Moreover, baseball should be a year-round job.
- *On the Field:* "We are going to stress fundamentals. We will have a Giants Way. We will be better conditioned and we will work harder. We will be better prepared."[29]
- *Off the Field:* Players are "heroes with a lot of money." But they are also "professionals," which brings a lot of responsibility. The players are "ambassadors for the game and Giants."[30]

For the business and front-office side, Neukom identified ten items:

- *Strategic Planning:* Neukom integrated general manager Brian Sabean (and his key lieutenants) much more into the overall business operation. "Traditionally the baseball side has had a kind of autonomy from the enterprise," Neukom said. "That is less and less true in modern baseball. Brian Sabean and all of his people understand that they are one group in a tightly connected network." On the other hand, the general manager's sphere of influence was increased to include input on other areas: "[In the past] Brian would come to an investor meeting and give his report and leave. I would look around and say that's silly. He's as smart as we are. Now he contributes in discussions in other parts of the enterprise."[31]
- *Listening:* "Central to the Giants Way is listening to and serving our customers."[32]
- *Performance Management:* "We'll establish a culture of merit. . . . If you perform well, if you work hard and smart and if you've

got the skill set that matches your job you will achieve your potential."[33]

- *Smart Work:* And Neukom emphasized, outwork the competition as well. "It's important we have better scouts and better statistical analysis. We just have to outwork people, whether it's in the conditioning room, down the dirt roads in Middle America or in front of the (computer) screen."[34]
- *Communication:* Neukom wanted to make sure the communication between the baseball and business sides of the enterprise was working well. Moreover, he wanted to make sure that all the latest information technology was available to the baseball side.
- *Teamwork:* Neukom believed in deflecting credit to coworkers.
- *Innovation:* As he learned in the high-tech world, Neukom told his employees not to be afraid of failure, but to use it as a learning opportunity.
- *Mistakes:* Neukom believed in acknowledging mistakes and learning from them.
- *Respect*
- *Ethics*

At first glance many of these precepts sound like generalities and platitudes, but Neukom was determined to succeed with his Giants Way. Soon after taking over he offered particulars as to what the Giants needed and what had failed in the recent past, detailed enough on the baseball side that it even appeared as if he was impinging on Sabean's sphere. "Our analysis was that we had very good pitching," Neukom said early in the 2009 season.

And if we could catch the ball and play good defense we ought to generate enough runs to be a much better team this year than last year without shooting the moon and spending more than we want to and without putting frankly a lid on talent which we finally have some of in the farm system. Our plan is to bring up homegrown talent. It's cheaper and they've been taught to play baseball the way it should be played and fans are attached to homegrown talent the way they never are to someone who comes in as a free agent. So there's every reason in the world to develop our farm system. We have neglected it for a while with good reason. I'm not second-guessing that strategy. I was a part of it. You have Barry Bonds and you have the best ballpark in America you should have done what we did and we rode that horse as far as we could. We probably should have had a better transition plan, succession plan earlier than we had. But now we have some good draft picks. We better have some talent in our system because we had the picks to get them.[35]

Neukom's commitment to the Giants Way was more than just a re-emphasis, but Sabean and his staff had also established a couple of key advantages in the Magowan years. For one, the team had been effective in drafting young pitchers. Matt Cain (a three-time All-Star) had been drafted in 2002, Jonathan Sanchez in 2004, Tim Lincecum (Cy Young Awards in 2008 and 2009) in 2006, and Madison Bumgarner in 2007. Along with Zito these four would anchor the rotation when the Giants broke through in 2010. Sabean deflected much of the credit for these young pitchers to his player-personnel chief: "We've been very lucky. Dick Tidrow and his staff should take a lot of credit for that.... We're above the norm as far as drafting, signing and developing these young guys, including getting them to be big league-ready and produce at a young age."[36]

To his credit Sabean, the longest-tenured general manager in baseball, developed a loyal and stable team of lieutenants. "Like Pat Gillick," wrote Jerry Crasnick, "Sabean is a firm believer in delegating authority and hiring good people and letting them do their jobs."[37] Besides Tidrow, who signed on as a scout in 1994, Sabean relied on Bobby Evans, who joined the front office the same year. Evans proved a valuable assistant, principally on the business side, helping to negotiate contracts, overseeing rules compliance, and assisting with budgets.[38] These two and scouting director John Barr, hired in 2008, sometimes joined Sabean at the investor meetings.[39]

But there is more to great pitching than simply drafting youngsters with live arms. A team needs to direct their development through the Minor Leagues and keep them healthy. The Giants understood that "having great statistics in the minors doesn't mean anything if you're getting hurt when you get to the big leagues."[40] When he first took over in 1996, Sabean put an emphasis on the health of his players, particularly pitchers. "We need to reduce our injuries," he told trainer Stan Conte. "All of a sudden," Conte remembered, "the medical department was involved in every aspect of decision making. We started with a healthier team, and we were able to keep it healthy."

At the time, there was little hard data on injuries (types, frequency, implications) to work with. "USA Today published a list of guys put on the DL [disabled list] every Tuesday," Conte recalled. "This was before everything was on the internet, so I was trying to track down every paper copy of that newspaper I could find." His research serendipitously became more complete one day while in the CFO's office when he noticed a big red volume on the desk. When he asked what it was, the CFO told him, "'Oh, the [insurance] company does a bunch of stuff and they send it out every year.' I look inside and it had everything: time lost, DL dates, dollars lost. It was unbelievable."[41] Conte followed up with the insurance company to get as many past volumes as he could. With Conte's involvement Sabean's initiative was successful: from 1997 to 2001 the Giants lost fewer games to the disabled list than any other team in baseball.[42]

The Giants continued to refine and stress their injury-prevention ideas and research so that by 2010, their top four starting pitchers all started at least 33 games, and in 2012 the team's top five starting pitchers started 160 of the 162 games. Being able to count on one's top pitchers game after game is a huge advantage over a 162-game season. "You start early with these guys," said Sabean. "Keep them in a basic state of general health, and you're way ahead of the game."[43] And then the medical people remain involved with the team daily. "The trainers are on top of us," Cain said. "Guys take advantage of learning what they can do. And they aren't set on what they have done in the years past."[44]

The team also granted statistical analysis a more meaningful part of the evaluation process.[45] Jeremy Shelley, a vice president charged with pro scouting and player evaluation, and Yeshayah Goldfarb, the director of Minor League operations and quantitative analysis, both took on enhanced roles within the organization. As Baer described Goldfarb, "He's one of our 'Moneyball' guys if you will."[46] Neukom added, "They are not just crunchers who give you some funny numbers. They love the game and have an opinion, and they stand up to Brian and the scouts and Tidrow and say, 'This is not the guy you want for these reasons' or 'this is what you might not have caught on this guy.'"[47]

Greatly to Sabean's credit, he accepted input from Shelley and Goldfarb. The ongoing debate between scouts and statistical analysts, fueled by the publication of *Moneyball* in 2003, had significantly died down by the time Neukom took over but still simmered in many baseball quarters. Sabean, who spent his formative front-office years in scouting and player development, would naturally have resented the way Michael Lewis portrayed scouts and the superiority of statistical analysis. Instead, he adapted.

The ball club that Neukom inherited after the 2008 season had one predominant strength: a pitching staff that included excellent young starting pitchers in Lincecum and Cain and a useful contributor in twenty-five-year-old Jonathan Sanchez. But the team was burdened with significant weaknesses, predominantly among its position players. No player on the team with more than 150 at bats had an OPS over .800. As a consequence, the team averaged less than four runs per game, well below the league average of just over four and a half. And they were not making up for it on the defensive side. By defensive efficiency, a simple but relatively reliable metric that measures the percentage of balls in play turned into outs, the Giants ranked twelfth in the league. Over the next two and a half years, Sabean and his staff completely rebuilt the lineup without surrendering any key contributors.

Before the 2009 season Sabean signed White Sox infielder Juan Uribe and Triple-A outfielder Andres Torres, and in midsummer he swapped two Minor Leaguers to the Pirates for veteran second baseman Freddy Sanchez. More important, the club gave the third base job to twenty-two-year-old Pablo Sandoval, signed out of Venezuela in 2003, and the youngster responded by hitting .330 with twenty-five home runs. With the improved offense, and great pitching from Lincecum and Cain, in 2009 the Giants advanced to eighty-eight wins and third place in the NL West.

Buster Posey, the Florida State catcher taken with the fifth overall pick in the 2008 draft, spent just over a year in the Minor Leagues before he became the club's starter and franchise player and captured the 2010 Rookie of the Year Award. Other key additions in 2010 were first baseman Aubrey Huff, signed as a free agent before the season; outfielder Pat Burrell, signed in May after his release from Tampa Bay; and outfielder Cody Ross, claimed off waivers in August.

The team's position players, once a weakness, were no longer a liability: the offense was now close to the league average, and the team's defensive efficiency record was the league's best. Neukom praised the Giants' front office for uncovering these underappreciated players: "They deserve a lot of credit for burning the midnight oil all the way through the midseason. They looked at hundreds of possibilities of ways to reinforce this team. And they obviously found some good ones."[48] One writer aptly described this approach: "Baseball executives say there are specific traits they look for: position players with several years of experience and a high work ethic, and healthy relief pitchers with a decent track record who have been struggling—and thus may simply be unlucky and due for improvement."[49]

More specifically, an AL executive said: "We take a closer look at a player if he gets both a scouting recommendation and a statistical recommendation. If we have either of those, that triggers taking a hard look." An AL scout expanded on this: "You really have to do your homework. You have to dig to find that extra bit of information, especially on guys who've been around a long time. . . . You have to see past the label. You have to get that info."[50] Sabean and his staff did so.

Sabean also reinforced the bullpen, anchored by 2003 draftee Brian Wilson. The Giants had signed Jeremy Affeldt after the 2008 season and Santiago Casilla after 2009 and traded for Javier Lopez and Ramon Ramirez at the 2010 trading deadline. The latter two combined to allow only 24 hits in 175 batter plate appearances over the final two months of the season. The young starters, now also including 2007 draftee Madison Bumgarner, matured over the intervening years and, combined with a rebuilt competent bullpen, led the league in ERA in 2010.

These Giants pickups performed beyond any reasonable expectation, and manager Bruce Bochy guided his squad efficiently. Certainly, some good fortune was involved, but the combination of scouting, analytics, and technology helped Sabean and his team uncover some undervalued, still-capable ballplayers.

With this restructured squad the 2010 Giants won the NL West with a record of 92-70. In the NLCS the team overcame the defending champion Phillies and capped the season by beating the Texas Rangers, giving San Francisco its first World Series title. The Giants' strategy had not been unique, but they executed it to perfection.

The Giants could not repeat in 2011, dropping from ninety-two wins to eighty-six, principally because the patchwork offense fell apart. The Giants finished last in runs scored, as many of the overachieving players of the previous year regressed to their historical averages, and Posey was seriously injured in a home plate collision. Of the twelve players with at least 230 plate appearances, eight had an OPS below .700, and only Sandoval was a productive hitter.

Late in the disappointing 2011 season the Giants board promoted president Larry Baer to CEO, and although the club behaved as if Neukom had willingly stepped aside, there was some chatter otherwise. The other owners reportedly felt that Neukom had not sufficiently included them in spending decisions, particularly some of the higher-dollar free-agent signings.[51]

Moreover, as Mark Purdy wrote in the *Mercury (CA) News*, "Neukom's falling-out with the Executive Committee, the baseball sources said, began over how to spend the additional millions of dollars that flowed into team coffers after the World Series championship. . . . Neukom, it is said, believed that this was his money to spend as he saw fit—and he did so, increasing payroll and buying new technology for the baseball department, among other expenditures. Instead, the Executive Committee wanted the money to be put in a 'rainy-day fund' for use in leaner times."[52] (To the last point Neukom responded that "in any normal business sense of the word 'rainy-day fund,' we have a rainy-day fund, and it's more than adequate.")[53] Nonetheless, Neukom was out.

Though the Giants still had a nucleus of good young players under team control, Sabean had a difficult rebuilding task for 2012 with his underperforming offense. Once again he turned over more than half his regulars in a short time. To play shortstop the team had promoted Brandon Crawford in 2011 and hoped he would hit better in 2012. The team also expanded the role of Brandon Belt, a 2009 draftee, making him the regular first baseman over the course of the 2012 season. To round out the infield Sabean signed veteran free agent Ryan Theriot to play second. He rebuilt his outfield by trading for Angel Pagan and Melky Cabrera, the latter later suspended in August for testing positive for performance-enhancing drugs while second in the league in batting average. At the trading deadline he added outfielder Hunter Pence and veteran second baseman Marco Scutaro.

The team's offense rebounded to finish sixth in runs scored. The pitching staff slumped slightly, primarily due to Lincecum's off year, and fell to fifth in ERA. The bullpen, now anchored by Sergio Romo, an amateur free-agent signing, and Santiago Casilla, remained a strength. With the revamped offense, the Giants won ninety-four games and the city's second World Series in three years. The professional management initiated by Neukom in 2008, combined with Sabean's stellar execution and Bochy's managing, gave San Francisco one of baseball's best-run organizations and its first two titles.

The Giants' success in these years can be traced in large part to the management philosophy put in place by Bill Neukom and embraced by Brian Sabean and his staff. In an era when new ideas and information are available as never before, the Giants were both receptive and innovative. The use of video is one example. In the same way that integrating statistical analysis with traditional scouting created an inflection point in the evaluation of ballplayers, marrying video downloads with high-powered computing is creating another. And like with the analysis of injuries, the Giants were at the forefront.

The best known of the new video technologies is PITCHf/x, an installation of purposefully placed cameras in every Major League stadium to track the exact trajectory, location, and speed of every pitch. First introduced in a playoff game between Oakland and Minnesota in 2006, by 2008 the application was operating in all Major League stadiums.[54] Developed by Sportsvision, a company based in nearby Mountain View and perhaps best known for devising the yellow first-down line that appears on football telecasts, PITCHf/x is revolutionizing the way that teams evaluate pitchers.

The Giants were one of the early proponents of the technology, which can be used to evaluate a pitcher's "stuff" and his injury propensities. "In 2008 the club was among the first to delve into using three-dimensional video to monitor the mechanics of their pitchers' motions," wrote Matthew Futterman in the *Wall Street Journal*, "so that everyone on the staff learned how to maintain what Sabean called a 'healthy arm action.'"[55] As Sportsvision CEO Hank Adams sees it, a "holy grail" of the technology is recognizing injured or potentially injured pitchers, even before the pitcher himself knows.[56] "The Giants were also the first team to adopt motion sensor suits," wrote Peter H. Lewis for the *New York Times*, "the same technology used to digitize human movement in video games and movies, to capture the nuances of a pitchers motion or hitter's swing on a computer."[57]

The Giants continued their pioneering approach with the next generation of the technology, FIELDf/x, introduced into their ballpark in 2009 to effectively measure and quantify just about everything that happens on the field. The full impact of this technology is limited only by the huge amount of video data that must be processed to create usable information. "You will be able to measure all these things you weren't able to measure before," said Bill Schlough, the Giants' chief information officer. "How fast a ball is thrown, how fast does a runner run, how far did a runner have to move to catch a ball, and what was your reaction time if you tagged up on a fly ball."[58] It also helped that the team's video operations coordinator, Danny Martin, dubbed "the unblinking eye" by Neukom, knew the game and could hold his own when working with the scouts and coaches.[59]

Like with the consequences of the analytical revolution, the influence of advanced video technology dramatically impacted the relationship between the front office and the field staff. Once a team has properly analyzed the data, the club can use it to position fielders, defend against base runners, and direct players on the base paths. The boundary between the front office and the field will continue to blur in the coming years, and the teams that manage this convergence most efficiently will gain an advantage.

Adams believes that this revolution in on-field video "is like Moneyball 2.0."[60] And the San Francisco Giants, who won two World Series in this period, were at the forefront. The Giants "applied a mixture of tech and baseball savvy that helped the baseball and business side. . . . [Y]ou might call it Techball," wrote USA Today.[61] By 2013 this included many firms promoting both advanced video and statistical analytics capabilities.[62] To administer and process Techball, the Giants employed three programmers and two statistical analysts and engaged more than ten firms to supply "the best available data, video, and technology."[63]

The Giants also understood, however, that any head start due to early adoption of technology could quickly be lost. "All clubs have access to the same information, it's how you digest it," said assistant general manager Bobby Evans. "It's a classic combination of scouting, tech and analysis."[64] Baseball had come a long way in the decade since the controversies over *Moneyball*.

22 Modern Game

It used to be that there were guys like myself that, if you played the game, you ran a baseball team. It's like saying to be a jockey you have to be a horse first. The best thing about the last 10 years is that now really bright people are running baseball teams, which is the way it should be.—BILLY BEANE, baseball executive

In October 2013 baseball's World Series matched two of its most storied franchises, the Boston Red Sox and the St. Louis Cardinals. When it was over, the Red Sox winning in six games, the two clubs had won half of the previous ten championships and were widely hailed as two of the best organizations in the game. Both clubs had undergone large changes during the decade, changing players, managers, GMs, and even organizational philosophies, with the one constant a firmly entrenched and involved ownership group. Reviewing their recent histories is instructive for understanding today's more complex front-office environments.

John W. Henry made his fortune in the 1980s and 1990s as a financial investor, developing an objective mechanical strategy for buying and selling that reacted to, in Henry's words, "what is, not what should be," and that precluded discretionary input.[1] He bought the struggling Florida Marlins in 1999, but sold them so that he could form a syndicate to buy the Boston Red Sox in 2002. With baseball's analytical revolution in its infancy, there were few owners anywhere more receptive to data-driven strategies than Henry.

The Red Sox ownership group was publicly represented by three men: Henry, as principal owner; Tom Werner, as chairman, largely concerned with the team's ownership of the New England Sports Network; and Larry Lucchino, president and CEO, who ran the club day to day. Lucchino had previously run the Orioles and Padres with some success and made his most lasting mark in Baltimore by envisioning and helping to create Oriole Park at Camden Yards, which opened in 1992 and stood as the model for two decades of ballpark design.

The Red Sox played in Fenway Park, built in 1912, and the team's owners had been trying to drum up public support to replace it for decades. The park had deteriorated badly by 2002, but Henry's group soon realized that public support was not coming. Lucchino hired Janet Marie Smith (who had worked on Camden Yards) to plan major renovation and expansion of the facility. Within a few years they had spent millions on the park, added five thousand more seats, and derived huge revenue from what had suddenly become one of the city's crowning jewels. In 2003 they started a sellout streak that lasted nine years, helping to keep the Red Sox near the top of baseball in revenue.

Henry had conquered Wall Street by exploiting unorthodox approaches and wanted his team to be on the forefront in data-driven thinking. He hired Bill James, easily the most famous and accomplished baseball analyst, as an adviser. After the 2002 season Henry nearly hired Billy Beane away from the A's, a saga retold in *Moneyball* when it was released the following spring. Beane agreed to terms with the Red Sox but backed out because of the disruption it would cause his California-based family. Instead, partly because of a glowing recommendation from Beane, the Red Sox hired twenty-eight-year-old Theo Epstein, a Yale-educated local kid who had been brought to the Red Sox from the Padres by Lucchino.

At the time of Beane's withdrawal, there was speculation that the Red Sox would have a difficult time finding an established GM willing to work under the aggressive, hard-driving Lucchino. "Larry is president and CEO of the Red Sox," Henry said at the time. "Everyone within the Red Sox organization reports to him directly or indirectly. The GM reports to Larry. That won't change."[2] But the local media would continue to resent Lucchino and his role with the team. "In no other industry," he said, "do they call it meddling when a CEO tries to stay active and involved in all facets of his company."[3]

After Epstein took over he repeatedly said that he wanted to build a "$100 million player development machine" to provide athletic young talent to the big-league club, depth to deal with injuries or poor performance, and assets to deal to fill in developmental holes. It all started, Epstein felt, with the amateur draft and young international free agents.[4] His farm director, Ben Cherington, managed the machine, and he and Epstein worked closely together for the next nine years.

As it happened the Red Sox won the World Series in 2004, before Epstein's development machine began churning out prospects. The championship, the team's first in eighty-six years, was celebrated in the city like the end of a world war, and the parade attracted three million people from around the world. Epstein's principal contribution to the club was a series of brilliant trades and signings that landed players such as David Ortiz, Bill Muellar, Kevin Millar, Curt Schilling, and Keith Foulke. As a so-called *Moneyball* Team, the Red Sox' success was often credited to their finding undervalued players who might strike out a lot and have low batting averages, but with on-base skills and power. Epstein was a hero in Boston and also in an analytical community that considered him their surrogate in the battle with the old guard.

But even as the team was winning, Epstein and his staff believed they needed to keep their focus on player development. "We decided that it was going to be fundamental to our approach," Epstein recalled, "and that in order to win the World Series we needed to develop home grown players and in order to develop home grown players we wanted to shift as many of our resources as we could to the draft, not only scouting resources and our time and our attention, but to a certain extent and to the extent the rules permitted, dollars and draft picks." (As an aside, the changes in the 2012 collective bargaining agreement have made this strategy much more difficult. According to Epstein, one "can't really choose how much you want to emphasize the draft anymore."[5] Additionally, the new agreement increased revenue sharing among the teams, further curbing the advantages of the high-revenue clubs.)

In the two off-seasons following their 2004 championship, the Red Sox lost several high-priced free agents, including Pedro Martinez, Derek Lowe, Orlando Cabrera, and Johnny Damon, while gladly cashing in the additional draft picks they received as compensation. Meanwhile, Cherington's organization was developing the next generation of stars. The Red Sox drafted Jon Lester in 2002, Jonathan Papelbon in 2003, Dustin Pedroia in 2004, and Clay Buchholz and Jacoby Ellsbury in 2005. By 2007 all five were in the big leagues and, along with a few more trade acquisitions and free-agent signings, helped the Red Sox win another World Series.

Off the field the Red Sox had developed a software program, called "Carmine," that provided ownership, baseball operations, and field staff with access to a myriad of data, scouting reports, and analysis (including future projections) on players in and out of the Red Sox system. Francona used this program often and pushed back only when baseball ops (or, on occasion, Henry himself) tried to tell him who should play. Once the media found out about the program, it became another data point in the story of baseball analytics supposedly taking over the game.[6]

Meanwhile, a strain had developed in the relationship between Epstein and ownership. Epstein had resigned after the 2005 season, though Henry convinced him to return three months later. Excessive interference seemed to be the problem, though a philosophical split within the organization occurred as well.

This schism came to a head again after the Red Sox' first-round playoff exit in 2009, made worse when the hated Yankees won the World Series. Epstein knew that the team had aged and needed some holes filled. He believed that the organization would be able to fill them as it had leading up to 2007, but that the solutions were not quite ready: "We still think that if we push some of the right buttons, we can be competitive at the very highest levels for the next two years. But we don't want to compromise too much of the future for that competitiveness during the bridge period, and we all don't want to sacrifice our competitiveness during the bridge just for the future. So we're just trying to balance both those issues."[7]

The next day Dan Shaughnessy angrily ripped the Red Sox in the *Boston Globe*, writing, "It's nice that Theo has a passion for player development, but asking fans to take a year off is outrageous. Henry is a billionaire and the Sox are making bundles of money."[8] As Shaughnessy saw it, and many other fans and writers seemed to agree, the Red Sox had the highest ticket prices in baseball and were swimming in cash, and now they were unwilling to open the bank for the annual free-agent crop. What Epstein saw as patiently waiting for the next bounty from the player-development machine, Shaughnessy and others saw as ripping off the fans.

Red Sox ownership also had no interest in Epstein's bridge. "I think he made a rare mistake saying that," said Tom Werner. "I think Theo would be the first to say it wasn't his finest Winston Churchill moment."[9] Looking back years later, Epstein thought the moment telling. "It underscores the conflict between the approach we wanted to take in baseball ops and the inherent tension with what the Red Sox became—the public image, the expectations, the dollars, the bigger-better-now mentality. It was a truthful moment, and I think demonstrated how we'd gotten too big."[10]

The Red Sox had been losing TV viewers since their 2004–7 peak, and Werner would later tell Epstein and Francona, "We need to win in a more exciting fashion."[11] Within a few weeks the Red Sox signed John Lackey (five years, $82.5 million), Adrian Beltre, Mike Cameron, and Marco Scutaro. After the Red Sox, with the second-highest payroll in baseball, failed to make the postseason in 2010, the team opened the vault even more, signing Carl Crawford (seven years, $142 million) and trading for Adrian Gonzalez and extending his contract (seven years, $154 million). Several of the signings cost the team draft choices, and the Gonzalez deal cost them three of the best players in their system.

The Red Sox were hailed as a superteam heading into the 2011 season, and they played like it for five months. At the end of August they had an 83-52 record, one and a half games ahead of the Yankees. They crashed to 7-20 in September, losing the division race and, on the final day of the season, the wild card as well. After this stunning collapse and multiple stories concerning turmoil in the clubhouse, Francona, sensing ownership had lost faith in him, resigned. A couple of weeks later Epstein followed suit, taking a job as president of the Cubs.

"It was my fault," Epstein lamented later. "I fucked up by giving in to [the trades and signings]. There was always a tension between the scouting and development approach and what I call 'The Monster.' Talk about the arc of the decade. I think our group was really good at fighting that Monster and being true to our approach in the early and middle years, then toward the end—and I blame myself for this—we sort of gave in to it."[12] With the Cubs Epstein had more power and was determined to build his machine and fight for it.

To replace Epstein the Red Sox promoted Cherington, a longtime assistant whose background was heavily steeped in player development as a scout and farm director. His tenure as GM got off to a rocky start when he was not allowed to find his own manager. Instead, he hired Lucchino's choice, the mercurial Bobby Valentine, who had spent the past several years as a manager in Japan and as a television commentator in the United States. The Red Sox had lost their edge, Lucchino felt, because Francona had allowed his players to become lazy and selfish, and the tough-talking Valentine would straighten them out. Instead, Valentine spent the summer criticizing individual players to the media, and by July many of the players hated him. The team had a terrible run of injuries—to Pedroia, Ortiz, Ellsbury, Lackey, and others—and finished 69-93, their worst record in forty-seven years. The team was suddenly terrible, old, and expensive. Valentine was an obvious casualty, replaced by John Farrell, who the players knew and liked.

Cherington helped secure the club's future in August when he worked out a remarkable deal with the Dodgers. In exchange for Crawford, Gonzalez, Josh Beckett, and Nick Punto (who were owed more than $250 million on their current contracts), the Dodgers gave them first baseman James Loney and a few prospects. The return was not important—Loney left after the season, and the prospects were not close to the Majors—but the deal allowed Cherington to reset the team. The team got worse—Gonzalez in particular was one of the team's better players—but Cherington suddenly had the financial flexibility to try to fix it.

After the season he made a series of smaller short-term free-agent investments, finally implementing Epstein's bridge. Ownership, perhaps humbled with the last-place finish, left Cherington alone and kept mum while he did not recruit expensive slugger Josh Hamilton, whom the media and many fans craved. "We had gotten into this cycle," Cherington acknowledged, "of retaining high-profile veteran players and trying to extend our success that way." Henry, too, recognized the need for change: "We went back to what had made us great for a very long time."[13] Nevertheless, the team's farm system was not quite ready to help out (still recovering from the prospects and draft picks lost in the 2009–11 spree), so Cherington brought in several players on short-term contracts to tide them over until the prospects emerged. In fact, partially as a result of their analytical approach, the signings—Mike Napoli, Shane Victorino, Stephen Drew, Koji Uehara, Jonny Gomes, Ryan Dempster—were tremendously valuable contributors in 2013. In addition, many of the hurt and ineffective players from 2012 rebounded, and the team shocked everyone by winning ninety-seven games and their third World Series title in a decade.

The path the Red Sox traveled was unusual, but their organization appeared to be in great shape looking ahead. They had a talented baseball operations staff, a top-notch farm system, a market that gave them a revenue advantage, committed ownership, and a talented core with no long and onerous contract obligations. Like Epstein, Cherington wants to build a team through the farm system first and fill in with trades and free-agent signings as needed. This approach requires that the system produce talent, obviously, but also that ownership and baseball operations are in sync when it comes to waiting for it to do so. The Red Sox are an illustration of how conflict in the front office can materially affect a team's performance and also how it can work.

In 1995 Anheuser Busch sold the St. Louis Cardinals for $150 million to a group headed by Bill DeWitt Jr., who had made his fortune as a private investor. DeWitt was the son of a famous baseball executive, but he did not get involved in baseball until after his father's death and following three decades in private business.

The father, Bill DeWitt Sr., had spent more than fifty years in the game, crossing paths with many of the executives profiled in this book. He began working for the Cardinals as a teenager, before becoming the GM of the St. Louis Browns in the 1930s. He presided over the only Browns pennant winner in 1944, bought the club after the war, struggled on and off the field for a few years, and then sold out to Bill Veeck Jr. in 1951.

DeWitt Sr. next became an assistant to George Weiss in New York for several years and then the GM of the Detroit Tigers in the late 1950s (making excellent trades for Rocky Colavito and Norm Cash).

In 1960 he succeeded Gabe Paul as the GM of the Cincinnati Reds and won the pennant the very next year. DeWitt bought the Reds from the Crosley foundation after the season and held the club for another five years. During his tenure the team drafted or signed Pete Rose, Johnny Bench, and Tony Perez, but DeWitt sold the Reds in 1966 to a group led by Francis Dale, who hired Bob Howsam to run the team.

Meanwhile, DeWitt Jr. earned economics and business degrees from Harvard and Yale and began making his way in private business. He was part of the ownership group (with George W. Bush) that bought the Rangers in 1988 and later was a major investor in Peter Angelos's group that purchased the Orioles in 1994. The next year he sold his shares to Angelos and bought the Cardinals.

DeWitt inherited general manager Walt Jocketty and soon lured Oakland manager Tony LaRussa to be the Cardinals' skipper. The Cardinals won the division title in 1996 and then made the playoffs six times in the next decade, losing the World Series to the Red Sox in 2004 and beating the Tigers in 2006. Jocketty kept the team contending mainly by making notable trades for star veterans, such as Mark McGwire, Edgar Renteria, Darryl Kile, Fernando Vina, Jim Edmonds, Woody Williams, Scott Rolen, and Larry Walker. The team had generally mediocre drafts in this period but made up for most of them when they nabbed Albert Pujols in the thirteenth round in 2000. Jocketty was named the *Sporting News* Executive of the Year in 2000 and 2004.

Despite the team's success, DeWitt came to believe that the team needed to rethink how it found its talent. "We had great teams in that era," he recalled, "but I knew that that wasn't sustainable because as that group aged, we would need younger players. . . . [W]e made a conscious decision . . . that we were going to throw a lot of resources and make every effort to build from within. . . . Rather than giving up draft choices, we tried to accumulate draft choices."[14]

In 2003 DeWitt hired Jeff Luhnow as vice president for baseball development. Luhnow had no baseball background—he had degrees in engineering and economics from Penn and a master's in business administration from Northwestern and had worked for McKinsey as a management consultant. Born to a New York advertising executive living in Mexico and fluent in Spanish, after joining the Cardinals

Luhnow opened a baseball academy in the Dominican Republic and expanded scouting efforts in Venezuela. He took charge of the team's amateur draft beginning in 2005, and in the next few years he and his staff selected Colby Rasmus, Jaime Garcia, Allen Craig, Jon Jay, and Lance Lynn. By 2006 Luhnow was in charge of the team's farm system and scouting.

Luhnow was hired in the aftermath of *Moneyball* and brought an analytical mind-set to the Cardinals. Luhnow reported directly to DeWitt, which undercut Jocketty and set up rivalries within the front office. This discord was seen as part of the cold war created by *Moneyball*, with different writers weighing in, depending on how they felt about the new guard.

The club won the World Series in 2006, but after a disappointing 2007 season, DeWitt fired Jocketty, citing divisions in the front office. Speaking for many, Bill Madden wrote that the firing was "just another example of the growing trend of meddling owners reducing the powers of the general manager and shifting the emphasis of baseball operations to statistical analysis."[15]

To be the new GM, DeWitt hired Jocketty's assistant John Mozeliak, at least partly because he had worked so well with both factions in the divided office. "I think a lot of that's been overrated," Mozeliak said. "I will say this: My working relationship with Jeff has been outstanding. What he's done to this point has allowed us to make better decisions as we move forward and it would be ludicrous for me to ignore that."[16]

Luhnow drafted Lance Lynn in 2008 and the next year had one of the greatest drafts in recent memory, selecting Shelby Miller, Joe Kelly, Matt Carpenter, Trevor Rosenthal, and Matt Adams. As an example of how the Cardinals melded scouting and analytics, the selection of Adams represented a collaboration between area scout Brian Hopkins and analyst Sig Mejdal. Hopkins watched Adams play at Slippery Rock University in western Pennsylvania, while Mejdal devised a player-projection technique for Division II colleges. Both liked Adams and jointly advocated for him.[17]

The Cardinals won the NL Central in 2009 and then won the World Series as a wild-card team in 2011. Unlike the great teams from 2004 to 2006, the 2011 champions were the first payoff of DeWitt's strategic shift to homegrown talent. "I knew it was the right strategy, but you have to execute the strategy, too," he said. "Fortunately, our guys did that. They have a really good staff, and I give them a lot of credit for doing that. But you have to plan it, and when it plays out the way it has, it's really pretty rewarding."[18]

The winter after the 2011 World Series was another one of transition for the Cardinals. LaRussa retired after thirty-three years as a manager, sixteen of them in St. Louis. Pujols, the team's best player for a decade, signed with the Angels as a free agent, the Cardinals opting not to compete with the ten-year, $240 million winning bid. And Luhnow was hired away to be the Astros' general manager, going from the world champions to the worst team in baseball. DeWitt, however, had built an organizational foundation that would withstand any person's departure, even men as talented as LaRussa, Pujols, and Luhnow.

Under Mozeliak, the club resurrected the Cardinal Way, a concept whose roots went back to Branch Rickey in the 1920s. As Ben Rieter described it in *Sports Illustrated*: "Upon signing with the organization players receive a package in the mail that includes a shiny Cardinals jacket as well as an 86-page handbook called *The Cardinal Way*. It's both a meticulously detailed instruction guide and a crash course rich in Cardinals tradition." Young pitcher Michael Wacha assured Reiter that it was more than just a formality: "This organization is all about attention to detail—they hammer this stuff home constantly, and if you don't pay attention, someone's going to call you out."[19]

Mozeliak recognized the need for constant adaption. "We understand that we're going to have to zig and zag to stay successful," he said. "We can't ever just get complacent and think we've figured it out. The moment we do that we're going to get passed." One of their most significant advantages was their ability to draft and develop pitchers. "In the draft we decided to emphasize not just pitchers who were throwing hard at the time, but guys we thought might throw harder in the future. The club focused on systematically evaluating prospects' mechanics to identify those who not only had mid-90s potential but who could also deliver it without breaking down."[20]

To enhance the Cardinal Way, Mozeliak created a baseball development department to house several analytical projects. The group created a software program to be used for scouting reports, game reports for Minor League managers, and player-development project reports. They also built an internal website where the front office and field staff can have instant access to everything about every player: medical reports, playing record, scouting reports, and more. The group collects data that they can use to create graphs and charts for coaches, hitters, pitchers, and fielders.

Critically, the entire organization from top to the bottom adopted the analytical program, and the managers and coaches in the Minors and Majors all use the same tools and the same instruction. This unified philosophy goes back to Rickey with the Cardinals, later brought to the Dodgers and expanded by their organization. "We rely on the fact," said assistant GM Michael Girsch, "that all of our coaches are good at their jobs, communicate with each other, and are on the same page. As the player moves up in the system, we know he's getting the same message; it's just coming from a different voice."[21]

The Cardinals came within a game of returning to the World Series in 2012, before making it back the next year. Remarkably, the 2013 postseason roster included just five players (and no pitchers) from the 2011 team. The Cardinals were loaded with hard-throwing young hurlers, the envy of the other twenty-nine organizations. Manager Mike Matheny drew criticism for hardly using twenty-two-year-old favorite Shelby Miller in the playoffs, reportedly to conserve his workload, but he did use twenty-one-year-old phenom Wacha, who won four postseason starts. "To have our minor league system be able to produce and really sort of define this club, I think it said a lot about the organization," Mozeliak said. "When you think about creating that sustained model to always be competitive, year in and year out, it really does start with how you procure the talent and how you develop it."[22]

The 2013 Cardinals were not a perfect team—they had a hole at shortstop, and their outfield defense was suspect, with no ready prospects to solve these problems—but their track record gave their fan base confidence that the team would solve these problems. In late November Mozeliak traded for center fielder Peter Bourjos and signed shortstop Jonny Peralta. They appeared ready for 2014.

In the first eighteen years of DeWitt's ownership, the team made the playoffs eleven times and won four pennants, finishing below .500 just three times. With a young team, a great farm system, respected executives in baseball operations, and a committed ownership all working together, in 2014 the Cardinals' organization remained baseball's gold standard.

By 2013 Billy Beane had returned the A's to competitiveness through a balance of great scouting and cutting-edge analytics. The 2003 publication of *Moneyball* had come in the middle of a great run for Oakland—the club made four straight playoff appearances beginning in 2000 and won more than one hundred games in both 2001 and 2002. Although the book focused attention on Billy Beane's reliance on statistics at the expense of scouts, these great teams were largely built by old-fashioned scouting and player development. In the 1990s the A's drafts included Jason Giambi, Eric Chavez, Tim Hudson, Mark Mulder, and Barry Zito, and they signed Dominican Miguel Tejada as an amateur free agent. This terrific group of players led the A's on their great run.

Grady Fuson, a longtime A's scout and national cross-checker who served as scouting director from 1997 to 2001, deserves much of the credit for their drafts and signings. In 2001 Fuson left to take a promotion with the Texas Rangers, before the book came out depicting him and his scouts as out-of-touch old dinosaurs. "If he wants to show no appreciation to the team he had in place, it's his prerogative," said Fuson in 2003.[23] In the ensuing years the A's gradually slipped out of contention, with only one playoff appearance the rest of the decade and no more than eighty-one wins between 2007 and 2011. Much of the falloff can be attributed to the lack of success from Oakland's college-centric drafting philosophy (or its execution). From 2002 to 2009 the A's drafts produced only three players who have turned in more than ten career WAR, with only Nick Swisher above twenty, though closer Sean Doolittle, originally drafted as a first baseman, could still get there. In total, their draft picks during these eight years generated just sixty-five WAR. And due to their small market size and intelligent use of expiring contracts to land compensatory picks, Beane had amassed a total of twenty-one first-round picks (including supplemental choices) in these years.

In 2010 Fuson returned to the A's as a special consultant to Beane, surprising many observers. "Do we disagree on things?" asked Beane. "That's part of a business relationship. But when it is over it's over. I have a tremendous respect for his work ethic and his ability to lead a department, and I think he likes the fact that our approach (in Oakland) is that we all work together, at every level, to get the job done." Moreover, Fuson was persuaded that Beane recognized that the A's had become overreliant on stats.[24]

In 2012 and 2013 the Athletics returned to the top with back-to-back division titles and posted their best two records since the year *Moneyball* came out. It was a team filled with players Beane had acquired cheaply in trades, a testament to the A's ability to discover underappreciated talent. In 2013 their payroll of $69.4 million was twenty-fourth of thirty teams in baseball and was dwarfed by two teams in their own division: the Texas Rangers ($138.3 million) and the Los Angeles Angels ($112.5 million). The A's recent success, like their accomplishments a decade earlier, was a testament to Beane, his scouting organization, and his analytical staff, all working together.

In the 1950s, when George Weiss's Yankees won pennants nearly every season, the American League afforded a much less competitive environment than its twenty-first-century version. Among the seven teams Weiss competed with, the undercapitalized Browns, Athletics, and Senators had no chance at the pennant and no hope of rebuilding with better players. Their farm systems were dwarfed by New York's, and they had no money to buy players from other teams. In 1952 the Yankees took in total revenues of nearly $4 million, while none of the three aforementioned brought in more than $1.6 million.[25]

The Chicago White Sox were still run by the Comiskey family, which had not won a pennant since the Black Sox scandal of 1919. In Detroit the Tigers had deteriorated since the death of Frank Navin in 1945. Only Cleveland and Boston offered any realistic competition to the Yankees, and the Red Sox wasted much of Tom Yawkey's money on untried bonus players. The Yankees of Webb, Topping, Weiss, and Stengel deserve credit for winning consistently and creating a dynasty, but their efforts were considerably aided by the underwhelming, uncommitted, and financially compromised competition.

In the 1955 annual baseball guide,[26] the Yankees listed two owners and eight men in their front office, three of whom were concerned with what we now call "baseball operations": Weiss as general manager, Bill DeWitt Sr. as his assistant, and Lee MacPhail as farm director. The Boston Red Sox, in their 2013 media guide, have photos and bios for twenty-four vice presidents, many of them involved in the ever-growing legal and business sides of the club.[27] There were at least twenty people working in baseball operations, including software developers and video coordinators. Whereas the Yankee scouts in the 1950s would have reported to Weiss or MacPhail, the modern Red Sox employed three scouting directors (amateur, professional, and international) and three assistants. In order to compete and win in the modern game, a front office needs to run and manage a complex business and do it as well or better than everyone else.

The most forward-thinking organizations are always looking for a competitive edge. What can they do to find, develop, and deploy the best players? The various answers have significant implications. Simply being smarter than one's competitors may succeed in the short term but is not a model for sustainable excellence. There will always be someone else smarter coming along. More directly, front-office executives and scouts frequently move from one organization to another, making it extremely difficult to maintain inside knowledge.

Yet many organizations have succeeded over long periods, and knowledge seems to diffuse among the teams more slowly than one might expect. Pat Gillick's Blue Jays won at least eighty-six games a season for eleven consecutive years because of his genius in running a franchise and his "many rivers into one" approach for finding players. His uncanny success in the Rule 5 Draft was testament to his brilliance, but his relationship with Epy Guerrero and their efforts in institutionalizing an advantage in Latin America generated the opening for long-term success.

Jacob Ruppert's early adoption of professional management and Billy Beane's integration of analytics each created an inflection point in the administration of front offices. Similarly, Ruppert and Branch Rickey introduced the farm system, a systematic way to acquire and develop amateur talent. Being first with these initiatives created an advantage, as other clubs were slow to give up the existing orthodoxies, and once they did they still needed to work out implementation.

Some inflection points are caused by forces beyond the initiatives of any one or two teams. The first-year player draft put more of a premium on finding and ranking top amateurs; offering more money or selling the benefits of one's organization to amateur free agents was no longer enough. Free agency created a new dynamic, as star players in the prime of their career could now be acquired without sacrificing any of one's own talent. The new stadium spree of 1990s and 2000s also created a new revenue reality in which a team needed to adapt or fall behind.

Winning in any environment requires certain skills on the part of management: an ability to hire good people, a willingness to delegate and listen to one's staff without sacrificing ultimate responsibility, persistence in pursuing the defined goals, the capacity to adapt to changing circumstances, and an enthusiastic environment to make everyone in the organization work a little harder.

But to create a long-term successful organization, management must also discover and institutionalize a competitive advantage, either by creating or by responding to an inflection point in the way the business operates. Competition in the mid-2010s is as strong as it has ever been; only by marrying the soft skills with institutionalized advantages can a team hope to be consistently successful.

EPILOGUE

The 2016 World Series—a tight, back-and-forth seven-game series eventually won by the Chicago Cubs—was quickly lauded as one of the most exciting ever played. For an observer of team building, it was even more so—a battle between two of the game's most innovative baseball operations staffs.

This was not lost on the mainstream press. One of the central narratives of the World Series was the supposed brilliance of the two front offices and how they had each rebuilt their organization into a model franchise. The Cleveland Indians were justly celebrated for their innovative and intelligent approach to building a pennant winner, but it was the victorious Cubs and their president of baseball operations, Theo Epstein, that received the bulk of the accolades.

Topping the honors, in early 2017 *Fortune* magazine placed Epstein at the pinnacle of its ranking of the world's greatest leaders, just ahead of Jack Ma, head of the Chinese digital conglomerate Alibaba; Pope Francis; Melinda Gates, cohead of the Gates Foundation; and Jeff Bezos, founder and chief executive of Amazon—heady company indeed.[1] To his credit, Epstein himself remained admirably humble and grounded throughout the off-season of praise. Epstein's humility notwithstanding, baseball operations had clearly reached a new level of popular appreciation.

In fact, Epstein's rebuilding of the Cubs *was* remarkable, all the more so because he was fairly transparent about his strategy. When he took over the Cubs in October 2011, negotiations for a new collective bargaining agreement were ongoing. The contract that emerged, while making it harder to accumulate extra draft picks, still allowed a team to profitably redirect a disproportionate share of its resources toward amateurs and prospects. Epstein and his staff, which included GM Jed Hoyer, concentrated on rebuilding with young positon players through trades and the draft.

"One of the reasons we've invested heavily in position players in the draft, international markets, and trades," Epstein recently explained, "is because they're good bets to return value. We've identified a core of players we really believe in, who have gotten here and helped us win a championship already. . . . You can't necessarily develop all your position players and all your pitchers both homegrown. And the plan all along was to take some of the position players and turn them into pitchers."[2]

Trading proven veterans for prospects is a long-established practice in baseball, as discussed throughout this book, and Epstein understood the trade-offs and risks perfectly: "As a rule, if you're the team that's selling—if you're out of it and you're trading with a team that's in it—you usually have the pick of just about their whole farm system with a few exceptions. You should hit on the guys you get back."[3]

To make sure the Cubs were finding and successfully developing the best position player prospects, Epstein built up the organization's scouting, statistical analysis, video, medical, neuroscience, and sports science departments into a terrific player development machine. By the end of 2016 the organization had expanded to fifty-three amateur and international scouts—a small increase—and enlarged the pro scouting department to twenty-six people, more than twice as many as when Epstein came in.[4] Testifying to the team's medical expertise, the Cubs' top five starting pitchers in 2016 started 152 games. Not having to continually reach for a substitute starting pitcher gives a team a great chance to win every time out.

Nevertheless, Epstein stressed the need to further extend the organization's capabilities. "The big thing for us is starting pitching," Epstein acknowledged. "We're supremely confident in our ability to identify and develop position players, and waves of position players. We have not done nearly as good a job with starting pitching—pitching in general. And that has to change. We've built some of the best pitching staffs in baseball the last couple of years, statistically, but it hasn't been through our system, and eventually we're going to need that."[5] Despite building a great starting pitching staff through trades and free agency, the Cubs realized there was room for improvement.

Epstein, though, reached his lofty *Fortune* ranking not just for his technical ability to build a dominant baseball club but for his ability to lead people and understand the importance of character and chemistry. As Cubs owner Tom Ricketts explained: "The reason [Epstein's] successful is he has a great leadership style and eye for talent, but an eye not so much for how a slider breaks, but for people who work collaboratively, and he engages them. There's an element of those skills that would cause some people on the baseball side to roll their eyes, because he's very concerned about the character of players he signs and the atmosphere in the clubhouse. Is the player going to be additive or does he subtract?"[6]

As Epstein has looked for new market inefficiencies in his pursuit of players, he has hypothesized that innovation may come on the people side of the business: "If we can't find the next technological breakthrough, well, maybe we can be better than anyone else with how we treat our players and the relationships we develop and how we put them in positions to succeed. Maybe our environment will be the best in the game, maybe our vibe will be the best in the game, maybe our players will be the loosest, and maybe they'll have the most fun, and maybe they'll care the most. It's impossible to quantify."[7] In just one example of this strategy, the Cubs built a relatively small, circular clubhouse to foster relationships between the players.[8] There can be little doubt, though, that the Cubs owe the bulk of their success to the great scouting, analysis, and development machine that Epstein fashioned (which, of course, is not mutually exclusive with enhancing the players' environment).

As much as the buzz has focused on Epstein—and to a lesser extent manager Joe Maddon and general manager Hoyer—the Cleveland Indians' story is at least as fascinating from a front office perspective. The organization has been a wellspring of front office talent over the past two decades. Since John Hart rebuilt the front office in the early 1990s, the Indians have groomed the greatest collection of front office talent ever assembled. Thirteen members of Cleveland's recent front offices have gone on to become general managers, nine of whom were GMs or heads of baseball operations in 2017: Hart (Atlanta), Ross Atkins (Toronto), Mark Shapiro (Toronto), Derek Falvey (Minnesota), David Stearns (Milwaukee), Neal Huntington (Pittsburgh), Mike Hazen (Arizona), Mark Chernoff (Cleveland), and Chris Antonetti (Cleveland); others who were no longer GMs were Josh Byrnes, Paul DePodesta, Ben Cherington, and Dan O'Dowd.[9]

Jed Hughes, vice chairman of the executive search firm Korn Ferry, which helped place Falvey in Minnesota and Stearns in Milwaukee, praised the Indians' pedigree: "General Electric turns out a lot of good people. There's a reason. They teach leadership. They train people how to do it. The Green Bay Packers under Ron Wolf—same thing. So you look for trees of how people are developed. There's a history of people that have come out of that [Indians] organization."[10]

One of baseball's most innovative organizations, the Indians have consistently been able to restock their baseball operations department with passionate, bright analysts. In one novel approach, they have hired a number of writers from the baseball online and magazine community. In just three examples, assistant GM Matt Forman came from *Baseball America*, principal data scientist Keith Woolner was hired from *Baseball Prospectus*, and director of pro scouting Victor Wang was discovered through his writings in the statistical newsletter of the Society of American Baseball Research and the *Hardball Times* website while still in high school. Once employed, some join the operations department as analysts while others are schooled in scouting.[11]

The Phillies are another organization that searches for front office talent from nontraditional sources. Principal owner John Middleton recently said the team was looking to establish a "sustainable competitive advantage." He went on to elaborate that "the best way to achieve that goal is to combine people who are thoroughly grounded in baseball and baseball analytics, Matt [GM Klentak] and Ned [assistant GM Rice], with extraordinarily bright people who can think critically and creatively and have a proven track record in analytical jobs outside baseball." Recent analytic hires include an executive who worked as a quantitative analyst and on product enhancements at YouTube, another with experience in photo sharing app development and enterprise architecture for a bank, and one with a background as an aerospace systems engineer.[12] Many other organizations have taken a similarly broad approach to talent sources.

The specifics of what each team is doing to gain a lasting advantage are not public—no club wants to give away any lead it has in this area—but Cleveland has been very much at the forefront of strategic initiatives. The team first designed and implemented the now ubiquitous all-inclusive player database in 2000, well before the *Moneyball* enthusiasm. On the playing field (starting with manager Terry Francona) they redefined the usage of relief pitchers, as best demonstrated by Andrew Miller in the 2016 postseason, and designed a roster that gave the team's hitters the platoon advantage more than any other team in 2016. To get buy-in from players for the new analytic concepts, the club was highly deliberate about condensing the extensive reports it prepared into a format players could act upon. Cleveland was also a leader in many high-tech and advanced training techniques, particularly for pitchers, including mental skills testing and training. The club also developed models to help identify and develop late bloomers. Moreover, Cleveland was one of the first to focus on process, learning from a broad array of well-run organizations from the Navy SEALS to the St Louis Cardinals.[13]

Mark Shapiro, who left the Indians to become president of the Blue Jays, summarized the emphasis on process and all the associated elements: "A good GM stewards a decision by gathering information, all the variables that exist—makeup, character, personality, medical, objective analysis, subjective analysis—they steward all the process, they arrive at a strong recommendation, and ultimately I think if that process is good, my job to approve the decision is easy. It's an easy decision. It's all about the process."[14]

Another Cleveland front office alumnus, David Stearns, took over as GM of the Brewers after the 2015 season. He drilled down a little more on what the process needs to deliver: "The philosophy of building a sustainable playoff team is not a secret. You need to acquire, develop and keep controllable, young talent. . . . The trick is to develop a process and a system that allows you to continually regenerate that pipeline, even as you're competitive at the major league level."[15]

No matter how diligently one follows a process, however, no matter how well executed, there are twenty-nine other teams with their own plan and no guarantee of success. Of course, once in a while success can ensue even if the process isn't fully realized. After the Minnesota Twins won the 1987 World Series, personnel director Bob Gebhard observed, "We were just trying to get organized, and we won it."[16]

Since the first release of this book in 2015, the focus on technology and the associated possibilities for scouting and player development has grown exponentially. The expanding frontier of technology and the potential benefits are transforming team building and front office organization. Teams' technological efforts fall into roughly three categories: large, comprehensive databases; analysis of Statcast data; and sports science, broadly defined.

As the databases became larger, more sophisticated, and encompassed a wider range of information on teams' own and opposing players, their importance in decision-making grew considerably. Highlighting the sensitivity and value of this information, the urge to hack into other teams' systems to steal their knowledge overcame one front office employee on the Cardinals. Scouting director Chris Correa accessed the database of the Astros—whose GM Jeff Luhnow and other executives had recently jumped from the Cardinals—on approximately fifty separate occasions in 2013 and 2014 according to reports. The appropriated information included scouting reports on players for the upcoming draft, scouts' ranking of those players, notes on Astros trade discussions with other teams, information on the Astros' various research projects, and international player scouting reports, among other items. Much of the hacked data ended up later being leaked. This was a significant breach that offered Correa an extremely valuable inside look at the Houston organization. For this violation, in 2016 Correa was sentenced to forty-six months in prison, and the Cardinals were required to pay a $2 million penalty to the Astros and forfeit to them their two highest draft picks in the 2017 draft, which turned out to be numbers 56 and 75.[17]

Luhnow later discussed the fallout from the hacking. "At the time when it happened a year ago, it was like coming home and seeing your house has been broken into," he said. "You feel violated when someone does that without permission. As far as whether it affected our ability to execute our plan? It's difficult to assess the effect, but we have continued to execute our plan and we are making progress. I had to call the other 29 GMs and apologize that private notes our organization had made had been made public. Those were not fun calls to make. But I've made several trades since then, and I've had no problems getting anybody on the phone."[18]

Statcast is Major League Baseball's all-embracing tracking system, completed and installed in every Major League ballpark since the first publication of this book. It is based on high-resolution cameras, Trackman, and high-speed computing that can track the baseball, the fielders, and the batter simultaneously. In effect the system can break down nearly every event occurring on the field. For batters, key elements like exit velocity (how fast the ball comes off the bat) and launch angle can be quantified, measurements that provide important insights into the success or failure of a hitter.

Similarly, pitchers can be evaluated by more than just velocity and traditional scouting techniques—by factors such as spin rate and arm slot. Moreover, teams are trying to figure out how to use this data to benchmark and measure arm stress to reduce injuries. Fielders, too, can now be assessed on how fast they move toward a batted ball and how efficiently they cover the ground getting to it. These and many other insights can be distilled from the data, most obviously for player evaluation. From the teams' perspective, Statcast only provides the data—each team needs to do the work to analyze and make use of it.

The Statcast information can also assist in player development. Several hitters, such as Josh Donaldson, J. D. Martinez, Justin Turner, and Daniel Murphy, improved dramatically after changing their approach to hit more fly balls, though this is not a universally applicable strategy—again testifying to the complexity of player development. Similarly, by reviewing in detail the specific readings of various offerings in a pitcher's repertoire, coaches can recommend a modification in the frequency of the pitches thrown. Journeyman hurler Collin McHugh was signed by the Astros after the 2013 season because the team liked the spin rate on his curveball. They encouraged him to throw it more often, and McHugh has since turned into a valuable pitcher. More recently the Astros had similar success with another nondescript pitcher, Charlie Morton. In this instance, rather than focus on his breaking ball, the Astros recognized and augmented his increase in velocity.

Despite the myriad uses to which teams are applying the Statcast output, the system has only been fully operational in all ballparks since 2015, and teams are still learning how to take advantage of the gigantic data sets being generated. According to Greg Cain, senior director of sports data at MLB Advanced Media, each game produces about eighty gigabytes of compressed data or around seven terabytes uncompressed.[19] Multiply this over roughly 2,500 games per year, and one can see why teams are bringing in video and database experts to distill useful knowledge from all this data.

And it's not yet evident what additional revolutionary insights may ensue. PITCHF/x, a Statcast precursor designed to quantify pitch information for pitchers, including the exact location of each pitch, actually turned out to be a great instrument for evaluating catchers. Pitch framing—how well catchers get pitches at the edge of the strike zone called strikes—is now one of the essential skills on which catchers are scouted and developed. How effectively teams implement big-data approaches to Statcast's vast digital output will go a long way to determine who will be successful over the next generation.

Sports science—the use of technology in scouting, injury prevention and rehab, and player development—has become ubiquitous at all levels of baseball. Devices include wearable technologies for pitchers that measure various arm and body torques and stresses, camera-based imaging systems that can track in detail pitcher and batter motions, and bat sensors to calculate swing planes and other elements of the batting action for hitters. In just one example of the effect of new training techniques on pitching, the average fastball velocity has increased almost every year over the past dozen years: in 2002 the average fastball velocity was 89.0 mph; in 2016 it was up to 92.3 mph.[20] In another realm, Mookie Betts was drafted as high as he was by the Red Sox due to his scores on the team's neuro-scouting platform.[21]

Teams are looking beyond technological answers as well. Traditional scouting is now regarded as a potential source of sustained advantage much more than in the past. Like the Cubs, many teams have grown their scouting staffs, and they see an ever-increasing proprietary benefit in the information they gather and how they evaluate a prospect. As a result, after more than forty years, the Major League Scouting Bureau (which Blue Jays general manager Pat Gillick opted out of many years ago) was restructured with a diminished role. Originally conceived to help teams save money in their scouting budgets by delivering scouting reports on the current year's prospect class, the bureau was restructured along more administrative lines, such as collecting medical information and video on prospects and spotting younger prospects, which the clubs then evaluate themselves.[22]

Organizational structure and staffing remains a focus too. Ever since teams introduced the general manager role in the 1920s, they have been tinkering and transforming to find the best structure. In Toronto, for instance, Shapiro introduced a high-performance division to his baseball operations staff. He hired a performance expert from IMG Academy to run the group, beefed up by specialists in mental performance, sports science, strength training, and nutrition.[23] Oakland hired one-time big league third baseman Ed Sprague as their coordinator of instruction, a new position created to translate analytics into something players can use and understand. Not surprisingly, one of the most significant challenges with all the new information is packaging it in a way that allows players to take advantage of it. As an ex–big league player, Sprague could help be a "liaison and an educator to players about analytics."[24] To minimize the player development disruption caused by the occasional minor league affiliate shuffle, the Brewers reassessed their long-held practice of not owning their minor league clubs and were negotiating to purchase their high Class A affiliate in the Carolina League.[25]

In another new structural evolution, the Los Angeles Dodgers created a "pitching department" of roughly six specialists to oversee organization-wide pitcher development, as opposed to the single pitching coordinator practice used by most teams. "We view part of our responsibility running baseball operations is to evaluate how the game and the industry have changed and adapt our own organization," GM Farhan Zaidi said. "Particularly with pitching, there's so much more information out there. . . . I mean if every organization was scrapped and started from scratch, I think you'd see bigger pitching departments than exist today."[26]

As we have stressed throughout the book, context matters, and the new collective bargaining agreement, approved in December 2016, markedly curbed several of the established pathways open for stocking up on amateur talent: draft pick compensation for losing a free agent was reduced, penalties for exceeding bonus limits on international amateur free agents were boosted significantly, while the draconian consequences of overspending allotted bonus pools in the amateur draft remained in place. Within the CBA, small-market teams received a modest rebuilding boost in the form of slightly better draft pick compensation when losing a free agent, a slightly higher international bonus pool allotment, and an additional draft pick at the end of the first or second round. Big-spending clubs were further cramped by small increases in the competitive balance tax (better known as the "luxury tax") over the term of the agreement and the amplified penalties for exceeding it.

Now, nearly all of the resourceful ways teams stockpiled amateur talent over the previous couple of decades—tools Epstein especially used with the Red Sox in the mid-2000s—no longer exist. But whether through scouting technology, player development insights, medical breakthroughs, discovering a new source of baseball talent, fashioning a new organizational structure, or some other still unforeseen innovation, the top franchises will continue to uncover new strategic advantages.

As the opportunities for areas of inquiry and application have proliferated, the role of "general manager" (the term we have used generically throughout the book to designate the head of baseball operations) has evolved considerably, even in the few years since the release of the first edition of *In Pursuit of Pennants*. Most notably, front offices have multiplied in size and now include large analytic staffs, video editors and programmers, medical evaluators and performance analysts, database management personnel, sports science experts, nutritionists, neuroscience and mental skills evaluators and support staff, and a large increase in scouting staffs. In one study that counted the number of baseball operations employees working in analytics, relatively narrowly defined, the authors concluded that number had grown from 44 in 2009, to 75 in 2012, to 156 in 2016.[27]

Obviously, such a surge in personnel necessitated an expansion of executive staffs to manage everyone. Many franchises have assistant general managers or other senior executives taking on additional responsibilities. As of the beginning of the 2017 season, eleven teams had moved to a more formalized two-headed structure, with a senior baseball executive (typically titled president of baseball operations) sitting above the general manager. In June 2017 the Cardinals also adopted this model, promoting John Mozeliak to president of baseball operations and Mike Girsch to GM. Another two teams have presidents of baseball operations without formal general managers under them—Boston and Miami didn't fill their GM positions when they became vacant.

Moreover, some of the larger-market teams with sizeable staffs have brought in ex-GMs in roles that are more than simply advisory. For example, after the departure of GM Mike Hazen, Boston still retained former GMs Allaird Baird and Frank Wren as senior advisors.

As potential advantages multiply for front offices and the monetary stakes continue their seemingly inexorable climb, baseball's owners have become increasingly impatient with their front office executives. Unlike years ago, when general managers were often old friends of the owner and kept their jobs for many years, today the turnover is startlingly rapid. Between the 2014 All-Star break and the start of the 2017 season (roughly two and a half years) eighteen teams, or 60 percent of the franchises, brought in new general managers. A couple of these moves involved promoting the existing GM to a president of baseball operations–type role and an internal candidate to GM, but even so, the number of executive-level changes in Major League front offices is startling.

Furthermore, owners are not bringing in ex-players or longtime baseball men to oversee their front offices. More and more, they are looking for young, exclusively educated men who have proven themselves over several years in baseball operations departments—people like Theo Epstein. Of the thirty top baseball executives at the start of the 2017 season (identified somewhat subjectively), thirteen have degrees from Ivy League schools, while several others are from elite universities like Amherst, Georgetown, and Notre Dame. Only two—Oakland's Billy Beane and Seattle's Jerry Dipoto—played in Major League Baseball. By contrast, through the first third of the 2017 season, of the 1,052 players who had appeared in a Major League game, just 6 had graduated from an Ivy League school.[28]

These new front offices come at a time of increased cachet for baseball operations. When Dave Dombrowski told his eighth grade teacher as part of a student survey that he wanted to be a big league GM, she advised him, "I can't put that down. Nobody wants to do that." Today it seems nearly everyone wants to work in a baseball front office. Young men (and women) from exclusive schools with advanced degrees and potentially high-paying jobs awaiting them are instead opting for low-paying internships in baseball.

The Baseball Hall of Fame has also shown a renewed appreciation for the significance of general managers within the baseball ecosystem. In 2017 the Hall inducted longtime Atlanta and Kansas City GM John Schuerholz. He and Pat Gillick, inducted in 2011, are the only GMs recently recognized by the Hall, after years of the position being overlooked by the prevailing voting committee.

This pursuit of the next great, young GM forged in an elite college or university has paradoxically narrowed the overall inventory of candidates. As of the start of 2017, there were only four minority general managers or heads of baseball operations, and two of those—Michael Hill in Miami and Farhan Zaidi in Los Angeles—went to Harvard and MIT, respectively. Women, too, remain woefully underrepresented in baseball front offices. Jean Afterman of the Yankees and Raquel Ferreira of the Red Sox were the only two women with vice president–level titles in baseball operations with a Major League team.[29]

The monetary and notoriety rewards for success for both owners and GMs along with the elevated demands from teams' fan bases for success on the field—or at least an apparent plan to get there—have raised the stakes for baseball operations groups. Recent postseason runs by small-market and long-suffering franchises have shown that any well-run team can succeed in today's environment, further increasing the pressure to win. As general managers try to meet these challenges, turnover in front offices and innovation in team building strategies, technologies, and organizational approaches will accelerate.

The 2017 World Series further cemented the primacy of the modern baseball front office. Both the Houston Astros and Los Angeles Dodgers are among the most data-savvy organizations in the sport, not only building championship rosters but using their information to redefine the game on the field. The Astros hired GM Jeff Luhnow from the Cardinals in 2011 and followed the Cubs' model. Trading current wins for future wins, they suffered through several terrible seasons before emerging as a contender in 2015 and a champion two years later.

When Andrew Friedman joined the Dodgers as head of baseball operations in October 2014, he inherited a first-place team with one of the largest payrolls in the game. Friedman and his staff rebuilt their team around a young core, winning four straight division titles and reaching the World Series for the first time in twenty-nine years.

Whether the seven games the Astros and Dodgers played represent an evolution of the sport remains to be seen. But whatever lies ahead over the next few years, as teams look to find and exploit new advantages, we can be sure that the Dodgers and Astros will be near the forefront.

APPENDIX A

Front Office Awards and Recognition

The *Sporting News* Executive of the Year

1936	Branch Rickey	St. Louis Cardinals
1937	Ed Barrow	New York Yankees
1938	Warren Giles	Cincinnati Reds
1939	Larry MacPhail	Brooklyn Dodgers
1940	Walter Briggs	Detroit Tigers
1941	Ed Barrow	New York Yankees
1942	Branch Rickey	St. Louis Cardinals
1943	Clark Griffith	Washington Senators
1944	Bill DeWitt	St. Louis Browns
1945	Phil Wrigley	Chicago Cubs
1946	Tom Yawkey	Boston Red Sox
1947	Branch Rickey	Brooklyn Dodgers
1948	Bill Veeck	Cleveland Indians
1949	Bob Carpenter	Philadelphia Phillies
1950	George Weiss	New York Yankees
1951	George Weiss	New York Yankees
1952	George Weiss	New York Yankees
1953	Lou Perini	Milwaukee Braves
1954	Horace Stoneham	New York Giants
1955	Walter O'Malley	Brooklyn Dodgers

1956	Gabe Paul	Cincinnati Redlegs
1957	Frank Lane	St. Louis Cardinals
1958	Joe L. Brown	Pittsburgh Pirates
1959	Buzzie Bavasi	Los Angeles Dodgers
1960	George Weiss	New York Yankees
1961	Dan Topping	New York Yankees
1962	Fred Haney	Los Angeles Angels
1963	Bing Devine	St. Louis Cardinals
1964	Bing Devine	St. Louis Cardinals
1965	Calvin Griffith	Minnesota Twins
1966	Lee MacPhail	Commissioner's Office
1967	Dick O'Connell	Boston Red Sox
1968	Jim Campbell	Detroit Tigers
1969	Johnny Murphy	New York Mets
1970	Harry Dalton	Baltimore Orioles
1971	Cedric Tallis	Kansas City Royals
1972	Roland Hemond	Chicago White Sox
1973	Bob Howsam	Cincinnati Reds
1974	Gabe Paul	New York Yankees
1975	Dick O'Connell	Boston Red Sox
1976	Joe Burke	Kansas City Royals
1977	Bill Veeck	Chicago White Sox
1978	Spec Richardson	San Francisco Giants
1979	Hank Peters	Baltimore Orioles
1980	Tal Smith	Houston Astros
1981	John McHale	Montreal Expos
1982	Harry Dalton	Milwaukee Brewers

1983	Hank Peters	Baltimore Orioles
1984	Dallas Green	Chicago Cubs
1985	John Schuerholz	Kansas City Royals
1986	Frank Cashen	New York Mets
1987	Al Rosen	San Francisco Giants
1988	Fred Claire	Los Angeles Dodgers
1989	Roland Hemond	Baltimore Orioles
1990	Bob Quinn	Cincinnati Reds
1991	Andy MacPhail	Minnesota Twins
1992	Dan Duquette	Montreal Expos
1993	Lee Thomas	Philadelphia Phillies
1994	John Hart	Cleveland Indians
1995	John Hart	Cleveland Indians
1996	Doug Melvin	Texas Rangers
1997	Cam Bonifay	Pittsburgh Pirates
1998	Gerry Hunsicker	Houston Astros
1999	Billy Beane	Oakland Athletics
2000	Walt Jocketty	St. Louis Cardinals
2001	Pat Gillick	Seattle Mariners
2002	Terry Ryan	Minnesota Twins
2003	Brian Sabean	San Francisco Giants
2004	Walt Jocketty	St. Louis Cardinals
2005	Mark Shapiro	Cleveland Indians
2006	Terry Ryan	Minnesota Twins
2007	Mark Shapiro	Cleveland Indians
2008	Andrew Friedman	Tampa Bay Rays
2009	Dan O'Dowd	Colorado Rockies

2010	Walt Jocketty	Cincinnati Reds
2011	Dave Dombrowski	Detroit Tigers
	Doug Melvin	Milwaukee Brewers
2012	Billy Beane	Oakland Athletics
2013	Ben Cherington	Boston Red Sox
2014	Dan Duquette	Baltimore Orioles
2015	Alex Anthopoulos	Toronto Blue Jays
2016	Theo Epstein	Chicago Cubs

Source: "Baseball Awards," http://www.baseball-almanac.com/me_award.shtml.

Baseball America Major League Executive of the Year

1998	Doug Melvin	Texas Rangers
1999	Jim Bowden	Cincinnati Reds
2000	Walt Jocketty	St. Louis Cardinals
2001	Pat Gillick	Seattle Mariners
2002	Billy Beane	Oakland Athletics
2003	Brian Sabean	San Francisco Giants
2004	Terry Ryan	Minnesota Twins
2005	Mark Shapiro	Cleveland Indians
2006	Dave Dombrowski	Detroit Tigers
2007	Jack Zduriencik	Milwaukee Brewers
2008	Theo Epstein	Boston Red Sox
2009	Dan O'Dowd	Colorado Rockies
2010	Jon Daniels	Texas Rangers
2011	Doug Melvin	Milwaukee Brewers
2012	Brian Sabean	San Francisco Giants

2013	Billy Beane	Oakland Athletics
2014	Dan Duquette	Baltimore Orioles
2015	Sandy Alderson	New York Mets
2016	Chris Antonetti	Cleveland Indians

Source: "Baseball America," http://www.baseballamerica.com/news/baseball-america
-awards/#0igWz6x0bsGw7RYD.97.

Baseball America Organization of the Year Award

1982	Oakland Athletics
1983	New York Mets
1984	New York Mets
1985	Milwaukee Brewers
1986	Milwaukee Brewers
1987	Milwaukee Brewers
1988	Montreal Expos
1989	Texas Rangers
1990	Montreal Expos
1991	Atlanta Braves
1992	Cleveland Indians
1993	Toronto Blue Jays
1994	Kansas City Royals
1995	New York Mets
1996	Atlanta Braves
1997	Detroit Tigers
1998	New York Yankees
1999	Oakland Athletics
2000	Chicago White Sox

2001	Houston Astros
2002	Minnesota Twins
2003	Florida Marlins
2004	Minnesota Twins
2005	Atlanta Braves
2006	Los Angeles Dodgers
2007	Colorado Rockies
2008	Tampa Bay Rays
2009	Philadelphia Phillies
2010	San Francisco Giants
2011	St. Louis Cardinals
2012	Cincinnati Reds
2013	St. Louis Cardinals
2014	Kansas City Royals
2015	Pittsburgh Pirates
2016	Chicago Cubs

Source: "Baseball America," http://www.baseballamerica.com/news/baseball-america
-awards/#0igWz6x0bsGw7RYD.97.

Major League General Managers in the Hall of Fame

Ed Barrow	New York Yankees
Warren Giles	Cincinnati
Pat Gillick	Toronto, Baltimore, Seattle, Philadelphia Phillies
Larry MacPhail	Cincinnati, Brooklyn, New York Yankees
Lee MacPhail	Baltimore, New York Yankees

Branch Rickey	St. Louis Cardinals, Brooklyn
John Schuerholz	Kansas City Royals, Atlanta
George Weiss	New York Yankees

Source: "Hall of Famers," http://www.baseballhall.org/hall-famers.

Major League Owners in the Hall of Fame

Charles Comiskey	Chicago White Sox
Barney Dreyfuss	Pittsburgh
Clark Griffith	Washington Senators
Walter O'Malley	Brooklyn–Los Angeles Dodgers
Jacob Ruppert	New York Yankees
Albert Spalding	Chicago White Sox
Bill Veeck Jr.	Cleveland, Chicago White Sox
Tom Yawkey	Boston Red Sox

Source: "Hall of Famers," http://www.baseballhall.org/hall-famers.

APPENDIX B

The Top Thirty General Managers

In early 2015, as this book was going to press, we used our blog to count down the twenty-five greatest general managers in big league history. Every weekday for five weeks we posted a short biography of a GM, from number 25 down to number 1. The individual posts allowed us to explore some of the themes covered in our book and also to tell some new stories. With the publication of the new edition of *In Pursuit of Pennants*, we present a new ranking, revised based on further conversation and the passage of three years' worth of events. We won't repeat all of the bios here, but feel free to go to our blog if you want to read more.

To produce our rankings we considered a number of factors, including the success of the GM's teams, given the resources and authority at his disposal; the job the GM was asked to do (such as a rebuild versus maintaining a winning team); the strength of the entire organization, including the farm system; and the length of a GM's tenure or tenures. Importantly, we also gave a lot of weight to innovation, to GMs who either created or exploited a strategic advantage before the competition had done so.

A couple of notes on eligibility: The GM role was created around 1920—before then players were signed or acquired either by the owner or the manager. For the purposes of this exercise, we are not considering GMs who were also owners or managers of the team. If we did, John McGraw (a manager in charge of the New York Giants' roster for thirty years) and Barney Dreyfuss (who owned the Pirates for thirty-two years and built several champions himself) would each be in the top 10. Also, we are ranking the men (so far, they are all men) who have run what we now call "baseball operations," regardless of the person's actual title. As of 2017, Theo Epstein is the president of baseball operations for the Chicago Cubs, while Jed Hoyer is the GM. For our purposes, we are crediting Epstein for the Cubs' performance, since he is in charge.

We also, somewhat arbitrarily, chose to require a ten-year career. Cedric Tallis, featured in this book, is regretfully left out. Once they accumulate a few more years, men like Jeff Luhnow and Mike Rizzo will likely join this list—as we have written on a number of occasions, we are living in a Golden Age for general managers. Similarly, all active GMs will see their status rise (or fall) based on their remaining careers.

30. DICK O'CONNELL

The two-time pennant winning general manager of the Red Sox, O'Connell rebuilt the franchise and is profiled in chapter 11.

29. BING DEVINE

Achieving his greatest success with his building of the 1960s Cardinals, Devine is the main character in chapter 10.

28. GABE PAUL

A front office boss over four decades, Paul's place in history rests with his brilliant build of the 1970s Yankees, a job that required difficult dealings with his mercurial boss. Paul's tenure in New York is examined in chapter 17.

27. ANDY MACPHAIL

The son and grandson of Hall of Fame baseball executives, MacPhail won two World Series with the Minnesota Twins and has subsequently run baseball operations for the Orioles, Cubs, and Phillies with more modest results.

26. JIM CAMPBELL

In his long run leading the Detroit Tigers, Campbell built the club that won the 1968 World Series and most of the team that won in 1984. He is profiled in chapter 11.

25. JOHN QUINN

In his thirty-year career as general manager, Quinn won three pennants with the Braves (1948 in Boston and 1957–58 in Milwaukee) and built an excellent 1964 Phillies team, which unfortunately stumbled in September.

24. DAN DUQUETTE

After building a talented Montreal Expos team in the early 1990s, Duquette moved to Boston, where he reached three postseasons and left behind most of the team that won the 2004 World Series. Unable to get another job for a decade, Duquette finally surfaced as GM in Baltimore in late 2011, taking over a team that had been out of the postseason for fourteen years. Playing in the always strong AL East, the Orioles made three playoff appearances in Duquette's first six seasons.

23. JON DANIELS

Taking over the Rangers after the 2005 season, Daniels has made five postseason appearances with Texas, losing the 2010 and 2011 World Series, the latter a heart-breaking seven-game affair to the Cardinals. Just twenty-eight when he got the job, Daniels quickly became one of the more respected GMs in the game.

22. WALT JOCKETTY

After taking over a St. Louis team that had been out of contention for several years, Jocketty ran the Cardinals for thirteen years, winning two pennants and the 2006 World Series. He later made multiple postseasons with the Cincinnati Reds.

21. JOHN HART

Though he later led front offices in Texas and Atlanta, Hart's place is based on his brilliant turnaround of the hapless Cleveland Indians franchise in the 1990s, the large number of future GMs that have come out of the Cleveland front office, and his shrewd strategy to extend the contracts of his young talent early to ensure a longer run of contention.

20. JOHN MOZELIAK

Mozeliak was promoted after the 2007 season because owner Bill DeWitt wanted the club to place a greater influence on analytics. His ascension to GM is examined in chapter 22.

19. LEE MACPHAIL

MacPhail had success in several jobs throughout his long career in the game. Much of MacPhail's career is considered in chapter 14.

18. ANDREW FRIEDMAN

Friedman took over the long moribund Tampa Rays in 2005 and built the club that won the 2008 AL pennant and made three other playoff appearances. After the 2014 season he moved over to run the LA Dodgers and has proved himself equally adept at running a big-market club.

17. BRIAN CASHMAN

Cashman is a particularly challenging person to rank, since he took over one of history's greatest teams, the 1998 Yankees. While his detractors can point to the huge revenue advantage he enjoyed for a decade or more, it is hard to set aside his fifteen playoff appearances and four championships. That the club appears to have recently retooled with young players without truly bottoming out is to his credit as well.

16. SANDY ALDERSON

One of the first innovative, analytical general managers, Alderson created some great clubs in Oakland, where he gave Billy Beane his first front office job. Alderson later ran baseball ops in San Diego and with the New York Mets, where he won another pennant.

15. BILLY BEANE

Beane's great success with a small budget led to a best-selling book and movie; more recently the job has proven tougher as the big-budget teams have amped up their own analytical thinking. Beane is discussed in chapters 20, 21, and 22.

14. AL CAMPANIS

The owner of one of the most impressive front office resumes in baseball history, Campanis demonstrated excellence in scouting, instruction, development, and as a general manager. He is a primary subject in chapter 7.

13. BRIAN SABEAN

The winner of four pennants and three World Series with the Giants, Sabean's fascinating evolution is detailed in chapter 21.

12. JOE L. BROWN

Running the Pirates for twenty-one years, Brown oversaw many great and beloved teams, including the 1960 and 1971 champions and several division winners.

11. DAVE DOMBROWSKI

After successful tenures in Montreal, Florida (where he won the 1997 World Series), and Detroit, Dombrowski is currently leading the Boston Red Sox.

10. FRANK CASHEN

Cutting his teeth as the president of the Orioles in their glory years of 1966–71, Cashen later had his own success as GM in Baltimore before his brilliant build of the Mets in the 1980s.

9. HARRY DALTON

A longtime farm director with the Orioles under Lee MacPhail, Dalton took over the club in late 1965 and won four pennants and two World Series with one of history's greatest teams. His multiteam career is explored in chapter 11.

8. BUZZIE BAVASI

As Dodgers GM he won eight pennants (with two pennant playoff losses) and four World Series in eighteen years and oversaw one of the most respected organizations in baseball history. Bavasi's long tenure with the Dodgers is described in chapter 7.

7. JOHN SCHUERHOLZ

Although the 1990s Braves are often remembered for their postseason disappointments, it's hard to fault the GM who, after earlier winning the 1985 Series with the Royals, built a team that made fourteen postseason appearances and won five pennants and the 1995 World Series.

6. GEORGE WEISS

If one considers his fifteen years running the great Yankees farm system, Weiss would rank higher. Judged solely as a GM, Weiss's nine pennants in eleven years are unmatched. We tackle his Yankees years in chapter 8.

5. BOB HOWSAM

The architect of the Big Red Machine, one of history's greatest teams, Howsam's story is fascinating because it is so methodical and relentless, with hardly a missed step for an entire decade. His career is profiled at length in chapter 13.

4. THEO EPSTEIN

As the man primarily responsible for ending the game's two most famous championship droughts, with the 2004 (and 2007) Red Sox and 2016 Cubs, Epstein has assured himself a plaque in Cooperstown. The Red Sox' version of his story is explored in chapters 20 and 22, while the Cubs' version is ongoing.

3. ED BARROW

Barrow was one of the first to hold the job we have come to label "general manager." He performed it masterfully for nearly twenty-five years, effectively defining the role for several generations. Barrow's front office career is presented in chapters 3, 4, and 6.

2. PAT GILLICK

Gillick was asked to run a baseball team four times, and he succeeded masterfully every time, winning three World Series and earning induction to the Hall of Fame. His story is extensively explored in chapters 18, 19, and 21.

1. BRANCH RICKEY

Had Rickey not brilliantly orchestrated the integration of the game with his signing of Jackie Robinson, he *still* would be the best GM in history based on all his other accomplishments and innovations. What he did with Jackie was his greatest act and makes this an easy choice. Rickey is discussed throughout the book, especially in chapters 3, 5, 7, 9, and 10.

NOTES

INTRODUCTION

1. Ernest R. May, *Knowing One's Enemies: Intelligence Assessment before the Two World Wars* (Princeton NJ: Princeton University Press, 1986), 4.
2. Andrew S. Grove, *Only the Paranoid Survive* (New York: Currency, 1999), 33.

1. OWNER-OPERATOR

1. Lee Allen, *Cooperstown Corner* (Cleveland: SABR, 1990), 164.
2. Fred Lieb, *The Pittsburgh Pirates* (New York: G. P. Putnam's Sons, 1948), 41.
3. *Sporting Life*, May 8, 1897, 9.
4. Joe King, "The 'Wonder Man' of Pittsburgh: The Story of Fred Clarke, Part 2," *Sporting News*, March 21, 1951, 16.
5. Thanks to Bill Lamb for his feedback on the ownership factions.
6. "Savannah Sayings," *Sporting Life*, May 5, 1894, 6.
7. Ronald T. Waldo, *Fred Clarke: A Biography of the Baseball Hall of Fame Player-Manager* (Jefferson NC: McFarland, 2011), 16–17.
8. Waldo, *Fred Clarke*, 16–17.
9. Lieb, *The Pittsburgh Pirates*, 62.
10. Fred Lieb, "Pittsburgh Mourns Early Star Fred Clarke," *Sporting News*, August 24, 1960, 13.
11. Waldo, *Fred Clarke*, 23–24.
12. Waldo, *Fred Clarke*, 24.
13. "Association Meet," *Sporting Life*, July 12, 1890, 9.
14. Edward Lyell Fox, "Finding the Stars of Baseball," *Outing*, August 5, 1913.
15. Dennis DeValeria and Jeanne Burke DeValeria, *Honus Wagner* (New York: Henry Holt, 1995), 41.
16. "Wagner, Winner," *Sporting Life*, December 28, 1907, 3.
17. William Hageman, *Honus: The Life and Times of a Baseball Legend* (Champaign IL: Sagamore, 1996), 11–12.
18. "Wagner, Winner," *Sporting Life*, December 28, 1907, 3.
19. Daniel R. Levitt, *Ed Barrow: The Bulldog Who Built the Yankees' First Dynasty* (Lincoln: University of Nebraska Press, 2008), 32.
20. *Sporting Life*, January 8, 1898, 4.
21. Mark Armour, "Tommie Leach," SABR's Baseball Biography Project, http://sabr.org/bioproject.
22. Robert Peyton Wiggins, *The Deacon and the Schoolmaster* (Jefferson NC: McFarland, 2011), 19.

23. *Sporting Life*, November 26, 1898, 9.
24. Mark L. Armour and Daniel R. Levitt, *Paths to Glory* (Washington DC: Brassey's, 2003), 7–12.
25. *Sporting Life*, September 2, 1899.
26. *Sporting Life*, April 22, 1899.
27. *Sporting Life*, October 14, 1899, 7.
28. The six other players were Cliff Latimer, Walter Woods, Patsy Flaherty, Elton Cunningham, Conny Doyle, and Mike Massit.
29. Daniel Ginsburg, "Ginger Beaumont," SABR's Baseball Biography Project, http://sabr.org/bioproject.
30. Waldo, *Fred Clarke*, 43.
31. Waldo, *Fred Clarke*, 45.
32. King, "'Wonder Man' of Pittsburgh," 16.
33. King, "'Wonder Man' of Pittsburgh," 16.
34. Honus Wagner, "Honus Wagner's Story," *Los Angeles Times*, June 14, 1924, B2.
35. William F. Lamb, "A Fearsome Collaboration," in *Base Ball: A Journal of the Early Game* 3, no. 2 (2009): 11.
36. Waldo, *Fred Clarke*, 75.
37. Waldo, *Fred Clarke*, 76.
38. Lieb, *The Pittsburgh Pirates*, 95.
39. Lieb, *The Pittsburgh Pirates*, 46.
40. Lawrence S. Ritter, *The Glory of Their Times: The Story of the Early Days of Baseball Told by the Men Who Played It* (New York: Vintage Books, 1985), 75–76.
41. Levitt, *Ed Barrow*, 212–13.
42. Bill Lamberty, "George Sisler," SABR's Baseball Biography Project, http://sabr.org/bioproject.
43. "Sam Dreyfuss Dead: A Baseball Notable," *New York Times*, February 23, 1931.
44. "Dreyfuss, 66, Dead: Owner of Pirates," *New York Times*, February 6, 1932.
45. Lieb, *The Pittsburgh Pirates*, 47.

2. FIELD MANAGER

Epigraph: Randy Roberts, "When the Bear Left for Bama," *Wall Street Journal*, September 13, 2013, D10.
1. Harold Seymour and Dorothy Seymour Mills, *Baseball: The Golden Age* (New York: Oxford University Press, 1971), 24–25; Harry Pulliam, letter to Barney Dreyfuss, May 23, 1905, August Herrmann Papers, National Baseball Library; Dreyfuss affidavit, May 24, 1905, August Herrmann Papers, National Baseball Library.
2. King, "'Wonder Man' of Pittsburgh," 16.
3. Frank Graham, *The New York Giants* (Carbondale: Southern Illinois University Press, 2002), 35.

4. Armour and Levitt, *Paths to Glory*.
5. Chris Jaffe, *Evaluating Baseball's Managers: A History and Analysis of Performance in the Major Leagues, 1876–2008* (Jefferson NC: McFarland, 2010), 106; Armour and Levitt, *Paths to Glory*, 95.
6. Edward Mott Wolley, "The Business of Baseball," *McClure's*, July 1912, 244.
7. Leonard Koppett, *The Man in the Dugout: Baseball's Top Managers and How They Got That Way* (New York: Crown, 1993), 34.
8. Koppett, *Man in the Dugout*, 50.
9. Daniel R. Levitt, *The Battle That Forged Modern Baseball: The Federal League Challenge and Its Legacy* (Lanham MD: Ivan R. Dee, 2012), 178–79.
10. Charles C. Alexander, *John McGraw* (New York: Penguin, 1989), 238.
11. Harold Kaese, *The Boston Braves, 1871–1953* (Boston: Northeastern University Press, 2004), 181; Seymour and Mills, *Baseball: The Golden Age*, 32.
12. David Pietrusza et al., eds., *Baseball: The Biographical Encyclopedia* (Toronto: Sport Classic Books, 2003), 1273.
13. Jim Sandoval, "Dick Kinsella," SABR's Baseball Biography Project, http://sabr.org/bioproject.
14. Lee Allen, *The Cincinnati Reds* (New York: G. P. Putnam's Sons, 1948), 126.
15. John Lardner, "That Was Baseball: The Crime of Shufflin' Phil Douglas," *New Yorker*, May 12, 1956, 140.
16. Lardner, "That Was Baseball," 143.
17. Pietrusza et al., *Baseball: The Biographical Encyclopedia*, 384–85; *Sporting News*, March 24, 1973, 54.
18. *Sporting News*, October 29, 1984, 57.
19. Jude Novi, "A Hall of Famer Recalls the Game 50 Years Ago," *Baseball Digest*, June 1978, 44.
20. Pietrusza et al., *Baseball: The Biographical Encyclopedia*, 51.
21. Alexander, *John McGraw*, 228–29; Daniel E. Ginsburg, *The Fix Is In: A History of Baseball Gambling and Game Fixing Scandals* (Jefferson NC: McFarland, 1995), 168; David Pietrusza, *Judge and Jury: The Life and Times of Judge Kenesaw Mountain Landis* (South Bend IN: Diamond Communications, 1998), 180–82; *New York Times*, February 20, 1920.
22. Leonard Koppett, *The Rise and Fall of the Press Box* (Toronto: Sport Classic Books, 2003), 197.
23. *New York Times*, December 7, 1921; Pietrusza, *Judge and Jury*, 183; Allen, *The Cincinnati Reds*, 156.
24. Pietrusza, *Judge and Jury*, 183.
25. *Sporting News*, July 18, August 4, 1921; Pietrusza, *Judge and Jury*, 185–86; Frank Graham, *The New York Yankees: An Informal History* (Carbondale: Southern Illinois University Press, 2002), 80–81; Lieb, *The Pittsburgh Pirates*, 190–91.
26. *New York Times*, July 27, 1921; Alexander, *John McGraw*, 235.
27. Alexander, *John McGraw*, 236.

28. Lardner, "That Was Baseball," 151.

29. *Sporting News*, December 9, 1959.

30. Arthur Nehf, "World's Series and My Friend McGraw," *Baseball Magazine*, November 1926, 533.

31. Nehf, "World's Series and My Friend McGraw," 533.

32. *Sporting News*, January 1, 1989; Peter Williams, *When the Giants Were Giants: Bill Terry and the Golden Age of New York Baseball* (Chapel Hill NC: Algonquin Books, 1994), 39–45.

33. Alexander, *John McGraw*, 255.

34. *New York Times*, February 26, 1934.

35. Alexander, *John McGraw*, 281–82; Steve Steinberg, correspondence with author.

3. GENERAL MANAGER

1. Alfred D. Chandler Jr., *Strategy and Structure: Chapters in the History of the American Industrial Enterprise* (Cambridge MA: MIT Press, 1998), 19.

2. Chandler, *Strategy and Structure*, 40.

3. Peter Drucker, *The Essential Drucker: The Best of Sixty Years of Peter Drucker's Essential Writings on Management* (New York: Collins Business, 2005), 5.

4. Lee Lowenfish, *Branch Rickey: Baseball's Ferocious Gentleman* (Lincoln: University of Nebraska Press, 2007), 83.

5. Craig Lammers, "Bob Quinn and the Farm System," SABR's Baseball Biography Project, http://sabr.org/bioproject.

6. Correspondence with Steinberg.

7. Harry Neily, "Hard-Fisted Policies Only Masked Human Side of Veeck," *Sporting News*, October 26, 1933.

8. James Crusinberry, "General Managers," *Baseball Magazine*, June 1950, 219.

9. Lowenfish, *Branch Rickey*, 150.

10. Bill James, *The New Bill James Historical Baseball Abstract* (New York: Free Press, 2003), 128; David Anderson, "Billy Evans," SABR's Baseball Biography Project, http://sabr.org/bioproject; Franklin Lewis, *The Cleveland Indians* (New York: G. P. Putnam's Sons, 1949), 157; *Sporting News*, February 1, 1956, 21.

11. *Reach Official American League Baseball Guide, 1928* (New York: A. J. Reach, Wright & Ditson, 1928), 23.

12. John Kieran, "Big-League Business," *Saturday Evening Post*, May 31, 1930, 17.

13. John Drebinger, "The Changing Trend," *Baseball Magazine*, February 1940, 402.

14. Drebinger, "The Changing Trend," 401.

15. Warren Brown, *The Chicago Cubs* (New York: G. P. Putnam's Sons, 1946), 134.

16. *"Sporting News" Record Book for 1938* (St. Louis: Sporting News, 1938).

4. EXECUTIVE

Epigraph: Branch Rickey, *Branch Rickey's Little Blue Book* (New York: Macmillan, 1995), 4.

1. "Bachelor Apartment," unidentified article in Jacob Ruppert's file at the Baseball Hall of Fame.
2. George Perry, *Sporting News*, March 2, 1939.
3. Letter from Tillinghast Huston to Jacob Ruppert and other documents included in Robert Edward Auctions May 18, 2013, lot 1284; Levitt, *Ed Barrow*, 181. Years later it was occasionally reported that the American League contributed fifty thousand dollars toward the purchase by Ruppert and Huston. We have found no contemporary evidence of this, and given the strained baseball finances of the time, it is highly unlikely.
4. The purchase prices and Yankee player salaries come from the New York Yankees' financial records on file at the Baseball Hall of Fame.
5. *Sporting News*, October 12, 1933, 4.
6. Timothy R. Hylan et al., "The Coase Theorem, Free Agency, and Major League Baseball: A Study of Pitcher Mobility from 1961 to 1992," *Southern Economic Journal*, April 1996, 1029.
7. Jay Maeder, "Jacob Ruppert the Old Ball Game," *New York Daily News*, March 2, 1999.
8. Alva Johnston, "Beer and Baseball," *New Yorker*, September, 24, 1932.

5. FARM SYSTEM

1. Craig Lammers, "Bob Quinn and the Farm System," http://sabr.org/bioproject.
2. Lammers, "Bob Quinn and the Farm System."
3. U.S. House of Representatives, *Report of the Subcommittee on the Study of Monopoly Power of the Committee on the Judiciary: Organized Baseball*, 82nd Cong., 2nd sess. (1952), 63.
4. U.S. House of Representatives, *Report of the Subcommittee on the Study of Monopoly Power*, 63.
5. U.S. House of Representatives, *Report of the Subcommittee on the Study of Monopoly Power*, 989.
6. U.S. House of Representatives, *Report of the Subcommittee on the Study of Monopoly Power*, 65.
7. Jonathan Frazer Light, *The Cultural Encyclopedia of Baseball*, 2nd ed. (Jefferson NC: McFarland, 2005), 312.
8. U.S. House of Representatives, *Report of the Subcommittee on the Study of Monopoly Power*, 66.
9. U.S. House of Representatives, *Report of the Subcommittee on the Study of Monopoly Power*, 1582.
10. U.S. House of Representatives, *Report of the Subcommittee on the Study of Monopoly Power*, 1035–36.

11. Henry D. Fetter, *Taking on the Yankees: Winning and Losing in the Business of Baseball, 1903–2003* (New York: W. W. Norton, 2003), 163.
12. U.S. House of Representatives, *Report of the Subcommittee on the Study of Monopoly Power*, 1559.
13. All the data for this graph were derived from SABR's Minor League database as shown at http://baseball-reference.com/minors.

6. ORGANIZATION

Epigraph: Drucker, *Essential Drucker*, 5.
1. Unidentified newspaper article, Joe McCarthy's file at the Baseball Hall of Fame, September 20, 1938.
2. *Washington Post*, December, 2, 1937.
3. In 1931 the Yankees paid Connery forty thousand dollars for Jack Saltzgaver, a player Ruppert later came to believe the Yankees already owned the rights to.
4. Levitt, *Ed Barrow*, 277–79.
5. Levitt, *Ed Barrow*, 325; *Sporting News*, November 12, 1936, 5; December 3, 1936, 1; *New York Sun*, January 13, 1939.
6. *New York World-Telegram*, February 21, 1938.
7. Levitt, *Ed Barrow*, 309.
8. Chris Lamb, "L'Affaire Jake Powell: The Minority Press Goes to Bat against Segregated Baseball," *J&MC Quarterly* (Spring 1999).
9. *Sporting News*, January 19, 1939.
10. Mark Armour, *Joe Cronin: A Life in Baseball* (Lincoln: University of Nebraska Press, 2010), 119.
11. Pat Gillick, phone interview, October 2, 2012.

7. DODGER WAY

1. Jim Murray, "Busy Buzzie," *Los Angeles Times*, September 9, 1962.
2. Buzzie Bavasi and Jack Olson, "The Real Secret of Trading," *Sports Illustrated*, June 5, 1967.
3. Buzzie Bavasi and John Strege, *Off the Record* (Chicago: Contemporary Books, 1987).
4. Andy McCue, *Mover and Shaker: Walter O'Malley, the Dodgers and Baseball's Westward Expansion* (Lincoln: University of Nebraska Press, 2014), 33.
5. Mark Stewart, "Pete Reiser," SABR's Baseball Biography Project, http://sabr.org/bioproject.
6. Kevin Kerrane, *Dollar Sign on the Muscle* (New York: Beaufort Books, 1984), 9.
7. Charles Maher, "Bavasi: Baseball's Smartest Operator," *Los Angeles Times*, March 7, 1967.
8. Charles Maher, "Bavasi's First Love Was Giants," *Los Angeles Times*, March 8, 1967.

9. Hugh Bradley, "Bavasi . . . He's the Dodger Buzz-Saw," *New York Journal-American*, October 20, 1963.
10. Charles Maher, "Bavasi Breaks in Baseball as Winner—Loses Money," *Los Angeles Times*, March 9, 1967.
11. Murray, "Busy Buzzie."
12. Bavasi and Olson, "Real Secret of Trading."
13. Myron Cope, "How the Dodgers Are Building a Dynasty," *Sport*, July 1961, 50.
14. Andy McCue, "A Half-Century of Springs: Vero Beach and the Dodgers," in *From McGillicuddy to McGwire: Baseball in Florida and the Caribbean* (Cleveland OH: SABR, 1999), 8–13.
15. Frank Graham Jr., "Spanish-Speaking Al Campanis Lures Latin Talent for Dodgers," *Sporting News*, January 12, 1955, 21.
16. Ben Gould, "Dodgers, Not Senators, Top Favorites in Latin-America, Campanis Finds," *Sporting News*, October 22, 1952, 6.
17. Al Campanis, *The Dodgers' Way to Play Baseball* (New York: E. P. Dutton, 1954).
18. *The "Sporting News" Official Baseball Guide, 1951* (St. Louis: Charles C. Spink & Son, 1951), 151.
19. *The "Sporting News" Official Baseball Guide, 1953* (St. Louis: Charles C. Spink & Son, 1953), 97.
20. *"Sporting News" Official Baseball Guide, 1953*, 97.
21. Kerrane, *Dollar Sign on the Muscle*, 17.
22. Bavasi and Olson, "Real Secret of Trading." More recent scholarship by Stew Thornley calls into question whether the Dodgers were really trying to "hide" Clemente from discovery by other teams. Stew Thornley, "Roberto Clemente's Entry into Organized Baseball: Was He Hidden in Montreal?," http://milkeespress.com/clemente1954.html.
23. Bavasi and Olson, "Real Secret of Trading."
24. Brent Kelley, *Baseball's Biggest Blunder* (Lanham MD: Scarecrow Press, 1997).
25. Bradley, "Bavasi . . . He's the Dodger Buzz-Saw."
26. Cope, "How the Dodgers Are Building a Dynasty," 50.
27. Cope, "How the Dodgers Are Building a Dynasty," 50.
28. Cope, "How the Dodgers Are Building a Dynasty," 50.
29. *New York World Telegram & Sun*, August 29, 1955.
30. Cope, "How the Dodgers Are Building a Dynasty," 85.
31. Arnold Hano, "The High-Octane Confidence of Willie Davis," *Sport*, December 1962, 18.
32. John Roseboro with Bill Libby, *Glory Days with the Dodgers—and Other Days with Others* (New York: Atheneum, 1978), 226.
33. Jerry Hicks, "Baseball and His Daughter Keep Myers' Name Alive," *Los Angeles Times*, May 2, 1996.

34. Rick Obrand, "The Sandlot Mentors of Los Angeles," in *The National Pastime*, edited by Jean Hastings Ardell and Andy McCue (Phoenix: SABR, 2011), 27.

35. Bill James, *The Bill James Guide to Baseball Managers* (New York: Scribner, 1997), 208.

36. Mark Armour, "Frank Howard," SABR's Baseball Biography Project, http://sabr.org/bioproject.

37. Paul Hirsch, "Ron Fairly," SABR's Baseball Biography Project, http://sabr.org/bioproject.

38. Murray, "Busy Buzzie."

39. Maher, "Bavasi: Baseball's Smartest Operator."

40. *New York World Telegram & Sun*, May 26, 1961.

41. Maher, "Bavasi: Baseball's Smartest Operator."

42. Maher, "Bavasi: Baseball's Smartest Operator."

43. McCue, *Mover and Shaker*, 313–16.

8. DYNASTY

Epigraph: Earl Lawson, "Reds Sail to Gold, Glory with Howsam at Helm," *Sporting News*, October 30, 1976.

1. Levitt, *Ed Barrow*, 361.

2. Many years later a plausible explanation surfaced for the Yankees' seemingly inexplicable sale of Borowy to the Cubs. It was, the theory went, Larry MacPhail's repayment to Chicago general manager Jim Gallagher for the 1941 deal that brought Billy Herman to Brooklyn.

3. G. Richard McKelvey, *The MacPhails* (Jefferson NC: McFarland, 2000), 75.

4. J. G. Taylor Spink, "Battle of the Biltmore: Victory Brawl," *Sporting News*, October 15, 1947, 1, 4.

5. Spink, "Battle of the Biltmore," 1, 4.

6. Spink, "Battle of the Biltmore," 1, 4.

7. Spink, "Battle of the Biltmore," 1, 4.

8. Spink, "Battle of the Biltmore," 1, 4.

9. Dan Daniel, "Bombers to Ban Ballyhoo in New Regime," *Sporting News*, October 15, 1947.

10. Stanley Frank, "Yankee Kingmaker," *Saturday Evening Post*, May 24, 1948, 110.

11. Levitt, *Ed Barrow*, 350–51.

12. *Sporting News*, November 29, 1945.

13. Tom Meany, *The Yankee Story* (New York: E. P. Dutton, 1960), 144.

14. *Baseball Digest*, April 1959, 64.

15. Charles Maher, "Bavasi: Baseball's Smartest Operator," *Los Angeles Times*, March 7, 1967.

16. Meany, *The Yankee Story*, 145.

17. Jack Mann, *The Decline and Fall of the New York Yankees* (New York: Simon and Schuster, 1967), 174–75.

18. *Newsweek*, July 15, 1957, 62.
19. Lee MacPhail, *My Nine Innings: An Autobiography of 50 Years in Baseball* (Westport CT: Meckler, 1989), 52–53.
20. George Weiss with Robert Shaplen, "The Best Decision I Ever Made," *Sports Illustrated*, March 13, 1961, 32.
21. *Sporting News*, July 19, 1961, 2.
22. George M. Weiss with Robert Shaplen, "The Man of Silence Speaks," *Sports Illustrated*, March 6, 1961, 48.
23. MacPhail, *My Nine Innings*, 49; *Sporting News*, November 25, 1949, 18.
24. U.S. Senate, *Organized Professional Team Sports: Hearings Before the Subcommittee on Antitrust and Monopoly of the Committee on the Judiciary*, 85th Cong., 2nd sess. (July 1958), 648.
25. Robert Shaplen, "The Yankees' Real Boss," *Sports Illustrated*, September 20, 1954.
26. *New York Times*, October 6, 1953.
27. Stanley Frank, "Boss of the Yankees," *Saturday Evening Post*, April 16, 1960, 111.
28. *New York Times*, November 3, 1960, 50.

9. INTEGRATION

1. For a more complete look at this subject, see Mark Armour, "Integration, 1947–1986," SABR's Baseball Biography Project, http://sabr.org/bioproj.
2. Jules Tygiel, *Baseball's Great Experiment* (Oxford: Oxford University Press, 1983), 329–30; Jules Tygiel, email correspondence, May 2007.
3. Tygiel, *Baseball's Great Experiment*, 286.
4. *Chicago Defender*, May 24, 1952, 17.
5. Nick Miroff, "After 50 Years Cuba Says Its Baseball Players Can Go Abroad," http://npr.org/blogs, November 28, 2013.

10. COMMITMENT

Epigraph: *Philadelphia Daily News*, April 2, 2007.
1. David Halberstam, *October 1964* (New York: Villard, 1994), 57–58. Historian Bill Lamb has pointed out that in the 1950s, *black* was a pejorative slur and that Busch more likely used the term *colored* or *Negro*, which at the time were more commonly used on television and in polite society. Regardless of the exact word, Busch's message was clear.
2. Peter Golenbock, *The Spirit of St. Louis* (New York: Spike, 2000), 399.
3. *New York Times*, February 21, 1953, 1.
4. Burton A. Boxerman and Benita W. Boxerman, *Ebbets to Veeck to Busch* (Jefferson NC: McFarland, 2003), 181.
5. Boxerman, *Ebbets to Veeck to Busch*, 183.
6. Golenbock, *Spirit of St. Louis*, 405.
7. *New York Times*, May 27, 1953, 32.

8. *Christian Science Monitor*, October 8, 1953.

9. Halberstam, *October 1964*, 21–22.

10. Charles Maher, "Bavasi: Baseball's Smartest Operator," *Los Angeles Times*, March 7, 1967.

11. Bob Vanderberg, *Frantic Frank Lane: Baseball's Ultimate Wheeler-Dealer* (Jefferson NC: McFarland, 2013), 72–73.

12. Golenbock, *Spirit of St. Louis*, 416–17; Steve Treder, "Frantic Frankie Lane," *Outside the Lines* (newsletter of SABR's Business of Baseball Committee), October 19, 2008, 1.

13. Bing Devine, *The Memoirs of Bing Devine* (Champaign IL: Sports Publishing, 2004), 62–82.

14. *Washington Post*, November 6, 1957, A21; *New York Times*, November 22, 1957, 28; Dick Schaap, "What They Say in the Dugouts About: The St. Louis Cardinals," *Sport*, August 1958, 72.

15. Tommy Holmes. "Boyer Is Doing It Now," *Sport*, July 1957, 60.

16. Devine, *Memoirs of Bing Devine*, 4.

17. Devine, *Memoirs of Bing Devine*, 141.

18. Bob Burnes, "Why Solly Hemus?," *Sport*, April 1959, 18.

19. Phil Pepe, "How Flood Finally Made It," *Sport*, November 1962, 4.

20. Russ J. Cowans, "Russ's Corner," *Chicago Daily Defender*, March 17, 1958, 23; Bill Lee, "With Malice toward None," *Hartford (CT) Courant*, March 28, 1958, A23.

21. Devine, *Memoirs of Bing Devine*, 89–90.

22. Barry Gottehrer, "Bill White Is a Hitter," *Sport*, September 1960, 47.

23. Bob Gibson and Lonnie Wheeler, *Stranger to the Game* (New York: Viking, 1994), 52–53; Curt Flood, *The Way It Is* (New York: Trident, 1971), 67.

24. Halberstam, *October 1964*, 110.

25. Flood, *The Way It Is*, 70–71.

26. *Chicago Defender*, August 15, 1962, 22.

27. *New York Times*, October 30, 1962, 55; Devine, *Memoirs of Bing Devine*, 14–16; *Washington Post*, November 6, 1962, A17.

28. *Washington Post*, November 7, 1962, D4.

29. Devine, *Memoirs of Bing Devine*, 17.

30. Shirley Povich, "This Morning," *Washington Post*, April 2, 1963, A17; Arthur Daley, "Sports of the Times," *New York Times*, March 15, 1963, 16.

31. *Chicago Daily Defender*, October 30, 1963, A24.

32. Larry Williams, "That McCarver Is a Bulldog," *Sport*, May 1964, 40.

33. *Sports Illustrated*, April 13, 1964, 52–53.

34. Halberstam, *October 1964*, 219–22; Gibson, *Stranger to the Game*, 59–60.

35. Halberstam, *October 1964*, 37.

36. Golenbock, *Spirit of St. Louis*, 454–55.

37. Golenbock, *Spirit of St. Louis*, 459.

38. Golenbock, *Spirit of St. Louis*, 457–58.

39. Devine, *Memoirs of Bing Devine*, 18–19.
40. Leo Durocher, *Nice Guys Finish Last* (New York: Simon and Schuster, 1975), 335–47.
41. Bob Gibson with Phil Pepe, *From Ghetto to Glory: The Story of Bob Gibson* (Englewood Cliffs NJ: Prentice Hall, 1968), 87.
42. Gibson, *From Ghetto to Glory*, 87.
43. Robert Lee Howsam, *My Life in Sports* (self-published, 1999), 73.
44. Gibson, *From Ghetto to Glory*, 101.
45. *Hartford (CT) Courant*, October 17, 1964, 35.

11. EXCELLENCE REWARDED

1. Ken Coleman and Dan Valenti, *The Impossible Dream Remembered* (Lexington MA: Stephen Greene Press, 1987), 289.
2. "Rising Dynasty for the Birds?," *Sports Illustrated*, April 17, 1967, 76.
3. Kerry Keene, "Dick O'Connell," SABR's Baseball Biography Project, http://sabr.org/bioproject.
4. All transaction details from http:// Retrosheet.org.
5. Dave Williams, "Mike Ryan," SABR's Baseball Biography Project, http://sabr.org/bioproject.
6. Dick Williams and Bill Plashke, *No More Mr. Nice Guy* (San Diego: Harcourt, Brace, Jovanovich, 1990), 72.
7. Leigh Montville, *Why Not Us: The 86-Year of the Boston Red Sox Fans from Unparalleled Suffering to the Promised Land of the 2004 World Series* (New York: PublicAffairs, 2004), 55.
8. Dan Ewald, *John Fetzer: On a Handshake; The Times and Triumphs of a Tiger Owner* (Champaign IL: Sagamore, 1997), 83.
9. Jeanne Mallett, "Jim Campbell," SABR's Baseball Biography Project, http://sabr.org/bioproject.
10. Mallett, "Jim Campbell."
11. Tim Wendel, *Summer of '68: The Season That Changed Baseball—and America—Forever* (Cambridge MA: Da Capo, 2012), 139.
12. Warren Corbett, *The Wizard of Waxahachie: Paul Richards and the End of Baseball as We Knew It* (Dallas: Southern University Press, 2009), 174.
13. John Eisenberg, *From 33rd Street to Camden Yards: An Oral History of the Baltimore Orioles* (New York: Contemporary Books, 2001), 68.
14. Corbett, *Wizard of Waxahachie*, 114.
15. Brent Kelley, *Baseball's Biggest Blunder: The Bonus Rule of 1953 to 1957* (Lanham MD: Scarecrow Press, 1997), 67.
16. Eisenberg, *From 33rd Street to Camden Yards*, 70.
17. Eisenberg, *From 33rd Street to Camden Yards*, 67.
18. Eisenberg, *From 33rd Street to Camden Yards*, 70.
19. Eisenberg, *From 33rd Street to Camden Yards*, 132.
20. Eisenberg, *From 33rd Street to Camden Yards*, 137.

21. Farm Department Memo, February 23, 1961, Harry Dalton Papers, Baseball Hall of Fame Library.
22. Eisenberg, *From 33rd Street to Camden Yards*, 233.
23. MacPhail, *My Nine Innings*, 79.
24. MacPhail, *My Nine Innings*, 80.
25. Paul Wilkes, "Don Buford and the Dignity of a Dirty Uniform," *Sport*, December 1968.
26. Eisenberg, *From 33rd Street to Camden Yards*, 233.
27. Eisenberg, *From 33rd Street to Camden Yards*, 76.
28. Eisenberg, *From 33rd Street to Camden Yards*, 233.
29. See Dalton Papers, Baseball Hall of Fame Library.

12. AMATEUR DRAFT

Epigraph: Carrie Muskat, "Epstein Addresses Manager, Other Topics," MLB.com, October 26, 2011.
1. *The "Sporting News" Official Baseball Guide, 1965* (St. Louis: Charles C. Spink & Son, 1965), 168–69.
2. We use WAR from http://baseball-reference.com. All data courtesy of Sean Lahman's database.
3. Harry Dalton, note to Frank Cashen dated October 19, 1971, from the Dalton Papers at the National Baseball Hall of Fame Library.

13. THE MACHINE

1. Greg Rhodes and John Erardi, *Big Red Dynasty: How Bob Howsam & Sparky Anderson Built the Big Red Machine* (Cincinnati: Road West, 1997), 113.
2. Howsam, *My Life in Sports*, 39.
3. Rhodes and Erardi, *Big Red Dynasty*, 47.
4. Howsam, *My Life in Sports*, 40.
5. MacPhail, *My Nine Innings*, 55.
6. Rhodes and Erardi, *Big Red Dynasty*, 47.
7. Howsam, *My Life in Sports*, 61–63.
8. Howsam, *My Life in Sports*, 75–76.
9. Dick Kaegel, "Howsam Happy with Revamped Cards," *Sporting News*, November 29, 1965, 1.
10. Howsam, *My Life in Sports*, 77.
11. Associated Press, "Red Hire Bob Howsam as Manager," *St. Josephs (MO) Gazette*, January 23, 1967.
12. Lawson, "Reds Sail to Gold."
13. Howsam, *My Life in Sports*, 100.
14. Rhodes and Erardi, *Big Red Dynasty*, 55–56.
15. Earl Lawson, "Hypnosis, Motivation: Howsam Probing Deeply," *Sporting News*, January 6, 1973, 48.
16. Rhodes and Erardi, *Big Red Dynasty*, 54–55.

17. Earl Lawson, "Forecast by Pappas Comes Oh So True in Six Player Deal," *Sporting News*, June 22, 1968, 16.

18. Associated Press, "Atlanta Swaps with Cincinnati to Bolster Pitching," *Gadsen (AL) Times*, June 12, 1968, 11.

19. "National Nuggets," *Sporting News*, September 7, 1968, 28.

20. Earl Lawson, "Reds to Transplant Rose Again—to CF," *Sporting News*, October 26, 1968, 22.

21. Rhodes and Erardi, *Big Red Dynasty*, 57.

22. Rhodes and Erardi, *Big Red Dynasty*, 61.

23. Rhodes and Erardi, *Big Red Dynasty*, 76.

24. Daryl Smith, *Making the Big Red Machine: Bob Howsam and the Cincinnati Reds of the 1970s* (Jefferson NC: McFarland, 2009), 55–56.

25. Lawson, "Reds Sail to Gold."

26. Pat Harmon, "Reds Are a Team on Rise; Reason Is Howsam," *Sporting News*, October 24, 1970, 47.

27. Rhodes and Erardi, *Big Red Dynasty*, 109.

28. Rhodes and Erardi, *Big Red Dynasty*, 115.

29. Rhodes and Erardi, *Big Red Dynasty*, 111.

30. Smith, *Making the Big Red Machine*, 59.

31. Rhodes and Erardi, *Big Red Dynasty*, 116.

32. Earl Lawson, "Howsam in Top Fielding Form on Questions from Reds Fans," *Sporting News*, January 29, 1972, 29.

33. Howsam, *My Life in Sports*, 119–20.

34. Armour and Levitt, *Paths to Glory*.

35. Howsam, *My Life in Sports*, 119–20, 124.

36. Earl Lawson, "Minor Deals Made Howsam Top Major Exec," *Sporting News*, December 8, 1973, 29.

37. Bob Hertzel, "Racial Prejudice a Definite Stranger to Reds," *Sporting News*, April 28, 1973, 7.

38. Howsam, *My Life in Sports*, 127.

39. Rhodes and Erardi, *Big Red Dynasty*, 167.

14. LONG ROAD BACK

Epigraph: David Haugh, "Tigers' Dombrowski Knows How to Build a Winner," *Chicago Tribune*, June 12, 2012.

1. Richard Goldstein, "George Steinbrenner, Who Built Yankees into Powerhouse, Dies at 80," *New York Times*, July 13, 2010.

2. Matt Schudel, "George Steinbrenner Dies at 80; Yankees Owner Built Billion-Dollar Empire," *Washington Post*, July 13, 2010; David Kozo, "Yankees Owner George Steinbrenner Dies," *Wall Street Journal*, July 13, 2010.

3. Jane Leavy, *The Last Boy: Mickey Mantle and the End of America's Childhood* (New York: Harper, 2010), 270.

4. Jim Bouton, *Ball Four: My Life and Hard Times Throwing the Knuckleball in the Big Leagues*, edited by Leonard Shecter (New York: World, 1970).

5. Leavy, *Last Boy*, 270–72.

6. Mann, *Decline and Fall of the New York Yankees*, 19.

7. Hal Bock, Associated Press, "Yankee Housecleaning Begins at Top with Dan Topping," *New London (CT) Day*, September 20, 1966, 13.

8. William Reel, "The Go-Getter of Sports and Business Isn't Going to Stop until He's Got the Yankees Playing Like Yankees Again," *New York Daily News*, July 8, 1967, 98.

9. "Yankee Broadcaster Have Brighter Future," *Miami News*, September 21, 1966, C1.

10. Red Smith, "Red Had to Go," *New London (CT) Day*, September 29, 1966, 26.

11. Associated Press, "Yanks Hire MacPhail to Do Rebuilding Job," *Meriden (CT) Morning Record*, October 14, 1966, 13.

12. Milton Gross, "Operation Trio," *St. Petersburg (FL) Independent*, October 18, 1966, A16.

13. Joe Falls, "What's Ahead for the Yankees," *Baseball Digest*, January 1967, 47.

14. Edgar Munzel, "N.L. Prexy Giles' Persuasion Blocked More Deals with A.L.," *Sporting News*, December 31, 1966, 28, 34.

15. "Scorecard," *Sports Illustrated*, June 5, 1967.

16. Peter Carry, "The Yankees Are Coming, or So They Hope," *Sports Illustrated*, April 6, 1970.

17. Reel, "Go-Getter of Sports and Business," 98.

18. Mann, *Decline and Fall of the New York Yankees*, 226.

19. Jimmy Cannon, "Only Burke Can Save Baseball," *Los Angeles Herald-Examiner*, December 16, 1968, D2.

20. MacPhail, *My Nine Innings*, 118.

21. MacPhail, *My Nine Innings*, 119.

22. Peter Carry, "Dreamy Times for Mini-Bombers," *Sports Illustrated*, June 22, 1970.

23. Jim Ogle, "Yanks' MacPhail Lashes at Baying Wolves," *Sporting News*, June 17, 1972.

24. *Sports Illustrated*, August 22, 1972.

25. Jim Ogle, "Yanks Terrific, Soul-Searching Reveals," *Sporting News*, August 19, 1972.

26. Joseph Durso, "Mets Send Agee to the Astros for Pair; Yanks Trade Four to Get Graig Nettles," *New York Times*, November 28, 1972, 57.

27. Howard Cosell, "Mike Burke: A Great Man Who Cared," *New York Daily News*, February 11, 1987.

28. "They've Got The Race Right Here: American League East," *Sports Illustrated*, April 9, 1973.

29. William Johnson, "Yankee R[x] Is Good Therapy," *Sports Illustrated*, February 12, 1973.

30. Howard Cosell, "Mike Burke: A Great Man Who Cared," *New York Daily News*, February 11, 1987.

31. William Leggett, "Pinstripes Are Back in Style," *Sports Illustrated*, July 2, 1973.

32. MacPhail, *My Nine Innings*, 124.

15. EXPANSION

1. Dave Nightengale, "Free-Agent Draft: It Was a Farce," *Sporting News*, November 28, 1981, 53.

2. Dickson Terry, "Kaycee 'Will Never Lose This Team,'" *Sporting News*, January 27, 1968, 23–24.

3. Allan T. Demaree, "Ewing Kauffman Sold Himself Rich in Kansas City," *Fortune*, October 1972, 101.

4. Anne Morgan, *Prescription for Success: The Life and Values of Ewing Marion Kauffman* (Kansas City MO: Andrews and McMeel, 1995), 266.

5. Demaree, "Ewing Kauffman Sold Himself," 100.

6. Mark Mulvoy, "KC Is Back with a Vengeance," *Sports Illustrated*, May 26, 1969.

7. "Army Captain Gets G.M. Post," *Sporting News*, February 18, 1948, 23; "Near Riot at Thomasville," *Sporting News*, June 23, 1948, 36.

8. "Henry Aaron Aims at RBI Mark," *Sporting News*, June 24, 1953, 33.

9. Keith Mathews, "Tallis Drafts Plan for New Coast League," *Sporting News*, September 18, 1957, 9.

10. "Mounties Seek Home-Grown Talent, Hold Six-Day Clinic," *Sporting News*, August 13, 1958, 34.

11. Hy Zimmerman, "G.M. Tallis Resigns His Seattle Post," *Sporting News*, October 12, 1960, 24.

12. Earl Lawson, "Tallis, Ex-Boss of Seattle, Top Choice for Post," *Sporting News*, November 2, 1960, 5.

13. Ross Newhan, "Angel Finale—Chavez Quiet as Tomb," *Sporting News*, October 9, 1965, 15.

14. Bill Madden, *Steinbrenner: The Last Lion of Baseball* (New York: HarperCollins, 2010), 202; Jack McKeon and Kevin Kernan, *I'm Just Getting Started: Baseball's Best Story Teller on Old School Baseball, Defying the Odds, and Good Cigars* (Chicago: Triumph, 2005), 106.

15. Lou Gorman, *High and Inside: My Life in the Front Offices of Baseball* (Jefferson NC: McFarland, 2008), 117.

16. Bob Andelman, *Stadium for Rent: Tampa Bay's Quest for Major League Baseball* (Jefferson NC: McFarland, 1993), 77.

17. Charlie Metro with Tom Altherr, *Safe by a Mile* (Lincoln: University of Nebraska Press, 2002), 331; Gorman, *High and Inside*, 81–82.

18. Gorman, *High and Inside*, 94.

19. Metro, *Safe by a Mile*, 12–13, 132, 133.

20. Joe McGuff, "Metro Goes to Bat for Sunken Bases," *Sporting News*, May 2, 1970; Joe Falls, unidentified article from Charlie Metro's Hall of Fame file, June 6, 1970.
21. Metro, *Safe by a Mile*, 320.
22. John Schuerholz, interview with Dan Levitt, March 11, 2013.
23. Unidentified clipping, Cedric Tallis Hall of Fame file.
24. Gorman, *High and Inside*, 83; Allan Simpson, ed., *The Baseball Draft: The First 25 Years, 1965–1989* (Durham NC: American Sports, 1990), 65.
25. Steve Treder, "The Royals of Sir Cedric," http://www.hardballtimes.com, December 21, 2004.
26. Metro, *Safe by a Mile*, 327–28, 330, 344.
27. Schuerholz interview.
28. Metro, *Safe by a Mile*, 330, 333.
29. Frank Deford, "It Ain't Necessarily So, and Never Was," *Sports Illustrated*, March 6, 1972.
30. Joe McGuff, "Kauffman Goal: Flag in Five Years; Royals' Boss Weighs Daring Plan," *Sporting News*, June 7, 1969, 16.
31. Metro, *Safe by a Mile*, 335–36; Syd Thrift and Barry Shapiro, *The Game according to Syd: The Theories and Teachings of Baseball's Leading Innovator* (New York: Simon and Schuster, 1990), 33.
32. Joe McGuff, "Royals Will Build Florida Academy; Cost Is $3 Million," *Sporting News*, September 27, 1969, 20; Spike Claassen, "42 Survive Cuts for Royals' Academy," *Sporting News*, September 5, 1970, 42.
33. William Leggett, "School's In: Watch Out for Baseball Players," *Sports Illustrated*, August 23, 1971; Spike Claassen, "K.C. Baseball Academy Dedication on March 21," *Sporting News*, February 27, 1971, 31.
34. Thrift, *Game according to Syd*, 27; Morgan, *Prescription for Success*, 253.
35. Richard J. Peurzer, "The Kansas City Royals' Baseball Academy," in *The National Pastime* (Cleveland: SABR, 2004), 3; Claassen, "42 Survive Cuts for Royals' Academy," 42; Claassen, "K.C. Baseball Academy Dedication on March 21," 31.
36. Peurzer, "Kansas City Royals' Baseball Academy," 10; *The "Sporting News" Official Guide* (St. Louis: Sporting News, 1972), 579.
37. Thrift, *Game according to Syd*, 33; Metro, *Safe by a Mile*, 332; Gorman, *High and Inside*, 109.
38. Joe McGuff, "Pay Cuts on Tap for Royals Who Slumped in 1970," *Sporting News*, January 30, 1971.
39. Peurzer, " Kansas City Royals' Baseball Academy," 10; Gorman, *High and Inside*, 113; Joe McGuff, "Kaycee Academy Grooms Rejects, but Cost Is High," *Sporting News*, April 21, 1973, 17.
40. McGuff, "Kaycee Academy," 17.
41. Frank White with Bill Althaus, *One Man's Dream: My Town, My Team, My Time* (Olathe KS: Ascend Books, 2012), 51.

42. Jesse W. Markham and Paul V. Teplitz, *Baseball Economics and Public Policy* (Lexington MA: Lexington Books, 1981), 148, 151; McGuff, "Kaycee Academy," 17.

43. Peurzer, "Kansas City Royals' Baseball Academy," 12.

44. Metro, *Safe by a Mile*, 323.

45. Joe McGuff, "Royals Take Stock after Milkes' Jab," *Sporting News*, August 16, 1969.

46. Gorman, *High and Inside*, 100; Metro, *Safe by a Mile*, 321.

47. Joe McGuff, "Tallis' Shrewd Trades Fuel Royals' Fast Start," *Sporting News*, June 26, 1971.

48. Metro, *Safe by a Mile*, 323–24; Gorman, *High and Inside*, 101–2; McGuff, "Tallis' Shrewd Trades."

49. Gorman, *High and Inside*, 105; Metro, *Safe by a Mile*, 337.

50. Metro, *Safe by a Mile*, 324–35; Gorman, *High and Inside*, 116.

51. Ralph Ray, "Instead It's No Season," *Sporting News*, June 27, 1981.

52. Associated Press, "Royals Air Dirty Laundry as Lemon Is Dismissed," *St. Joseph (MO) News-Press*, October 4, 1972.

53. Joe McGuff, "'Blame Me for Lemon's Exit,' Says Kauffman," *Sporting News*, October 21, 1972; Joe McGuff, "Tallis-Kauffman Split Linked to Lemon Firing," *Sporting News*, July 6, 1974.

54. McKeon, *I'm Just Getting Started*, 107. In his first book, *Jack of All Trades* (Chicago: Contemporary Books, 1988), Jack McKeon attributed the accusation of lying to Gorman.

55. Metro, *Safe by a Mile*, 332; Gorman, *High and Inside*, 128–29.

56. Gorman, *High and Inside*, 128–29.

57. Joe McGuff, "McKeon Sees Red over Royal Dearth of Deals," *Sporting News*, June 30, 1973.

58. Metro, *Safe by a Mile*, 336–37.

59. Sid Bordman, "Royals Promote Burke to G.M. Post," *Sporting News*, June 29, 1974.

60. "Joe Burke Joins Royals," *Sporting News*, September 22, 1975.

61. Morgan, *Prescription for Success*, 260.

62. Joe McGuff, "Royals Remain on Roller-Coaster," *Sporting News*, June 22, 1974.

63. Morgan, *Prescription for Success*, 261.

64. Joe McGuff, "Player Yelps Follow Bouncing of Lau," *Sporting News*, October 19, 1974.

65. Herm Weiskopf, "Baseball's Members in Good Standing," *Sports Illustrated*, December 19, 1983.

66. McGuff, "Tallis' Shrewd Trades."

67. Joe McGuff, "Tallis' Work with Royals Earns Executive Accolade," *Sporting News*, December 4, 1971.

16. FREE AGENCY

Epigraph: Peter Bavasi, email to author, January 19, 2013.

1. *The "Sporting News" Official Baseball Guide, 1968* (St. Louis: Sporting News, 1968), 175; Ken Harrelson with Al Hirshberg, *Hawk* (New York: Viking Press, 1969), 200–204.
2. John Helyar, *The Lords of the Realm: The Real History of Baseball* (New York: Villard Books, 1994), 149.
3. *"Sporting News" Official Baseball Guide, 1968*, 300.
4. Earl Lawson, "'Arbitration Too One-Sided'—Morgan," *Sporting News*, January 31, 1976, 46.
5. Ralph Ray, "Camps Delayed: Player-Owners Gap Still Wide," *Sporting News*, March 6, 1976, 12.
6. Mike Haupert, Haupert Baseball Salary Database, private collection.
7. Marvin Miller, *A Whole Different Ball Game: The Sport and Business of Baseball* (New York: Birch Lane Press, 1991), 248.
8. Miller, *Whole Different Ball Game*, 252.
9. Jesse W. Markham and Paul V. Teplitz, *Baseball Economics and Public Policy* (Lexington MA: Lexington Books, 1981), 147, 150; U.S. House of Representatives, *Report of the Subcommittee on the Study of Monopoly Power*, 1603, 1607; Travis Sawchik, "Production Shift Changes MLB Free Agency," November 2, 2013, http://triblive.com/sports/pirates/4962321-74/free-players-agency#axzz3BMxnV1jB.
10. Markham and Teplitz, *Baseball Economics and Public Policy*, 147; Matt Snyder, "Report: MLB Revenues in 2012 Were $7.5 Billion," http://CBSSports.com, December 9, 2012.
11. Sawchik, "Production Shift."

17. THE ZOO

1. Ed Linn, *Steinbrenner's Yankees* (New York: Holt, Rinehart, and Winston, 1982), 63.
2. Steve Jacobson, *The Best Team Money Could Buy* (New York: Atheneum, 1978), 14–15.
3. Marty Appel, *Pinstripe Empire: From before the Babe to after the Boss* (New York: Bloomsbury, 2012), 394–95.
4. Joseph Durso, "Yankees Hire Williams, Risking Legal Struggle," *New York Times*, December 14, 1973, 1.
5. Associated Press, "Angry Yanks Criticize Trade," *Washington Post*, April 27, 1974.
6. Madden, *Steinbrenner*, 61–62.
7. Red Smith, "Teacher Sends George Home," *New York Times*, November 29, 1974.
8. Appel, *Pinstripe Empire*, 398; Madden, *Steinbrenner*, 62–63.

9. UPI, "Giants Trade Bonds for Yanks' Murcer," *Wilmington (NC) News*, October 21, 1974, 38.

10. Phil Pepe, "Bonds, Hunter—and Good Times Come Again," *Sporting News*, March 8, 1975, 3.

11. Ron Fimrite, "A City on Pinstripes and Needles," *Sports Illustrated*, April 21, 1975.

12. "Gillick Brings Master Farm Talent to Yankee Job," *Sporting News*, September 14, 1974.

13. John Schuerholz, *Built to Win: Inside Stories and Leadership Strategies from Baseball's Winningest GM* (New York: Warner Books, 2006), 127–28.

14. Madden, *Steinbrenner*, 96–97.

15. Phil Pepe, "Yankees Adopting 3-R Plan: Rivers, Randolph—and Runs," *Sporting News*, December 27, 1975, 44.

16. Pepe, "Yankees Adopting," 44.

17. Madden, *Steinbrenner*, 98.

18. Murray Chase, "Yankees Claim Messersmith; Pitcher Denies Deal," *New York Times*, April 1, 1976, 54.

19. UPI, "Messersmith Is a Free Agent All over Again," *Los Angeles Times*, April 4, 1976.

20. Associated Press, "Aftershocks Rattle Baseball World," *Spokesman (WA) Review*, June 16, 1976, 54.

21. Linn, *Steinbrenner's Yankees*, 67.

22. Linn, *Steinbrenner's Yankees*, 74.

23. Linn, *Steinbrenner's Yankees*, 74; Murray Chass, "Yanks Stalking Jackson Instead of Grich," *New York Times*, November 21, 1976, 181.

24. Robert Ward, "Reggie Jackson in No-Man's Land," *Sport*, June 1977.

25. Linn, *Steinbrenner's Yankees*, 124.

26. Linn, *Steinbrenner's Yankees*, 143.

27. Linn, *Steinbrenner's Yankees*, 162, 172.

28. Terry Pluto, *The Curse of Rocky Colavito: A Loving Look at a Thirty-Year Slump* (New York: Simon and Schuster, 1994), 206.

29. Linn, *Steinbrenner's Yankees*, 66.

18. MANY RIVERS

Epigraph: Whitey Herzog and Kevin Horrigan, *The White Rat: A Life in Baseball* (New York: HarperCollins, 1987), 85.

1. "The Press: New Owner," *Time*, February 21, 1955.

2. Larry Millson, *Ballpark Figures: The Blue Jays and the Business of Baseball* (Toronto: McClelland and Stewart, 1987), 137.

3. Stephen Brunt, *Diamond Dreams: 20 Years of Blue Jays Baseball* (Toronto: Viking, 1996), 191.

4. Millson, *Ballpark Figures*, 133.

5. Brunt, *Diamond Dreams*, 53; Millson, *Ballpark Figures*, 119–22.
6. Brunt, *Diamond Dreams*, 55; Millson, *Ballpark Figures*, 121.
7. Unidentified article, Peter Bavasi Hall of Fame file, January 27, 1973.
8. Tom Weir, USA *Today*, October 9, 1985.
9. Millson, *Ballpark Figures*, 125.
10. Brunt, *Diamond Dreams*, 55.
11. Peter Bavasi, email correspondence with author, January 19, 2013.
12. Millson, *Ballpark Figures*, 134.
13. Bavasi, email.
14. Millson, *Ballpark Figures*, 134.
15. Bavasi, email.
16. Bavasi, email.
17. Frank Fitzpatrick, "In College, Pat Gillick Discovered His Baseball Savvy," *Philadelphia Inquirer*, July 23, 2011
18. Philippe van Rjndt and Patrick Blednick, *Fungo Blues: An Uncontrolled Look at the Toronto Blue Jays* (Toronto: Seal, 1985), 196.
19. Michael P. Geffner, "Orioles G.M. Pat Gillick Is His Usual Stressed-Out Self in His Quest to Reach Baseball's Top Perch Once Again," *Sporting News*, April 22, 1996.
20. Unidentified clipping, Pat Gillick Hall of Fame file.
21. John Wilson, "Cesar Cedeno . . . the Next Superstar?," *Sporting News*, August 19, 1972.
22. Bob Elliott, "The Skill to Find the Talent," *Memories and Dreams*, April 2013, 20.
23. Millson, *Ballpark Figures*, 75–78.
24. Terry Pluto, *The Curse of Rocky Colavito: A Loving Look at a Thirty-Year Slump* (New York: Fireside, 1995), 262.
25. Pat Gillick, interview with Levitt, October 2, 2012.
26. Bavasi, email.
27. Gillick, interview.
28. Brunt, *Diamond Dreams*, 76.
29. Bavasi, email.
30. William Plummer, "Baseball Scout Epy Guerrero Looks for Rough Diamonds amid Hunger and Poverty," *People*, April 10, 1989; Jim Sandoval in Jim Sandoval and Bill Nowlin, eds., "Epy Guerrero: Super Scout," in *Can He Play? A Look at Baseball Scouts and Their Profession* (Phoenix: SABR, 2011), 103.
31. Jim Kaplan, "How to Succeed in the Baseball Business: A Blueprint for Major League Expansion Teams," in *Bill Mazeroski's Baseball, 1991* (annual preview magazine): 13.
32. Ian Thomsen, "Do They Hate Danny Boy," *Sporting News*, March 21, 1988, 10; Paul Attner, "Remodeling the Redskins," *Sporting News*, September 8, 1986, 12–14.

33. Millson, *Ballpark Figures*, 161–62.

34. Bavasi, email.

35. *Sporting News*, undated article in Peter Bavasi's Hall of Fame file.

36. Jim Kaplan, "Ringing in the New," *Sports Illustrated*, January 10, 1977.

37. Dave Stieb with Kevin Boland, *Tomorrow I'll Be Perfect* (Toronto: Doubleday, 1986), 27–32.

38. Alison Gordon, *Foul Balls: Five Years in the American League* (Toronto: McClelland and Stewart, 1984), 57.

39. *Toronto Globe and Mail*, quoted in Tom Cheek, *Road to Glory: Sixteen Years of Blue Jay Fever* (Toronto: Warwick, 1993), 122; *Sporting News*, October 13, 1979, 36.

40. Gordon, *Foul Balls*, 60.

41. Gordon, *Foul Balls*, 62.

42. Bob Elliott, "The Skill to Find the Talent," *Memories and Dreams*, April, 2013, 20.

43. Millson, *Ballpark Figures*, 32.

44. Cheek, *Road to Glory*, 135–36.

45. Brunt, *Diamond Dreams*, 125.

46. Millson, *Ballpark Figures*, 140.

47. Millson, *Ballpark Figures*, 140.

48. Brunt, *Diamond Dreams*, 127.

49. Cheek, *Road to Glory*, 131.

50. Gillick, interview.

51. Millson, *Ballpark Figures*, 33.

52. Herzog and Horrigan, *White Rat*, 106.

53. Cheek, *Road to Glory*, 167.

54. Gillick, interview; Brunt, *Diamond Dreams*, 158.

19. WINNING NOW

1. Cheek, *Road to Glory*, 198.

2. Peter Gammons, "Toronto Blue Jays," *Sports Illustrated*, April 6, 1987.

3. *Sporting News*, December 19, 1988, 56.

4. Ernie Whitt and Greg Cable, *Catch: A Major League Life* (Scarborough ON: McGraw-Hill, 1989), 218–21.

5. George Bell and Bob Elliot, *Hardball* (Toronto: Key Porter, 1990), 121–22; Brunt, *Diamond Dreams*, 183; Cheek, *Road to Glory*, 233.

6. Art Thiel, *Out of Left Field: How the Mariners Made Baseball Fly in Seattle* (Seattle: Sasquatch, 2003), 85–86.

7. Franz Lidz, "Birdland," *Sports Illustrated*, September 11, 1989.

8. Lidz, "Birdland."

9. "Forbes Valuations of the 30 Clubs in MLB," http://bizofbaseball.com.

10. Bob Elliott, "The Skill to Find the Talent," *Memories and Dreams*, April 2013, 20.

11. Brunt, *Diamond Dreams*, 291–92.

12. Brunt, *Diamond Dreams*, 232.

13. Steve Wulf, "The Blue Jay Way," *Sports Illustrated*, November 2, 1992.

14. Bavasi, email.

15. Larry Stone, "Big Deals Could Determine Who Wins Baseball's Stretch Run," *Seattle Times*, July 19, 2003.

16. Frank Fitzpatrick, "Before Hall, Gillick Talks of Phils," *Philadelphia Inquirer*, July 16, 2011.

17. Wulf, "The Blue Jay Way."

18. Tim Kurkjian, "The Blue Days," *Sports Illustrated*, July 11, 1994.

19. The usatoday.com salary database is available at http://content.usatoday.com/sportsdata/baseball/mlb/salaries/team/1993.

20. Martin O'Malley and Sean O'Malley, *Game Day: The Blue Jays at SkyDome* (Toronto: Viking, 1994), 126–45.

21. *Sporting News*, December 13, 1993, 34.

22. Pat Gillick, email correspondence with author, August 19, 2014.

23. *Sporting News*, December 11, 1995, 54.

24. Roland Hemond, interview with Levitt, February 28, 2013.

25. John Eisenberg, *From 33rd Street to Camden Yards: An Oral History of the Baltimore Orioles* (New York: Contemporary Books, 2001), 435.

26. Tim Kurkjian, "One Quick Fix," *Sports Illustrated*, February 21, 1994.

27. Eisenberg, *From 33rd Street to Camden Yards*, 437.

28. Eisenberg, *From 33rd Street to Camden Yards*, 451.

29. *Sporting News*, December 11, 1995, 54.

30. Bob Cohn, "Mariners' Gillick Builds Baseball's Best," *Washington Times*, May 22, 2001.

31. Eisenberg, *From 33rd Street to Camden Yards*, 455.

32. *Sporting News*, June 10, 1996, 12; Eisenberg, *From 33rd Street to Camden Yards*, 456–57.

33. Tom Verducci, "Losing Their Way," *Sports Illustrated*, April 26, 1999.

34. Eisenberg, *From 33rd Street to Camden Yards*, 458.

35. Tom Verducci, "Liar's Poker," *Sports Illustrated*, August 25, 1997.

36. *Sporting News*, October 28, 1996, 12; Eisenberg, *From 33rd Street to Camden Yards*, 460–62.

37. Gerry Callahan, "In Flight," *Sports Illustrated*, May 19, 1997.

38. Pat Gillick, interview with Levitt, October 2, 2012; Eisenberg, *From 33rd Street to Camden Yards*, 465–66.

39. Callahan, "In Flight."

40. *Sporting News*, November 10, 1997, 38; Eisenberg, *From 33rd Street to Camden Yards*, 473–77.

41. Eisenberg, *From 33rd Street to Camden Yards*, 485.

42. Eric Young, "One-on-One with Giants CEO Larry Baer," http://www.bizjournals.com, October 4, 2012.

43. Eisenberg, *From 33rd Street to Camden Yards*, 477.
44. Joe Strauss, "Murray, O's Chat," *Baltimore Sun*, October 26, 1999.
45. Jon Wells, *Shipwrecked: A Peoples' History of the Seattle Mariners* (Kenmore WA: Epicenter, 2012), 84.
46. Wells, *Shipwrecked*, 68.
47. Thiel, *Out of Left Field*, 184.
48. Thiel, *Out of Left Field*, 187–90.
49. Laura Vecsey, "Mariners' Gillick Will Get Players, Not Played," *Seattle Post-Intelligencer*, July 25, 2000; Linda Tischler, "Seattle Mariners: (Re) Build It and They Will Come," *Fast Company*, June 14, 2002.
50. Wells, *Shipwrecked*, 141.
51. John Heyman, "Thanks to Gillick, Seattle Boasts a Slew of New Talent," *Sporting News*, January 24, 2000.
52. Gillick, interview; Thiel, *Out of Left Field*, 204.
53. Thiel, *Out of Left Field*, 203.
54. John Hickey, "Gillick Seeks No. 1 Starter," *Seattle Post-Intelligencer*, June 9, 2001.
55. Tom Verducci, "Crunch Time," *Sports Illustrated*, August 27, 2001.
56. Phil Rogers, "Mariners Won't Add to Payroll," Knight Ridder/Tribune News Service, July 27, 2002.
57. Rogers, "Mariners Won't Add to Payroll."
58. *Hearing Before the Committee on the Judiciary House of Representatives on HR 3288*, 107th Cong., 1st sess. (December 6, 2001), 230.
59. Larry Stone, "Mariners Are among Baseball's Money Men," *Seattle Times*, http://community.seattletimes.nwsource.com/archive, December 4, 2001.
60. Blaine Newnhan, "M's Climb Is a Wondrous Achievement," *Seattle Times*, http://community.seattletimes.nwsource.com/archive, July 1, 2001.
61. "Mariners Keep Most Crucial Piece on the Board," *Seattle Times*, http://community.seattletimes.nwsource.com/archive, October 10, 2002.
62. Wells, *Shipwrecked*, 153.
63. Bob Finnigan, "Gillick to Turn over the Reins: M's General Manager Steps Down," *Seattle Times*, http://community.seattletimes.nwsource.com/archive, October 1, 2003.
64. Finnigan, "Gillick to Turn over the Reins."
65. Zack Zolecki, "Gillick's Mission: Complex Challenges Already Awaiting Phils' General Manager," *Philadelphia Inquirer*, November 3, 2005.

20. ANALYTICS

Epigraph: "Emotional Breakdown," *Economist*, April 6, 2013.
1. Michael Lewis, *Moneyball: The Art of Winning an Unfair Game* (New York: W. W. Norton, 2003), 37.
2. Joel Sherman, *Birth of a Dynasty: Behind the Pinstripes with the 1996 Yankees* ([Emmaus PA]: Rodale, 2006), 76.

3. Jack Etkin, "At Last, Rockies Have Mile High Math," *Yahoo Sports*, April 19, 2000.

4. Larry Stone, "A's, M's Not Quite on the Same Page," *Seattle Times*, http://community.seattletimes.nwsource.com/archive, September 19, 2003.

5. Stone, "A's, M's."

6. Larry Stone, "Inside Pitch: Paying the Price of 'Moneyball,'" *Seattle Times*, http://community.seattletimes.nwsource.com/archive, April 18, 2004.

7. Stone, "A's, M's."

8. Stone, "A's, M's."

9. Farhan Zaidi, interview with David Laurila, http://fangraphs.com, March 18, 2013.

10. Edward Grant Barrow with James Kahn, *My Fifty Years in Baseball* (New York: Coward-McCann, 1951), 126.

11. Brian Costa, "Never Managed? You're Hired!," *Wall Street Journal*, December 12, 2013.

12. Lewis, *Moneyball*, 154.

13. Terry Francona and Dan Shaughnessy, *Francona: The Red Sox Years* (New York: Houghton Mifflin Harcourt, 2013), 161, 247.

14. Andrew Keh, "Mets' Latest Weapon, So They Hope," *New York Times*, March 22, 2013.

15. Paul Swydan, "Covert Tracking," *ESPN the Magazine*, September 2, 2013, 28.

16. Matthew Leach, "Track to the Future: The Game's New Metrics," May 20, 2014, http://mlb.com.

17. "Supercomputers: Game On," *Babbage* (blog), *Economist*, May 10, 2014, http://www.economist.com.

18. Jonah Keri, *The Extra 2%: How Wall Street Strategies Took a Major League Baseball Team from Worst to First* (New York: ESPN Books, 2011), 187–203.

19. Steve Melewski, "Rick Peterson Brings Biomechanical Analysis to the Orioles," http://www.masnsports, January 20, 2012.

20. Jim Summers, interview with David Laurila, http://fangraphs.com, May 3, 2013.

21. "Cubs, Bloomberg Sports to Partner on New Baseball Analytic Technology Solutions System," http://mlb.com, January 12, 2012.

22. Brian Peterson, interview with David Laurila, http://fangraphs.com, February 3, 2012.

23. Brian Costa, "Steel City's Alternate Universe Is Reality," *Wall Street Journal*, October 1, 2013, D6.

24. Travis Sawchik, "Aggressive Defensive Plan Has Led to Pirates' Turnaround," http://www.triblive.com, September 14, 2013.

25. Tom Verducci, "Stephen Strasburg Shut Down Is Right Decision by Rizzo," *Sports Illustrated*, September 4, 2012; Matt Gelb, "Phillies Continue to Rely More on Scouting than Sabermetrics," *Philadelphia Inquirer*, March 29, 2013.

26. Adam Kilgore, "The Nationals and Analytics, Extended Cut," http://www
    .washingtonpost.com, March 28, 2013.

21. POST-*MONEYBALL*

1. "Phillies Fire GM Wade after Eight Seasons," http://ESPN.com, October 10,
   2005.
2. Jim Salisbury, "One More Kick at the Can," *Philadelphia Inquirer*, February
   12, 2006.
3. Salisbury, "One More Kick at the Can."
4. Zolecki, "Gillick's Mission."
5. Rich Hofmann, "Still Itching for Some Pitching," *Philadelphia Daily News*,
   January 11, 2006.
6. Rich Hofmann, "2007: A Year to Forget," *Philadelphia Daily News*, July 31,
   2006.
7. Gillick, interview.
8. Marcus Hayes, "Reconstruction Era," *Philadelphia Daily News*, April 2, 2007.
9. Bill Evans, "Phillies Tenure Capped Gillick's Hall of Fame Resume," http://
   www.nj.com, July 24, 2011.
10. Gillick, interview.
11. John R. Finger, "Gutsy Moves Put Pat Gillick in the Hall of Fame," http://
    www.CSNPhilly.com, July 22, 2011.
12. Gillick, interview.
13. Paul Hagen, "In Hiring Pat Gillick as GM, Phillies Made a Hall of a Choice,"
    Philadelphia Daily News, July 22, 2011.
14. Ray Ratto, http://www.csnbayarea, September 15, 2011.
15. Ann Killion, "A Giant Leap," *Stanford Magazine*, July–August 2011.
16. "Talkin' Baseball (and More) with Neukom," http://www.pressdemocrat
    .com, May 31, 2009.
17. Lowell Cohn, "Bill Neukom Speaks about Himself and the Giants," http://
    cohn.blogs.pressdemocrat.com, May 30, 2009.
18. William Neukom biographical information from Conor Dougherty, inter-
    view with Bill Neukom, "From Windows to Box Seats," http://wsj.com, Au-
    gust 27, 2009; Cohn, "Bill Neukom Speaks"; Andrew Baggarly, "Bill Neu-
    kom Articulates the 'Giants Way,' and Yes It Includes a Bit of 'Moneyball,'"
    http://blogs.mercurynews.com, October 7, 2008; Ray Ratto, "Bill Neukom
    Redefines the Giants' Approach," http://www.sfgate.com, October 8, 2008;
    "Talkin' Baseball"; Killion, "A Giant Leap"; Lloyd Duhaime, "Bill Neukom,
    Lawyer Biography," http://www.duhaime.org/LawFun/LawArticle-1220
    /Bill-Neukom-Lawyer-Biography.aspx.
19. Baggarly, "Bill Neukom Articulates."
20. Dougherty, interview with Neukom, "From Windows to Box Seats."
21. Rick Wartzman, "Peter Drucker's Winning Team," *Business Week*, April 10,
    2008.

22. Bill Neukom, interview with Levitt, December 16, 2013.
23. Baggarly, "Bill Neukom Articulates."
24. The outline list of four points under the players, their development, and their game on the field and the ten points under the business–front office side come from slides shown as part of Neukom's presentation at the Santa Clara Law Sports Law Symposium, September 16, 2010, available at http://www.youtube.com/watch?v=9kxFjqVCNGA, http://www.youtube.com/watch?v=kXMDuX-6xt4, http://www.youtube.com/watch?v=po_YKTj4EiU, http://www.youtube.com/watch?v=WDCusog1pt4.
25. Andrew Baggarly, "New Giants Boss Neukom Lays Out His Vision," http://www.mercurynews.com, October 7, 2008.
26. Baggarly, "Bill Neukom Articulates."
27. Dougherty, interview with Neukom, "From Windows to Box Seats."
28. Neukom presentation.
29. Baggarly, "Bill Neukom Articulates."
30. Neukom presentation.
31. Dougherty, interview with Neukom, "From Windows to Box Seats."
32. Baggarly, "Bill Neukom Articulates."
33. Cohn, "Bill Neukom Speaks."
34. Baggarly, "Bill Neukom Articulates."
35. Cohn, "Bill Neukom Speaks."
36. Chris Haft, "Front Office Enjoying Fruits of Its Labor," http://mlb.com, October 26, 2010.
37. Jerry Crasnick, "Bringing the Giants Forward, from Behind," http://ESPN.com, November 15, 2010.
38. San Francisco front-office bios at http://mlb.com.
39. Chris Haft, "Neukom Puts His Stamp on Giants," http://mlb.com, February 27, 2009.
40. Mathew Futterman, "The Warm-Body Theory," *Wall Street Journal*, October 17, 2012, D6.
41. Molly Knight, "The Hurt Talker," http://ESPN.com, August 13, 2012.
42. Peter Keating, "Son of Moneyball," *ESPN the Magazine*, October 13, 2004.
43. Futterman, "The Warm-Body Theory"
44. Futterman, "The Warm-Body Theory"
45. Colin Wyers, "BP Unfiltered: Do the Giants Signal the End of Moneyball?," http://baseballprospectus.com, October 30, 2012.
46. Andy Altman-Ohr, "Unknown Hero Helps Make Giants World Series Champions," http://jweekly.com, November 4, 2010.
47. Haft, "Neukom Puts His Stamp."
48. Haft, "Front Office Enjoying Fruits of Its Labor," http://mlb.com, October 26, 2010.
49. Darren Everson, "Where Did That Guy Come From?," *Wall Street Journal*, April 28, 2009.

50. Matt Eddy, "Clubs Use Dual Criteria to Find Potential Fits," http://baseball america.com, May 9, 2009.

51. Gwen Knapp, "Neukom's Ouster a Misplay by Giants' Ownership," *San Francisco Chronicle*, September 16, 2011.

52. Mark Purdy, "Bill Neukom Out as S.F. Giants Honcho," *Mercury (CA) News*, September 14, 2011.

53. "Baer Takes Giants Reins; Neukom Denies Management Friction," *San Francisco Chronicle*, September 15, 2011.

54. Mike Fast, "What the Heck Is Pitch F/X," in *Hardball Times Baseball Annual, 2010* (Skokie IL: ACTA Sports, 2009), 153; Darren Everson, "Baseball's Nerd Machine," *Wall Street Journal*, May 23, 2008.

55. Futterman, "The Warm-Body Theory."

56. Hank Adams, http://mlb.com, March 12, 2012.

57. Peter H. Lewis, "For the Love of the Technology, the Bay Area Is Reinventing Baseball (Again)," *New York Times*, April 26, 2012.

58. John Boudreau, "AT&T Leading the Way in Digitally Enhanced Baseball," *Mercury (CA) News*, July 17, 2009.

59. Neukom, interview.

60. Peter H. Lewis, "For the Love of the Technology."

61. "San Francisco Giants Ride Techball to the Top," *USA Today*, March 31, 2013.

62. "Info Hungry Baseball Teams' Secret Sauce: Data," *USA Today*, March 31, 2013.

63. "San Francisco Giants Ride Techball to the Top."

64. "San Francisco Giants Ride Techball to the top."

22. MODERN GAME

Epigraph: Brian MacPherson, "Ten Years after 'Moneyball,' Billy Beane Both Pleased, Dismayed There's No Longer 'Low-Hanging Fruit,'" *Providence (RI) Journal*, April 23, 2013.

1. Casey Ross and Callum Borchers, "John W. Henry, Soft-Spoken Businessman with an Appetite for Risk," *Boston Globe*, August 8, 2013.

2. Seth Mnookin, *Feeding the Monster: How Money, Smarts and Nerve Took a Team to the Top* (New York: Simon and Schuster, 2006), 166–67.

3. Mnookin, *Feeding the Monster*, 174.

4. "Theo Epstein Chat," http://bostondirtdogs/boston.com, February 6, 2003.

5. WEEI, "Theo Epstein Talks about His Time in Boston and Building World Championship Teams," http://audio.weei.com/a/87165587/theo-epstein -talks-about-his-time-in-boston-and-building-world-champion-teams.htm.

6. Francona and Shaughnessy, *Francona*, 163.

7. Amalie Benjamin, "Steering It from the 'Bridge,'" *Boston Globe*, December 9, 2009.

8. Dan Shaughnessy, "Sox Have a Bridge to Sell Us," *Boston Globe*, December 10, 2009.

9. Francona and Shaughnessy, *Francona*, 252.
10. Francona and Shaughnessy, *Francona*, 252.
11. Francona and Shaughnessy, *Francona*, 264.
12. Francona and Shaughnessy, *Francona*, 277–78.
13. Joshua Green, "John Henry and the Making of a Red Sox Baseball Dynasty," *Bloomberg Businessweek*, April 24, 2014, http://www.businessweek.com.
14. Tyler Kepner, "Cardinals' Strategy Replaces Big Names with Ingenuity," *New York Times*, October 19, 2013.
15. Bill Madden, "Walt Jocketty Gets Axed from Cards Because of Numbers Crunch," *New York Daily News*, October 7, 2007.
16. "Mozeliak Replaces Former Boss Jocketty with Cardinals," http://ESPN.com, October 31, 2007.
17. http://sportsillustrated.cnn.com/mlb/news/20130424/matt-adams-cardinals/.
18. Kepner, "Cardinals' Strategy."
19. Ben Reiter, "Birds on a Power Line," *Sports Illustrated*, May 27, 2013.
20. Reiter, "Birds on a Power Line."
21. David Laurila, "Q&A: Michael Girsch, St. Louis Cardinals Assistant General Manager," http://fangraphs.com, November 21, 2013.
22. Derrick Goold, "2014 St. Louis Cardinals Top 10 Prospects," http://baseballamerica.com, November 20, 2013.
23. Tracy Ringolsby, "Fuson, Beane Reunite for Sake of A's," http://www.foxsports.com, March 4, 2010.
24. Ringolsby, "Fuson, Beane Reunite for Sake of A's."
25. U.S. Senate, *Organized Professional Team Sports: Hearings*, 650.
26. *"Sporting News" 1955 Baseball Guide* (St. Louis: Charles C. Spink and Son, 1955), 10.
27. *Boston Red Sox 2013 Media Guide* (St. Louis: STATS, 2013).

EPILOGUE
1. "World's Greatest Leaders," *Fortune*, April 1, 2017, 47–50.
2. Gordon Wittenmyer, "Cubs Plan to Divest Stock," *Baseball America*, January 13–27, 2017.
3. Tyler Kepner, "Epstein's Moves Fortify the Cubs with Impact Players," *New York Times*, October 23, 2016.
4. Kyle Glaser, "Cubs Build from Ground Up to Title," *Baseball America*, December 9–30, 2016.
5. Gordon Wittenmyer, "Cubs Have Arm Urgency," *Baseball America*, June 17–July 1, 2016.
6. Tom Verducci, "The Rainmaker," *Sports Illustrated*, December 19, 2016, 114–16.
7. Tom Verducci, "Theo Epstein," *Fortune*, April 1, 2017, 50.
8. Jared Diamond, "The Chicago Cubs' Circle of Trust," *Wall Street Journal*, May 23, 2017.

9. Anthony Castrovince, "Cleveland's 'Dream Team' Front Office," sportsonearth .com/article/161217636/1998-indians-front-office-executives-tree, January 7, 2016; Tyler Kepner, "Cleveland Indians, a School for Executives, Face Mark Shapiro, a Top Alumnus," nytimes.com/2016/10/13/sports/baseball/cleveland -indians-a-school-for-executives-face-mark-shapiro-a-top-alumnus.html, October 12, 2016.

10. Mike Berardino, "Twins' Search Firm Looked at 70 People: Here's Why Derek Falvey Got the Job," twincities.com/2017/02/21/korn-ferry-exec -jed-hughes-says-derek-falvey-has-the-right-stuff, February 21, 2017.

11. R. J. Anderson, "Baseball's Next Moneyball Concept: Turning Internet Writers into Prospect Scouts," cbssports.com/mlb/news/baseballs-next -moneyball-concept-turning-internet-writers-into-prospect-scouts, March 29, 2017; Phil Bencomo, "The Once and Future Baseball Man," thebaseballchronicle .com/reporting/the_once_and_future_baseball_man; Jared Diamond, "The Indians' Brain Trust: Baseball Writers," *Wall Street Journal*, March 31, 2017; Vince Gennaro, email correspondence.

12. Matt Gelb, "Why the Phillies Built an Analytics Think Tank with Non-Baseball Brains," philly.com/philly/sports/phillies/20170309_Why_the _Phillies_built_an_analytics_think_tank_with_non-baseball_brains.html, March 8, 2017.

13. Michael Bode, "Fully Immersed: Diving into Baseball's Player Development Culture," waitingfornextyear.com/2016/01/cleveland-indians-player -development, January 6, 2016; Daniel Barbarisi, "Cleveland Thrives on Split Decisions," *Wall Street Journal*, October 12, 2016; Ben Reiter, "Ready to Party," *Sports Illustrated*, August 8, 2016; August Fagerstrom, "The Game Plan: How the Indians Almost Won It All," fangraphs.com/blogs/how-the -indians-built-the-game-plans-that-nearly-won-it-all, November 4, 2016.

14. Shi Davidi, "Big Tests Await New Jays Regime," *Baseball America*, January 1–15, 2016.

15. Tom Haudricourt, "Stearns Cites Sustainability as Key to New Plan," *Baseball America*, November 20–December 4, 2015.

16. Patrick Reusse, "MacPhail Works Magic on Cubs," *Minneapolis Star Tribune*, April 30, 1995.

17. Mike Axisa, "We Now Know Extent of Cardinals Hack and the Unprecedented Penalties from MLB," cbssports.com/mlb/news/we-now-know-extent -of-cardinals-hack-and-the-unprecedented-penalties-from-mlb, January 30, 2017; Lindsey Adler, "Feds: Cardinals Hacker Probably Leaked to Deadspin as Revenge for Astros' *Sports Illustrated* Cover," deadspin.com/feds-cardinals -hacker-probably-leaked-to-deadspin-as-r-1791778599, January 30, 2017; "Ex-Cards Scouting Director Chris Correa Sentenced to Prison for Hacking Astros," espn.com/mlb/story/_/id/17101079/chris-correa-former-st-louis -cardinals-scouting-director-sentenced-jail-hacking-houston-astros, July 19, 2016; David Barron and Jake Kaplan, "As MLB Ruling Nears, New Details of

Cardinals' Hacking of Astros Account," chron.com/sports/astros/article/As
-mlb-ruling-nears-new-details-of-Cardinals-10891605.php, January 28, 2017.

18. Ben Reiter, "Exclusive: Astros GM Jeff Luhnow Speaks Out about Hacking
Scandal," si.com/mlb/2015/06/18/jeff-luhnow-cardinals-astros-hacking
-scandal, June 18, 2015.

19. Barb Darrow, "Live from Fenway Park, a Behind-the-Scenes Look at MLB
Statcast," fortune.com/2015/09/04/mlb-statcast-data, September 4, 2015.

20. See Fangraphs, fangraphs.com/leaders.aspx?pos=all&stats=bat&lg=all&qual
=0&type=4&season=2017&month=0&season1=1901&ind=0&team=0,ss&rost
=0&age=0&filter=&players=0&sort=3,d.

21. Peter Gammons, "Draft Helped Remake Red Sox," *Baseball America*, July 1–
15, 2016.

22. Michael Lananna, "Under Bavasi Scouting Bureau Will Restructure," *Baseball America*, February 12–16, 2016.

23. Peter Gammons, "Chip on Sculpted Shoulder, Bautista Flips Away Doubts,"
Baseball America, March 25–April 8, 2016; John Manuel, "Changes Likely
After Playoff Run," *Baseball America*, November 4–18, 2016.

24. Casey Tefertiller, "A's Tap Sprague for Analytics," *Baseball America*, February 14–March 10, 2017.

25. Tom Haudricourt, "Brewers Stay Clear of Shuffle," *Baseball America*, March
10–24, 2017.

26. Bill Plunkett, "Pitching Department Is Born," *Baseball America*, March
24–April 7, 2017.

27. Ben Lindbergh and Rob Arthur, "Statheads Are the Best Free Agent Bargains in Baseball," fivethirtyeight.com/features/statheads-are-the-best
-free-agent-bargains-in-baseball, April 26, 2016.

28. John Rosengren, "The Smartest Man in Baseball," *City Pages*, July 5–11,
2017.

29. Andrew Marchand, "Will Jean Afterman Be Baseball's First Female GM?
The Sport Should Be So Lucky," http://www.espn.com/mlb/story/_/id
/19103117/will-new-york-yankees-jean-afterman-baseball-first-female
-gm-sport-lucky, April 12, 2017; Gordon Edes, "Raquel Ferreira, Earning
Her Respect," medium.com/@gedes/raquel-ferreira-earning-her-respect
-d9f663e4dcbc.

INDEX

Illustrations are indexed by figure number.

Aaron, Henry, 136, 138
Abell, Gus, 12
Abreu, Bobby, 364
Adair, Jerry, 172, 173, 182, 192
Adams, Babe, 26
Adams, Hank, 383, 384
Adams, Matt, 393
advance scouts, 207
advantages of successful teams, xiv–xvi
Affeldt, Jeremy, 380
African American players: Cardinals and, 138–42, 146, 149–50, 159–60, 417n1; Dodgers and, 102, 104–5, 108; integration into Major Leagues, 135–39; Red Sox and, 164, 169, 174; Tigers and, 175; Yankees and, 130–31, 237. *See also specific players*
agency, free. *See* free agency
Ainge, Danny, 310
Alderson, Sandy, 330–31, 358
Alexander, Charles, 45
Alexander, Cliff, 114
Alexander, Doyle, 191, 195, 291, 292, 315, 316, 321–22
Allen, Johnny, 85, 101
Allen, Lee, 3
Alomar, Roberto: with Blue Jays, 327, 329, 330, 331; with Orioles, 334, 336, 337, 338
Alomar, Sandy, 284, 288
Alou, Felipe, 242, 243, 244
Alou, Matty, 243, 244

Alston, Tom, 142
Alston, Walter, 104, 106, 118
Altman, George, 152, 155
Amaro, Ruben, 236
Amaro, Ruben, Jr., 362
amateur draft. *See* draft, amateur
American Association, 4, 5, 71, 200. *See also specific teams of*
American League: expansion of, 62, 249, 300, 307; general managers in, 59, 60; integration and, 138; post–World War II, 125; profits distribution in, 66; start-up of in majors, 18, 20–21, 22–24; team attendance in, 20, 164. *See also specific teams of*
Americans, Boston, 25, 32
Amoros, Sandy, 106–7, 108, 110
Anaheim Angels. *See* Angels, Anaheim
analytics. *See* statistical analysis
Anderson, Brady, 334, 335
Anderson, Sparky: about, 213; with Dodgers, 114, 213; with Reds, 198–99, 206, 213–14, 216–18, 223, 225–27
Andrews, James, 359
Andrews, Mike, 170–71, 192
Angelos, Peter, 332–34, 335, 336, 337, 338–39, 392
Angels, Anaheim, 368
Angels, California, 214–15, 289, 293–94
Angels, Los Angeles, 188, 189, 252, 253, 255, 397
Anheuser-Busch, 140–41, 391

Aparicio, Luis, 184

Arbuckle, Mike, 362

Armstrong, Chuck, 339, 342, 349

Ash, Gordon, 323, 330–31

Asia, as a source for players, 139, 344, 355, 368

Astrodome, 219

Astros, Houston, 218–20, 281, 305–6, 359, 394

Athletics, Kansas City, 130, 191, 249, 275

Athletics, Oakland: in the 1960s, 221–22; in the 1970s, 191, 220–21, 263, 275, 282–83, 291–92; in the 2000s, 352, 354, 356, 396–97; statistical analysis and, 352, 354–57, 356, 396

Athletics, Philadelphia, 58, 72, 78

Atlanta Braves. *See* Braves, Atlanta

Auten, Phil, 18

Autry, Gene, 249

Baer, Larry, *fig. 30*, 338–39, 369, 378–79, 381

Bahnsen, Stan, 241, 242

Bailor, Bob, 308

Baker, Frank, 64

Baker, William, 40, 44

Ball, Phil, 54, 56

Ball Four (Bouton), 236

Baltimore Browns, 141

Baltimore Orioles. *See* Orioles, Baltimore

Bancroft, Dave, 40, 43, 48

Bando, Sal, 191, 222

Banks, Ernie, 136, 138, 144

Barber, Red, 98, 99, 238

Barber, Steve, 182, 184, 185

Barfield, Jesse, 311, 314, 315, 316, 323, 324

Barnes, Jesse, 36, 39, 40, 48

Barnes, Virgil, 49

Barr, John, 377

Barrow, Ed, *fig. 6*; about, 6, 57; with Minor League teams, 6, 9–10; with

Red Sox, 57; with Tigers, 55; with Yankees, 57, 66–69, 80–87, 89, 92–93, 120–21, 356

Baseball Academy. *See* Kansas City Baseball Academy

Baseball America: Executive of the Year Awards of, 404; farm system rankings of, 334, 338, 341, 350; Organization of the Year Awards of, 405–6

Baseball Digest, 128

Baseball Magazine, 20

Bauer, Hank, 129, 184, 186

Bavasi, Buzzie, *figs. 7, 9*; about, 104; with Brooklyn Dodgers, 97–98, 103–7, 110–12; with Dodger farm clubs, 104–5; on Frank Lane, 143; with Los Angeles Dodgers, 97–98, 115–18, 239; with Padres, 275–76, 301; Peter Bavasi and, 301–2

Bavasi, Peter, *fig. 27*; about, 119, 301–2; with Blue Jays, 302–4, 306–7, 308–11, 313; with Indians, 371; with Padres, 301–2; on team operations, 274, 328, 371

Baylor, Don, 195, 280, 293

Beane, Billy, *fig. 29*; 352, 354–57, 385, 386, 396–97, 399

Bears, Denver, 199–201

Bears Stadium, 199, 201

Beauchamp, Jim, 208–9

Beaumont, Clarence "Ginger," 15, 16, 17, 19, 22, 24

Beene, Fred, 284

Beeston, Paul, 300, 302, 303, 311, 313, 323, 328–29

Bell, David, 347, 368

Bell, Gary, 172, 192

Bell, George, 310, 315, 316, 322–24, 326–27

Belt, Brandon, 382

Bench, Johnny: draft and, 189; in farm system, 208, 210; with Reds, 211, 213, 215, 217, 220, 228

Bender, Sheldon "Chief," 202, 205, 217, 225

Benswanger, William, 28

Bentley, Jack, 48

Bergesch, Bill, 314

Berra, Yogi, 128, 129, 138, 234, 235

Big League, 5–6

Big Red Machine nickname, 213, 215, 227

Billingham, Jack, 115, 219, 220, 224, 227

Birnbaum, Phil, 349

Black, Joe, 106

black players. *See* African American players

Blomberg, Ron, 241–42, 286

Bloomberg Sports, 359

Blue, Vida, 191, 280, 291–92

Blue Jays, Toronto: overview of, 398; under Pat Gillick (1982–85), 313–18, 321, 326; under Pat Gillick (1986–90), 321–26; under Pat Gillick (1991–94), 327–32; under Peter Bavasi, 308–13; startup of, 300–301, 302–4, 306–7

Blues, Kansas City, 200

Bochy, Bruce, 380, 382

Bonds, Barry, 368–69

Bonds, Bobby, 285, 286, 288–89

Bonilla, Bobby, 334, 335, 336

bonus players, 109–11, 164, 180–81, 188–89

Boone, Bret, 345, 346, 349

Booth, Clark, 174

Boras, Scott, 345

Borbon, Pedro, 214–15

Borders, Pat, 326

Bordick, Mike, 336

Borowy, Hank, 122, 416n2

Boston Americans, 25, 32

Boston Braves. *See* Braves, Boston

Boston Globe, 388–89

Boston Red Sox. *See* Red Sox, Boston

Bourjos, Peter, 395

Bourn, Michael, 365, 367

Bouton, Jim, 234, 236, 240, 265

Bowen, Joe, 206, 217

Bowen, Rex, 206–7, 217

Bowie, Robert R., xiii–xiv

Boyer, Clete, 234, 240

Boyer, Ken, 143, 145, 148, 151, 153, 159, 161, 203–4

Boys of Summer, 105

Bradley, Alva, 58

Brandon, Darrell, 169, 171–72, 173

Bransfield, Kitty, 18, 19

Braves, Atlanta, 160–61, 290, 317–18, 329

Braves, Boston, 36, 38, 47, 84, 127

Braves, Milwaukee, 138

Breadon, Sam, 57–58, 75–76, 100, 101

Brett, George, 267, 269, 272–73

Brett, Ken, 193, 288–89, 292

Briggs, Spike, 175

Briggs, Walter, 175, 401

Bristol, Dave, 207, 209, 210, 211, 213

Broaca, Johnny, 85

Brock, Lou, 156, 159

Broeg, Bob, 158

Broglio, Ernie, 147, 149, 150, 153, 154, 156

Broncos, Denver, 201

Brooklyn Dodgers. *See* Dodgers, Brooklyn

Brown, Bob, 182

Brown, Gates, 177, 178, 197

Brown, Joe, 263, 288–89

Brown, Kevin, 333, 334

Brown, Warren, 59

Browns, Baltimore, 141

Browns, St. Louis, 12, 54, 56, 141, 162, 391

Brush, John, 6, 21–22, 23–24, 29, 32, 33, 35

Buchholz, Clay, 387

Buford, Don, 186, 194, 305

Bumgarner, Madison, 377, 380

Bunker, Wally, 183, 184, 185–86, 261

Bunning, Jim, 175

Burdette, Lew, 153, 154

Burke, Joe, 268, 269–70, 287–88

Burke, Mike, *fig. 19*, 233, 237–41, 244–48, 290

Burkett, Jesse, 12, 46

Burkett, John, 335

Burnitz, Jeromy, 335

Burns, George, 43, 45

Burns, Harlan, 369

Burrell, Pat, 363, 365, 380

Busby, Steve, 267, 269–70

Busch, August "Gussie," Jr., *fig. 12*; about, 140; as Cardinals owner, 140–44, 146–47, 150–52, 157–60, 201, 204, 417n1

Busch Stadium, 141, 203

Buskey, Tom, 284, 312

Butler, Bill, 196, 261

Byrne, Tommy, 130

Cabrera, Melky, 382

Cain, Matt, 377, 378, 379

California Angels. *See* Angels, California

Camacho, Ernie, 371

Cameron, Mike, 343, 344, 347, 389

Camilli, Dolph, 99, 101

Campanella, Roy, 102, 104, 105, 107, 138

Campanis, Al, *fig. 8*, 106, 107–12, 117, 118, 191

Campanis, Jim, 119

Campbell, Jim, *fig. 14*, 175–79, 197, 402

Campusano, Sil, 323, 324

Candiotti, Tom, 327

Cannon, Jimmy, 241

Caray, Harry, 140, 157, 158

Carbo, Bernie, 194, 214, 215, 217

Cardenas, Leo, 212

Cardinals, St. Louis: about and overview of, xiii, 100, 385, 391–92, 396; under Bing Devine (1957–1961), 144, 145–50; under Bing Devine (1962–1964), 150–59; under Bob Howsam, 158–60, 161, 201–5; under Branch Rickey, 56–59, 74–76, 78, 98–101, 391; farming system of, 74, 75–76, 78, 98, 99, 100, 393; under Frank Lane, 143–45; under John Mozeliak, 393–95; player integration and, 138–39, 140–42, 146, 159–60, 417n1; under Walt Jocketty, 392–93

Cardinal Way (concept), 394–95

The Cardinal Way (handbook), 394

Carey, Max, 27, 28

Carmine, 388

Carroll, Clay, 210, 211, 215, 220

Carroll, Parke, 130

Carter, Joe, 327, 329, 337

Carty, Rico, 308

Cash, Norm, 177, 178, 196, 197, 391

Cashen, Frank, 185, 195–96, 301, 402

Casilla, Santiago, 380, 382

Cater, Danny, 194, 243

Caudill, Bill, 315, 316

Causey, Wayne, 181

CBS (Columbia Broadcasting System), 235, 237, 238, 245–46, 247

Cedeno, Cesar, 219, 305–6

Celler, Emanuel, 132

Cepeda, Orlando, 148, 161, 204, 372

Cerone, Rick, 308

Chambliss, Chris, 270, 284, 291, 292, 295, 298

Chance, Dean, 183

Chandler, Alfred, 53, 54

Chandler, Happy, 123, 131

Chaney, Darrel, 212

Charlton, Norm, 337–38, 340

Chase, Hal, 37–38

Chavez, Eric, 354, 396

Cheek, Tom, 313, 315, 322

Cherington, Ben, *fig. 31*, 387, 390–91, 404

Chesbro, Jack, 15, 16, 17, 19, 20, 22–23

Chicago Cubs. *See* Cubs, Chicago

Chicago White Sox. *See* White Sox, Chicago

Cimoli, Gino, 115, 147

Cincinnati Reds. *See* Reds, Cincinnati

Clancy, Jim, 307–8, 316

Clarke, Fred, 28: Barney Dreyfuss and, 5, 6; with Colonels, 7–8, 9, 10, 12, 13, 14, 16; on John McGraw, 30; with Modocs, 6–7; with Pirates, 15, 17, 19–20, 24, 26

Clemens, Doug, 155, 156

Clemente, Roberto, 110–11, 136, 415n22

Cleveland Indians. *See* Indians, Cleveland

Cleveland Pipers. *See* Pipers, Cleveland

Cleveland Spiders. *See* Spiders, Cleveland

Click, James, 358–59

clinics, baseball, 108, 110, 251–52

Cloninger, Tony, 210, 211, 213, 215

Coase, Robert, theorem, 65

Cochrane, Mickey, 84

Colavito, Rocky, 177, 391

Colborn, Jim, 344–45

Coleman, Jerry, 236

Coleman, Ken, 163

collective bargaining agreements, 276, 277, 280, 387

Collins, Dave, 314, 315

Collins, Eddie, 59, 165

Collins, Jimmy, 8

Colonels, Louisville, 4–8, 10–11, 12–16

Colorado Rockies. *See* Rockies, Colorado

Columbia Broadcasting System (CBS), 235, 237, 238, 245–46, 247

Columbus Redbirds. *See* Redbirds, Columbus

Combs, Earle, 68, 90

Comiskey, Charles, 51, 54, 83, 406

Concepcion, Dave, 215, 216, 227, 228

Cone, David, 329

Conigliaro, Tony, 166, 171, 172, 173–74, 192

Connery, Bob, 81, 414n3

Conte, Stan, 378

Continental League, 201

contract status, 278

Cook, Earnshaw, 256

Cooper, Cecil, 192–94

Coors Field, 353

corporate structure of baseball teams, 237, 328, 371–74

Corrales, Pat, 210, 371

Cox, Billy, 103

Cox, Bobby, 287, 312–18, 321

Craig, Allen, 393

Craig, Roger, 113, 114, 155

Crasnick, Jerry, 377

Crawford, Brandon, 382

Crawford, Carl, 389, 390

Cromie, Adam, 361

Cronin, Joe, 27–28, 80, 164, 283

Crosetti, Frank, 68, 85, 89

Crosley, Powel, 98, 281

Crowe, George, 147, 148

Cubs, Chicago: about, 133, 156, 346; statistical analysis and, 359; under William and Phil Wrigley, 54, 56–57, 59; in World Series, 82, 88

Culver, George, 209

Cunningham, Joe, 147, 148

Cuyler, Kiki, 27, 28

Cy Young Awards, 294, 298, 377

Dahlgren, Babe, 87, 89

Dal Canton, Bruce, 263

Dale, Francis, 204–5, 219, 229, 392

Dalton, Harry, *fig.* 15, 179–83, 185–87, 194–95, 293–94, 402

Dalton Gang, 182

Daniel, Dan, 125

Daniels, Bennie, 149

Daniels, Jon, 367–68, 404

Davis, Curt, 100, 101

Davis, Eric, 336, 337

Davis, Lefty, 19, 22

Davis, Tommy, 111, 115–16

Davis, Willie, 113, 116

Dedeaux, Rod, 305

Demaree, Allan, 250

Demeter, Don, 168–69, 172, 177

Dempsey, Rick, 291

Dent, Bucky, 294–95

Denver Bears. *See* Bears, Denver

Denver Broncos. *See* Broncos, Denver

DePodesta, Paul, 352, 354–55

Devery, William, 63

Devine, Bing, *fig. 13*; about, 144; with
    Cardinals, 144–47, 149–53, 155–60,
    161, 201–2, 402; with Mets, 160–61

Devine, Joe, 27–28, 86

DeViveiros, Bernie, 177

Devlin, Art, 39

DeWitt, Bill, Jr., 332, 391, 392–94, 396

DeWitt, Bill, Sr., 127, 175, 177, 204,
    281, 391–92, 401

Dickey, Bill, 69, 85, 86, 89, 122

DiMaggio, Joe, 86, 87–88, 89–90

DiMaggio, Vince, 127

disabled lists, 378

Dobson, Pat, 178, 194, 246, 267, 284,
    311, 336

Dodgers, Brooklyn: bonuses and,
    109–11; under Branch Rickey, 97–
    98, 99, 100, 101–3, 104–5, 107–8;
    under Buzzie Bavasi, 97–98, 103–
    4, 105–7; integration and, 135, 138;
    under Larry MacPhail, 99–100,
    101–2, 103; overview of, 12, 97–98,
    118–19, 401; scouting and, 108,
    110, 111–15, 191

Dodgers, Los Angeles, 405; under
    Buzzie Bavasi, 97–98, 107, 110–18,
    402; draft and, 191; scouting and, 128

Dodger Stadium, 116, 118

The Dodgers' Way to Play Baseball
    (Campanis), 108–9

Dodgertown, 107–8

Dodger Way, 107–9, 114, 118–19

Doheny, Ed, 20, 22, 24

Dombrowski, Dave, 233, 335, 404

Dominican Republic: scouting from,
    xvi, 305, 309, 315, 368, 393

Donald, Alty, 87

Donovan, Bill, 57, 64, 126

Donovan, Patsy, 15

Double A circuits of Minor Leagues,
    71–72, 355

Douglas, Phil, 38–39, 40, 45, 46–47

Downing, Al, 234, 241

Doyle, Larry, 33, 36, 43

Drabek, Doug, 337–38

draft, amateur, 188–97; about, 188–
    91, 355, 387, 399; Athletics and,
    221–22, 396–97; Blue Jays and, 311,
    331; Cardinals and, 392–93, 394; Gi-
    ants and, 374–75, 377; Orioles and,
    194–96; Red Sox and, 192–94, 387;
    Royals and, 254–55, 257; Tigers
    and, 196–97; Yankees and, 241–42

draft, minor league, 70–73. *See also*
    Rule 5 Draft

Draft, Rule 5. *See* Rule 5 Draft

drafts, expansion, 222, 255, 307–8

Drago, Dick, 261, 263–64

Drebinger, John, 59

Dressen, Charlie, 106, 178

Dreyfuss, Barney, *fig.1*; about, xvii, 3–
    4, 28, 406; with Colonels, 4–11, 12–
    15; John McGraw and, 29; with Pi-
    rates, 14–15, 18–21, 22–28, 72, 75

Dreyfuss, Sam, 28

Driessen, Dan, 223–24, 226, 227

Drucker, Peter, 55, 80, 371

Drysdale, Don, 111, 115, 117–18

Duffy, Frank, 216–17

Duffy, George, 45

Dugan, Joe, 44, 65, 90
Durocher, Leo, 99, 158

Eastern League, 126
Ebbets, Charlie, 12, 99
Ebbets Field, 99
Eckert, William, 160–61, 184, 238
Economist, 352
Edwards, Johnny, 210
Ehlers, Arthur, 182
Ehret, Red, 10
Eichhorn, Mark, 333
Eliot, John, 358–59
Ellis, Dock, 289, 291, 295, 296
Ellis, John, 339, 342
Ellsbury, Jacoby, 387
Ely, Bones, 16, 19
English, Gil, 127
Ennis, Del, 143–44, 147
Epstein, Theo, 188, 353, 359, 386–90, 404
Erickson, Scott, 334, 337
Essick, Bill, 68, 86, 87
Etchebarren, Andy, 183, 185
Evans, Billy, 58
Evans, Bobby, 377, 384
Evans, Darrell, 191
Executive of the Year Awards, 200, 252, 401–4
Exhibition Stadium, 308

Fairly, Ron, 114, 116, 305
Fall Instructional League, 129
Falls, Joe, 239
Farley, James, 121
farm systems: Blue Jays and, 308, 312, 331; Cardinals and, 74, 75–76, 78, 98, 99, 100, 393; Dodgers and, 98, 100–102, 104–5, 109; Giants and, 376–77; Mariners and, 341, 346, 350; origination and evolution of, 56, 58, 74–79, 399; Orioles and, 179–80, 182–83, 185, 333, 334, 338, 339; Reds and, 205–6, 208, 227; Red Sox and,
166, 390–91; Royals and, 259, 260; Tigers and, 197; Yankees (1920s–1930s) and, 68, 77–78, 81, 83, 85–87, 91, 126; Yankees (1950s–1970s) and, 77–78, 126, 128–29, 234, 239, 242
Farrell, Frank, 63
Farrell, John, *fig. 31*, 390
Federal League, 40, 54, 64, 74
Feeney, Chub, 118
Felix, Junior, 324, 327
Fenway Park, 64–65, 386
Fernandez, Chico, 108, 175
Fernandez, Tony, 315, 316, 323, 327, 330, 331
Ferrell, Rick, 175
Fetter, Henry, 76
Fetzer, John, 175–76
FIELDf/x, 383
field managers, about, 55, 57
Figueroa, Ed, 289, 291, 292, 295, 298
Fingers, Rollie, 222, 280, 291
Finley, Charlie, 188, 221–22, 275, 280, 282–83, 291–92
first-year player draft. *See* draft, amateur
Fleischmann family, 53
Flood, Curt, 146–47, 148, 149, 151, 153, 159, 274
Florida Marlins, 385
Fontaine, Bob, 303–4
Forbes Field, 26–27
Ford, Whitey, 128, 129, 138, 234, 235, 240
Fortune, 250
Foss, Joe, 333, 335, 338
Foster, George, 216–17, 226–27
Foy, Joe: with Red Sox, 167–68, 170, 171, 173, 192; with Royals, 255, 262
Francona, Terry, 357, 388, 389, 390
Franklin, Pete, 299
Frazee, Harry, 64–65, 69, 90
free agency: about, 65, 274–80, 316, 399; Blue Jays and, 327–28, 329;

free agency (*continued*)
    expansion draft and, 307–8; first
    year signing of, 292–94; Mariners
    and, 342–43, 344, 346–48, 350; Ori-
    oles and, 337; Phillies and, 364–66;
    Red Sox and, 387–88; Yankees and,
    291–94
Freedman, Andrew, 6, 11, 12, 21, 23, 32
Freehan, Bill, 177, 178, 197
Frick, Ford, 103, 104
Frick, Fred, 104
Frisch, Frankie, 39, 43, 45, 48, 49
front offices: analysis revolution and,
    353, 356, 383, 395; evolution of, 4,
    55, 57, 59, 328, 371–76, 398–99; im-
    portance of efficient, xvi–xvii
Fuchs, Judge Emil, 84
Fuson, Grady, 396, 397
Futterman, Matthew, 383

Gallagher, Jim, 416n2
Gamble, Oscar, 294
game fixing, 41, 46–47
Gammons, Peter, 174
Garcia, Damaso, 308, 312, 322
Garcia, Freddie, 341–42, 344, 346, 347,
    367
Gardner, Rob, 243
Gaston, Cito, 325
Gehrig, Lou, 67, 69, 85, 86, 89
Geishert, Vern, 214–15, 216–17
general manager (GM) position, 53–
    61; origination of, xv, 53–61; role
    and duties of, xvii, 30, 55, 60–61,
    328
general superintendents position,
    53–54
Gentile, Jim, 184
Geronimo, Cesar, 219, 220, 223, 227,
    228
Giants, New York: integration and,
    138, 142; under John McGraw
    (1901–1919), 26, 29–30, 32–40, 50;

under John McGraw (1920–1932),
    40–51, 66; ownership of, 23, 30, 35–
    36, 58–59; in playoffs with Dodg-
    ers, 106, 116, 117; trades of, 11, 26,
    147–48, 184, 217; 1936 World Series
    and, 86
Giants, San Francisco: under general
    manager Brian Sabean, 368–69,
    377–82; Latino players and, 317;
    under managing general partner
    William Neukom, 369, 370–72, 374–
    81, 382–84; operations evolution
    of, 338–39, 372–74; trades of, 285
Giants Way, 374–77
Gibson, Bob, 148, 149–50, 153, 154–57,
    159–60
Gibson, George, 26
Giles, Bill, 301, 362
Giles, Warren, *fig. 12*, 98, 239, 281,
    401, 406
Gilhousen, Rosie, 268
Gilliam, Jim, 106, 115
Gillick, Pat, *fig. 28*; about, xvi, 304–6,
    321, 332, 339, 351, 398; as Blue Jays
    executive president (1982–1990),
    313–18, 320–26; as Blue Jays execu-
    tive president (1991–1994), 327–32;
    as Blue Jays vice president of op-
    erations, 310–13; as Blue Jays vice
    president of player personnel, 303–
    4, 306–7, 308–10; with Mariners,
    339, 342–50, 354; with Orioles,
    332, 334–39; with Phillies, 362–68;
    quotes of, 93, 140; statistical analy-
    sis and, 354–55, 368; with Yankees,
    287, 288–89, 303–4, 306
Girsch, Michael, 395
Goldfarb, Yeshayah, 378–79
Gomez, Lefty, 68, 85, 86, 87, 90
Gonzalez, Adrian, 389, 390
Gordon, Alison, 311–12
Gordon, Joe: as manager, 254, 261–62,
    265; as player, 87, 88, 91, 123

Gorman, Lou, *fig. 24*, 253–56, 258–59, 263, 265, 268

Gotay, Julio, 152

Gott, Jim, 310, 316

Graham, Charley, 86

Graham, Charley, Jr., 370

Graham, Frank, 30

Grammas, Alex, 147, 215, 220

Granger, Wayne, 212, 220

Grant, George Washington, 36

Greason, Bill, 142

Greenberg, Hank, 69

Grich, Bobby, 256, 292–94

Griffey, Ken, 224, 226–27

Griffey, Ken, Jr., 339, 340, 341–42, 343, 344, 366

Griffin, Alfredo, 308, 312, 314, 315

Griffith, Clark, 58, 80–81, 401

Grimes, Burleigh, 51

Grimsley, Ross, 196, 224, 225–26

Groat, Dick, 152–54, 157, 159, 161, 203–4, 206

Groh, Heinie, 43–44, 45–46, 50

Grove, Andrew S., xv

Grove, Lefty, 72, 83

Gruber, Kelly, 310, 322, 323, 326

Guerrero, Epy, 305–6, 309, 315, 398

Guidry, Ron, 242, 295, 298, 309

Guillen, Carlos, 341, 345, 347

Gulf Coast League, 258, 259

Gullett, Don: with Reds, 215, 217, 227, 228, 280; with Yankees, 293, 295, 298

Gura, Larry, 270, 284

Guzman, Juan, 327, 329, 330

Hairston, Jerry, 338

Halama, John, 341–42

Halberstam, David, 149

Hall of Famer owners and managers, 406–7

Hamels, Cole, 364, 365, 366

Hamey, Roy, 234

Hamilton, Josh, 390

Haney, Fred, 252, 402

Hanlon, Ned, 12, 31, 33

Hardy, Peter, 313

Harper, Tommy, 193, 209

Harrah, Toby, 256

Harrelson, Ken, 172, 193, 275

Harris, Luman, 182

Harrris, Bucky, 122, 131–32, 165

Hart, James, 6, 14

Hart, Jim Ray, 266–67

Hartsfield, Roy, 307, 311–12

Harwell, Ernie, 179

Healy, Fran, 270, 272

Helms, Tommy, 208, 219, 220

Hemond, Roland, 332–34, 402, 403

Hempstead, Harry, 35–36

Hemus, Solly, 147, 148–50, 159

Henderson, Rickey, 330–31

Hendricks, Elrod, 186, 291

Henke, Tom, 316, 325, 326–27

Henrich, Tommy, 87, 88, 90, 91

Henry, John W., 353, 357, 385–86, 388, 390

Herman, Billy, 106, 166, 167–69

Herrmann, Garry, *fig. 1*, 23–24, 44, 53

Hershberger, Willard, 127

Hertz, John, 120

Herzog, Whitey, 270, 300, 315

Heydler, John A., 28, 37–38

Higbe, Kirby, 100, 251

Higgins, Mike, 165–66

Highlanders, New York, 62

Hiller, John, 177, 178, 197

Hirschbeck, John, 336

Hitchcock, Billy, 183–84

Hodges, Gil, 103, 105, 114, 115, 142–43, 161, 283

Hoffberger, Jerry, 184–85

Holland, John, 156

Holtzman, Ken, 280, 291, 292

Hopkins, Brian, 393

Hornsby, Rogers, *fig. 4*, 51

Horton, Tony, 167, 168, 170, 171, 172

Horton, Willie, 177, 178, 197

Houk, Ralph, 200, 234–36, 238, 244, 247–48, 282–83

Houston Astros, 218–20, 281, 305–6, 359, 394

Howard, Elston, 130, 138, 172, 235, 237, 240, 282

Howard, Frank, 114, 115–16

Howard, Ryan, 363, 364

Howsam, Bob, *fig. 17*; about, xv, 199, 228, 257, 392; with Cardinals, 157, 158, 159, 161, 201–4; free agency and, 226, 228, 276, 280, 402; quote of, 120; with Reds (1967–1968), 204–13; with Reds (1969–1972), 198–99, 213–21, 222–23, 265–66; with Reds (1973–1977), 223–28, 280; with Reds (1983–1985), 228–29; Western League and, 199–201

Howser, Dick, 298

Hoy, Dummy, 10

Hubbell, Carl, 50

Huff, Aubrey, 380

Huggins, Miller, *fig. 5*, 57, 64, 66–67, 82, 93

Hunter, Bob, *fig. 7*

Hunter, Jim "Catfish," 222, 275–76, 285–86, 291, 295

Huston, Tillinghast L'Hommedieu, 54, 57, 62, 63–64, 66–67

Hutchinson, Fred, 145, 147

Iglehart, Joe, 181

The Impossible Dream Remembered (Coleman and Valenti), 163

Indians, Cleveland: about, 132–33, 138, 245, 281, 299, 337, 346, 371; trades of, 58, 87, 99, 123, 172, 308

inflection points, xv–xvi, 382, 399

information, importance of when team constructing, xiii–xiv

injury-prevention, 359, 378, 383

Inside Edge, 359

integration of players, 135–39; Cardinals and, 138–39, 140–42, 146, 150, 159–60, 417n1; Dodgers and, 102, 138; Major Leagues and, 130, 135–39, 164; Tigers and, 175; Yankees and, 130–31

International League, 43, 71, 72. *See also specific teams of*

Jackson, Larry, 147, 149, 150, 151–52

Jackson, Mike, 340

Jackson, Reggie, 191, 222, 280, 294–98

Jackson, Travis, 35, 48, 49

Jacobs, Eli, 332

Jacobson, Steve, 282

James, Bill, 352–53, 386

James, Charlie, 155

Japan, players from, 343, 344–45, 348, 368

Japanese Pacific League, 344

Javier, Julian, 151, 153

Javier, Stan, 344, 347

Jaworski, Leon, 285

Jocketty, Walt, 392–93, 403, 404

Johnson, Alex, 211, 213, 214

Johnson, Arnold, 130

Johnson, Ban, 21, 22–23, 31, 32, 54, 72

Johnson, Bob, 210, 211, 262, 263, 272

Johnson, Cliff, 314, 316, 321

Johnson, Davey, 185, 332, 334, 336, 337, 339

Johnson, Deron, 208–9, 266–67

Johnson, Ed, 199

Johnson, Johnny, 236

Johnson, Mike, 223

Johnson, Randy, 330, 331, 339, 340, 341–42

Jones, Fielder, 56

Jones, Mack, 208, 209

Jones, Sam, 65, 90, 147, 148

Jongewaard, Roger, 354

Kalas, Harry, 218

Kaline, Al, 111, 175, 177, 178, 196, 197

Kalk, Josh, 358–59

Kamieniecki, Scott, 337

Kansas City Athletics. *See* Athletics, Kansas City

Kansas City Baseball Academy, 257–61, 264–65, 269, 272–73

Kansas City Blues, 200

Kansas City Royals. *See* Royals, Kansas City

Kapstein, Jerry, 293–94

Karsay, Steve, 330–31

Kasko, Eddie, 167, 193

Katalinas, Ed, 177

Kauff, Benny, 40–41

Kauffman, Ewing, *figs. 21, 23*; about, 249, 250; Peter Bavasi and, 303; as Royals owner, 249–51, 256–61, 263–65, 268–70, 271, 273

Keane, Johnny: with Cardinals, 144, 150–60; with Yankees, 160, 235, 236

Keener, Sid, 123

Keller, Charlie, 87, 90, 91, 92

Kelly, George, 35, 39–40, 43, 45, 49, 51

Kennedy, Brickyard, 24

Kent, Jeff, 329, 368

Keri, Jonah, 358–59

Kerr, William, 14, 18

Kerrane, Kevin, 101

Key, Jimmy, 315, 316, 321, 329, 336, 337

Kiddie Corps, 182

Kieran, John, 51, 58

Killilea, Henry J., 25

Kinsella, Dick, 37, 50

Kirby, Clay, 224–25, 226–27

Kittredge, Malachi, 13

Klein, Jeff, 328

Kline, Steve, 245, 284

Kluszewski, Ted, 214

Kluttz, Clyde, 282, 286

Knorr, Fred, 175

Koenig, Mark, 68, 81, 90, 91

Kolb, Gary, 155

Koppett, Leonard, 33–34

Koufax, Sandy, 108, 111, 115, 117–18

Krichell, Paul, 67–68, 69, 85, 87

Kroc, Ray, 302, 308

Kubek, Tony, 129, 234, 236

Kuhn, Bowie, 241, 277, 280, 285, 290, 291–92, 306

Labatt Breweries, 300–301, 302, 304

Lackey, John, 389, 390

LaMacchia, Al, 306, 323, 330

Lambs Club incident, 41–43

Landis, Kenesaw: Minor League draft and farming and, 72, 74–75, 77, 99; rulings of, 41, 44, 87, 88, 99; Yankees ownership and, 120

Lane, Frank, 143–45, 402

Lardner, John, 38

LaRussa, Tony, 392, 394

Lary, Lyn, 68, 76

Lasorda, Tommy, 114, 118

Latin America, scouting from, 108, 110, 137, 139, 305, 309, 317, 398

Latino players, 135–39, 309, 317, 331. *See also specific players*

Lau, Charlie, 269–70

Lavelle, Gary, 316

Lawrence, Brooks, 142

Laws, Brick, 251

Lawson, Chris, 339

Lawson, Earl, 205

Lazzeri, Tony, 68, 69, 80, 86, 90

Leach, Tommie, 11, 13–15, 16, 19, 22–23, 24

Leavy, Jane, 236

Lee, Manny, 317, 323, 327

Leever, Sam, 15, 16, 20, 24–25

LeFevre, Dave, 299

Leishman, Edwin, 301

Lemon, Bob, 263, 264

Levine, Thad, 353

Lewis, Johnny, 155

Lewis, Michael, 352–57, 362, 379

Lewis, Peter H., 383
Lidge, Brad, 365, 367
Lieb, Fred, 4, 7, 26, 28
Lincecum, Tim, 377, 379, 382
Lincoln, Howard, 339, 342, 348, 349
Lindsay, John, 244
Lindstrom, Fred, 35, 48, 49, 50
Linn, Ed, 282, 298
Locklear, Gene, 223
Lolich, Mickey, 177, 178, 179, 197
Lonborg, Jim, 169, 171–72, 173, 174, 175, 192–93
Loney, James, 390
Lopat, Eddie, 129, 234
Los Angeles Angels. See Angels, Los Angeles
Los Angeles Coliseum, 115
Los Angeles Dodgers. See Dodgers, Los Angeles
Louisville Colonels, 4–8, 10–11, 12–16
Lucchino, Larry, 333, 385–86, 390
Luhnow, Jeff, 359, 392–94
Lyle, Sparky, 194, 243, 245, 284, 295–96, 298
Lynn, Lance, 393

MacFayden, Danny, 83
Mack, Connie, 17, 57, 58, 64, 83
Mack, Jones, 208–9
MacPhail, Bill, fig. 18
MacPhail, Larry, figs. 10, 11, 18; about, 98, 406; Bob Howsam and, 200; Dodgers and, 97–100, 101–2, 104, 401; Yankees and, 120–25, 416n2
MacPhail, Lee, fig. 18; about, 127, 238, 406; free agency and, 275; with Orioles, 181–82, 183–85; with Yankees as farm director, 129, 131, 200; with Yankees as general manager, 233, 238–39, 240, 241–45, 246–48
Madden, Bill, 393
Maddox, Elliot, 196, 283, 284, 286
Madison Square Garden, 246

Maglie, Sal, 107
Magowan, Peter, 369
Major League Scouting Bureau, 269, 306
Malone, Kevin, 334, 338
Maloney, Jim, 208, 213
Malzone, Frank, 167
Manager of the Year Awards, 160, 337. See also Executive of the Year Awards
Mann, Les, 46
Mann Act, 37
Mantilla, Felix, 167
Mantle, Mickey, 128, 138, 234, 235–36, 240–41
Mariners, Seattle: as expansion team, 300, 307, 309; ownership of, 339; under Pat Gillick, 339, 342–50, 354; under Woody Woodward, 339–42
Marion Laboratories, 249, 250, 268
Maris, Roger, 161, 204, 234, 240
market, free. See free agency
Marlins, Florida, 385
Marquard, Rube, 27, 47
Marquez, Luis, 131
Marshall, Bill, 138
Martin, Billy, 287, 293, 294, 297–99, 309
Martin, Danny, 383
Martinez, Buck, 271, 314
Martinez, Edgar, 339, 341, 346
Martinez, Tino, 339, 340
Martinez, Tippy, 291
Matheny, Mike, 395
Mathewson, Christy, fig. 3, 32, 37–38
Matlack, Jon, 224, 262
Mattick, Bobby, 306, 310, 312, 330
Mauer, Joe, 279
May, Lee, 208, 211, 214, 218, 220
May, Rudy, 284, 291
Mayberry, John, 264, 267, 271, 272, 314
Mays, Willie, 144, 372, 373

McAuliffe, Dick, 177, 178
McCann, Gene, 87
McCarthy, Joe, *fig. 6*, 57, 68, 82–87, 88, 120, 122
McCarver, Tim, 153–55, 159
McCloskey, John, 7, 8
McClure's, 33
McDaniel, Lindy, 151–52, 242, 245, 268, 272, 283
McDonald, John, 124
McDougald, Gil, 129, 234
McDougall, Don, 300, 301, 328
McDowell, Sam, 247, 266–67
McFarlan, Claude, 9
McGinnity, Joe, 32
McGlothlin, Jim, 214–15, 223
McGraw, John, *figs. 2, 3*; about, 30–31; Barney Dreyfuss and, 29; farm systems and, 75; George Duffy and, 45; with Giants (1902–1919), 23, 26, 29–30, 32–33, 35–40; with Giants (1920–1924), 40–49; with Giants (1925 and on), 50–51; Lambs Club and James Slavin incident and, 41–43; management style and success of, xiv, 30, 33–35, 49–50, 52; with Orioles, 30–32; Phil Douglas and, 46–47; Yankees and, 63; young player development and, 34–35, 48, 49, 50
McGregor, Scott, 242, 291
McGriff, Fred, 314, 322–23, 325, 327
McHale, John, 175, 177, 402
McKeever, Ed, 99
McKeon, Jack, 264–65, 266–67, 269–70
McKinney, Rich, 242, 243
McLain, Denny, 177, 178, 179
McLaughlin, Jim, 179–80, 182, 206
McLemore, Mark, 344, 345
McMahon, Don, 169, 172
McMullen, Ken, 115, 262
McNally, Dave, 183, 185–86, 194, 274, 289

McQuinn, George, 87, 123
McRae, Hal, 214, 215, 216, 222–23, 265–67, 272
Medich, George "Doc," 242, 284, 288–89
Medwick, Joe, 100, 101
Mejdal, Sig, 393
Melvin, Bob, 350
Mercury (CA) News, 381
Merkle Boner, 34
Merritt, Jim, 212, 213, 217
Messersmith, Andy, 274, 289–90
Metro, Charlie, *fig. 24*; about, 213, 251; with Mounties, 251; with Reds, 208, 209; with Royals, 253–56, 258–59, 261, 262–63, 268
Mets, New York: Bing Devine and, 160–61; compared to Yankees, 239–40, 242–43, 290; league championships and World Series of, 224, 242; statistical analysis and, 358; trades with Cedric Tallis and, 262
Meusel, Irish, 44–45, 48
Meyer, Dick, 141, 143, 144, 146, 151, 204
Michael, Gene, 299, 353
Microsoft, 370
Mile High Stadium, 199
Milkes, Marvin, 250, 252, 255, 261
Miller, Eddie, 127
Miller, Marvin, 275–77
Miller, Ray, 336, 337–38
Miller, Shelby, 393, 395
Milwaukee Braves. *See* Braves, Milwaukee
Minnesota Twins. *See* Twins, Minnesota
Minor Leagues, draft and optional assignment from, 35, 67, 68–69, 70–73. *See also* farm systems
Minoso, Minnie, 143
Mitchell Report, 369
Mize, Johnny, 129–30, 234

Modern Baseball Strategy (Richards), 181

Molitor, Paul, 329–30

Monbouquette, Bill, 167

Monday, Rick, 191, 222

Mondry-Cohen, Samuel, 361

Moneyball (Lewis), 352–57, 362, 368, 379, 386, 393, 396

Montgomery, Dave, 362

Montgomery Minor League team, 7, 251

Montreal Royals. *See* Royals, Montreal

Moon, Wally, 115, 143, 147

Morehead, Dave, 165, 167, 169, 171

Morgan, Joe, 218–20, 226–27, 228, 280

Morris, Jack, 327, 329, 330, 331

Moseby, Lloyd, 311, 312, 314, 315, 316, 324

motion sensor suits, 383

Mounties, Vancouver, 251–52

Moyer, Jamie, 340, 342, 343, 364, 365, 366–67

Mozeliak, John, 393–94, 395

Mulliniks, Rance, 314, 322

Munson, Thurman, 242, 244, 247, 284, 291, 295–98

Murcer, Bobby, 241, 242, 244, 247, 284, 285

Murphy, Johnny, 69, 85–86, 87, 262, 402

Murray, Dale, 314

Murray, Eddie, 195, 335

Murray, Jim, 97, 105, 116

Murtaugh, Danny, 263

Musial, Stan: as general manager, 161; as player, 143, 144, 145, 147, 148, 151, 153

Mussina, Mike, 334, 337

Myer, Buddy, 80

Myers, Brett, 363, 365

Myers, Kenny, 113–14

Myers, Randy, 334, 337

National Agreement, 70–72

National Association, 70–71

National Association for the Advancement of Colored People (NAACP), 139

National Commission, 27, 73–74

National League: in the 1890s, 5, 11–12, 14–15; from 1900 to 1913, 18, 32–33; expansion of, 150, 249; general managers in, 59, 60; integration and, 138–39; threat of American League start-up and, 18, 21–24. *See also specific teams of*

Nationals, Washington, 360–61

Navin, Frank, 53, 55–56, 64, 75, 76, 84, 397

Nee, Johnny, 69, 87

Negro Leagues, 131, 139

Nehf, Art, 38–39, 45, 47

Nelson, Jeff, 340, 345

Nelson, Roger, 222, 223, 255, 261, 265

Nettles, Graig, 243–44, 247, 284, 291, 295, 296, 298

Neukom, Bill, *fig. 30*, xv, 369–71, 374–77, 378–81, 382

Neun, Johnny, 122

Newcombe, Don, 102, 104–5, 106, 107

New Haven team, 126

New York Giants. *See* Giants, New York

New York Highlanders. *See* Highlanders, New York

New York Mets. *See* Mets, New York

New York Times, 51, 133, 233, 383

New York Yankees. *See* Yankees, New York

Nightengale, Bob, 334

Nintendo, 339

Nippert, Louis, 229

no-farming rule, 73–74

Nolan, Gary, 208, 211, 215, 223, 224

Nordbrook, Tim, 293–94

Norman, Fred, 223, 224, 227

Northrup, Jim, 177, 178, 197

Oakland Athletics. *See* Athletics, Oakland

Oaks, Oakland, 76, 251

Oates, Johnny, 333

O'Connell, Dick, *fig. 16*; about, 165–66; with Red Sox, 163, 165–70, 172, 174, 192–94, 402

O'Connell, Jimmy, 46

O'Connor, Jack, 22

O'Connor, Leslie, 75

O'Dowd, Dan, 353, 403, 404

Oglivie, Ben, 192–94

Olerud, John, 326–27, 330, 331, 344

Oliver, Bob, 263

Oliver, Gene, 153

O'Malley, Peter, 118–19

O'Malley, Walter, *figs. 7, 9*; about, 119, 142–43; Buzzie Bavasi and Fresco Thompson and, 97, 103–4, 105, 112, 118; Dodgers move to Los Angeles and, 107; Dodgers ownership and, 103, 112, 117, 118; Dodgertown and, 107–8

Only the Paranoid Survive (Grove), xv

optional assignment, 73

Orenstein, Josh, 358

Organization of the Year Awards, 405–6

organizations, importance of building efficient, xvi–xvii

organized baseball defined, 70

Oriole Park, 333, 386

Orioles, Baltimore: from 1890s to 1920s, 12, 23, 30–31, 72, 126; from 1953 to 1968, 162, 171, 173, 179–87, 235, 238; in the 1970s, 291, 298; in the 1990s, 332–39, 341; attendance and, 333; biomechanical studies and, 359; draft and, 194–96; farming system of, 179–80, 182–83, 185, 333, 334, 338, 339; George Weiss and, 126; ownership of, 332, 392

The Oriole Way to Play Baseball (Pries), 186–87

Orix team, 344–45

Orta, Jorge, 314

Osinski, Dan, 167

Ostrowski, Joe, 130

Otis, Amos, 192–93, 262, 264, 267, 271, 272

O'Toole, Marty, 27, 72

Ott, Mel, 50

Oyler, Ray, 177, 178

Pacific Coast League, 71. *See also specific teams of*

Padres, San Diego, 118, 223, 301–2

Pafko, Andy, 106

Paley, William S., 245

Palmer, Jim, 183, 185–86, 194, 255–56

Pappas, Milt, 182, 184, 185, 208, 210

Paschal, Ben, 68

Patek, Freddy, 263, 264, 271, 272

Paths to Glory (Armour and Levitt), 31, 221

Patterson, Red, 127

Pattin, Marty, 193

Paul, Gabe, *fig. 26*; about, xvi, 281; on Cedric Tallis, 253; with Indians, 299; with Yankees (1973–1974), 246, 281–86, 402; with Yankees (1975–1977), 285–89, 291–92, 294–95, 297–99

payments by Major Leagues to Minor Leagues, 72–73

Pedroia, Dustin, 387, 390

Pennant Park, 51

Pepitone, Joe, 234–35, 240, 241

Percentage Baseball (Cook), 256

Perez, Tony, 207–8, 211, 213, 215

Perry, George, 63

Pesky, Johnny, 165, 166

Peterson, Brian, 360

Peterson, Fritz, 241, 245, 284

Peterson, Rick, 359

Petrocelli, Rico, 166, 170, 171, 192
Philadelphia Athletics. *See* Athletics, Philadelphia
Phillies, Philadelphia: in the 1920s, 40, 44; under Ed Wade, 362, 363; farm systems and, 78; under Pat Gillick, 362–68
Phillippe, Charles "Deacon," 11, 13, 15, 16, 20, 24–25
Phillips, Lefty, 111, 114
Pilots, Seattle, 255, 261, 300
Piniella, Lou: as Mariners manager, 339, 341, 344, 345, 349; as player, 261, 267, 268, 272, 283, 286, 298; with Yankees, 324–25
Pinson, Vada, 146, 207, 212, 213
Pipers, Cleveland, 245–46
Pirates, Pittsburgh: in 1899, 14–17; from 1900 to 1903, 16–20, 22–25; from 1905 to 1932, 26–28, 45; in the 2000s, 360; Branch Rickey and, 103, 155; Roberto Clemente and, 110; World Series of, 25, 26, 28, 133, 195
PITCHf/x, 358, 382–83
pitching distance, 5–6
pitching rubber, 5
Pittsburgh Leader, 17
Pittsburgh Pirates. *See* Pirates, Pittsburgh
Pittsburgh Tribune-Review, 279
Players League, 4
players strike. *See* strike, players
player's union, 264, 275–76
Podres, Johnny, 106–7
Ponson, Sidney, 338
Posey, Buster, 379–80, 381
Powell, Boog, 183, 184, 186
Powell, Jake, 88–89
Power, C. B., 17
Power, Vic, 131
Pries, Don, 186–87

professional management beginnings in baseball, overview of, xv, 54–55, 60–61, 399
profits, team: of Blue Jays, 311; of Cubs, 133; of Dodgers, 99; of Giants, 33, 50, 66; of Indians, 132–33; of Mariners, 348; of Orioles, 133; Paul Beeston on, 300; of White Sox, 132–33; of Yankees, 66, 132–33
Pujols, Albert, 392, 394
Pulliam, Harry: Colonels and, 8–10, 11, 15; as National League president, 23–24, 29; Pirates and, 15, 18
Purdy, Mark, 381

Queen, Mel, 208, 211
Quinn, Bob, 3, 56, 403

racism in baseball, 88–89, 146, 149, 169, 218
Rainiers, Seattle, 252
Randolph, Willie, 288–89, 291, 295, 298
Rangers, Texas, 260, 287, 345, 367–68, 392, 397
Rapp, Goldie, 43–44
Raudman, Bob, 209
Rays, Tampa Bay, 358–59
Reach Guide, 58
Redbirds, Columbus, 98
Reds, Cincinnati: under Bill DeWitt, 252, 392; under Bob Howsam (1967–1968), 198–99, 204–13; under Bob Howsam (1969–1977), 213–21, 222–28, 265, 280; under Bob Howsam (1983–1985), 228–29; Curt Flood and, 146–47; farming system of, 205–6, 208, 227; free agency and, 228, 280; under Gabe Paul, 281; Heinie Groh and, 44–45; under Larry MacPhail and Warren Giles, 98; ownership of, 23, 53, 204, 228, 392; WAR and, 190; World

Series of, 90, 220, 227, 228, 280, 292, 339

Red Sox, Boston: in 1967, 163, 171–72, 191–92; in the 2000s, xiii, 385–91, 398–99; about and overview of, 162–63, 164–65, 166, 397–98; under Dick O'Connell, 165, 166–74, 191–94; draft and, 191–94; farm system of, 166, 390–91; integration and, 137, 169, 174; ownership of, 55, 56, 83, 385; sale of players to Yankees, 64–65; statistical analysis and, 353, 386, 388; World Series of, xiii, 64, 163, 227, 353, 385, 387

Red Wings, Rochester, *fig. 13*, 281

Reese, Jimmy, 68, 76

Reese, Pee Wee, 99, 105, 107

Regan, Phil, 333

Reichardt, Rick, 188–89

Reilly, Raymond, 257–58

Reiser, Pete, 99

Repulski, Rip, 143

reserve clause, 71, 274, 276

revenues, baseball, 260, 277–78, 325–26, 348–49, 397

Reynolds, Allie, 123, 129

Rhodes, Arthur, 343, 344, 364

Rice, Jim, 193, 194, 297

Richards, Paul, 179–83

Richardson, Bobby, 129, 234

Richardson, Spec, 218–19, 402

Rickey, Branch, *fig. 10*, 62, 401, 406; Bob Howsam and, 200–202, 203; with Browns, 56; with Cardinals, 57–58, 74–76, 99–101, 151–52, 155, 157–58, 160; with Dodgers, 97–98, 99, 100–105, 107–8, 110; farm systems and, 74, 75–76, 78, 99, 100–101, 399; Larry MacPhail and, 123–24; as talent evaluator, 3, 101

Rieter, Ben, 394

Ripken, Cal, 333, 334, 336

Ritchey, Claude, 10, 13, 14, 15, 16, 19

Ritchie, Jay, 208–9

Riverfront Stadium, 215–16, 217

Rivers, Mickey, 289, 291, 295, 298

Rizzo, Mike, 360

Roberts, Robin, 109, 184

Robinson, Brooks, 181, 182, 184, 185

Robinson, Eddie, 305

Robinson, Frank, 136, 185, 186, 194, 195

Robinson, Herk, 254

Robinson, Jackie, 89, 102–3, 105, 107, 111, 135, 138

Robinson, Wilbert, 64

Robison, Frank, 11–12, 14, 21

Robison, Stanley, 11–12

Rochester Red Wings, *fig. 13*, 281

Rockies, Colorado, 353, 365

Rodriguez, Alex, 340, 341–42, 344, 345, 366

Roe, Preacher, 103

Rogers, Jim, 8

Rogers, John I., 6

Rohr, Billy, 170, 171–72, 173

Rojas, Cookie, 262, 263, 267, 269, 272

Rolfe, Red, 85, 89

Rollins, Jimmy, 363, 365

Rose, Pete: with Reds (1967–1971), 207, 211, 213, 215, 216, 217; with Reds (1973–1985), 223, 227, 228, 280

Roseboro, John, 113

roster limits, 73, 74, 75, 77

Rothstein, Arnold, 36

rowdyism, 14, 23, 31

Royals, Kansas City, 213; Baseball Academy and, 257–61; under Cedric Tallis, 222–23, 253–56, 261–69, 270–73; Ewing Kauffman and, 249–50, 256–58, 260–61, 268–69, 273; under Joe Burke, 268–70, 287–88; World Series 1985 and, 268–70, 287–88

Royals, Montreal, 105
Royals Stadium, 249, 267
Rudi, Joe, 222, 280, 291, 293
Ruffing, Red, 85, 86, 90
Rule 4 Draft. *See* draft, amateur
Rule 5 Draft, 309–10, 312, 316–17, 331, 368
Ruppert, Jacob, *fig. 5*; about, xv, 62–63, 88, 89, 120, 407; on Barney Dreyfuss, 28; purchase of Yankees by, 54, 62, 63; as Yankees owner, 57, 63–68, 76–77, 80–89, 92–93, 399, 414n3
Ruppert Brewery, 62, 65–66
Russell, Lefty, 27
Russo, Jim, 180, 182
Russo, Marius, 87
Ruth, Babe, 45, 48, 49, 57, 65–68, 82–85
Ryan, Mike, 168, 171
Ryan, Rosy, 43

Sabean, Brian, *fig. 30*, 368–69, 375, 377–83, 403, 404
sabermetrics, 353, 357, 361. *See also* statistical analysis
Sadecki, Ray, 149, 153, 159, 204
Safeco Field, 340, 342
Saigh, Fred, 138–39, 140
Sain, Johnny, 130, 178
Saints, St. Paul, 27, 43, 81, 105, 127
salaries, player, 6, 131, 277–78
Sanchez, Jonathan, 377, 379
San Diego Padres. *See* Padres, San Diego
Sandoval, Pablo, 379, 381
Sanford, Fred, 129
San Francisco Giants. *See* Giants, San Francisco
San Francisco Seals. *See* Seals, San Francisco
Sasaki, Kaz, 343, 344
Schaal, Paul, 261

Scheinblum, Richie, 222, 265, 272
Scherger, George, 214
Schlough, Bill, 383
Schoendienst, Red, 143, 145, 203, 209
Schott, Marge, 228
Schroeder, Jay, 310
Schuerholz, John, 254, 256, 287–88, 403
Schupp, Ferdie, 39
scientific baseball, 6
Scott, George, 168, 171, 173–74, 192–94, 263
Scott, Jack, 47
scouting: African American and Latino players, 137, 141–42; Blue Jays and, 306, 309; Branch Rickey and, 100–101; Cardinals and, 141, 145, 393; Colonels and, 5, 8–9; Dodgers and, 108, 110, 111–15, 191; draft and, 189; Giants and, 380; Orioles and, 180, 182–83; Pirates and, 27; Reds and, 206–7; Royals and, 259, 269, 271, 273; statistical analysis and, 352–54, 360–61, 379, 380; Tigers and, 176–77; Yankees and, 67–69, 87, 92, 129
Scutaro, Marco, 382, 389
Seals, San Francisco, 86
Seattle Mariners. *See* Mariners, Seattle
Seattle Pilots. *See* Pilots, Seattle
Seaver, Tom, 161, 224, 228
Sebring, Jimmy, 24
Seitz, Peter, 274, 275, 276, 289
Sele, Aaron, 343–44, 348
Selkirk, George, 85, 90
Senators, Washington, 49, 60, 80, 85, 268
service-time provision, 276, 348
Shannon, Mike, 157, 204
Shaughnessy, Dan, 388–89
Shawkey, Bob, 64, 82
Shea Stadium, 224, 239, 244, 285, 290
Shelley, Jeremy, 378–79

Shepard, Larry, 214
Sherry, Norm, 113–14
Shore, Ray, 207, 211, 215, 217, 218, 222, 226
signing bonuses, 109–11, 164, 180–81, 188–89
Simmons, Curt, 109, 149, 150, 159, 203
Simpson, Dick, 185, 209–10
Simpson, Wayne, 206, 215, 217, 222, 265
Sinclair, Harry, 40, 54
Singer, Bill, 309
single trust company plan of National League, 21–22
Sisler, Dick, *fig. 20*
Sisler, George, 27
Skinner, Bob, 155–56
Skowron, Bill, 129
SkyDome, 325, 333
Slavin, James, 42–43
Smith, Billy, 293, 294
Smith, George, 167, 168
Smith, Janet Marie, 386
Smith, John, 103
Smith, Mayo, 178–79
Smith, Red, 141, 238, 277, 285
Smith, Reggie, 170–71, 174, 192
Smith, Tal, 282, 287, 303–4, 306, 402
Snider, Duke, 102, 105, 115
Snyder, Frank, 38, 39
Soden, Arthur, 6, 21
Solway, Herb, 300, 313
Somers, Charles, 21, 22
Sparma, Joe, 177, 178
Sparrow, Harry, 57
Spiders, Cleveland, 12
Spikes, Charlie, 242, 243
Spink, J. G. Taylor, 65
Splittorff, Paul, 254–55, 267, 273, 298
Spoljaric, Paul, 330, 340
Sport, 296–97
Sporting Life, 5, 6, 14
Sporting News, 5; Larry MacPhail and, 125, 238; Major League Executive

of the Year awards, 401–4; Mariners and, 345; Minor League Executive of the Year awards, 200, 252; Minor League Player of the Year awards, 168; on Pat Gillick, 288
Sports Illustrated, 97, 163, 242–43, 345, 394
Sportsman's Park, 141
Sportsvision, 382–83
St. Louis Browns, 12, 54, 56, 141, 162, 391
St. Louis Cardinals. *See* Cardinals, St. Louis
St. Louis Star-Times, 123
St. Paul Saints. *See* Saints, St. Paul, 27, 43, 81, 105, 127
stadium boom, 325–26, 357, 399
Stange, Lee, 169, 173
Stanky, Eddie: with Cardinals, 141, 142, 145, 152, 202; with Dodgers, 103; with Mets, 158
Stanley, Fred, 292
Stanley, Mickey, 177, 178–79, 197
statistical analysis, 352–61; Athletics and, 354–57, 396; Cardinals and, 394–95; Dodgers and, 112–13; early uses and discussions of, 112–13, 256–57, 352–56; effects on front office and manager relations of, 356–57, 383, 393; Giants and, 378–79; Red Sox and, 353, 386, 388; Royals and, 256–57, 273; scouting and, 352–54, 360–61, 379, 380; twenty-first century uses of, 357–61
Steinbrenner, George: about, 233, 245–46; Cedric Tallis and, 250; illegal campaign contributions and, 284–85; Pat Gillick and, 304, 306, 314, 324; purchase of Yankees and, 245–46; Yankees (1974–1975) and, 281–82, 285–90, 306; Yankees (1976–1993) and, 290, 292, 294–99, 314

Stengel, Casey, 44, 46, 130, 132, 133, 234

Stewart, Dave, 329, 330

Stieb, Dave, 311, 314, 315, 316, 325, 327

Stoneham, Charles, 36, 51, 66

Stoneham, Horace, 59, 401

Stottlemyre, Mel, 234, 241, 242, 284, 327

Stottlemyre, Todd, 324–25, 330

Strasburg, Stephen, 360

strike, players, 228, 264, 277

Stucky, Thomas Hunt, 10–11

success, requirements for team, xiv–xv, 399

Sukeforth, Clyde, 110

Sullivan, Haywood, *fig. 16*

Summers, Jim, 359

Superbas, Brooklyn, 12, 13, 22

Suzuki, Ichiro, 344–45, 346

Swango, Bruce, 180–81

Swift, Bob, 178

Sydex Sports, 359

Tallis, Cedric, *figs. 20, 24, 25*; about, 249–50, 251–53; with Royals, 253–55, 258–59, 261–69, 270–73; with Yankees, 287–88, 299

Tammany Hall, 21, 63

Tampa Bay Rays. *See* Rays, Tampa Bay

Tannehill, Jesse, 15, 16, 17–18, 20, 22

Tartabull, Jose, 169

Taylor, Joe, 146

team building: about, xiii–xvi, 60; free agency and, 274; pre-farming systems and, 70–73. *See also* draft; minor league; farm systems

Tebbetts, Birdie, 146, 287, 295

Tejada, Miguel, 354, 396

Temple, Johnny, 145

Tenace, Gene, 191, 222

Terry, Bill, 48, 49, 57, 58–59

Thomas, Lee, 146, 167, 403

Thomasville, Tigers affiliate club in, 176, 202, 251

Thomasville Orioles training camp, 181

Thompson, Fresco, *fig. 9*, 105, 107, 113, 115, 117, 118

Thornley, Stew, 415n22

3-D tracking systems, 358

Thrift, Syd, *fig. 23*, 254, 256, 257–59, 333, 334

Tidrow, Dick, 284, 295, 377

Tigers, Detroit: 1960s rebuilding of, 174–79; American League pennants of, 84; draft and, 196–97; under Frank Navin, 55–56, 76; ownership of, 53, 162; statistical analysis and, 359–60

Time, 300

Tolan, Bobby, 212, 213, 215, 218, 220, 223, 224–25

Toney, Fred, 37, 39, 41, 47, 50

Topping, Dan, Jr., 133, 236, 238

Topping, Dan, Sr., *fig.11*; from 1945 to 1960, 121, 124–25, 129–30, 133, 234; from 1961 to 1966, 234–38, 402

Toronto, Red Sox farm team in, 169–71

Toronto Blue Jays. *See* Blue Jays, Toronto

Torrez, Mike, 196, 295, 298

TrackMan, 358

Traynor, Pie, 27, 28

Treder, Steve, 255

Tresh, Tom, 234, 240, 241

Triple Crowns, 168, 173, 185

Trouppe, Quincy, 141

Truitt, Charles, 268

Tucker, Leonard, 141

Turner, Ted, 318

Twins, Minnesota, 279

Tygiel, Jules, 137

Uecker, Bob, 155

United Press International (UPI), 160

Upshaw, Willie, 309, 312, 314, 322, 323

USA Today, 378, 384

Utley, Chase, 363, 364–65, 366

Valenti, Dan, 163

Valentine, Bobby, 191, 390

Vaughan, Arky, 28, 100, 101

Veeck, Bill, Jr., 391, 407

Veeck, Bill, Sr., *fig. 4*, 56–57, 59, 65, 157, 401, 402

Venezuela, scouting from, 288, 379, 393

Verducci, Tom, 335

Victorino, Shane, 364, 365, 391

video technology, 258, 358, 359, 382–84

Vincent, Al, 180

Virdon, Bill, 143, 283, 285, 287

Virgil, Ozzie, 175

von der Horst, Harry, 12

Wacha, Michael, 394, 395

Waddell, George "Rube," 13, 15, 16, 17, 19

Wade, Ed, 362

Wagner, Dick, 202–3, 205, 228

Wagner, Honus: about, 9, 28; with Colonels, 9–10, 13, 15, 16; with Pirates, 15, 17, 19, 20, 22, 24

Walker, Dixie, 99, 101, 102

Walker, Harry, 144, 145, 152, 218–19

Walker, Jerry, 181, 182

Walker, Jimmy, 63

Wall Street Journal, 233, 383

Waner, Lloyd, 27–28

Waner, Paul, 27–28

Ward, Duane, 322, 325, 329–27, 330

Ward, Robert (Federals owner), 54

Ward, Robert (writer), 296–97

Warwick, Carl, 155

WAR (wins above replacement) from drafted players, 189–90, 193–95; Athletics and, 396; Blue Jays and,

331; free agency and, 278–79; Phillies and, 365; Pilots and, 255; Reds and, 226; Royals and, 255, 271, 272

Washington, Ron, 260, 265

Washington, U. L., 260

Washington National League club, 12, 15

Washington Nationals. *See* Nationals, Washington

Washington Post, 233, 361

Washington Senators. *See* Senators, Washington

Weaver, Earl, 183, 184, 186–87, 305

Webb, Del, *fig. 11*, 121, 124–25, 131, 235, 237

Webster, R. Howard, 300

Weeghman, Charles, 54

Weiss, George: about, 81–82, 126, 127–28, 162, 406; Bob Howsam and, 200; with Mets, 160–61; with Yankees post Jacob Ruppert, 121, 124, 125, 127–34, 234, 401–2; with Yankees under Jacob Ruppert, 81–86, 93

Wells, David, 326–27, 334–35, 336

Wendel, Tim, 179

Werner, Tom, 385, 389

Wert, Don, 177, 178

Werth, Jayson, 338, 364, 365, 366–67

Western League, 199–200

Whitaker, Steve, 236, 261, 272

White, Bill: with Cardinals, 148, 151, 153, 154, 156, 159, 203–4; with Giants, 148; with Phillies, 161, 203; Solly Hemus and, 148

White, Devon, 327

White, Frank, *fig. 22*, 259–60, 265, 272

White, Roy, 240, 242, 244, 291, 295, 298

White Sox, Chicago, 83, 132–33, 138, 143, 326, 397

Whitfield, Fred, 209

Whitt, Ernie, 193, 308, 314, 323, 326

Widdrington, Peter, 301
Wilhelm, Hoyt, 184, 255, 272
Williams, Dick, *fig. 16*, 114, 163, 164, 169–72, 173, 282–83
Williams, Edward Bennett, 285
Williams, Edwin, 177
Williams, Jimmy, 15, 16, 17, 18–19
Williams, Jimy, 210, 321–24
Wills, Maury, 116, 206, 239
Wilson, Earl, 167, 168–69, 177, 178, 196
Wilson, Hack, 49, 50–51
Wilson, Owen "Chief," 26
Winfield, Dave, 328, 329
wins above replacement (WAR). *See* WAR (wins above replacement) from drafted players
Woodward, Woody, 210, 211, 212, 339–42
World Series: from 1903 to 1919, 25, 26, 36, 57; in the 1920s, 28, 45, 48–49, 65, 67, 75, 77; in the 1930s, 76, 80, 82, 86, 87, 88, 90; in the 1940s, 101, 123, 132, 201; in the 1950s, 105, 106, 107, 132, 200; from 1960 to 1966, 117–18, 133, 159, 185–86; from 1967 to 1969, 160, 161, 163, 179, 196, 242; from 1970 to 1974, 118, 191, 194, 195, 215, 220; from 1975 to 1979, 118, 227, 228, 292, 298; in the 1980s, 118, 270, 317; in the 1990s, 327, 329, 331; from 2002 to 2004, 162, 353, 368, 387, 392; from 2006 to 2010, 353, 365, 381, 388, 392; from 2011 to 2013, xiii, 382, 385, 391, 393
Wrigley, Phil, 59, 60, 401
Wrigley, William, *fig. 4*, 54, 56–57
Wyatt, John, 169

Wyatt, Whitlow, 99, 101
Wynn, Jimmie, *fig. 8*, 218

Yamauchi, Hiroshi, 339
Yankees, New York, in the 1910s, 54, 57, 62–64; in the 1920s, 45, 48–49, 57, 65–68, 90–91; from 1930 to 1938, 59, 77–78, 80–89, 94, 126–27; from 1939 to 1949, 78, 89–92, 122–26, 131–32; in the 1950s, 126–33, 138, 397–98; from 1960 to 1973, 133, 233; from 1974 to 1975, 281–90; from 1976 to 1977, 233, 290–99; in the 2000s, 278–79, 353; farming system of, 234, 239, 242; under general manager Ralph Houk, 234–37; under general manager Roy Hamey, 234; ownership of, 235, 237, 245–46; under president Mike Burke, 237–48
Yankee Stadium, 243; building of, 66, 67, 287, 290; remodels and upgrades of, 122, 244, 247, 287, 290
Yastrzemski, Carl, 166, 171, 173–74, 191–92, 194
Yawkey, Tom, 55, 80, 83, 121, 137, 164–66, 401, 407
Yawkey, William Clyman, 55
Yawkey, William H. "Bill," 53, 55–56
Young, Nick, 6, 22
Youngs, Ross, 35, 36–37, 39, 40, 45, 48, 50
Youse, Walter, 183

Zaidi, Farhan, 356
Zimmer, Chief, 13, 14, 15, 16, 17
Zimmer, Don, 114, 206
Zimmerman, Heinie, 41
Zito, Barry, 369, 377, 396

CPSIA information can be obtained
at www.ICGtesting.com
Printed in the USA
LVHW07s1932230218
567708LV00003B/250/P